ELEVEN VERSE PLAYS

MAXWELL ANDERSON

1929-1939

HARCOURT, BRACE & WORLD, INC.

BY ARRANGEMENT WITH ANDERSON HOUSE

CONTENTS

I · ELIZABETH THE QUEEN

CHARACTERS

(In the order of appearance)

SIR WALTER RALEIGH
PENELOPE GRAY
A CAPTAIN
SIR ROBERT CECIL
LORD ESSEX
FRANCIS BACON
QUEEN ELIZABETH
LORD BURGHLEY
LORD HOWARD
THE FOOL
CAPTAIN ARMIN
MARY
ELLEN
TRESSA
MARVEL
A COURIER
A HERALD
BURBAGE
HEMMINGS
FALSTAFF
PRINCE HENRY *Players in the*
GADSHILL *scene from*
PETO *Henry IV*
POINS

Also GUARDS, MEN-AT-ARMS, MAIDS-IN-WAITING,
and others

ACT ONE

SCENE I

SCENE: *An entrance hall before a council chamber in the palace at Whitehall. The entrance to the council room is closed and four GUARDS with halberds stand at either side. A small door at the left of the entrance is also shut. It is early morning. The guards stand immobile.*

First Guard. The sun's out again, and it's guineas to pounds the earl comes back this morning.

Second Guard. I'll be glad of it, for one. You get nothing but black looks about the court when he's away.

First Guard. You'll get little else now he's back, my bully. They quarrelled too far for mending, this time.

Third Guard. Tut! They quarrel no more than the cock with the hen. The earl's been sick.

First Guard. Sick of the queen's displeasure. It's a disease a favorite can die of, and many have.

Fourth Guard. He's no sicker of her displeasure than she of his, if a man may judge. Once the earl's gone there's no dancing, no plays, no feasting . . . nothing to do nights but sleep. The very scullery-maids grow cold, and go to bed alone; like the queen.

First Guard. There are some even a scullery-maid would seldom kiss, save in moments of great excitement. Poor Wat looks forward to feast nights.

Fourth Guard. I've had my luck.

3

First Guard. You've had what was coming to you. Muckle-mouth Jean, of the back kitchen.

Fourth Guard. You'd have been glad of her yourself if you could have had her.

First Guard. Consider, man. She may not have been true. When she wouldn't play with you, mayhap she was playing with somebody else. And if the queen could live without her Earl of Essex, it may have been because Sir Walter had a new suit of silver armor.

Third Guard. And there's a handsome man.

Fourth Guard. God defend me from speaking lightly of the queen!

First Guard. Eh? God defend you? Let no man accuse me of speaking lightly of the queen, nor of any other woman . . . unless she be a light woman, in which case, God defend me, I will speak lightly of her if I choose.

Third Guard. What say you of the queen?

First Guard. Of the queen? I say she is well-known to be the virgin queen, I say no more.

Second Guard. But do you think she is a virgin?

First Guard. She has doubtless been a virgin, bully, for all women have been virgins, but the question is: First, when . . . and, second, where?

Second Guard. Where?

First Guard. Where, bully, where?

Third Guard. Would you not say, in the proper place?

First Guard. No. I would not say in the proper place. Because it is hard to say if there is a proper place wherein to be a virgin . . . unless it be in church, and, God defend me, I do not go to church.

Second Guard. You do not go to church?

First Guard. No, for my sins, I do not go to church . . . or, if you like, I do not go to church for my sins.

Second Guard. Does it follow that the church is a proper place for virgins?

First Guard. It does. Did I not tell you I do not go there for my sins?

Fourth Guard. They say the queen's getting to be an old woman but I swear she looks younger than my wife, whom I married a young thing, six years come Easter.

Third Guard. It would age a girl fast, just the look of you.

First Guard. As for the queen, powder and paint accounts for some of it. To say nothing of the earl. A young lover will do much for a lady's face.

Fourth Guard. Now God defend me. . . .

First Guard. Aye, aye . . . God defend poor Wat.

   [*A* Nobleman *enters in silver armor. It is* Sir Walter Raleigh, *no other*]

Raleigh. Has the queen come forth yet?

First Guard. No, Sir Walter.

Raleigh. The Earl of Essex . . . is he here?

First Guard. No, my lord.

Raleigh. When he comes send me word. I shall be in the north corridor.

[*He turns*]

First Guard. Good, my lord.

[PENELOPE GRAY *comes in from the right, passing through*]

Raleigh.

[*Meeting her*]

Greetings, lady, from my heart.

Penelope. Good-morrow, lord, from my soul.

Raleigh. I take my oath in your face that you are rushing to the window to witness the arrival of my lord of Essex.

Penelope. And in your teeth I swear I am on no such errand . . . but only to see the sun-rise.

Raleigh. The sun has been up this hour, my dear.

Penelope. The more reason to hurry, gracious knight.

Raleigh. Do you think to pull the bag over my head so easily, Penelope? On a day when the earl returns every petticoat in the palace is hung with an eye to pleasing him. Yours not the least.

Penelope. I deny him thrice.

Raleigh. I relinquish you, lady. Run, run to the window! He will be here and you will miss him!

Penelope. Is there a lady would run from Sir Walter in his silver suiting? Since the sun is up . . . I have no errand.

Raleigh. Is there no limit to a woman's deception, wench? Would you go so far as to appear pleased if I kissed you?

Penelope. And no deception.

[*He kisses her*]

I call the Gods to witness . . . did I not blush prettily?

Raleigh. And meant it not at all. Tell me, did the queen send you to look out the casement for news of her Essex, or did you come at the prompting of your heart?

Penelope. Shall I tell you the truth?

Raleigh. Verily.

Penelope. The truth is I cannot answer.

Raleigh. Both, then?

Penelope. Both or one or neither.

Raleigh. Fie on the baggage.

Penelope. Is it not a virtue to be close-mouthed in the queen's service?

Raleigh. If you kept the rest of your person as close as your mouth what a paragon of virtue you would be!

Penelope. Indeed, my lord, I am.

Raleigh. Indeed, my lady? Have there not been certain deeds on dark nights?

Penelope. Sh! Under the rose.

Raleigh. Meaning under covers . . .

Penelope. Fie on my lord, to make me out a strumpet!

Raleigh. It is my manner of wooing, fair maid! I woo by suggestion of images . . .

Penelope. Like small boys on the closet wall . . .

Raleigh. Like a soldier . . .

Penelope. Aye, a veteran . . . of encounters . . .

Raleigh. I will have you yet, my love; I will take lessons from this earl . . .

Penelope. Take this lesson from me, my lord: You must learn to desire what you would have. Much wanting makes many a maid a wanton. You want me not . . . nor I you. You wear your silver for a queen.

> [*A* CAPTAIN *enters from the left*]

Captain. Good-morrow, Sir Walter. Is the queen still under canopy?

Raleigh. I know not.

Captain. The earl is here and would see her.

Raleigh. Bid him hurry if he wishes to find her abed as usual.

Penelope. She is dressed and stirring, captain, and awaits my lord.

Raleigh. And many another fair maid awaits him likewise, captain. Take him that message from me. Run, girl, run. Tell the queen.

> [*The* CAPTAIN *goes out left*]

Penelope.

> [*Going*]

You make yourself so easily disliked.

> [*She goes right.* CECIL *enters, passing her*]

Cecil. He is here?

Raleigh. So. The heavenly boy, clad in the regalia of the sun, even now extracts his gallant foot from his golden stirrup and makes shift to descend from his heaving charger. Acclamation lifts in every voice, tears well to every eye . . . with the exception of mine, perhaps, and yours, I hope. . . .

Cecil. I am at a pass to welcome him, myself. This Elizabeth of ours can be difficult on her good days . . . and there have been no good ones lately.

[*Two* MEN-AT-ARMS *enter with silver armor in their arms*]

Raleigh. And what is all this, sirrah?

First Man. Armor, my lord.

Raleigh. For whom?

First Man. We know not.

Raleigh. Now by the ten thousand holy names! Am I mistaken, Robert, or is this armor much like my own?

Cecil. Very like, I should say. Is it sterling?

Raleigh. And the self-same pattern. Has the earl gone lunatic?

Cecil. He means to outshine you, perhaps.

Raleigh. Has it come to this? Do I set the style for Essex? That would be a mad trick, to dress himself like me!

[BACON *appears in the doorway at right*]

What do you know of this, Sir Francis?

Bacon. Greeks, my lord, bearing gifts.

Raleigh. To hell with your Greeks! The devil damn him!
This is some blackguardry!

[*Two more* MEN-AT-ARMS *enter, carrying armor*]

There's more of it! Good God, it comes in bales!
I say, who's to wear this, sirrah? Who is it for?

[ESSEX *enters from corridor between the two files of soldiers,
pushing them aside as he does so, and crosses to right of*
RALEIGH, *speaking as he enters*]

Essex. Their name is legion, Sir Walter. Happily met!
Felicitations on your effulgence, sir!
You're more splendid than I had imagined! News came
of your silver
Even in my retreat! I was ill, and I swear it cured me!
You should have heard the compliments I've heard
Passed on you! Sir Walter's in silver! The World's out-
done
They said—the moon out-mooned. He gleams down
every corridor
And every head's turned after him. The queen
Herself has admired it—the design—the workmanship!
There's nothing like it this side of Heaven's streets.
And I said to myself—the great man—this is what we
have needed—
More silver everywhere—oceans of silver!
Sir Walter has set the style, the world will follow.
So I sent for the silver-smiths, and by their sweat
Here's for you, lads, tailored to every man's measure—
Shall Raleigh wear silver alone? Why, no,
The whole court shall go argent!

Raleigh. Take care, my lord.
  I bear insults badly.

Essex. And where are you insulted?
  For the queen's service you buy you a silver armor.
  In the queen's service I buy you a dozen more.
  A gift, my friends, each man to own his own,
  As you own yours. What insult?

Raleigh. Have your laugh,
  Let the queen and court laugh with you! Since you are
    envious
  You may have my suit. I had not thought even Essex
  Bore so petty a mind.

Essex. I misunderstood you
  Perhaps, Sir Walter. I had supposed you donned
  Silver for our queen, but I was mistaken . . .
  Keep these all for yourself. The men shall have other . .
  Some duller color.

Raleigh. I have borne much from you
  Out of regard for the queen, my lord of Essex.

Essex. And I from you.
  By God . . .

Cecil. You have forgotten, Sir Walter,
  A certain appointment . . .

Raleigh. And you will bear more, by Heaven! . . .

Cecil. He is going to the queen,
  Remember. And we have an errand.

Essex. You presume to protect me,
   Master Secretary?

Cecil. I protect you both, and our mistress.
   There can be no quarrelling here.

Raleigh. That's very true. Let us go.
   [CECIL *and* RALEIGH *go out right*]

Bacon. And this armor? What becomes of it?

Essex. I have given it.
   Would you have me take it back?

Bacon. There has seldom been
   A man so little wise, so headstrong, but he
   Could sometimes see how necessary it is
   To keep friends and not make enemies at court.
   But you . . . God knows.

Essex. Let him make friends with me.
   He may need friends himself.
      [*To the* GUARDS]
   These are your armors.
   Keep them, wear them, sell them, whatever you like . . .
   Or your captain directs you.

First Guard. We thank you.
      [*They retire to examine the armor*]

Bacon. You are going to the queen?

Essex. Yes. God help us both!

Bacon. Then hear me a moment . . .

Essex. Speak, schoolmaster,
   I knew it was coming. You've been quiet too long.

Bacon. Listen to me this once, and listen this once
To purpose, my lord, or it may hardly be worth
My while ever to give you advice again
Or for you to take it. You have enough on your hands
Without quarrelling with Raleigh. You have quarrelled
    with the queen
Against my judgment . . .

Essex. God and the devil! Can a man
Quarrel on order or avoid a quarrel at will?

Bacon. Why certainly, if he knows his way.

Essex. Not I.

Bacon. You quarrelled with her, because she wished to keep
    peace
And you wanted war . . .

Essex. We are at war with Spain!
But such a silly, frightened, womanish war
As only a woman would fight . . .

Bacon. She is a woman and fights a womanish war;
But ask yourself one question and answer it
Honestly, dear Essex, and perhaps you will see then
Why I speak sharply. You are my friend and patron.
Where you gain I gain . . . where you lose I lose . . .
And I see you riding straight to a fall today . . .
And I'd rather your neck weren't broken.

Essex. Ask myself
What question?

Bacon. Ask yourself what you want:
To retain the favor of the queen, remain

Her favorite, keep all that goes with this,
Or set yourself against her and trust your fortune
To popular favor?

Essex. I'll not answer that.

Bacon. Then . . . I have done.

Essex. Forgive me, dear friend, forgive me.
I have been ill, and this silly jackanapes
Of a Raleigh angers me with his silver mountings
Till I forget who's my friend. You know my answer
In regard to the queen. I must keep her favor.
Only it makes me mad to see all this . . .
This utter mismanagement, when a man's hand and
    brain
Are needed and cannot be used.

Bacon. Let me answer for you;
You are not forthright with yourself. The queen
Fights wars with tergiversation and ambiguities . . .
You wish to complete your record as general,
Crush Spain, subdue Ireland, make a name like Cæsar's
Climb to the pinnacle of fame. Take care.
You are too popular already. You have
Won at Cadiz, caught the people's hearts,
Caught their voices till the streets ring your name
Whenever you pass. You are loved better than
The queen. That is your danger. She will not suffer
A subject to eclipse her; she cannot suffer it.
Make no mistake. She will not.

Essex. And I must wait,
Bite my nails in a corner, let her lose to Spain,
Keep myself back for policy?

Bacon. Even so.

Essex. I come of better blood than Elizabeth.
My name was among the earls around King John
Under the oak. What the nobles have taught a king
A noble may teach a queen.

Bacon. You talk treason and death.
The old order is dead, and you and your house will die
With it if you cannot learn.

Essex. So said King John
Under the oak, or wherever he was standing,
And little he got by it, as you may recall.
What the devil's a king but a man, or a queen but a
    woman?

Bacon. King John is dead; this is Elizabeth,
Queen in her own right, daughter of a haughty line
There is one man in all her kingdom she fears
And that man's yourself, and she has good reason to fear
    you.
You're a man not easily governed, a natural rebel,
Moreover, a general, popular and acclaimed,
And last, she loves you, which makes you the more to be
    feared,
Whether you love her or not.

Essex. I do love her! I do!

Bacon. My lord, a man as young as you—

Essex. If she were my mother's kitchen hag,
Toothless and wooden-legged, she'd make all other
Colorless.

Bacon. You play dangerously there, my lord.

Essex. I've never yet loved or hated
For policy nor a purpose. I tell you she's a witch—
And has a witch's brain. I love her, I fear her,
I hate her, I adore her—

Bacon. That side of it you must know
For yourself.

Essex. I will walk softly—here is my hand.
Distress myself no more—I can carry myself.

Bacon. Only count not too much on the loves of queens.

Essex. I'll remember.

[CECIL *and* RALEIGH *reappear in the doorway at the right.*
RALEIGH *is wearing ordinary armor and carries his silver suit.*
ESSEX *looks at him, biting his lip*]

Sir Walter, take care of your health!

Raleigh. My health, sir?

Essex.
[*Going out*]
Wearing no silver, in this chilly weather.

Raleigh.
[*Tossing his silver armor into the pile*]
Put that with the others.

First Guard. Are we to wear them, sir?

Raleigh. No. Melt them down and sell the silver. And thus
see for yourself how soon a fool is parted from his
money. Take station in the outer hall and carry this
trash with you.

First Guard. Yes, sir.

    [*The guards go out right.*

Raleigh.

    [*To* BACON]

    And you, sir, you are his friend . . .

Bacon. And yours, Sir Walter . . .

Raleigh. It's the first I've heard of it, but if you're mine
    too, so much the better. Carry this news to him: his
    suits go to the melting-pot.

Bacon. Willingly, my lord, if I see him. You have done
    quite properly.

Raleigh. I do not ask your commendation!

Bacon. No, but you have it.

    [*He bows low and goes out to left*]

Raleigh. There's the viper under our flower, this Francis.
    He should be on the winning side.

Cecil. He will be yet . . .
    Like all wise men. For myself, I no longer
    Stomach Lord Essex. Every word he speaks
    Makes me feel queasy.

Raleigh. Then why put up with him?

Cecil. The queen, my friend, the queen. What she wants she
    will have,
    And she must have her earl.

Raleigh. Which does she love more,
    Her earl or her kingdom?

Cecil. Yes, which? I have wondered.

Raleigh. Then you're less sapient
  Than I've always thought you, Cecil. She loves her
    kingdom
  More than all men, and always will. If he could
  Be made to look like a rebel, which he's close to being . . .
  And she could be made to believe it, which is harder,
  You'd be first man in the council.

Cecil. And you would be? . . .

Raleigh. Wherever I turn he's stood
  Square in my way! My life long here at court
  He's snatched honor and favor from before my eyes . . .
  Till his voice and walk and aspect make me writhe . . .
  There's a fatality in it!

Cecil. If he could be sent from England . . . we might have
    a chance
  To come between them.

Raleigh. Would she let him go?

Cecil. No . . . but if he could be teased
  And stung about his generalship till he was
  Too angry to reflect . . . Suppose you were proposed
  As general for the next Spanish raid?

Raleigh. He would see it,
  And so would she.

Cecil. Then if you were named
  For the expedition to Ireland?

Raleigh. No, I thank you.
  He'd let me go, and I'd be sunk in a bog

This next three hundred years. I've seen enough
Good men try to conquer Ireland.

Cecil. Then how would this be?
We name three men for Ireland of his own supporters:
He will oppose them, not wishing his party weakened
At the court. Then we ask what he suggests
And hint at his name for leader . . .

Raleigh. Good so far.

Cecil. He will be angry and hint at your name; you will offer
To go if he will.

Raleigh. No. Not to Ireland.

Cecil. Yes!
Do you think he'd let you go with him and share
The military glory? It will go hard,
Having once brought up his name, if we do not manage
To ship him alone to Dublin.

Raleigh. We can try it, then,
Always remembering that no matter what
Is said . . . no matter what I say or you . . .
I do not go. You must get me out of that,
By Christ, for I know Ireland.

Cecil. I will. Be easy.

Raleigh. When is the council?

Cecil. At nine.

Raleigh. You'll make these suggestions?

Cecil. If you'll play up to them.

Raleigh. Count on me. I must look after
   These silver soldiers.

Cecil. At nine then.

Raleigh. Count on me.
   [*They go out in opposite directions*]

CURTAIN

ACT ONE

Scene II

Scene: *The queen's study, which adjoins her bed-chambers and the council hall. It is a severe little room, with chairs, a desk and a few books, huge and leather-bound.* Penelope *comes in from the bed-chamber and looks out through a curtain opposite. She returns to the chamber, then re-enters to wait.* Essex *enters.*

Penelope.
[*Rising*]
Good-morrow, my lord.

Essex. Good-morrow, Penelope. Have I kept the queen?

Penelope. If so, would I acknowledge it?

Essex. I commend me to your discretion.

Penelope. Only to my discretion?

Essex. Take her what message you will . . . only let it be that I am here.

Penelope. May I have one moment, my lord? She is not quite ready.

Essex. As many as you like. What is it, my dear?

Penelope. Do you love the queen?

Essex. Is that a fair question, as between maid and man?

Penelope. An honest question.

Essex. Then I will answer honestly. Yes, my dear.

Penelope. Dearly?

Essex. Yes.

Penelope. I would you loved someone who loved you better.

Essex. Meaning . . . whom?

Penelope. Meaning . . . no-one. Myself, perhaps. That's no-one. Or . . . anyone who loved you better.

Essex. Does she not love me, sweet?

Penelope. She loves you, loves you not, loves you, loves you not . . .

Essex. And why do you tell me this?

Penelope. Because I am afraid.

Essex. For me?

Penelope. I have heard her when she thought she was alone, walk up and down her room soundlessly, night long, cursing you . . . cursing you because she must love you and could not help herself . . . swearing to be even with you for this love she scorns to bear you. My lord, you anger her too much.

Essex. But is this not common to lovers?

Penelope. No. I have never cursed you. And I have good cause.

Essex. But if I were your lover, you would, sweet. So thank God I am not.

Penelope. I must go and tell her you are here.
   [*She lifts her face to be kissed*]
   Goodbye.

Essex. Goodbye, my dear.
  [*He kisses her*]
  And thank you.

Penelope. Will you beware of her?

Essex. Lover, beware your lover, might well be an old
  maxim.
  I will beware.

Penelope. For I am afraid.
  [*A* MAID-IN-WAITING *appears in the doorway*]

Maid. Her Majesty is ready.

Penelope. I will tell her my lord is here.
  [*She runs out hastily.* ELIZABETH *enters, signing imperiously
  to the maid, who disappears. There is a moment's
  silence*]

Elizabeth. When we met last it was, as I remember,
  Ill-met by moonlight, sir.

Essex. Well-met by day,
  My queen.

Elizabeth. I had hardly hoped to see you again,
  My lord of Essex, after what was vowed
  Forever when you left.

Essex. You are unkind.
  To remind me.

Elizabeth. I think I also used
  The word forever, and meant it as much, at least . . .
  Therefore, no apology. Only my Penelope
  Passed me just now in the door with eyes and lips

That looked the softer for kissing. I'm not sure
But I'm inopportune.

Essex. She's a crazy child.

Elizabeth. A child! That's for me, too, no doubt! These children
Have their little ways with each other!

Essex. Must we begin
With charges and counter-charges, when you know . . .

Elizabeth. Do I indeed? . . .
   You have been gone a week, at this Wanstock of
      yours . . .
   And a week's a long time at court. You forget that I
   Must live and draw breath whether I see you or not . . .
   And there are other men and women, oh yes, all fully
   Equipped for loving and being loved! Penelope . . .
   You find Penelope charming. And as for me
   There's always Mountjoy . . . or Sir Walter . . . the
      handsome,
   Sir Walter, the silver-plated . . .

Essex. He'll wear no more
Silver at your door.

Elizabeth. What have you done . . . come, tell me.
I knew this silver would draw fire. What happened?

Essex. Nothing . . . but the fashion's gone out.

Elizabeth. No, but tell me!

Essex. He happened to be in the way
When the upstairs pot was emptied.
He's gone to change his clothes.

Elizabeth. You shall not be allowed
  To do this to him. . . .

Essex.

    [*Moving toward her*]

  You shall not be allowed
  To mock me, my queen.

    [*He kisses her*]

Elizabeth. Isn't it strange how one man's kiss can grow
  To be like any other's . . . or a woman's
  To be like any woman's?

Essex. Not yours for me,
  No, and not mine for you, you lying villain,
  You villain and queen, you double-tongued seductress,
  You bitch of brass!

Elizabeth. Silver, my dear. Let me be
  A bitch of silver. It reminds me of Raleigh.

Essex. Damn you!

Elizabeth. Damn you and double-damn you for a damner!
  Come some day when I'm in the mood. What day's
    this? . . .
  Thursday? Try next Wednesday . . . or any Wednesday
  Later on in the summer . . . Any summer
  Will do. Why are you still here?

Essex. Oh, God, if I could but walk out that door
  And stay away!

Elizabeth. It's not locked.

Essex. But I'd come back!
  Where do you think I've been this last week? Trying,
  Trying not to be here! But you see, I am here.

Elizabeth. Yes, I see.

Essex. Why did you plague me without a word?

Elizabeth. Why did you not come?

Essex. You are a queen, my queen. You have proscribed
  me,
  Sent formal word I'd not be admitted if I came.

Elizabeth. I may have meant it at the time.

Essex. I think I have a demon, and you are it!

Elizabeth. If ever a mocking devil tortured a woman
  You're my devil and torture me! Let us part and
  quickly,
  Or there'll be worse to come. Go.

Essex. I tell you I will not.

Elizabeth. Come to me, my Essex. Let us be kind
  For a moment. I will be kind. You need not be.
  You are young and strangely winning and strangely
  sweet.
  My heart goes out to you wherever you are.
  And something in me has drawn you. But this same
  thing
  That draws us together hurts and blinds us until
  We strike at one another. This has gone on
  A long while. It grows worse with the years. It will end
  badly.

Go, my dear, and do not see me again.

Essex. All this
Is what I said when last I went away.
Yet here I am.

Elizabeth. Love someone else, my dear.
I will forgive you.

Essex. You mean you would try to forgive me.

Elizabeth. Aye, but I would.

Essex. What would you have to forgive?
I have tried to love others. It's empty as ashes.

Elizabeth. What others?

Essex. No one.

Elizabeth. What others?

Essex. Everyone.

Elizabeth. Everyone?

Essex. That too has been your triumph! What is a cry
Of love in the night, when I am sick and angry
And care not? I would rather hear your mocking
laughter—
Your laughter—mocking at me—defying me
Ever to be happy—with another.

Elizabeth. You have done this to me?

Essex. You have done this to me! You've made it all
empty
Away from you! And with you too!

Elizabeth. And me—what of me while you were gone?

Essex. If we
   Must quarrel when we meet, why then, for God's sake,
   Let us quarrel. At least we can quarrel together.

Elizabeth. I think if we are to love we must love and be
     silent—
   For when we speak—

Essex. I'll be silent then.
   And you shall speak—

Elizabeth.
     [*Her finger to her lips*]
   Hush!

Essex. If you would sometimes heed me—

Elizabeth. Hush!

Essex. Only sometimes—only when I'm right. If you would
   Say to yourself that even your lover might be
   Right sometimes, instead of flying instantly
   Into opposition as soon as I propose
   A shift in policy!

Elizabeth. But you were wrong! You were wrong!
   A campaign into Spain's pure madness, and to strike at
     Flanders
   At the same moment . . . think of the drain in men
   And the drain on the treasury, and the risks we'd run
   Of being unable to follow success or failure
   For lack of troops and money . . . !

Essex.
     [*Letting his arms fall*]
   But why lack money . . .

And why lack men? There's no richer country in Europe
In men or money than England! It's this same ancient
Unprofitable niggardliness that pinches pennies
And wastes a world of treasure! You could have all
    Spain,
And Spain's dominions in the new world, an empire
Of untold wealth . . . and you forgo them because
You fear to lay new taxes!

Elizabeth. I have tried that . . .
    And never yet has a warlike expedition
    Brought me back what it cost!

Essex. You've tried half-measures . . .
    Raids on the Spanish coast, a few horsemen sent
    Into Flanders and out again, always defeating
    Yourself by trying too little! What I plead for
    Is to be bold once, just once, give the gods a chance
    To be kind to us . . . walk through this cobweb Philip
    And take his lazy cities with a storm
    Of troops and ships!
    If we are to trifle we might better sit
    At home forever, and rot!

Elizabeth. Here we sit then,
    And rot, as you put it.

Essex. I'm sorry . . .

Elizabeth. It seems to me
    We rot to some purpose here. I have kept the peace
    And kept my people happy and prosperous.

Essex. And at what a price . . .
    What a cowardly price!

Elizabeth. I am no coward either.
    It requires more courage not to fight than to fight
    When one is surrounded by hasty hot-heads, urging
    Campaigns in all directions.

Essex. Think of the name
    You will leave . . . They will set you down in histories
    As the weasel queen who fought and ran away,
    Who struck one stroke, preferably in the back,
    And then turned and ran . . .

Elizabeth. Is it my fame you think of,
    Or your own, my lord? Have you not built your name
    High enough? I gave you your chance at Cadiz,
    And you took it, and now there's no name in all England
    Like yours to the common people. When we ride in
        the streets
    Together, it's Essex they cheer and not their queen.
    What more would you have?

Essex. Is it for fear of me
    And this hollow cheering you hold me back from Spain?

Elizabeth. It's because I believe in peace, and have no faith
    In wars or what wars win.

Essex. You do not fear me?

Elizabeth. Yes, and I fear you, too! You believe yourself
    Fitter to be king than I to be queen! You are flattered
    By this crying of your name by fools! You trust me no
        more
    Than you'd trust . . . Penelope . . . or any other woman
    To be in power! You believe you'd rule England better
    Because you're a man!

Essex. That last is true. I would.
　And that doesn't mean I don't love you . . . remember
　　that.
　I love you, my queen, madly, beyond all measure,
　But that's not to say I cannot see where you fail
　As sovereign here, and see that why you fail
　When you do is merely because a woman cannot
　Act and think like a man.

Elizabeth. Act and think like a man . . . !
　Why should I
　Think like a man when a woman's thinking's wiser?
　What do you plan? To depose me, take over the king-
　　dom?

Essex.
　[*Smiling*]
　You are a touchy queen.

Elizabeth. I had bad bringing up.
　I was never sure who my mother was going to be
　Next day, and it shook my nerves.

Essex. You're your father's daughter,
　I'll swear to that. I can tell by your inconstancy.

Elizabeth. I wish you had need
　To fear for me . . . or at any rate that I'd never
　Let you see how much I'm yours.

Essex. But why?

Elizabeth. Tell me, my dear,
　Do you tire of me . . . do I wear upon you a little?

Essex. Never.

Elizabeth. But you'd have to say that, you can see . . .
   You'd have to say it, because you wouldn't hurt me,
   And because I'm your queen. And so I'll never know
   Until everyone else has known and is laughing at me,
   When I've lost you. Wait, let me say this, please . . .
     When the time
   Does come and I seem old to you, and you love
   Someone else, tell me, tell me the first . . .

Essex. You are not old! I will not have you old!

Elizabeth. Will you do that, in all kindness, in memory
   Of great love past? No. You could not, could not.
   It's not in a man to be kind that way, nor in
   A woman to take it kindly. I think I'd kill you,
   In a first blind rage.

Essex. Kill me when I can say it.

Elizabeth. Love, will you let me
   Say one more thing that will hurt you?

Essex. Anything.

Elizabeth. Your blood's on fire to lead a new command
   Now that you've won so handsomely in Spain,
   And when I need a general anywhere
   You'll ask to go. Don't ask it . . . and don't go.
   You're better here in London.

Essex. Was this all you wanted?

   [*Stepping back*]

   To make me promise this?

Elizabeth.

  [*Softly*]

  Not for myself,
  I swear it, not because I think you reckless
  With men and money, though I do think that,
  Not because you might return in too much triumph
  And take my kindgom from me, which I can imagine,
  And not because I want to keep you here
  And hate to risk you, though that's also true . . .
  But rather . . . and for this you must forgive me . . .
  Because you're more a poet than general . . .
  And I fear you might fail, and lose what you have gained
  If you went again.

Essex. God's death! Whom would you send?

Elizabeth. I asked you not to be angry.

Essex. Not to be angry!
  How do you judge a leader except by whether
  He wins or loses? Was it by chance, do you think,
  That I took Cadiz?

Elizabeth. Very well. You shall go.
  Go if you will. Only I love you and I say
  What would be wiser.

Essex. You choose the one thing I must have
  And ask me not to ask it! No. Forgive me.

Elizabeth. I'll not say it again.

Essex. But if I'm more poet than
  General, why poets make better generals
  Than generals do, on occasion.

Elizabeth. You've proved it so
  One more than one occasion.
    [*A clock strikes. She rises*]
  There's the chime.
  The council's waiting, and we shall hear about Ireland,
  If Cecil has his way. One thing remember,
  You must not go to Ireland.

Essex. No. That's a war
  I'm content to miss.

Elizabeth. Thank God for that much then. I've been afraid
  Ireland might tempt you. And one more thing remem-
    ber . . .
  I'll have to oppose you in the council on
  The Spanish hostages . . . You'll have your way . . .
  But I'll have to oppose you, lest they think it's your
    kingdom . . .
  Will you understand . . . ?

Essex. I'll play my part perfectly.
    [*He kisses her hand, then her lips*]

Elizabeth. Now what can come between us, out of heaven
    or hell,
  Or Spain or England?

Essex. Nothing . . . never again.

CURTAIN

ACT ONE

Scene III

Scene: *The same as Scene I, save that the doors to the council room have been thrown back, revealing a chair of state for the queen, and beneath it a table at which her councillors sit. The* Guards *are placed at left and right. The* Queen *sits in her chair.* Raleigh, Cecil, Essex, Burghley, Howard, *and one or two others are at the table. The queen's* Jester *sits cross-legged on at mat.* Burghley *is speaking.*

Burghley. It is quite true we shall have an enemy
  In Spain while Philip lives and his state has power
  To wage war on us, but there is little he can do
  Against an island as well walled as ours.
  He has tried his best, and failed. My lord of Essex
  Says it costs more to fight Spain every year
  In this chronic fashion than it would to throw
  A challenge down, raid the Escurial
  And sack the empire. With this the weight of the council
  Disagrees, and we may hold it settled
  That our tactics continue defensive till the queen
  Rule otherwise.

Elizabeth. You'll wait some time for that.

Burghley. But in the matter
  Of the Spanish ransoms it appears to me
  Lord Essex has right on his side. The English soldiers
  Who brought their prisoners home from the last raid
  Deserve their prize money. By immemorial custom
  The ransom belongs to the taker of the prisoner
  And not to the state.

35

Elizabeth. That I intend to change,
    That same immemorial custom. I thought you had been
    Informed, Lord Burghley, that it was my will
    That the Spanish ransoms be paid to the treasury.

Burghley. But my lord of Essex . . .

Elizabeth. My lord of Essex does not speak for me.
    I was told this expedition into Spain
    Would be paid for in booty. The cost, so far,
    Has not been made up; and since there are Spanish
        nobles
    To be ransomed, I think they should pay it.

Essex. Your Majesty,
    I do not speak for myself . . . I took no prizes . . .
    But only to redeem my word. I assured
    My followers that they would have for their own
    Whatever ransoms they earned.

Elizabeth. And by what right
    Did you make this promise?

Essex. By this same ancient custom
    Of which Lord Burghley speaks. A custom so well
    Established there's not a soldier anywhere
    But takes it for granted.

Elizabeth. Your word is pledged?

Essex. It is.

Elizabeth.
    [*Smiling*]
    And if the state should confiscate these ransoms
    You would make them good to the captors?

Essex. No. To speak frankly . . .

   [*He smiles*]

   No.

Elizabeth. Then the issue lies between the queen
   And her soldiers . . . and your lordship need feel no
   Concern in the matter.

Essex. When I made these promises
   I spoke for Your Majesty . . . or believed I did.

Elizabeth. Master Cecil, advise us; am I as queen
   Bound by Lord Essex' promise?

Cecil. No, my liege;
   It is well-known a regent may repudiate
   Treaty or word of a subject officer.
   The throne is not bound.

Essex. If it comes to repudiation,
   The throne can, of course, repudiate what it likes.
   But not without breaking faith.

Elizabeth. I fear we are wrong, Sir Robert;
   And what has been promised for me and in my name
   By my own officer, my delegate in the field,
   I must perform. The men may have their ransoms.
   The state will take its loss; for this one time
   Only, and this the last. In the future a prisoner
   Is held in the name of the state, and whatever price
   Is on his head belongs to the crown. Our action
   Here is made no precedent. What further
   Business is there before us?

Cecil. There is one perpetual
　　Subject, Your Majesty, which we take up
　　Time after time, and always leave unsettled,
　　But which has come to a place where we must act
　　One way or another. Tyrone's rebellion in Ulster
　　Is no longer a smouldering coal, but a running fire
　　Spreading north to south. We must conquer Ireland
　　Finally now, or give over what we have won.
　　Ireland's not Spain.

Elizabeth. I grant you.

The Fool. I also grant you.

Elizabeth. Be quiet, fool.

The Fool. Be quiet, fool.
　　　　[*He slaps his own mouth*]

Elizabeth. Lord Burghley,
　　You shall speak first. What's to be done in Ireland?

Burghley. If my son is right, and I believe him to be,
　　We can bide our time no longer there. They have
　　Some help from Spain, and will have more, no doubt,
　　And the central provinces are rising. We must
　　Stamp out this fire or lose the island

Elizabeth. This means
　　Men, money, ships?

Burghley. Yes, madam.

Cecil. And more than that . . .
　　A leader.

Elizabeth. What leader?

Cecil. A Lord Protector
  Of Ireland who can carry sword and fire
  From one end of the bogs to the other, and have English
     law
  On Irish rebels till there are no rebels.
  We've governed Ireland with our left hand, so far,
  And our hold is slipping. The man who goes there now
  Must be one fitted to master any field . . .
  The best we have.

Elizabeth. What man? Name one.

Cecil. We should send,
  Unless I am wrong, a proved and able general,
  Of no less rank, say, than Lord Howard here,
  Lord Essex, Sir Walter Raleigh, Knollys, or Mount-
     joy . . .
  This is no slight matter, to keep or lose the island.

Elizabeth. I grant you that also.

The Fool. I also grant you. Be quiet,
  Fool!
     [*He slaps his mouth*]

Elizabeth. I ask you for one and you name a dozen,
  Sir Robert.

Raleigh. Why should one go alone, if it comes
  To that? Why not two expeditions, one
  To Dublin, one into Ulster, meeting half-way?

Elizabeth. Are there two who could work together?

Cecil. Knollys and Mountjoy.
  They are friends and of one house.

Essex. Yes, of my house.

Elizabeth. Essex, whom would you name?

Essex. Why, since Lord Cecil
Feels free to name my followers, I shall feel free
To name one or two of his . . .

Elizabeth. In other words,
You would rather Knollys and Mountjoy did not go?

Essex. I would rather they stayed in England, as Sir
Robert knows.
I have need of them here. But I will spare one of them
If Lord Cecil will let Sir Francis Vere go with him.

Elizabeth. Let Vere and Knollys go.

Cecil. Lord Essex names
Sir Francis Vere because he knows full well
I cannot spare him, my liege.

Elizabeth. Is this appointment
To wait for all our private bickerings?
Can we send no man of worth to Ireland, merely
Because to do so would weaken some house or party
Here at court?

The Fool. Your Majesty has said . . .

Elizabeth. Be quiet . . .

The Fool. Fool!

Elizabeth. Be quiet!

The Fool. Fool!

Elizabeth. Be quiet!

> [*The* FOOL *forms the word "fool" with his lips, but makes no sound*]

Cecil.

> [*Rising*]

I hope I betray no secret, Sir Walter,
If I tell the council that I spoke with you
Before the session, and asked you if you would go
Into Ireland if the queen requested it . . . and that you said
Yes, should the queen desire it.

Burghley. That would answer.

Cecil. But I believe, and Sir Walter believes, there should be
More than one hand in this . . . that if he goes
Lord Essex should go with him.

Elizabeth. With him?

Essex. In what
Capacity?

Cecil. Leading an equal command. Two generals
Of coeval power, landing north and south
And meeting to crush Tyrone.

Essex. Would you set up
Two Lord Protectors?

Cecil. It was my thought that we name
Raleigh as Lord Protector.

Essex. And I under him?

Cecil. Since the Azores adventure
  Which my Lord Essex led, and which came off
  A little lamer than could be wished, but in which
  Sir Walter showed to very great advantage,
  It has seemed to me that Raleigh should receive
  First place if he served in this.

Essex.
  [*Rising*]
  This is deliberate,
  An insult planned!

Cecil. It is no insult, my lord,
  But plain truth. I speak for the good of the state.

Essex. You lie! You have never spoken here or elsewhere
  For any cause but your own!

Elizabeth. No more of this!

Essex. The good of the state! Good God!
  Am I to swallow this from a clerk, a pen-pusher . . .
  To be told I may have second place, for the good of the
      state?

Cecil. Were you not wrong at the Azores?

Essex. No, by God!
  And you know it!

Elizabeth. Whoever makes you angry has won
  Already, Essex!

Essex. They have planned this!

Cecil. I say no more.
  Raleigh will go to Ireland as Lord Protector

And go alone, if the queen asks it of him,
And since you will not go.

Essex. I have not said
I would not go. But if I were to go I would go
Alone, as Lord Protector!

Elizabeth. That you will not.
I have some word in this.

Essex. If this pet rat
Lord Cecil wishes to know my mind about him,
And it seems he does, he shall have it! How he first crept
Into favor here I know not, but the palace is riddled
With his spying and burrowing and crawling under-
    ground!
He has filled the court with his rat friends, very gentle,
White, squeaking, courteous folk, who show their teeth
Only when cornered; who smile at you, speak you fair
And spend their nights gnawing the floors and chairs
Out from under us all!

Elizabeth. My lord!

Essex. I am
Not the gnawing kind, nor will I speak fair
To those who don't mean me well . . . no, nor to those
To whom I mean no good! I say frankly here,
Yes, to their faces, that Cecil and Walter Raleigh
Have made themselves my enemies because
They cannot brook greatness or power in any but
Themselves! And I say this to them . . . and to the
    world . . .
I, too, have been ambitious, as all men are

Who bear a noble mind, but if I rise
It will be by my own effort, and not by dragging
Better men down through intrigue! I admit
Sir Walter Raleigh's skill as a general
And Cecil's statecraft! I could work with them freely
And cheerfully, but every time I turn
My back they draw their knives! When Cecil left Eng-
     land
I guarded his interests as I would my own
Because he asked me to . . . but when I left,
And left my affairs in his hands . . . on my return
I found my plans and my friends out in the rain
Along with the London beggars!

Cecil. I did my best . . .

Essex. Aye . . . the best for yourself! For the good of the
     state!

Raleigh. If Lord Essex wishes
     To say he is my enemy, very well . . .
     He is my enemy.

Essex. But you were mine first . . .
     And I call the gods to witness you would be my friend
     Still, if I'd had my way! I take it hard
     That here, in the queen's council, where there should be
     Magnanimous minds if anywhere, there is still
     No trust or friendship!

Elizabeth. I take it hard that you
     Should quarrel before me.

Essex. Would you have us quarrel

Behind your back? It suits them all too well
To quarrel in secret and knife men down in the dark!

Burghley. This is fantastic, my lord. There has been no
    knifing.
Let us come to a decision. We were discussing
The Irish protectorate.

Cecil. And as for Ireland,
    I am willing to leave that in Lord Essex' hands
To do as he decides.

Essex. Send your Sir Walter
    To Ireland as Protector! And be damned to it!

Cecil. As the queen wishes.
    It is a task both difficult and dangerous.
I cannot blame Lord Essex for refusing
To risk his fame there.

Essex. There speaks the white rat again!
    Yet even a rat should know I have never refused
A task out of fear! I said I would not go
As second in command!

Cecil. Then would you go
    As Lord Protector?

Elizabeth. You have named your man . . .
    Sir Walter Raleigh.

Raleigh. I'll go if Essex goes.

Essex. What! Is our Raleigh
    Afraid to go alone?

Raleigh. I don't care for it . . .
    And neither does our Essex!

Essex. Why, what is this
  That hangs over Ireland? Is it haunted, this Ireland?
  Is it a kind of hell where men are damned
  If they set foot on it? I've never seen the place,
  But if it's a country like other countries, with people
  Like other people in it, it's nothing to be
  Afraid of, more than France or Wales or Flanders
  Or anywhere else!

Cecil. We hear you say so.

Essex. If I
  Am challenged to go to Ireland, then, Christ, I'll go!
  Give me what men and horse I need, and put me
  In absolute charge, and if I fail to bring
  This Tyrone's head back with me, and put the rebellion
  To sleep forever, take my sword from me
  And break it . . . I'll never use it again!

Elizabeth. Will you listen . . . ?

Essex. They've challenged me!

Elizabeth. If you volunteer
  To go to Ireland there is none to stop you.
  You are first soldier here, first in acclaim
  And in achievement, but since the decision lies
  With yourself alone, reflect a little.

Essex. My queen,
  I can see that Raleigh and Cecil have set themselves
  To bait me into Ireland! They know and I know
  That Ireland has been deadly to any captain
  Who risked his fortunes there; moreover, once

I'm gone they think to strip me here at home
Ruin me both ways! And I say to them "Try it!"
There are men who are greater than Ireland or their
     chicane . . .
Since this is a challenge I go, and go alone,
And return victorious, and, by God, more of a problem
To Cecils and Raleighs than when I went!

    [*The* FOOL *rises and approaches* ESSEX *from behind*]

Burghley. If Essex
Will go, it solves our problem, Your Majesty.
We could hardly refuse that offer.

Elizabeth. No.

Essex. I will go,
And I will return! Mark me!

The Fool.
    [*Touching* ESSEX]
My lord! My lord!

Essex.
    [*Turning suddenly with an instinctive motion that sweeps the*
        FOOL *to the floor*]
Take your hands off me! You touch me for a fool?
    [*He helps the* FOOL *up*]
Get up!

The Fool. Do not go to Ireland!

Essex.
    [*Impatiently*]
You too?

The Fool. Because, my lord, I come from Ireland.
   All the best fools come from Ireland, but only
   A very great fool will go there.

Essex. Faugh!

The Fool. It's not too late yet!

Elizabeth. Break up the council, my lords.
   We meet tomorrow.

Burghley. And this is decided?

Essex. Yes!

Elizabeth. Yes, if you wish it. Go now.
      [*The council rises when the queen does and files out silently,
         leaving* ESSEX *and* ELIZABETH]
   You should have had
   The fool's brain and he yours! You would have bettered
   By the exchange.

Essex. I thank you kindly, lady.

Elizabeth. What malicious star
   Danced in my sky when you were born, I wonder?

Essex. What malicious star danced in the sky
   Of Ireland, you should ask.

Elizabeth. Oh, my dear,
   You are a child in council. I saw them start
   To draw you into this, and tried to warn you . . .
   But it was no use.

Essex. They drew me into nothing.
   I saw their purpose and topped it with my own.
   Let them believe they've sunk me.

Elizabeth. You will withdraw.
  I'll countermand this.

Essex. And give them the laugh on me?
  I'll have the laugh on them yet.

Elizabeth. Better they should laugh
  A little now than laugh at you forever.

Essex. And why not win in Ireland?

Elizabeth. No man wins there.
  You're so dazzled
  With the chance to lead an army you'd follow the devil
  In an assault on heaven.

Essex. No, but I'd lead him.
  Heaven is always taken by storm. That's one thing
  The devil doesn't know. Ireland is only
  A country, and this is superstition.

Elizabeth. I know.
  You were quite right. I thought so as you said it.
  Only somehow here in my breast something con
     stricts . . .
  Is it the heart grows heavy? I must let you go . . .
  And I'll never see you again.

Essex. Mistrust all these
  Forebodings. When they prove correct we remember
     them,
  But when they're wrong we forget them. They mean
     nothing.
  Remember this when I'm back and all turns out well . . .
  That you felt all would turn out badly.

Elizabeth. Oh, my love,
Come touch me, tell me all will happen well.

Essex. And so it will.

Elizabeth. Do you want to go?

Essex. Why yes . . .
And no. I've said I would and I will.

Elizabeth. It's not yet
Too late. There are no announcements made, no orders
Given. If you win, that will divide us . . .
And if you lose, that will divide us too.

Essex. I'll win, and it will not divide us. Is it so hard
To believe in me?

Elizabeth. No . . . I'll believe in you . . .
And even forgive you if you need it. Here.
My father gave me this ring . . . and told me if ever
He lost his temper with me, to bring it to him
And he'd forgive me. And so it saved my life . . .
Long after, when he'd forgotten, long after, when
One time he was angry.

Essex. Darling, if ever
You're angry rings won't help.

Elizabeth. Yes, but it would.
I'd think of you as you are now, and it would.
Take it.

Essex. I have no pledge from you. I'll take it
To remember you in absence.

Elizabeth. Take it for a better reason. Take it because

The years are long, and full of sharp, wearing days
That wear out what we are and what we have been
And change us into people we do not know,
Living among strangers. Lest you and I who love
Should wake some morning strangers and enemies
In an alien world, far off; take my ring, my lover.

Essex. You fear
You will not always love me?

Elizabeth. No, that you
Will not love me, and will not let me love you.
    [*She puts the ring on his finger*]

CURTAIN

ELIZABETH THE QUEEN
ACT TWO

ACT TWO

Scene I

Scene: *The queen's study.* Penelope *is sitting reading. The* Fool *enters. She does not see him.*

The Fool. Sh! Make no noise.

Penelope. What do you mean?

The Fool. Silence! Quiet!

Penelope. I am silent, fool.

The Fool. You silent? And even as you say it you are talking!

Penelope. You began it.

The Fool. Began what?

Penelope. Talking.

The Fool. Oh, no. Talking began long before my time. It was a woman began it.

Penelope. Her name?

The Fool. Penelope, I should judge.

Penelope. Fool.

The Fool.
    [*Looking away*]
No, for with this same Penelope began also beauty and courage and tenderness and faith . . . all that a man could desire or a woman offer . . . and all that this early Penelope began has a later Penelope completed.

55

Penelope.

[*Rising*]

It lacked only this . . . that the court fool should make love to me.

The Fool. I am sorry to have been laggard. But truly I have never found you alone before.

Penelope. How lucky I've been!

The Fool. Are you angered?

Penelope. At what?

The Fool. At my loving you.

Penelope. I've learned to bear nearly everything.

The Fool. A lover's absence?

Penelope. Among other things.

The Fool. The presence of suitors undesired?

Penelope. That, too.

The Fool. I am not a suitor, my lady. I ask nothing. I know where your heart lies. It is with my lord Essex in Ireland. I do not love you.

Penelope. Good.

The Fool. I lied to you. I do love you.

Penelope. I am sorry.

The Fool. You will not laugh at me?

Penelope. No.

The Fool. Then there is yet some divinity in the world . . .

while a woman can still be sorry for one who loves her
without return.

Penelope. A woman is sadly aware that when a man loves
her it makes a fool of him.

The Fool. And if a fool should love a woman . . . would it
not make a man of him?

Penelope. No, but doubly a fool, I fear.

The Fool. And the women . . . how of the women?

Penelope. They have been fools, too.

The Fool. The more fool I, I tried to save Lord Essex from
Ireland . . . but he needs must go . . . the more fool he.

Penelope. Let us not talk of that.

The Fool. May I kiss you?

Penelope. No.

The Fool. Your hand?

Penelope. Yes.

    [*He kisses her hand*]

The Fool. I thank you.

    [*She touches his fool's cap gently with her hand*]

Penelope. The more fool you, poor boy.

    [ROBERT CECIL *enters from the left*]

Cecil. This is hardly a seemly pastime, Mistress Gray.

Penelope. And are you now the judge of what is seemly,
Sir Robert?

Cecil.
> [*To the* Fool]

Be off with you!

> [*To* Penelope]

The queen is expecting Master Bacon here?

> [*The* Fool *goes*]

Penelope. I am set to wait for him.

Cecil. You will not be needed.

Penelope. Excellent.

> [*She goes out right, passing* Raleigh, *who enters*]

Cecil. This Bacon keeps himself close. I have been unable to speak with him. She has this news?

Raleigh. Yes.

Cecil. She believes it?

Raleigh. Burghley himself believes it.

Cecil. Then she does.

Raleigh. Beyond question.

> [*The curtains part at the left and* Bacon *enters*]

Cecil. Good-morrow, Master Bacon.

Bacon. And to you, my lords.

Cecil. I have sent everywhere for you, sir, this three hours . . . and perhaps it was not altogether by accident that I could not find you.

Bacon. I was not at home. You must forgive me.

Cecil. You are here to see the queen?

Bacon.

> [*Bowing*]

The queen has also been good enough to send for me.

Cecil. It was my wish to speak with you first . . . and it is my opinion that it will be the better for all of us, if I do so now . . . late as it is.

Bacon. I am but barely on time, gentlemen.

Cecil. You need answer one question only. You have been in correspondence with Lord Essex in Ireland?

Bacon. Perhaps.

Cecil. The queen has this morning received news warning her that Lord Essex is allied with the Irish rebels and is even now leading his army back to England to usurp her throne. Had you heard this?

Bacon. No.

Cecil. Do you credit it?

Bacon. It is your own scheme, I believe.

Cecil. That Essex should rebel against the queen?

Bacon. Even so.

Raleigh. You accuse us of treason?

Bacon. If the queen were aware of certain matters she would herself accuse you of treason.

Cecil. What matters?

Bacon. I prefer that the queen should question me.

Cecil. Look to yourself, Master Bacon. If you intend to

accuse any man of the suppression of letters written by Essex to the queen, or of the suppression of letters sent by the queen to Essex, you will be unable to prove these assertions and you will argue yourself very neatly into the Tower.

Bacon. My lord ... I had no such business in mind.

Raleigh. Then what? ...

Bacon. I hope I can keep my own counsel. The truth is, my lords, you are desperate men. You have overreached yourselves, and if wind of it gets to the royal ears you are done.

Raleigh. We shall drag a few down with us if we are done, though, and you the first.

Cecil. You have but a poor estimate of me, Master Bacon. If you go in to the queen and reveal to her that her letters to Essex have not reached him ... as you mean to do ... the queen will then send for me, and I will send for Lord Essex' last letter to you, containing a plan for the capture of the city of London. It will interest you to know that I have read that letter and you are learned enough in the law to realize in what light you will stand as a witness should the queen see it.

Bacon. I think it is true, though, that if I go down I shall also drag a few with me, including those here present.

Cecil. I am not so sure of that, either. I am not unready for that contingency. But to be frank with you, it would be easier for both you and us if you were on our side.

Bacon. You must expect a man to side with his friends.

Cecil. And a man's friends . . . who are they? Those who can help him to what he wants.

Bacon. Not always.

Cecil. When he is wise. You have served Lord Essex well and I believe he has made you promises. But the moment Essex enters England in rebellion, he is doomed, and his friends with him.

Bacon. One word from the queen to him . . . one word from him to the queen . . . one word from me, revealing that their letters have been intercepted, and there can be no talk of rebellion. There has been some underhand traffic with the couriers between here and Ireland. Their letters have been lost, you have induced the queen to promulgate arbitrary orders . . . and since they are both proud, you have bred distrust in her and defiance in him. Your machinations have been so direct, so childish, so simple . . . and so simply exposed . . . that I wonder at you!

Cecil. My friend, a child could trip him. Not so simple as your own. I have news this morning that Lord Essex has already landed in England and set up his standard here. He is a rebel, and when a man is once a rebel, do you think there will be any careful inquiry into how he happened to become one?

Bacon. Essex in England!

Cecil. In England.

Raleigh. And has neglected to disband his army.

Cecil. You speak of explanations between the queen and

Essex. Unless you betray us there will be no explanations. They are at war and will never meet again.

Bacon. That is, if your plan succeed.

Cecil.

[*Standing aside*]

Very well, then. Go in. You have chosen your master I have done with you.

Bacon.

[*Not moving*]

And if I say nothing?

Cecil. Then . . . whatever you have been promised, whatever you have desired, that you shall have. There is no place in the courts you could not fill. You shall have your choice. If you need excuse, no-one should know better than you that this Essex is a danger to the state, a danger to the queen, a danger to liberty.

Bacon. If I need excuse I shall find one for myself.

[*There is a pause. Then the curtain parts to the right and* PENELOPE *enters. She holds the curtain back*]

Penelope. Yes, Your Majesty; he is here.

Elizabeth. Why was I not told?

[*She enters*]

Is this an ante-chamber, Sir Robert? Am I never to look out of my room without seeing you?

Cecil. Your pardon, Your Majesty. I was just going.

Elizabeth. Then go. You need not pause to explain why you came. I am weary of your face!

Cecil. Yes, Your Majesty.

[CECIL *and* RALEIGH *bow and depart*]

Elizabeth. I have heard that you are a shrewd man, Master
    Bacon.

Bacon. Flattery, Majesty, flattery.

Elizabeth. I have heard it,
    And in a sort I believe it. Tell me one thing . . .
    Are you Cecil's friend?

Bacon. I have never been.

Elizabeth. He is a shrewd man; he's
    A man to make a friend of if you'd stand well
    In the court, sir.

Bacon. It may be so.

Elizabeth. Why are you not
    His friend then?

Bacon. We are not on the same side.

Elizabeth. You follow Lord Essex?

Bacon. Since I have known him.

Elizabeth. There's
    A dangerous man to follow.

Bacon. Lord Essex?

Elizabeth. Lord Essex.

Bacon. I am sorry, madam,
    If I have displeased you.

Elizabeth. You have displeased me.

Bacon. I repeat then . . .
   I am sorry.

Elizabeth. You will change, then? You will forget
   This Essex of yours?

Bacon. If you ask it . . . if there is reason . . .

Elizabeth. Well, there is reason! He has taken up arms
   Against me in Ireland.

Bacon. You are sure of this?

Elizabeth. I have reports. Is it so hard to believe?

Bacon. Without proofs, it is.

Elizabeth. I have proof.

Bacon. May I ask of what sort?

Elizabeth. Proof good enough. You know the punishment
   For treason? From what I have heard
   Of late both you and Essex should remember
   That punishment.

Bacon. Madam, for myself I have
   No need to fear, and if Lord Essex has
   I am more than mistaken in him.

Elizabeth. I am very sorry
   That I must do this . . . but all friends of Essex
   Go straightway to the Tower. I have sent for you
   To give you a last chance to change your mind
   Before this blow falls. Are you still his friend?

Bacon. Yes, Majesty.

Elizabeth. I am sorry for it.

Bacon. That is all?

Elizabeth. Why, no. You do not believe me?

Bacon. I do not.

Elizabeth. And why?

Bacon. I neither believe our Essex a rebel
　Nor that you believe so. If you intended to place me
　In the Tower . . . I would be in the Tower . . . and no
　　talk about it.

Elizabeth. You are shrewd indeed.

Bacon. I am Essex' friend.

Elizabeth. If that
　Were true . . . if I could speak to you . . . if there were
　　only
　The sound of one honest voice!
　. . . I must rule England,
　And they say he is rebel to me . . . and day and night,
　Waking, sleeping, in council, there is still always
　One thing crying out in me over and again . . .
　Waking and sleeping I hear it crying: He cannot,
　Cannot fail me! But I have written him my love
　And he has not answered. What you know of this
　Answer me truly, truly . . . bitter or not,
　And you shall not lose!

Bacon. He has not answered?

Elizabeth. No.

Bacon. If I
　Knew why I would know much. Have you angered
　　him . . .
　Sent arbitrary orders?

Elizabeth. I have ordered him to disband
His forces and return. I have cut off
Revenue and supplies.

Bacon. But this was rash . . .
To send a popular leader out with an army
And then check him suddenly, heap disgrace upon
  him . . .
He has great pride.

Elizabeth.
  [*Getting up*]
He has rebelled then?
I wrote him lovingly.

Bacon. And he answered? . . .

Elizabeth. Nothing.

Bacon. That could not be excused.

Elizabeth. And it cannot be. It's true. It will not be!

Bacon. Dear queen, I fear
I have turned you against him!

Elizabeth. No, no! I needed that!

Bacon. And if there were something wrong . . .
Some misunderstanding? . . .

Elizabeth. No, no . . . don't try comfort now . . .
He had my letters. That could not go wrong.
Did he not have my letters?

Bacon. Could it be otherwise?

Elizabeth. You would know that. You would know if he
  had not.
You've had word from him?

Bacon. Yes.

Elizabeth. He has written you,
But not me! Or are you traitor to him also? . . .
I think you are! I think you lie to me! I am
Encompassed by lies! I think you, too, betray him . . .
But subtly, with infinite craft, making me believe
First that you would not wrong him! No, no . . . I'm
   gone mad
Pacing my room, pacing the room of my mind.
They say a woman's mind is an airless room,
Sunless and airless, where she must walk alone
Saying he loves me, loves me, loves me not,
And has never loved me. The world goes by, all shadows,
And there are voices, all echoes till he speaks . . .
And there's no light till his presence makes a light
There in that room. But I am a queen. Where I walk
Is a hall of torture, where the curious gods bring all
Their racks and gyves, and stretch me there to writhe
Till I cry out. They watch me with eyes of iron
Waiting to hear what I cry! I am crying now . . .
Listen, you gods of iron! He never loved me . . .
He wanted my kingdom only . . .
Loose me and let me go! I am yet a queen . . .
That I have! That he will not take from me.
I shall be queen, and walk his room no more.
He thought to break me down by not answering . . .
Break me until I'd say, I'm all yours . . . what I am
And have, all yours! That I will never, never,
Never say. I'm not broken yet.

Bacon. Nor will be, majesty.

Elizabeth. We must not follow him.
We must forget him, break him as he would break us,
Bow that bright head . . . I shall be as I was.
See him no more, my friend,
He walks on quicksand. Avoid him.

Bacon. Yes, my queen.

Elizabeth. Go, my friend.
You have done well. I trust you.

Bacon. I thank Your Majesty.

> [*He goes out.* ELIZABETH *claps her hands twice. After a moment*
> CAPTAIN ARMIN *enters*]

Elizabeth. Captain Armin, keep a watch on Master Bacon,
On his house and on his correspondence.
I wish to know all he knows.

Armin. Yes, Your Majesty.

Elizabeth. Wait. I have found you true of word,
And sure of hand. Moreover, you can keep counsel—

> [ARMIN *bows. She beckons him to come to her. He does so*]

What we say now is forever secret between us—
Between us two—not one other.

Armin. I'll hold it so.

Elizabeth. It is reported there is an army risen
Against me—

Armin. God forbid!

Elizabeth. It is so reported. The rebellion I speak of's the
force
Lord Essex has brought back with him from Ireland.

I wish to make this preparation for it: Whatever orders
You receive from your superiors, whatever broils
Occur, he is to have free access to my presence.

Armin. There would be danger to your person, madame.

Elizabeth. I will risk that.

Armin. You would be hostage if he were in command.

Elizabeth. Be ready for danger—and if need be, death.

Armin. Yes, Majesty.

> [*He goes out.* ELIZABETH *stands motionless for a moment.
> There is a sudden burst of girls' laughter in an adjoining
> room, and the* FOOL *runs in with a garment in his hand.
> Three* GIRLS *run after him, the foremost tripping him
> so that he falls in a corner and is instantly pounced
> upon by all three*]

Mary.
> [*Entering*]

Thief! Thief! Stop thief!

Ellen. Kill the slobber thief! Fall on him!

Tressa. Can a maid not keep a silk smock?

The Fool. Help! Salvage! Men-at-arms to the rescue! I am
boarded by pirates!
> [*They tickle him*]

Ellen. Tear it from him! He will exhibit it!

Tressa. No, no! Don't tear it!

The Fool. If you sit on me in that fashion, darling, you will
regret it. There will be issue!

Ellen. What issue?

The Fool. Twins! Seven or eight!

> [ELLEN *slaps him*]

Mary. Rise! Rise quickly! The queen is here. Rise!

> [*They all get up in confusion*]

Tressa. We are sorry, Your Majesty.

> ELIZABETH *looks at them without seeing them and goes out to her bedroom*]

Ellen. What is it? She seemed not to see.

Mary. It's not like her not to strike us.

Tressa. We'll be whipped.

The Fool. No, no. She strikes instantly or not at all.

Tressa. Give me that.

> [*She snatches her smock from the* FOOL]

Mary. Come.

> [*They tiptoe out*]

CURTAIN

ACT TWO

SCENE II

SCENE: *The interior of Essex' tent on the coast of England.* ESSEX
sits in the light of a candle, reading dispatches. A GUARD
stands in the shadow. MARVEL, *an aide, enters.*

Marvel. There is a courier from the queen, my lord.

Essex. At last, then.

Marvel. You will see him at once?

Essex. Yes . . . Wait. Bring him in and stay here while I
read the dispatches. If I give orders to torture or kill
him, show no surprise. You understand?

Marvel. You will not torture him?

Essex. Am I not tortured? And you, too, sirrah. You will
remember?

The Guard. Yes, my lord.

Essex. Good.

> [MARVEL *goes out.* ESSEX *rises and stands out of the light,*
> *waiting.* MARVEL *enters with the* COURIER, *who falls*
> *on his knee before* ESSEX]

The Courier. My lord of Essex?

Essex. Yes.

Courier. Dispatches from the queen.

Essex. When did you leave London?

Courier. Four days ago, my lord. We were delayed.

Essex. What delayed you?

Courier. Robbers.

Essex. And they took what from you?

Courier. Our horses and money.

Essex. And the letters? . . .

Courier. Were returned to me untouched.

Essex. When did this happen?

Courier. This side of the ford. There were four armed men against us two.

Essex. Give me the letters.
  [*The* Courier *does so.* Essex *reads briefly*]
This is all?

Courier. Yes, my lord.

Essex. You are sure you have lost nothing?

Courier. Indeed yes, my lord. There was but one missive and the seal was returned unbroken. The cut-throats told us they cared the less about our letters for they could not read.

Essex. You are a clever liar, sirrah, and you are the third liar who has come that same road to me from London. You are the third liar to tell this same tale. You shall pay for being the third.

Courier. My lord, I have not lied to you.

Essex. Take his weapons from him, lieutenant.
  [Marvel *obeys*]

Set him against the post there. Not so gently. He shall lose his ears first and then his lying tongue.

Courier. Your lordship does not mean this?

Essex. And why not? We shall then cut him in pieces . . . But gradually, with infinite delicacy.

> [MARVEL *approaches the* COURIER *with a knife. The* GUARD *holds him*]

Courier. No, no, no, no! Oh, God! Oh, my lord! My lord!

Essex. What are you waiting for?

Marvel. We must tie him to the pole first, sir.

Essex. Then tie him!

Courier. No, no . . . oh, God, no! What do you want of me? I swear to you I haven't lied to you! I swear . . . ugh!

> [*He is choked*]

Essex. Let him speak. What do you swear?

Courier. My lord, I have not lied . . . I speak truth . . .

Essex. Tie him up.

Courier. Let me speak . . . I can . . . ugh . . .

Essex. Silence him. We know too well what you have done, sirrah. We need no evidence of that. What we ask is that you tell us who set you on . . . and your accomplices. Tell us this and I want no more of you. You shall have your freedom . . . and this . . .

> [*He tosses a clinking bag at his feet*]

Speak.

Courier. My lord, if I knew . . .

Essex. Bind him. Truss him up and cut him open. Dispense
with these niceties. Have you no knife?
[*He is bound*]
We have heard enough! Take out his tongue!
[*They approach him. He becomes calm*]

Courier. My lord, I am not a coward, though it may seem
to you
I am, for I have cried out . . . but I cried out
Not so much for pain or fear of pain
But to know this was Lord Essex, whom I have loved
And who tortures innocent men.

Essex. Come, silence him!

Courier. Come then. I am innocent. If my lord Essex
Is as I have believed him, he will not hurt me;
If he will hurt me, then he is not as I
And many thousands believe him, who have loved him,
And I shall not mind much dying.
[*A pause*]

Essex. Let him go.
[*They unbind the* COURIER]
I thought my letters had been tampered with.
You'd tell me if it were so.

Courier. My honored lord,
By all the faith I have, and most of it's yours,
I'd rather serve you well and lose in doing it
Than serve you badly and gain. If something I've done
Has crossed you or worked you ill I'm enough punished
Only knowing it.

Essex. This letter came
    From the queen's hands?

Courier. It is as I received it
    From the queen's hands.

Essex. There was no other?

Courier. No other.

Essex. Take this and go.
    [*He tosses the bag to the* Courier]

Courier. I have brought misfortune . . .

Essex. You bring good news. We break camp tomorrow for
    London . . . Go . . . take that news with you. They'll
    welcome you outside. Remain with my guard and return
    with us.
    [*The* Courier *goes out*]

Marvel. We march tomorrow?

Essex. Yes.

Marvel. Under orders?

Essex. No.
    [*He reads*]

"Lord Essex is required to disperse his men
And return to the capital straightway on his own
Recognizance, to give himself up."

Marvel. And nothing with this?

Essex. Give out the necessary orders, we shall
    Move at daybreak.

Marvel. Yes, my lord.

Essex. And it is
    As well it falls out this way! By right of name
    And power and popular voice this is my kingdom . . .
    This England under my feet, more mine than hers,
    As she shall learn. It is quite as well.

Marvel. There is no man
    But will think so. There is victory in your path,
    My lord. The London citizens will rise
    At the first breath of your name.

Essex. Yes . . . that I'm sure of.

Marvel. And with London in your hands . . . well . . . it's
    your world then . . .
    As far as you like.

Essex. And I am glad for England.
    She has lain fallow in fear too long! Her hills
    Shall have a spring of victory. Goodnight.

Marvel. Goodnight.

Essex. And for this order, I received it not.
    [*He tears the paper*]

CURTAIN

ACT TWO

Scene III

SCENE: *The council hall of Act I is cleared here for a court assembly. Those who attended the council are present, save for ESSEX, also the* FOOL, ELLEN, MARY, TRESSA, PENELOPE. BACON *and other* LORDS-AND-LADIES-IN-WAITING. BURGHLEY *and* CECIL *are standing to one side in earnest talk. Across from them a group made up of* RALEIGH, BACON, *the* FOOL *and a number of others.*

Burghley. These players should be put down with an iron hand. They have neither conscience nor morals. They will make any display for money. In my young days they were allowed only interludes and instructive entertainment. The queen has been too lax . . .

Cecil. Have you seen this play of Richard II?

Burghley. I see no plays.

Cecil. It's high treason. Richard is deposed in it. High treason.

Bacon. Treason to depose a king? Not if you succeed.

Cecil. No, but treason to teach treason.

Bacon. What is treason?

Raleigh. Said jesting Pilate.

Cecil. Is it not treason to depose a king?

Raleigh. What if it makes a king of you?

The Fool. It would then be treason not to have done it.

77

Bacon. The Fool is a Jesuit.

The Fool. In truth, he was deposed. It is treason to all his successors to deny it.

Bacon. An excellent Jesuit.

The Fool. What? I a Jesuit? Jesu!

Penelope. And a wit.

Bacon. Bad.

Penelope. Very bad.

Raleigh. Unutterably bad. What? Jesu-wit! Poisonous! Shall we allow this?

Penelope. I am guilty. I surrender.

Raleigh. What did you do with the body?

Penelope. There was none. I did eat my words.

Raleigh. A cannibal, a monster, a word-swallower!

The Fool. A man-eater.

Penelope. Nay, nay!

Bacon. Do you eat your men with butter or salt?

Penelope. With salt if they are buttery and with butter if they are salty.

Raleigh. Ready then. Here comes a salty man to be buttered.

Penelope. A butter-in.

The Fool. A salt-butter.

Bacon. A cheese . . . a whole cheese.

Tressa. Full of holes, holey.

Ellen. Pitted.

Penelope. What? Am I pitted against a cheese?

Raleigh. Let but this cheese roll into your pit, lady . . .
and you are answered.

Penelope. No . . . you are answered. You are answered no.

Burghley.
> [*To* CECIL]

There can be no doubt the Essex faction sent money to
the actors to purchase a performance of Richard. It is
an old play; it would draw no public.

Cecil. The actors are then accessory.

Burghley. Think you so?

Cecil. They could hardly be unaware of the purposes of the
Essex party.

Bacon. Is it so certain that Essex has a purpose?

Cecil. He has led his army into London.

Bacon. The men live in London. Moreover the order to
disperse on landing may not have been received. Such
things have happened.

Cecil. Yes?

Bacon. Aye, indeed.

Cecil.
> [*To* BURGHLEY]

You are to see these actors?

Burghley. They are sending spokesmen today.

The Fool. Let them put on the play for us.

Tressa. Yes . . . the deposition scene. It may convince us. We may all turn rebel.

Burghley. Tut!

The Fool. Tut? What does this mean . . . this tut?

Burghley. Will you learn manners, sirrah? In my young days there was no such loose speaking about the court.

The Fool. There was no tutting, neither.

Penelope. You are mistaken. There used to be tutting parties. They all brought their tutting.

The Fool. Fie on you! Also pooh on you!

Penelope. Yes . . . there were fieing and poohing parties also.

Raleigh. True, true. Well I remember the old days when all the young people would get together and try which could make the greatest pooh.

Tressa. There was such laughter and jesting!

Raleigh. Ah, yes, at the old Tut, Fie and Pooh Tavern! It's torn down now, but what a place it was!

The Fool. The game went out of fashion, alas, when it was discovered that a virgin could always pooh farther than anybody else.

Tressa. Tut!

Mary. Fie!

Ellen. Pooh!

The Fool. I beg pardon. I had forgotten there were virgins present.

Penelope. We are all virgins.

Raleigh. The proof then, quickly. Show me.

Penelope. It is nothing that can be seen, my lord.

Raleigh. They say seeing is believing.

Penelope. Virginity is rather a state of mind.

Ellen. Nay . . . a state of preservation.

The Fool. I have seen these preserved virgins.

Raleigh. You have seen them?

The Fool. Seen them? I've been bothered by them. The whole court used to be driven indoors by them regularly on our progress through Middlesex.

Raleigh. They are worse at night, I believe? Middlesex . . . Middlesex . . .

Penelope. Change the subject, gentles. This virginity begins to wear thin.

The Fool. It has worn clear through, and a great hole appears in the center.

Penelope. A hole in your wit.

Raleigh. His Jesuit.

Penelope. His half-wit.

[*A* HERALD *enters and speaks to* CECIL]

The Herald. My lord, there are two fellows here who ask for audience with the queen.

Cecil. Who are they?

Herald. Players, my lord.

Cecil. Tell them to wait. The queen will see them presently.
[*The* HERALD *goes out*]

Burghley. To my mind it was one of these same players writ the ballad that was posted up at St. Paul's.

Cecil. No, no . . . the man has been discovered . . . and will have his ears cropped for it.

Burghley. But he could not have written it . . . he was but an instrument. The actors are too devilish ingenious at writing ballads. I cannot put it out of my mind they are all treasonous scoundrels.

Raleigh. Is this the ballad on the Earl's return?

Cecil. Aye . . .
"When England needeth victories
She calleth Essex on . . ."
And more to the same purpose. What I cannot understand is that the queen should take no steps to put the city in a posture of defense. Essex draws near with his army . . . and we swing the gates as usual.

Bacon. Is that a symptom of danger . . . that an English general should return with his army to the English capital?

Cecil. Are you not aware that Essex' house in the Strand

is a camp brimming full of armed nobles going and coming?

The Fool. It is much more likely to be brimming with
drunken nobles going and coming brim full.

Cecil. Be quiet!

The Fool. Fool.

> [CECIL *lays a hand on his sword angrily. The* FOOL *points to
> his own breast and repeats:*]

Fool.

> [CECIL *turns away. There is a rustling among those present.
> Several rise. At the rear the* QUEEN *appears silently,
> two* LADIES *following her. She comes forward without
> speaking, her eyes seeking for someone. She fixes on*
> LORD BURGHLEY]

Elizabeth. Is it true, then, my dear Burghley, that you
have taken to attending the Theatre?

Burghley. No, madam.

Elizabeth. It was not you, then, who forbade the per-
formances of Richard II without asking my advice?

Burghley. It was, madam.

Elizabeth. On what ground?

Burghley. Your Majesty, the play is treasonous. It shows
the deposition of a king, and its performance was pro-
cured by rebels.

Elizabeth. Rebels? What rebels?

Burghley. I know not, madam. I have sent for the players
to discover that.

Elizabeth. You have sent for them?

Burghley. Aye, madam . . . and they are here.

Elizabeth. They will laugh at you, dear Burghley.

Burghley. Others have laughed at me, Majesty.

Elizabeth. They will laugh at you, sir, and you will deserve it. Is my kingdom so shaky that we dare not listen to a true history? Are my people so easily led that the sight of a king deposed in play will send them running thither to pull the queen out of her chair? Have we not passion plays in every little town showing the murder of our Lord? You are nervous, Lord Burghley. Let these children play their plays.

Cecil. Your Majesty, I very much fear they are not all children, and that they mean to do harm.

Elizabeth. Then let them. Let them do all the harm they can. Are we too stupid to see that to prohibit a rebellious play is to proclaim our fear of rebellion? Who is there here who fears a rebellion against me? I do not.

Cecil. It is dangerous to let these mutterings grow, dear queen.

Elizabeth. It is dangerous to touch them. Let them mutter, if they will. Let them cry out . . . let them run the streets, these children! When they have worn themselves weary running and crying "Up with Essex!" "Down with Elizabeth!" and got themselves drunk on mutual pledges, they will go to bed and sleep soundly and wake up wiser. Let me speak to these players. Bring them to me.

Burghley. Here, madam?

Elizabeth. Here.

Cecil. Majestas, adsunt legati de curia Galliæ. Placetne eos recipere antequam . . .

Elizabeth. Cras illos recipiam.

Cecil. Sed maxime præstat . . .

Elizabeth. Si bene mihi videbitur, cras redituros recipiam! Nay, I can bang you in Latin too!

    [CECIL *goes out*. ELIZABETH *sits and turns to the* FOOL]

You, sirrah . . . I hear that you have fallen in love. Do you wish to be whipped?

The Fool. I would rather have been whipped, madam; much rather.

Elizabeth. Why?

The Fool. It would hurt less.

Elizabeth. Good. You shall be whipped.

The Fool. Madam, if you can whip it out of me I will give you my lucky shilling.

Elizabeth. You shall be whipped and keep your shilling.

The Fool. You would better take it, madam queen.

Elizabeth. Your shilling?

The Fool. Yes, madam queen, to buy another whip with for yourself. Nay, you had perhaps better buy several. But in truth, dear queen, I have not fallen in love, only a pretty little strumpet has fallen in love with me and I beg leave that we be allowed to marry.

Elizabeth. Is she of the court?

The Fool. Yes, madam.

Elizabeth. What, are there strumpets at court?

The Fool. Oh, they are all strumpets here at court. Some
are here because they are strumpets and some are strumpets because they are here, but strumpets they all are.

Elizabeth. Which is it you wish to marry?

The Fool. It is not that I wish to marry her, madam, but
she wishes to marry me.
   [*Walking about to choose finally pointing to* TRESSA]
This one, Majesty.

Tressa.
   [*Leaping at him*]
Scoundrel! . . .

The Fool.
   [*Pointing to* ELLEN]
No, no . . . I mean this one.

Ellen. You dog! You . . .
   [*The* FOOL *passes* PENELOPE *by*]

The Fool.
   [*Pointing to Mary*]
Or that one . . .

Mary. What!

The Fool. I feel sure it was one of them, Majesty . . . but it
was dark at the time . . . and in truth I gave her my
word of honor in the dark that I would make an honest

woman of her by daylight. It is thus that most marriages
are made.

Elizabeth. How, fool?

The Fool. In the dark, my lady. Quite in the dark.

Elizabeth.
  [*To a soldier*]
Take this fool, captain, and put him in the dark for
three days with but little bread and water. I have a distaste for this fooling.

The Fool. No, no, madam.

Elizabeth. I am tired of your strumpets! And let him not
see his lady Penelope meanwhile. You will be sure of
that, mistress?

Penelope. I have no desire to see him.

Elizabeth. Whom do you desire to see?

Penelope. No-one, your Majesty.

Elizabeth. You lie! This Mistress Gray, take her too! Let
her have bread and water!
  [*She looks at* PENELOPE *with hatred*]

Penelope. Your Majesty . . . what is this?

Elizabeth. I am weary to death of you! I am weary of all
men and women, but more of you than any! You have
written. You have had letters! I say, take her out of
my sight!
  [*The soldiers start to take out* PENELOPE *and the* FOOL]
Whip them first, whip them both!
  [*The two are taken to the door*]

Nay, leave them here, leave them, knaves . . . leave
them! Damn you, do you hear me! You are too quick
to obey orders! You like this whipping too well, sirrah!
You have an itch for laying on! You beef-witted bastards! And now let us have entertainment, gentle lords!
Let us be merry! The players are here! Let us have a
play!

[*A* HERALD *runs in to the queen without ceremony, calling out
as he comes*]

The Herald. Your Majesty, Your Majesty! Lord Scroop
sends me from the city to tell you there is a rising in
London! There is a mob rising in the city!

Elizabeth. What . . . is this one of the players? Are you
playing Richard II for us?

The Herald. No, no, Your Majesty! A great number of
people came through Fleet Street . . . and they have
sacked a grocer's and broken into a wine-merchant's
cellar! It is said they will break into Fleet Prison and
set all free . . .

Elizabeth. Not they. If they've broken into a wine-cellar
they'll get no farther. We're a marvellous people, we
English, but we cannot hold liquor. Now if they were
Scotch one might worry. What are they saying, these
wine drinkers?

The Herald. I cannot tell you that, Your Majesty.

Elizabeth. Are they not crying "Up with Essex!" "Down
with Elizabeth!"?

The Herald. Yes, madam!

Elizabeth. Why surely. What else would they be crying? "Up with Essex!" Viva! "Down with Elizabeth!" À bas! The queen is dead, long live the king! If I were there I would cry it myself! It has a marvellous ring! "Up with Essex!" "Down with Elizabeth!"

Burghley. What are we to do, madam?

Elizabeth.

[*To the* HERALD]

What is the Lord Mayor doing about this?

Herald. Nothing, madam.

Elizabeth. How like a Lord Mayor and how sensible. That's the first principle of government. Never do anything. Let the others make all the mistakes.

Cecil. But madam . . . there are five hundred of the royal guard at the Tower . . .

Elizabeth. Let the mayor of London look out for his people. If he allows them to run up and down breaking into wine-cellars, it's his own affair.

Burghley. But if it spreads to the palace, Majesty?

Elizabeth. Why yes . . . let them bring their revolution here to me. I should be amused to see it. They are children, Burghley, drunken children. Would you fire on children?

Burghley. Then let me go into London, madam . . .

Elizabeth. And call out the guard and put down these traitors with powder and ball? No! They are to be al-

lowed to get quite drunk and then go to sleep. Where
are these players?

[CECIL *enters with* BURBAGE *and* HEMMINGS]

Cecil. Here, madam.

Elizabeth. Ah, yes, bold Burbage and handsome Hemmings. Well, my masters, I understand that you have
come to me to have your noses slit and your thumbs
branded? Is it so?

Burbage. Only if unavoidable, Your Majesty.

Elizabeth. You have put on a play, I believe?

Burbage. Many, Your Majesty.

Elizabeth. You have revived the old play of Richard II,
including in it the deposition scene which was censored
on its first presentation, and you have done this to foster
treasonous projects.

Burbage. No, Your Majesty, I swear it.

Elizabeth. You have not played this play?

Burbage. But not to foster treason, that I swear.

Elizabeth. If you played Richard with that pot-belly it was
treason indeed. Then for what purpose?

Burbage. To make money.

Elizabeth. On an old play?

Burbage. We were paid in advance . . .

Elizabeth. By whom?

Burbage. By Lord Southampton.

Burghley. You see? A friend of Essex.

Elizabeth. You have much too handsome a nose for slitting, Master Hemmings, yet you say nothing.

Hemmings. There is only this to say, Your Majesty . . . that we knew nothing of any traitorous intent in the matter . . . and that, had we known of such intent, we would not have given the performance.

Elizabeth. I think you are all traitorous knaves and rascals, as a matter of fact, in league with Essex and Southampton and the smoothest liars in Christendom. Is there something in this?

Hemmings. No, madam.

Elizabeth. You know Essex and Southampton?

Hemmings. We know Lord Southampton.

Elizabeth. How much were you paid for the revival of Richard?

Hemmings. Three pounds, Your Majesty.

Elizabeth. No more?

Hemmings. No more.

Elizabeth. Play it again this afternoon, masters, play it at my request this afternoon, and you shall have ten pounds for it. Lord Cecil, pay Master Burbage ten pounds from the royal exchequer for one performance of Richard. And let it stand in the record.

Cecil. Yes, madam.

Elizabeth.

> [*To* HEMMINGS]
>
> And tell Lord Southampton when you see him that I paid ten to his three. Will you tell him?

Hemmings. Yes, Your Majesty.

Elizabeth. And when you have all this treason out of your systems be ready to play Sir John Falstaff for me at the end of the week. I should like to see your Falstaff again, sir.

Burbage. Yes, Your Majesty.

Elizabeth. You may go.

> [BURBAGE *and* HEMMINGS *go out*]

Cecil.

> [*Waiting till they are gone*]
>
> You are mad, Your Majesty! This is a rebellion, and you play into their hands. The outer court is thronging with messengers from the city! Half the town is in uprising!

Elizabeth. I know.

Cecil. Madam . . .

Elizabeth. Little man, little man, let me alone.

Cecil. This much I must tell you. Lord Essex has been seen with an armed force in the city.

Elizabeth. Lord Essex?

Cecil. With an army. Where he is now no-one can say.

Elizabeth. And if one were to guess?

Cecil. He is on his way hither.

Elizabeth. So I think. I shall be glad to see him. Let him bring his revolution here. How long think you it will last after I have looked on it?

Burghley. Madam, the palace is unprotected from the waterside. The guard must be drawn up.

Elizabeth. With your permission, my lord, I would rather not.

Cecil. I took the liberty of ordering a guard posted along the river.

> [*A door is opened without and a sudden snarl of angry voices breaks in on the conference*]

The Voices. "Who has given these orders?"
"Back there . . . back!"
"Not the queen, by God!"
"The queen . . . the queen! Defend the queen!"
"An Essex!"
"Hold your mouth!"
"Stand back, fellow!"

Essex.

> [*Outside*]

I say the queen will see me! Stand back!

> [*There is a clank of armor in the hallway and* ESSEX *appears in the doorway, soldiers following him*]

Elizabeth. You come with a file of soldiers at your back, my lord of Essex.

Essex. Do I need them, Your Majesty?

Elizabeth. No.

Essex. Then be off with you. Follow my orders . . . They
told me you would not see me.

Elizabeth. They were wrong. I will see you. It seems you are
in rebellion,
My good lord. Enter and state your grievance,
If you have grievance. For myself, I have
A great affection for rebels, being one myself
Much of the time.

Essex. I am no rebel, Your Majesty . . .
But, newly arrived from Ireland, and bearing news
Of your subjects there, I venture to come to see you,
No more.

Elizabeth. And your army? . . . You have an army with
you?

Essex. I have brought my men home to London.

Elizabeth. You received
My orders, no doubt, directing you to disband?

Essex. I believed them to be mistaken. To disband on the
coast
And leave my expedition there, seemed strange,
And dangerous to the country. An army turned loose
Becomes a mob.

Elizabeth. And you tell me this! You are informed in these
matters
But I am not!

Essex. Indeed, that is quite true . . .
I do know about armies . . . and you do not.

Elizabeth. Oh, yes . . .
  Oh, indeed. And who paid them then? I believe
  Your supplies were cut off?

Essex. I have paid them.

Elizabeth. They are then
  In your service?

Essex. In my service and therefore
  Devoted yours.

Elizabeth. And Ireland? How of Ireland?

Essex. I could have conquered Ireland had you given me
    time.
  I left it worse than I found it.

Elizabeth. An honest answer,
  At any rate.

Essex. Why should I lie? The fault,
  If any, was yours. To conquer Ireland requires
  More than the months you gave me. Years, perhaps.

Elizabeth. You were engaged in subduing the rebels, then,
  When I summoned you home?

Essex. Just so.

Elizabeth. You were not, by chance,
  Joined with the rebels?

Essex. Never.

Elizabeth. You held no parleys
  With our friend Tyrone?

Essex. I did. They were part of my plan.

Elizabeth. Your plans! Your plans! Why did you write me
  nothing
  Of these your plans? Am I a witch to find out
  What happens on the far side of the Irish Sea
  Without being told?

Essex. I wrote you . . .

Elizabeth. Masterly letters,
  Brief, to the point, wasting no words, in short,
  Nothing.

Essex. I know not what Your Majesty means
  By that. I wrote you fully, and in answer
  Received no reply.

Elizabeth. You wrote me?

Essex. Many times.

Elizabeth. And had no letters from me?

Essex. None.

Elizabeth. Before God,
  If the couriers were tampered with there shall be
  Some necks stretched here! My lords, I wish to speak
  With Lord Essex here alone! Leave us.

Cecil. Dear queen,
  Do you think it safe . .

Elizabeth. Leave us!

  [BURGHLEY *makes a sign and the stage is silently emptied
    save for the* QUEEN *and* ESSEX. *A pause*]

What did you write me?

Essex. I wrote you my love—for I thought you loved me
    then—
    And then I pled with you not to bring me home
    In the midst of my mission—and then at last angrily—
    For I had not heard—but always to say I loved you—
    Always.

Elizabeth. But is this true?

Essex. Would I lie?

Elizabeth. Some one
    Has lied and will pay with his life if this is true!—
    Before God and hell—Some one will pay for this.

Essex. What did you write me?

Elizabeth. I wrote—my love—
    God keep you safe—I know not—and then, not hearing
    I wrote God knows what madness—as to a rebel—
    Thinking you no longer mine—faithless!
    Thinking—

Essex. I would I had known—I was in torment—
    I—forgive me—

Elizabeth. You should never have gone away.
    God, how I've hated you!—

Essex. No!

Elizabeth. Planned to put you to torture!

Essex. I have been in torture!
    [*He steps toward her*]

Elizabeth. Not yet—I can't breathe yet—I can't breathe—
    Or think or believe—

Essex. Nor I.

Elizabeth. Can we ever—
  Believe again? Can it be as it used to be?

Essex. We can make it so.

Elizabeth. Come, kill me if you will. Put your arms round
    me—
  If you love me. Do you still love me?

Essex. Yes.

Elizabeth. Yes, yes—
  If this were false, then, then truly—then I should die.
  I thought because I was older—you see—some one
    else—

Essex. No one—never a breath—

Elizabeth. Is it all, all as before?

Essex. We have not changed.

Elizabeth. No. Yes, a little, perhaps.
  They have changed us a little.

Essex. Not I. I have not changed.

Elizabeth. Can I trust you now?

Essex. Sweet, think back, all those months,
  All those hideous months! No word, no love.
  And when word did come, it was to make me prisoner!
  Christ, I have pride!
  And though I came here in defiance, I came truly to
    find you
  Who have been lost from me.

Elizabeth. Do you ask forgiveness?
  It is all forgiven.

Essex. Then, why then, hell's vanished—
  And here's heaven risen out of it, a heaven of years
  In the midst of desolate centuries.

Elizabeth. We have so few years.
  Let us make them doubly sweet, these years we have,
  Be gracious with each other, sway a little
  To left or right if we must to stay together—
  Never distrust each other—nay, distrust
  All others, when they whisper. Let us make this our pact
  Now, for the fates are desperate to part us
  And the very gods envy this happiness
  We pluck out of loss and death.

Essex. If two stand shoulder to shoulder against the gods,
  Happy together, the gods themselves are helpless
  Against them, while they stand so.

Elizabeth. Love, I will be
  Your servant. Command me. What would you have?

Essex. Why nothing—

Elizabeth. Take this my world, my present in your hands!
  You shall stand back of my chair and together we
  Shall build an England to make the old world wonder
  And the new world worship!—What is this doubt in
    your brow?

Essex. I am troubled to be dishonest. I have brought my
    army

Here to the palace—and though it's all true what we've
    said—
No letters—utter agony over long months—
It is something in myself that has made me do this,
Not Cecil—nor anyone. No one but myself.
The rest is all excuse.

Elizabeth. Speak what you will.

Essex. If you had but shown anger I could have spoken
Easily. It's not easy now, but speak I must!
Oh, I've thought much about this
On lonely marches and in distant tents,
Thinking of you and me. I say this now
Without rancor—in all friendliness and love—
The throne is yours by right of descent and by
Possession—but if this were a freer time,
And there were election, I should carry the country be-
    fore me,
And this being true, and we being equal in love,
Should we not be equal in power as well?

Elizabeth. We are equal.
I have made you so.

Essex. Yes, but still it's all yours—
Yours to grant me now or take away.

Elizabeth. How could this well be otherwise?

Essex. Am I not—and I say this too in all love—
As worthy to be king as you to be queen?
Must you be sovereign alone?

Elizabeth. You are young in policy,

My Essex, if you do not see that if I
Should grant high place to you now it would show ill to
   the kingdom—
It would be believed that you had forced this on me,
Would be called a revolution. It would undermine
All confidence. What is built up for years
In people's minds blows away like thistledown
When such things get abroad.

Essex. But is this your reason
  Or have you another? Would you trust me as king?

Elizabeth. No.

Essex. And are you still reluctant to give up
  Your prerogatives?

Elizabeth. Yes.

Essex. Then now, when the country is mine, the court in
   my hands,
  You my prisoner, I must send my men away,
  Disband my army, give back your kingdom to you,
  And know I have been king for a moment only
  And never will be again?

Elizabeth. I am your prisoner?

Essex. The palace and the city are in my hands.
  This England is mine now for the taking—

Elizabeth. This is your friendship! This is your love!

Essex. As water finds its level, so power goes
  To him who can use it, and soon or late the name
  Of king follows where power is.

Elizabeth. Oh, my Essex,
　You are a child in war as you are in council.
　Why all this talk of power? No army opposed you
　When your troops came the road from Ireland. No guard
　　was set
　To stop your entrance with your thousand halberds.
　Shall I tell you why? Because I wished to keep
　A semblance of peace between us. And for that,
　I am your prisoner!

Essex. Yes. My dear prisoner.

Elizabeth. Now I do know at least
　What it was you wanted. You wanted my kingdom. You
　　have it.
　Make the best of it. And so shall I.
　What are your plans?

Essex. I have none.

Elizabeth. The Tower, the block—
　You could hardly take a queen prisoner and have no
　　thought
　Of her destiny. I am my mother's daughter,
　I too can walk the path my mother walked.

Essex. These are heroics. You know you are free as air.

Elizabeth. If I do as you ask.

Essex. Is it so hard to share your power with your love?
　I could have all—and I offer to share with you.

Elizabeth. Let's have no more pretending.
　I'd have given all—but you came with an army, de-
　　manding—

In short, you don't love—nor trust me—no—nor want
me—

Essex. God knows I have wanted you. I have wanted
power—
Believed myself fitted to hold it—but not without you.

Elizabeth. If you had wanted me would you rise and strike
At me with an army? Never, never! You'd have come
To me quietly, and we'd have talked of it together
As lovers should—and we'd both have our way—
And no one the wiser. But now, to take the palace,
Hold me prisoner—no—what you wanted you've
taken—
And that is all you shall have. This is your kingdom—
But I—I am not yours.

Essex. But I am yours
And have been.

Elizabeth. Who will believe that? Not the world,
No, and not I. I'd rather go to the Tower
Than share my place on terms like these. Put me where I
Will do least harm.

Essex. I cannot, could not, will not.

Elizabeth. If I could have given freely—
But not now. Not surrendering. Not to a victor,

Essex. I am no victor if I lose you. The only gift
That I could take from you, is that we are equals.

Elizabeth. Yes, but not now.

Essex. I ask one word from you.
Give me this word—this one word—and these soldiers
Shall leave, and you shall be free.

Elizabeth. I'll believe that
When it happens.

Essex. I'll believe you when you promise.

Elizabeth. Then you have my promise.
You shall share the realm with me. As I am queen,
I promise it.

Essex. Then this is my answer.
[*He kisses her, then calls*]
Marvel!—Marvel!
[MARVEL *enters*]
Carry out the order of release. Dismiss my guard—
Return the palace into the queen's hands.
Retire with all our forces to the Strand.
Release all prisoners. Release the queen's guard
And send them to their stations.
[MARVEL *goes out*]
The palace will be
Returned as quickly as taken. This is our last quarrel.

Elizabeth. Yes—our last.

Marvel's Voice.
[*Offstage*]
Form for retire!

Another Voice. Form for retire!

A More Distant Voice. Form for retire!

A Voice.
  [*In the distance*]
  Ready to march!

Another Voice. Ready to march!

Another. All ready!

Another. Ready, captain!
  [MARVEL *enters*]

Marvel. The order is obeyed, my lord.

Essex. Follow your men.

Marvel. Yes, my lord.
  [*He goes out*]

Essex. It is as I planned. They are leaving the palace.
  Now let us talk no more of this tonight—
  Let us forget this matter of thrones and kingdoms
  And be but you and me for a while.

Elizabeth.
  [*Immobile*]
  Yes—yes—
  Let us forget. Have you kept your word indeed?

Essex. I have kept my word.

Elizabeth. If I clapped my hands
  Would my guard come now—or yours?

Essex. Yours only. Shall I call them?

Elizabeth. No—I'll call them.
  [*She claps her hands four times.* CAPTAIN ARMIN *appears in
  the entrance followed by four* BEEF-EATERS *with halberds. They stand at attention in the entrance*]

To be sure I have a guard
Once more.
The palace has been returned? It is in
Our hands?

Captain. Yes, Majesty.

Elizabeth. I have ruled England a long time, my Essex,
And I have found that he who would rule must be
Quite friendless, without mercy, without love.
Arrest Lord Essex!
Arrest Lord Essex! Take him to the Tower
And keep him safe.

Essex. Is this a jest?

Elizabeth. I never
Jest when I play for kingdoms, my lord of Essex.

Essex. I trusted you.

Elizabeth. I trusted you,
And learned from you that no one can be trusted.
I will remember that.

Essex. Lest that should be all
You ever have to remember, Your Majesty,
Take care what you do.

Elizabeth. I shall take care.

[ESSEX *unsheathes his sword, breaks it across his knee, flings
it at the foot of the throne, turns and walks out between
the two files of guards*]

CURTAIN

ELIZABETH THE QUEEN
ACT THREE

ACT THREE

SCENE: *The queen's apartments in the Tower, a square and heavy room, long and with a raised stone platform at one end of which stands a regal chair. It is dawn, the light filtering in coldly.* ELLEN *stands in the doorway at the left, weeping, with one arm before her face.* THE FOOL, *who has been sleeping wrapped in the draperies of the queen's chair, uncoils himself fron among them and rolls over to rub his eyes.* TRESSA *hurries in.*

Tressa. Come back quickly, dear, quickly! She's sorry she hurt you. She'll have no one else read to her.

Ellen.

[*Weeping*]

I can't read now. I'm—I don't mind if she strikes me—only—it wasn't my fault—We're all so weary.

Tressa. She's sorry—

The Fool.

[*Waking*]

One, two—there should be three.

[MARY *comes to the door*

Mary.

[*Very low*]

Ellen—

The Fool. Three.

Mary. Ellen! She wants you at once.

[ELLEN *runs out*]

The Fool. Where am I?

Mary. Yes—and what are you doing there?

The Fool. Trying to sleep.

Mary. Sleep? In the Tower?

The Fool. Come and help me. I have heard that you are perfect at lying down.

> [MARY *and* TRESSA *go out.* THE FOOL *looks about him sleepily, then remembers something and hunts for it under a chair. When he extracts it it proves to be a roasted bird on a wooden platter, covered with leaves. He examines it, then replaces a large leaf over it.* PENELOPE, *fully dressed, comes in from the rear*]

Penelope?

Penelope. Yes?

The Fool. Have you slept?

Penelope. No.

The Fool. Then you should break your fast. You are hungry?

Penelope. No. I can't eat.

The Fool.

> [*Showing his capon*]

Look.

Penelope. What's that?

The Fool. Breakfast. I brought it from Whitehall.

Penelope. Eat it then.

> [*She sits on a step disconsolately*]

The Fool. You won't have any?

Penelope. No.

The Fool.
> [*Pushing the food away*]
I'm not hungry either.

Penelope. Eat it, poor fool.

The Fool. I don't want it. I brought it for you.

Penelope. I know. But eat it.
> [*She wipes her eyes*]

The Fool. Why should you weep?

Penelope. God knows. He never wept for me.

The Fool. The earl's not dead yet, remember.

Penelope. No.

The Fool. And she'll never let it happen.

Penelope. The clock's struck five. He's to die at six.

The Fool. Why has she not sent to him?

Penelope. She has. We were awake all night. She has sent messages but he's not answered. She's been waiting for word from him. But he's as silent as if he wanted to die.

The Fool. Will she let them kill him if he says nothing?

Penelope. She's a strange woman. She wants him to beg her pardon . . . or something like that.

The Fool. Would you beg her pardon if you were he?

Penelope. No.

The Fool. Then he won't. For I think he's as proud as you.

Penelope. He has not said a word or sent a message since his arrest.

The Fool. And the queen has not slept?

Penelope. No.

The Fool. Nor you?

Penelope. No.

The Fool. God help these women.

Penelope. She says she gave him a ring once. If he ever
wanted forgiveness he was to send the ring. And he sits
there stubbornly with the ring on his finger. Oh, God,
will nothing happen?

> [*The* Fool *has absent-mindedly pulled the capon toward him
> again, and begins to eat.* Elizabeth *emerges from the
> rear*]

Elizabeth. Penelope?

Penelope. Yes.

Elizabeth. Have the players come?

Penelope. Not yet.

> [*The* Fool *has pushed the food guiltily behind him*]

Elizabeth. These cheating grooms! I'll have them carbo-
nadoed for this dallying! I shall go mad here! Bring me
the little book of prayers . . . from the window-sill. No
. . . leave it. The gods of men are sillier than their kings
and queens . . . and emptier and more powerless. There
is no god but death, no god but death!

> [*She sees the food the* Fool *has been hiding*]

Gnaw your bones somewhere else!

> [*The* Fool *goes out left*]

Come here, my dear. I heard the clock strike five.

Penelope. Yes. I heard it.

> [*They sit together on the steps, and* PENELOPE *puts her arm round* ELIZABETH]

Elizabeth. Do you love him well, my dear?

Penelope. Yes, Your Majesty.

> [ELIZABETH *bows her head wearily on* PENELOPE]

Elizabeth. I love him. He has never loved me.

Penelope. Yes, yes. He does love you. I've been madly jealous of you.

Elizabeth. Of me? Poor child.

Penelope. But he loved you . . . and never me at all.

Elizabeth. How do you know?

Penelope. He told me.

Elizabeth. What did he say?

Penelope. He said, "I love her dearly." I wanted him for myself, and I warned him against you. He laughed at me. He said, "I love her very dearly."

Elizabeth. You tell me this because you want to save him.

Penelope. No, dear queen. It's true.

Elizabeth. This is the end of me, dear. This is the end.
It comes late. I've been a long while learning,
But I've learned it now. Life is bitter. Nobody
Dies happy, queen or no. Will he speak, think you?
Will he send to me?

Penelope. No. Not now.

Elizabeth. You see,
  This is the end of me. Oh, I shall live,
  I shall walk about and give orders . . . a horrible
  while . . .
  A horrible old hag.

Penelope. You must send for him.
  He's proud as you are, and you have the upper hand.
  He'll say nothing. You must send for him, bring him
  here.
    [*The chimes ring the quarter hour*]

Elizabeth. Not yet. Not yet.
    [*She rises*]
  Where are the players? I sent
  For the players hours ago! They shall pay for this,
  The insolent servants! Mary . . . Tressa, God's head!
  I'm bestially served! Ellen!
    [ELLEN *looks in, partly dressed*]
  Find out if the players
  Are here? And be quick.

Ellen. Yes, madam.
    [*She disappears*]

Elizabeth. Where's my fool?

The Fool.
    [*Looking in with a bone in his hand*]
  Here, madam.

Elizabeth. Where are you when I need you?
  Look at the oaf! Say nothing! You're funny enough

The way you are with your capon in your mouth!
Eat! Eat! Let me see you!

The Fool. I don't seem to be hungry!

Elizabeth. Eat, I say!

The Fool. Yes, madam.
[*He tries to eat*[

Elizabeth. Now wipe your fingers.
Here, take my napkin, child. Come here! You're dis-
gusting!
[*She gives him a kerchief*]
Can you not clean your face?

The Fool. With this?

Elizabeth. Aye, with that.
[*She takes his bone and throws it*]
Why do you make mouths at it? It's clean.

The Fool. Yes, madam!
[*He begins to wipe his mouth, then starts to cry, and sitting
down on the step, sobs heavily, his head in his hands*]

Elizabeth. What is it now? What good's a fool that cries
When you need comfort? What's the matter?

The Fool. Please,
I don't know. You aren't like the queen.

Elizabeth. I am
The queen, though.

Tressa.
[*Looking in*]
The players, madam.

Elizabeth. Bring them here.

Penelope. The time's grown short. Will you send for him?

Elizabeth. Wait . . . he may come.

Penelope. No, no. He won't. You'll let it go too long
Watching the players.

Elizabeth. Let them come in.
[TRESSA *is seen at the doorway with the actors*]

Penelope. You should eat
A little something first.

Elizabeth. No, no. Bring them in.
[*The* ACTORS *enter*]
Come in, my masters, let us have a play . . .
Let us have revels and amusements quickly . . .
If ever you played play now. This is my bad
Quarter of an hour.

Penelope. Please, please . . .

Elizabeth. Quick! Quick . . .
You are late, sirs . . . never mind . . . some scene from
Falstaff . . .
The one where he lies to the prince about running away
And the prince catches him . . .

Hemmings. Where, Majesty?

Elizabeth. There, anywhere. Come, sit down. Sit down.
[*The girls and the* FOOL *group about her*]
Begin, Falstaff! "I call thee coward! I'll see thee
Damned ere I call thee coward!"

Falstaff. I call thee coward! I'll see thee damned ere I call thee coward: but I would give a thousand pound I could run as fast as thou canst.

Prince Henry. What's the matter?

Falstaff. What's the matter! there be four of us here have ta'en a thousand pound this day morning.

Prince Henry. Where is it, Jack? where is it?

Falstaff. Where is it! taken from us it is: a hundred upon poor four of us.

Prince Henry. What, fought ye with them all?

Falstaff. All! I know not what ye call all; but if I fought not with fifty of them, I am a bunch of radish: if there were not two or three and fifty upon poor old Jack, then am I no two-legged creature.

Elizabeth. Come, come . . . this is not to the purpose . . . I had thought this witty . . .

   [*The Players pause*]

Play! Play!

Prince Henry. Pray God, you have not murdered some of them.

Falstaff. Nay, that's past praying for: I have peppered two of them; two I am sure I have paid, . . . two rogues in buckram suits. I tell thee what, Hal, . . . if I tell thee a lie, spit in my face, call me horse. Thou knowest my old ward . . . here I lay, and thus I bore my point. Four rogues in buckram let drive at me . . .

Prince Henry. What, four? thou saidst but two even now.

Falstaff. Four, Hal; I told thee four.

Poins. Ay, ay, he said four.

Falstaff. These four came all a-front, and mainly thrust at me. I made me no more ado but took all their seven points in my target, thus.

> [*The* QUEEN *walks from place to place, restlessly*]

Prince Henry. Seven? why, there were but four even now in buckram.

Poins. Ay, four in buckram suits.

Falstaff. Seven, by these hilts, or I am a villain else.

Prince Henry. Pr'ythee, let him alone; we shall have more anon.

Falstaff. Dost thou hear me, Hal?

Prince Henry. Ay, and mark thee too, Jack.

Elizabeth. Aye, aye . . . we are listening . . .
Play!

Falstaff. Do so, for it is worth the listening to. These nine in buckram that I told thee of . . .

Prince Henry. So, two more already.

Falstaff. Began to give me ground: but I followed me close, came in foot and hand; and with a thought seven of the eleven I paid.

Prince Henry. O monstrous! eleven buckram men grown out of two!

Falstaff. But, as the devil would have it, three misbegotten knaves in Kendal green came at my back and let drive at me . . . for it was so dark, Hal, that thou couldst not see thy hand.

Prince Henry. These lies are like the father that begets them . . . gross as a mountain, open, palpable. Why, thou clay-brained guts, thou nott-pated fool, thou whoreson, obscene, greasy tallow-ketch . . .

Falstaff. What, art thou mad? art thou mad? is not the truth the truth?

Prince Henry. Why, how couldst thou know these men in Kendal green, when it was so dark thou couldst not see thy hand? come, tell us your reason: what sayest thou to this?

Poins. Come, your reason, Jack . . . your reason.

Falstaff. What, upon compulsion? Give a reason on compulsion! if reasons were as plenty as blackberries I would give no man a reason on compulsion, I.

Prince Henry. I'll be no longer guilty of this sin; this sanguine coward, this bed-presser, this horse back-breaker, this huge hill of flesh . . .

Falstaff. Away, you starveling, you elf-skin, you dried neat's tongue . . . O for breath to utter what is like thee! . . . you tailor's yard, you sheath, you bow-case, you vile standing-tuck . . .

Prince Henry. Well, breathe awhile, and then to it again: and when thou hast tired thyself in base comparisons, hear me speak but this.

Poins. Mark, Jack.

Prince Henry. We two saw you four set on four; you bound
them, and were masters of their wealth . . . Mark now,
how a plain tale shall put you down . . . Then did we
two set on you four; and, with a word, out-faced you
from your prize, and have it: yes, and can show it you
here in the house: . . . and, Falstaff, you carried your
guts away as nimbly, with as quick dexterity, and roared
for mercy, and still ran and roared, as ever I heard bull-
calf. What a slave art thou, to hack thy sword as thou
hast done, and then say it was in fight! What trick, what
device, what starting-hole, canst thou now find out to
hide thee from this open and apparent shame?

Poins. Come, let's hear, Jack; what trick hast thou now?

Falstaff. By the Lord, I knew ye as well as He that made
ye. Why, hear ye, my masters: was it for me to kill the
heir-apparent? Should I turn upon the true prince?
Why, thou knowest I am as valiant as Hercules: but beware instinct; the lion will not touch the true prince.
Instinct is a great matter; I was a coward on instinct. I
shall think the better of myself and thee during my life;
I for a valiant lion, and thou for a true prince. But, by
the Lord, lads, I am glad you have the money. What,
shall we be merry? Shall we have a play extempore?

Elizabeth. My God, my God . . . can one not forget for a
moment?
Who are these strangers? What is this interlude?
Go! Go! It's a vile play and you play it vilely!
Go! By my God, will no-one deliver me from this tor-
ment?
[*The players start out*]

Take your trappings and go!
[*They leave. The chimes strike*]
Again . . . the half-hour . . .
[CECIL *enters*]
Yes?
[*To* PENELOPE]
Was I not wise to wait? He has spoken first! Yes?

Cecil. Your Majesty, a citizen rabble has gathered
To protest the execution of Essex. The captain
Begs permission to use your guard. There's no other
Force at hand to disperse them.

Elizabeth. It's your day, Cecil
I daresay you know that. The snake-in-the-grass
Endures, and those who are noble, free of soul,
Valiant and admirable . . . they go down in the
     prime,
Always they go down . . .

Cecil. Madam, the guard
Is needed at once . . .

Elizabeth. Aye . . . the snake-mind is best . . .
One by one you out-last them. To the end
Of time it will be so . . . the rats inherit the earth.
Take my guard. Take it. I thought you brought word
     from . . .
Go, call Lord Essex for me
From his cell . . . and bring him thither! I'll wait no
     longer!

Cecil. Lord Essex is prepared for execution.
The priest has been sent to him.

Elizabeth. Bring him here, I say,
And now . . . at once!

[CECIL *bows and goes out*]

Go out from me, all of you,
All save Penelope. Go quickly, quickly . . .
All . . .

[*They leave*]

Penelope, bring my robe, the one
Laid out . . .

[PENELOPE *goes.* ELIZABETH *seats herself in the royal chair.*
PENELOPE *returns with the robe*]

Look here in my face, Penelope. He's so young,
And I'm old, girl, I'm old. It shows in my eyes.
Dear, you're so young. Do not be here when he
comes . . .
Do you mind? You'll look so young.

Penelope. Yes, madam . . . but you . . .
You're beautiful.

Elizabeth. Beautiful still? But I was once . . . I was . . .
You'd not believe it now.

Penelope. Oh, yes . . .
You're always beautiful. You've always been.

Elizabeth. Thank you,
My dear. Go now. He'll come.

Penelope. Yes.

[*She goes out to the rear. After a moment* ESSEX *enters from
the left with a Guard. The Guard leaves him and steps
out.* ESSEX *is dressed in black and is very pale*]

Essex. You sent for me?
  Or so they said.

Elizabeth. Yes.

Essex. It would have been kinder
  To leave me with my thoughts till the axe came down
  And ended them. You spoil me for death.

Elizabeth. Are you
  So set on dying?

Essex. I can't say I care for it.
  This blood that beats in us has a way of wanting
  To keep right on. But if one is to die
  It's well to go straight toward it.

Elizabeth. You must have known
  I never meant you to die.

Essex. I am under sentence
  From Your Majesty's courts. There's no appeal that
    I know of.
  I am found guilty of treason on good evidence,
  And cannot deny it. This treason, I believe,
  Is punishable with death.

Elizabeth. God knows I am proud . . .
  And bitter, too . . . bitter at you with much cause,
  But I have sent for you. I've taken the first step
  That way. Do not make me take the next!

Essex. The next is to the scaffold. It's only a step
  Now, and I've made ready.

Elizabeth. Aye, you are bitter,
  Too; we have let it go late; we've both

Waited for the other. But it was I who spoke
First . . . Will you make me tell you first how much
I've longed for you? It's hard for me.

Essex. My dear,
You can tell me so gracefully, for you
Have nothing to gain or lose by me . . . but I
Have life and love to gain, and I find it less
Than fitting to speak like a lover, lest you suppose
I do it to save my head.

Elizabeth. It's true that you never
Loved me, isn't it? You were ambitious, and I
Loved you, and it was the nearest way to power,
And you took the nearest way? No, no . . . one mo.
    ment . . .
This is an hour for truth, if there's ever truth . . .
I'm older than you . . . but a queen; it was natural
You'd flatter me, speak me fair, and I believed you.
I'm sorry I believed you. Sorry for you
More than for me.

Essex. Why, yes . . . that's true enough.
Now may I go? This dying sticks in my mind,
And makes me poor company, I fear.

Elizabeth. It was true.
It was true then?

Essex. If you wish to make me tell you
What you well know, how much I used to love you,
How much I have longed for you, very well, I will
    say it.

That's a small victory to win over me now,
But take it with the rest.

Elizabeth. You did love me?

Essex. Yes.

Elizabeth. And love me still?

Essex. Yes. You should know that, I think.

Elizabeth. You kept my ring. You never sent my ring.
I've been waiting for it.

Essex. You may have it back
If you have use for it . . . I had thought to wear it
As far as my grave, but, take it.

Elizabeth. I'd have forgiven
All that had passed, at any hour, day or night,
Since I last saw you. I have waited late at night
Thinking, tonight the ring will come, he will never
Hold out against me so long, but the nights went by
Somehow, like the days, and it never came,
Till the last day came, and here it is the last morning
And the chimes beating out the hours.

Essex. Dear, if I'd known . . .
But I could not have sent it.

Elizabeth. Why?

Essex. If I'd tried
To hold you to a promise you could not keep
And you had refused me, I should have died much more
Unhappy than I am now.

Elizabeth. I'd have kept my promise.
   I'd keep it now.

Essex. If I offered you this ring?

Elizabeth. Yes . . . even now.

Essex. You would pardon me, set me free,
   Cede back my estates to me, love me as before,
   Give me my place in the state?

Elizabeth. All as it was.

Essex. And what would happen to your throne?

Elizabeth. My throne?
   Nothing.

Essex. Yes, for I'd take it from you.

Elizabeth. Again?
   You'd play that game again?

Essex. The games one plays
   Are not the games one chooses always. I
   Am still a popular idol of a sort.
   There are mutterings over my imprisonment,
   Even as it is . . . and if you should set me free
   And confess your weakness by overlooking treason
   And setting me up in power once more, the storm
   That broke last time would be nothing to the storm
   That would break over you then. As for myself,
   I played for power and lost, but if I had
   Another chance I think I'd play and win.

Elizabeth. Why do you say this?

Essex. I say it because it's true.
I have loved you, love you now, but I know myself.
If I were to win you over and take my place
As it used to be, it would gall me. I have a weakness
For being first wherever I am. I refuse
To take pardon from you without warning you
Of this. And when you know it, pardon becomes
Impossible.

Elizabeth. You do this for me?

Essex. Why, yes,
But not altogether. Partly for England, too.
I've lost conceit of myself a little. A life
In prison's very quiet. It leads to thinking.
You govern England better than I should.
I'd lead her into wars, make a great name,
Perhaps, like Henry Fifth and leave a legacy
Of debts and bloodshed after me. You will leave
Peace, happiness, something secure. A woman governs
Better than a man, being a natural coward.
A coward rules best.

Elizabeth. Still bitter.

Essex. Perhaps a little.
It's a bitter belief to swallow, but I believe it.
You were right all the time.
    [*The chimes ring three-quarters*]
And now, if you'll pardon me,
I have an appointment near-by with a headsman.
He comes sharp on the hour.

Elizabeth. You have an hour yet.
  It's but struck five.

Essex. It struck five some time since.

Elizabeth. It cannot go this way!

Essex. Aye, but it has.
  It has and will. There's no way out. I've thought of it
  Every way. Speak frankly. Could you forgive me
  And keep your throne?

Elizabeth. No.

Essex. Are you ready to give
  Your crown up to me?

Elizabeth. No. It's all I have.
    [*She rises*]
  Why, who am I
  To stand here paltering with a rebel noble!
  I am Elizabeth, daughter of a king,
  The queen of England, and you are my subject!
  What does this mean, you standing here eye to eye
  With me, your liege? You whom I made, and gave
  All that you have, you, an upstart, defying
  Me to grant pardon, lest you should sweep me from
    power
  And take my place from me? I tell you if Christ his
    blood
  Ran streaming from the heavens for a sign
  That I should hold my hand you'd die for this,
  You pretender to a throne upon which you have

No claim, you pretender to a heart, who have been
Hollow and heartless and faithless to the end!

Essex. If we'd met some other how we might have been
  happy . . .
But there's been an empire between us! I am to die . . .
Let us say that . . . let us begin with that . . .
For then I can tell you that if there'd been no empire
We could have been great lovers. If even now
You were not queen and I were not pretender,
That god who searches heaven and earth and hell
For two who are perfect lovers, could end his search
With you and me. Remember . . . I am to die . . .
And so I can tell you truly, out of all the earth
That I'm to leave, there's nothing I'm very loath
To leave save you. Yet if I live I'll be
Your death or you'll be mine.

Elizabeth. Give me the ring.

Essex. No.

Elizabeth. Give me the ring. I'd rather you killed me
Than I killed you.

Essex. It's better for me as it is
Than that I should live and batten my fame and fortune
On the woman I love. I've thought of it all. It's better
To die young and unblemished than to live long and
  rule,
And rule not well.

Elizabeth. Aye, I should know that.

Essex. Is it not?

Elizabeth. Yes.

Essex. Goodbye, then.

Elizabeth. Oh, then I'm old, I'm old!
  I could be young with you, but now I'm old.
  I know now how it will be without you. The sun
  Will be empty and circle round an empty earth . . .
  And I will be queen of emptiness and death . . .
  Why could you not have loved me enough to give me
  Your love and let me keep as I was?

Essex. I know not.
  I only know I could not. I must go.

Elizabeth.
    [*Frozen*]
  Yes.
    [*He goes to the door*]
  Lord Essex!
    [*He turns*]
  Take my kingdom. It is yours!
    [*Essex, as if not hearing, bows and goes on.* PENELOPE *runs
      in, meeting him*]

Penelope. My lord! She has forgiven you?

Essex. Goodbye, my dear.
    [*He kisses her*]

Penelope. No, no! She loves you! Go to her.
    [*Essex goes out*]
  Run to her! She waits you still! See, if you turn

She waits you still! Dear queen, would you let him
go?
He goes to his death! Send, send after him!

[*The* QUEEN *lifts her head and shows a face so stricken that*
PENELOPE, *who has gone to her, says no more. The clock*
strikes six. ELIZABETH *bows her head on* PENELOPE'S
knees, her hands over her ears]

CURTAIN

II · NIGHT OVER TAOS

CHARACTERS

(In the order of their appearance)

Indian Slave

Donna Veri

Valeria

Maria

Raquel

Conchita

Nuna

Lita

Carlotta

Cristina

Graso

Donna Josefa

Father Martinez

Diana

Diego

Federico

Narciso

Captain

Don Hermano

Don Miguel

Felipe

Santos

Pablo Montoya

Andres

Don Fernando

Don Mario

Mateo

1st Trapper

2nd Trapper

3rd Trapper

Peons

ACT ONE

Scene: *The great hall in the residence of* Pablo Montoya *at Taos,*
New Mexico, in the year 1847.

The room is long and low, its adobe walls white-washed to the
beamed ceiling and covered with red tapestries to a height of
four or five feet. A long table, homemade, as is all the furniture,
occupies the center, flanked with benches and chairs. There is a
large fire-place at the right and an entrance to the inner rooms
behind it. At the left a gigantic entrance door with small altars
on either side. Candles burn before both. At the rear are three
small and low windows, sunk deep in the four-foot wall and not
glazed, but covered with translucent parchment. A large hour-
glass sits on a stand near the fireplace. It is evening and dark
save for candle light.

A number of women and young girls, two or three of whom have
been setting the table, are weeping quietly while they exchange
news in awed voices. Those who were supposed to be carrying
in dishes have set down their trays. An Indian Slave *has been*
cleaning ashes from the fireplace into a wooden bowl. Donna
Veri, *an old woman, has turned from giving him directions to*
listen to the women.

Maria. And Estevan, too, is dead?

Nuna. I don't know. He didn't say.

Maria. Yes, dead. I knew it.

Lita. Yes, dead. I knew it.

Raquel. Who told you this?

Nuna. Santos. Graso heard him.

Carlotta. But is Taos defeated?

Cristina. Defeated? How could Taos be defeated?

Lita. Yes. How could it be?

Nuna. He didn't say that . . .

   [Graso, *an old peon, enters*]

Graso. Someone must speak to Donna Josefa . . .

Maria. Graso! What was this news?

Cristina. Graso . . .

    [*The Indian goes out with the ashes*]

Graso. Someone must speak to Donna Josefa at once. Santos, the coward, brings word and runs away! He will not come in! No, he must leave it to me!

Raquel. But what has happened?

    [*A wailing song is heard from without*]

Graso. Mind you, it comes from Santos, not from me. Santos said there was a great battle, and General Montoya taken prisoner, and a great trampling and running in the snow . . . for, you see, it snowed there in the pass where they were . . .

Cristina. General Montoya taken! . . .

Graso. It's not my news . . . it's Santos brings it . . . and you must tell Donna Josefa. . . . Run in and tell her, Maria.

Maria. No, no, not I.

Raquel. Conchita will go. Run in, Conchita, and tell her.

Conchita. But what shall I tell her?

Christina. That there's been a battle, and Graso is here . . .

Graso. No . . . say nothing about me.

    [Conchita *goes out*]

Raquel. Graso . . . what more did he say?

Graso. No more. . . .

Raquel. Yes yes . . . there was something about Pedros!

Graso. Who would believe a great liar like that when he says General Montoya is taken prisoner by gringos . . . and if we cannot believe him in regard to the one thing is it likely he spoke truth in respect to the other?

Raquel. Graso, for the love of our mother, is my Pedros killed?

Graso. Pedros?

Raquel. Yes, Pedros! For God's love, say!

Graso. What you have heard.

Raquel. He's dead!

Graso. If one wishes to believe a great liar.

Maria. And Estevan?

Graso. Why, as to Estevan, no . . . I heard nothing.
[*He turns*]

Cristina. Graso, look at me . . . speak not what we wish, but what is true.

Lita. Is it Americans we fight with, Maria?

Maria. Be quiet! Yes, Americans.

Graso. You must repeat the message to Donna Josefa . . . and tell her it is lies . . . only she must hear it. . . .
[*He goes to the door*]

Veri. Stay and tell her yourself!

Graso. I . . . I bring no news!
[Conchita *returns*]

Conchita. Donna Josefa wishes to see Graso!

Christina. Graso . . .

Graso. Have I prophecy? . . . I know no more! Tell her I had gone.

　　[*He goes out*]

Cristina. Nunita!

Nuna. I don't know, Cristina.

Cristina. No one will tell me, I see. I must find him myself.

Carlotta. Where is Santos?

Nuna. He went on down to the village.

Raquel. But if Montoya's prisoner, then they're all taken prisoner, or dead!

Carlotta. We'll go after him.

Cristina. Yes.

　　[*They go toward the door*]

Veri. How they weep, the little fat-brains! How they drip! Tender hearts, broken hearts!

Conchita. And why not, then? Is it any time for laughing?

Veri. Don't spit at me, little brimstone image. I know them and their race. They've no sooner one man killed over them than they've crawled under another, and more likely than not an Americano! More than once I've wondered whether the pure blood of Spain is more likely to turn dark with Indian or white with the northerners.

Cristina. We haven't all traveled your path, Veri.

Lita. You hear that, Veri? You hear?

Veri. You've been more places than the stations of the cross, little lambs of God!

Carlotta. Let her talk.
[*She starts to go*]

Veri. Only take care Mateo doesn't come home at the wrong moment, Carlotta.

Carlotta. What do you mean?

Veri. Nothing.

Carlotta. If you mean . . .

Veri. I do mean! And why not? Let the conquerors conquer! Only I've never had a gringo under my skirts, chiquita.

Nuna. Come, mother, let her alone.

Carlotta. But she lies!

Veri. Was there not one tall hunter from the north who escaped when they killed the governor?

Cristina. Come, Carlotta, nobody believes her.

Carlotta. It's all lies, lies, lies . . .

Veri. I won't say a word, I promise you.

Nuna.
[*Aghast*]
She's . . . she's wicked. She's as wicked as she is dirty.

Veri. All I say is you've been more places than the stations of the cross . . .
[Donna Josefa *enters*]

. . . and little brimstone here is the fruit of one of your trips! And Nuna is another!

Josefa. What is all this noise? Why are you in the hall at this hour?

Raquel. Forgive us, Donna Josefa. We followed Nunita in because she brought news of the battle.

Josefa. What news?

[*There is silence*]

What news? Nuna?

Nuna. It was Graso that brought it, Donna Josefa.

Josefa. Yes . . . but . . . what was it? And where is Graso?

Nuna. It seems they both ran, Donna Josefa, both sides. And it was fought in darkness and there was snow falling on the mountain, so that nothing is sure.

Josefa. Is that all? Come . . . what else?

[*Another pause*]

Raquel. It is said that a number of the men of Taos have been killed, Donna Josefa, and a number taken prisoner, among them General Montoya himself . . . but we know this to be untrue.

Josefa. How do you know it to be untrue?

Raquel. We cannot believe that, if you please.

Lita. Did you know that we fight with Americanos, Donna Josefa? It's true. Just now they told me.

Josefa. Nuna, who brought this news?

Nuna. Santos.

Josefa. Bring him to me.

Nuna. He has gone to the village.

Josefa. Bring him . . . have him found. And stop that
music. Tell them to take their wailing further away. Out
now, all of you.

[*All go except* VERI *and* JOSEFA]

Veri. Well, if it be so you're at least rid of him before you
have to take second place in his house. The gringos
spare no prisoners.

Josefa. Take out your ashes and beware you don't spill
them!

Veri. In all humility, yes, madonna.

Josefa. What were you saying to the women?

Veri. I was only reminding them, since they are so young
and so fat-brained, that the women of a country never
change, Donna Josefa. Lo, if a mare but answer the bit
softly and remember her paces, what matters a change
of riders now and then?

Josefa. Empty your ashes.

Veri. Oh, it was nothing about madonna . . . not the lightest word.

Josefa. You have spoken too many covert insults about me,
Veri. I'm not compelled to hear them.

Veri. No, truly? I was once in a position to repel insults
myself, dear lady. I was his first love . . . his second bore
him two sons . . . you are the third . . . and a fourth
trembles now into his waiting arms. Bear insults, Josefa!

You will yet bear ashes like myself and Diana will give you orders.

Josefa. When I live to take her orders!

Veri. That was what I said! But I lived . . . and I took orders . . . even from you!

[FATHER MARTINEZ *has entered from within*]

Josefa.

[*Pointing*]

Quick!

[VERI *goes through the outer door*]

Martinez. Good evening, Donna Josefa.

Josefa. Good evening, father. I was not aware that we had a guest.

Martinez. I have only now come up the path . . . and I heard the women crying. . . .

Josefa. There's news of a battle . . .

Martinez. Yes. Rumors have reached the village.

Josefa. A soldier was here . . . Santos.

Martinez. He's below now . . . with a crowd around him.

Josefa. It's his story? That Pablo's a prisoner?

Martinez. His among others.

Josefa. Do you believe it?

Martinez. Remember this was a battle fought at night and in great confusion. Those who ran away would need a good story to tell.

Josefa. Yes . . . but it shakes one . . . it might happen.

Martinez. Don't let their hysteria take hold on you. The peons are a credulous lot and their wives are worse. They believe the worst to avert misfortune. There'll be better news tonight.

Josefa. God send it soon.

Martinez. Pablo Montoya is an old hand at mountain warfare. He's never been defeated or even checked. He's not the man to be beaten in a first skirmish, nor to be taken prisoner at any time.

Josefa. But suppose it were worse than that ? What happens to you . . . or me . . . or to this house?

Martinez. Worse than that? Worse than prisoner? Ask what would happen to Taos . . . and New Mexico? We are the farthest arm of an old civilization here. . . . We are rich, and there are great houses on our hills. . . . But there has been only one man of all the ricos, who dared face the north and fight it. And that is your husband. He must return.

Josefa. And he will?

Martinez. Yes . . . and he will.

Josefa. Only . . . you say that out of a great need to have it so.

Martinez. Perhaps.

Josefa. And there's something else behind it.

Martinez. No.

Josefa. Yes. You don't trust me. You know that if Pablo were dead there'd be some power in my hands. And you want to know what I'd do with it.

Martinez. Would you answer such a question?

Josefa. Not till I know what power I'll have.

Martinez. Let us be honest. It has occurred to you as well as to me that if Pablo were dead on the mountain, Federico would inherit his place and his power. Also that you are not much older than Federico . . . and he looks on you with friendly eyes.

Josefa.

   [*Angry*]

If you were not a priest!

Martinez. Forget who I am! When things happen one faces them! You are Pablo's wife and Federico is his son. Nevertheless, if Pablo's dead you'll go to Federico. . . .

Josefa. You should have thought of that before you encouraged Pablo to set a new wife over me!

Martinez. But I haven't, Josefa!

Josefa. You knew of it! He wouldn't go about it without telling you! It's like him to pick out a slave I gave orders to, and plan to make her mistress over me!

Martinez. But I had no part in it. He will do as he pleases in this as in other things. If any man could influence him I might . . . but it was hopeless.

Josefa. Did you try?

Martinez. I did. Not so much for you, it may be, but to keep his weakness from the world. When we all depend so heavily on one man it's dangerous to allow laughter at him. And after all, he's sixty . . . she's not yet twenty. No matter how much power a man wields they always laugh a little at that . . . in corners. . . .

Josefa. I had my laugh . . . but it was a bitter one.

Martinez. His father was lord of life and death before him, and he's been a god so long here in the valley that he thinks he's a god in fact. That's his strength, too, though it sometimes makes him a fool.

Josefa. I hate him! Hate him!

Martinez. Well . . . that part of it's done. If he lives he's earned your hatred. But if he's dead, what are we to do, Josefa?

Josefa. It's not for me to decide.

Martinez. Federico will decide it. Help me with that, Josefa! We cannot retreat . . . must not be defeated. Help me to hold Federico to what his father would have done!

Josefa. Father, if Pablo Montoya is dead on the mountain, it won't matter much who rules in Taos . . . or who influences the ruler! Federico could never hold back the Americanos. It's senseless to think so.

Martinez. Montoya's son—

Josefa. And don't be misled about me! Much as I hate Montoya, I hate the Americanos more! May he live to kill them! I'll be a slave in his house if I must, with his new woman over me . . . but may he live to kill them! Does that answer you?

Martinez. Josefa . . .

> [DIANA, *a girl of eighteen, comes in, finds that she is intruding, and goes on toward the outer door*]

Diana. I'm sorry. I thought I heard someone calling. Was there news . . . of the battle?

Josefa. No. Nothing.

Diana. Oh.

> [*She goes on*]

Martinez. There have been conflicting reports, Diana, but nothing we can count on.

Diana. Thank you, father.

> [*She goes out*]

Josefa. There walks his new lady, a skin with ten years less wear . . . and that's all she has.

Martinez. I've always thought her a gentle child.

Josefa. Does a woman tempt without intending it? She'll be fat, though, fat before I am, and uglier when she's forty than I'll be at fifty.

Martinez. And less faithful. He may discover that—

Josefa. That she loves Felipe?

Martinez. You know that, too?

Josefa. Only that I've seen it in their eyes!

Martinez. Felipe is his heart's darling, his stainless son. And

Felipe loves the girl he intends to marry. I think this
may make the marriage more than doubtful.

Josefa. No. He'd kill Felipe.

Martinez. He'd be in no mood for marrying.

> [*There is a sudden loud cry outside from the crowd of peons,
> then a silence followed by a babble of voices.* DIEGO, *a
> peon, enters*]

Diego. Don Federico is returning!

Martinez. Federico!

Diego. His troop is climbing the trail!

Martinez. We'll know from him.

Diego. Excuse me, father! Excuse me, madonna.

> [*She runs out*]

Martinez. But you spoke truth concerning Pablo? You'd
rather take a lower place in his household than see him
defeated?

Josefa. If I can bear it! If I find I can bear it!

Martinez. Then remember this, Donna Josefa: if he has
been defeated, and we are never to see him again, we
must still go on without him. Federico will have to step
into his place. Whatever has happened, help me to keep
up Federico's courage.

Josefa. I'll do what I can.

> [FEDERICO *enters with* TWO SOLDIERS *and many women
> and peons listening for news.* DIANA *slips in among
> them. The men are dressed in black buckskin, with silver
> buttons. Serapes are thrown over the soldiers' shoulders.*

FEDERICO'S *hunting-shirt, however, is of white buck-skin, the mark of the men of the* MONTOYA *family*]

Federico. Greetings, Donna Josefa . . . greetings, father!
We're back from the wars! Clear out of here, you trash!
Nobody's killed so far as I know, I tell you . . .
They ran like hell, the pack of them . . . they never
Got close enough to get killed! Get out! Get out!

> [*The crowd clears out, the soldiers with them.* DIANA *goes toward the inner door*]

Are we alone? The news is bad enough
In conscience. My father's dead. He was cut off
At the pass by a posse of trappers. We tried to reach him
But they were all massacred there. Keep this from the peons
Till something's decided. They may take to the hills
If they hear of it.

Martinez. And so . . . Montoya's dead . . .

Federico. We waited as long as there seemed any chance . . .
But these trappers take scalps like Indians; they wouldn't neglect
A trophy like Pablo Montoya's.

Martinez. And how are we left?

Federico. We're left as we always were . . . hanging on by our eye-lids.
They met us with five hundred men . . . we had,
Say, fifteen hundred. They were trappers with rifles
And a few troops . . . they've sworn to get revenge
For the massacre at Taos. The man who ordered
The American governor killed brought this on us

And we'll all pay for it . . . the ones who've paid already,
They're the lucky ones.

Martinez. You were defeated?

Federico. God love you!
   What do you expect? Fifteen hundred with spears
   And bows and arrows, and a few old-fashioned muskets
   Go out to meet troops from the north, and trappers who
      hunt
   For a living! Is it likely we'd win? If it hadn't been dark
   With a heavy snow falling, just when it bothered them
      most
   They'd be here now in possession, and we'd be hidden
   Somewhere in the rocks with the catamounts.

Martinez. And why,
   If I may ask, are they not here, these victors?

Federico. Because the snow sent them back. They hadn't
      counted
   On two feet of snow in the trail, and they returned
   To reorganize for the weather. But not for us,
   Let me assure you. We didn't hinder them.

Martinez. There's only one pass. You met them there?

Federico. Holy father,
   What's a pass to a trapper? They went around it, be-
      hind it
   Under it, any way but through it . . . the troops
   Tried a charge at the summit, and a few were killed,
   But that was their only error.

Josefa. What can we do?

Federico. Before they break through and exterminate us all
    To pay us out in kind, someone who can speak
    Had better speak for the valley, and speak quickly
    While there's still time to negotiate.

Martinez. Never.

Federico. Well,
    Perhaps you want to die, but I don't. Not yet.
    The United States has formally taken over
    This region of ours, and sent a governor . . .
    We killed him and killed every northerner we could find
    Along with him in Taos. Now vengeance may be
    Delayed sometimes . . . bad weather can block the roads
    And even cool the blood, but a governor
    Was killed, and that's a first-rate challenge to
    The northerners' sovereignty!

Martinez. It was meant to be.

Federico. Exactly . . . and it was . . . and they'll roll down
    On us, like the mills of God. It may take time,
    But it's sure as that . . . New Mexico is lost
    To Spain and to Mexico, and to you and me.
    It's as sure as death . . . and the only thing we can hope
    To save out of it is our lives . . . if we're in time. . . .

Martinez. You are the elder son
    Of Pablo Montoya, Federico . . . it will be presumed
    That you speak for Taos and New Mexico
    In your father's absence . . . but before you speak
    Give me a word with you in private.

Federico. Surely . . .
  Any number.

Martinez. Now?

Federico. When I've disposed
  My troops and given a few last orders. Then
  I shall be at your service. Give me this room alone
  A little while, Josefa.

Josefa. Very well.
  [MARTINEZ *and* DIANA *go out*]

Federico. I shan't need you, Narciso: Tell the men
  To meet at dawn at the church for a muster call.
  Till then they can sleep.

Narciso. Yes, captain.

Federico. And, on your way,
  Send in the prisoner to me.
  [NARCISO *goes out*]

Josefa. I give you welcome,
  And my love, Federico.

Federico. Thank you, Josefa.

Josefa. No more?

Federico. This is desperate business. I have no time.

Josefa. We have this moment.

Federico. When I'm trying to snatch
  Some safety from the wreck . . . bear this in mind,
  We must not be seen together.

Josefa. When have I
    Forgotten that?

Federico. Also it's necessary
    For both of us to forget whatever's past
    Between you and me.

Josefa. And why?

Federico. Because, for one thing,
    You are my father's wife.

Josefa. You thought little of that
    A day or two ago. And if, as you say,
    Pablo is dead, there's less reason to think of it now.
    What are you trying to think yourself into? What wrong
    Have I done, that wasn't done me first? A woman
    Has a right to any revenge she can take!

Federico. That's true.
    Take any revenge you can, then. But not with me.

Josefa. Why, yes . . . I see it. You're to be in power
        here . . .
    And I'm not chosen. Not now. Who is it, then?
    Who is it?

Federico. No one.

Josefa. Diana? I think it is.
    She's snared you too. I've seen you look after her . . .

Federico. It's no one.

Josefa. It is Diana. May she burn
    In hell, and all three with her!

Federico. Will you go now?

> [*An* OFFICER, *dressed as a trapper is brought to the door by* TWO SOLDIERS]

Leave him alone with me.

> [JOSEFA *goes within. The* TWO SOLDIERS *go through the out-side door, closing it.* FEDERICO *closes the door behind* JOSEFA]

The devil's in these priests,
And the women, too.
What happened at the pass?

Officer. It worked as planned.

Federico. And my father . . . ?

Officer. It's pretty certain.
There was nobody left alive there.

Federico. You do your work thoroughly.

Officer. You weren't
Exactly in this for his health, were you? Be thankful
He's out of your way. He'd put you out of his
Fast enough.

Federico. I know that. It can't be helped.
I'll have to go through with it.

Officer. Good. What is it you want?

Federico. I want to govern Taos . . . with your guarantee

Officer. You have little to offer.

Federico. I've already given
More than you'll find it easy to repay.

You'd have walked into the old man's trap, and your
  nose
Would be two feet under snow if I hadn't stopped you.
Do you find that little?

Officer. No.
  But that's done . . . that's past. We did win, and I think
  You'll agree the war's over.

Federico. And that's what a word of honor means to Ameri-
  canos!
  The war's over,
  And whatever you promised is wiped out.

Officer. I don't say that . . .
  But I do say, don't ask too much, don't hope
  To get all your father had and our guarantee
  Behind you to keep it. No one can guarantee
  You'll keep your job if you muff it, also my powers
  Are limited here. I'll be doing well for you
  If I save your property for you, and that of your friends.
  Or even part of it.

Federico. Be on your way then!
  If that's how much you trust me, and all you're trusted
  At home, I've no more to say!

Officer. There's no use being touchy
  And turning Castilian on me at this stage.
  I can use you and you can use me, but kindly
  Don't ask too much . . . or you'll ask more than I've got
  And you'll get nothing. This is the way we stand:
  Taos has been defeated, and Taos is due
  To be ground under. You murdered our governor

And very likely you'll have to produce a scape-goat
To stand the gaff for that. But when that's over
We'll want somebody in power here that understands
The peons and the ricos . . . and you could have it
And keep your father's property to boot
If you're willing to take orders, and keep order among
Your aristocratic friends.

Federico. Oh, I'm to take orders.

Officer. You're damn right you'll take orders! You'll be glad
Of the chance to live unmolested on your land.
You've had it soft here, you and your class. Your peons
Jump when you speak. The king of Spain couldn't ask
More than your father got in the way of service.
But that's all past. Times change. But I'll save your ranch,
And my price for this is exactly half your holdings.

Federico. Half my land?

Officer. I could take all, but I leave you half of it,
Being generous to a fault.

Federico. A Yankee peddler . . .
That's what I have to deal with!

Officer. I could make it
Two-thirds, now I've been insulted, but I won't,
I'll stick to half.

Federico. And I'd live neighbor to you
And see you lining your nest with what you've stolen.
No, by God, I can't do that!

Officer. I have no more desire to live next door

To you than you to me. I won't live here.
I'll put an agent in charge.

Federico. Why, then, I'll take it. . . .
Provided I don't have to see you again.

Officer. Good. Then . . .
You'll be willing to sign this paper before I go.

Federico.
   [*Reading it*]
No, I will not. This takes the house from me.

Officer. Sign it, my good lad, sign it . . . and I'll try hard
To save the estate from appropriation by
The new governor. Your father was a rebel
Against our government, and his land's forfeit . . . yes,
All of it . . . but I think I can save it.

Federico.
   [*He sits down and signs the paper*]
If I'd known what this would come to you could all be
   damned.
And I'd go with you, before I'd touch this!

Officer. I swear I've done you a favor. One more thing . . .
I want a map of this place.

Federico. What place?

Officer. The estate . . .
I want to know what I've got. It's a peddler's notion . . .
But I want to see it.

Federico. There is none.

Officer. Draw one then . . .
  I want to see it.
    [FEDERICO *goes to a case near the fireplace, takes out papers
      and brings a map. The* OFFICER *looks at it*]
  How many acres in all?

Federico. Eighteen thousand.

Officer. Why, that's enough for both,
  Plenty for both. I'll take this with me, and have
  A copy made.

Federico. I may need it.

Officer. I'll bring it back,
  Or another just as good, showing your half.
  You see I'm a man of my word. I stick to half.
  Do you want the place you're offered?

Federico. I'll take it.

Officer. Remember
  This is no child's play. If you show any sign
  Of treachery . . . and you'll be watched . . . you go
  By a quick route. You won't be popular
  With the new citizens you'll have.

Federico. I know . . .
  And better than you can tell me, what's left to me,
  And what my place will be.

Officer. Get the ricos out then . . .
  See to it there's no resistance, or not enough
  To make us trouble, and I'll do my part . . .

Federico. Well, I'll do mine.
  You'll find me here alone when you march on Taos.

Officer. Goodnight, then.

Federico. Goodnight.

> [*He leads to the inner door*]

Go this way. The small door there sharp to your right.
It leads to an alley-way, and that will take you
To a little gate. Open it. There's a path
Straight down the hill.

> [*The* OFFICER *goes out.* FEDERICO *returns to the table. The
> women have begun their wailing song again outside.*
> FEDERICO *listens for a moment, then makes a gesture of
> impatience and strikes a bell.* GRASO *enters*]

Graso. Yes, senor.

Federico. Tell them to take that tune of theirs further
away.
What's the matter with them now?

Graso. Some of your men, senor, brought confirmation of
deaths, and the women are mourning.

Federico. They'll have to do their mourning outside the
plaza tonight. I've heard too much of it. Tell them that.

Graso. Yes, senor. Also Don Hermano and Don Miguel
have returned and wish to speak with you.

Federico. Let them come in.

> [GRASO *goes out.* FATHER MARTINEZ *enters from within*]

Martinez. We've seen many torches across the valley,
Federico.
They were near Don Hermano's hacienda.

Federico. He's here,
And Don Miguel with him.

Martinez. Good. They may perhaps help me
  With what I wanted to say. I wanted to see you
  Before you were committed to a course
  Toward the Americanos.

Federico. It doesn't follow, you know,
  That because I'm my father's son, I'll do as he did,
  Or that his friends will be mine.

Martinez. I have no wish
  To be an inherited friend.
  But if we can help each other, why not?

Federico. I doubt
  That you can help me. If, in any way,
  I can help you . . . why, speak.
    [Don Hermano *and* Don Miguel *enter. They are ricos
      proudly dressed*]

Hermano. You're here before us,
  Don Federico.

Federico. You're welcome, Don Hermano,
  And you, Don Miguel.
    [*They embrace*]

Miguel. Thank you. Now, God be praised.
  There's one Montoya here!

Hermano. No word of your father?

Federico. None.

Miguel. Nor of Felipe?

Federico. Yes, he was seen
  After the battle.

Hermano. He'll be with us then,
And that will help. Good-evening, father.

Martinez. Good-evening,
Don Hermano . . . and to you, Don Miguel . . .
I saw the lights around your gates and found them
Most reassuring.
[*They bow to* MARTINEZ, *who returns the salutation*]

Miguel. It was reassuring to be there . . .
And to find I had some neighbors left.

Martinez. You led your men home with you?

Miguel. What remained of them.
There were some missing. Hermano overtook me
And brought me along . . . We mean to see this through.

Hermano. Whatever we do we must do together now . . .

Martinez. I knew we could count on you.

Hermano. And whatever has happened
To Pablo Montoya . . . we pledge ourselves, and I think
We can pledge all the ricos that return,
To stay with you to the end.

Miguel. It's touch and go;
We must face that, for Montoya was our man . . .
But if there's still Federico to lead them, and they
Aren't given a moment to think, or consult their wives,
We can herd them into one last dash, and catch
The Americans off their guard.

Federico. It might be done.

Hermano. Can you think of a better way?

Federico. I can think of nothing
That won't be fatal in the end.

Hermano. You'd surrender?

Federico. No.
What good would it do to surrender? We're under death
sentence . . .
All of us if we stay here.

Martinez. Suppose your father
Were now alive, what plan would he follow?

Federico. If you
Are fortunate enough to know, why answer?

Martinez. The Yankees
Are on the way back to Santa Fe. They find it
Rather hard going. They'll be camped tonight
Not far from where you met them. At the pass.
They'll be cold and sleep sound, and keep a poor guard,
Not having much discipline. They're at your mercy.
Your father'd be there before morning.

Federico. And suppose we slaughtered four
Or five hundred, and the rest got away
To tell the story, well, then, what have we gained?
Only another massacre to set
Against our names and rouse the Americans.

Martinez. They wouldn't march so readily this way
Next time, if they left five hundred men on the hills.

Federico. Are you honest in this, and crazy, or cunning and
sane?
You have a brain, you must know, if you lie awake

And think in the night, that we can't win over a nation.
We're a broken end of an empire here, cut off
And dying . . . Mexico's a republic, and we're
Disowned at Mexico City. The United States
Has men and arms and armies. Do you want to die?
Have you set your heart on dying?

Martinez. No.

Federico. Well, then
   You must be cunning . . . you must see your way
   To send me against the north to wreak your vengeance
   While you escape, and let the rest of us pay.
   My father's paid already . . .

Martinez. Your father needed
   No urging.

Federico. Then you're innocent of his death.
   But it's still true that you knew when he went
   That it was hopeless . . . you knew when the massacre
   Was planned that it would all turn out as it has . . .
   You knew they'd send an army against us then
   And we couldn't stop it . . .

Martinez. It seems to have stopped . . .

Federico. Not for long!
   If it took them a hundred years they'd have to wipe out
   The blood that was spilled here . . .

Martinez. Are you so sure
   The north will beat us?

Federico. I wish I were as sure
   Of living through the next year, as I am of that.

Beat us? Our hundreds against their millions?
Our muskets against their rifles! Beat us!

Martinez. When
Your father was alive, would you have dared
To tell him that?

Federico. What's that to do with it?

Martinez. This: the reason you couldn't tell him then
Was that it wasn't true then. While he was alive
We couldn't be conquered. Yes, while there was one
In this whole region that would not bow, they were helpless
To set up their sovereignty—here.

Federico. They set it up.

Martinez. And he tore it down! The strength
Of a state is not in its numbers but in faith.
I have seen your father stand at the plaza gate
And look out over the valley . . . and every peon
Looking up from the fields, and every neighbor
On the adjoining hills, knew while he stood there,
Stood firm and would not falter, their world was safe;
The rulers to the north
Knew that, and when they had to make a gesture,
Urged on by those behind, they made it slyly,
Reluctantly and in fear! This governor
They sent out over us, he was a man of straw
Set up to try the wind and see how much
We could be made to endure. We endured nothing.
Pablo Montoya turned on them. They died
Before an order was issued.

Federico. And Pablo Montoya
   Is also dead.

Martinez. Even so, they've retreated.
   Even so, I feel all about us still the spirit
   Of Pablo Montoya. His courage
   Is over us like a mantle, and it falls
   Inevitably to your shoulders.

Federico. No.

Martinez. But it does!
   Take up the lance he dropped, call on us to follow . . .
   Believe in us and our cause and the great days
   We've lived through in the past, and this enemy
   You think so well of dissolves to a rabble before you
   And lets you through! The man who is his son
   Has greatness in him! Wherever he went
   He carried with him the center of an age,
   The center of a culture, and people's hearts,
   Clung to him like vines to rock! You, too, are this
     man . . .
   His other self, his heir . . . all eyes are on you . . .
   When you are in your house the people will say . . .
   He is in his house, we are secure . . . he thinks for us . . .
   We can sleep tonight. When you ride on a journey
   The people's gaze will go with you anxiously . . .
   And scan the horizon for your return! But beware,
   If you betray this.

Federico. Yes . . . he was such a man . . .
   And I might be.
     [*He rises*]

Even tonight, even now,
I could strike at them . . .

Miguel. You could do more than strike.
You could finish them . . . make an end to them.

Federico. No.
  [*The thought of his bargain has come back on him*]

Hermano. Think . . .
Think what we have to lose. Nowhere on this earth
Will we find a life like ours, or ever again
Live as we live here. Ours is a little clan.
But we stem from a great nation; this is worth defending
From gringos who have nothing.

Federico. Is he padre or wizard . . .
To turn the truth inside out? We're struck to the heart,
And the wound's mortal. It's too late for courage.
You know it as well as I.

Miguel. Too late! We've fought
One indecisive battle!

Federico. Too late because
We're out of fashion! Our guns are out of fashion,
Also our speech and our customs and our blood.
They're the new race with the new weapons!

Miguel. We must fight them or die.

Federico. We can retreat.

Hermano. And abandon Taos to them?

Martinez. Is that your counsel . . .
To abandon Taos?

Federico. I can think of nothing better.

Miguel. I believe you mean this.

Federico. I do.
> [*A pause*]

Miguel. Why, then, let's go.
I had some hope when I came here.

Federico. Don't think I'm happy
To say this to you. I like it no more than you do.

Hermano. No . . . but to leave our houses, our flocks, to turn
The peons adrift . . . I'd rather make a stand
And die for it. And you would!

Federico. No. I would not.

Miguel. Will you go now?

Hermano. Yes. Goodnight, Don Federico.

Federico. Goodnight, Don Hermano. Goodnight, Don Miguel.

Miguel. Goodnight.

Federico. What are your plans?

Hermano. I have none. We'll need
No plans for what's left to do.
> [Don Hermano *and* Don Miguel *go out*]

Martinez. And what are yours?
If I may ask.

Federico. To salvage what I can carry.

Martinez. What can one carry that's of any value?
   What we have is Taos. Losing our city,
   We have nothing left . . .
      [NUNA *comes to the door, bringing* SANTOS]

Federico. If you'll pardon me,
   I have much to do.

Nuna. Is Donna Josefa here?

Federico.
      [*Stepping toward the inner door*]
   What do you want?

Nuna.
      [*Frightened*]
   She sent me for Santos.

Federico. Must you track through the hall?
      [*He goes through the inner door*]

Nuna. She was here . . . she sent . . . He's angry at me.

Martinez. She may have sent you, dear child, but you are
   obviously not wanted now. Nor I either, you might add.
   . . . Come along, and bring Santos with you.
      [*He goes through the outer door.* DIANA *enters from within*]

Nuna. Senorita!

Diana. Yes.

Nuna. Is Donna Josefa within?

Diana. I don't know.

Nuna. She sent me . . . I was to bring old Santos . . .

Diana. Nunita, tell me . . . can you be true . . . and silent?

Nuna. Yes, senorita . . .

Diana. Could you be a friend to me?

Nuna. But I am a servant . . . I'll be your servant.

Diana. No . . . it's more than that. If I ask you a question, you'll never tell that I asked it?

Nuna. Never.

Diana. Then . . . tell me . . . Is Senor Felipe alive?

Nuna. Yes, senorita, they think so.

Diana. But they're not certain?

Nuna. No.

Diana. He'd be back if he were alive . . . don't they say that? . . . I thought I heard them say that, from a window . . .

Nuna. He's late coming, but that might be. Santos?

Diana. No . . . no!

Nuna. I'll be careful. Santos . . .

　　[Santos *comes forward*]

Santos. Yes, Nunita.

Nuna. Did anyone go back along the pass to look at the faces of the slain?

Santos. No, no, it was dangerous. You could not.

Nuna. But if any were wounded . . . they would be cared for?

Santos. Girl, how can I tell? . . . Am I not brought here to speak with the Donna Josefa?

Nuna. You speak with Senorita Diana, pig, and she is even greater than Donna Josefa!

Santos. Is she indeed? I did not know.
[*He takes off his cap*]

Nuna. The senorita wishes to know if the wounded of Taos will be cared for.

Santos. Ah, that is with God!

Nuna. One can see that it is not with Santos.

Santos. But senorita!

Nuna. Would you go back along that trail for her?

Santos. But when one has escaped by miracle with his life would he tempt the good God by returning?

Nuna. Our Santos is afraid . . . afraid of Americanos!

Santos. No . . . No! Who would be afraid of Americanos? They are a small and weak nation, compared with the people of Taos . . . but they have rifles, and rifles are deadly.

Nuna. Then that's all, Santos . . .

Santos. But the Donna Josefa . . .

Nuna. She won't see you today.

Santos. If I have incurred displeasure . . .

Diana. No . . . no . . . only that's all now.
[SANTOS *withdraws, cringing*]

Nuna. But I would go.

Diana. Where?

Nuna. Back along the trail.

Diana. We'd never find it . . . You'd go with me?

Nuna. Yes.

Diana. We'd never find it.

Nuna. No, it's true. We wouldn't. It's dark and cold . . . and a long way.

Diana. Only . . . there are men lying there at this moment.

Nuna. You love him?

Diana. No! . . . say nothing of this! . . . run away! . . . Oh, Nuna, Nuna . . . I can't talk to you . . . nor to anyone . . . but you know what hangs over me.

Nuna. I know. We have all heard.

Diana. And what do the women say?

Nuna. They say you're lucky mostly.

Diana. He may be dead.

Nuna. They say he is . . . and they say Felipe's alive.

Diana. Oh, God . . . if that could be true!

[VERI *enters carrying linen through*]

Veri. You're wanted, Nuna.

[*She goes up to* DIANA]

And this is the piece of flesh he had in his eye. This is his dish.

[*She pulls* DIANA'S *shawl away from her breast*]

Curds and cream for the old goat!

Nuna. Let her alone!

[*She drags* Veri *away*]

Veri. From what I hear he'll keep warm with the jackals tonight . . . not with my lady.

Diana. What have you against me, Veri?

Veri. That he should want you . . . that's all!

Nuna. You'd better go make those beds!

Veri. Before God, this one's putting on airs now . . . and she's pretty, too. She'll be marrying Don Federico and running the house. Well . . . when it happens remember I spat on you once . . . pht!

[*She goes in.* Nuna *is grave for a moment, then is unable to restrain a smile*]

Nuna. Forgive me.

[*A loud clear voice is heard outside calling a name,* "Felipe!"]

Martinez.

[*Outside*]

Now God be praised . . . Felipe! It is Felipe!

Felipe.

[*Outside*]

Good evening, father. It's Felipe. You're not mistaken

Martinez.

[*Outside*]

Wounded?

Felipe.

[*Outside*]

Enough to hurt. That's all.
[DIANA *sits*]

Martinez.
[*Outside*]
Let me see.

Felipe.
[*Outside*]
I'm well.

Martinez.
[*Outside*]
You come late.
[FELIPE *and* MARTINEZ *enter*]

Felipe. I went back over the ground to look for my father;
We found some dead and some dying; on both sides . . .
But not the man we were looking for.
[NUNA *goes out backwards, all eyes*]

Martinez. He was gone.

Felipe. He must be dead, or wounded too badly to answer.
We called his name . . . and I got this scratch on my pains.
Some of the trappers shot at us from the rocks,
Where they'd taken shelter. It's a moonless night,
And the snow fell so fast the bodies were covered
Before we reached them. And yet I can't believe
He's there among them.

Martinez. I hope not!

Felipe. I hope not. Good evening, senorita.

Diana. Good evening, senor.

Felipe. Federico's returned?

Diana. Yes, unwounded.

Felipe. I must speak to him.
I came upon real panic in the village.
They've heard of my father's death, but they're not
    mourning.
They've put away their guitars, and the burros
Are loaded for a flight to the mountains. Look, from that
    window.
You can see the lights of lanterns in the street
Gathering like fireflies. When these people are silent
They're badly frightened.

Martinez. Federico's here.
I'll tell him you've come.
    [*He goes within*]

Felipe. Diana.

Diana. Yes. Yes, senor.

Felipe. I break a bond with myself when I speak to you
Alone. I've sworn I would not.

Diana. Yes . . . I've known it.

Felipe. But now we have only a moment, and whether we'll
    ever
Be given another . . .
    [*He breaks off*]
Should my father not return
You'll have enemies here . . .

Diana. Yes.

Felipe. Count on me to help you
  In any way I can.

Diana. Then . . . he won't return?

Felipe. I did what I could to find him. If he were alive
  It seems there'd have been some trace . . . or a hint
    somewhere.
  Yet in my heart I think he lives.

Diana. And I . . .
  I think so.

Felipe. Why, Diana?

Diana. Because I fear it.

Felipe. I'm sorry . . . I fear . . . the other.

Diana. If he
  Had failed to see me, I could have loved him too.

Felipe. What plans we can make for you should be made
    at once.
  I think they'll lay this valley desolate . . .
  The Americans . . . and those of us whose lot
  Is cast with Taos will go with our city. But you
  Have northern blood in your veins . . . you came here
    by chance,
  A prisoner . . . and there's no reason why you should
    add
  One life more to the slaughter. There must be some way
  To send you where you'll be safe, and can find friends
  Before the worst happens. That much I can do.

Diana. Do you want me away?

Felipe. I want you to be safe.

Diana. And you stay here to be killed?

Felipe. That's the price one pays
For being a Montoya in Taos. There's no such reason
Why you should remain . . . Diana . . . if this were
    said . . .
This that's between us . . . if it were ever in words
You'd be mine in my heart . . . not his . . . I'd go mad
To take you in my arms . . . and it would be mad-
    ness . . .
Because I'd want him dead . . . my father . . . the man
I've loved and honored above all others . . . and still
Do love and honor.

Diana. If you must die with Taos . . .
Felipe, Felipe!

Felipe. Try not to say it!

Diana. Then I . . .
I must die here too.

Felipe. So long as one loves
In silence it can be borne . . . as much as before
My father stands between us.

Diana. Not if he's dead!

Felipe. But he's not . . . I feel it and know it. He'll be here
And take you from me. And how can I bear that now,
Now that I know? I should have left this house
And stayed away till it all burned out . . . but that

Was impossible . . . so I lived here, and loved you more
And fought against it. But always when I saw you
It's been the same.

Diana. I'm glad.

Felipe. We know it now.
We must be content with that.

Diana. But don't ask me to go.

Felipe. You're the one thing in my world
I can save out of it, and I must save it. You'd be
A needless sacrifice.

Diana. It's all needless, Felipe,
Needless and useless for you as well as for me.
You must not die, Felipe.

Felipe. But there's one thing
A man can't do . . .

Diana. What is it?

Felipe. Desert in danger.
I'm my father's son, Diana. We have a strict code.
I can't break with it, nor with him. I'm a Spaniard,
And I honor my line and my name.

Diana. But if all here
Are to die?

Felipe. Yes, even if he
Were dead, and I knew it, I couldn't leave Taos. Not
If I were to keep respect for myself and believe
Myself worth saving. But I could wish I'd been born
In the north like you! . . . Then I'd say, let all the rest

Go where they like . . . let Taos and the Rio Grande
Dissolve like a mist and leave me fatherless
Alone by a strange river . . . if you'd come with me!
In the north no questions are asked; a man and a maid
May come and go as they like. We could make our own
    kingdom
Somewhere among them.

Diana. And this defeat could mean freedom!

Felipe. Yes.

Diana. Felipe!

Felipe. Yes?

Diana. To think and act . . .
    To love as one wills . . . to speak and walk like a queen
    Freely in a free land . . . to love where we love
    And no one to forbid us. Why, that's no kingdom,
    Felipe, it's heaven!

Felipe. Heaven we can never have.

Diana. Are those the ways of the north?

Felipe. Yes.

Diana. And young
    And old go their own paths, and no one is bound
    To love except from his heart?

Felipe. Yes.

Diana. If these are my people,
    And their blood is mine, and their ways are better than
        these,
    Could you not live by them?

Felipe. No.

Diana. He's dead, Felipe.
    And all this is dead around us . . . dead or dying . . .
    He would have taken me from you when I loved you . . .
    Would still if he were here!

Felipe. If Taos is dying
    Put your love elsewhere, Diana, for I'm part of Taos . . .
    And my blood's strong in me. You look abroad and see
    The earth as a maze of many roads and cities,
    All open to you . . . and yours to choose . . . but I
    Am born to one world, and share its destiny
    Whether it's good or bad. If my father's dead
    I still belong to Taos. It's not a choice.
    It's the only thing I can do.

Diana. Then I have no choice.
    I'll stay here with you.

Felipe. You'd do that . . . to be near me?

Diana. I have no more choice than you.

Felipe. Diana, if
    I put my arms once round you, I'll lose all sense
    Of what I have to do . . .
        [*He goes to her and takes her in his arms*]
    And so I lose it.

Diana. There's someone watching.
        [*She draws away from him.* FEDERICO, JOSEFA *and* MARTINEZ
        enter from within]

Josefa. Give them your blessing, father. She takes them
all . . .
Our chaste Diana! Father, sons, Holy Ghost . . .

Federico. Be silent! Greetings, Felipe.

Felipe. Greetings, brother.

Federico. You're wounded.

Felipe. It's not a wound. It's not that much.
[*The brothers embrace*]

Federico. Well . . . we've come out of this.

Felipe. In some fashion or other.

Federico. Yes . . . not too luckily . . .
Not with our father gone.

Felipe. I looked for him.

Federico. It was useless?

Felipe. No one had seen him.
No one knew what had happened to him. And still
I'm certain somehow he is alive.

Federico. If he were alive we'd have heard from him.
We'll have to get on without him.

Felipe. If he were dead
The world would be one thing . . . but if he returns
Something quite different. Whatever plans we make
Must fit with both.

Federico. My plans do fit with both.
[NARCISO *enters with a* SOLDIER]

Narciso. Don Federico, pardon me . . . I think you're
    needed
    Below . . . they're panic-stricken, both men and women
    . . .

Felipe. When I came through the village the peons were
    packing
    And ready to leave for the range. You must make some
    announcement
    Or they'll walk out from under us. Just now it looks
    Like the flight into Egypt down there . . . on a vast
    scale . . .
    Only the Josephs are mounted on the donkeys
    And the Marys are walking behind.

Federico. There's no danger tonight,
    Go down and quiet them, Narciso. Tell them
    I'll give them a leader, and let them go before morning.

Narciso. They won't believe me. The town's a caravan.

Federico. Wait then. I'll go down and talk to them.

Felipe. You'll give them
    A leader . . . and let them go?

Federico. I mean to stay here
    With a few friends who've made their minds up to it . . .
    And stand the attack when it comes. They'll over-run us,
    Of course, but someone must stay behind to delay them,
    And to wait for Pablo. He might come. The peons
    And those who wish to live are to take the trail
    And make their escape. I give you charge of that.

Felipe. You ask me to lead them?

Federico. Yes.

Felipe. That's a hard sentence . . .
  To lead a retreat from Taos at a time
  When men are needed here.

Federico. Brother, men are needed
  Most, where they'll do most good. If we all stay
  The siege might be prolonged, but it would end
  Exactly the same way. You're younger than I am
  And it's better that you should live and use what talents
  You have to find new lands for the citizens
  And slaves who are driven out.

Felipe. This may be necessary . . .
  But not till we know what's happened to our father.

Federico. You'll wait till morning, and then set out.

Felipe. I don't like it.
  It's a coward's job. If the peons must stampede,
  Let them go. The fight's as much mine as yours.

Federico. Brother, if we had one chance of holding out,
  I'd say try it . . . all of us . . . but since it's hopeless
  Before we start, I forbid it. It's noble to die,
  No doubt, when you have a noble cause to die for,
  But when you have no cause, when your cause is lost,
  The fewer lives lost the better.

Felipe. I don't like the role you
  Cast me for. Lead the retreat yourself,
  And leave me in Taos.

Federico. No.

Felipe. But I can say no
  As well as you, Federico. I won't go.

Federico. I've made it a command.

Felipe. I don't understand you, Federico.
  It's not like you to insist so firmly on dying . . .
  Forgive me for saying so.

Federico. Don't puzzle about it.
  I have my reasons for wanting you out of the house,
  And our father would have them if he were here.
  You say he's alive and will return. If he does
  He'll ask for Diana. I'd rather not have to tell him
  To look for her with you.

Felipe. And that's your reason?

Martinez. These orders of yours fit oddly with what you
    told me
  A while ago, Federico. You said, I believe,
  That others might die if they cared to, defending Taos,
  But you'd rather not.

Federico. It may be I've changed my mind.

Martinez. I don't think so. I think as Felipe does
  That there's something odd about it.

Federico. By God, he'll go,
  Or I won't answer for him!

Felipe. This is strange talk
  For a brother, Federico.

Federico. And you have strange manners

With the woman betrothed to your father! You're to go
And Diana stays here.

Felipe. And now I quite understand you.
You mean to make peace and save what's left for yourself . . .

Federico. You're a little mad, I think, to make such a
charge,
Mad with love, no doubt. Diana belongs
To Pablo Montoya, and he may return!
Meanwhile, to guard her honor, the least I can ask
Is that you take the road.

Josefa. He lies, Felipe.
He's done all this for Diana. Now strike at me!
But it's the truth!

Felipe. You hear?

Federico. Are we to listen
To women? My charge against you is just, and you
Retort with another. It's you who've been traitorous . . .
But I've given you a chance for life. Will you take com-
mand
Of the expedition to the south, as I've ordered you,
Or are you an enemy?

Felipe. I don't trust you.

Federico. Arrest him . . .
Arrest him, Narciso.

Martinez. You anticipate a little,
Federico. You're not yet master here.

Federico. You'll wait
  A long time for another. Arrest him!

Martinez. Narciso!
  Mind what you do!

Federico. If you ask for it I'll find
  A way to quiet you, too! I need no priest's leave
  For taking what I want. If I remain
  Your master here, Diana is mine to give
  And I take her for myself.

Felipe. Yes?

Federico. Let her learn to love
  Where she finds it necessary. As things stand you've
    nothing
  To offer her, and I have!
    [NARCISO *approaches* FELIPE]

Felipe.
    [*Brushing him aside*]
  May God pardon me.
    [*He draws his sword*]

Federico. Lay your hands on him!

Felipe. Give me fair play! You're not my father's son . . .
  I won't believe it!
    [FEDERICO *draws*]

Federico. Let him alone, then! I warn you!
  You're a novice at this business! I've made you an offer,
  And you'd be wise to take it!

Felipe. I'll take nothing!

[*The swords clash.* MARTINEZ *leaps between them, catches the blades under his arm and breaks* FEDERICO's *sharp off.* FEDERICO *drops the useless weapon and draws his dagger.* FELIPE *tosses his sword back over his shoulder and draws his dagger also. They manoeuver for position slowly and silently*]

Federico. Narciso!

Narciso. Yes!

[*He draws his sword and springs to* FEDERICO's *side.* FELIPE *stoops and picks up his sword. There is a sudden sharp shout in unison from a distance:* "Montoya! Pablo Montoya!" *After a pause this is repeated:* "Montoya! Pablo Montoya!"]

Martinez. That comes from the village! Wait!

Federico. What are they saying?

The Crowd. Montoya! Pablo Montoya!

Martinez. They're calling Pablo Montoya!

Josefa. He's returned!

Felipe. Yes. He's returned.

Diana.

[*At the window*]

They're coming up from the village . . . along the road.

[*She looks at* FELIPE, *and he at her. There is a silence, then* THE CROWD *can be heard singing*]

Federico. If he has come back we'll say no more about this.

[FELIPE *looks at him without answering*]

You've made a groundless charge against me, Felipe,

And I was angry. But I'm willing to forget it
If you are.

Felipe. What do you think it matters to me
Who you've betrayed or when?

[*He goes quickly to* DIANA *and bends over her*]

Martinez. We shall all do well,
I think, to forget whatever passed in this room.

[*The singing becomes audible again as* THE CROWD *rounds a
corner of the hills, and a patter of feet is heard.* CON-
CHITA *comes in hurriedly*]

Conchita.

[*Breathless*]

It's . . . he's come!

Martinez. Yes . . . we're waiting for him.

[*The singing stops and nothing is heard save the trampling of
feet.* TWO *or* THREE WOMEN *come to the door and edge
in silently. They are followed by* BOYS *and* MEN. *The
stage is filled, all looking back at the doorway as they
pause.* PABLO MONTOYA *enters, a solid, burning-eyed
man of sixty, his hair gray, his face intent. He stops to
take in the room, then comes to the center.* OTHERS *enter
behind him.* MONTOYA'S *glance lights up as he sees*
FELIPE. *He lays a hand on his arm and then turns
toward* FEDERICO *to greet him also. But he stops when
he notices the broken sword*]

Montoya. Whose sword was that?

Federico. Mine, Pablo.

Montoya. Take it up! It offends me! If swords must be
broken
Let them break in a gringo's throat, against the bone,

Not in our houses!

[FEDERICO *picks up the sword.* MONTOYA *looks round the room again*]

Men of Taos, I have come home, and I bring
Only a doubtful victory. Women of Taos,
What victory we have, little though it is,
Has saved us from slavery, and those we must thank
    for that
Lie now on the mountains. They chose rather to die
Than live not free. First, let us mourn for them.
Mourn with me, women of Taos. They were my friends,
And your heart-break's mine. But our mourning must
    be brief,
And forgotten in anger. Let the women go out.
All save Diana.

[*The women go*]

This was no defeat! We were betrayed at the pass,
Betrayed from within. If that were not so
We'd have spilled them like water, and not one death
Would have been needed!

Hermano. Betrayed!

Montoya. Just that!

I went back over their march. They'd followed the trail
Through every pass till they came to the one where we
    waited . . .
And then they went round to attack our flank! They
    knew
Where we were waiting for them! I read the story
There in the snow. It was plain. And somewhere among
    us

Some Indian-livered dog-spawn crouches that traded
Our plans to the north! Yes, by our God, and I'll find
   him
Before this night's out! If he stands here and hears me
Let him breathe deep, and taste the air! It's good,
This mountain air . . . and it's the last he'll have!
It happens I've taken an opportune prisoner or so,
And I know how to make them talk! We'll have that
   vengeance
Before we strike again!

Hermano. We attack tomorrow?

Montoya. This was no victory for the Americans,
   Remember! They had our plans . . . they attacked from
     the flank!
   Where they knew we were unprepared. And they came
     to punish
   The people of Taos. Instead we've crippled them
   And sent them limping home! Punish Taos! They go
     back
   To Santa Fe without seeing Taos! They left
   Their own dead too on the mountain, and they'll look
     twice
   Before they leap at our throats again! Why, look . . .
   This was no defeat . . . but a victory that will lead
   To victory again! They'll never touch Taos . . .
   They'll never push us back . . . no . . . rather we
   Will push them out of Santa Fe, and northward
   Back to their English mothers! We'll pledge to that.
   Let each man pour himself a glass of wine,

And fill it full, for we drink death to the Yankees!
  [*The men fill their glasses*]
But before we drink we must know what more we drink
  to.
My ears are good. I have heard it said here and there
That Spain is old and I am old, and the dogs
Of the north will have their day. Do you believe this?
  [*There is a slight pause, then a murmur of* "no, no," "no, no"]
And if you did what place would you have in the world?
None. You'd be the dogs of slaves, you'd be
The slaves of dogs. We come of an old, proud race,
From that part of the earth where the blood runs hot,
  and the hearts
Of men are resentful of insult. We are either lords
And masters of ourselves, or else we die.
And who are these conquerors who intend to take
Our places and our rights? For this is our place,
We wrought it out of a desert, built it up
To beauty and use; we live here well, we have
Customs and arts and wisdom handed down
To us through centuries. They would break this up,
And scatter it, these tricksters from the north.
They come here penniless, homeless, living with squaws
For women, vagabond barbarians, with hardly
A language, no laws, no loyalty . . . traders . . . what-
  ever
They have they'll sell . . . behind each other's backs
They've sold me a thousand rifles! And I have them!
And when next we fight you'll use them.

  [*The men lean forward*]

And are these the men
To lop off an arm of Spain? Oh, brothers in blood,
If you are proud, take pride now in what we are!
It is said that Spain has abandoned us here, that we live
Cut off from allegiance . . . under an ancient banner
That's lost its meaning . . . but Spain has never gone
    back!
It's now three long centuries since Cortes led
His hundreds into Mexico. Had you listened
Then, you'd have heard Spain's enemies whispering . . .
She spreads too far, her power will weaken soon . . .
We'll wait . . . then strike! They waited a hundred
    years . . .
Then struck at Brazil! Two hundred years ago,
That was! And Spain roused and shook them off, and ran
The Dutch from her colonies, and invaded Flanders
And wrote on their doors with blood! And if you had
    listened
Behind those doors you'd have heard them whispering
    again:
Wait! Spain is old . . . she has endured too long . . .
We'll strike a little later! And they did wait.
Two hundred years they waited before Napoleon
Dared cross the border, and lost Europe crossing it!
And again they say Spain is old . . . she's ruled too long,
These stragglers from the north! She has ruled so long
That they are a race of children . . . and their plans
Are a child's plans, playing with sticks and mud. We
    have never
Gone back, our people . . . we never will! We'll push

These scavengers north, these eaters of dirt . . . we'll
    thrust them
North to the Lakes, take the St. Lawrence from them,
And leave them the eastern seaboard only so long
As they can hold it! That is what we drink to!
Who drinks with me?
    [*The men are motionless for a moment, then come forward to
        fill the glasses*]
There is a play that we perform at New Year's . . .
In which the men of Taos, retaliating
Against the Comanches, don Comanche war-paint,
Trail feathers in their hair, and charge like Indians,
And return victorious. And there's a final scene
That shows a silent field, with fallen men.
I was a young man then but I fought in that battle,
And others who fought there are still here. It's grown
To be a legend . . . but it was more than legend.
Out to the east a hundred miles there lies
A ring of bones still whitening in the wind
Where you can count them. Seven hundred men
And not one left alive. The Comanche nation
Never struck back. It was never a nation again.
Tomorrow the Americanos camp at Cordova.
They won't get farther. And before they wake we sur-
    round them,
This time with rifles, and a hundred years from now
Our children's children, passing through that valley,
Will count the white-picked skeletons and remember
Who turned the Americans. If any pause,
Thinking this is not without risk, some will die, why
    true,

But it's death if we wait for them here! We struck them
    first,
And we'll not be forgiven! If any man say in his heart:
I have too much to lose, I dare not die,
Let him remember this is my wedding night,
I go from a bride's arms to battle. No man risks more.
Who drinks with me?

> [*Each man lifts his glass. Suddenly they give a thunderous cry:*
>   "Montoya! Pablo Montoya!" *They raise the glasses*
>   *to their lips*]

CURTAIN

NIGHT OVER TAOS
ACT TWO

ACT TWO

Scene: *The same room a little later the same evening. The men have eaten and drunk and the remains of the food are on the table. A stack of long-barrelled rifles has been placed at the outer door, and the guests are beginning to file out toward them.*
A Few Women, *among them* Raquel, *come in to clear away.* Diana *is not in the room.* Martinez *is seated, waiting.*

Montoya. Let each man take his rifle as he goes. I take mine now.

    [He does so]

Sleep as long as you like tonight, as long as you can tomorrow. At sundown we start for Cordova, and it would be well to be fresh when we arrive. We should have drunk deeper if it were not for that, for the laws of the church run backward for me this evening, and I am to be married at midnight. All those of noble blood will return at that hour for the wedding. Goodnight to the rest.

The Men.

    [As they go out]

Goodnight, Don Pablo.

Montoya. Goodnight, and sleep sound.

    [He turns toward an inner door and the assembly is dispersing quietly. A woman's voice is heard calling outside]

The Voice. Don Pablo! Don Pablo! Let me come in!

    *[*Montoya *pauses and the others listen]*

Don Pablo!

Montoya. Let her in.

The Voice. In the name of God, justice! He's killed my daughter!

[*A* MIDDLE-AGED WOMAN *enters, the men standing aside. She is followed by a* SOLDIER *who leads* MATEO, *a Spaniard, the latter wearing a bandage round his head.* NUNA *comes in after them*]

The Woman. Don Pablo . . . will you hear me?

Montoya. What is it, Valeria?

Valeria. My daughter's murdered!

Montoya. By whom?

Valeria. Carlotta's murdered! Mateo killed her!

Montoya. Mateo?

Mateo. Why, yes, I killed her.

Montoya. Why?

Mateo. For no reason.

Montoya. Answer me.

Mateo. Why does a man kill a woman? Let the others answer!

Valeria. He had no reason! He came home and greeted us . . . and then he went to her room and strangled her!

Montoya. Mateo?

Mateo. That is so.

Montoya. You're ready to die for it?

Mateo. I have no defence. Do what you like with me.

Montoya. Who knows what lies behind it? Come . . . there
are women here. What was the cause?

[*There is no answer*]

Maria?

Maria. Don Pablo . . . she was Mateo's wife.

Montoya. Mateo won't touch you. What gossip have you
heard?

Maria. Don Pablo . . .

[*She pauses*]

Montoya. Yes?

Maria. At the time of the massacre one gringo escaped. It
was supposed he carried news to the north.

Montoya. We know that.

Maria. It is said Carlotta warned him.

Montoya. Nothing more? There should be more than that.

Maria. Nothing more was certain.

Cristina.

[*Under her breath*]

It was certain enough.

Montoya. Cristina?

Cristina. She brought all this on us. And she deserved it.

Nuna. They lied about her . . . lied!

Montoya. Be quiet, Nunita! How? What have you known?

Cristina. I've heard her talk.

Montoya. What did she say?

Cristina. She came to the market one day not long since, when Mateo had beaten her . . . and said she'd have her satisfaction.

Montoya. Well?

Cristina. She said that she had borne bastards to Mateo in the past and would bear him bastards again. She said that the men of the north thought all women angels and treated them so, but the Spaniards believed all women devils and therefore made devils of them . . .

Nuna.
    [*Whispering*]
    Lies, lies!

Montoya. That was all?

Cristina. No. We taxed her with knowing too well how the northerners treated a woman . . . and she said we would all bed with northerners before the year was out, and be glad of the change.

Montoya. Who else heard this?

Cristina. Raquel.

Montoya. Raquel?

Raquel. It was what she said. I heard it.

Montoya. Nunita . . . she was your mother. What judgment shall I lay upon Mateo?

Nuna. They lied about her, always!

Montoya. And shall Mateo be punished? I make you judge

of this. What you say shall be carried out. Does he live
or die?

Nuna. You make me the judge?

Montoya. Yes.

Nuna. Then kill him! . . . No, no . . . it was true . . . Oh,
God, now I know it was true about her! Let him go! . . .
Let me go now!

Montoya. Yes, go, Nunita.

 [NUNA *goes out*]

And you, Mateo, take your rifle from the stand. You are
no less one of us than before. If my wife had done as
yours or spoken as yours did, I'd use the same measures.
Let those women beware whose eyes have wandered.
Wait! What was the name of the man who escaped
through Carlotta?

Cristina. They called him Captain Molyneaux.

Montoya. We were betrayed then. And through Carlotta.
Mateo, there was more reason than you knew for what
you've done. It was Carlotta's doing that we were surprised at the pass. The blood of every man killed was
on her head. We were beaten by treachery, not by the
north! By God, it's true!

Hermano. It is true! And you were right!

Miguel. You knew this all the while.

Montoya. We've put our finger on the traitor, Miguel! And
we know there was a traitor . . . and by that same token
we know the next time we meet them will be another
story.

Hermano. She may have had an accomplice.

Montoya. There's no doubt of it. And we must find him, too. That's what I want to do now.

Hermano. We'll leave you, then.

Montoya. But I'll see you?

[*He gives his hands to* Miguel *and* Hermano]

Hermano. Yes.

Montoya. And you, Don Miguel . . . and Don Fernando?

Don Fernando. Within the hour?

Montoya. Near midnight.

Don Miguel. Expect us, Don Pablo.

[*The ricos go out, leaving* Montoya, Martinez, Andros, Felipe, Federico, Maria *and* Raquel. Montoya *sits, seeming weary. The women continue clearing the table*]

Felipe. Pablo, you ate nothing. I watched you. Be mortal for a few minutes now . . . and touch some meat and wine.

[*He offers a plate*]

Montoya. No, no. Let the others eat. I think more clearly without it. Wait . . . lest it should be said that I have refused you anything . . .

[*He takes a morsel of meat with his fingers and washes it down with a gulp of wine*]

No more.

Felipe. Come now. I was famished. You're still hungry.

Montoya. Not when I'm about to fight, Felipe. Have the
sons of Montoya never felt it . . . a fever in the liver so
devouring that food is impure? No, no . . . you're young.
There's an ancient belief that wisdom comes with age,
and the twenties are the time of passion. It's for that
reason they choose old men as judges . . . men who will
have outworn the lusts of flesh and blood and be willing
to rule impartially over the sins of youth. But all this
is a fallacy. For wisdom and justice we must depend on
the young; for madness in devotion to a cause, for all
madness, you must go among their elders.

Federico. You say this to reprove us.

Montoya. Tonight let us have no reproof among the Montoyas. No, I said it in excuse for you both, Federico.
When a man is first a man a little fire is kindled in him
for his race and his cause. If he is a man worthy the name
he blows this fire to a flame . . . and it burns up in
him to a conflagration. It burns in me now so white-hot
and steady that I look at my hand in wonder seeing that
it doesn't tremble . . . there's such a roaring of living
fire inside, such a war of seething heat that sweeps my
brain and nerves. It's a thought for your state should
you ever govern, Felipe. Make no old men judges.

Andros. General Montoya . . .

Montoya. Wait. Make the old men soldiers. Old men are
swift, violent, crafty, lecherous, unscrupulous in winning, relentless in defeat, putting their cause before their
affections. Young men are much too tender, much too
true. When I was lost on the hills tonight, and some

thought me dead, I was hidden in a cave with three companions, because the rifles of the trappers had swept the trail. And I heard a voice calling my name. Up and down the pass it went, calling my name. It was your voice, my son, and you were risking your life needlessly. Had I tried to reach you I should have been killed, and I lay there, nursing my wrath at the enemy, knowing when next we met them our rifles would outnumber theirs. Had I been young as you I would have tried to warn you and been slain for my trouble. And I learned then that in a battle youth is too tender and too true. You should have known that if I were dead it would do me no harm to lie a night in the snow, that if I were alive I would find my way alone.

Felipe. And if you were wounded?

Montoya. Then better one wounded than two. But if you dream I might hold this against you, my Felipe, you are wrong. You are a kind and loving son. Only, when you are older, as old as Federico, you will not take these chances. Federico is already wiser. He came home, and he was here before you.

Federico. I'm not good at riddles. Am I to gather that I've displeased you, sir?

Montoya. I am never displeased by superior wisdom. With what could I be dissatisfied, Federico?
  [*He lays a hand each on his sons' shoulders*]
  These are tall brothers, in every way worthy. Go, and make yourselves ready for the wedding. Lie down if you are weary. It will not be for an hour yet. Tomorrow, too,

you can rest . . . we won't start till evening. And whatever happens, this has been true . . . that I have been proud of you both, and have trusted you. That I have looked forward to an old age which you would lighten, one on either side.

[*He turns.* FELIPE *and* FEDERICO *start to go.* RAQUEL *suddenly throws herself at* FELIPE'*s feet.* JOSEFA *enters and stands near the door*]

Felipe. What is it? Who is this?

Raquel. Ask him for me, in God's mercy. Ask him.

Felipe. Who are you?

[*He raises her face with his hand*]

It's Raquel. What shall I ask him?

Raquel. Only ask him, and let him say.

Felipe. About Pedros?

Raquel.

[*In agony*]

Yes.

[FELIPE *turns to* MONTOYA]

Montoya. Pedros? You've had no news?

Raquel. Nothing.

Montoya. Federico, he was your officer.

Federico. He hasn't returned. I know nothing further about him.

Raquel. Pablo Montoya, you know. I can take your word.

[FEDERICO *goes out.* JOSEFA *looks at him. He avoids her eyes*]

Montoya. I should say that Pedros would be alive. Yes . . .
if I know Pedros.

Raquel. Then he is.

[*She rises*]

Thank you, senor.

[*She goes out, and the other servants follow her*]

Montoya. Andros?

[FELIPE *goes*]

Andros. You wanted me?

Montoya. Bring me the three prisoners.

Andros. Yes, Don Pablo.

[*He goes.* JOSEFA *comes forward*]

Josefa. If I can be of use, Pablo, only let me know what
you would like to have and it will be done. There may be
preparations no one else could make so well as I.

[*He is silent*]

I am no longer angry, Pablo. You will do as you will . . .
and I shall consider it just. Even this wedding . . . I will
help with it if I can. It is your house. The women in it
are yours . . . If I rebelled at first, you must forgive that.
It has not been easy, but I accept it now.

Montoya. There will be no preparations. One thing you
can do. Tell Diana that I wish to see her.

Josefa. Yes, Pablo.

[*She goes out*]

Montoya. What devil has poured his unction on that bitch?
She wish me well? There's something in this house . . .

I knew it when I came in . . . there's some snake's pur-
pose
Under this crawling. Federico, too.
He looked at me smiling, but there was that in his eyes
That wished someone dead and damned. Have you
talked to him . . .
Or to her? What have they said?

Martinez. Nothing that's secret.

Montoya. Meaning you won't tell me. Because you think
It's better I shouldn't know. But, by God, I will.

Martinez. You imagine this!

Montoya. Friend, I imagine nothing. I see and act.
I've seen two things that I'll find the bottom of
Before tomorrow . . . I saw that I was betrayed
At the pass by someone within my ranks . . . and I saw
When I came home . . . that it was only my coming
That balked another betrayal!

Martinez. As to the pass,
I know nothing of it . . . if we were betrayed
God help you find the traitor . . . but for the other . . .

Montoya. The other I'm sure of. If Federico glanced
About him like Felipe, and took my hand
With the same pressure . . . but no, his conscience eats
Into his brain . . . and he crawls, and Josefa crawls . . .
Felipe's done nothing he regrets. His eyes
Look back at you clear as a lake. And I think I know
What's bitten Federico. He's looked too long
At Diana, and wants her. And that explains Josefa.

I've watched her with Federico. She's willing that I
Should marry Diana and cut Federico off
From hope of her. And now I have one son.
One son only.

Martinez. Pablo, when a man grows gray,
Loves a young girl, he peoples the wind with rivals.
But even if this were true of Federico,
Isn't it natural enough? If she should love him
Could she be blamed? I could swear it isn't true,
But if it were . . .

Montoya. He's a man, I believe! Son or not,
My path has never been crossed! I'd cut him down
Like cactus!

Martinez. Pablo, youth turns to youth
Inevitably as water seeks a level.

Montoya. And a son to a father's wife when she's young?

Martinez. She's not
Your wife yet!

Montoya. She will be.

Martinez. At our age men may have lust, but the day of
love
Is over with us. A woman as young as Diana
Wants more than desire.

Montoya. Why, then, you know more than I do,
About women's needs, my priest. So far as I've known
What they want's desire, and when they get it they're
happy,
And also they're in love. I've heard these lectures

From churchmen on the subject of lust. But I know
And you know, too, there's nothing a man's more proud
  of
Than his lust for a woman, and nothing a woman prizes
More highly in a man. Since before the beginning
Of knowledge women have given where gifts were re-
  quired.
A woman goes to the stronger, as land and nations
Go to the stronger. There's not one title to land
Or possession in any empire that isn't based
On a thousand murders . . . not one life in a nation
That wasn't nursed in a thousand conquered women!

Martinez. You are the people's idol, Pablo. They look
  On you to free them, and keep them free. This marriage
  Detracts from you a little. It's something to smile at
  When they meet to gossip.

Montoya. Let them laugh if they like.
  They won't laugh in my face! The drivelling bas-
    tards . . .
  You saw how they climbed on their asses and made for
    the hills
  When they thought I was done for! No village of half-
    wits will set
  My laws for me! I take the woman I choose,
  And God can't help him who gets in my way!

Martinez. God won't help him
  Who gets in the way of what's coming.

Montoya. Of what that's coming?

Martinez. The times are changing. Mexico's a republic.

The English to the north broke from their kings. We're
  here
Like a little island of empire, and on all sides
The people have a share in what happens.

Montoya. And that's what you've meant
  By your printing press ... and your teaching the peons
    to read!
  Do you want a republic here?

Martinez. I want to save
  What we have, Pablo. They're not all peons. They look
  To the north and south, my friend, and take stock of
    themselves,
  A little, and wonder why one class of men,
  Or one man out of that class, has it all his own way
  In the province of Taos.

Montoya. If so, it's because you've taught them
  To think they can think.

Martinez. Not so. It came without asking,
  Like an infection. There's only one cure for it,
  And that's to seem to offer them from within
  What's offered them outside. Give them books and
    schools,
  And the franchise if they want it.

Montoya. You're my friend, José,
  And have been, but this difference between us
  Is deep as hell, and as wide. You fight the north
  Because you want to keep your place. In your heart
  You want what the north wants! But I fight the north

Because I despise what it stands for! Why should they
  think
About government, these peons? They're happier
With someone thinking for them! Why should the young
Take rank above their elders?

Martinez. We must give them the shadow
  Or they'll want the substance.

Montoya. Begin to make concessions
  And they turn to a mob and tear you to pieces! Show
    them
  You're afraid of them, and they're wolves! But let them
    see
  That you're the better man and they're sheep, and your
    dogs
  Can herd them without fences! . . . And shall women
    choose men?
  Are they so much wiser? All your reforms fall in
  With this plague from the north that enfeebles us! God's
    name,
  I think you mean well! You've been my friend, but what
  You teach is poison to me!

Martinez. An enlightened people
  Could be ruled more simply . . .

Montoya. All rule is based on fear . . .
  On fear and love . . . but when they know too much
  They neither fear you nor love you! Teach them too
    much
  And you tear your empire down, and what you have left
  Is what there was before there were empires! This

Is all your progress . . . and they won't thank you for it.
Nor will the women. They don't want freedom! But
    they'll take it,
And laugh at you for giving it!
>   [*The* TRAPPER *and* TWO OTHER PRISONERS *are brought in
>   guarded*]

Martinez. Then the marriage goes forward?

Montoya. Must we have this again?
>   [MARTINEZ *bows and goes out*]
>   [*To the* 1ST TRAPPER]
>   What is your name?

1st Trapper. Senor, I have no intention
Of telling you my name nor anything else.
If you insist on one I'll give you the wrong one.

Montoya. Good, you have spirit. You're the leader then.
That's what I wanted to know. Your name, sir.

2nd Trapper. James.

Montoya. What kind of name is that?

2nd Trapper. If you want my full name
It's Humphrey James.

Montoya. Were you at the pass tonight?

2nd Trapper. Yes. I was there.

Montoya. Have you searched them?

Andros. We took their arms.
That's all there was.

Montoya. Let me see them.
  [*An armful of weapons is brought forward*]
  And who are you?

3rd Trapper. I'm a prospector. I wasn't with the others.

Montoya. So this one's a coward.
  [*He turns to the weapons*]
  Whose dagger is this?

Andros.
  [*Pointing to the* 3RD TRAPPER]
  It was his.

Montoya. And now I know you're a liar.
  I know this dagger. Where did you get it?

3rd Trapper. I bought it . . .
  In Santa Fe.

Montoya.
  [*To himself*]
  This dagger belonged to Pedros . . .
  And I heard Pedros' voice after the battle.
  He was alive then. There could hardly be two like this.
  It's impossible. This one's a coward and liar.
  And Pedros is dead. Search them again. Take off
  That hunting shirt.
  [*To the* 1ST TRAPPER]

1st Trapper. I think not.

Montoya. Take it off him!
  [*The guards peel the shirt from the* 1ST TRAPPER]

Toss it here.

[*They toss it to his feet. He touches it with his foot*]

Put it on. Must I bring it to you?

[*The* 1ST TRAPPER *takes up his shirt*]

Search the next.

[*They search the* 3RD TRAPPER]

Take that shirt off him.

[*The shirt is tossed to him. He examines it with his foot*]

Look through it. There's a paper in it.

[ANDROS *rips the shirt with a knife and takes out a map,
    which he hands to* MONTOYA]

By God, I was right!

They've been in my house. They were leaving here when
    we met them.

Where did you get this?

3rd Trapper. I didn't know it was there!

Montoya.

[*Taking up the man's dagger*]

Where did this come from? This is Pedros' dagger.

Do you want to die the way he did?

3rd Trapper. He gave it to me.

Montoya. Who?

3rd Trapper.

[*Indicating* 1ST TRAPPER]

He did.

Montoya. What's his name?

3rd Trapper. Captain Molyneaux.

Montoya. What else did he give you?

3rd Trapper. Nothing.

Montoya. Did he tell you
   Why you were to carry this? Quick . . . speak.

3rd Trapper. No, senor.

Montoya. Were you in this house?

3rd Trapper. No.

Montoya. Tell me, senor Captain,
   Who gave you this map?
      [*The* OFFICER *smiles without reply*]
   You are all three to die,
   You know . . . unless there is one of you who is willing
   To tell more about this.

Officer. We'll die anyway, boys,
   So keep your mouths shut.

Montoya. Even to an enemy
   I keep my word.
      [*To the* 3RD TRAPPER]
   Do you want to live or not?

3rd Trapper. The Captain was in the house. He brought
      two papers . . .
   And gave one to me to carry, and one to him . . .
   And we went separate ways.

Montoya. Search this man again.

2nd Trapper. Search me all you like. There was a paper,
   But you won't find it. I burned it.
      [ANDROS *searches the* 2ND TRAPPER]

Andros. There's nothing on him.
  It's true he burned something.

Montoya. When?

Andros. Outside in the jail.

Montoya. You sons of fools!

Andros. He threw it on the fire.

Montoya. What was in that paper?

3rd Trapper. Senor, I don't know . . .

Montoya. But you have an idea . . .
  Come, we shall get along, we two. I promise you,
  You'll live, and I don't lie.

3rd Trapper. They were talking about
  A settlement . . . the captain was going to arrange
  Not to destroy the town . . . because he owned it.

Montoya. Not to destroy Taos?

3rd Trapper. Yes, senor, because
  This house was his.

Montoya. And who had signed that paper?

3rd Trapper. Senor, I don't know . . . and that's the truth.

Montoya.
  [*To the* OFFICER]
  Someone had signed away this house to you,
  And in return you were to pacify
  The officials at Santa Fe.

Officer. The lad's a fool,

Don Pablo. He'll tell you anything you ask for,
He's making this up to save his hide.

Montoya. With whom
Did you make this agreement?

Officer. If you want a story from me
I can tell one fast enough. I negotiated
With a priest called Martinez.

Montoya. That is a lie . . .
Go on. If you tell enough lies I'll know the truth.

Officer. Senor Montoya, I know the fix I'm in
As well as you can tell me. You're a hard man,
But I never met a Spaniard harder than I am . . .
And you won't frighten me. The worst you can do
Is kill me or torture me. Well, the Indians tried that,
And they know the game, but I kept my mouth shut.
    You
Can say or do what you will, I give no one away . . .
And I tell nothing. But if you have the time
I'd like to speak a word about this business,
Quite without malice.

Montoya. Good. You wish to advise me.
Proceed. Advise.

Officer. You've killed the governor
And a number of our citizens. Now, by what right
The government at Washington first laid hold
Of New Mexico I don't know. So far as I see
This land belonged to you Spaniards, but you were
    adrift

From Mexico . . . and you're not protected by Spain . . .
There's nobody helping you but yourselves. Whatever
Your rights may be you'll lose. The government sent
A force to put you down, and it had to go back.
It wasn't sufficient. Well, they'll send another . . .
An if necessary another . . . they'll send an army
If they find they have to . . . and the more you resist
The worse it'll be. Taos will be destroyed,
With every man, woman and child, if you hold out,
And there's no point in it. It's a fertile valley,
And a handsome town, and it's rich. If you were willing
To lay down your arms, and concede some part of the
  place
To American ownership you could keep the rest
And the war would be over . . . and a lot of lives saved,
  too.
If it goes on it's plain murder.

Montoya.
  [*To* 3RD TRAPPER]
One more question.
Where did you get this dagger?

3rd Trapper. He let me have it.
  [*Indicating the* OFFICER]

Montoya. You took it off a corpse?

3d Trapper. Yes.

Montoya. Then who killed him?

3rd Trapper. Killed himself.

Montoya. More lies?

3rd Trapper. No, no, it's true . . . he killed himself!

Montoya. Pedros killed himself?

3rd Trapper. I don't know his name . . .
  He brought a message to the captain before the bat-
    tle . . .
  And afterward, after the battle, he came again,
  And pretended he had a message, only this time
  He tried to kill the captain. He had no message
  This time. It was a ruse. They took him out
  To shoot him, but he was too quick for them.

Montoya. What did he say?
  Remember what he said.

3rd Trapper. When?

Montoya. Any time . . .
  Whatever he said.

3rd Trapper. I wasn't near enough
  The first time he was there, but afterward,
  After the battle, when he'd drawn his knife on the cap-
    tain
  And we were taking him out, he said he'd thought
  He was bringing a message to mislead us, but tnen
  He found he'd betrayed his own people, so he came back
  To kill Captain Molyneaux. He called that back
  To the captain when we were taking him away,
  And then he killed himself.

Montoya. Pedros was true then . . .
  Captain Molyneaux, will you tell me the name
  Of the man who betrayed me?

Officer. No.

Montoya. You can have your life,
  I have no interest in taking it.

Officer. No.

Montoya. And whether
  You tell me or not I'll find it out.

Officer. I say no!
  And no's my answer!

Montoya. This is strange behavior
  For a man about to die. Are there other gringos
  As stubborn as you?

Captain. Well, get it over with!
  If you think I'm stubborn you've got a lot to learn!
  You're used to peons and Indians!

Montoya. You prize your stiff neck
  More than your life, it seems! You're proud of that,
  And in your country it may be that the dogs
  Are better than their masters . . . but not here!
  Here you bend your neck or you don't live long.
  Goodnight to you.

  [*He goes to* ANDROS *and they speak a few words*]

3rd Trapper. Senor! Your promise! Senor!

Montoya. You may live,
  But it's no compliment. Send in Narciso,
  I saw him outside.

  [*The prisoners are led out.* NARCISO *enters*]
  Narciso, Raquel has asked me
  For word of Pedros. Was Pedros lost?

Narciso. I don't know,
  Don Pablo.

Montoya. But he's not here.

Narciso. No.

Montoya. And I'm quite certain
  I heard his voice after the battle. He was, I think,
  Federico's officer?

Narciso. Yes.

Montoya. You've taken his place?

Narciso. Yes.

Montoya. When were you appointed?

Narciso. An hour ago,
  Or a little more.

Montoya. Narciso, I'm sorry to say this,
  But there's something strange about Pedros' disappear-
    ance,
  And it reflects on you.

Narciso. Pablo, I'm also sorry.

Montoya. And that's all?

Narciso. Why . . . no. Pablo, perhaps I know
  Where Pedros is, but it's something I'd keep from saying
  As long as I could.

Montoya. Where is he?

Narciso. I think he crossed
  The line to the Americans.

Montoya. Why do you think so?

Narciso. He quarrelled with Federico after the battle
And set off across country alone.
[*There is a long pause*]

Montoya. With Federico. And what was said
In this quarrel with Federico?

Narciso. I don't know that.
I didn't hear it . . . but they were very angry
And almost came to blows. I heard the noise.

Montoya. You heard not one word from this quarrel?

Narciso. Let me remember . . .
No . . . not a word. I couldn't make out at the time
What they were incensed about.
[DIANA *comes to the door. She has changed her dress*]

Montoya. Come in, Diana.
That will do, Narciso. Your name is cleared.
But send Federico to me. Tell him I wish
To lay our plans for Cordova.
[NARCISO *goes out.* MONTOYA *takes up the map and puts it in
its place. The dagger he puts in his belt. He brings out a
casket and sets it on the table*]
This is a holiday dress. You are ready?

Diana. Yes.

Montoya. It becomes you. I wish a man might look
Behind a woman's eyes, Diana, and see
What lies there. You veil your eyes from me.

Diana. Now?
[*She looks at him*]

Montoya. Even now.

Diana. I'm sorry.

Montoya. No, don't be sorry, but this is a world
No man can trust much, even at best . . . and when
He gives his name to a woman, he must know as near
As he can how much he can trust her. Those closest to us
Have most to betray. I've been betrayed tonight . . .
Virtue's gone out of me, and out of this house.
Let me see your eyes again. Diana?

Diana. Yes?

Montoya. What can you say?

Diana. I don't know.

Montoya. Are you afraid?

Diana. Yes.

Montoya. Afraid of Pablo Montoya?

Diana. Yes.

Montoya. Is it because I'm older than you . . . and have
power?

Diana. Yes.

Montoya. Yes, perhaps. Let me see your eyes again.
I think that's what it is . . . This dress becomes you.
Whatever you wear looks its best on you, Diana.
That's why I want you to wear a few jewels tonight
That haven't been worn since this house was built.
They are waiting
For someone to wear them who'd be worthy of them
  [*He takes out a tiara*]

Take down your hair.

   [*She loosens her hair*]

This is to be your own . . .

And it's a dowry to be proud of.

   [*He fastens it on her*]

No matter

What the future may bring for me or you . . .

Keep it for your fortune.

Diana. I do thank you.

Montoya. Thank me better. Have you no better thanks?

Diana. Yes.

Montoya. Take my hands. Kiss me.

   [*She does so*]

If I have sensed

What happiness lay in you . . . I was wrong . . . you
   are richer,

Sweeter than I could know. Let me look at you . . .

I want to see what bride it is I take

Before the others are here. This is your hair.

This is your hand. You stand thus. Now

Could you kiss me, and kiss me as a lover kisses?

Diana. Yes. Must it be tonight?

Montoya. You are a gentle girl, Diana. Perhaps

One takes advantage of that, and assumes that you

Will understand what's strange, forgive what's left out

In the way of courtesy.

Diana. It's not that.

Montoya. For the rest,
   You have known a long while what was destined for you.
   You came here a captive child, with other captives,
   And played at my feet as a child, and, watching you,
   And weary of tongues and unfaith, and women who seem
   To love where they hate, I lost myself in dreaming
   Of a child-wife, who would love where she seemed to love
   And give herself purely. You grew in beauty, too . . .
   Grew maiden-like, flower-like, woman-like, and still
     kept
   Your candid eyes that never lied, and I knew
   If you were mine, you'd be wholly mine. I could rest
   In that. You come of an alien race, somewhere
   From the north . . . I've lost trace of where, but a
     woman's mind
   And heart are in her eyes . . . and you could be trusted.
   And so I told you of this, and you were troubled
   As a maiden is . . . but I wanted the world to know
   Where I had chosen, and wanted to prepare you
   Softly as might be. If I come suddenly now
   To fulfill my promise, it's not as I would have had it,
   But we run risk of death tomorrow, and I
   Should not be willing to die before I'd tasted
   For once, this one happiness. Am I forgiven
   Now, for my abruptness?

Diana. I've made myself ready.

Montoya. There are two kinds of happiness, to win
   In battle, because that makes you one with those
   Who are your people, and to share a love
   With one who loves you . . . because then, for an instant

A man is not alone. But when one shares
Himself and all he has and then discovers
Too late, that he was mocked, and the woman mocked
    him,
There's no such loneliness on earth. I've loved
And given, but without return. Always I've known
Too late that I was alone.

Diana. Could that have been . . .
Don Pablo, because you demanded . . . instead of ask-
    ing . . .
Because you took as your right, whatever you wanted,
Instead of wooing for it?

Montoya. But not with you!
With you I have been gentle . . . Only give me all
Your faith, and you shall have mine! Will you give me
    that?

Diana. I have no wish to rule . . . !
I don't care for that! Let me live where I can,
Humbly, anywhere . . . and marry humbly
And be forgotten! You have many things
In your life! I could be forgotten!

Montoya. You said you would give me
What you could.

Diana. Yes.

Montoya. I won't ask more than that.
You are a child still, and I seem grim to you
And you're afraid. But as for running from me
And hiding from the world, and marrying humbly . . .
That you don't mean.

Diana. Oh, yes.

Montoya. There was never a woman
Worthy to be a woman, who wouldn't choose
A man she could honor rather than a handsome face
Growing on a peon. Yes, a woman will take
One-tenth of a man she can honor, and share him with
others
Rather than breed with his servants. You, too, will know
that
When you are older . . . and love me, and be proud.

Diana. I thought I could bear it. But I can't! Pablo Mon-
toya,
Have pity! You are great! You won't need me. Oh, for
God's love,
Have pity on me!

Montoya. Child, I love you. If you
Had ever been in love you would know there was one
thing
A love cannot do. It cannot let go.

Diana. But I could.
If I were in love I could take all my life in my hands
And give it to him I loved, and turn away
And never see him if he asked it!

Montoya. Yes,
But you are a woman. And something in what you say
Teaches me you are more of a woman than you could be
If your heart were empty. Who do you love?

Diana. No one!

Montoya. You love my son! I had evidence of this before
But I wouldn't believe it. When Josefa came to me
Smiling, to hurry the wedding, I knew it then.
She wishes you married to me. What has there been
Between you and Federico?

Diana. Federico!
Nothing.

Montoya. No . . .
But there would have been had I not interrupted it
By returning awkwardly. You've been untrue
Already to me at heart. You're like the others,
A woman, inconstant, deserving of no better
Than the others, and giving no better. But know this
    about him . . .
If there were no other reason that he should die
He'd die for this, but there are other reasons.
He's sold us out here, or tried to, and he fought
Against us at the pass, like the whelp he is,
And my nest shall be cleaned of him! I loved him
    well . . .
Stood ready to share my name and fortune with him,
And he sneaks like a jackal in his father's house,
Stealing his wife and his place, surrendering
To thieves that he might share! Go, and be ready . . .
But guard yourself . . . for I know you now . . .
Look not
To right or left from me. For I swear to you
That if the son I love were to lift his hand
Toward yours, he'd die . . . and as for Federico . . .

Count him dead. Go! Why should you look on my torment?

> [DIANA *goes out. The village is heard singing far-off the same
> song with which they welcomed* MONTOYA *back. He sits
> listening.* FEDERICO *comes to the door*]

Federico. Their spirits have come back. You hear them?

Montoya. Yes. They'll follow tomorrow, and gladly, too,
If we can keep them singing.

Federico. They sing enough.
Too much sometimes.

Montoya. Is there something on your heart,
Federico?

Federico. No. I think not.

Montoya. You start queerly
Sometimes, as if the opening of a door
Might bring ill-fortune. As if something lurked
In corners here.

Federico. It may be I'm not so easy
When things are happening, as I will be later
When I've seen more.

Montoya. Are you clear enough in your mind
To lead one section of the attack tomorrow
Without failing me?

Federico. I think so. What are the plans?

Montoya. If we can time ourselves to reach Cordova
Just before dawn, before the horses wake
To graze, we'll find the troops camped in the valley
Along the stream. They'll have to take the trail

That brings them there . . . and they'll stop there, for
the water
Is hard to reach further on. If we attack
From one side or the other, they'll have the trail
Before them, and they'll escape, or most of them . . .
But if we make a division of our forces . . .
Attack with half the rifles on this side
And meanwhile plant an ambush on the other
Where they'll run into it unprepared, we'll have them
As neatly bottled as could be wished. Now I
Can't be on both side of the camp. If you
Will lead one-half our men around Cordova
And wait where the gulch is narrow, our campaign's
planned
And we can sleep tonight.

Federico. That's excellent.
It's almost certain victory.

Montoya. More than that,
It may be that not one will get away.
That's what I want . . . to take them by surprise,
And leave not one alive.

Federico. That's possible,
But not too likely . . . they can climb like goats . . .
These hunters. Some would escape.

Montoya. Which would you choose . . .
To make the first attack at this side, or lead
The detachment round for the ambush?

Federico. Let me have

The post of danger. I'll go on ahead
And wait for them where it's narrow.

Montoya. And you're sure
You can hold them there?

Federico. Trust me.

Montoya. Your Officer . . .
Narciso, is it?

Federico. Yes.

Montoya. I could wish it were Pedros.
We lost out best man in Pedros.

Federico. He was hardy.

Montoya. And faithful, too. One could trust him always.
I wonder at his being killed. I could have sworn
I heard his voice after the battle, among your men
As plainly as yours now.

Federico. You heard his voice?

Montoya. It must have been an illusion. Such things do
happen . . .
Voices come back from the dead . . . to testify
Or complain, perhaps, if their owners died unhappy.
And this is strange . . . I took this dagger from
A trapper prisoner. Was that Pedros' dagger?

Federico. I think it was. From a trapper?

Montoya. Yes

Federico. That's like them . . .
To rifle the bodies.

Montoya. Well . . . Narciso will do . . .
   But don't depend on him too much.

Federico. I'll see
   To every order myself. And let me thank you
   For laying this trust on me.

Montoya. I think you'll be worthy
   Of the trust I give you. Federico,
   It's been borne in on me of late that I've taken
   Too much to myself, and allowed no scope for the play
   Of younger minds and hands. The estate is large
   And I've kept too much to myself in its supervision . . .
   I can't do everything well. If I should give you
   Half share in the ranch, would you stay here with me
      and keep it
   As jealously as I have?

Federico. I would indeed.
      [*A marriage song begins outside*]
   But this . . . you don't mean this?

Montoya. Why, indeed I do.
   I do mean it. And lest we let it go
   And you think it out of mind, let us get the map
   And make our choices.

Federico. Let it go till later.

Montoya. No, bring it . . . bring the map.

Federico. I can't accept it
   Till you've had time to think.

Montoya. I've thought a whole life-time!
      [*A pause*]

Federico. After we meet them tomorrow.

    [*He turns*]

Montoya. Very well.

  We'll let it go till later.

    [FEDERICO *starts to go*]

  No, wait,

  Good God, **let's settle** this little matter! We'll have

    The map!

    [*He goes to chest and brings it out*]

  Four thousand acres this side of the river,

  And fourteen thousand in the flat, beyond. It's enough

  To make a Yankee covetous, I admit.

    [FEDERICO, *terrified, is rooted where he stands*]

  But is that reason enough to cause a Montoya,

  An elder son, trusted, acknowledged heir,

  To draw a line down the center, and auction off

  His father and his brother, and a whole village

  To keep his skin from danger?

    [MARTINEZ, FELIPE, DIANA *and* JOSEFA *come in*]

Martinez. This is the time you set,

  Is it not, Pablo?

    [*The marriage song comes nearer*]

Montoya. Why yes, it is time. Come in . . .

  Come in, Felipe! Come in all of you

  And watch his face while I read him a history

  Of what he's done! Look at him!

    [*The* NOBLES *of the village, four or five in number enter with
their wives. They are ushered in by* NUNA, *who goes out
at once*]

Federico. What do you mean?
   What have I done?

Montoya. Be patient. I'll tell you. This map
   Has a line drawn across it . . . a line dividing
   Your share from the man you sold out to . . . you were
      to get
   Immunity to live here for that share!
   Look at this dagger, too! Look hard at it
   And let nothing show in your face when you remember
   Whose dagger it was, and how much a better man
   Pedros was than you are! Pedros is dead.
   He killed himself when he knew what you were about
   And what he'd helped you with. It was Pedros who car-
      ried
   The word to the other side to avoid the pass
   And strike us on the flank. And the man who sent him
   Was Federico.

Felipe. It was true then?

Federico. Someone has lied
   To you about this.
      [*There is a volley outside, then two more in quick succession*]

Montoya. Someone told me the truth,
   And that's his reward for it. The Yankee trader
   Who traded with you is dead. Look, look, Felipe . . .
   That was my eldest . . . that one there with the face
   That twitches . . . but the deed is cancelled now.
   The party of the second part is dead,
   And the party of the first part's dying.

      [ANDROS *and* NARCISO *enter*]

Federico. But it was annulled when you came back! And
    think . . .
    You hadn't returned . . . it was supposed you were lost,
    And I knew no other way to save our lives
    And the lives in the village . . . was it treasonous
    To take command when I thought I must?

Montoya. Look, Felipe . . .
    Whatever love or promises I gave him . . .
    Whatever was his as my eldest son, is yours,
    Stand at my shoulder now . . . let me believe
    One can trust a son . . . this is not easy, to send
    A son to death. I'll try to forget that he's lived
    And remember only Felipe. Why, look, he's not
    And never was a Montoya . . . See, he crawls . . .
    Crawls again!

Federico. I think you're wrong!

Montoya. That's better . . .
    Stand up and fight me, at least. If I must kill you
    At least die like a man!

Felipe. Perhaps he's not
    So much to blame as you think.

Montoya. I know the story
    From beginning to end. It was his plot that brought us
    Defeat on the mountain. Even then he was in touch
    With the northerners . . . and even then he was wooing
    The woman I'd chosen to marry. Weren't there enough
    half-breeds
    To help you populate the valley, that you

Must approach my woman, and win her over to you
And away from me?
    [*To* DIANA]
How proud of your choice are you now . . .
Now that you know him?

Federico. I won Diana from you?

Montoya. Yes . . . that too.

Federico. You fool! It was Felipe.
She loves Felipe now!

Montoya. Yes, tell your tales . . .
Lie out of it if you can.

Josefa. It's true, Don Pablo . . .
She loves Felipe!

Montoya. And you, too, have your reasons
For wanting me to think so!
    [*To* ANDROS]
Take out Federico
And chain him at the plaza gate, let him feel
What it's like to hang in irons before we hang him
The last time for the buzzards!
    [ANDROS *and* NARCISO *start to lead* FEDERICO *out*]

Felipe. You won't do that!

Montoya. By God, I will!
He could hang a thousand years, and it wouldn't pay me
For what he's done!

Felipe. But I say you won't!

Montoya. Why not?

Felipe. He's your son . . . my brother . . . you can't stake
  him out
  Like a bear to be tortured . . . !

Montoya. Only I will!

Martinez. Don Pablo . . . !

Montoya. Get on with him! Get him out before this knife
  Of Pedros' finds a home in him!

Martinez. Don Pablo!
  [*They take* FEDERICO *out*]

Montoya. Damn you! One thing I could bear . . . that he'd
  betray me . . .
  I'd swallow that . . . I'd have let him live . . . a coward . . .
  But the other I won't take!

Josefa. Then why do you send
  The wrong man out to be chained?

Montoya. You fiend . . . be quiet! . . . Felipe!
  This is not true?
  [*A pause*]

Felipe. It's true that I love Diana.
  I can't deny that.

Montoya. And she loves you.
  [FELIPE *is silent*]
  You do love him?

Diana. No, no . . . I swear it . . .
  There's been nothing, nothing . . .

Montoya. And you've been willing
  To let Federico suffer . . .

Diana. Oh, Pablo, believe me . . .
  I'll be a true wife to you.
    [*She goes to him*]
  I'll be true and faithful,
  And do all you can ask.
    [*She kneels*]
  Forgive me if I
  Have been silent when I might have spoken, or seemed
  To turn away when you came to me. It's true
  I'm young, and you are older . . . and I've been fright-
    ened . . .
  That I couldn't help . . . but I'll be kinder
  And give you all you ask . . .

Montoya. Do you love Felipe?
    [*She is silent. There is the beginning of a babble of voices outside
    that increases in volume slowly*]

Montoya. Speak! Do you love Felipe?

Diana. But it's not his fault!
  I loved him first, and he never spoke to me . . .
  And there's been no crime . . . no touch . . .

Josefa. She lies . . . we found them together . . .
  In each other's arms!

Diana. Only when you were lost
  And hadn't returned! Punish me, Pablo. Felipe
  Is your son . . . and wouldn't dishonor you!

Montoya. I'm blessed
  With dutiful sons, it seems. They think of me only . . .
  And of my wife!
   [*The voices outside are louder*]

Diana. Pablo . . .

Montoya. Be silent! You'll drive me
  To something I must keep my hands from, pleading . . .
  Are you so hot for him?

Martinez. This not more or less
  Than you could hope for, Pablo. Since it comes now
  Before this marriage, it won't come later on.
  If you'd been married, every year that went by
  Would have brought it nearer, inevitably. Somewhere,
  Some time, she would have loved and been loved where
    her youth
  Was certain to lead her . . .

Montoya. What are you mumbling?

Martinez. I say
  There's no crime in it except your own.

Montoya. You knew this!

Martinez. It was certain to come.
   [*There is a shout outside. It trails off into single voices, indis-
   tinctly heard:* "What does he say?" "They've sworn
   to destroy the village!" "Three hundred thousand
   men" "He talked with the northerners." "Will you
   listen to him or his father?" "He's a Montoya, as
   much as Don Pablo!" "I say, loose him!" "Let him
   go!" "Damn you, come no nearer!" *There is silence,
   then* FEDERICO *is heard as if a door had been opened in
   the passage*]

Federico.

    [*Outside*]

    You have seen a village

    When it was in ruins . . . no life, the people living

    Somewhere in the hills! . . . But this will be worse . . .

        they're in thousands,

    These Americans . . . they'll come like locusts . . .

        flies . . .

    They'll come when you least expect it . . . not one

        escapes . . .

    And they could be placated . . . my father's mad . . .

    Crazy . . . he wants to die . . . wants you all to die . . .

    And you've been fools and followed him because

    He gave you rifles! . . . Why, if he gave you warpaint

    Like the Indians you'd do as well!

    [*The crowd breaks into a louder babble*]

    [ANDROS *enters*]

Andros. I'm sorry, Don Pablo,

    But I think you should interfere before your soldiers

    Listen to more of it. Federico's surrounded

    By a great crowd at the gate . . . and when they asked

        him

    How he came there, he told them that he had arranged

    A peace with the north which you had repudiated . . .

    Also that you intend to execute him

    To keep this knowledge from them.

Montoya. Say that again.

Andros. Federico's spreading sedition at the gate.

    They've all surrounded him because of his chains,

And he tells them they can never win against
The English of the north . . . many believe him . . .
Or at any rate, they're shaken.

Montoya. You will stay here
And wait for me . . . all save Andros.

> [MONTOYA *and* ANDROS *go out. Soon afterward the noise of the crowd is suddenly hushed*]

Diana. Felipe . . . you . . .
Go quickly . . . I won't see you . . . but I'll love you . . .
Go . . . the other door . . .

Felipe. You must think lightly
Of me, Diana. Would I go, and leave you?

Diana. Felipe . . .

Felipe. Will you come with me?

Diana. If we were caught
You would be killed . . .

Felipe. But we wouldn't be caught . . .

Diana. Yes . . . yes . . . there's only a moment, Felipe
. . . you waste
Your whole life waiting . . . !

Felipe. Come then . . .

Diana. And bring your death on you?
You'll die if you stay here now . . . you'll die if I go
Along with you . . . but you alone could escape . . .
He'll let you go if I'm here . . . but if I were with you
He'd never forgive you, and he'd never give up
Till he'd hunted us down!

Martinez. All this is true, Felipe . . .
  Be off, and swiftly . . . and I'll tell him I advised it.

Montoya.
  [*Outside*]
  Stand back from him! Stand back!

Diana. Quick! Now, Felipe! Oh, God, will you wait for
  him . . .
  Till he comes back? You must live . . . If he should kill
  you
  And I were to blame, how could I live?
    [*There is a great shriek from the crowd . . . then silence and one
    voice*]

The Voice. Don Pablo!
  Don Pablo! Your son!
    [*There is complete silence, then the steps of* MONTOYA *returning
    slowly in the corridor. He comes to the door and enters,
    his head bowed, the dagger in his hand. As he comes to
    the center a great splash of scarlet is seen to have ap-
    peared on the front of his white hunting-shirt.* NUNA
    and RAQUEL *appear silently in the doorway, a few*
    OTHERS *behind them.* RAQUEL'S *face is a tragic mask.*
    MONTOYA *stands with bowed head for a moment, then
    tosses the dagger to the center of the table, where it sticks
    trembling, and turns his eyes toward* FELIPE]

CURTAIN

NIGHT OVER TAOS
ACT THREE

ACT THREE

SCENE: *The same. The act opens some minutes after the close of Act II.*

FELIPE *and* DIANA *are guarded and about to be led out.* MONTOYA *stands near the table, breathing as though he had come through a scene of violent altercation.* MARTINEZ *faces him, evidently his antagonist. The* RICOS *have drawn nearer. The rear door is open and* MANY PEOPLE *have collected silently to listen, unnoticed by the* RICOS.

Montoya.

> [*To* MARTINEZ]

> I say he dies!

> [*There is a slight gasp and motion among the people.* MONTOYA *notices them*]

> Andros, clear out those slaves!

Andros. Out that way, Narciso. Take them with you.

> [*The crowd murmurs*]

Santos. What's he done?

Graso. He's done nothing.

Diego.

> [*Loudly*]

> Pablo, what's the charge against Felipe? We want to know.

Andros. Are you going?

> [*The crowd is put out and the door closed. Only* RAQUEL *and* CRISTINA, *who were making preparations for the marriage, remain behind*]

Montoya.

> [*Quietly, to* MARTINEZ]

I say he dies.

> [*To* FELIPE]

A woman hated me once
And tried to poison me. It happens it was your mother,
Yours and Federico's. She had loved me at first
And borne me two sons, but she grew to hate me then
As fiercely as she'd loved. I knew this. She tried
To hide it with soft words, but one night at supper
She turned her back for a moment, pouring my wine,
And then set a glass for me, and one for herself.
I looked in her eyes, and changed the goblets, and drank,
And she took the challenge and drank . . . she was no
    coward . . .
And died before my eyes. I have this poison
Of hers. It's quick and painless, and stops the heart.
I found it, and still keep it. There's enough left
To end her generation! You were all three traitors,
All three in different ways. It's fitting to end it
With her own potion. And go on alone.
Take them out.

> [DIANA *and* FELIPE *are led out.* MONTOYA *faces* MARTINEZ]

In the future, Father Martinez,
Remember that your business is with the church.
Your authority stops there!

Martinez. What you do tonight
Concerns not you alone, but all Taos. I plead
For our city . . . not for the church, not for myself . . .
And I say call back Felipe!

Montoya. Have I lived so long
  That I hear a priest give me orders?

Martinez. Things are not as they were!
  From now on you'll listen to more than yourself!

Montoya. You heard
  What was charged against Federico, heard his reply!
  I heard it . . . and rather than any other hand
  Should be lifted against him, I killed him. He was my
    son.
  His life was mine. It's not what a man would choose . . .
  To strike down his own son . . .

Martinez. No man has challenged
  The death of Federico! But to kill Felipe
  Endangers us all!

Montoya. He also is my son,
  And his life's mine!

Martinez. Then the north does win!

Montoya. It wins if he lives!

Martinez. Whether he's guilty or not
  To kill him means we're beaten. You'd never gather
  Your army round you tomorrow. There'd be no army;
  Your leadership depends on the trust they have
  In your strength and wisdom. If you execute Felipe
  They'll no longer respect you. The news will spread
  That Pablo Montoya's raving in his house
  And murdering his sons. Can you command them
  With that in their minds?

Montoya. Is this happening to me . . . to Pablo Montoya,

To hear this mouthing! Not since I was a man
Has my rule in this house been questioned . . . nor in
this city!
Am I likely to accept it now?

Martinez. I remind you only
To think of Taos first . . .

Montoya. The north wins in Felipe
If he has his way! When sons turn against their fathers
And get their will by it, all our rule goes down
And order with it. Our state's built on that . . . but no
more . . .
Not if Felipe can defy me, and keep
What he got by defiance! You fool, the north itself
Attacks us from within, and if it conquers
In Taos, what will it matter if Taos is taken
And conquered from the outside?

Martinez. Don Miguel . . . Hermano . . .
You must see this!

Miguel. Martinez, in these days
An anarchy drifts down from the north upon us,
Even here where we guard ourselves, and some give
credit
To new strange gods, and deny our ancient customs.
The rights of the old, the rights of fathers give way
To the rights of sons. Children look up with envy
At family possessions, and snatch when they can;
And some say, "Good. Let the old men look to them-
selves."
And some say justice should be dealt by the rabble

On young and old, on rich and poor alike.
So thought Federico. You see where it led him.
You see where it leads us all.

Hermano. I have a house
Of my own, and I have sons, and I'd rather they gave
No orders to me.

Fernando. Nor I.

Martinez. There have been two things
I wanted . . . that we might save the house of Montoya,
And that we should save Taos. Perhaps we can't have
both.
In that case it's best to save Taos, Pablo Montoya
Can sign his own death warrant, and yours, Don Miguel,
And every rico's, but not mine, and not
The city's.

Fernando. You're one of us, Martinez, you
Will go as we all go!

Martinez. No.

Fernando. From the very beginning
You sat in our councils.

Martinez. We part over this!

Montoya. Let him go.

Cristina.
  [*Whispering*]
  Now, Raquel.

Raquel. Don Pablo!

Montoya.
  [*Without looking at her*]
  What is it?

Raquel. I'm only
  A woman, Don Pablo . . . but I've lost a husband . . .
  I've lost Pedros, and he was true to you
  When others failed you. Remember that and forgive
  me . . .

Montoya. Forgive you what?

Raquel. For saying this: Felipe
  Must not die, Don Pablo! Whatever he's done
  He must not!
    [Montoya *is silent, looking at* Martinez]

Josefa. You've been dismissed! Is once not enough?
    [Raquel *and* Cristina *go out*]

Hermano. What do you mean to do? Where will you go?

Martinez. I go with your peons outside . . . and ask what
    they ask!
  They're right this time, and you're wrong . . . and they
    have the power
  To say what you must do!

Montoya. Let him go!

Martinez. I followed
  Pablo Montoya, believing that through his strength
  And leadership we dared take up the challenge
  The north threw down. I believed there was a chance
  Of making this province too costly for them. But when
  Montoya tosses his leadership away

And tears his house down quarrelling with his son
It's time to think of my people.

Montoya. Your people?

Martinez. Yes, mine!
They're no longer yours! You abandon them to keep
Your pride! We all know what hangs over us!
We're at war with a nation that outnumbers
Our little state by millions! This counter-stroke
You've planned might make them wary, hold them
    off . . .
Make them regret what they've started! But fail in that,
Lose the next battle, lose the people's confidence,
And your history's ended! Kill Felipe, and you do
    fail . . .
Keep him with you, and you may win!

Montoya.
    [*Coldly*]
Think more clearly, Martinez.
Suppose Felipe lived, and lived in my house.
She would be Felipe's or mine. Suppose she were mine,
And I knew she had loved Felipe. Is that a thing
A man can bear? Or suppose I gave her up,
As I might, and she were Felipe's, and lived with him
Here in my house. Is that a thing a man could
Bear, and live? Not I.

Martinez. The city of Taos
Will live on, then, and the church . . . and I myself . . .
But this is the end of the ricos.

Fernando. You intend to betray us?

Martinez. What could I betray? They know who leads here
   And who's committed with him. I'm no friend to
   The north, and I'll never be . . . but I can live with it
   If I have to . . . and so can the peons! Go fight your
      battle,
   And when you're broken, I'll gather what's left of our
      city
   And we'll live here as we can! But, good God, what's a
      woman
   To weigh one way or another when the question's only
   How to save the house of Montoya, and saving that,
   Save all of you?

Hermano. And why should our winning or losing
   Depend on Felipe? He's but one man among us
   And a young soldier . . .

Martinez. You haven't seen that yet?
   That Montoya no longer governs Taos? . . . That
      you . . .
   All of you . . . hold your places here only so long
   As the peons think you worth fighting for? You heard
   What Raquel said . . . Felipe must not die!
   You thought nothing of it. She was only a woman . . .
   Unworthy to give you counsel, but she spoke for all
      Taos . . .
   And all Taos waits at your gate to hear the answer . . .

Montoya. They heard my answer!

Miguel. Pablo, there's truth in this.

Montoya.
> [*To* MARTINEZ]
> I think you'd rather the ricos
> Were gone, and the town was yours to rule as you
>   pleased,
> Federico-fashion!

Martinez. Have you known me so long,
> Pablo . . . and you can believe that?

Hermano. It's true, if Felipe
> Could live, Don Pablo . . .

Montoya. Am I alone among you?
> Fernando?

Fernando. Speak to Felipe, Don Pablo. Too much
> Depends on this.

Montoya. I am alone.

Fernando. It's true
> They govern us now. If they find us unworthy to die for,
> Why should they die for us? And they won't do it.

Miguel. No.
> [MONTOYA *regards his guests silently, making up his mind*]

Josefa. How can you ask it of him? How can you dare
> to ask this of Montoya?

Montoya. Be silent.

Josefa. I know
> When to be silent. I've hated him in my time,
> And also I've loved him . . . but there's not a man
>   among you,

And not one outside, with half his strength or cour-
age . . .
And yet you dare ask him to humble himself before
His people and his son!

Montoya. Every man asks
What he must to save himself. Well . . . I can give up
To Felipe . . . to save the city. I've lived enough
To face that much. I'd rather Felipe lived.
This is no longer my city, but Felipe's.
Arrange it as best you can. I leave this to you,
Hermano. Call him in.

    [*He turns slowly and goes out*]

Hermano.

    [*To* ANDROS]

Bring Diana first.

    [ANDROS *goes out and returns with* DIANA]

You must not be frightened,
Diana. Stand here . . . and let me ask you only
Two or three questions. You're not to be punished,
neither
You nor Felipe. It's not a thing forgiven
Easily, that you've forgotten a pledge
Sworn to Montoya, but there's nothing for us to do
But erase what's happened. Can you forget Felipe?
Utterly, Diana?

Diana. No.

Hermano. But you
Will promise to be a true wife to Pablo Montoya

In word and deed?
　　[*There is no answer*]
You must answer yes to that
Or we can't save him.

Diana. Yes.

Hermano. And whatever has passed between you and
　　Felipe
　　Is cancelled and ended?

Diana. Yes.

Hermano. Why, see now, the world
　　Is yours again to live in. This is not so bad,
　　You'll find . . . to trade a first maiden inclination
　　For a whole world. Let us have Felipe, Andros.
　　　　[ANDROS *goes out*]
　　You need not stand now, Diana. That's the last ques-
　　tion,
　　And Felipe's to live.
　　　　[*She sits*]

Martinez. Are you so sure of that
　　Montoya meant to give Diana up
　　To Felipe. He said as much. Do you mean by these
　　questions
　　That Diana goes to Pablo?

Hermano. I do mean that.
　　And why not? What we want is to save Felipe . . .
　　Does it matter how?

Martinez. Diana will promise whatever

She must to help him . . . but he won't surrender
  her . . .
He'll choose to die . . .

Hermano. I think not.

Martinez. He'll choose to die . . .
  And you'll be driven to threaten him. If he still
  Refuses . . .

Hermano. He won't refuse.
  [FELIPE *is brought in*]
  Felipe, it's been decided
  That we must go back to where we were . . . blot out
  What was said here . . . and what led to it. If we do
    that
  Our lives can go on as before . . . if not, this night
  Will leave terrible scars on all of us. What we could do
  To palliate your offense, we've done, and will do,
  Not only for your sake, but for your father,
  And the name you bear in this province. If you will
    promise
  To put Diana out of your mind . . . why then
  Nothing will be held against you. I'm delegated
  To put this to the question. Answer wisely, and keep
  Your place in our hearts and our city. You'll do this?

Felipe. Yes, if I can.

Hermano. Then first . . .

Fernando. Ask him first what there's been
  Between him and Diana.

Felipe. Senors, if my father

Questions me I'll answer whatever he asks.
Let him ask me himself.

Hermano. He left this to us.

Felipe. As to Diana . . . I knew she was my father's . . .
But I did love her . . . and do.

Hermano. She loves you?

Felipe. Yes.

Hermano. But you're willing to relinquish her?

Felipe. I am a prisoner,
   Don Hermano. Why should I be asked
   To relinquish Diana willingly, when you know
   You can compel me to do whatever you like?
      [MONTOYA *re-enters and waits in the rear*]

Fernando. Because you must live. And your father and you
      must both live,
   And live here in this house! She will be his wife!
   Say something that will make us understand
   That this sickly love is ended, before it ends
   Our hopes in you!

Felipe. How can a man promise that?

Fernando. He can promise whatever he has to!

Felipe. I have no heart
   To oppose my father . . .

Fernando. Then why do you oppose him?
   That's what you're doing. We ask only your promise!

Felipe.
> [*Impatient*]
> I give it!

Montoya. Never mind his promise . . . I ask
> No promise from him, nor from her. I have this to say,
> Which I should have said before. Let the north come
> down . . .
> And all the devils to fight on its side . . . Let the peons
> Yell at my gate till they're speechless . . . Let all of you
> Warn me as you have . . . this is still my place
> And my house and my city! Let him promise or not
> As he likes, he'll do what's required of him while he's
> here,
> And Diana likewise! Let the north come down!
> I'll be as I've always been . . . and live as I've lived . . .
> And fight as I've fought . . . ! Let Felipe live! You
> might
> Have spared your promise. I meant to let you live,
> Promise or not . . .
> > [*He turns*]

Felipe. Pablo, let me speak to you!

Montoya. Why, speak.

Felipe. I?

Montoya. Yes.

Felipe. You've forgotten my name then, Pablo?

Montoya. What do you want to say?

Felipe. Why have we grown

So far apart? When I looked for you on the mountain . . .
I loved Diana then . . .

Montoya. You looked for me hoping
You'd never find me.

Felipe. Pablo . . .

Montoya. Are you afraid?
Another Federico?

Felipe. We were always friends,
Pablo . . . even tonight . . . tonight in this room,
And though I seem to blame for what's come between us,
I can't help trying to tell you . . . that I'm sorry . . .
And I wish we could be as we were . . .

Montoya. He is a coward.

Felipe. And I'm no coward!
I tell you that when I sought you on the mountain
I sought you because I loved you! I sought you as you
Might have looked for me if I'd been lost! If I'd found
you
Dying there in the snow I'd have given my life
To save you! Yet I knew then that I loved Diana . . .
And more than I loved you . . . and that if you lived
You'd keep her from me! . . . It was you who were
wronged
By my loving her . . . not I . . . but I never chose it!
Never in my life have I wanted to hurt you
Or thwart your wishes! Only, now, since we're caught
In this thing together, and neither can help it, why
Are you suddenly a stranger?

Montoya. Because I know
What happens when two men meet face to face
And want the same woman! Brothers they may be,
Or father and son, but they hate each other! You
Both hate and defy me.

Felipe. Pablo, does what I say
Sound like defiance?

Montoya. I have no more desire than you
For a feud between us. I loved you as you loved me.
I want to love you now. But there's no tie
Between two men that holds when both of them love
A woman, and one has her. This will happen to us . . .
Be sure of it. It happens now in your eyes.
You wished me dead in the snow. You tried not to wish
   it,
But you wished me dead.

Felipe. It's true. I tried not to wish it,
But I did wish you dead.

Hermano. He's given his word,
Don Pablo, and he'll keep it. Give him your hand.
He's a better son than you think. Let it go at that.

Montoya.
   [*Turning away*]
Yes. Let it go.

Felipe. And I'd rather not give my hand,
And rather it didn't end this way. My father
Has an instinct in such matters.

Miguel. What do you mean?

Felipe. I'm a son of Taos. I've been loyal to Taos,
  And its ways are deep in my blood, but still it's true
  That I'm a rebel at heart. Somewhere within me
  Something cries out: Let us go! Let us be free
  To choose our own lives! Sometimes, if you let me live,
  It will be the worse for Taos that I'm alive . . .

Hermano. Damn you, be still!

Felipe. No . . . I tell you my father
  Makes no mistakes in such matters! I'd be a traitor
  To my house and my cause if I lived. I tell you that
  To save you from it!

Miguel. Do you want to talk yourself
  Into dying quickly?

Felipe. It may be a better death
  Than I'd have later, better than I think's likely
  To come your way, Don Miguel . . . or any of you!
  I don't know when it will come . . . you'll have victories,
  Perhaps, for a while, but before they're through with you
  The armies of the north will crush you in
  And drive a last few of you to this crag to die
  And keep you here till it's ended! Till it's all ended,
  The last of Taos, the last of Spanish power
  North of Mexico city!

Fernando. And you're for the north,
  That's what you mean?

Felipe. How could I be for the north
  When all my people, all my friends, and my life
  Are rooted in Taos? I've fought on your side and mine,

And I'd do it again . . . but still I'm not so blind
But what I can see that if the laws of the north
Were to judge between us, my father would be in the
      wrong,
And I'd be held right! And it would be just! But here
A girl goes where he's sent by her father, and when
She's chosen by an old man who can pay for her
Or who has her at his mercy, she's his, and a slave,
And all the women are slaves here! (That's why you
      can't trust them!)
And the men are slaves! Yes, I am myself no better
Than a peon, nor any of you! I've earned the right
To say this. I'll die for it!

     [DIANA *rises*. MONTOYA *turns on* FELIPE]

Montoya. When a woman once bears a bastard
She'll bear more than one, count on it! Federico's
      mother
Was also yours, and all three hated me,
And all three tried to betray me! You think I don't dare
To send you after them . . . you think we'll pick
Some justification for you, and cover it over
Because you're only half guilty. If you were a man
Worth saving you'd be one thing or the other. This
Is too cowardly to be treason! Half-coward, half-traitor.
More snake-like, more deadly, more to be despised
Than Federico himself. You've chosen sides
Against a man who can take a handful and make it
An army by what he dares! They'll come to me . . .
Come fawning to me, they'll crowd under my banner
And fight against their own, these northerners,

When they know the man I am! You should have known
   it,
And you've failed as a man and my son! Hermano!

Hermano. Felipe!
Do you want to drag us all down?

Felipe. Let him free Diana
To make her choice! And remember that Federico
Was right about the north!
   [*A silence*]

Hermano. Are we in accord in this?
   [MIGUEL *and* FERNANDO *assent silently.* HERMANO *turns to*
   MONTOYA]

Montoya. Leave them to me.
   [*The stage empties of all save* MONTOYA, FELIPE *and* DIANA]
Why, yes, Diana may choose.
Do you choose Felipe . . . or me?

Diana. To go with Felipe.

Montoya. You know what it means?

Diana. Yes.

Felipe. There's no question of that.

Montoya. She'll choose for herself.

Felipe. Diana!

Diana. Would you have me live . . .
And live on after you, a slave? They say
I'm a northerner by birth! A woman of the north
Chooses the man she'll follow! I have my own right
To choose to die!

Montoya. And since you choose Felipe . . .
  I was a traitor to myself to want you
  With your northern blood and face. It's just as well.
    [*He sets out a carafe and glasses*]
  It's fitting to end it
  With her own potion . . . and go on alone.
    [*He pours two glasses and takes out a little phial*]
  Drink quickly! Let me see the last of her spawn
  Put under ground!
  Take with you my own treachery to myself . . .
  This woman that stands here . . . and let me go out
    alone
  To face my world again!
    [*He lifts the phial, but instead of pouring it in the glasses,
      holds it in his hand*]
  Wait, wait, I'd forgotten!
    [*He sits*]
  There's something I'd forgotten. It was a dream.
  Is this a dream that we were standing here
  And I had sentenced Felipe? I've dreamed it before.
  There's something unreal about it. Don't drink, I said,
  It may be poisoned!
    [*He starts up*]
  Do you know what's true?
  I'm old and alone, and my people fall away,
  And the race is old and nerveless. The village is eaten
  With doubt of me and my purpose. They're all decayed
  Under the skin. They bloom like health, but they're
    rotten
  And dying out. Why should they fight the north?

They'd rather surrender, and live here under Mar-
    tinez . . .
And so would Felipe. I killed Federico, but that
Was a last effort, desperate. No strength.
Till now I thought I was young. I've always been young,
The first man in the field . . . in any assembly
First there too. To youth and strength belong
The whole of the earth, and I've believed them mine
Because I was strongest. The eagle lives long, but at last
He grows old, his sight is dimmed, he misses
His stroke, and goes hungry on his crag. This thing
Comes to them all, eagle and kite alike,
And now it come to me. I had a dream
That Spain was old, and her arts and ways were worn
To mockery, threadbare . . . her power was taken
    away . . .
Her kings were impotent on her throne, her people
Impotent at home. The barbarians
Lifted new standards . . . that which once was right
Was right no longer, but wrong. The children's words
Were taken for truth . . . the old men stood aside
And listened to this new wisdom. A new race came
And said, There is a God over you who sets
A term to all things, to man and nation alike,
And your term is up. Felipe came to me
And said, love is not bartered in the new lands . . .
Give me back my love. But this was no dream,
Or else my dreams are true. Our race is done.
The Spanish blood runs thin. Spain has gone down,
And Taos, a little island of things that were,

Sinks among things that are. The north will win.
Taos is dead. You told me this before,
But I wouldn't believe it. I believe it now.
Yes, and it's right. It's right
Because what wins is right. It won't win forever.
The kings will come back, and they'll be right again
When they win again. Not now. The gods are weary
Of men who give orders, playing at God. And why
Should a man, an old man, looking forward to nothing,
Take pride in breaking men to his will? Meanwhile
The years creeping up at his feet, and all he has
Going down around him? And then to stand there, alone,
Helpless . . . an old man, playing at God. Go out,
Leave me, be together, be free! In all Taos
There's only one man who could not surrender and live,
And his heritage is darkness. I drink to your mother.
She had her way.

    [He drinks from the phial]

Felipe. Pablo!

Montoya. And you have yours.

Felipe. Never! Pablo, believe me! Hermano, Miguel.

    [He goes to the door]

Montoya. Stay here . . . I need no crowd around me to die!
  What do you want to do?

Felipe. To bring help . . .

    *[*Martinez* enters]*

Montoya. It's useless . . .
  If that's what you mean. I'd rather you were here,

Felipe. Forgive me. It begins to blind me already.
   [*He reaches for a chair and sits*]

Felipe. If I could help you . . .

Diana. Or I.
   [*She kneels beside his chair*]

Montoya. You'd be wrong. If I lived
   We'd be enemies, and I'd kill you. This is what death's
      for—
   To rid the earth of old fashions. Forgive me, too,

Diana. I was wrong. I was caught between
   The old days and the new, and what I did
   Would have been right once—yes, all the life I lived
   Was new and fresh and right—when I was young
   And Taos was young with me. Ah, yes, Martinez—
   I leave you my world. Save it, keep it alive,
   There are those who care to live.
      [*He shudders and is still*]
   They have been too proud,
   Too proud—these Montoyas.

CURTAIN

III · MARY OF SCOTLAND

CHARACTERS

(In the order of their appearance)

First Guard, JAMIE
Second Guard
Third Guard
JOHN KNOX
JAMES HEPBURN, Earl of Bothwell
CHATELARD
MARY STUART
DUC DE CHATELHERAULT
MARY BEATON
MARY SETON
MARY LIVINGSTONE
MARY FLEMING
ELIZABETH TUDOR
LORD BURGHLEY
HENRY, LORD DARNLEY
LORD GORDON
DAVID RIZZIO
JAMES STUART, Earl of Moray
MAITLAND of Lethington
LORD HUNTLEY
LORD MORTON
LORD ERSKINE
LORD THROGMORTON
A Porter
LORD RUTHVEN
LORD DOUGLAS
Young RUTHVEN
First Sentinel
Second Sentinel
A Sergeant
A Warden
Soldiers and others

ACT ONE

Scene I

Scene: *A half-sheltered corner of the pier at Leith. It is a sleety, windy night, and the tall piles of the background and the planks underfoot shine black and icy with their coating of freezing rain. Long cables stretch away into the dark. The only light comes from the lantern of two iron-capped* Guards *who are playing cards morosely on the head of a fish-tub in the lee of a great coil of rope.*

First Guard. Na, na, put them away. I'm fair clabbered with cold.

Second Guard. Aye, you'd say that, wi' ma siller-piece laced in your brogues!

First Guard. Gie me the hand, then. But man, it's an unco bitter nicht for indoor pleasures.

Second Guard.
   [*Throwing out cards*]
   It's a blastit wonner—

First Guard. Put out, put out!

Second Guard.
   [*Laying down a coin*]
   Aye.

First Guard. And we'll just stop now, forbye to go on 'ud strain your two-year credit.
   [*He shows his hand*]

3

Second Guard. Dod, mon, ye hae luck wi' the titties. Ye'll no refuse me ma revenge, Jamie?

[*A tall bearded* FIGURE, *muffled in a cloak, has come in from the left*]

First Guard. When ye can afford it. No earlier.

Second Guard. Ye see yoursel', Jamie. I'm gouged out clean—-

First Guard. And is that a reason I should risk my gains—?

The Old Man. Aye, dicing, gaming, cards, drinking, dancing, whoring, and all the papistical uses of the flesh—they run before her like a foul air—

Second Guard. It's the Master—wheest—put them awa'.

First Guard. An' what of it? I'm na member of his congregation.

[*A third* GUARD *runs in from the right*]

Third Guard. I was right, Jamie! 'Tis the Queen's ship!

First Guard. The Queen's ship, you goik! How could it be the Queen's ship? She's to come in a galley, and she's none due this month yet.

Third Guard. My word on it, Tod, I rid out wi' the fishermen, and she's a galley wi' oars, and by God she carries the oriflamme!

Second Guard. Would the queen's ship dock without notice to the lords, and no retinue at the pier?

Third Guard. There it lies—yon wi' the lights!

First Guard. She's lights aplenty, afore God. Aweel, we've no orders aboot it.

Third Guard. But we can do no less than give her what
escort we can—

First Guard. We're set to guard the pier, and for nowt else.
—And why are you so hot for a Romish sovereign to set
foot on Scottish soil, do you mind if I ask?—For myself,
I'm no member of the congregation, I'm a sojer doing
what I'm set to, but it runs in my head we've had enough
of the Guises and their Holy Father. Let them stick to
their warm climates where they're welcome—and may
they come to a hotter place before they set up another
standard here!

The Ola Man. Ye may be na member of the congregation,
friend, but you will be if you keep in that opinion. For
her or against her it's to be in this land, and no half-way
to stand on. The kirk of Christ or the hussy of Rome,
drowned in wine, bestial with fornication, corrupt with
all diseases of mind and blood—

Second Guard. Is it the queen's galley, Master?

The Old Man. Aye, is it.

Second Guard. For there's been no herald of it, nor anyone
told—

The Old Man. I have my ways of knowing. And, hearing
of it, I came myself to see this white face they speak of,
and these taking graces, and to tell her to that white face
of hers and despite her enchantments that we want
and will have none of her here. For whatever beauty
she may possess, or whatever winning airs, they are
given her of the devil to cozen us, they are born solely

of the concupiscence of hell and set upon her like a
sign. They say when she speaks she drips honey and she
smells sweet with boughten perfumes, but I say the man
who tastes of her or the people who trust in her will
chew on dry ashes in the last day and find no remedy for
that thirst! I say she comes with a milk-white body and
a tongue of music, but beware her, for she will be to
you a walking curse and a walking death!

Third Guard. You will say this to the queen?

The Old Man. I will say this to her whey face!

    [BOTHWELL *enters from the right*]

Bothwell. Leg it over to the inn, one of you lads, and fetch
a chair—

First Guard. We're on guard here, my lord.

Bothwell. Damn your guard duty! The queen of Scotland's
stepping out of a boat 'n velvet shoes—

Third Guard. I doubt there's a chair nearer than Edinburgh
town—

Bothwell. There's one at the Leith inn, as ye well know—

First Guard. We'd need the silver for that, in any case—

Bothwell. My mannie, if I was to lay a fist to the side of
that iron pot of yours I doubt the dinge would come out
in a hurry—. What the devil do ye mean bauchling over
a dirty chair? Seize it, seize it in the queen's name!

Third Guard. I'll fetch it, sir.

    [*He starts out*]

Bothwell. And do you go with him. I suspect ye of being a psalm-singer with that face.

    [*The first* GUARD *goes with the third*]

A verra braw evening to you, Master Knox.

The Old Man. And to you, my lord.

Bothwell. It seems some here heard of her coming, though not perhaps those she'd have chosen. You're not here, by chance, to greet the daughter of Mary of Guise?

The Old Man. If I have aught to say to her, it will be for her own ears.

Bothwell. No doubt, no doubt. And I have a little observe to make to you about that, too, sir. Whatever it is you have to say to her you won't say it.

The Old Man. And why not? Are the Papists muzzling the ministers of God?

Bothwell. I'm no Papist, as ye're aware, Master Knox, and if I were I'm no such fool as to try to muzzle a minister, nevertheless, whatever it was you were going to say, you won't say it, that's my observe to you—

Knox. I shall say what I have come to say.

    [BOTHWELL *follows the Soldiers. A man's voice, speaking French in a light tenor comes in from the right*]

Chatelard.

    [*Outside*]

It is a badge of honor, I assure Your Majesty.

Mary.

    [*Outside*]

Still, when next you toss your cloak in the mud. take
note whether there are any watching to report it—

Chatelard.

[*Outside*]

But if my queen and lady note it—ah, what other
advertisement would a man desire?

[MARY *the Queen enters with* CHATELARD, CHATELHERAULT,
and the FOUR MARYS-IN-WAITING]

Mary. Tut, if it were not known, or suspected, that I was
queen, I should have stepped in bog like a drover's
daughter—

Chatelard. Madame, that you are queen would be known if
the world were stripped of subjects. The very trees and
frozen mountains would bow down to you!

Mary.

[*Laughing*]

I can well imagine.
Body o' me, I could wish the clouds would stoop less
to their queen in my native land.

Chatelherault. One forgets how damn dismal this Scotland
can be.

Mary. Dismal? Traitor, have you never plucked a gowan
in spring—a fairy fresh gowan—?

Chatelherault. Late—it comes late here—

Mary. Or gorged with bright thorn-apples in mid-August?

Chatelherault. Is there an August in this heathenish
climate? God, I can't remember it!

Mary. They are sweeter here than in France, as I recall, and all fruits are sweeter here, of those that grow—and the summer's sweeter—

Chatelherault. They're short enough, God knows.

The Old Man. And when they come they will bring excellent devices of masks and ornament to deceive the eye, and soft words and stenches to cumber the senses of mankind. Adulterers, jig-masters and the like will come in authority, and their counsel will be whoring and carousing, the flowers and fruits of evil, of that great sin, that sin that eats at the heart of the world, the church of abominations, the church of Rome.

[*He pauses.* MARY *stops to look back at him*]

Mary. Chatelherault, I have been long away, and the speech of Scotland falls strangely on my ears, but is this talk usual among my people?

The Old Man. Yet is there a place reserved for them, where the fire is unending and abates not, even as their desires abate not, where their tender flesh shall be torn from them with white-hot pincers, nor shall rank or station avail them, whether they be queens or kings or the lemans of queens and kings—!

Mary.

[*Tremulous*]

Surely this is some jest, sir. Surely this is not said in welcome to me.

The Old Man. And what other welcome shall we give the

whore of Babylon—the leprous and cankerous evangel of the Beast!

[BOTHWELL *returns from the right*]

Bothwell. Your Majesty, they are preparing a room at the inn, and the chair will be here at once. If you would deign to take my cloak for your shoulders—

[*He lays his cloak around her*]

Mary. Thank you. I wish to speak to this gentleman—

Bothwell. This is Master John Knox, of whom your Grace may have heard.

Mary. Nay, then I have heard of him, and I wish to speak to him. Master Knox, it is true that I am Mary Stuart, and your queen, and I have come back from France after many years away, to take up my rule in this country. It is true, too, that I am sad to leave the south and the sun, and I come here knowing that I shall meet with difficulties that would daunt many older and wiser than I am—for I am young and inexperienced and perhaps none too adept in statecraft. Yet this is my native place, Master Knox, and I loved it as a child and still love it—and whatever I may lack in experience, whatever I may have too much of youth, I shall try to make up for, if my people will help me, in tolerance and mercy, and a quick eye for wrongs and a quick hand to right them—

The Old Man. Aye, they told me you spoke honey—

Mary. And cannot you also—you and your people and those you know—cannot you too be tolerant toward me a little space while I find my way? For it will be hard enough at the friendliest.

The Old Man. Woman, I remember whose daughter and whose voice you are—

Mary. If I were your daughter, Master Knox, and this task before me, would you think it fitting to lay such hard terms on me, beast and whore and I know not what? For I am not a whore, I can say truly, but the daughter of a prince, softly nurtured and loving honor and truth. Neither is my body corrupt, nor my mind Nay, I am near to tears that you should think so, and I was not far from tears before, finding myself unexpected on this coast, and no preparation to receive me. What you have said comes as very cold comfort now when I need greeting and reassurance.

Bothwell. Your Majesty, if the old goat has said anything that needs retracting—

Mary. He shall retract nothing in fear! I would have all men my friends in Scotland!

Bothwell. I'm afraid that's past praying for.

Mary. Look on me, sir—and judge my face and my words. In all fairness, am I the evangel of the Beast? Can we not be friends?

The Old Man. I fear not, madam.

Mary. I strongly desire it. I have no wish for any enemy of mine except that he become my friend. You most of all, for I have met you first, and it is an augury.

The Old Man. Your Majesty, I have said what I came to say.

Mary. But you no longer mean it! See—I give you my hand, Master Knox—it is a queen's hand, and fair—and I look at you out of honest eyes—and I mean well and fairly—you cannot refuse me! Do you still hesitate? It is clean.

> [*She smiles. He bows stiffly over her hand*]

And will you come to see me at Holyroodhouse, and give me counsel? For God knows I shall need counsel —and I shall listen, that I promise.

The Old Man. Your Majesty, I should be untrue to myself and my calling if I refused counsel where it is asked.

Mary. You will come?

The Old Man. I will come.

Mary. I will send for you, and soon.

> [*Her words are a kindly dismissal*]

The Old Man. Good night, Your Majesty—

Mary. Goodnight, Master Knox.

> [Knox *goes to the left*]

Now I wonder, will he hate me more or less?

Bothwell. More, probably. However, it's just as well to have him where you can watch him.

Mary. You're an outspoken man yourself, Captain.

Bothwell. I am.

Mary. You will forgive, me, but so far I have not heard your name.

Chatelherault. The Captain is James Hepburn, madame—the Earl of Bothwell.

Mary. Ah—you fought ably for my mother.

Bothwell. I have been of some slight service here and there.

Mary. You have indeed! Tell me, my lord of Bothwell, have I done well so far? Shall I not make this Scotland mine?

Bothwell. Madame, it is a cold, dour, sour, bastardly villainous country, and the folk on it are a cold, dour, sour, bastardly lot of close-shaving psalm-retching villains, and I can only hope no harm will come here to that bonny face of yours, and no misery to the spirit you bring.

Mary. Now here's a new kind of courtesy!

Bothwell. You'll hear far and wide I'm no courtier, madame—but I have eyes, and I can see that the new sovereign is a sonsie lass and a keen one, and I was for her from the first I saw her face—but from my heart I could wish her a better country to rule over—

Mary. Now, will no one speak well of this poor Scotland of mine—?

Bothwell. Your Majesty, shall I praise it for you—as high as it deserves—?

Mary. Say whatever good you can!

Bothwell. Then this is Scotland, my lady: To the north a few beggarly thousands of Highland Catholics who have not yet learned the trick of wearing britches, and to the south a few beggarly thousands of Lowland Protestants whose britches have no pockets to them—Their pleasures are drinking and fighting, both of which they do badly, and what they fight about is that half of them are willing to sell their souls for a florin, whereas the other half has no expectation of getting so much. What business they have is buying cheap and selling dear, but since none of them will sell cheap, and none will pay dear, the up- shot is there's no business done—

Mary. Enough, enough!—solemnly and truly, sir—it may be they are not a happy race, but they have beliefs—and what they believe they believe from the heart! Even this Master Knox—

Bothwell. He? He believes whatever's to his own advantage, and prophesies whatever will line his nest if it comes to pass. He makes his living yelling nonsense into the lugs of these poor, benighted, superstitious savages—he's split the country wide open over your coming and leads the pack against you, brawling from his dung-hill! We'll have bloodshed over it yet—

Mary. Blood-shed?

Bothwell. And plenty.

Mary. No. If I thought that I should turn now and bid the mariners hoist sail and put back for France. I shall win, but I shall win in a woman's way, not by the sword.

Bothwell. Let us hope so.

Mary. Hope so! But I shall!

Bothwell. I am no courtier, madame. I say, let us hope so.

Mary Beaton. The chair has come, madame.

Mary. Yes, and in time. We're chilled to the heart here.
   Come.
   [*She goes out with* BOTHWELL, *the others following. The first
   and third* GUARDS *return*]

First Guard. Did the old man spit his venom?

Second Guard. You'll not believe it. He kissed her hand.

Third Guard. She's a witch, then.

Second Guard. Aye, is she. The kind a man wouldna mind
   being bewitched by.

Third Guard. No.

Second Guard. I tell you she fair wenched him. The old
   man doddert a bit and then bent over like a popinjay.

First Guard. She's tha' kind then?

Second Guard. She's tha' kind.

CURTAIN

ACT ONE

Scene II

Scene: *A corner of Queen Elizabeth's study at Whitehall. It is morning, but the sun has not yet risen. She is up early to go over plans with* Lord Burghley, *who sits opposite her at a small table on which an hour-glass stands like a paper-weight on their notes. She is a young woman, still beautiful, with a crafty face. Tall candles burn behind them in a sconce. Outside the circle of light the scene is indefinite.*

Burghley. It still lacks something of dawn, Your Majesty.

Elizabeth. We have one more hour before the palace will be stirring. You said, I believe, that you have made memoranda in regard to Mary Stuart?

Burghley. I have set down the facts as we must face them, and alternative policies.

Elizabeth. Read them, if you will. And turn the glass. It's run out.

Burghley.

[*Turning the glass and taking up a paper*]

They are not in order, but the main points are covered. First, Mary Stuart has crossed from France to Scotland against your advice and without your safe-conduct. This is in itself a slight to Your Majesty, and almost a challenge, though not one of which you can take public cognizance.

Elizabeth. Yes.

Burghley. Second, she has been crowned queen of Scotland, this also against your wish and in defiance of your

16

policy. This may be construed as an open breach of friendship, or may be overlooked, as Your Majesty may desire—and as it may seem best.

Elizabeth. Yes.

Burghley. Third, she is a Catholic and related by blood to the most powerful Catholic house in France, which constitutes her a public danger to Protestant England. Fourth, she is next heir after Your Majesty to the throne of England, and is held by Catholic Europe to be the rightful queen of England at the present time, Your Majesty being regarded by all Catholics as a pretender, unjustly seated on your throne.

Elizabeth. True. Proceed. You have more on that point. They believe me a bastard and say so. Very well, let us face that, too.

Burghley. Fifth, then—you are held by the Catholic Europe to be the illegitimate daughter of Henry the Eighth, the divorce of Henry from Catherine of Aragon being unrecognized by the Church of Rome and his marriage to your mother, Anne Boleyn, deemed invalid. Sixth, these things being true, Your Majesty must not allow Marie Stuart to succeed as Queen of Scotland. For in so far as she is secure in Scotland you are insecure in England. Your Majesty will forgive my bad habit of setting down in writing what is so obvious, but it is only by looking hard at these premises that I am able to discover what must be done.

Elizabeth. Out with it then. What must be done?

Burghley. She must be defeated.

Elizabeth. How?

Burghley. Is there more than one way? We must pick our quarrel and send an army into Scotland.

Elizabeth. Declare war?

Burghley. Perhaps not openly—but we have excuse for it.

Elizabeth. And reason?

Burghley. She must be defeated.

Elizabeth. Truly, but not so quick, not so quick with wars and troops and expenses. Have you no better counsel?

Burghley. In all my reading I have found no case of a sovereign deposed without violence.

Elizabeth. And in all those voluminous notes of yours you have set down no other method save warfare? The last resort, the most difficult, costly and hazardous of all?

Burghley. It is the only sure method, and you cannot afford to fail.

Elizabeth. My dear Burghley, in any project which affects England and our own person so nearly we have no intention of failing. But you have overlooked in your summary two considerations which simplify the problem. One is the internal dissension in Scotland, half Protestant, half Catholic, and divided in a mortal enmity—

Burghley. Overlooked it! Madame, it is the main argument for an immediate declaration of war—Edinburgh would rally to your arms overnight! This is our opportunity to unite England and Scotland!

Elizabeth. A war would unite Scotland against us—unite Scotland under Mary. No—it is necessary first to undermine her with her own subjects.

Burghley. And how would that be accomplished?

Elizabeth. This brings me to the second consideration which you overlook—the conduct and reputation of Mary herself.

Burghley. Would that affect our policy?

Elizabeth. It will make it. Merely to remind us, will you read over again the report of Mary's character in Randolph's latest budget of news?

Burghley. This? "As for the person of Marie, our new Queen, I must say in truth that she is of high carriage, beautiful in a grave way—"?

Elizabeth. So—go on.

Burghley. "Beautiful, in a grave way, somewhat gamesome and given to lightness of manner among her lords as well as with other company, very quick-witted to answer back, and addicted to mirth and dancing, wherewith she hath made many converts to her cause among those most disaffected, though there be also those found to say her manners might more beseem the stews or places of low resort than so ancient a palace and line—"

Elizabeth. You see, she is a Stuart.

Burghley. "Moreover, she hath allowed herself to be seen much in the company of certain men, among them the

Earl of Bothwell, and hath borne herself among these men, they being known of somewhat loose report, in such fashion as to give scandal to the stricter sort here, she not scanting to lend her eyes or hands or tongue to a kind of nimble and facile exchange of smiles and greetings which might better become the hostess of an alehouse, seeking to win custom. Natheless she is liked, and greatly liked by those on whom she hath smiled closely, they being won not as a wise sovereign wins subjects, but as a woman wins men."

Elizabeth. Yes, a Stuart.

Burghley. "Yet to be true again I must say also that she is of noble mind, greatly religious in her way, and the whispers against her name not justified by what she is in herself, but only by her manners, which she hath brought from France."

Elizabeth. She has won our Randolph among others. He shall go north no more.

Burghley. "And in addition she hath borne her power thus far with so discreet and tolerant a justness, impartial to north and south, to Catholic and Protestant alike, that if she persevere in this fashion she is like to reconcile the factions and establish herself firmly on the throne of Scotland. For vast numbers who thought to curse her now remain her fast friends."

Elizabeth. Have you yet seen what we must do?

Burghley. I find in this only a graver and more malicious danger.

Elizabeth. And you would still make war?

Burghley. Your Majesty, it will be war whether we like it or not—and there is imminent danger, danger to your throne and life. The more suddenly you act the less effort will be needed—

Elizabeth. My lord, my lord, it is hard to thrust a queen from her throne, but suppose a queen were led to destroy herself, led carefully from one step to another in a long descent until at last she stood condemned among her own subjects, barren of royalty, stripped of force, and the people of Scotland were to deal with her for us?

Burghley. She would crush a rebellion.

Elizabeth. She would now, but wait. She is a Catholic, and for that half her people distrust her. She has a name for coquetry and easy smiling, and we shall build that up into a name for wantonness and loose behaviour. She is seen to have French manners; we shall make it appear that these manners indicate a false heart and hollow faith.

Burghley. Can this be done?

Elizabeth. She is a woman, remember, and open to attack as a woman. We shall set tongues wagging about her. And since it may be true that she is of a keen and noble mind, let us take care of that too. Let us marry her to a weakling and a fool. A woman's mind and spirit are no better than those of the man she lies under in the night.

Burghley. She will hardly marry to our convenience, madame.

Elizabeth. Not if she were aware of it. But she is next heir to my throne; she will hope for children to sit on it, and she will therefore wish to marry a man acceptable as the father of kings. We can make use of that.

Burghley. Only perhaps.

Elizabeth. No, certainly. She is a woman and already jealous for the children she may bear. To my mind the man she marries must be of good appearance, in order that she may want him, but a fool, in order that he may ruin her, and a Catholic, in order to set half her people against her.

Burghley. We know that she is seen much with Bothwell.

Elizabeth. And he is a Protestant.

Burghley. He is a Protestant. Now suddenly it occurs to me. If she were to marry a Protestant and turn Protestant herself, would she not make an acceptable ally?—

Elizabeth.

  [*Rising*]

I do not wish her for an ally! Have you not yet understood? I wish her a Catholic and an enemy, that I may see her blood run at my feet! Since Bothwell is a Protestant, the more reason for dangling some handsome youngster instantly in the north, as if by accident, nay, as if against my will, some youngster with courtly manners, lacking in brain, a Catholic, and of a blood-strain that would strengthen pretensions to the throne of England.

Burghley. You have thought of someone?

Elizabeth. I have thought of several. I shall even let it be rumored that I oppose such a marriage. I shall let it go abroad that I favor someone else.

Burghley. Who is the man?

Elizabeth. I have thought of Darnley.

Burghley. But after herself Darnley is in fact heir to the English throne. An alliance with him would actually strengthen her claim to succeed to your place.

Elizabeth. The better, the better. He is handsome, and of good bearing?

Burghley. Yes.

Elizabeth. And a fool?

Burghley. A boasting, drunken boy.

Elizabeth. And a Catholic.

Burghley. As you know.

Elizabeth. If I give out that I am determined against it, she will marry him, and he will drag her down, awaken her senses to become his slave, turn her people against her, make her a fool in council, curb this pretty strumpetry that gains her friends, haul her by the hair for jealousy, get her big with child, too, and spoil her beauty. I tell you a queen who marries is no queen, a woman who marries is a puppet—and she will marry—she must marry to staunch that Stuart blood.

Burghley. This will take time.

Elizabeth. It may take many years. I can wait.

Burghley. And we shall need many devices.

Elizabeth. You shall not find me lacking in devices, in the word to drop here, the rumor started there. We must have constant knowledge of her, and agents about her continually, so that her acts and sayings may be misconstrued and a net of half-lies woven about her, yes, till her people believe her a voluptuary, a scavenger of dirty loves, a bedder with grooms. Aye, till she herself think ill of herself and question her loves, lying awake in torment in the dark.—There is a man called Knox who can be used in this.

Burghley. But that—to accomplish that—

Elizabeth. We live in a world of shadows, my lord; we are not what we are, but what is said of us and what we read in others' eyes. More especially is this true of queens and kings. It will grow up about her in whispers that she is tainted in blood, given over to lechery and infamous pleasures. She will be known as double-tongued, a demon with an angel's face, insatiable in desire, an emissary of Rome, a prophetess of evil addicted to lascivious rites and poisonous revenges. And before all this her own mind will pause in doubt and terror of what she may be that these things should be said of her—she will lie awake in torment in the dark—and she will lie broken, nerveless there in the dark. Her own people will rise and take her sceptre from her.

Burghley.

  [*Rising*]

But Your Majesty—you—

Elizabeth. However, I am not to appear in this. Always, and above all, I am to seem her friend.—You would say that I am in myself more nearly what will be said of her.

Burghley. No, no—

Elizabeth. Why, perhaps. But that is not what is said of me. Whatever I may be, it shall be said only that I am the queen of England, and that I rule well.

CURTAIN

ACT ONE

Scene III

SCENE: *A great hall in Mary Stuart's apartments at Holyroodhouse. The room is rectangular with wide fireplaces glowing to the left and right. An entrance door opens to the right, and two doors at the left lead, one to Mary's study, and the other to her bedroom. The stone of the walls is largely covered with stamped leather hangings. A chair, slightly elevated, stands in the middle of the rear wall, the royal arms of Scotland draped above it. The floor is stone with a few Eastern rugs. There are two high, heavily draped windows at the rear, on either side of the queen's chair.*

MARY BEATON, MARY SETON, *and* MARY LIVINGSTONE *are concerning themselves with the hanging of the ensign behind the chair, and* LIVINGSTONE *has stepped upon a stool to reach a fold of it.* LORD DARNLEY *and* LORD GORDON *are warming themselves at one of the fires, having just come in.*

Beaton.

[*To the men*]

It's to hang there because she wants it there. Isn't that enough?

Gordon. I've heard my father say the kings of Scotland were always plain folk, but queens are a fancy breed, and their ways are fancy.

Darnley. A thought higher with that fold, my dear—just a thought higher.

Livingstone.

[*Turning*]

And why?

26

Darnley. Dod, lady, it's a neat turn of ankle you show when you reach up. Reach a bit higher.

Livingstone.

   [*Back to her work*]

  Look your eyes full if it does you any good, my Lord Darnley.

Darnley. Man, man, but that's a pretty foot!

Gordon. Aye.

Darnley. Ye have heard it said, no doubt, what they say about a woman's foot?

Gordon. Aye.

Seton. What do they say?

Darnley. About a woman's foot? Only that it's, in a sort, a measure of her capacities.

Beaton. Oh, is it, indeed? I've heard the same in respect to a man's nose, and I can only say if it's true your nose is no great advertisement for you.

Darnley. The nose is a fallible signal, my lady, as I'll prove to you—you naming your own place and time.

Beaton. I to name the place?

Darnley. It is your privilege.

Beaton. Your own bed-chamber, then.

Livingstone. Beaton!

Darnley. Accepted! Accepted! My own bed-chamber! And the time?

Beaton. The night of your wedding, by God!

Darnley. My dear lady—

Gordon. She has you there, Darnley.

Beaton. Moreover, if there is one kind of a man a woman dislikes more than another it's one so little experienced that he goes peeping at ankles for lack of better satisfaction.

Darnley. Stop there! I will furnish you with data—

Beaton. Unless indeed it be the kind of man whose experiences with women have been like nothing so much as those of a dog with lamp-posts—

Livingstone. Beaton!
  [MARY FLEMING *enters from the queen's study*]

Beaton.
  [*Clapping a hand to her mouth in mock chagrin*]
  Oh, what have I said, what have I said?

Seton. A great plenty!

Darnley. Mistress Fleming, is it true our sovereign is inaccessible this day?

Fleming. Quite true, I fear.

Darnley. God help the man who tries to woo a queen.

Fleming. And so he might if your Lordship prayed to him with any serious intent.

Darnley. Perhaps. And yet I doubt it might do more good if a man were to have studied in France.

Fleming. Studied?

Darnley. The arts. The arts of Ovid. The arts of pleasing a maid.

Beaton. They are the same in France as elsewhere, no doubt.

Darnley. No doubt, says she, and a very pretty innocence.

Gordon. Aye, as though she'd never been there.

Fleming. We're not denying that we've been in France.

Darnley. Then don't tell us that the art of Love is the same there as in England and Scotland, for the report runs different.

Gordon. It's a kennt thing that French love is none the same.

Livingstone. Will you tell us how?

Gordon. Eh, we're to tell you who've lived among them?

Fleming. Aside from better manners the people of France are like the people of Scotland, both in love and war.

Darnley. It's not an easy matter to go into with my lady's bevy of beauty, nevertheless they say there are no virgins there above four years old.

Livingstone. Then they lie who say it, and you're fools to believe it.

Darnley. Nay, it may be a bit exaggerated, but I'd lay no more than a groat on any piece of French virginity. They have summat to tell in confession; they have had their three of a night; they have had their what-for, and come up all the fresher and more lisping for it.

Beaton. I must say I've never met nastier minds than here-about, and that's something for John Knox to ponder on, too.

Gordon. Will ye come, man? Ye'll have no sight of the queen today, and these trollops have no time for plain Scotchmen.

Darnley. Aye.

Fleming. Lord Darnley is to remain within call. It is her Majesty's pleasure.

Darnley. Ah, well that's something.

Gordon. It's dangling, to give it a plain name.

[BOTHWELL *enters from the right*]

Livingstone. Oh, my lord Bothwell.

Bothwell. By God, my name's remembered, and that's a triumph,
Tell the sweet queen Lord Bothwell would see her alone.

Livingstone. Sir, she is closeted with her secretary—
We are not free to speak with her.

Bothwell. Closeted? So?
I like not that word closeted. Who is there here
Who can speak with her and tell her?

Fleming. My Lord, she has spaced
This day off into hours, so many to each,
And I fear your name is not scheduled.

Bothwell. Distrust your schedule,
Then, my prim, for I'll see her.

Fleming. The ambassador
From England arrives today, for his audience,
And before that Her Majesty plans to hold
A conclave with the lords.

Darnley. We've been sloughed off
Much the same way, my lord

Bothwell. Run along then, and practise
Wearing that tin sword you've got hung on you,
Before it trips you.

Darnley. Trips me?

Bothwell. Aye, run and play!
This one's been used. The nicks along the edge
Were made on tougher than you. Tell my lady queen
I wish to see her now.

Fleming. I cannot myself.
I might speak to Master Rizzio.

Bothwell. Then do that. Is Scotland grown so formal
That a man's received like a money-lender?
     [FLEMING *goes out*]

Livingstone. No,
But these matters must be arranged.

Bothwell.
     [*To* DARNLEY]
Are you still here?

Darnley. Still here.

Bothwell. I knew a pimp in Paris had much your look,
But the women he brought me were foul.

Darnley. But good enough,
  I daresay.

Bothwell. You might have thought so.
    [RIZZIO *enters,* FLEMING *following*]

Rizzio. Oh, my lord Bothwell,
  There's such great pressure on our time today—
  Matters that must be seen to; if you could come
  Tomorrow—

Bothwell. Well, I cannot come tomorrow.
  Tomorrow will not do. I am here today.
  And will not be here tomorrow. Is that understood?
    [RIZZIO *pauses*]

Darnley. Let him run his suit into the ground.

Gordon. Aye, and himself.
    [DARNLEY *and* GORDON *go out*]

Rizzio. My orders are strict, my lord. Her Majesty
  Has great problems of state—

Bothwell. And they concern me
  More than some others. Now, before Christ, I've
    argued
  Enough with women and women-faced men! A room's
    a room
  And a door's a door! Shall I enter without warning
  Or will you announce me to her? Great pressure on
  Our time! Our time, he says! My fine Italian—
    [MARY STUART *enters. There is sudden quiet*]

Mary. I will speak with my lord alone.
    [*One by one, and silently,* RIZZIO *and the girls go out*]

Do I find you angry?

Bothwell. At these pests and midges.

Mary. You saw me yesterday.

Bothwell. I have been standing since this early morning—
I and some hundred crows, out in the coppice
On the cliff's edge, waiting for the smoke to rise
From your breakfast chimney. And by the Lord these
    crows
Are a funny company. I've had four full hours
To study them.

Mary. You come to tell me this?

Bothwell. I come to tell you
I've never shown such patience for a woman,
Not in my life before.

Mary. Did you call it patience
On a time when I could not see you, to wreck an inn,
Leave mine host in the road with a broken head
And lie with his daughter?

Bothwell. That was not true. Or at least
I had her good will for it.

Mary. And another time
To besiege the governor's house with your border
    knaves
And rouse all Edinburgh? Are you a man
Or a storm at sea, not to be brought indoors?

Bothwell. When I would see my girl, why I must see her
Or I am a storm, and indoors, too.

Mary. Your girl? Give me leave,
　Since I am a queen, with a kingdom to reign over,
　To queen it once in a while.

Bothwell. I tell you truly
　I've the manners of a rook, for we're all crows here,
　And that's what's understood in this town, but I
　　could
　Be tame and split my tongue with courtly speeches.
　If I could be sure of you—if I could know from one
　　day
　To another what to make of your ways. You shut
　　yourself up
　With secretaries and ministers, harking for weeks
　On end to their truffle—while I perch me on the rocks
　And look my eyes out.

Mary. When I was but thirteen
　A pretty lad fell in love with me; he'd come,
　Oh, afternoons, late midnight, early dawn
　Sopping with dew-fall; he'd stand there, waiting for a
　　glance—
　I've never had such tribute.

Bothwell. This is no boy.
　This is a man comes beating your door in now.
　It may be you're too young to know the difference,
　But it's time you learned.

Mary. You've had your way, my lord;
　We've spoken together, though I had no time to give,
　And now, with your pardon—

Bothwell. You'll go about the business

Of marrying someone else. That's what this mangy
Meeting of councillors means, and that's what por-
    tends
From Elizabeth's ambassador! I warn you,
Make no decisions without me!

Mary. I cannot marry you.
    I beg you, ask it not; speak not of it. Our day
    Has come between us. Let me go now.

Bothwell. My lady,
    I will speak softly. Have no fear of me
    Or what I intend. But there have been days I remember
    When you had less care what hostages you gave
    The world. I think you showed more royally then
    Than now, for you loved then and spoke your love,
        and I
    Moved more than mortal for that while. Oh, girl,
    If we would be as the high gods, we must live
    From within outward! Let the heavens rain fire
    Or the earth mud. This is a muddy race
    That breeds around us. Will you walk in fear of mud-
        slingers,
    Or walk proudly, and take my hand?

Mary. I am a queen.

Bothwell. They've made a slave of you,
    This bastard half-brother of yours, this fox of a Mait-
        land,
    This doddering Chatelherault! They frighten you
    With consequences. They're afraid of men's tongues
    And they've made you afraid. But what they truly fear

Is that you'll win the country, be queen here truly.
And they'll be out of it. What they'd like best of all
Is to wreck you, break you completely, rule the country
  themselves,
And why they fear me is because I'm your man alone,
And man enough to stop them.

Mary. Yes. You are man enough.
  It's dangerous to be honest with you, my Bothwell
  But honest I'll be. Since I've been woman grown
  There's been no man save you but I could take
  His hand steadily in mine, and look in his eyes
  Steadily, too, and feel in myself more power
  Then I felt in him. All but yourself. There is aching
  Fire between us, fire that could take deep hold
  And burn down all the marches of the west
  And make us great or slay us. Yet it's not to be trusted
  Our minds are not the same. If I gave my hand
  To you, I should be pledged to rule by wrath
  And violence, to take without denial,
  And mount on others' ruin. That's your way
  And it's not mine.

Bothwell. You'll find no better way.
  There's no other way for this nation of churls and
    cravens.

Mary. I have been queen of France—a child-queen and
    foolish—
  But one thing I did learn, that to rule gently
  Is to rule wisely. The knives you turn on your people
  You must sometime take in your breast.

Bothwell. You know not Scotland
  Here you strike first or die. Your brother Moray
  Seeks your death, Elizabeth of England
  Seeks your death, and they work together.

Mary. Nay—
  You mistrust too much—and even if this were true
  A sovereign lives always with death before and after,
  And many have tried to murder their way to safety—
  But there's no safety there. For each enemy
  You kill you make ten thousand, for each one
  You spare, you make one friend.

Bothwell. Friends? Friends? Oh, lass,
  Thou'lt nurse these adders and they'll fang thee—
    Thou'rt
  Too tender and too just. My heart cries for thee—
  Take my help, take my hands!

Mary. I would I could take both.
  God knows how I wish it. But as I am queen
  My heart shall not betray me, what I believe
  And my faith. This is my faith, dear my lord, that all
    men
  Love better good than evil, cling rather to truth
  Than falseness, answer fair dealing with fair return;
  And this too; those thrones will fall that are built on
    blood
  And craft, that as you'd rule long, you must rule well—
  This has been true, and is true.

Bothwell. God help thee, child.

Mary. Be staunch to me. You have been staunchest of all.

Let me not lose your arm. No, nor your love—
You know how much you have of mine. I'm here
Alone, made queen in a set, hard, bitter time.
Aid me, and not hinder.

Bothwell. So it shall be.

Mary. And give me the help I'd have.

Bothwell. That I can't promise.
   I'll help thee and defend thee. Lady dear,
   Do you use guile on me?

Mary. No, sweet, I love thee,
   And I could love thee well.
      [*She goes to him. He kisses her hand and then her lips*]
   Go now, and leave me.
   We've been seen too much together.

Bothwell. You must lay this hand
   In no one's else. It's mine.

Mary. I have but lease on it,
   Myself. It's not my own. But it would be yours
   If it were mine to give.
      [Mary Livingstone *comes to the right hand door*]

Livingstone. Your Majesty,
   The Lords of the council are here.

Mary. Let them be admitted.
      [Livingstone *goes out*]

Bothwell. Has Your Majesty forgotten
   That I am of the council, under your seal?

Mary. I could wish you were elsewhere. These are the men
    I least
Have wanted to find us alone. But stay, now you're here.
    [*She goes pensively to her chair of state and seats herself.* LORD
    JAMES STUART, *Earl of Moray,* MAITLAND OF LETH-
    INGTON, *the* DUC DE CHATELHERAULT, HUNTLEY,
    MORTON, *and* ERSKINE *are ushered in by* MARY
    LIVINGSTONE, *who withdraws. There is a brief silence*]

Maitland. We have not interrupted Your Majesty?

Mary. No. The Earl of Bothwell is of the council.
I have asked him to take part.

Maitland. There was some agreement
That since the Earl's name might come up, it would
    be as well
If he were not here.

Bothwell. And then again, since my name .
May be mentioned, and there's none so able as I
To defend it, it may be as well that I'm here.

Maitland. My lord,
There was small thought to attack you.

Bothwell. Less now, perhaps,

Mary. Lord Bothwell will remain.

Moray. Sister, it may be that Bothwell will be offended
By something said.

Mary. You are courtier enough
To couch it not to offend, my brother.

Maitland. Nay, then,
What we have come to say must be softly said,

But meant no less strictly. The question of our queen's
    marriage,
Of which everyone has spoken, let me add,
But which we have avoided here, must now come up
Whether or no we like it.

Mary. Be not so tender
    With me, dear Maitland. I have been married. I am
    A widow, and free to marry again.

Huntley. That's the lass!
    They say widows are always ready.

Mary. Do they say that?
    Do they not say ready but—wary?

Huntley. Aye, that too.

Mary. But the truth is I should prefer my own time for
    wedding.
    I know of no prince or king whose hand is offered,
    And whose hand I'd take.

Maitland. It's not to be treated lightly
    I'm much afraid. The thrones of all the world
    Are shaken with broils even as we stand here. The
    throne
    On which you sit, our sovereign, is shaken, too,
    Though Your Majesty has done more than I'd have
    dreamed
    Could be done to still the factions. It's our belief
    That a marriage, if the right one, would seat you more
    firmly,
    Put an end to many questions.

Mary. There's more of this?

Maitland. That's all we wish—to see you safe on your
throne
So that we may be safe in our houses. Until men know
What alliance we're to make, what hangs over us
In the way of foreign treaties, the clans will sleep
With dirks in their brogans, and a weather eye still open
For fire in the thatch. And yet to choose the man—
That's a point we can't agree on.

Mary. I'm with you there.
For you see, I'm hard to please.

Maitland. And more than that,
Of princes that offer, or have been suggested, each one
Commits us to some alliance of church or state
We'd find embarrassing. Philip of Spain, the Duke
Of Anjou—these are Catholic—

Bothwell. Has it crossed your mind
That there are lords in Scotland?

Maitland. And there, too—
If the choice were to fall on a Scottish earl, the houses
Passed over would take it ill—and it might well lead
To a breach in our peace—

Bothwell. Yes?

Maitland. Nay, even to civil war.

Mary. I cannot give myself out
As a virgin queen, yet our cousin Elizabeth's plan
Has virtues. Must I marry at all?

Morton. Your Majesty,
  We have not yet said what we came to say,
  And it needs saying bluntly. The people of Scotland
  Are given to morals almost as much as to drink.
  I'll not say they're moral themselves, but they'll insist
  On morals in high places. And they've got in their heads
  That you're a light woman.
    [MARY *rises*]
  I don't know how it got there,
  And I daresay it's not true—

Mary. Thank you. For your daresay.

Maitland. I could have wished to speak more delicately
  Of this, but it's before us, and can't be denied.
  Your Majesty, when you came to us from France
  And I saw you first, I said to myself in my heart,
  All will be well with Scotland. What I thought then
  I can say now, for you are wiser even
  Than I had supposed, and you have dealt more justly
  Than any could have hoped, yet still it's true
  Some spreading evil has gone out against you,
  A crawling fog of whispers.

Mary. Who believes them?

Maitland. I'll not say they're believed. I'm not sure they
    are.
  But there was the episode of the boy who was hidden
  In your bed-chamber

Erskine. Chatelard.

Maitland. Aye, he, and
  That may have begun it. I believed at first it stemmed

From John Knox's preaching, for he holds all Catholics
To be the devil's own, but there's more than that—
A much more seeded, intentional crop of lyings
Planted here, till I've wondered if Chatelard
May not have been an agent, or one of many.

Mary. Planted by whom?

Huntley. Why, by Elizabeth.
Who else?

Maitland. But that's not certain, either.
Chatelard came from France, and in all this scurril
I've traced no word to London.

Mary. It's what they say.
Not what they believe.

Huntley. You've lent them some color for it,
Your Majesty. You've been no statue.

Mary. No,
Nor wish to be. My lord of Lethington,
What you have said of me, how I was when you saw me,
How I seem to you now, I swear to you, you were not
wrong.
I have not betrayed myself as woman or queen.

Maitland. I would swear that, too.

Mary. And since I know that is true,
I have thought very little of whispers. For there is
judgment
Somehow in the air; what I am will be known, what's
false

Will wash out in the rains.
  [*She seats herself again*]

Maitland. My sovereign, you are yet young.
  I once believed that. But I have lived long enough
  To see error grow up and prosper, and send its roots
  A century deep. There's force enough in these winds
  Of malice to blow us all down—

Mary. I'll try to be serious,
  For I see you are. It's your thought, then, that a marriage
  Would end the rumors?

Maitland. Aye.

Mary. But as to whom I'll marry—
  Happily, that's not decided for me yet.

Morton. By God.
  If it was we'd see you to bed with him tonight.

Mary. Has the woman no voice in such matters?

Morton. Not in such cases.

Mary. And what is my case, may I ask?

Morton. Why, we've said nothing
  About my Lord Bothwell. It's his name's coupled with yours;
  His young Rizzio's.

Bothwell. I've thought often, Morton,
  One of us would die before the other. Now
  I'm sure of it. And soon.

Morton. I have you.

Mary. My lords,
   Will you quarrel in council over your queen's virtue?
   Let me defend my own honor, and let you
   Defend your own. Do I understand that I
   Am accused with Bothwell or Rizzio? Or both?

Maitland. You are accused of nothing.

Morton. You are not accused,
   Your Majesty. Moreover, you are queen
   Of Scotland, and therefore no man here would dare
   Accuse you—

Mary. Oh, speak out, man! Are you afraid?
   When have I punished plain dealing?

Morton. Why, then, you are queen,
   And may set your own customs, but if my wife were seen
   Abroad as you are, and half so free of contact
   With young and old as you are, I'd not answer
   For what was said about her!

Mary. I'm no man's wife.

Morton. No. And the sense of this council
   Is that it might be better if you were,
   Better for your good name and better for Scotland.

Mary. I will answer these things: as for Rizzio,
   He is my secretary; if I spend time
   In private with him, that is the reason. If I
   Had not liked him, he would not be my secretary.
   As for Lord Bothwell, he has put more strength
   Behind what I wished to do than any among you,
   And at times when I had despaired. He is my good
      friend.

We were here alone before this conference
And we differed in opinion. To wipe that out
I went to him of myself and kissed his lips.
We had kissed but once before, may not kiss again,
But that's at my option, not yours.

Huntley. Lassie, ye've been
Too honest for your own good.

Mary. Why, if so much weight
Is placed on a kiss in Scotland, come now, each one
And take your kiss—or if that's no recompense
Come to me then in private, and you shall have,
Each one, one kiss.

Morton. And after that, there are kisses
Elsewhere—and when you've finished, whether you'll
marry
Or not may not be the question, but whether we can find
A prince who'll have you.

Mary.
[*Rising and taking a step down*]
And having heard that word—
My lords, when you wish to talk with me again
As civilized men, and not barbarians,
You shall have audience. This Scottish kirk of yours
Has misled you as to the meaning of kisses. I am
Unsullied and young, and have my own faith to plight
And more to think of than these maunderings
Over pantry gossip. I shall not marry till
I find it wise, nor until I have made quite sure
What effect it will have on my inheritance

Of the throne of England. You come here in high con-
clave
And spend three-farthing's worth of wit to chaffer
Over a kiss in my audience-chamber! The question
Is not to save my name, I hope, nor my throne,
But how best to meet the destiny that has made me
Full heir to all this island.—Scotland is mine,
And England will come to me or to the child
I hope to have. It's this that makes my marriage
A matter of moment.—And this—with your good
pardon—
Will be the last for today.
  [*She goes into her study*]

Moray. Morton, I warned you
  To leave all speech to Lethington.

Morton. She sits on that throne
  Only so long as we want her there, no longer.

Bothwell. If my lord of Morton
  Would care to lose those black feathers from his crest
  I await his pleasure.
  [*He goes out*]

Moray. I'm for that, too. Settle it between you,
  And may you both win. We'll all be the better for it.
  [LIVINGSTONE *enters from the right*]

Livingstone. Lord Throgmorton is here from England
  With embassies for the queen.

Maitland. She's gone to her study.
  She'll wish to admit him.

Livingstone. Yes.

> [*She goes to the queen's study.* MORTON *goes out the other door*]

Maitland. We get no further
Today then,

> [*He goes to the door*]

Huntley. No. Erskine, a word with you.

> [ERSKINE *and* HUNTLEY *go out.* THROGMORTON *enters*]

Maitland. Come in, Lord Throgmorton. You've been announced within.

Throgmorton. Greetings, my lord, fair greetings.

Maitland. We can have speech later.

Throgmorton. We shall.

> [MAITLAND *goes out.* THROGMORTON *and* MORAY *are alone*]

Greetings also to my Lord James Stuart,
In fine, the best of greetings.

Moray. From Elizabeth?

Throgmorton. I'm burdened with them—and more to you
than any.

Moray. May I know the drift?

Throgmorton. This is hardly the place for that,
But this much for now: Elizabeth has determined
That you are to reign in Scotland, if not as king,
Then as regent again.

Moray. Well, that's news.

Throgmorton. She bids me to tell you
As if from herself, you are not to be disturbed

If her policy seems at variance with her mind.
It's a wide arc of intrigue, but she carries
These schemes in her head like a gambit, and she means
To play it to the end. Your sister Mary
Is not acceptable to her.

Moray. But this scheme of hers?

Throgmorton. Later, later. You're a silent man, I know.
No word.

Moray. None.
[MARY *enters*]

Mary. Lord Throgmorton?

Throgmorton. Your Majesty.
[*He kneels. She comes to him and gives him her hand to kiss*]
From one great queen to another, happiness.

Mary. A courtier in the grand style.

Throgmorton. Nay, Majesty,
A plain man of business.

Mary. Let us to business, then.
[*She motions him to rise, and he does so*]
My brother, did you wish further word with me?

Moray. No, madame, only that I may see you tomorrow.

Mary.
[*Goes to her chair*]
At your own time.
[MORAY *bows low and goes out*]
You had more to say?

Throgmorton. Much more. My poor brain's taxed with re-
   membering.
   But to begin, Queen Elizabeth sends her love
   To her cousin of Scotland, wishes her well, and a reign
   Both long and easy, and proffers to that end
   Whatever friendship and amity between thrones
   Your Majesty will accept.

Mary. Tell Elizabeth
   She will not find me niggard of friendship or love.

Throgmorton. I shall report Your Majesty so. Then, further,
   I'm bid to say, what Elizabeth most desires
   Is that all briars of discord that have grown
   Between this city and England, be wed away,
   And leave a path for peace.

Mary. I desire that, too.
   Does she put a name to these briars?

Throgmorton. Your Majesty, I am
   Permitted to speak quite frankly?

Mary. I beg you to.

Throgmorton. You are next heir to the throne of England,
   and you
   Are a Catholic. This is a danger to you
   As well as Elizabeth. Were you to turn Protestant
   Elizabeth would at once recognize in you
   Next heir to her succession.

Mary. I should think she might,
   Since I am next heir.

Throgmorton. Forgive me for speaking plainly.

Mary. Oh, forgive me!

Throgmorton. If this seems difficult, I am bid to remind you
That Elizabeth was a Catholic, but became
A Protestant for political reasons.

Mary. That
I could never do. Nor do I see that one's faith
Should be touched by politics.

Throgmorton. Why, not politics,
My gracious queen! God forbid me that I should bring
That word into such a context! We know, of course,
How one clings, shall we say for sentimental reasons,
To the rituals of his youth! Aye, and even a prince,
We admit, would rather say his pater nosters
The way he learned them when he was a child. And yet
Must we take these childish things so gravely now,
When war or peace hangs on them? There are Catholics
In England still. They still plot against our queen.
Were she struck down by one of them you'd take
Her throne and rule us. It follows that your faith
Is a challenge to her—yes, if your Grace will pardon
The word—a defiance.

Mary. You were bid to say this to me?

Throgmorton. Madame, it was said so smoothly by my
    queen
There was no offense in it, but I have no gift
Of language. I must say things out.

Mary. Your manner
Is packed with the most magniloquent impudence
That's come my way. Do you or your queenly mistress

Deem me an inferior, to be given orders blithely,
With a high hand?

Throgmorton. No, madame.

Mary. Say three words more
In this cavalier offensive style of yours
And you'll find yourself in the courtyard.

Throgmorton. Madame, I—

Mary. Come down to earth, and speak without swaggering.

Throgmorton. I've been in the wrong.

Mary. That's better.

Throgmorton. It's true that I'd
Rehearsed my song and dance. Your wit is quicker
Than's been supposed in London.

Mary. Quick enough
To perceive an insult, I hope.

Throgmorton. Your Majesty,
There was none intended, but I might have spoken
more wisely
Had I known your mettle. Elizabeth is concerned,
As I have said, with the differences that are certain
To arise over your religion. Further than that,
What arrangements may be made to avert a breach
In the present concord, if we may discuss these things
Frankly, and you will make frank replies, I have
No other mission.

Mary. Now you talk sense. And frankly.
I will not change my faith.

Throgmorton. And, frankly again,
  There was little hope that you would. There is some
    hope,
  However, that when Your Majesty seeks a consort
  You will not do so to bolster up your claim
  To the English crown, which is strong enough already,
  To cause us uneasiness in London.

Mary. That
  Had not occurred to me.

Throgmorton. But surely your choice in marriage
  Will imply your attitude?

Mary. I have no intention
  Of plighting my troth at once, but if I had
  I've received advice already on that point,
  A mort of it—and I'm tender.

Throgmorton. Say no more,
  Madame, and I'll say no more.

Mary. Oh, out with it now,
  Give the advice. I won't take it.

Throgmorton. Why, it's only this:
  If Your Majesty were to marry a Protestant lord
  Of no royal pretensions, it would indicate
  That you meant no danger to our Elizabeth.

Mary. She has chosen for me, I daresay? She has some lord
  Of the sort in mind?

Throgmorton. You embarrass me to go on.
  She mentioned a name.

Mary. Yes?

Throgmorton. Madame, The Earl of Leicester.

Mary. I hope her ears burn now. Leicester? Her cast-off!—
Her favorite—the one she's dangled? This is an affront—
She named Lord Leicester?

Throgmorton. Nay, nay—only to show you
What it was she had in mind. The kind of match.

Mary. I would hope so.

Throgmorton. For, you see, Your Majesty,
She had a fear of this—the young Lord Darnley
Has come north against her will. Why he's here we don't
know.
Nor whether by invitation, nor what your plans
Might be concerning him.

Mary. I have none.

Throgmorton. Then, if you will,
Forget what I've said. It was only that this Darnley
Combines to exactness what Elizabeth dreads
In case you marry. After you he's next to her throne,
And he's a Catholic. Should you marry Lord Darnley
And call up Catholic Europe to your back—
Well, we'd be ringed in steel.

Mary. I have offered your queen
My friendship and love. I meant that offer.

Throgmorton. But even
If there were no quarrel, and you should marry Darnley
And have a son by him—he'd be heir to England—
And I think the plain fact is that Elizabeth
Would rather choose her own heir.

Mary. Now God forgive me!—
  I am heir to the throne of England, and after me
  Whatever children I have—unless by some chance
  The virgin queen should bear sons! Is it part of her love
  To cut me off from my right?

Throgmorton. It must be remembered
  That England is Protestant, and it might come hard
  To accept a Romish sovereign. In brief, my queen
  Has wished that you might choose Bothwell, or perhaps
    some other
  Of Protestant persuasion!

Mary. And that's the message.
  We're down to it at last. My lord Throgmorton,
  I marry where I please—whether now or later,
  And I abate not one jot of my good blood's lien
  On the English throne. Nay, knowing now the gist
  Of Elizabeth's polity toward that claim, I shall rather
  Strengthen it if I can. The least worthy sovereign
  Has a duty toward his blood, not to weaken it
  Nor let it decline in place.

Throgmorton. This will hardly please.

Mary. I could hardly expect it would. But I too am a
    power,
  And it matters what pleases me. This was all?

Throgmorton. This was all
  I'm commissioned with.

Mary. I shall see to your safe-conduct.

Throgmorton. I thank your Majesty.

> [*He goes out.* MARY *is alone a moment, brooding.* RIZZIO *enters*]

Mary. Oh, Rizzio, Rizzio,
They make a mock of me! It was as you predicted
To the utter syllable.

Rizzio. A warning, then.

Mary. We'll expect no friendship from England.
She cuts me off, me and my line.

Rizzio. May I say that this
Is only her wish, not accomplished?

Mary. Aye, and not to be.
I'd have stood her friend, Rizzio, meant to be her friend,
But now—this is not to be borne! Go and find Lord
    Darnley.

Rizzio. Your Majesty—you have made a decision?

Mary. Yes.

Rizzio. Now I thank you. Now, God helping us, we'll win.
She'll not stamp you out.

Mary. So I think. And now find him.

Rizzio. Yes.

> [MARY BEATON *comes to the outer door*]

Beaton. Will your Majesty see a gentleman calling himself
Lord Bothwell?

> [BOTHWELL *comes to the door*]

Mary. He's in again?

Beaton. There's no keeping him out.

Bothwell.
  [*Entering*]
  The doxy invited me in herself. She's a slut.
  This Beaton of yours.
  [RIZZIO *goes out the outer door*]

Mary. Oh, I know.

Beaton, May I put in a word
  For this gentleman, madame? Of all who come calling
    on you
  He's the most ill-favored. It may be that he's honest,
  I hope so, to go with that face. You're not afraid
  To be left alone with him?

Mary. You may go. Beaton.

Beaton. Yes, Majesty.
  [*She curtseys hurriedly, and goes out*]

Bothwell. Now, what an inexperienced queen you are
  To surround yourself with such taking bitches!

Mary. My lord,
  I have heard from England.

Bothwell. Mary, my queen what you heard
  I could have guessed. She's your demon. She bodes you
    ill.

Mary. I believe it now.

Bothwell. And moreover, between the two,
  This cormorant brother of yours, and that English harpy
  They'll have the heart out of you, and share it. Trust

Not one word they say to you, trust not even the anger
Their words rouse in you. They calculate effects.

Mary. Where is Lord Morton?

Bothwell. Lord Morton is not well.
  [*He is very serious*]
  A sudden indisposition.

Mary. Bothwell, Bothwell—
  You've fought with him!

Bothwell. A mere puncture. What men think
  I cannot punish, nor what they say elsewhere but when
  I hear them, by Christ, they'll learn manners.

Mary. I forbade it.

Bothwell. Forbade it! My dear, not God nor the holy angels
  Forbid me when I'm angry.

Mary. I say I forbade it
  It's I who's responsible for my kingdom—not you—
  You were bound to keep the peace!

Bothwell. When my lady's slandered?
  I'll teach them to hold their peace where you're con-
  cerned.
  Or find their sweet peace in heaven.

Mary. Would God I'd been born
  Deep somewhere in the Highlands, and there met
  you—
  A maid in your path, and you but a Highland bowman
  Who needed me.

Bothwell. Why, if you love me, Marie,
  You're my maid and I your soldier.

Mary. And it won't be.

Bothwell. Aye, it will be.

Mary. For, hear me, my lord of Bothwell.
  I too have a will—a will as strong as your own,
  And enemies of my own, and my long revenges
  To carry through. I will have my way in my time
  Though it burn my heart out and yours. The gods set us
    tasks,
  My lord, what we must do.

Bothwell. Let me understand you.
  The gods, supposing there are such, have thrown us
    together
  Somewhat, of late.

Mary. Look, Bothwell. I am a sovereign,
  And you obey no one. Were I married to you I'd be
  Your woman to sleep with. You'd be king here in
    Edinburgh,
  And I'd have no mind to your ruling.

Bothwell. They'll beat you alone.
  Together we could cope them.

Mary. Love you I may—
  Love you I have—but not now, and no more. It's for me
  To rule, not you. I'll deliver up no land
  To such a hot-head. If you'd been born to the blood
  I'd say, aye, take it, the heavens had a meaning in this,
  But the royal blood's in me.— It's to me they turn

To keep the peace, patch up old quarrels, bring home
Old exiles, make a truce to anarchy. Escape it I cannot.
Delegate it I cannot. The blame's my own
For whatever's done in my name.—I will have no master

[BOTHWELL *is silent when she pauses*]

Nay, I am jealous of this my Stuart blood.
Jealous of what it has meant in Scotland, jealous
Of what it may mean. They've attacked that blood, and
        I'm angry.
They'll meet more anger than they know.

Bothwell. And who
Has angered you? Not I?

Mary. Elizabeth.

Bothwell. I thought so.
She's afraid, if I'm half a prophet,
That you'll marry me.

Mary. Her fears run the other way.
She's afraid I'll marry a Catholic and threaten her
        throne!
She threatens disinheritance! Offers me Leicester!
Her leavings!

Bothwell. Yes, by God, that's a cold potato.

Mary. And means to choose another heir for her throne!
I may never sit on it, but the Stuart line
Shall not suffer by me!

Bothwell. Will you tell me what that means?

Mary. I mean if I have a son he'll govern England.

Bothwell. And so he might, if he were mine, too.

Mary. Nay, might—
But it must be!
She dares to threaten my heritage!

Bothwell. Does that mean Lord Darnley
   [*She is silent*]
Aye, lady, will you stoop so low to choose
A weapon? This is not worthy of the girl
I've known. Am I to be ousted by a papejay
Who drinks in the morning and cannot carry his drink?
An end of mouldy string? You take too much
On yourself of the future. Think of us, and the hours
Close on us here we might have together. Leave some-
   thing
To the gods in heaven! They look after lovers!

Mary. Oh, what's a little love, a trick of the eyes,
A liking, to be set beside the name
You'll have forever, or your son will have?

Bothwell. Well, it's been nibbling at you this long while,
And now it's got you, the blight of Charlemagne—
The itch to conquer.

Mary. I have an itch to conquer?

Bothwell. It goes deep, too, that itch. It eats out the brain.

Mary. Well, and my love for you, how worthy is that?
It's my body wants you. Something I've fought against
Comes out in me when you're near. You've not held it
   sacred,

You've taken others. I've known. And then come
wooing.
It would happen again.

Bothwell. It's a man's way. I've loved you
None the less.

Mary. You don't offer enough, Lord Bothwell.
You're not true in it, and I'm not true to myself
In what I feel for you.

Bothwell. I'm no lute-player
To languish and write sonnets when my lady
Says me nay. Faith, I've lived rough on the border.
And cut some throats I don't forgive myself
Too easily, when I look back, but I tell you
If I give my pledge to you it's an honest pledge,
And I'll keep it. Yes, and when the tug begins
Around your throne, you'll be lost without me. Try
No threats toward England.—It will tax a hardy man
All his time to hold what you have.

Mary. We differ there, too.
What I have I'll defend for myself.

Bothwell. If you marry this Darnley
I take away my hand.

Mary. Before God, he believes
He's held me up so far, and I'd fall without him!

Bothwell. I believe it, and it's true! Darnley, sweet Christ!
No miracle could make him a king! He's a punk,
And he'll rule like a punk!

Mary. We shall see. Lord Bothwell.

Bothwell. Well I'm sped. My suit's cold. But, dod, lady—
 Darnley—
 He sticks in my craw—I can't go him. You'll find few
 that can.
 Think twice about that. Let him not cross my way,
 Or he'll lose his plumes like Morton!

Mary. Will you learn, Lord Bothwell,
 That this is not your palace, but mine? Or must you
 Be taught that lesson?

Bothwell. There's been a bond between us
 We'll find it hard to forget.

Mary. You may. Not I.
 I've set my face where I'm going.

   [RIZZIO *enters.* DARNLEY *is seen behind him*]

Rizzio. Lord Darnley is here,
 Your Majesty.

Mary. Let him enter.

   [DARNLEY *enters from the doorway*]

Bothwell. Lass, lass, God fend thee.
 You've seen the last of me.

Mary. I've given no leave
 For departure, Lord Bothwell

Bothwell. I need no leave, nor leave-taking.
 You see no more of me.

   [*He goes out.* RIZZIO *bows and follows him.* MARY *crosses the*
 room away from DARNLEY *and looks for a moment in*
 the fire. Then she turns to him]

Mary. I have sent for you.
Lord Darnley, to tell you your suit has prospered.
  You've asked
My hand in marriage, and I grant it.

Darnley. Your Majesty—
I hardly hoped—I haven't dared—this is fortune
To take one's breath!
  [*He comes forward and falls to one knee*]
I shall love you, keep you, defend you!

Mary. We shall face troubled times.

Darnley. We'll meet them bravely.
This is some dream—or a jest. It can't be.

Mary. Aye. I feel that.
And yet it's true.

Darnley. I'm to hold you in my arms!

Mary. Not yet. And yet, if you like, come, kiss me.

Darnley. They say
A kiss seals the bargain!
  [*He rises, staggering slightly*]

Mary. I've heard so.
  [*He crosses to her*]
You've drunk too much.

Darnley. Nay, only a morning cup. Oh, Lady, lady—
When you're kind the whole world's kind!

Mary
  [*She faces him, then draws back a step in repulsion*]
You're a boy, a child.

Darnley. Older than you, though.
  It's a bargain, then?

Mary. Yes.
  [*He puts out his arms to her. Her eyes hold him off*]
  Let the kissing go. Let it go till the bond's sealed.

Darnley. Aye, madame.
  [*He drops his arms. They stand looking at each other*]

CURTAIN

MARY OF SCOTLAND
ACT TWO

ACT TWO

Scene I

Scene: *The hall in the palace. Evening.* Mary *and the* Four
    Mary's-in-Waiting *are sitting near the fire, listening as*
    Rizzio *sings to his lute.*

Rizzio. My heart's in the north,
    And my life's in the south
    False I've pledged with my hand,
    False I've kissed with my mouth.

Oh, would we might lie
    Where we lay by the firth,
    With one cloak about us,
    To keep us from earth,

With hand caught to hand
    And the rain driving blind,
    As the new years have driven
    Old love out of mind.

Mary. What is the line, False I've pledged with my hand?

Rizzio. False I've pledged with my hand,
    False I've kissed with my mouth.

Mary. Where did you come by the song?

Rizzio. It's one I made.

Mary. I thought so. Well, it's too true—and past time for
    crying.

Beaton. These poets make much of false pledges and false
    kisses—but they often turn out quiet as well.

Mary. Nay, they turn out badly. If you should love, Beaton, give yourself where you love.

Beaton. There's one of these silly hackbuteers I could have a mind to but I gather he has his penny a day and no more.

Mary. Then if I were you I'd take him.

Livingstone And live on a penny a day?

Mary. Or anything.

Rizzio. My lady, I shall never forgive myself.

Mary. It was my own doing.

Rizzio. My counsel weighed with you. I favored Darnley because he was of my faith. And he's our weakness, not our strength.

Mary. None could have known that.

Rizzio. I should have known. Bothwell would have been better.

Livingstone. Bothwell!

Rizzio. Aye, Bothwell. He'd have held them off. There's no trifling with him.

Livingstone. We do well enough without him.

Rizzio. Well enough perhaps.

Mary. Let's have no talk of Bothwell.

Livingstone. He's better away. The country's been much quieter since he left it. Hasn't it, madame?

Mary. Much quieter.

Fleming. You will have a child, your Majesty. You will have an heir, and then you will be happier.

Mary. With Darnley's child?

Fleming. He will change, too. The man changes when there are children.

Mary. We must hope so.

Seton. His Majesty will return tomorrow?

Mary. He was to have returned three days since. But the hunting may have been delayed.

Beaton. The hunting! He does his hunting o' nights.

Mary. Nay, Beaton.

Beaton. Nor do I take much joy in hearing him called His Majesty.

Seton. But it's the correct address. Lord Darnley has been crowned.

Beaton. Is that a reason for giving him any deference among ourselves? He's a baby, and a spoilt one, and it would give me small pain if I never saw his foolish face again.

Seton. I think that's very treacherous talk!

Mary. It is, too.

Beaton. I'm true to my queen, and I'll be true to none else.
[*She goes to* MARY *and leans her head against her knee*]

Mary. Not even your hackbuteer?

Beaton. Not even him.

Rizzio. Your Majesty, I have a request which you have denied before, but which I must make again. It is necessary for me to leave Scotland.

Mary. David, David!

Rizzio. I grow lonely for Italy.

Mary. And who will write my letters?

Rizzio. There are many who could write letters.

Mary. Can you name one—both efficient and to be trusted?

Rizzio. Maitland.

Mary. Would you trust him?

Rizzio. I think I should go, Your Majesty.

Mary. We know why, David, and I won't have it. I won't have my friends driven from me.

Rizzio. I think it's best.

Mary. Has His Majesty spoken to you?

Rizzio. Only by the way.—I'm not wanted here—you know that.

Mary. The king is full of these whims and fancies, my dear Rizzio. If I gave way to one I should have to humor him in all. You and I know that I am quite innocent with you, and you with me. And I can't spare you.

Rizzio. God knows you are innocent, madame, and I too unless it be a crime to love you. I do love you, I can't deny that.

Mary. Nor do I hold it a crime.

Rizzio. Majesty, I tell you honestly it's torture to speak of going away—and yet—oh, I want no harm to come to you through me!

Mary. And none will. The king is jealous, of everyone, my Rizzio, everyone, I see or have seen. It's a brainsick notion. I know that he has acted and spoken foolishly in many such matters. But as for danger, there is none.

Rizzio. I hope there is none.

[*There is a clatter of armor in the hall to the right*]

Mary. Say no more of going.

Rizzio. My queen, I am too easy to convince in this! Too much of me cries out to stay—and yet—say no more and let me go!

Mary. Why, very well.

Rizzio. But not angrily—not in anger.

Mary. Not in anger.

Rizzio. I thank your Majesty.

[A PORTER *comes to the door at the right*]

Porter. Master Rizzio?

Rizzio. Yes.

Porter. Lord Maitland of Lethington and Master John Knox are here.

Mary. They are to come in.

[RIZZIO *makes a gesture to the* PORTER *who goes out. The* QUEEN *rises.* RIZZIO *goes to the door and ushers in* MAITLAND *and* KNOX, *then goes out.* KNOX *stands at the door*]

Maitland. Ah, Your Majesty—I was to bring Master Knox—

Mary. Yes, I remember.

Maitland.

[*Looking about*]

I gather that he wishes to speak with you in private.

Mary. I doubt that we shall find the subject makes it necessary. Master Knox, will you come closer to the fire?

Knox. I am very well here, I thank your Majesty.

Mary. You come—was it the word?—to make a protest?

Knox. Would it be convenient that I speak with you alone?

Mary. When we last spoke alone, sir, there was some talk to the effect that I had used arts on you. I could wish to avoid a repetition of that.

Knox. Why, then, I have but one thing to say and I shall make shift to say it quickly. You are a Catholic queen in a Protestant land, your Majesty—

Mary. Only in part Protestant.

Knox. Protestant in great majority—

Mary. Yes.

Knox. You have taken a Catholic husband and set him on the throne beside you, giving him what is called in the courts of this world the crown matrimonial. You have also set up an altar in this your palace, where the mass and other idolatrous rites are said for you. In these ways you encourage Lord Huntley and the

Highland Catholics of the north in their heathenish practices, and in so doing bring grave dissension among your people. I come to warn you.

Mary. To warn me of what, Master Knox?

Knox. That the forms and appurtenances of the Romish faith cannot be thrust upon us. That this will not be borne by the defenders of the Lord's word and church.

Mary. I ask no one to subscribe to my faith, sir. But it has been mine from a child, and I keep it.

Knox. You seek to gain it a foothold here, and build it up about you. I wish no evil to you nor to this kingdom and I say the celebration of the mass must cease, for there are those among us to whom it is abhorrent. And though it cost civil war and the slaughter of brother by brother it will not be borne.

Mary. And are you among those who will not bear it?

Knox. I am.

Mary. Do you find it written that all men must worship in one fashion?

Knox. There is but one true faith and one true fashion of worship.

Mary. And would you enforce it with the sword?

Knox. There is no tolerance for the idolator nor the adulterer. They are to be weeded out—and even now—before they come to the great pit and are given over to his unending fire—a fire not to be quenched nor remedied nor appeased.

Mary. I understand your attitude toward the idolator, Master Knox, but do you consider it apposite to bring adulterers also into this conversation?

Knox. The idolator, the adulterer, the priests of Baal, they shall be uprooted, seed and seedling, and cast into the burning—

Mary. But Master Knox, Master Knox, let us have a meeting of minds! An idolator is not the same as an adulterer. Confine yourself to some meaning!

Knox. They come among us in one person—the priests of the flesh and the worshippers of the flesh—

Mary. If you would but leave off prophesying for a moment and speak sense! Who is the idolator here?

Knox. Have you not set up an altar?

Mary. A very little one, sir. Nothing to what I could wish. And does that make me an idolator?

Knox. Will you deny it?

Mary. I do deny it. And now tell me who is the adulterer.

Knox. Let them search in their hearts who came from France.

Mary. I have searched in mine, and find no adultery there. And shall not those who live in Scotland search in their hearts also?

Maitland. Your Majesty, I have brought Master Knox here only because I am convinced that he voices an attitude which must be seriously considered.

Mary. But I try to take him seriously and he speaks in
parables. I ask him to define his words and he talks
of a great fire. To him a priest is a priest of Baal, an
idolator is the same as an adulterer, and those who
come from France run especial danger of damnation.
What can one say to such a man? Master Knox, I believe you mean well, but can you not see that I also
mean well, and that there might be more than one
opinion concerning the worship of Our Lord?

Knox. There will be but one opinion held in that last day—
when he comes with his armies, and driveth before him
those who are not his children!

Mary. Look, what can one say to him? You ask him a
question—and he threatens you with the Last Judgment! You see, Master Knox, you are not the judge who
will sit over us in the Last Judgment! You are instead
an elderly gentleman of provincial learning and fanatical
beliefs, lately married to a niece of your own some forty
years your junior, and one who conducts his conversa-
tions almost exclusively in quotation from the Old
Testament. If you will talk sensibly with me I shall talk
sensibly with you, but if you come here to frighten me
I shall regard you as a most ridiculous antediluvian
figure, and find you very funny. Which shall it be?

Knox. Well I know you hold the Lord God as a jest and a
mockery!

Mary. Do not confuse yourself with Lord God again!
There's a difference!

Knox. I am His spokesman.

> [RIZZIO *comes to the door*]

Mary. Indeed. Will you show me your commission?

Knox. I call ruin to fall on this house, the shelter of the great beast—!

Mary. And there again! Maitland, can you, by any stretch of the imagination, look upon me as the great beast?

Rizzio. Your Majesty, Lord Huntley is here

Mary. Come in, Lord Huntley!

> [HUNTLEY *enters*]

Sir, I have just heard myself likened to the great beast of Revelations. Can you see any similarity there?

Huntley. Why, lass, I'd say at the least it's an exaggeration.

Maitland. If Your Majesty wishes to give audience to Lord Huntley—

> [*He starts to withdraw*]

Mary. Nay, why should you go? And why should John Knox and Lord Huntley not meet face to face in one room? I am aware that Master Knox is a Protestant and that Huntley is a Catholic, but they dwell in the same small kingdom, and it would be well if they understood each other.

Knox. I am loath to say it, but I am of a mind that there can be no understanding between him and me, no, nor between myself and Your Majesty, lest I betray my Lord.

Huntley. Madame, it's my opinion we understand each other dom well. Too dom well.

Mary. But since you must both live in this kingdom and one must be Catholic and one Protestant, surely it were wiser to be amiable over small matters, Maitland?

Maitland. Aye, it would be wiser.

Knox. Not for what you have said to me or of my person, for that unto seventy times seven those who follow him forgive, but because the air of this house is offensive in his nostrils, I call ruin on it! Nor will I commune in it further, neither with those who make their beds here nor with those who come here for counsel! Yea, if there are any here who would avoid the wrath, let them turn now, for it is upon you and your servants!

Mary. Well—it would seem there's little to be done about that. You are dismissed if you wish to go.

    [MAITLAND *and* KNOX *turn to leave*]

Maitland. I offer my apologies, Your Majesty.

Mary. Oh, surely.

Knox. Yea, those who breed and take their ease in the places of the annointed, turn, turn now, before the axe fall quickly and be followed by silence! For now it is not too late, but no man knows when he cometh, nor of the wings of what morning!

    [MAITLAND *and* KNOX *go out.* RIZZIO *rejoins the group at the fire*]

Mary. You are duly impressed by this talk, sir?

Beaton. Why, the solemn ass! He should have been booted!

Huntley. My dear, you've been too easy with him, and if you continue to be easy we'll pay for it.

Mary. And in what way, sir.

Huntley. You and I are alone here, Your Majesty, so far as Catholicism's concerned. My Highlanders are Catholic, it's true, and there's a plenty of them, and they're tough, but the rest are all against us, every noble and man of note. They're John Knox's men, and you heard yourself what he said.

Beaton. He with the persimmon-colored whiskers?

Huntley. Aye, he. And he means it.

Mary. What does he mean?

Huntley. Ruin to this house.

Mary. Is this a house to be blown down with windy talk?

Huntley. My birdie—I canna call you Ye're Majesty and all that—

Mary. You need not.

Huntley. Then, my bird, they draw their nets tight about us. I told you before, and it's coming.

Mary. And who draws the net?

Huntley.

   [*Looking at the others*]
   Lady—

Mary. These five know my secret heart. They'll say nothing.

Huntley. Lady, there's only one defence. Attack them first. And there's but one proper place for John Knox. He should be in Edinburgh Castle—and all those with him who are of his mind.

Mary. You'd imprison him?

Huntley. He and some twenty others.

Mary. And then?

Huntley. Then you can go to work. You're not safe here and I'm not safe here while a sect of Protestant lords divide your dominion with you. You rule by sufferance only.

Mary. They are here by my sufferance, Huntley.

Huntley. You have heard of the sheep nursed the wolf-pups till they tore her to pieces.

Mary. But we're not sheep and wolves, my lord. There's room for all of us here, and for whatever faiths we may choose to have.

Huntley. Never think it, my bird, never believe it! It's never yet happened that a state survived with two religions in it. Never. Elizabeth knows that. She's behind this Knox. He'd never dare be so bold if she weren't behind him.

Mary. But it's my thought that in Scotland, though it be the first time in the world, we shall all believe as we please and worship as we list. And Elizabeth may take it as she sees fit.

Huntley. She uses it against you, my dear, and uses John

Knox against you. Ladybird, I'm willing to beg it of you, take heed of me now or we're both done!

Mary. Rizzio?

Rizzio. You know my mind. I'm with Lord Huntley in this.

Mary. But how can I bring myself to imprison men for no wrong they've done, on suspicion only, imprison them for their faith—?

Huntley. It's more than faith. It's works. You heard John Knox!

Mary. It cuts athwart every right instinct I have, my lord! Every fibre I have that's royal shrinks at such penny-wise petty doings! And John Knox—a doddering imbecile, drooling prophecy!

Huntley. He threatened you, lady.

Mary. No, no, I can't. Even if it were wisdom to do it, and it's not.

[*The right-hand door opens suddenly and* DARNLEY *stands in it.* MARY *turns toward him*]

My lord!

[DARNLEY *walks slowly to the middle of the room and lays a hand on the table*]

Darnley. I'm unexpected, perhaps? Too early? A thought Too early? I'll retire. Come when I'm wanted.

Mary. No,
My lord, you've been long expected, and more than welcome.

Darnley. Why, a pretty wife, a huswife with her maids;
A pretty sight, and maybe a cavalier

Or two, for the maids' company. Dod, sit down all!
Damn me if I'll intrude!

Mary. Will you speak to Lord Huntley?

Darnley.
[*Focussing on* HUNTLEY]
Right. That's right. Lord Huntley, give me your hand.
I thank you for watching over the pretty wife here.
I've been away.

Huntley.
[*Turning*]
Your Majesty, you've a wife
Such as I wish I'd had when I was young.

Darnley. Right—You have right. They all say that. I'd say
it myself.
Only I know her better.
[*He turns to the door*]
I know her too well,
And not well enough. She wouldn't care to hear it.
Not from me.

Mary. Darnley.

Darnley. She sleeps alone.
At least as far as I know.

Huntley. I'll take my leave,
My lady.

Mary. Yes.

Darnley. Stay, stay, I'm going. I only
Tell you she sleeps alone as far as I know.

A pretty wife. These women—they get with child,
You never know how—and then they won't sleep with
you.
[Huntley *bows to* Mary, *turns deliberately, and goes out the
door to the right, closing it*]
What's the matter with him? He's an old married man.
He knows these things.

Mary. You're tired, my lord. Will you wish
Some service, something to eat and drink?

Darnley. She sends me
Off to bed, you note. You note it, Rizzio?
There's a service she could do me, but I doubt
She'll offer it. And I'm a king, by God, a king,
And you're a clark by office!

Mary. My lord, I hoped
You'd have some other word for me when you
Returned.

Darnley. My pink, if I gave you the word you've earned
The room would smell. I've been at the hunting. We
had
Something to drink. Alban! Alban! Allons!

Mary. You call someone?

Darnley. Alban! God's right! St. Andrew! Alban!
I'm drunk, you see.

Mary. I think not.

Darnley. Yes, but I am.
Alban! Christ his sonties, am I left
Alone here! God and St. Andrew!
[*The right hand door opens and* Ruthven *enters in full armor*]

Mary. What is this?
  [*To* Ruthven]
You will retire, sir. Who are you?

Darnley. My good friend Ruthven.

Mary. Is this a place for armor? I will receive
Lord Ruthven another time.

Darnley. The callant's there,
Ruthven.

Ruthven. Aye.

Mary. I had heard that Lord Ruthven was ill,
And thought to go to him, not to see him here.

Ruthven. I am ill, and it's mortal, but I've sworn to be
    mortal
To another first.

Mary. This is my apartment, sir,
And I ask you to go.
  [Douglas *appears behind* Ruthven]

Mary. I demand little courtesy,
But that little I must have. Are these your friends?
If so, take them elsewhere.

Darnley. Aye, I'm to have my friends
In my apartment—and you're to have yours here.
I say no—they're to mingle.—
  [*He points to* Rizzio]
You see that grig
With the kinked hair there? He with the lady's hands

And feet? Where does he sleep nights? That's he, that's
 the one
We have in question!

Mary. My lord, when you've been drinking
 I have little taste for your company, and tonight
 Less, perhaps, than ever.

Darnley. He, he, I tell you!
 That Italian spawn!
  [Rizzio, *trembling, steps back toward the queen's study*]

Mary.
  [*Stepping in front of* Rizzio]
 Go into my study.
  [Lord Morton *enters*]
 Lord Morton,
 Whatever you have in hand here, put no faith
 In this king I've crowned and set beside me! His word
 Is a paper shield.

Darnley. I'm king in this country, mistress—
 And I know my rights.

Mary. Beaton, why were these men
 Not stopped at my door?

Darnley. They came with me.
  [*Facing* Morton]
 Will you tell me
 What you want with the queen?

Morton.
  [*His dagger drawn*]

Damme, do you want this bodkin
Through that bodice of yours?

[*She shrinks back.* RIZZIO, *having reached the study step by
step, opens it and reveals a* GUARD, *a drawn claymore
in his hand*]

Rizzio. Let me pass!

The Guard. Nay, lad.

Fleming. Your Majesty,
They've broken into your rooms

[MARY *turns and sees the guard*]

Mary. Lord Darnley, was that
By your order?

Rizzio.

[*Hardly able to speak for fear*]

Save me, my queen, save me!

Mary. Aye, Rizzio.

[*The five women retreat before the armed men, covering* RIZZIO
from them]

Morton. Look to the women-folk, Darnley. We'll care for
him.

[RIZZIO *turns suddenly and leaps behind the heavy drapes of
the high window down-stage.* MORTON, DOUGLAS *and*
RUTHVEN *follow him,* DOUGLAS *with his dagger raised*]

Mary. Douglas, I'll remember this!

[*A fall is heard behind the curtains, but no cry.* MARY *runs
toward the window, but is met by* RUTHVEN, *sheathing
his dagger*]

You've murdered him!
You pack of filthy cowards!

Ruthven. Yea, and done well.

Mary. Done well! Oh, fools and cowards!

> [*She runs to the curtain and with* MARY BEATON *pulls it back
> from* RIZZIO, *then bends over him and draws back again.
> in terror*]

Oh, David, David,
It was I wouldn't let you go!

Darnley.

> [*Looking away*]

You might cover that sight.

Mary. Is he dead, Beaton?

Beaton. Yes, madame.

Mary. Oh, you do well, you do well.
All of you!

> [*She conquers her repulsion, and tries to loosen* RIZZIO's *ruff.*
> FLEMING *comes to help her*]

We'll help him if we can,
Fleming.

Fleming. Yes.

Mary. You were too gentle for them,
David. They couldn't bear it—these boors and swine—
Your kerchief, Fleming! He bleeds so—

Fleming. It's useless, Madame.

Mary.

> [*Rising*]

Yes.

> [*To the lords*]

To take him unarmed, and poniard him—
One who had never hurt you!

Ruthven.
   [*Sinking to a chair*]
   Well, the work's done,
   And my queen's wiped clear of him.

Mary. Wiped clear! You believed
   I was guilty with him!

Ruthven. Were you not?

Mary. No!

Ruthven. I'd be sorry
   If you were not. I struck him down for that.

Mary. I was not guilty. But will you tell me now
   Who'll believe me innocent? You've branded me deep
   With this murder, and you've killed a guiltless man!
   Why do you sit in my presence?

Ruthven. Because I'm ill
   And dying. I should be sorry if this thing
   I've done were in error—for it's the last I'll do.

Mary. You'll stand in my presence! Whose order was it?

Ruthven. Why, ask His Majesty that—
   And Morton there, and Moray.
   [*He rises with difficulty*]

Mary. Moray too?

Ruthven. Yea, your brother. For me— let me go home.

Mary. Go. Morton and Douglas, I give you three days
   To leave this kingdom.

Morton. And the king? I have the king's seal
    For what I've done.

Mary. Is that true?

Darnley. Aye.

Mary. The worse for you.
    The worse for you all.

Darnley. My lady, this long while past
    You've denied me your chamber, and when I've seen you
        there's been
    This Rizzio with you.

Mary. Never again while I live
    Will you see me alone. I bear your child in me
    Or you'd answer for this!

Darnley. There'll be no answering!
    We know what we know about you!

Mary. I would I knew
    In what strange dark chamber of your oafish brain
    You found reasons for Rizzio's death. If I saw you
        seldom
    Remember how often you drank yourself imbecile
    Before you came to me. You've slain your last friend, sir.
    It was Rizzio's counsel put you where you are
    And kept you there. These are not your friends, these
        three,
    Nor Moray. They wanted Rizzio out of the way,
    And they wanted to drag you down, and drag me
        down,
    And you play into their hands. I've never been

Unfaithful to you, but we're at an end, we two.
From this time forward if I touch your hand
May God blight me and my child!

Darnley. I wanted you!
You kept away from me, and it drove me mad!

Mary. You won't mend it now. Look, young Rizzio's dead.
You've blackened me, blackened yourself, thrown a
     black doubt
On the child who'll be your heir. The lords look on
And smile, knowing they've trapped you. You'll never
     climb
From the pit where you've fallen, and I may fall with
     you. Lord Moray
Weaves his web round us. You've helped him.

Darnley. God knows I wanted
Only my right.

Mary. You pitiful dolt! To think
Such a calf should rule, and at my choosing! God
May forgive you—not I. Nor forgive myself.—And
     Rizzio.—
Take yourselves out! You pollute the dead to stand
     there!
He wanted to go to Italy.

Fleming. Yes.

Mary. Will you go?

  [MORTON *beckons the guards, and they cross from the study to
      the outer door*]

Ruthven.

> [*At the door*]

> You'll want some help, mayhap.

Mary. None of yours. I've noticed
> It's men that kill, but women that wash the corpse
> And weep for it. May none ever weep for you.

Ruthven. None will. I've been in the wrong.

Mary. I'm sorry, Lord Ruthven.
> It's an ill thing to have on your heart when you die.

Ruthven. Aye, is it.

> [*He goes out, and the men follow him.* DARNLEY *looks back as if
> he wished to speak to the queen, but goes silently*]

Mary. And now we're alone. The lords have shown their
> hand.
> Rizzio's gone—and Darnley, what there was to go.
> We've been not long in Scotland, but time enough
> To show I can lose it, have lost it in their minds
> Already. We must lay the poor lad somewhere.
> Could we lift him together?

Seton. Oh, madame, I'm afraid?

Mary. Of what?

Seton. I've never seen one dead before.
> I've not known it was like this.

Mary. It's poor Rizzio.
> No one to hurt us. And you and I will lie
> Sometime like this, and folk will be afraid
> Because we lie so still. How strange it is

That he should frighten us who wished us well,
And would still if he lived. We must take him up
And lay him on my bed. I'll sleep with Beaton
Tonight.

    [*She takes a step toward* Rizzio]

Beaton. Madame, the blood will stain your dress.

Mary. If that were all. This will bring more blood after.
Now I see it. Before I reign here clearly
There will be many men lie so for me
Slain in needless quarrel. Slain, and each one
With blood to spill but once, like his. And yet
One steps on into it—steps from life to life
'Till there are thousands dead, and goes on still
Till the heart faints and sickens, and still goes on
And must go on.

    [*An iron gate clangs outside.* Beaton *parts the curtains to
      look out*]

I tell you, Fleming, my soul
Is aghast at this blood spilled for me, and yet
It hardens me, too. These are their manners, this
Is the way they go to work. I shall work on them,
And not too lightly. They think of me as a girl,
Afraid of them. They shall see.—And yet my mind
Believes nothing of what I say; I'm weak as grief,
Stripped and wept out before them. They press me close,
And I have no one to send.

    [*There is a rattle of staves in the courtyard*]

Beaton.

    [*Turning back*]
It's the provost, madame,

I heard them call his name.

Mary. He's not to enter.
Let no one enter.

　　[BEATON *goes out right*]

No one. In all this kingdom
I can trust only five, and one's myself,
And we're women, all of us.—If they go scot-free
After this indignity I'm no queen. For Ruthven
He'll pay his own score. He's dying. Morton and Douglas
Must die too.

Fleming. They were under Lord Darnley's orders.

Mary. He was under theirs. It won't save them.

Fleming. Your Majesty,
They've left the city by now. They should have been
　　taken
While they were in your hands.

Mary. I know. It's true.
They've fled to raise troops. When next we find them
　　they'll meet us
With culverins.

　　[BEATON *enters*]

He's gone?

Beaton. Yes. But there's one
Below from France—says he has news.

Mary. From France?
Tomorrow, though. I wish I were still in France
And had never seen these stone walls.

Livingstone. And so do I.

Mary. What is his name?

Beaton. He gave me
This token for you, no name. It's a crow's feather.

Mary.
[*Takes the feather, then pauses*]
Tell my Lord Bothwell I have no wish to see him
Now or later.

Beaton. Madame, you'll see him? I brought him
Along with me.

Mary. No. Not now. Not ever.
There's nothing to say between us now.

Beaton. He came
From France to see you.

Mary. Tell him.
[Lord Bothwell *is seen standing in the doorway*]

Bothwell. Your Majesty,
You've had unwelcome company this hour,
If I've heard aright, and I care not to be another,
But I come to make an offer I made before—
To be your soldier.

Mary. I have no time to talk,
Lord Bothwell. Nor do I wish to see you. The time's
Gone by.

Bothwell. My queen, my queen, turn not away
Your friends. You've few enough, too few it seems
To prevent what's happened.

Mary. Go.

Bothwell. Does he still lie here?
I'll lay the poor boy away for you at least,
And then I'll go, since you wish it.
  [*He crosses to* Rizzio]
Aye, they made sure,
Lad—and their dirks were sharp. Shall I place him
  within?

Mary. Yes.
  [Bothwell *picks up* Rizzio *and carries him into Mary's
  chamber*]
Must you betray me, too?

Beaton. I wished only—
If you'd but follow your heart!

Mary. We two must twain,
My Beaton. You take too much on you. Lord Bothwell,
May be your friend, not mine.

Beaton. Forgive me.

Mary. What warrant
Have you been given to vouch for my heart, or judge
Whether I should follow it?

Beaton. None.

Mary. Oh, God, this vice
Of women, crying and tears! To weep, weep now
When I need my anger! Say my farewells for me,
I've gone to my study.
  [*She turns.* Bothwell *enters*]

Bothwell. Goodnight, my queen.

Mary. Goodnight.
I'm not unkind. But I'm cut off from you.
You know that.

Bothwell. Yes. There's no need to hide your weeping.
He was over-young to die.

Mary. It's not for him.
No, it's for all I wanted my life to be,
And is not.

Bothwell. Majesty, you have a fortunate star.
It will come well yet.

Mary. If I have a star at all
It's an evil one. To violate my room,
Kill my servant before my eyes—How I must be hated!

Bothwell. They'll pay for that.

Mary. Perhaps.

Bothwell. I've taken an oath
They'll pay for it. Your Majesty, I wearied
Of France and exile, wearied of sun and wine,
And looked north over the water, longing for fog
And heather and my own country. Further, the news
Was none too happy from Scotland. They want your
throne
And plan to have it. But I mean to live in this land
And mean you to be queen of it. The Earl of Bothwell
Is home, and spoiling for a fight. Before
Day dawns they'll hear from me.

Mary. My lord, I thank you—

Bothwell. Give me no thanks. I like a fight too well
    To pretend it's a virtue. Moreover, if I'm to live here
    I'd rather you were my liege than Moray. I'm none
    So fond of your half-brother. This night's work
    Should show you he's what I knew him, half-bred, half-
      faced
    And double-tongued.

Mary. You have no army.

Bothwell. I have
    My border men. Lord Huntley's joined with me
    With his Highland kilties. If you'd call your clans
    We could drive them to the wall.

Mary. It's a war then.

Bothwell. It's war,
    Already. They've turned your Darnley against you.
      They'll use him
    As long as they need his seal. Once they've got you out
    They'll set Moray up as regent. They fear one chance:
    That you and I should league together and balk them.
    I've come back in time, not too soon.

Mary. I think you have.
    My lord, I had no heart to face you. The fault
    Was mine when we parted.

Bothwell. It's not too late. I've come
    Only just in time, but in time.

Mary. It is too late—
    For you and me. These faults we commit have lives
    Of their own, and bind us to them.

Bothwell.

> [*Pointing toward her bedroom*]
> Yon was Darnley's work.
> Are you still his?

Mary. Am I not?

> [BEATON *gathers up the three others with a look and goes into
>   the queen's study with them silently*]
> I'm to bear his child.
> I cannot hate my child.

Bothwell. It's in the wind
> This Darnley's not to live long.

Mary. I'd have no hand
> In that—nor you!

Bothwell. It happens he's a pawn
> In the game the lords are playing. They'll sacrifice him
> When the time comes. It's no plot of mine.

Mary. But he lives
> And I'm his wife, and my babe is his. I must drink
> My cup down to the rinse. It was I that filled it,
> And if there's grief at the bottom it's mine. I'll name you
> My officer, but only if you can pledge
> No harm will come through you to Darnley.

Bothwell. Lady,
> I need you, and you need me, but I'll be damned
> If Darnley's needed on this earth. I have
> No project against him, but I'll give no pledge
> To block me if I should have. There be men
> Who wear their welcome out in this world early
> And Darnley's one of them.

Mary. You have never yet
  Learned how to take an order.

Bothwell. And never will—
  From man or woman living, sovereign or knave,
  Judge or vicegerent. I have not been conquered
  And will not be. But I offer you my fealty,
  And it's worth the more for that.

Mary. You must make your own terms—
  I'm but a beggar here.

Bothwell. Nay, nay, it's I
  That sue, a beggar for what's impossible,
  With this Darnley standing between us.
    [*She pauses again*]

Mary. You shall be
  My Lord Admiral and act for me. Yes, and to that
  Let me add how my breath caught when I knew you
      here,
  Hoping I know not what, things not to be,
  Hopes I must strangle down. Oh, Bothwell, Bothwell!
  I was wrong! I loved you all the time, and denied you!
  Forgive me—even too late!

Bothwell. I tell you we
  Shall be happy yet.

Mary. No, for I think I've been
  At the top of what I'll have, and all the rest
  Is going down. It's as if a queen should stand
  High up, at the head of a stair—I see this now
  As in a dream—and she in her dream should step

From level to level downward, all this while knowing
She should mount and not descend—till at last she walks
An outcast in the courtyard—bayed at by dogs
That were her hunters—walks there in harsh morning
And the dream's done.

Bothwell.

[*Stepping toward her*]

You're weary. You've borne too much.
They shall pay for this.

Mary. Come no nearer, my lord. It's not ours
To have. Go now.

Bothwell. Yes, your Majesty.

[*He turns*]

Yet
I tell you we shall be happy. And there will be nothing
Not ours to have.

[*He goes out*]

CURTAIN

ACT TWO

Scene II

Scene: *Elizabeth's study at Whitehall.* Burghley *and* Elizabeth *are seated across a table. A* Third Figure *approaches from the side.*

Burghley. This will be Lord Throgmorton.

Elizabeth. You're early, sir.

Throgmorton. Madame, I rode all night.—I've news from the north.
Darnley's been murdered.

Elizabeth. How?

Throgmorton. Kirk o' Field was blown up.
The castle's in ruins.

Elizabeth. Now that was a waste of powder—
And of castles too. But he's dead—

Throgmorton. Yes, madame—they found him
It was no accident. He'd been strangled.

Elizabeth. So there's no more king in Scotland.
Who took this trouble?

Throgmorton. Moray, and Morton, no doubt—perhaps Maitland—

Elizabeth. Not Bothwell?—

Throgmorton. No—though he must have known of it—

Elizabeth. And the queen—
The queen weeps for her Darnley?

102

Throgmorton. Madame—

Elizabeth. Ah, yes—
  She'll weep and wear black—it becomes her. A second
    time
  She's a widow now. And she's borne a child. She begins
  To wear a little, no doubt? She must ponder now
  What costumes may become her?

Throgmorton. Nay, truly, your Grace,
  I'd say she charms as ever.

Elizabeth. Would you say so?
  But she weeps and puts on mourning?

Throgmorton. No, madame, Bothwell
  And the queen are friends again—or more than that.
  They'd be married already, I think, only Moray's
    against it
  And the earls behind him.

Elizabeth. Now in my day and time
  I have known fools and blockheads, but never, I swear,
  In such numbers as among these Scotch earls. Moray's
    against it?
  Against the queen's marriage with Bothwell?

Burghley. Your Majesty—
  If she were to marry Bothwell—we've opposed that, too,
  And even prevented it.

Elizabeth. Aye, times have changed,
  And we change along with them. She loves this Both-
    well?
  It's a great love—a queen's love?

Throgmorton. It is indeed.
　A madness, almost.

Elizabeth. Yes, yes—and it's well sometimes
　To be mad with love, and let the world burn down
　In your own white flame. One reads this in romances—
　Such a love smokes with incense; oh, and it's grateful
　In the nostrils of the gods! Now who would part them
　For considerations of earth? Let them have this love
　This little while—let them bed and board together—
　Drink it deep, be happy—aye—

Burghley. Madame, this Bothwell's
　No man to play with. If they marry she'll crown him
　　king—

Elizabeth. You did well to ride fast, Throgmorton! Turn
　　now
　And ride as fast back again; you can sleep later
　When we're old and the years are empty.—And tell my
　　lord Moray
　If he'd keep me a friend, let his sister marry Bothwell—
　Tell him to favor it—hurry it.

Burghley. And with Bothwell king
　Do you think to conquer Mary?

Elizabeth. Send next to John Knox,
　But do this cleverly, giving Knox evidence
　That Bothwell slew Darnley with the queen's con-
　　nivance
　And they bed together in blood. Have you wit enough
　To see this well done?

Throgmorton. I think so, Majesty.

Elizabeth. See to it.
  Who will deny that Bothwell murdered Darnley
  When he lives with the queen, and enjoys the fruits? Or
    who
  Will credit Bothwell's denial? Your brain, my Burghley!
  Where do you wear it, or what has it hardened into
  That you're so easily gulled?

Burghley. But is it wise
  To make a false accusation? This project hangs
  By a thread. Make but one error and we shall lose
  Whatever we've gained.

Elizabeth. Go and do these things—
  They are to marry—we sanction it—let none oppose it—
  She refused him before when he could have saved her—
  She'll take him now when it's fatal—Let her have this
    love
  This little while—we grant her that—then raise
  The winds against them—rouse the clans, cry vengeance
  On their guilty sleep and love—I say within
  This year at the very farthest, there's no more queen
  Than king in Scotland!

CURTAIN

ACT TWO

Scene III

Scene: *A hall in Dunbar Castle.* A Sentinel *is at his post near the outer gate, another at the guard-room door. There is a step on the cobbles outside. The* First Sentinel *swings round to the gate.*

Jamie.
   [*Outside*]
  Drop your point, man. Ye ken me.

First Sentinel. Eh, Jamie. What is it?

Jamie. I'm late. It was tough getting through. The queen's taken prisoner. Her army's gone.

First Sentinel. Nay! And Bothwell?

Jamie. Bothwell's free yet. Free and able to fight. We're to put the castle in posture of defense. Where's the sergeant?

First Sentinel. Call Graeme.

Second Sentinel. Graeme!—I told you this was no lucky battle to be in.

First Sentinel. Says John Knox!
   [Graeme *enters*]

Jamie. I've orders for the guard. We're to man the walls and be ready on the gates.

Graeme. It goes that way?
   [Beaton *enters from the stair*]

Jamie. That way and worse.
   [*They turn toward the gate*]

106

Beaton. Jamie, what brings you?

Jamie. Orders, lass.

Beaton. Quick, tell me!

Jamie. It goes badly with us, lass.

    [LORD HUNTLEY *enters*]

Beaton. My lord—

Huntley. There's to be a parley here. Make ready for it.

Jamie. Watch that outer post.

    [*The* SENTINELS *go out*]

Beaton. A parley—the battle's over?

Huntley. Aye, over and done. This is Moray's kingdom now.

Beaton. And the queen?

Huntley. The queen's a prisoner, lass. My men have deserted, her own men turned against her.

Beaton. My lord, you'll forgive me, but how could that be?

Huntley. This was John Knox's battle, lady. The auld limmer took a stance on a hill some half-mile to windward and there he stood haranguing like the angel Gabriel, swearing Bothwell killed Darnley to have the queen. And the queen's men listened to him, the psalm-singing red-beards, and then turned and made her prisoner and delivered her up to Lord Moray.

Graeme. Bothwell's returning.

Jamie. Upstairs with you, lass.

    [BEATON *goes up the lower stair*]

Graeme. Shall I set the guard?

Huntley. Wait a moment.

  [BOTHWELL *enters*]

Bothwell. We're not through yet, my lord. You'll stand by
  me?

Huntley. Aye,
  If it's any use. One may rally an army flying.
  But one that flies toward the enemy and makes friends—

Bothwell. Who spoke of rallying? They won by treachery,
  And we'll treat them some of the same!
    [*To* JAMIE]
  There were ninety men
  Left to guard the castle! They're here still?

Jamie. Aye sir.

Bothwell. They're under
  Lord Huntley's orders while this parley's on.
  Tell them to be ready. He'll join you.

Jamie. Aye.
  [*He goes into the guard-room*]

Bothwell. Sergeant, take the men you need and guard that
  arch—
  Let no one enter but the lords themselves.

Graeme. Aye, my lord.
  [*He goes out by the arch*]

Bothwell. I'll talk with these lords, and if they listen to
  reason
  They may keep their mangy lives, but if they refuse

To release the queen and give her back her kingdom
Then hell's their home! Watch my arm, and hark
For my sword on steel. They're outnumbered three to
one

Huntley. Kill them?

Bothwell. Cut their throats
If you like that better.

Huntley. That's plain murder.

Bothwell. Right,
And if they say no they've earned it.

Huntley. And we'd die, too.

Bothwell. Why, it might be we would. But I'd stake more
On our living long with them dead. If the queen's
deposed
Then I've lived long enough, and so have you.
Will you gamble with me?

Huntley. I will.

   [*They shake hands. A trumpet sounds outside*]

Bothwell. Wait for the signal.
My sword on steel.

   [HUNTLEY *goes into the guard-room. The voices of the Lords are
heard outside*]

Morton.
   [*Outside*]
Go carefully now. Not too fast.

Moray. Aye, you're the man to say that.

Morton. Let Maitland speak.

    [*They enter; one or two bow ironically*]

Bothwell. You may drop these scrapings. We know what we
    think of each other!

Morton. And that's true too!

Moray. We have little to gain, Lord Bothwell,
    By a conference with you. The battle is ours. The queen
    Is prisoner to us. But to spare ourselves further blood-
    shed
    And spare you bloodshed, we grant this respite, and ask
    That you surrender without conditions.

Bothwell. No.
    No, I thank you. Moreover if your tongue's
    To be foremost in this council, we'll stop now
    And argue the matter outside.

Maitland. Be patient, Lord Moray.
    We're here to make terms, as you are, Bothwell.
    The queen
    And you have been defeated. We made war on you
    Because you two were married, and because she planned
    To make you king.

Bothwell. You make war on us
    Like the pack of lying hounds you are, by swearing
    In public and in court that we killed Darnley
    So that we might marry! You know where that guilt lies.

Moray. Who killed Darnley
    We care not. Let the courts decide it.

Bothwell. It was you that killed him!
  And you fight us bearing false witness!

Moray. You wanted him dead.

Bothwell. I grant it. I wanted him dead. You killed him and
    managed
  To shift the weight on me. You've won with that lie,
  May your mouths rot out with it! And now what do
    you want—
  What do you ask of us?

Maitland. First, that you leave Scotland.

Bothwell. That's easily said;
  What else?

Maitland. Why, next that the queen should delegate
  Her powers to the lords of the council, those you see
  Before you—

Bothwell. Aye, I see them.

Maitland. And bind herself
  To act with our consent only.

Bothwell. No more?

Maitland. No more.

Bothwell. Then here are my conditions; I will leave,
  And trouble you no more, if you pledge your word
  That the queen's to keep her throne and her power
    intact,
  Without prejudice to her rights. But if you dare
  Encroach one inch on her sovereignty, guard your gates,
  For I'll be at them!

Morton. Aye, you make your terms!

Bothwell. Aye, I make mine; defeated, I still make mine—
  And you'll do well to heed them. I shall want leave also
  To see the queen for a moment.

Moray. You know our answer.

Bothwell. Then look to yourselves!
  [*He lays a hand on his sword*]

Maitland. Look now, Bothwell.
  It's you I rebel against. I'd lend no hand
  In this company, if the queen were to rule alone,
  And I've said as much to Lord Moray.

Morton. I speak for myself,
  And say no to it.

Moray. And I.

Bothwell. You've wanted my earldom,
  Lord Moray. Well, you may have it. I'll make it over.
  You shall choose a new earl of Bothwell. I'll disband my
    army.
  And threaten you no more. But on condition
  The queen reigns here as before.

Moray. We'll made our conditions—
  We have no time for yours.

Bothwell. My lines are not broken.
  I'll try conclusions yet, and you'll not sleep easy
  While I'm within these borders!

Maitland. Take his terms,
  My Moray.

Moray. Are we to fight a war and win
  And toss the spoils away?

Bothwell. Find some agreement,
  For I'm in haste, and if you say no to me
  I've other plans!

Erskine. Bothwell's been our one weapon
  Against the queen, Lord Moray. I believe it's wisdom
  To banish him, but remember the queen's a queen
  And it's dangerous to touch her. When he's gone
  You'll have no cause against her.

Moray. Why, damn you all!

Morton. Let him go, and leave her the throne.

Moray. And even Morton.

Morton. Gad, I want no long wars,
  I'm a married man. Send him on his way!
  He leaves his earldom.

Bothwell. Then this sword stays in the scabbard
  And lucky for all of you. Do you give your pledge?

Maitland. I give my pledge, Lord Bothwell, for all her.
    present.
  We have not rebelled against the queen, and will not
  If you are banished.

Bothwell. Then give me leave to speak
  Alone with her.

Maitland. With the queen?

Bothwell. Aye, for a moment.

Moray. No.

Maitland. There's no harm in that, Moray.

Erskine. We'll wait in the courtyard.
It's day and we have orders to give.

Morton. Gordon and Douglas,
You won't be needed. Intercept Lord Huntley's men
While there's yet time.

Maitland. The queen is here, Lord Bothwell,
And will be free to see you.

> [*The Lords go out. After a moment's pause,* QUEEN MARY
> *comes to the door—a soldier on either side. The guards
> retire, leaving* MARY *and* BOTHWELL *alone*]

Mary. Thank God you're safe!

Bothwell. And you are safe, my queen, safe and set free
And may keep your kingdom.

Mary. At what price?

Bothwell. They've made
A bargain with me. God knows whether they'll keep it,
But I think they will, for Maitland gave his word,
And he's been honest.

Mary. What bargain? You've sacrificed
Yourself for this. What have you offered?

Bothwell. Nothing
To weigh against what you'll keep. I've given my earl-
dom—
That's a trifle to what we save.

Mary. You shall have it back,
And more to put with it.

Bothwell. No. I've accepted exile.
I'm to leave the kingdom.

Mary. Why, then, I'm exiled too.
I'm your wife and I love you, Bothwell.

Bothwell. The bargain's made.
You may keep your crown without me but not with me.
Do you abdicate your throne? What's left?

Mary. Call in
The men of your guard, cut our way through and ride!
They'll never head us! We can rouse the north,
Ask help from France and England, return with an army
They dare not meet!

Bothwell. You'd raise no army, Marie.
You forget what a drag I am on you. The north
Is sullen as the south toward you and me.
What's left we must do apart.

Mary. What if we lost?
At the worst we'd have each other.

Bothwell. And do you vision the end of that?
A woman who was a queen, a man who was
The earl, her husband, but fugitives, put to it
To ask for food and lodging, enemies
On every road; they weary, heartsick, turning,
At last on each other with reproaches, she saying:
I was a queen, would be one now but for you,
And he, I have lost my earldom.

Mary. I betrayed you once
And betrayed my love, but I learned by that; I swear
Though it cost my kingdom, not again!

Bothwell. If you wish
To thrive, break that oath, betray me, betray your love,
Give me up forever—for you know as I know
We lose together. God knows what we'll ever win
Apart.

Mary. Nothing. Oh, Bothwell, the earth goes empty.
What worse could happen than parting?

Bothwell. Can I stay?
This once for the last I can save you from yourself,
And me. There's something wills it. I go alone.
This is your kingdom. Rule it.

Mary. You must not surrender
They'd serve you as they served Darnley.

Bothwell. I'll not surrender.
I'll see to my own banishment, find my guard,
Force my way out, and go.

Mary. We must say goodbye?

Bothwell. Aye, girl, we've spent what time we had,
And I know not when I'll see you. Let's have no pretense
Unworthy of us. It's likely, we'll not meet again
On this same star.

Mary. God help me and all women
Here in this world, and all men. Fair fall all chances
The heart can long for—and let all women and men
Drink deep while they can their happiness. It goes fast

And never comes again. Mine goes with you,
Youth, and the fund of dreams, and to lie a while
Trusted, in arms you trust. We're alone, alone,
Alone—even while we lie there we're alone,
For it's false. It will end. Each one dies alone.

Bothwell. I'll come
If I can. We've loved well, lass, could love better.
We've had but the broken fragment of a year
And whenever I've touched you, something that broods
    above us
Has made that touch disaster. This is not my choice.
Lest I bring you utter ruin we must wait,
Wait better times and luck. I'll come again
If I can.

Mary. Yes, if you can. Aye, among all tides
And driftings of air and water it may be
Some dust that once was mine will touch again
Dust that was yours. I'll not bear it! Oh, God, I'll not
    bear it!
Take me with you! Let us be slaves and pick
Our keep from kitchen middens and leavings! Let us
Quarrel over clouts and fragments, but not apart—
Bothwell, that much we could have!

Bothwell. Is there refuge in this world for you
And me together? Go far as we could, is there one
Turfed roof where we'd not be reminded of good days
And end in bitterness? Face these lords like a queen
And rule like a queen. I'd help you if I could
But I'm no help You must meet them now.

Mary. Yes I'll meet them
Can you break your way through? They're watching!

Bothwell. It's a chance.
Huntley! Huntley!

Huntley.
[*Outside*]
I'm here.

Bothwell. We ride at once
For Stirling. Be ready for a fight.

Huntley. We're ready.

Bothwell. I must take my moment.

Mary. I know.

Bothwell. Goodbye, sweet, but if they wrong you—if you
ever need me,
Look for me back.

[*He kisses her, and goes*]

Mary. Goodbye. To our two worlds.

[*There is a cry beyond the guard-room:* "BOTHWELL, *it's*
BOTHWELL!" *The alarm is taken up by the men at the
gate, who call:* "On guard there! Pistol him! Mount
and after him! Ride, you devils! On guard! Drop the
portcullis! He's gone!" *There is a sound of running
feet from the gate to the other side of the stage.* MARY
stands facing the guard-room door. GORDON *and*
DOUGLAS *run in through the arch*]

Douglas. Through the guard-room!

Gordon. He'll be over the wall—

Douglas. Out of the way, madam—

Gordon. Nay, it's the queen—

Douglas. Will you let us pass?

Mary. I guard this door, Lord Douglas.
　　You'll go the long way round!

Gordon. Your pardon, your majesty.
　　[*He bows.* BEATON *appears on the stairway.* LORDS MORTON,
　　　MORAY *and* MAITLAND *enter*]

Morton. This was hardly well done, your majesty.

Mary. Take care whom you question, sir.

Moray. You've sent Bothwell off!
　　That was your ruse!

Mary. Lord Bothwell will leave Scotland.
　　That was what you wanted.
　　[*Enter* LORD ERSKINE]

Moray. He's gone?

Erskine. Clean away!

Maitland. Madame, there was some understanding
　　You two would remain here.

Mary. None that I know of.

Morton. Eh, God, he'll wish he had.
　　[JOHN KNOX *appears in the archway*]

Mary. Remove that man from my presence! Is every
　　stranger
　　Free to enter my courts?

Knox. Though you be a queen
　　And have faith in thy gods and idols, yet in this day

It will not staunch nor avail! Bid the sea remove
From the castle front, and gnaw it no more, as soon
Will it obey thee. Pluck down the whore! Pluck her
    down,
This contamination of men!

Mary. Maitland, if there's to be counsel here, send out
This preacher and his ravings!

Maitland. He may stay, for me.

Moray. Madame, collect what necessities you require.
You will change your residence.

Mary. That is at my will, I think.

Morton. Do you think so?

Maitland. You are to be lodged
In Holyroodhouse for the time.

Mary. I am to be lodged—
And your faith? You pledged your faith and word,—
    all of you—
To leave my power untouched, leave me my throne
If Bothwell and I were parted.

Maitland. We'll keep it
When Lord Bothwell's surrendered to us.

Mary. Go out and take him!
Take him if you can! But for your queen,
I warn you, never since there were kings and queens
In Scotland, has a liegeman laid his hand
On my line without regret!

Morton. We'll take care of that.

Mary. My lords, if I go with you, expect no pardon,
  No clemency; I have friends, this farce will end.
  Once more, then, leave me in peace
  I have used you royally. Use me so.

Maitland. What you need,
  Gather it quickly.

Mary. This is betrayal at once
  Of your word and sovereign.

Morton. We know that.
    [*A pause*]

Mary. I need nothing.
  I am a prisoner, Beaton. Come after me
  To Holyroodhouse. I may have my own rooms there,
    perhaps?

Maitland. Yes, Madame.

Mary. You show great courtesy. For a liar and traitor.
  You lied to us, a black and level lie!
  Blackest and craftiest! It was you we believed!

Moray. Aye, sister. It was that we counted on.

Mary. Aye, brother.
    [MARY *turns from* MAITLAND *to* MORAY, *then walks to the
    archway and goes out*]

CURTAIN

MARY OF SCOTLAND
ACT THREE

ACT THREE

Scene: *A room in Carlisle Castle, in England. There are two windows at the right, both barred, a door at the rear and another, the hall-door, at the left. It is a prison room, but furnished scantily now for the queen's habitation. It is evening, but still light.*
Mary *sits at one of the windows, leaning her head against the bars.*
Beaton *is leaning over a table where* Fleming *has unrolled a map.*

Fleming. We came this way, through Cockermouth, and then took hired horses.

Beaton. If I had a thousand maps, I couldna tell you how I came. Jamie's acquent wi' the drovers and all the back ways. Seton and Livingstone, poor things, they're pining away back in Edinburgh Town.

Fleming. We might be as well off in Edinburgh ourselves, as it turns out. We'd looked forward to England for a free country, and strained toward it till our shoulders ached, trying to help the boat through the water. And here we are, and there's bars on the windows.

Beaton. But whose prisoners are we, Fleming?

Fleming. I would I knew. It's been a month now, and all I can tell you is we're prisoners, for we cannot leave.

Beaton. There's some mistake, Fleming.

Fleming. Aye, if it was a mistake, like, would it last a month? It's heartbreaking to escape one jailer and walk into the arms of another.

Mary. When does the guard change, Fleming?

Fleming. At ten, madame.

Mary. You're certain Jamie will come?

Beaton. Unless he's taken or dead, Your Majesty. He's true as one can have in a lad.

Mary. But they may unmask him.

Beaton. It's true, they may.

Fleming. Ye've more friends than a few in this castle, madame. They'd let us know if summat went wrong.

Mary. What friends?

Fleming. The two guards that go on for evening watch.

Mary. I fear they can't help much.

Fleming. They can always bring us news.

Beaton. And you've more friends than that, Your Majesty. Here and everywhere. As I came through the back roads I heard talk of you everywhere. I think they love their queen better now than before, now that she's shut away unjustly.

Mary. Do you think so?

Beaton. From what I heard I'd say the lords had worked their own ruin when they first betrayed you. If they could hear the buzzing against them they'd sleep badly there nights. And who rules Scotland now? Moray has no right to it, and nobody can give him the right save your own self.

Mary. Aye, that's so. He'll come begging yet.

Beaton. And for what he'll never have.

Mary. They've taken my son from me, though. If I have friends I would they'd hurry.

[*She turns toward the window*]

God know what Elizabeth means.

Fleming. You'll hear from Bothwell tonight, madame, or hear of him. I'm certain of it.

[A WATCHMAN *calls outside*]

Watchman. Ten o'clock, and all well. All well.

Beaton. Ten o'clock and still light.

Fleming. The days grow longer and longer.

Mary. They've grown so long that each is the whole time between a birth and a death—and yet they go so fast, too, that I catch at them with my hand. So fast that I watch the even light jealously, like a last candle burning. This is life, too, Beaton, here in this prison, and it goes from us quite as much as though we were free. We shall never see these same days again.

Fleming. And little will I want to.

Mary. But suppose you were to spend all your life in prisons? Might not one grow to love even prison-days—as better than none?

Beaton. We shall have better, though. These are the worst we shall have, and I think the last of them.

[*There is a rasping at the door*]

Your hear?—the signal—

[*There is a silence*]

Fleming. Nay, not yet.
   [*Another pause*]

Beaton. It's ten, and more.

Fleming. If we must wait again, then we must wait. He'll
   come at the latest, tomorrow.

Mary.
   [*Rising and pacing near her window*]
   But what could Elizabeth mean? What could she mean?
   She is my friend—over and over she writes she is my
   friend, I am her dear cousin, her sister sovereign, that
   she suffers when I suffer, that she would confine me on
   no pretext if it were not to secure me against my own
   enemies! Enemies! What enemies have I in her kingdom?
   What right has she to imprison a sovereign who takes
   sanctuary in England?

Fleming. Has anyone ever known Elizabeth's mind on any
   subject?

Mary. Writes, too, that she will come to see me, writes
   again to put it off, writes to say she cannot bear the
   week to pass without reassuring me of her good love.

Beaton. And yet I believe if all else fails Elizabeth will be
   found a friend and a good one at the end. If only for her
   own interest.

Mary. It may still be that she goes, in her own muddled
   and devious way, about the business of aiding me. It
   still may be.
   [*There is a rasping at the door again*]

Beaton. Yes?

> [*The door opens a crack, a chain clanging*]

Jamie.

> [*Outside*]

I may enter?

Beaton. Aye, come in.

> [JAMIE *steps in, closing the door*]

Jamie.

> [*Bonnet in hand*]

Your Majesty!

Mary. Good evening, Jamie.

Jamie. Ye'll forgive me. I was not sure I could jouk in, for the captain loitered about. However, the lad Mark keeps a look-out, and warns me if there's footsteps.

Beaton. Was there a messenger through, Jamie?

Jamie. Aye, I'll be quick, for I must, though a man hates to be quick wi' ill news. There's been a messenger, true enough, coming down wi' the drovers, as we cam'—and his tale is there was a battle at the Little Minch. Ma'am, it went badly for Bothwell, if the man says sooth, for he was defeated and taken.

Mary. Bothwell taken?

Jamie. Aye, madame. Aye, but there's some good, too. Kirkaldy of Grange has come over to Your Majesty's side and makes his threats against Moray.

Mary. But Bothwell, Bothwell was taken? How?

Jamie. That's the bare sum of it, madame. Just that he was prisoner to the lords. Only Kirkaldy has said Bothwell should be freed, and that he will see to it.

Mary. It's little comfort.

Jamie. Aye, so I feared. Though Kirkaldy was their best general, and they'll miss him.

Mary. I could have used him once.

Jamie. And now, if you'll pardon me, I must go. I had little liking to come—it's sore bad manners to leave folk wi' heavy hearts—

Mary. Nay, run no risk—only come again if there's any tidings.

Jamie. Yes, Your Majesty, and I pray God they be better.
   [*He turns*]

Beaton. Jamie.
   [*There is a sharp rap at the door*]

Jamie. Aye?
   [BEATON *goes up to him*]
Nay, lass, it's good just to see thee, but we'll not kiss afore Her Majesty.
   [*The rap again*]
It's for me. Keep thee, and all here.
   [*He opens the door and goes out, closing it softly. The chain clanks. There is silence*]

Mary. It's this that drives one mad, Beaton, to know
That on one certain day, at a certain hour,
If one had but chosen well, he'd have stood beside me

In a land all mine and his. Choosing wrong, I bring him
To fight a long war for me, and lose, bow his shoulders
To a castle keep.

Fleming. They'll not hold him long.

Mary. And that's
To remember too. He's not a man to hold
Easily, no, nor hold at all. I've seen him
When they thought him trapped, and well caught. His
    face goes cold,
Stern, and morgue under his morion. While he lives
And I live, they'll not jail us two apart,
Nor keep our due from us. Aye, it's something to love,
Even late, even bitterly, where it's deserved. Kirkaldy
Throws his weight on our side. There'll be others, too.
    Oh, Bothwell,
You've been my one hope! Bring me back to mind,
Now, as I bring you back!

> [*The chains of the door are undone, and the door opens.* A
> Guard *steps in*]

Guard. Your Majesty,
Lord Ruthven desires to see you.

Mary. Lord Ruthven's in Scotland.

Guard. No, Madame, he's here.

Mary. Why, I will see Lord Ruthven.
Yes, let him come in.

> [*The door swings wider and* Young Ruthven *enters. He bows*]

Sir, there've been days,
Not so far back when I'd have shifted somehow

To do without your face, or any visage
Among a certain congeries of lords
Of which you're one. Perhaps I'm tamed a trace
Sitting mewed at my window, for I'd accept
Any visitor from Scotland, bailiffs and hang-men
Not excluded, I'm that lonely.

Ruthven. Madame,
You hold against me much that was not my own.
I'm of a party, and one must swim or go down
With those of his interest.

Mary. Do you come now to see me
In your own person, then, or as representing
Those sharks you swam with last?

Ruthven. Why, Your Majesty,
It may be we're sharks. My mind's not made up. But
      I've come,
If you'll pardon me—and this is more truth, I think,
Than I'm supposed to say—because the lords
Who now hold Scotland had more hope you'd see me
Than any the others.

Mary. That's frank.

Ruthven. And I lend myself
To the embassy because, as things drift at home,
We verge on the rocks there. You are still queen of
      Scotland,
Yet you don't rule, and can't rule, being here,
A prisoner—and the upshot is we're not ruled.
There's anarchy in the air. It's necessary

That some approach be made between you and your
   brother
Before there's anarchy in the streets.

Beaton. We were saying
   That he'd come begging.

Mary. What does my brother ask—
   This good brother of mine?

Ruthven. That goes beyond
   My mission. To be frank still, I'm sent before
   To ask whether you will see him.

Mary. Let him ask my jailers
   Whether I may be seen.

Ruthven. He has asked already, madame.
   The request is granted.

Mary. Lord Moray is with you?

Ruthven. He is waiting.

Mary. Why, this is an honor. And others too, no doubt?
   A shoal of them?

Ruthven. Madame, as you have supposed
   They are all here.

Mary. It will please me vastly to view them,
   If only to know from them who gave permission
   To see me. For I swear, I guess not so far
   Whose prisoner I am, or who keeps my jail. I've moith-
   ered
   Over this a good deal.

Ruthven. I may call them?

Mary. If you'll be so good.

    [RUTHVEN *bows and goes out past the* GUARD]
Is it you, sir, who chain my door
So assiduously at night?

Guard. No, madame, the turn-key
Goes the rounds at twelve.

Mary. Will you ask him, then.
To make a thought less jangling if he can?
We try to sleep, you see, and these chimes at midnight
Are not conducive to slumber.

Guard. He shall be told;
I'm very sorry, Your Majesty.

Mary. Thank you.

    [MORTON *and* MORAY *come in, and behind them* MAITLAND
        and DOUGLAS. RUTHVEN *re-enters with* THROG-
        MORTON]
Gentlemen,
I greet you. You are all here, I see, the whole
Blood-thirsty race. But we lack John Knox. Now, surely,
John Knox should be with you.

Moray. Have your jest, my sister. For us
We're not here for jesting.

Mary. Oh, I'd have sworn you weren't.
You're no harbinger of merriment, my brother,
Nor of good fortune. The corbies from the wood
Presage more of that. And here's the Lord Throgmorton
Presses in among you! It should be a good day
When I'm crossed by this constellation!

Throgmorton. We pray it will,
  Your Majesty, and that things may be ironed out clean
  That have grieved us all.

Mary. Oh, do you know of grief,
  You who may take your meals in your own widehalls
  And walk in the rainy air? I had thought that grieving
  Was something found behind bars.

Maitland. This has lasted too long,
  This imprisonment, Your Majesty, and was never
  To any purpose. We come to offer you
  Release, and speedily.

Mary. The diplomat always, Maitland.
  Always the secret thought glancing behind
  The quick-silver tongue. You come to ask for much
  And give little for it, as ever.

Moray. We come to ask
  For what we have.

Mary. There, now it's brutally said,
  In my brother's plain-Scotch way, spoken plainly out of
  His plain Scotch face. He comes to ask, he says,
  For what he has, and he makes no doubt he'll get it.
  What is it you have, dear brother, and if you have it
  Why ask for it?

Maitland. Will Your Majesty give me leave
  To rehearse a brief history that may weary you
  Since you know it?

Mary. It will weary me, but go on.

Maitland. Forgive me: Your Majesty broke from prison
    in Scotland
And fled to England. This action was tantamount
To abandoning your throne.

Mary. Indeed it was not.
I came here for aid against you.

Maitland. We will pass that point.

Mary. Do. There's nothing gives me more pleasure, Lord
    Maitland,
Than passing a point.

Maitland. Then am I delighted to render
Your Majesty pleasure. Your wit is sharper than mine.
But to proceed: You were taken prisoner in England—

Mary. By whom, Lord Maitland—will you tell me that?
Who holds me here?

Maitland. That I'm not free to answer.
It remains that you're a prisoner, and that your realm
Is governed only by makeshift. Your son, the prince
    James—

Mary. Aye, what of him? My lords, I beg of you,
Whatever you must do, or think you must do,
To secure yourselves, he's but a babe, remember.
I can stand up and fight you for myself,
But use my child more kindly.

Maitland. The prince James,
Is well, and well cared for, and will be. The succession
Depends on him. We plan to make him king.
Your absence makes this necessary.

Mary. My absence
   Is not permanent, I hope. I am queen of Scotland
   And have not abdicated, nor do I intend
   To abdicate.

Morton. Will you tell us what you think
   To find, should you return?

Mary. If I return
   As I intend, I shall not find you there,
   Lord Morton, if you're wise. The country's fickle.
   For you, as it was for me. Now they've pushed their
      queen
   Aside, they begin to wonder if they were not wrong.
   And wonder too if they profit by the exchange,
   And give you side-long looks.

Maitland. If it's still in your mind
   That you might win your throne back, ponder on this:
   The lord of the isles has given you up, the north
   Is solidly with us, Bothwell has broken faith—

Mary. Aye?

Maitland. For the good of the kingdom, to secure your son
   His right to the throne, we ask you tonight to sign
   Your abdication, let us take it back with us.

Mary. Yes,
   But I catch you in two lies. Kirkaldy of Grange
   Has come over to me; you have taken Bothwell prisoner,
   But before he fights on your side you'll rot in the damp
   Under Edinburgh castle, and he'll see you do it!

Maitland. Madame,
  You've been misinformed.

Mary. I've been lied to and by you
  Specifically! Let me rehearse for you
  A history you may recall, you that stand before me:
  It was you killed Rizzio, and made capital of it
  To throw discredit on me. It was you
  Killed Darnley, and then threw the weight of that
  On Bothwell, saying through John Knox that I lived
  With my husband's murderer. It was you that promised
  To give me fealty if Bothwell and I were parted,
  And then cast me into prison! I escaped,
  As the truth will escape about you, and when it's known
  My people will drive you out. What you ask of me
  I refuse it, finally! I will not abdicate,
  Not to this off-scum that's boiled up around
  My throne to dirty me! Not now and not ever!

  [*The Lords are silent for a moment, and then* MORAY *nods an
      assent to* MAITLAND]

Maitland. Your Majesty, you asked me a moment since
  Who held you prisoner here. I cannot answer
  Still, but say there's another and higher judge
  Must pass on these charges of yours.

Mary. Nay, I know that.

Maitland. Oh, an earthly judge, Your Majesty, and yet
  High enough, I think. We wish you goodnight.

Mary. Goodnight.

  [*The Lords go out.* MARY *stands unmoving, watching the door.
      After a pause the* GUARD *pushes the door back and with-*

draws. ELIZABETH *comes to the doorway.* MARY *looks at her questioningly*]

I have seen but a poor likeness, and yet I believe
This is Elizabeth.

Elizabeth. I am Elizabeth.
  May we be alone together?

  [*At a sign from* MARY *the* MAIDS *go out the rear door.* ELIZA-
  BETH *enters and the hall-door swings to behind her*]

Mary. I had hoped to see you.
  When last you wrote you were not sure.

Elizabeth. If I've come
  So doubtfully and tardigrade, my dear,
  And break thus in upon you, it's not for lack
  Of thinking of you. Rather because I've thought
  Too long, perhaps, and carefully. Then at last
  It seemed if I saw you near, and we talked as sisters
  Over these poor realms of ours, some light might break
  That we'd never see apart.

Mary. Have I been so much
  A problem?

Elizabeth. Have you not? When the winds blow down
  The houses, and there's a running and arming of men,
  And a great cry of praise and blame, and the center
  Of all this storm's a queen, she beautiful—
  As I see you are—

Mary. Nay—

Elizabeth. Aye, with the Stuart mouth
  And the high forehead and French ways and thoughts—

Well, we must look to it.—Not since that Helen
We read of in dead Troy, has a woman's face
Stirred such a confluence of air and waters
To beat against the bastions. I'd thought you taller,
But truly, since that Helen, I think there's been
No queen so fair to look on.

Mary. You flatter me.

Elizabeth. It's more likely envy. You see this line
Drawn down between my brows? No wash or ointments
Nor wearing of straight plasters in the night
Will take that line away. Yet I'm not much older
Than you, and had looks, too, once.

Mary. I had wished myself
For a more regal beauty such as yours,
More fitting for a queen.

Elizabeth. Were there not two verses
In a play I remember:
Brightness falls from the air;
Queens have died young and fair—?
They must die young if they'd die fair, my cousin,
Brightness falls from them, but not from you yet; be-
lieve me,
It's envy, not flattery.

Mary. Can it be—as I've hoped—
Can it be that you come to me as a friend—
Meaning me well?

Elizabeth. Would you have me an enemy?

Mary. I have plenty to choose among as enemies—
And sometimes, as your word reached out to me

Through embassies, entangled with men's tongues,
It has seemed you judged me harshly, even denying
My right to a place beside you. But now you are here,
And a woman like myself, fearing as I do,
With the little dark fears of a woman, the creeping of age
On a young face, I see truer—I think I see truer,
And that this may be someone to whom I can reach a
    hand
And feel a clasp, and trust it. A woman's hand,
Stronger than mine in this hour, willing to help.
If that were so—

Elizabeth. Aye.

Mary. Oh, if that were so,
    I have great power to love! Let them buzz forever
    Between us, these men with messages and lies,
    You'll find me still there, and smiling, and open-hearted,
    Unchanging while the cusped hills wear down!

Elizabeth.
    [*Smiling*]
    Nay, pledge
    Not too much, my dear, for in these uncertain times
    It's slippery going for all of us. I, who seem now
    So firm in my footing, well I know one mis-step
    Could make me a most unchancy friend. If you'd keep
    Your place on this rolling ball, let the mountains slide
    And slip to the valleys. Put no hand to them
    Or they'll pull you after.

Mary. But does this mean you can lend
    No hand to me, or I'll pull you down?

Elizabeth. I say it
  Recalling how I came to my throne as you did,
  Some five or six years before, beset as you were
  With angry factions—and came there young, loving
    truth,
  As you did. This was many centuries since,
  Or seems so to me, I'm so old by now
  In shuffling tricks and the huckstering of souls
  For lands and pensions. I learned to play it young,
  Must learn it or die.—It's thus if you would rule;
  Give up good faith, the word that goes with the heart,
  The heart that clings where it loves. Give these up, and
    love
  Where your interest lies, and should your interest change
  Let your love follow it quickly. This is queen's porridge,
  And however little stomach she has for it
  A queen must eat it.

Mary. I, too, Elizabeth,
  Have read my Machiavelli. His is a text-book
  Much studied in the French court. Are you serious
  To rede me this lesson?

Elizabeth. You have too loving a heart,
  I fear, and too bright a face to be a queen.

Mary. That's not what's charged against me. When I've
    lost
  So far it's been because my people believed
  I was more crafty than I am. I've been
  Traduced as a murderess and adulteress
  And nothing I could have said, and nothing done

Would have warded the blow. What I seek now is only
My freedom, so that I may return and prove
In open court, and before my witnesses,
That I am guiltless. You are the queen of England,
And I am held prisoner in England. Why am I held,
And who is it holds me?

Elizabeth. It was to my interest, child,
To protect you, lest violence be offered to a princess
And set a precedent. Is there anyone in England
Who could hold you against my will?

Mary. Then I ask as a sovereign,
Speaking to you as an equal, that I be allowed
To go, and fight my own battles.

Elizabeth. It would be madness.

Mary. May I not judge of that?

Elizabeth. See, here is our love!

Mary. If you wish my love and good-will you shall have it
     freely
When I am free.

Elizabeth. You will never govern, Mary. If I let you go
There will be long broils again in Scotland, dangers,
And ripe ones, to my peace at home. To be fair
To my own people, this must not be.

Mary. Now speak once
What your will is, and what behind it! You wish me here,
You wish me in prison—have we come to that?

Elizabeth. It's safer.

Mary. Who do you wish to rule in Scotland,
   If not my Stuart line?

Elizabeth. Have I said, my dear,
   That I'd bar the Stuarts from Scotland, or bar your reign
   If you were there, and reigned there? I say only
   You went the left way about it, and since it's so
   And has fallen out so, it were better for both our king-
      doms
   If you remained my guest.

Mary. For how long?

Elizabeth. Until
   The world is quieter.

Mary. And who will rule in my place?

Elizabeth. Why, who rules now? Your brother.

Mary. He rules by stealth—

Elizabeth. But all this could be arranged,
   Or so I'm told, if your son were to be crowned king,
   And Moray made regent.

Mary. My son in Moray's hands—
   Moray in power—

Elizabeth. Is there any other way?
   [*A pause*]

Mary. Elizabeth—I have been here a long while
   Already—it seems so. If it's your policy
   To keep me—shut me up—. I can argue no more—
   No—I beg now. There's one I love in the north,
   You know that—and my life's there, my throne's there,
      my name

To be defended—and I must lie here darkened
From news and from the sun—lie here impaled
On a brain's agony—wondering even sometimes
If I were what they said me—a carrion-thing
In my desires—can you understand this?—I speak it
Too brokenly to be understood, but I beg you
As you are a woman and I am—and our brightness falls
Soon enough at best—let me go, let me have my life
Once more—and my dear health of mind again—
For I rot away here in my mind—in what
I think of myself—some death-tinge falls over one
In prisons—

Elizabeth. It will grow worse, not better. I've known
Strong men shut up alone for years—it's not
Their hair turns white only; they sicken within
And scourge themselves. If you would think like a queen
This is no place for you. The brain taints here
Till all desires are alike. Be advised and sign
The abdication.

Mary. Stay now a moment. I begin to glimpse
Behind this basilisk mask of yours. It was this
You've wanted from the first.

Elizabeth. This that I wanted?

Mary. It was you sent Lord Throgmorton long ago
When first I'd have married Bothwell. All this while
Some evil's touched my life at every turn.
To cripple what I'd do. And now—why now—
Looking on you—I see it incarnate before me—
It was your hand that touched me. Reaching out

In little ways—here a word, there an action—this
Was what you wanted. I thought perhaps a star—
Wildly I thought it—perhaps a star might ride
Astray—or a crone that burned an image down
In wax—filling the air with curses on me
And slander; the murder of Rizzio, Moray in that
And you behind Moray—the murder of Darnley, Throg-
    morton
Behind that too, you with them—and that winged
    scandal
You threw at us when we were married. Proof I have
    none
But I've felt it—would know it anywhere—in your
    eyes—
There—before me.

Elizabeth. What may become a queen
Is to rule her kingdom. Had you ruled yours I'd say
She has her ways, I mine. Live and let live
And a merry world for those who have it. But now
I must think this over—sadness has touched your brain.
I'm no witch to charm you, make no incantations;
You came here by your own road.

Mary. I see how I came.
Back, back, each step the wrong way, and each sign
    followed
As you'd have me go, till the skein picks up and we stand
Face to face here. It was you forced Bothwell from me—
You there, and always. Oh, I'm to blame in this, too!
I should have seen your hand!

Elizabeth. It has not been my use
  To speak much or spend my time—

Mary. How could I have been
  Mistaken in you for an instant?

Elizabeth. You were not mistaken.
  I am all women I must be. One's a young girl,
  Young and harrowed as you are—one who could weep
  To see you here—and one's a bitterness
  At what I have lost and can never have, and one's
  The basilisk you saw. This last stands guard
  And I obey it. Lady, you came to Scotland
  A fixed and subtle enemy, more dangerous
  To me than you've ever known. This could not be borne,
  And I set myself to cull you out and down,
  And down you are.

Mary. When was I your enemy?

Elizabeth. Your life was a threat to mine, your throne to
    my throne,
  Your policy a threat.

Mary. How? Why?

Elizabeth. It was you
  Or I. Do you know that? The one of us must win
  And I must always win. Suppose one lad
  With a knife in his hand, a Romish lad who planted
  That knife between my shoulders—my kingdom was
    yours.
  It was too easy. You might not have wished it.
  But you'd take it if it came.

Mary. And you'd take my life
And love to avoid this threat?

Elizabeth. Nay, keep your life.
And your love, too. The lords have brought a parchment
For you to sign. Sign it and live.

Mary. If I sign it
Do I live where I please? Go free?

Elizabeth. Nay, I would you might,
But you'd go to Bothwell, and between you two
You might be too much for Moray. You'll live with me
In London. There are other loves, my dear.
You'll find amusement there in the court. I assure you
It's better than a cell.

Mary. And if I will not sign
This abdication?

Elizabeth. You've tasted prison. Try
A diet of it.

Mary. And so I will.

Elizabeth. I can wait.

Mary. And I can wait. I can better wait than you.
Bothwell will fight free again. Kirkaldy
Will fight beside him, and others will spring up
From these dragon's teeth you've sown. Each week that
    passes
I'll be stronger, and Moray weaker.

Elizabeth. And do you fancy
They'll rescue you from an English prison? Why,
Let them try it.

Mary. Even that they may do. I wait for Bothwell—
  And wait for him here.

Elizabeth. Where you will wait, bear in mind,
  Is for me to say. Give up Bothwell, give up your throne
  If you'd have a life worth living.

Mary. I will not.

Elizabeth. I can wait.

Mary. And will not because you play to lose. This trespass
  Against God's right will be known. The nations will
    know it,
  Mine and yours. They will see you as I see you
  And pull you down.

Elizabeth. Child, child, I've studied this gambit
  Before I play it. I will send each year
  This paper to you. Not signing, you will step
  From one cell to another, step lower always,
  Till you reach the last, forgotten, forgotten of men,
  Forgotten among causes, a wraith that cries
  To fallen gods in another generation
  That's lost your name. Wait then for Bothwell's rescue.
  It will never come.

Mary. I may never see him?

Elizabeth. Never.
  It would not be wise.

Mary. And suppose indeed you won
  Within our life-time, still looking down from the heavens
  And up from men around us, God's spies that watch

The fall of great and little, they will find you out—
I will wait for that, wait longer than a life,
Till men and the times unscroll you, study the tricks
You play, and laugh, as I shall laugh, being known
Your better, haunted by your demon, driven
To death, or exile by you, unjustly. Why,
When all's done, it's my name I care for, my name and
    heart,
To keep them clean. Win now, take your triumph now,
For I'll win men's hearts in the end—though the sifting
    takes
This hundred years—or a thousand.

Elizabeth. Child, child, are you gulled
By what men write in histories, this or that,
And never true? I am careful of my name
As you are, for this day and longer. It's not what hap-
    pens
That matters, no, not even what happens that's true,
But what men believe to have happened. They will be-
    lieve
The worst of you, the best of me, and that
Will be true of you and me. I have seen to this.
What will be said about us in after-years
By men to come, I control that, being who I am.
It will be said of me that I governed well,
And wisely, but of you, cousin, that your life,
Shot through with ill-loves, battened on lechery, made
    you
An ensign of evil, that men tore down and trampled.
Shall I call for the lord's parchment?

Mary. This will be said—?
   But who will say it? It's a lie—will be known as a lie!

Elizabeth. You lived with Bothwell before Darnley died,
   You and Bothwell murdered Darnley.

Mary. And that's a lie!

Elizabeth. Your letters, my dear. Your letters to Bothwell
      prove it.
   We have those letters.

Mary. Then they're forged and false!
   For I never wrote them!

Elizabeth. It may be they were forged.
   But will that matter, Mary, if they're believed?
   All history is forged.

Mary. You would do this?

Elizabeth. It is already done.

Mary. And still I win.
   A demon has no children, and you have none,
   Will have none, can have none, perhaps. This crooked
      track
   You've drawn me on, cover it, let it not be believed
   That a woman was a fiend. Yes, cover it deep,
   And heap my infamy over it, lest men peer
   And catch sight of you as you were and are. In myself
   I know you to be an eater of dust. Leave me here
   And set me lower this year by year, as you promise,
   Till the last is an oubliette, and my name inscribed
   On the four winds. Still, STILL I win! I have been
   A woman, and I have loved as a woman loves,

Lost as a woman loses. I have borne a son,
And he will rule Scotland—and England. You have no
    heir!
A devil has no children.

Elizabeth. By God, you shall suffer
For this, but slowly.

Mary. And that I can do. A woman
Can do that. Come, turn the key. I have a hell
For you in mind, where you will burn and feel it,
Live where you like, and softly.

Elizabeth. Once more I ask you,
And patiently. Give up your throne.

Mary. No, devil.
My pride is stronger than yours, and my heart beats
    blood
Such as yours has never known. And in this dungeon,
I win here, alone.

Elizabeth.
    [*Turning*]
Goodnight, then.

Mary. Aye, goodnight.

> [ELIZABETH *goes to the door, which opens before her. She goes
>   out slowly. As the door begins to close upon her* MARY
>   *calls*]

Beaton :

Elizabeth.
    [*Turning*]
You will not see your maids again,
I think. It's said they bring you news from the north.

Mary. I thank you for all kindness.

> [ELIZABETH *goes out.* MARY *stands for a moment in thought,
> then walks to the wall and lays her hand against the
> stone, pushing outward. The stone is cold, and she shud-
> ders. Going to the window she sits again in her old place
> and looks out into the darkness*]

CURTAIN

IV · VALLEY FORGE

CHARACTERS

(In the order of their appearance)

ANDREW	A Brigadier
SPAD	SIR WILLIAM HOWE
ALCOCK	MARY PHILIPSE
TEAGUE	A Captain
MASON	FIELDING
JOCK	"THE WASHINGTON" (In masquerade scene)
OSCAR	
NICK	First Soldier
MINTO	Second Soldier
MARTY	Third Soldier
TAVIS	A Civilian
AUNTIE	GENERAL VARNUM
NEIL	GENERAL STIRLING
LIEUTENANT CUTTING	RAFE
ROVER	MR. HARVIE
LIEUT. COL. LUCIFER TENCH	MR. FOLSOM
An Aide	GENERAL CONWAY
GEN. GEORGE WASHINGTON	Five Ladies (In masquerade scene)
MARQUIS DE LAFAYETTE	
MAJOR ANDRE	Musicians and others

ACT ONE

Scene One

Scene: *A bunk-house at Valley Forge in January, 1778. The building is of logs, long, low and windowless. At the right is an entrance door, at the left a stone fireplace. Between the two, bunks are built against the wall in double tiers, constructed entirely of saplings, about twelve in all. Logs are heaped at the fireplace and a few cut logs are used as seats. A wash stand also stands not far from the fire, built of hewn timber, and a table, similarly made, is placed not far from the center of the room. The bunks are filled, over the sapling bottoms, with straw and pine needles, covered with what blankets the men have. It is evening; some candles burn on the table, and about half the bunks are occupied. Three or four of the men still have mess-dishes in their hands, out of which they eat with pen knives, or try to eat, for the food this evening is inedible.—The clothes of the men are dirty, torn, patched, threadbare, and in many cases almost nonexistent. There are no uniforms. The boots are worn out—many feet are on the floor. Socks are undreamed-of. A shirt is a rarity. Many of those still dressed wear coarse cloth or sacking tied on their feet for shoes, some wrap their legs with cloths in the manner of Russian peasants. What clothes are still recognizable were once Colonial homespun, and retain vestiges of the Colonial style. But most of the cocks have fallen on the hats, and many wear coonskin or other furred caps. One or two are dressed Indian style, in buckskin. These are the better dressed of the company. Long muskets are stacked in the corners, with pendant powderhorns.*

Spad, a round and red-faced Virginian, sits at the table with his tin of food. Teague, wearing hunters' clothes, leans at the doorway, a man of fifty-five, lean and corded. Alcock, a beefy man, wearing a blanket, is sitting on one of the log ends. Minto, an oldish, graying fellow, is at the fire, carefully preparing kindling with his knife and a piece of pine. Neil Bonniwell, a thin, handsome lad, with feverish eyes, lies in one of the bunks. His brother, Mason Bonniwell, sits beside him. Oscar, a stolid shipwright, is bending himself a snowshoe out of green wood. Marty, the feeble wit of the house, is lying back on his bunk, half asleep. Jock, a Scotchman, is combing his hair before the fire with a fine tooth comb. Andrew, Jock's brother, looks on and warms his hands.

3

Spad.

   [*Going to the door and pitching his food outside*]
   Peugh, it's no chaw for a white man.

Alcock. You should 'a' saved it for Teague, there; his pappy
was a Seminole brave—they won't eat meat till you can
stir it with a spoon.

Teague. Don't talk to me; you ate horse last week, you
horse-eating cannibal.

Alcock. Nobody could eat this carrion tonight. I wouldn't
set it down to a good dog.

Mason. That's Congress food, that is. Sent straight from
the Continental Congress to their Continental army.
And well they think of us, too.

   [*He pushes the food about on his plate with distaste*]

Jock. Toot—toot—speak na treason!

Mason. Treason—! Toward the gabble-mongers in Congress! 'T'd be a service to the cause of freedom to try out
the fat that's in them and use it for carriage grease.
Or flay the tough hides off them for a commodity of
shoes.

Alcock. What this army needs is pants. If I had a pair of
pants I might stand a chance of getting a pair of boots—
but you can't walk up to a lady's back door without
pants on—not for no purpose whatever.—And you can't
borrow a pair to stand sentry duty in! Teague, there—
wouldn't even loan me his leather britches at night when
he wasn't using 'em—

Teague. Who said I wasn't using 'em?

Alcock. And as a consequence I stood out from ten to six in a blizzard—with a magenta-colored behind pointing into the northeast wind. I got chilblains on my backside till I don't dare turn it toward a fire. You'd 'a' been honored to have a man inside those stinking clouts of yours—

Teague. If I was to sit on my bottom and wait for britches to come to it I wouldn't have any, either. I took these off an Injun seven years ago in revenge for his tommy-hawkin' my grandmother.—

Alcock. I'm surprised you had a grandmother! You've no heart and no balls of compassion—

Teague.
    [*Moving toward* ALCOCK]
I'll tear your cullions out of you, you roosting squab!

Mason. Let him alone! There's no gouging here to-night!

Teague. Why not?

Mason. Because my brother's sick, and it's not good for him.

Spad. There's a parcel of clothes coming down from New England, according to the Sergeant.

Jock. We wouldn't get 'em. Not i' this regiment.

Alcock. There's no clothes coming—you might know that. What happened was General Washington sent a requisition for pants to Congress. And Congress looked at the officer that brought the requisition and says: "Pants,

my dear man, is both dear and scarce. We can't send you
any pants. Moreover, the countryside around Philadelphia is full of Quakers with more pants on than they
need. Go out and take the pants off the Quakers." Two
or three weeks later the officer got back and reported to
General Washington. The air around the General's headquarters turned blue to an altitude of eighty foot and the
Schoolkill River ran backward a distance of some fourteen miles. This went on for quite a spell—and then the
General came to enough so's you could distinguish what
he was talking about. "You go back to Congress," says
he, "and ask 'em if they ever tried to take the pants off
a civilian.—Pants," he continues, "is one of the inalien-
able rights of man under the Declaration of Independence and the Ten Commandments. At this moment," he
says, "I have three thousand soldiers whose pants are
wide open from Genesis to Revelations, and while we remain in this defenceless condition there's nothing to stop
the British regulars from marching up to York and taking the pants off the Continental Congress, which I
rather hope they will do!" I was there when he said it,
and boys, I'd like to be there when he gets his answer
back.

> [*The door opens and two women come with a flurry of cold
> behind them.* TEAGUE *helps them shut the door against
> it. The woman who enters first is a slatternly work-
> woman in a thin dress covered with a worn homespun
> coat. She is known as* AUNTIE. *The second is fairly
> young and pretty, the widow of a soldier. She goes to*
> NEIL BONNIWELL's *bunk, carrying a wisp of black
> straw and a stone bottle*]

Jock. Aye—now maybe I could hae my shirt back.

Auntie. Oh, that's what it was—a shirt!

Jock. Am I to hae it—or not?

Auntie. How was I to know what it was—bucko?—The rag you gave me had no tails, no collar, no arms, and one button with no buttonhole to it!—And it's a shirt, is it?

Jock. Call it what you like, but I'll have it back, you travelling witch!

Auntie.
  [*Giving the shirt*]

You'd 'a' had it before, mannie, only there was no soap and no water and no fire. I think I got the itch washing it, besides. Let me see you putting it on, just for the entertainment.
  [Jock *dons his shirt, which does little toward covering him*]

Tavis.
  [*To* Mason]
My hands are cold—you'd best lift his head.
  [*He lifts* Neil *and she puts the straw under the blanket*]

There's hot broth in the bottle.—Now, God save you, boy, you've a fever.

Neil. How is it you—come twice in an evening?

Tavis. Twice?

Neil. Why—you were here before—with the great gold plate—and the flowers.—No, that's true, isn't it?

Auntie. You've been dreaming again—! Now where would she get a gold plate and flowers, soldier honey?

Neil. Was it—my mother, then—with the dirty wings—one of them dragged a little?

　[*A pause*]

There—I'm a fool—

Tavis. It's the fever, just—that's what makes your eyes so bright.

Spad. I suppose you saw the general orders this morning, Auntie?

Auntie. Now what would I want reading the general orders?

Spad. If you don't read 'em you'll hear about 'em. Hark ye.

　[*He turns to a handwritten scroll pasted on the inside of the
　　door jamb*]

"Owing to over-crowded conditions and the scarcity of provender for the troops of the encampment, each company commander is requested to inquire into the status of all camp followers and the like quartered in his vicinity, there appearing to be a remarkable number of women, and especially of pregnant women, established within the lines, and greatly in excess of the allotment for companies under our military articles. Commanders are reminded that six women are allowed to a company, for washing and other necessary duties, but under no circumstances more." What are these here—necessary duties?

Auntie. Who signed it?

Spad. Washington.

Auntie. Well, he can't say I'm pregnant! I haven't been pregnant this twenty years, and won't be—not while I know the signs of the zodiac.

Andrew. What's the receipt, Auntie?

Auntie. I'm not so young but I can stay away from it under a full moon, bucko.—Tavis, there, wouldn't take my advice, and as a result she looks to me to be coming in around the first of July.

Neil. I'll give you thanks not to joke about it, then! If she is, it's my doing, and the baby's mine, and I'll marry her!

Auntie. Nobody's keeping you from it, child—and the babe'll need a father—that's certain.

Tavis. Must you anger him now!—when it's too much for him?

Auntie. There, I'm sorry—and may you live like larks in a pie!

[*She hands a small bundle to* Oscar]

Those were socks once, God mend them.

[*To* Tavis]

I told you beforehand he looked to me like the last run of shad, but you've picked your straw and the next thing's to find a blanket for it.

[*She goes out.* Teague's *son,* Nick, *enters, and kneels to adjust his leggings*]

Neil. There's only one thing I want to ask you, Tavis. Don't let them take me to the pest house. It's bad enough to die, but a man doesn't want to be scared to death.

Mason. You'll stay here, and you won't die.

Tavis. Quit this talk about dying, and take some of the broth.
[*She runs her hand over his hair*]

Neil. All right, I will.
[*He sits up*]
Where did you get it?

Tavis. Stole it, dear—stole it, so I know it's good.

Spad. God damn this blasted army!

Alcock. This army? If God was to damn and blast this army every working day for a full year He couldn't do anything to it that hasn't been done. We've got everything from the itch to the purple fever, nothing to eat, nothing to wear, and the coldest son-of-a-bitch of a winter since the lake of Galilee froze over and Jesus walked on the water.

Spad. He could 'a' walked across Chesapeake Bay yesterday and hauled a fourteen-pounder behind Him.

Andrew. Will you quit talking about God for now? He might be listening.

Jock. Who's got a book?

Mason. You'll find the sermons of Jonathan Edwards under the slop-pail there. All about hell-fire.

Jock. Good. I could use a bit of hell-fire.

Teague. What's it like outside?

Nick. Fine and black. Coast's clear around by Mount Misery.

Teague. Eh, Minto?
   [*Taking up his gun*]

Minto. Coming, Teague.
   [*Rising and going to the corner*]

Spad. What's all this?

Teague. Just stepping out.

Spad. The Leftenant's coming in to-night.

Teague. For what?

Spad. Orders, you coonskin! Orders!

Teague. I'm going to get me something to eat.

Spad. I allow so.

Alcock. What's he doing? Absconding?

Spad. Um.
   [*The group looks on at the preparations in silence*]
   Don't count on me to put up a story for you. If you're gone you've decamped, that's all!

Teague. How long do you reckon any of you'll be here? I took a look around the commissary today. There's about enough grist there to make thin gruel for a clergyman's family, and that's all. They've been trading cavalry horses for shoats till they've dismounted two regiments, and there's no more shoats to be had. I aim to walk away from here while I've got strength to walk.

Alcock. All right, all right. I don't want to know anything about it.

Mason. There was a Hessian Johnny here to-day with
leather boots on—looking for a job as a general—or
maybe commander-in-chief. He stayed long enough to
soak in a few fair-sized impressions and then took out
for Philadelphia to join up with General Howe.

Spad. They eat over in Philadelphia.

Mason. Sure, the big-hearted patriots of Pennsylvania—
we fight for their liberty and they carry their butter and
eggs to Philadelphia in a steady stream to feed King
George's troops. And you can't stop 'em. Shoot 'em dead
and you can't stop 'em.

Alcock. King George pays cash and we pay in continentals.
Did you ever meet up with a Quaker that didn't prefer
a guinea in the hand to any amount of liberty in the
bush? You can shoot 'em, hang 'em, damn 'em, give
'em the water cure, rip their guts out and fill 'em up with
old iron, they go right on selling hogs to the English.

Teague. I'm no Quaker, son, and I'll fill anybody up with
old iron that says I'd sell out to General Howe! We're
going home, that's all.

Alcock. All right, all right. You've read the orders: the new
penalty for desertion is seventy-five lashes on the bare
back, well laid on—or hanging if there's treason connected with it. Don't get caught, that's all.

Teague. I've never been caught yet.

Alcock. How often have you taken French leave?

Teague. Whenever there's nothing to do here I go home.

Alcock. All right.

> [*The door opens and* Lieutenant Cutting *comes in. He is somewhat better dressed than the men and wears a neatly cocked and corded hat. A dog follows him in an goes instantly to the plate of food which* Alcock *has set beside him on the floor*]

Cutting. What dog's that?

Alcock. Hell, he came in with you, Leftenant.

Cutting. The cur's been following me all the way from the King of Prussia Inn.

Spad. You'd better avast from that mess, pup. It'll poison you.

Cutting. Time to bunk in if you want any sleep, Alcock. You're all to be on parade at five for manual of arms under Baron Steuben. After that you'll spend the day making cartridges.

Teague. Now what the hell good is a cartridge?

Alcock. Saves time and keeps your powder dry.

Teague. I'm willing to put it to a test with old Steuben himself! I can load and fire old Happy Thought with horn and charger three times to his two with those paper rigs of his. Watch here!

> [*He upends his gun and reaches for the powderhorn*]

Alcock. You shoot that thing in here and I'll have you cashiered, you mud-for-breakfast—

Teague. If I had mud for breakfast I got it here and not where I came from! I'd be damn glad to be cashiered and get my four months' back pay.

A Voice.
  [*Outside*]
  Hey, boy, what regiment's this?

Another Voice.
  [*Outside*]
  Who goes?

First Voice. You keep kind of an offhand guard here, soldier. If you must know it's Lieutenant Colonel Lucifer Tench, and I asked you a question.

Second Voice. First Virginia.

Tench. Good.
  [*He enters*]
  I didn't know whether that was a sentry you had out there or a prehistoric animal. He's standing with his feet in his hat and a blanket over his ears, making no sense whatever.
  [*Two or three of the men rise or half-rise out of respect*]
  Sit down! Sit down and put your feet in your hats if that's the latest fashion.

Mason. We've lost a couple of sentries with frostbite this month, sir, and the boy's shoes are none too good.

Tench. I'm sorry to hear it, because I'm looking for a squad with passable footwear. How many able-bodied men in your company, Leftenant?

Cutting. Seventy-two this morning.

Tench. How many with guns, shoes and equipment for a little stroll across country in the snow?

Cutting. Twenty-eight—or thereabout.

Alcock. Put me in! I'm going if I go in my shirt-tails!

Cutting. Twenty-eight.

Tench. Twenty-eight! It'll have to do. This is a raid on the hay islands below Darby under the personal supervision of the Commander-in-chief. We have information that Sir William Howe is running short of horse-fodder in Philadelphia and will shortly make an attempt to bring in the forage which was stored last fall on the islands of the Delaware. We mean to get their first with a party of horse to cut off his approach and a small party of pioneers to salvage the hay for ourselves or else dump it in the river. This company is made up of the kind of men we need for the work—hunters, farmers, fishermen, outdoor fellows and equal to anything.

Spad. Right.

Cutting. When are we supposed to start?

Tench. To-night. We must be there by three in the morning. Draw four days' rations for each man. We may be gone some time.

Cutting. We don't start to-night, though.

Tench. Sir!

Cutting. Not to-night, sir.

Tench. You heard the order, I believe!

Cutting. With my compliments, sir, it happens the thing is impossible. We've drawn the last ration for this regiment, such as it was. If that dog keeps it on his stomach he'll probably go to meet his maker before morning.

Tench. The supplies for your regiment were sufficient for ten more days.

Cutting. On paper, yes. But when they rolled out the last twenty barrels the meat was spoiled. As for the flour, they baked the remains of it this morning.

Tench. It appears to me you enjoy this situation.

Cutting. Not at all. Nor am I to blame for it. The blame, I believe, attaches elsewhere.

Tench. Do you wish to say where?

Cutting. I have said before and I say again that this is probably the worst managed army in the history of military operations.

Tench. Yes, I've heard you—and I say mismanaged by whom?

Cutting. When I served abroad there was never any doubt where the management of an army lay. It might be as well if you informed yourself on that head.

   [*A slight pause*]

Tench. It's of very little moment what you wish to say about me, Mr. Cutting—but there are certain names I don't care to hear insulted—

Cutting. I insult nobody!

Tench. Let me judge of that for myself!

   [*The door opens and an* AIDE *appears*]

The Aide. General Washington wishes to know if this matter is arranged, Colonel. He's in haste to reach General Wayne—

Tench. Will you say to General Washington that I've encountered unexpected difficulties, and would be glad if he could step in for a moment.—I'll tell him myself.

> [*He turns and goes out, followed by the* AIDE. *There is tension in the air. One or two of the men adjust their clothes. A tall, dark* FRENCH OFFICER *of nineteen or twenty enters in resplendent uniform.* WASHINGTON *comes in after him in shabby boots, a long, much-worn cloak, and an old cocked hat.* TENCH *reenters. The men have all risen save* NEIL *and* MARTY. NEIL *rises on one elbow and* SPAD *nudges* MARTY, *who gets up, open-mouthed*]

Washington. I'm distressed to hear of this shortage of supplies, Lieutenant, but happily we are not entirely without resource. A long-expected wagon train began to arrive this evening, and though the first wagons are loaded only with munitions there are eighteen long tons of flour and pork bringing up the rear, and it should be possible to victual your expedition by the time you can put yourselves in marching order.

Cutting. We shall make our preparations at once then. Is this the train which was sent on from Fishkill by General Putnam, sir?

Washington. It is. Though how you may have learned of that I'm at a loss to conceive.

Cutting. I supped this evening with General Conway, who had received a letter from Putnam. And if the information in the letter is correct I very much fear you will be disappointed of your expectations in regard to the salt pork and flour. Putnam was unable to locate mules or wagons to accommodate the food allotment.

Washington. Unable—?

Cutting. Completely unable, as he said.

Washington. You have information that the food was not sent?

Cutting. So it would seem.
   [*A pause*]

Washington. When did the letter arrive?

Cutting. I believe yesterday.

Washington.
   [*To* TENCH]
Can there be truth in this?

Tench. As a matter of fact the bills of lading failed to cover the food supplies, but I supposed them in error—

Washington. I should like to hope this report was erroneous, but some little experience with the commissary department has taught me to credit any amount of ill news from that quarter. It sticks in my crop a little, let me add, that I should receive important intelligence in a manner so singularly circuitous. General Putnam writes, not to me, but to General Conway, and General Conway conveys his intelligence, not to me, but to a junior officer with whom he has supped. Quite by chance I encounter this officer and in the course of conversation these little military details are relayed to me—

Cutting. Sir, I hope I have not offended—

Washington. Not in the least, sir. I am in your debt for the information, and can only congratulate you and General Conway on the celerity with which you receive dis-

patches which have not been vouchsafed to the Commander-in-chief.

[*He turns to* TENCH]

The expedition will be postponed or assigned to some
other company better prepared to move. Meanwhile
food must be obtained for this regiment if we have to
cut steaks off the members of the Board of War.
They're all prime, I've noticed.

[*He has turned to go*]

Lafayette.

[*Looking at the dog's collar*]

General, would you care to know whose dog this is?

Washington. We're in haste, Marquis.

Lafayette. Yes, but the inscription on this collar reads:
Rover, Sir William Howe. This rover has roved all the
way from Philadelphia. It is General Howe's dog.

Alcock. I was planning to skin him—and now I'll eat him.

Washington. I might have known by the fat on his ribs he
was no local product. We must see that he's returned.
Have you pen and ink here?

Spad. Yes, sir.

[*He sets an inkhorn and quill on the table*]

Washington. Lucifer!

[TENCH *crosses to take dictation at the table*]

"Sir Wm. Howe, British Headquarters, Philadelphia.
Dear Sir: The bearer of this note will return to you a
dog of which you appear to be the owner, since he wears
your name on his collar. May I say that I was the more

astonished to find him at Valley Forge because I believed the desertions to be going the other way. G. Washington." Choose a reliable man and send him to Philadelphia with a flag. The animal is to be delivered to the General himself with this note and my compliments.

[*Indicating* ALCOCK]

This is a man I know. Would the errand amuse you?

Alcock. I'm easy to amuse, General, but the fact is I haven't any britches.

Washington. Well, that can hardly be considered a defect of character. Choose a messenger, Lieutenant.

Cutting. Yes, sir.

Spad. I'd like to carry the note, sir.

Washington. If it's agreeable to your officer.

Cutting. Certainly.

Washington. Then take good care of the brute, and my thanks.

[*He hands the note to* SPAD]

Teague. General Washington!

Washington. Deliver both into Howe's hands.

Teague. General Washington!

Mason. Hark quiet, you fool!

Washington. What is it?

Teague. These here new regulations about men going home. Going home without leave. They say it's seventy-five lashes if they catch you now. Why is that?

Washington. The traditional penalty for desertion is shooting at sunrise. We've been more lenient here.

Teague. But look, General Washington, it don't make sense. It don't stand to reason—

Nick. Do you want to talk your neck into a rope?

Washington. Let him say what's on his mind.

Teague. Well, here it is: I'm going hungry here and my woman's going hungry at home. You let me go home for the winter, and you won't have to feed me, and that relieves the commissary; I rustle some wild meat for the younguns and the old woman, and they don't starve and I don't starve. More'n that, everybody knows there's two or three thousand men gone home already for that same reason, and if they was here now they'd be chewing the bark off the second-growth birch like so many cottontails. I don't hold it against you and I don't hold it against anybody because I don't know who in thunder to hold it against, but there's nothing to eat here.

Alcock. Stow it, will you? The dog ate the stuff, and he isn't dead yet.

Teague. It ain't that I'm afraid of a good fight. A good fight's ham and eggs to me. Me and my boy here, we make for home every winter when the grub gets scarce, and we come back every spring when the fighting starts. We're coming back next spring, and every spring, till we chase the god-damn red-coats clear out of Chesapeake Bay, and across the Atlantic Ocean and right up a lamp-post in London town! Fighting's fine, but sitting here and starving down to a hide and buttons—I don't savvy it.

Washington. What is your name, sir?

Teague. Teague, sir. Teague's my name.

Washington. Well, Master Teague, if they catch you they'll give you seventy-five lashes, and that's a good deal to take and live. On the other hand you're quite right from your own angle, and if I were you I'd feel as you do.—But this you should know, sir: if you go home, and we all go home this winter, you won't need to bother about coming back in the spring. There'll be no fighting to come back to.—General Howe will march out of Philadelphia and take over these states of ours. If he knew now how many have deserted, how many are sick, how many unfit for duty on account of the lack of food and clothes and munitions, he'd come out in force and wring our necks one by one, and the neck of our sickly little revolution along with us. So far we've kept him pinned in Philadelphia by sheer bluster and bluff and show of arms. We've raided his supplies and cut off his shipping and captured his food-trains and so bedeviled him generally that he thinks there's still an army here. But every able-bodied man, every man that owns a pair of dungareees for his legs and brogans for his feet, has to look like ten men if this nation's coming through the winter alive.—What are we in this war for? Are we tired of it? Do we want to quit?

The Men. No, sir. No.

Washington. I can't blame you if you sound a bit half-hearted about it.

Teague. I'm not half-hearted about it! Not me! I'm fighting to keep King George out of my backyard! I moved west three times to get away from his damn tax-collectors, and every time they caught up to me! I'm sick of tax-collectors, that's why I'm in it!

Washington. Then it may be you're here in error, and the sooner you discover it the better. You'll get death and taxes under one government as well as another. But I'll tell you why I'm here, and why I've hoped you were here, and why it's seemed to me worth while to stick with it while our guns rust out for lack of powder, and men die around me for lack of food and medicine and women and children sicken at home for lack of clothing and the little they need to eat—yes, while we fight one losing battle after another, and retreat to fight again another year, and yet another and another, and still lose more than we win, and yet fight on while our hair grows gray and our homes break up in our absence, and the best and youngest among us give their blood to swell spring freshets and leave their bones and marrow to flesh the hills. This is no lucky war for me. I thought it was at first. I wanted to astound the world as a military leader, but my head's grayer now and I've had enough of that. What I fight for now is a dream, a mirage, perhaps, something that's never been on this earth since men first worked it with their hands, something that's never existed and will never exist unless we can make it and put it here—the right of free-born men to govern

themselves in their own way.—Now men are mostly
fools, as you're well aware. They'll govern themselves
like fools. There are probably more fools to the square
inch in the Continental Congress than in the Continental
army, and the percentage runs high in both. But we've
set our teeth and trained our guns against the hereditary
right of arbitrary kings, and if we win it's curfew for all
the kings of the world.—It may take a long time, but
one by one, bolster themselves as they will, pour out
money as they may for mercenaries, make what victorious wars they can, they'll slip one by one from their
thrones and go out with the great wash through this
breach we make in their sea walls.—It may not be worth
the doing. When you deal with a king you deal with one
fool, knave, madman, or whatever he may be. When you
deal with a congress you deal with a conglomerate of
fools, knaves, madmen and honest legislators, all pulling
different directions and shouting each other down. So
far the knaves and fools seem to have it. That's why
we're stranded here on this barren side-hill, leaving a
bloody trail in the snow and chewing the rotten remains
of sow-belly on which some merchant has made his seven
profits.—So far our government's as rotten as the sow-
belly it sends us. I hope and pray it will get better. But
whether it gets better or worse it's your own, by God,
and you can do what you please with it—and what I
fight for is your right to do what you please with your
government and with yourselves without benefit of
kings.—It's for you to decide, Master Teague—you, and
your son, and the rest of you. This is your fight more

than mine. I don't know how long the Congress means to keep me where I am nor how long you mean to stay with me. If you desert they may catch you and they may not, but the chances are they won't, for the sentries are men as you are—hungry, shivering, miserable and inclined to look the other way. Make your own decision. But if we lose you—if you've lost interest in this cause of yours—we've lost our war, lost it completely, and the men we've left lying on our battle-fields died for nothing whatever—for a dream that came too early—and may never come true.

[*He pauses, looks round at the men, then at the officers*]

We mark time here, gentlemen, and there's much to do.

[*He goes to the door, followed by* LAFAYETTE *and the* AIDE]

Tench!

Tench. I'll follow you in a moment, sir.

[WASHINGTON, LAFAYETTE, *and the* AIDE *go out.* TEAGUE *and* NICK *look at each other briefly—then* TEAGUE *addresses* MINTO]

Teague. I guess the old woman'll get along. She's brought in her own bear meat before.

[MINTO *goes back to his place and sits down*]

Nick. Well, it's all right with me.

[*He straightens up, deliberately takes in another hole in his belt, crosses to a bunk, and lies back*]

Tench. And now, if you don't mind, we'll finish that conversation of ours.

Cutting. Fire when ready.

Tench. It's just occurred to me that dog's got General

Howe's name on his neck, and it may not be an accident that he's following you around.

Cutting.

[*Rising slowly*]

Now, by God, you will fight—

Tench. That's my intention.

Cutting. And if you mean I've been colloguing with General Howe or the English I'll tamp that lie down your throat and I'll do it now!

Tench. I don't know whether you have or not, but I say it's fitting and apropos that Howe's dog came in at your heels—

Mason. Gentlemen—

Cutting. Sir, before you lay charges of treason against me in this offhand manner, let me assure you there's no great mystery about the dog's appearance in our lines. An exchange of prisoners took place at General Conway's headquarters this evening, and the cur may have followed the British party into camp. I'm no friend to the English. If they win it will be because of you and those who side with you in your fanatic devotion to a gentleman whose leadership was long ago discredited.

Tench. Meaning General Washington.

Cutting. Meaning whom you will.

Tench. Name your new leader, then!

Cutting. Aye, you name him! I have no fancy for laying myself liable to court-martial.

Tench. It's as open as that, then.

Cutting. There's open dissatisfaction, if that's what you mean—and you're as well aware of it as I am. I've served as a brigadier-general under the French colors, and I'm cast here as a second lieutenant. There's no place in this army I couldn't fill, and I serve under a captain who sits at table in his stocking feet and got his experience fighting Indians on the Ohio. Why doesn't Benedict Arnold hold a commission? Why is Gates shunted into the northern department? Why are Lee and Conway pensioned off with minor commands—?

Tench. I thought we'd come to Conway.

Cutting. Why, because the army's run for the glory of a little inner clique, of which you happen to be one—

Tench. And you want it run for a little clique of adventurers that's served in every army in Europe, sworn allegiance to every king and cause in Christendom and turned your coats so often for money that you start undressing every time you see a shilling—

Cutting. You've served abroad, I believe!

Tench. I know a man when I see one! Washington's a man—and there isn't one among those you've named that he couldn't eat after dinner, with a little brandy and soda to wash down the taste. You may be a good officer, you may have served with all the duchies and principalities between Turkey and the Swedes, but take care how you align yourself with these foreign swashers who come over to cash in on this revolution—with nothing to recommend them but tarnished epaulets, tarnished reputations and a full set of military mustaches! We've had the clippings and sweepings of every European court dumped on us, mostly younger sons and bastard half-brothers, and leavings that were pitched out when the college of heraldry cleaned house!—I beg your pardon heartily if you're a bastard. I meant nothing personal.

Cutting. I think you did, though, and I'd take the trouble to quarrel with you if I thought it worth my while. It isn't. You can rate Conway and Lee and Gates as low as you like. They'll hold their commissions long after your Washington's gone back to planting tobacco along the Potomac. He's a beaten man. You heard his speech, and if that wasn't a valedictory I never heard one. He's tired and others are tired of him, and when he goes you'll go with him.

Tench. Come, come—this is news. When may we expect this happy sequel?

Cutting. I've said my say.

Tench. You have indeed—and you've said what I wanted to get out of you—

Cutting. No doubt you're a tale-bearer, too, to go with the rest of your Colonial virtues.

Tench. You may be right.

Cutting. Tell it then. I've said nothing that isn't said from here to Boston, and with added flourishes.

Tench. Good night, sir. Gentlemen, your pardon for a scene hardly calculated to instill respect and discipline. Good night.

[*He goes out. The men are silent.* SPAD *takes the dog by an improvised leash and goes to the door.* CUTTING *throws himself on a bunk*]

Mason. Starting now?

Spad. The least Sir William can give me's a square meal— and if I time it right I'll have beef and kidney pie tomorrow night for supper.

Alcock. I hope you over-eat yourself and regurgitate.

Spad. Thanks. Always a friend.

[*He goes out.* NEIL *sits up and swings his legs out of the bunk*]

Tavis. Lie still, sweet. Lie still and rest.

Neil. This is a poor death to die.

CURTAIN

ACT ONE

Scene Two

SCENE: *A ballroom in General Howe's headquarters in Philadelphia. Before the curtain rises a small string orchestra is playing one of Mozart's early minuets, and at its rise three or four furbelowed and periwigged couples are dancing to the music. SIR WILLIAM, who is dancing with a woman in a domino, leaves the group to talk with his partner. The end of the room is curtained off for amateur theatricals and there are boxes for spectators.*

Major Andre.

[*To his partner*]

This is the Mozart.

First Lady. Wolferl—the little one?

Andre. True, they called him Wolferl. He's older now.
   And they print him Wolfgang Amadeus. All the masters
   that ever set notes on paper meet in him
   or are vanquished by him.

First Lady. But he's so young.

Andre. My dear,
   I heard him play in London as a child.
   Music fell from him in cascades. These things
   are inexplicable, like windows to the unseen
   that open and show us marvels.

First Lady. Twenty years old!

Andre. Barely twenty, I think. There—the dominant—
   how fitly that's resolved!

[SIR WILLIAM *and his partner enter one of the boxes and draw*
the curtain. They are screened from the ballroom but
not from the audience]

A Brigadier. Our General
has made another conquest.

Second Lady. Nay, rather say
Sir William wins to lose. These victories
of his are Pyrrhic. The husbands get commissions—
a colonelcy at least.

Brigadier. For such a known beauty
he must make a brigadier.

Second Lady. Her husband's away—
a prisoner.

Brigadier. Ah, they play without forfeits.

Second Lady. She's not so young
that she has time to lose.
[*Fingers to lips they give the box a wide berth*]

Howe. Like pleated silk,
this music. It interweaves.

Mary Philipse. It is silken music.
Silken sad music.

Howe. Yes, sad too. These artists,
they know so well how to interweave love and death.

Mary. In tapestries—lutes, lovers, battles.

Howe. There's nothing
to break the heart like these same minuets
we use to dance to. You should have loved a soldier,
masked lady.

Mary. I married a soldier.

Howe. Yes? His name?

Mary. Is that to the purpose—to inquire names?

Howe. My dear,
    if I knew his name I'd be inclined to practice
    King David's stratagem. Poor man, I'd set him
    in the forefront of the battle, and then his widow—
    I'd keep her for myself.

Mary. And Mistress Loring,
    the lovely Mistress Loring?

Howe. A friend, I swear.
    Only a friend.

Mary. A bosom friend, then—one
    who gives her all?

Howe. Is a soldier to have but one,
    and she forever? May not a soldier weary
    and choose again—a fairer?
        [*He kisses her*]

Mary. You mistake me—

Howe. You are someone I know.

Mary. No, I think not.
    I'm no one you have seen—but you're forgiven
    for being misled. I smiled and led you on,
    and I'm not angry—but in truth I'm sad this evening
    for love of someone else.

Howe. Now, damn it all,
  why not for love of me?

Mary. Why, it just happens
  this once, you're not the man.

Howe. Someone outshines me
  in my own camp! Darkness and death and devils,
  shall this be borne? But tell me his name and place
  and you shall have him.

Mary. He's not at your dispose,
  Sir William; he serves elsewhere. No—in real truth,
  he serves on the other side, and what I wanted
  was leave to go out and see him.

Howe. Insult on insult!
  Not only a less than I am, an enemy!
  Sweet domino, you humble me my pride—
  but you shall have him, and my price is only
  that you doff this domino.
    [*She removes her mask*]
  And now I'm sorry
  I said I'd help you to him. The devil take him,
  some oaf of a musketeer! Would you be a rebel?

Mary. I've set my heart on it.

Howe. Never rebel, dear lady.
  God sets up kings, and all the prayer books teach us
  it's irreligious to fight against them.

Mary. Come—
  be serious—

Howe. With a woman?

Mary. Solemn, then, sad—
  doleful. I loved and lost when I was a child.
  I let my love go then, when I might have had him—
  and now it may be too late.

Howe. See the tears in my eyes—
  you have smitten the rock like Moses.

Mary. When I was a child
  a young man came wooing from Virginia way.
  And we fell in love, but my parents said, No, no—
  this is an Indian fighter; you are rich,
  and may turn out good-looking; let him go,
  and catch yourself a lord. And I let him go
  and caught myself a captain of marines
  or something of that kind. I've never loved him.
  I've wanted what I lost.

Howe. The Indian fighter.

Mary. Yes.

Howe. It's someone I know?

Mary. I doubt you've seen him,
  but you've heard of him; he's no less on the rebel side
  than you on this.

Howe. Washington?

Mary. I believe
  that was the name.

Howe. Is this some game you play?

Mary. It would be but a poor game. No, I'm deadly
    earnest,
  I'm not jesting now.

Howe. What a strange mad thing
　　is a woman's heart! To remember all this while
　　and brood on it, and remember. You'd go to him
　　and give up all that's civilized to live
　　on corn bread in log cabins?

Mary. Will it be so long
　　before we come to terms with the rebels? This
　　is the last year of their war.

Howe. A long-headed girl;
　　you've thought this through.

Mary. Oh, truly.

Howe. But then I've heard—
　　the man is married, is he not?

Mary. A widow.
　　When I refused him he married a widow with land
　　and a nest of children. Nasty ones, I hope,
　　with wipey noses.

Howe. Is there any other kind?
　　Strange that they're such a pleasure in the getting
　　and so damp to have about.—Why, no my dear;
　　the answer's no. As a gallant to a lady,
　　here in this ballroom, we may talk, look you,
　　of anything under heaven; but wars are something
　　which you have hardly imagined, here in this ballroom.
　　They're fought with blood and iron. I say, for your sake,
　　for yours alone, you're not to cross the lines.

Mary. I understand that. If you must refuse, why then,
　　you must refuse. You have your reasons. Still—
　　I shall go.

Howe. Without a pass?

Mary. If necessary.
  There comes a time when a woman's desperate
  to have her youth. It's come to me, and I'll have it
  though all the generals in hell should stand
  eyes front and bar my passage. Oh, believe me,
  I can make my way.

Howe. And, being warned, I shall find
  a way to prevent it.
      [*The orchestra begins to play Yankee Doodle*]
  Come; the masquerade
  is about to begin, and we're to be amused.

Mary. Surely.
      [*He pulls back the curtain. A number of couples have drifted in
      and* ANDRE *takes a central position with a paper in his
      hand*]

Andre. Ladies and officers, worshippers of beauty and
  beloved of the fair, it is now my sad duty to announce
  that the program will be taken over by General George
  Washington and his Continental army, whose services
  we have acquired for the evening at the expense of three
  shillings, sixpence, and three twists of local tobacco,
  very bad. In a personal interview, which I obtained with
  General Washington he said, in part, "Yes, sir, by gum,
  we'll be there, by gum, every man-jack of us, by gum!"
  Ladies and officers will now find seats or otherwise dispose themselves to view the entertainment. Warning is
  hereby issued that the committee is not responsible for
  possible depredations committed by General Washing-

ton's horse, a spirited animal and hard to hold! En avant!

> [*Amid cheers, jeers and hisses the curtains are pulled back, revealing three ragged soldiers, caricatures of the Continentals, and Washington as impersonated by a British officer on a broomstick hobbyhorse, with movable ears.* The Washington *raises his wooden sword*]

The Washington. Stop! Halt! Whoa! Give the password!

> [*At each command the horse wags an ear*]

First Soldier.

I am a soldier in a cause,
I march and fight for freedom;
I won't obey nobody's laws,
I never seem to need 'em.

Chorus.

> [*Sung, as* The Washington *does a clog dance*]
> Yankee Doodle has no shoes,
> Yankee Doodle Dandy;
> For ham and eggs he has no use,
> But he fills up on brandy!
> Clippetty, clippetty, clippetty, clippetty,
> clop, clop, clop, clop, clop; clip!

First Lady. I think he has a very intelligent face.

Andre. The horse? Yes, the horse keeps his countenance well.

Second Soldier.

When I was young I went to war
My freedom for to win, sirs,

Since then I've travelled fast and far
A-saving of my skin, sirs.

Chorus.

Yankee Doodle has no home,
From field and farm he's chased, sirs,
And if you ask us why we roam—
There's reason for our haste, sirs.
Clippetty, clippetty, clippetty, clippetty,
Clop, clop, clop, clop, clop! clip!

Mary. Oh, the poor little army! It's really sad.

Brigadier. Isn't it? One could almost weep.

Third Soldier.

I make my shoes of hempen bags;
I'm sorry that I come now,
Because I'm destitute of rags
To cover up my bum now.

Chorus.

Yankee Doodle, keep it up,
Yankee Doodle Dandy,
Mind the music and the step
And with the girls be handy!
Tootlety, tootlety, tootlety, tootlety,
Toot, toot, toot, toot, toot; peep!

The Washington. Eyes front! Manage your weapons! This
way, army! Face the war!

[*They face in different directions, muskets at every angle*]

Stock arms! Pull out rammer! Catch horn in left hand!
Charger in right hand! Fill charger! Empty charger in
bore! Grease patches!

Second Lady. But what are they doing?

Captain. They're getting ready to fire.

Second Lady. Oh, my dear!

The Washington. Patch on muzzle! Ball on patch! Ram ball down! Return rammer to gun! Ready! Aim!

[*They aim wildly in different directions, one gun pointing at* THE WASHINGTON, *who moves*]

First Lady. Oh, but this is serious!

[*Another woman gives a little scream*]

The Washington. Ready! Aim! Take aim!

[*He moves out of range; the gun follows him*]

Second Lady. The suspense is killing me!

The Washington.

[*To the soldier whose gun points at him*]

Will you do me the favor to turn your weapon in some other direction, sir? It may be loaded.

[*The soldier alters his aim*]

Take aim, men! Take aim! Fire!

[*They pull the triggers. One gun goes off with a terrific concussion, kicking its owner over backward. He falls against the other two, who go down likewise. They look about fearfully*]

A victory! An important victory! The Congress shall hear of this! Soldiers of the Continental army, this proves that our cause is righteous! We shall have liberty or death, probably death! Preferably death!

[SPAD *comes wandering onto the stage, leading the dog and watching the proceedings, at first with curiosity and then with growing resentment*]

Brigadier. Reenforcements are arriving!

Howe. Is that my dog he has there?

Spad. I'm looking for General Howe.

The Washington.

> Lift your eyes, my men, and greet the sunrise,
> > Soldiers, the dawn of liberty is ours!
> Long we've battled, long we've faced the foeman
> > To gain at least six feet of earth—and flowers.
>
> 'Twixt liberty and death we pause no longer,
> > No choice remains to disconcert the brave;
> Races are to the swift, power to the stronger—
> > Taxes we will not pay; we choose—the grave.
>
> I am that Washington on whom you've pondered;
> > My head is in the clouds, my feet—in mud.
> My socks are wet, my shirts are never laundered,
> > I grind the neighbors' children up for food.

Spad. Looky here, mister actor!

The Washington.

> In short to put it briefly, men and matrons.
> > I'm at the end of what I call my string;
> I'll trade this revolution, and its patrons,
> > For half a gill of rum—or anything.

Spad. You'll have to get up first then!

> [*He socks* THE WASHINGTON *in the jaw, and he sits down hard,*
> *very much surprised*]

Andre. What's all this? What's that man doing there?

Howe. Easy, easy! It may be part of the show!

Andre. Oh, no, sir! I wrote the play, and this is no part of it.

Howe. There may have been changes made in your manuscript, my dear author. These things happen!

Andre. I think not.

The Washington.
[*Getting up*]
What did you mean by that? Who are you?

Spad. I'm good enough for you!
[*They square off for a fight*]

Howe. Part them! Part them, some of you! Professional jealousy, that's all! Actors' jealousy!
[ANDRE *and another officer leap to the stage to hold the combatants*]

Andre. What are you doing on the stage?

Spad. I was sent here, wasn't I? Let go of me!
[*An officer appears from the wings in his shirt-sleeves*]

Andre. Did you let this madman loose in here?

Stage Manager. Wasn't he in this scene? He was dressed for it!

Andre. He's nobody I ever saw before. How did you get in here?

Spad. I'm bringing General Howe's dog back to him, that's all—and they pushed me in here. I've got a letter for General Howe.

Andre. From whom?

Spad. From General George Washington. And don't fool yourself—that don't look like him!

Andre. You have a letter from General Washington?
Spad. I have.

> [*He brings it out*]

And a dog. We found this dog at Valley Forge. There's the dog and there's the note, and that ends my business here. I'll go now, if you don't mind, because I don't think much of you—or of your gang!

Howe.

> [*Approaching*]

Let me see the note.

> [ANDRE *hands it to him*]

Spad. So that's all.

Andre. One moment, please.

Howe. Why yes. Quite right and to the point. Sir, I wish to thank you for the dog, for the note, and for your courtesy. I hope you will remain to be my messenger back again, for I wish to thank General Washington in writing for his consideration.

Spad. I wasn't instructed to wait for an answer.

Andre. Sir, this is no manner in which to address an officer.

Spad. Fine. You address him any way you like, and I'll address him any way I like.

First Lady. How sweet!

Andre. I shall not stand by quietly while some black-guardly curmudgeon of a rebel cheeks the commander of the British army.

Spad. When I came in here there was a blackguardly officer-of-the-line libelling George Washington as an eater of little children! I won't forget that!

Howe. No more of this, gentlemen! No more, please! My dear sir, even if you are unwilling to carry my thanks to General Washington you must not refuse some reward for your pains in returning my absent-minded canine.

Spad. No, thanks.

Howe. You will at least be my guest at a good dinner before you take the road, for you have come a long way, and I have heard that you fare but lightly along the Schuylkill.

Spad. Somebody's been lying like hell, then! They told you we were shy of victuals over at Valley Forge? Listen, last night I threw away more than I ate! I'm much obliged but I wouldn't be able to accommodate any dinner. I wouldn't want to take the last few mouthfuls away from a beleaguered army in straitened circumstances. No, thanks just the same, I'll go back to my own side, where the cooking's plentiful and excellent.

Howe. That must be as you wish, then. Captain, will you see that arrangements are made for this gentleman's safe return through our lines? And will you take the dog also into your custody?
   [*The* CAPTAIN *bows*]

Spad. I beg, your pardon, General, but I'd a little rather you didn't lump me in with your dog. If the dog rates an officer I rate one.

Howe. And a very fine feeling you have in the matter, too, sir. Again I beg your pardon. Fielding, I place the General's messenger under your protection.
   [*Another officer bows and* SPAD *goes out with him*]

Second Lady. And this is doubtless a sample of rebel etiquette!

Brigadier. At any rate we're rid of him.

Howe. I would we might be rid of all of them as easily. They're starving at Valley Forge, you know, and he refused food.

First Lady. A most disagreeable person.

Howe. Will you announce the next divertissement, Major? We must not interrupt our evening.

Andre. Ladies and gentlemen, this puts a rather unexpected period to our masquerade. Shall we retire to the refreshment tables in order to change the subject?
   [*The party begins to move toward the exits*]

Second Lady. But we'll dance again later?

First Lady. I must hear the Mozart Minuet once more.

Brigadier. Lady, we'll dance as long as there are officers afoot and ladies to face them.

Andre.
   [*To the musicians*]
The Mozart Minuet?

Howe. Major, if you'll remain a moment—

Captain. A fresh shipment of salt water delicacies, they say.
   [*The Minuet is played softly*]

Oysters from the Chesapeake, clams from Pamlico
Sound.

Second Lady. They run the blockade, then?

Captain. What blockade, madame? One mud fort and a
few chevaux-de-frise!

> [Howe *beckons to* Andre, *and the two are left alone save for*
> Mary *and the* Brigadier, *who are half-hidden at the*
> *far corner of the ballroom*]

Andre. Sir, at your service.

Howe. That lady is your guest, sir, I believe?

Andre. Yes, General—Mistress Morris, an old friend, and
my guest this evening. You'll remember that Major
Morris is unfortunately a prisoner?

Howe. You could vouch
for her loyalty, no doubt?

Andre. Why, with my life,
or anything you asked.

Howe. She tells some tale
of having been affianced to Washington,
or having come near it.

Andre. Why, that's no more than truth.
Her family broke it off. She told you that?
But I've heard it often.

Howe. Oh, she went much further—
wishes to see him—

Andre. Yes?

Howe. Oh, asked my help
to pass her through the lines.

Andre. It's not serious.

Howe. I think it is.

Andre. Well, it's hardly to be expected
you'd lend yourself to such a whim. I'm sorry
if she's been intrusive.

Howe, Not at all. It happens
I'd been casting about for expedients. I've had
bad news to-night.

Andre. Bad news?

Howe. The French alliance,
which we have feared, is imminent, or likely.—
Should the French lend their fleet and men to aid
the colonies, it will be a long war; it may
hurt England deep in the end. I've no heart for it.
I've seen too much blood shed.

Andre. Why, General—
you've won the last three battles!

Howe. Have I so?
If the French come in, and there's a hellish good prospect
they will, it'll be a long war. Perhaps five years more
of damn dull fighting, and every chance in the world
of losing after it all.

Andre. Losing? The British
lost to the Americans?

Howe. The longer it goes on
the more chance they have.—At this moment the war
is won.

Washington's army's a wraith. It lingers on
from month to month by miracle. And now,
now when I've won my war, the French drop on us
and botch the game.—I see one possible hope
of making an end of it. If Washington
can be reached, and convinced it's useless to go on,
the thing is done. He has reason to be discouraged
if ever a man had reason.

Andre. But this rumor from France,
  this will get to him too.

Howe, We've taken the packet
  that brought his letters. It will be some time
  before he learns of it. It's our cue to convince him
  there's no hope from France, and he's stuck alone
  at Valley Forge with his shambles of an army,
  and no help in sight. Suppose I sent this lady
  out of his youth with a message?

Andre. He'll see her, surely.
  She might persuade him.

Howe. Send off that talking ass
  she's dangling with, and bring her here. We'll see
  what mettle's in her.

Andre. But you'll not let her know
  of the French alliance?

Howe. We'd best lie to the lady
  on that one score. Tell her the French refused.
  It's fair enough.

Andre. Let her carry that lie to him?

Howe. Why yes. Why not?

> [ANDRE *goes to* MARY PHILIPSE, *who disengages herself from the* BRIGADIER *and returns with him.* HOWE *takes a pinch of snuff meanwhile and dusts his frill. The* BRIGADIER *goes out*]

Mary. You wished to see me, sir?

Howe. I've been revolving
this request you made, dear lady, and wondering
whether you might be of use.—If I could trust
a woman with a nation's destiny—

Mary. Forgive me,
I'm a woman, but I know where gossip ends.
It's safe with me.

Howe. And yet the bald fact is
you have an inclination toward one of the rebels,
and perhaps toward all.

Mary. It's not his quality
as rebel that attracts me, General.
I'd like him less so. If it could be managed
I'd make him less so for you.

Howe. Then perhaps—
if you still wish to see him—?

Mary. Oh, I'm not fickle.
But—you're willing to let me go?

Howe. I want your help.
I want this war to end. To-night we've learned
one fact that makes it perfect suicide
for the colonies to continue. The French alliance—
well—there's to be none.

Mary. You've learned this?

Howe. It's quite certain.
  And now what hopes have they?

Mary. None—none at all.

Howe. This Washington of yours,
  he's a Virginia squire at heart, he has
  about as much to gain as you or I
  out of this war. He likes to take his ease
  and hunt his foxes. If I had half an hour
  to talk things over with him, and make it plain
  how little they have to lose, how much to win
  by making terms, I'd have him on my side
  and there'd be no revolution.

Andre. You speak as if it lay
  with one man to decide. Let Washington
  be ever so discouraged, still there's Congress
  and the Boston merchants.

Howe. Sick of it, one and all. The Boston merchants
  and Massachusetts officers are plotting
  to put Gates in his place and sue for peace
  on any terms. They're ruined by the war,
  and losing money every day; no ships,
  no commerce, markets shot to fattrels, all
  the fat-backed Puritans screaming over taxes
  and retching with fear to think how big they signed
  their names to the Declaration. Washington—
  he's our man.

Andre. And is he open to reason?

Howe. He's a canny gentleman. He knows
  how bread is buttered.

Mary. Then—he will talk with you?

Howe. Well, that was where I thought you might come in,
Mistress Morris. You say he loved you once
and you wish to see him—well, that can be dished up
into some raggle-taggle gypsy tale,
all honey and moonlight—
how you sheer must—must see him; dashed away
forgetting husbands, wives, proprieties,
in one sweet sweep of passion—it's no man's brain
can find the seasoning, but you'll worm your way
into a friendly meeting—

Mary. I can say this truly,
with no help of seasoning. And then—?

Howe, Why then—
I have no speech prepared—but tell him this
in your own fashion: The war's gone on too long,
both sides lose, both are worn down till there's nothing
left to win should he win. One word from him
and we all forget and forgive—exchange general pardons,
live again like men. What beasts we've been,
we English-speaking brothers, to gash and stab
and drill each other's brains out all these years
over one kind of government or another
when they're all the same! I'm a liberal myself,
want to see men free, as he does—but, good Lord,
when has a king balked freedom, when has the lack
of a king guaranteed it?

Mary. But if I told him this
I should mean it, Sir William.

Howe. And I should mean it!

   [The music begins again]

   I mean it from my heart! You think because
I dance and take it lightly, and play about
with women, this damned war means nothing to me
but a Colonial interlude, a picnic
on military lines? I tell you and swear it,
if I could keep some semblance of victory
they could have their liberty for all of me!
Three years is much too much to give a cause
you never believed in!

Mary. Well—I'll go.

   [The dancers are returning]

Howe. And tell him
we in this camp know that he's lost, but are loath
to press our advantage home, having held him always
as a magnanimous gentleman and a soldier
just this side of miracle. You'll say this?

Mary. Yes.

Howe. And say, too, to give up hope of France.

Andre. The dancers are returning.

Mary. I'll say all this—
but with one difference—that I'll mean it all.

Howe. Our compact's drawn
and a kiss shall seal it. Shall we dance, my lady?

   *[HOWE and MARY take places in the Minuet and the scene ends
as it began, with several couples dancing to the Mozart
music]*

       CURTAIN

ACT ONE

SCENE THREE

SCENE: *Washington's headquarters. The parlor of a Colonial house. Windows and an entrance door to the left; to the rear a fireplace and a door to dining-room. A small desk is placed at the right, and rather formal chairs are spaced about the room. A large map hangs on the rear wall, showing Philadelphia, the Delaware below the city, and Valley Forge.* TENCH *is seated at the desk.* GENERALS VARNUM *and* STIRLING *are seated near him.* LAFAYETTE *is leaning at the rear doorway and* WASHINGTON *stands near the window, occasionally pacing back and forth.*

Washington. Now if you will read the minutes, sir.

Tench.

[*Reading*]

These sentences are to stand: Joseph Cutler, for repeated desertions from different regiments and companies, to be lashed and cashiered with infamy. A man known as Junius Morgan, one time a soldier in the Continental army, to be flogged at a cart's tail for selling provisions to the British and for the wounding of a sergeant when arrested. Abraham Toller, for selling farm produce to the British army, to be stripped of his remaining produce, the same to be turned over to the quartermaster's department. Samuel Jelliffe, who was sentenced to be hanged for espionage, to be reprieved, and returned to the officers' prison, in consideration of his having turned over to the commander of his regiment papers and documents of inestimable value, and made a full and free confession, accompanied by acts of contrition and promises of amendment.

52

I'd like to add to that, to my simple thinking
the only way to deal with a spy's to hang him,
not the second time, but the first.

Washington. I gave him my word,
and he kept his to me.

Tench. It's decided further
that Generals Stirling and Lafayette will lead
the raid on Howe's hay islands.

Washington. Let it be understood
that I leave the conduct of this expedition
in your hands who lead it, but only say once more
bring in what you can. What life's left in this camp
we live on hope of salvage. That was all?

Tench. That's all. Unless you've a minute to squander on
the puke-faced boy you saw in the entrance—

Washington. Who?

Tench. Damned if I know his name. I've booted him
some five or six times, but he's back again to-day
asking to see you. I'll pack him out if you like
but the poor calf had such a bleak look about him
I let him sit there this time.

Washington. Let him come in.

> [TENCH *goes out to the hall and a door is heard. He reenters
> with* NEIL BONNIWELL]

Tench. Spit it out and be terse about it. We've got
no time for a history.

Washington. Why are you here, sir?

Neil. Why,

I'll say it brief as I can. I've been in the army
nearly three years, sir. I joined it for three years,
and my time's nearly up.—I don't quite know how
to say what I came to say. The truth is, I'm dying.
They tell me it's ague, something wrong with my
    stomach
the doctors tell me; but I had two brothers die
just the same way. I've taken a consumption
and I'm near the end of it.

Washington. Colonel Tench will arrange
to send you home at once. I'm glad you came,
and sorry not to have seen you before.

Neil. Why, thank you,
but that's not what I wanted.

Washington. I'm afraid that's all
we have to offer.

Neil. It's harder than hell to say
what it is I wanted. I don't want to die.
Nobody wants to die—not young. But I will
whether I go or stay here. There are certain things
men have in this world, and I'll never have them. Damn
    it—
let me die for something! I've believed in this war
we're fighting—and you, I've believed in you! A man
doesn't like to go out forever and not one blow
struck for—it sounds like bluster—and that's what it
    is—
but one chance is all I can ever have—that's all
I could be remembered for—

Washington. I very much fear
   you're not fit for service—

Tench. Come on—if I'd had any notion
   what this was about—

Neil. Yes, death's a long way from you!
   You're alive—God, you're almost so much alive
   you can think you're immortal—but let me be on a field
   with a gun in my hands, and die there, not die retching
   my lungs and brains out!

Tench. There's no time for this.

Washington. One moment—

Neil. Will you try to see it, sir? A lot of men
   have died, and I'm only one, but we're dead a long time
   and we came to fight for something, my brothers and I—
   It was you we believed in!

Washington. We'll do what we can—
   You'll be looked after.

Neil. That's—all—?

Washington. That's all I can promise.
   Good night—and give me your hand.

Neil. Yes, sir. Good-night.
      [*He goes out with* Tench, *who returns at once*]

Washington. You have his name?

Tench. Yes.
      [*A pause*]

Washington. It's not accident,
   as you may have thought, that you four are here to-night.
   There's a question I ask myself so often now
   I must ask it of someone else. The reports before us
   show us we've neither food nor clothes nor arms
   for the maintenance of an army, nor defense
   if we're attacked. In my last letter to Congress
   I told them we must either starve or dissolve
   unless they sent instant aid. I've written before
   almost as urgently, receiving replies—
   friendly, cajoling, evasive, full of advice,
   mostly unworkable, and a thin stream of goods,
   sufficient, say, for half a regiment,
   and we've foraged for the rest. They're sending to-
      morrow
   two commissioners to investigate; by the time
   we've satisfied these stool-wits that we're dying
   the men who have gumption left to arise and walk
   will have walked away, and we'll muster nobody here
   but the sick and naked. It's begun already.
   Great bands of marauders shift away from camp
   and range the country like brigands. Some thousand or
      two
   have put out for home; it's reckoned another thousand
   have crossed the lines to Howe. One-third of our soldiers,
   and those the most able-bodied, have gone—the re-
      mainder—
   how they hold out, or why, I don't know.—We can't
      blame them
   if they follow their fellows.—Now when our army's gone,

as it seems to be going, Sir William Howe, who's waited
for just this chance, will stroll out in his fat-haunched way
to round us in and we're done for. My question's simply:
Does this end the adventure? Is the revolution over,
or is it worth trying to hold on into spring
when at least there's food to be had?—It will cost lives,
by hundreds, perhaps by thousands.—What it means to me
to say this, I think you know.—I ask General Varnum,
as first in rank, to speak first.

Varnum. Sir, I'm a soldier. If I were in command
of the Continental army, I'd say now
we can't go on. But I'm not in command.
I'm a soldier, and I take orders. And what I say
as a soldier, one who takes orders, is, now God help you,
you who bear this burden, to find some way
to command though we feed on dust and carrion,
and wear no pelts but our own, that we stick it out.—
What orders you give
may there be men left to follow!

Washington. And you, General Stirling?

Stirling. I'll string along with Varnum.
It's not on my conscience, I know, and it is on yours
if men die in a dead cause. As a way to die
it's early and unpleasant, and may come to nothing,
but I think you underestimate the number
who'll see it through with you, if you give the word,
till we've eaten the wolves extinct.

Washington. Enough, you think,
to hold the English till spring?

Stirling. No!
　　there would be enough—
　　now here I take up a sore subject, and one perhaps
　　there's no place for in this conference—but there'd be
　　　　enough
　　and then to spare, if those moth-eaten drones
　　who've served abroad, and spread their dog-eared com-
　　　　missions
　　in every company, to prove they've been in a war—
　　if they were dumped in the Schuylkill through the ice
　　till they'd mixed their brandy with water.
Washington. Let's stay with our subject.
　　There are many with us who served in England and
　　　　France,
　　and in Germany, too, before this war. There are some
　　of irreplaceable value—
Stirling. And some, by God,
　　who'd sell the cannon out of Valley Forge
　　for three Spanish dollars, paper! They'd sell you out
　　to Gates, or Lee, or any mother's son
　　who'd raise their rank by half-a-crown a year—
　　and stain their good right hands to the bone with ink—
　　not with blood, mind you—writing their peaching letters
　　to put you out, and Gates in! What disaffection
　　there is, they've started most of it!
Washington. Well, we have
　　no evidence of it, and this was not the theme
　　we met here to discuss—
Stirling. No evidence!
　　Take out some time for this: Three nights ago

I was drunk with a certain American general
who serves here in this valley. He was drunk, too,
and he boasted to me he'd written to General Gates
and to members of Congress, that in his ripest judgment
this war was lost unless you, Washington,
were superseded!

Tench. Who was this?

Stirling. Who? Why, Conway. He's a dirty traitor,
and there are plenty like him!

Varnum. That's talk in his cups—

Stirling. You think so?
It sobered me fast enough!

Washington. When you find such a letter
it will be time enough—

Stirling. Why, so I thought
when I was sober—and so thinking I saddled a horse
and rode me sixty miles till I caught the post
that carried that letter, and took it from him, and have it,
and there, with your leave, it is!
   [*He tosses the letter down*]

Washington. What does it say?

Stirling. What he boasted of, and more.

Washington. I shall see Conway.

Tench. And while you're about it see a Lieutenant Cutting
who runs his errands for him, and let me witness
what he said to me of the same.

Washington. We can take both later.
　　At the moment, who shall be head of this phantom army
　　is a question almost academic. I've asked
　　another question of you, and on your answers
　　it depends, largely, whether there is an army—
　　or will be one to-morrow, for Gates to covet
　　or me to say good-bye to. In a republic
　　treason is not exactly what it seems
　　under a king. There are rights of opinion here.
　　Friend Gates has been winning victories of late,
　　and it may be he'd be better.

Tench. Now if you meant that—

Washington. I don't, as it happens! This Conway's three-
　　quarters snake
　　and you'll see him squirm on a griddle!

Tench. Thank God for that.
　　A man can be over-patient.

Washington. I've asked your counsel
　　on another point, sir, not that.

Tench. And you want it now?

Washington. We're ready for it now.

Tench. Then I'd see the Congress
　　damned in hell, before I'd let them ruin
　　our campaign for us! Who is it sits at York
　　doling supplies out? A pack of puling grimsirs
　　with one testicle among them to keep their wives
　　in order and run the state! A school of prissies
　　thwarting the war and cadging on the side

to fur their gowns! This country'd come to you
with open arms if you said to them once for all:
I'll take just this and that, and I'll take it now
when it's needed! One word, one breath from you and
    you'd blow
the Congress from here to Maine!

Washington. A dictator?

Tench. Why,
are you so afraid of words? It's that or lose.

Washington. Has it escaped you, sir, that we fight this war
against usurpation of power? Should I usurp
the powers of Congress, which gave me what power I
    have,
I'd have nothing left to fight for.

Tench. I beg your pardon!
We're in rebellion against the king of England,
or so I thought.

Washington. It happens that our Congress
is the heart of what we fight for, good or bad,
and I uphold it. Now, keeping that in mind,
is it possible to go on?

Tench. No, it is not.
Last night there was mutiny in the Eighteenth; they
    objected
to their food, and little blame to them. The riot
was quelled only by scouring out the larders
of neighboring battalions. This will happen again
and spread. There's no holding men to discipline

when there's bread in the country, and boots, and bales
    of clothing
waiting for shipment, and nothing but plain damned
    fools,
sitting in legislature, withholds them! Who gives
a simple curse for Congress, or theories,
when his guts are rotted out with rotten food
and his toes fall off from freezing? I tell you now
a man would fight as hard for the porpoise turds
that float the Chesapeake, full of hot air, and with reason
quite as good, as for these fastidious wind-bags
that make our laws in session, and draw their pay,
and leave us to die here. I'm not a pious man;
I'm a soldier, as Varnum says he is, and a soldier's busi-
    ness
is to fight when he has to, run away when he can,
eat if he can get it, drink as much as there is,
and stay alive. I'll fight for the man I believe in,
but if I'm to fight to make Congress permanent
they can take their revolution and stick it back
in the bung it came from!

Washington. That's plainly said.

Tench. If it's too plain I'm sorry.

Stirling. Well, but pause a moment,
    my gentle Lucifer; there's treason enough
    without our adding to it.

Tench. If I speak treason,
    hell, make the most of it! The whole damned war
    is treason to King George! It all depends
    on the point of view, and whether you win!

Varnum. But still
    this war's for liberty; and the government
    we've set up freely for ourselves, we're here
    to defend it—for nothing else.

Tench. Well, when it comes
    to governments you'll have to let me out.
    They're all alike, and have one business, governments,
    and it's to plunder. This new one we've set up
    seems to be less efficient than the old style
    in its methods of plundering folk, but give them time;
    they'll learn to sink their teeth in what you've got
    and take it from you. To hell with the cause! I'll fight
    while I'm fed and paid, and I haven't seen much lately
    of either one.

Washington. This is new.

Tench. I've read your letters
    to Congress, and read their replies, and they've sickened
      me
    of our war for freedom!

Washington. Marquis?

Lafayette. I'm loath to speak,
    gentlemen, in this conference. I shall offend,
    I know, being but a young man, alien,
    the scion of an old kingdom, ancien régime
    in word and manner.

Washington. The more reason we should hear you.

Stirling. Let's have it, lad.

Lafayette. Shall I begin by saying
  something you know, but may have forgotten? This world
you have cut from a wilderness, is a new world, brighter
with sun in summer, colder with winter cold
than the world I knew. The air's strange-sharp, the voice
rings here with a hard ring. I find no man
but looks you in the eye and says his thought
in your teeth, and means it. This was not known before
on this star we inhabit. Europe has thirty kings
and a hundred million slaves. But here in this land
each man's a king, and walks like a king, each woman
bears herself regally, like a queen. You will find
this is not easy to throw away. The air
of this coast has fired your blood, and while three among you,
no more than three, hold hard against the old masters,
the kingdoms lessen and dwindle. They've felt your breath
and feared it, in the old world. Lose! Now the gods
in heaven hear me, you cannot lose! Bow down
and humble yourselves if you can! It's not in you to bow
nor to speak humbly. It's a trick you've never learned
and cannot learn in this air!—As for these thrones
that men have bowed to, I've come from them lately, and seen them,
how they're eaten down with old vices and slimed with worms
till they crumble into the moats! Lower your muzzles,
droop your flags! Even so the kingdoms falter
and go down of themselves!

Tench. And a very pleasant thought, too.

Lafayette. You must forgive me.
I have an unfortunate eloquence which betrays me
When I launch on this theme.

Tench. No, no—I meant that comment.

Lafayette. I shall curb it if I can, however, and save you
from the longeurs. But two facts I must state
before I end. The name of Washington
is magical in France. It conjures up
all we have hoped to dare, all our young men
have deemed worth dying for. France inherits a king,
a little king, shall I say, a Louis parvus,
to distinguish from Louis le Grand? And he views your
rebels
as the legendary bishop viewed the rats
who came to eat him. He would see your heads
in ten thousand wicker baskets, a dozen to each
and sold for cabbages. But I have a friend
named Beaumarchais, who guides the realm for the
moment,
looks on you as I do, has a deft hand
to manoeuvre policies. He has set himself
to send you men, money, ships. The little king
may scream, and cling to his velvet furniture
and stamp on his powdered wig, still he's dragged along
with Beaumarchais, and before the end of spring
you will have these men, money and ships.

Stirling. The end of spring.

Lafayette. You cannot wait. I know it. Not possibly.

Yet if you knew what dreams and faith rest on you
you would do this impossible. I'm a young noble, rich,
spoiled, and perhaps not wise. I'm twenty years old,
and I left a child wife in France whom I love. I came
because the best life in all this world lives here
in what *you* have to do. It's true that your Congress
has tied your hands with silly errors, true
that foreign captains, enlisted with your arms,
grumble at native generalship and slight
your leaders for advancement, true that the lives,
lost, and to be lost, may seem lost for nothing,
for a false dawn, a chimera; still, soberly,
in fact—in all soberness—not since Prometheus
drew the gods' fires in heaven and left them cold
to bring fire down to men, there's been no action
better worth risk of stapling to the rocks
with vultures at your liver, than your defiance
of Hanoverian kings! There—I've slipped again
into rhapsody—and again you must forgive me
since I meant each word.

Washington. You're quite forgiven.

Varnum. Yes, but the question's not what we want to do
but what we can.

Washington. What's on hand?

Tench. We might scratch up
by equalizing, three or four days' provision
for every corps.

Washington. Three days!
As for our high purpose,

we have it still, but the men, the men are mortal
and die around us so fast the heaviest work's
to bury the dead. Our slopes are honeycombed
with digging graves. The wards are crammed with sick
lying on logs without blankets. No medicine,
no food, no care; the farms around us swept
board-clean of grain this thirty miles. It's the men;
the men are human. They chop green wood for fires,
and shiver over them, stand their watch by night,
and drill by day, go to sleep supperless
and watch each other sicken. A stench goes up,
but whether it's from the living, dying or dead
it's too late to care. The lines of war we keep,
one middling wind would blow them with the leaves
and heap them in the gullies. Gentlemen,
looking back over what you've offered—each one of you
has said in his own way—even Lafayette—
there's no immediate hope.—And since I agree
that this is true—we should make our preparations
to break up camp and give over. We should—and yet—
since it's begun
and we're in it deep, while we have men and arms
and a government behind us and a gambler's stake
in what's to happen, we must still stand here
and take things as they come.

Lafayette. This is the man
we heard of overseas!

Washington. If you heard of a martyr
I fear I'll disappoint you. I'd rather live
and have my fun in my time, before my face hardens

into a mountain crag. I have no taste
for being stood into a hero: St. George and the dragon,
one foot on tyranny's neck, a long spontoon
glittering in my gripe! What's the king to me?
A customer for tobacco. But we have three days.
And the order's given. We gamble our three days
on a change of luck and face what brand of hell's
reserved for madmen.

    [*The officers rise*]

Tench. Our usual brand of hell,
only more of it.

Varnum. It will come to complete disaster,
very likely.

Stirling. And yet, if you'd said "We quit, to-night,"
I'd have walked to the other side of the glen
and blown my brains out.

Tench. You'd have taken a drink
and then another, and said, "All right, we quit."
And so would I.

Washington. All commanders
meet here at five in the morning.

Stirling. At five? The night's
half-shot already.

Washington. At five.

Tench. Drink one less bottle
and you'll come out plumb at five. Good-night.

Washington. Good-night, sir.

Varnum. Sleep well, and my thanks
    for taking it on yourself.

Washington. You'd have done the same.

Varnum. Not I.

Stirling. You might have, Varnum. The holder of power
    develops a conscience.
        [*He takes* WASHINGTON'S *hand*]
    If I'm drunk to-morrow, drop me.
    I'm your man.

Washington. Thanks, Stirling. Good-night.
Stirling. Good-night.
        [STIRLING, VARNUM *and* TENCH *go out*]

Washington. If I was short with you when you meant to
    praise me
    I hope to be forgiven, Marquis. This war
    is a democratic war, and one man's name—
    You see?

Lafayette. I understood, and I'll forgive you
    whatever you wish to say. Sometimes I feel
    I'm a difficult guest.

Washington. If I'd said what I meant
    I'd have told you how much you've upheld my hands
    when I was close to faltering. When a leader
    loses one battle he senses how his world
    begins to slide away from him. I've lost
    too many since winning one. We're more than a year
    from Trenton and Princeton; I've lost at Brandywine
    and Germantown since—and on the whole it's better

not to assume too much in company—
not on the record.

Lafayette. Well, to yourself I tell you
if France sends help, it's to you. No other name
counts much with us; and, to my understanding,
in a world that catches rumors while it whirls,
there's surprising justice in it.

Washington. Oh, I'm not humble.
I stand well in my own opinion. Still,
at the moment I'd trade, say, half-a-bucketful
of fame for a sound bucolic year of farming
with a good sleep thrown in.

Lafayette. It's past tattoo
even now, some four or five hours. I won't keep you.

Washington. No—
sleep's not a thing that comes on order. I'd rather
sit here and talk than lie awake. But you,
you'll need your rest if you leave at three in the morning,
for Howe's hay islands.

Lafayette. Bah! I shall not lie down!
It's not worth the undressing.

Washington. True. At nothing-and-twenty
all night means nothing.—There was something you said
that moved me strangely. You left a young wife in
France.
Does she mean so little to you?

Lafayette. Little? My friend,
if all the argosies of Spain blew toward me

and left me all treasure they've carried through all time
and took her away, they'd leave me beggared.

Washington. And yet,
loving her so, you left her?

Lafayette. It's a poor love
that belittles whom it loves, or would hold him back
from what's best and highest. If I wished to come
she would have me come.

Washington. You'll find few like her.

Lafayette. None.
None, I should think. And yet for every man
this should come once. Such a love. You must have known
what such a love could be.

Washington. No. Once perhaps.

Lafayette. It comes but once.

Washington. There was a girl one time—
when I was twenty-three—I might have loved so,
and might have loved me so. It's long ago.
It came out otherwise. A man begins
to lose his teeth and fear his eyes go bad
at forty-five—and wishes—well, it's trash.
Let it go with the rest.—Your fortune in a wife
has been our good fortune. You fall across our night
like a young star, all flame. Let's hope you're destined
to avoid our quenching.

Lafayette. Sir, the sun's quenched in ocean
and rises in the morning. I gauge my life
it will be so with you.

Washington. I'll rise in the morning,
    if that's what you mean.—Let's part no less good friends
    for an exchange of courtesies.

    [*They clasp hands.* TENCH *enters*]

Tench. Damn these females!

Washington. Yes, Lucifer?

Tench. There's an officer left over
    in the exchange of prisoners. A British major,
    or wears that uniform, but it's plain to see
    there's a woman inside.

Washington. It would seem hardly a problem
    for my attention.

Tench. The lady's on our hands.
    The escort's gone, and she asks to see Washington
    with a verbal message from Howe.

Washington. She carries no papers?

Tench. None. Not a scrap. But I must say she looks the
    lady.
    There's been money spent on her breeding.

Washington. Well—let her in
    if she comes from Howe.

    [*Tench goes out*]

Lafayette. I'll take myself away.

Washington. Stay, stay, you may help
    to end the interview.

    [TENCH *returns and stands at the door.* MARY PHILIPSE,
        dressed in a scarlet uniform, comes to the doorway, and
        pauses]

Come in. Come in.

[TENCH *goes out*]

Mary.

[*Advancing*]

You see before you, sir, one you've long forgotten,
but who's not forgotten you. I bring you a greeting
from Sir William Howe. The man who brought his dog
stayed for no message; it fell on me to return you
the General's kindest thanks.

Washington. I thank you, madame.
The General was welcome to his dog.

Mary. Such as it was?

Washington. It's not a breed I fancy.
I should remember you?

Mary. Oh, time long past
you swore not to forget; but love's time's drudge
and works but by the day.

[*A pause*]

Washington. Yes, I remember.

Lafayette. You'll pardon me. Good-night—

Mary. I drive you away!

Lafayette. No—I was going.

Washington. Wait—
I believe we had more to say—

Lafayette. I shall need my time,
if I may be excused.

[*He bows*, WASHINGTON *acknowledging the salute half-humorously.* LAFAYETTE *goes out*]

Washington. Yes I remember.
They say if one waits long enough all things
come round the circle.

Mary. I've heard so—and I waited,
then suddenly, it seemed too long to wait.
We grow old, we mortals.

Washington. At the risk of being
ungallant, may I ask why you're here? For truly
the dog will hardly serve.

Mary. I came to see you.

Washington. And this costume?

Mary. It's not becoming?

Washington. As to that—
it's worn by my enemies.

Mary. A woman's stratagem.
Is a woman never
to follow her heart, and run after him she loves
though she run back twenty years? You read no novels—
always the practical man—I can see it. This
    [*Indicating her uniform*]
is love's disguise. It passed me handily
in the exchange of prisoners.

Washington. Then you dealt with blind men
at either end.

Mary. Oh, a little pocket money.

properly placed, brings on astigmatism
or incipient cataract.

Washington. I'm afraid you mistake me.
A war's not quite a game of blind man's bluff,
nor am I a figure in grand opera
with love affairs between battles. It goes grimly
with me and mine. And, though it's true you meant
more than a heartbreak to me in my twenties,
still what treasure may lie there lies too deep
for dredging—nor have I heart nor hours nor patience
for nice romancing. I understand there's time
in plenty for all this in the camp you've left,
and wonder at your leaving.

Mary. There—I expected
just this rebuff, and have my answer ready.
In all these years, these twenty, there's been nothing
to feed a heart, save ashes. See, this is true—
I'll swear it. I'm not light, nor given to lightness—
nor have I come here lightly. The one thing worth having
in a brief life, I have still to seek. It was mine
once, for the taking. It came at your offering
and I tossed it away, believing like all young fools
it grew on every bush. I'm not young now
and I'd risk whatever name the world might give me
to have it back again.

Washington. You come from Howe.

Mary. I would have caught at any junketing
that brought me here. I came on chance. I ask
for nothing. But I'm here.

Washington. I shall seem ungracious.
  You married Captain Morris, and I am married.
  We're fixed in our two worlds. The time's run out
  for pleasantries. It's winter in my bones
  as well as in the year.
    [TEAGUE *enters with two bags, sets them down and goes out*]
  This is your baggage?

Mary. I'm afraid it is.

Washington. This will be somewhat awkward.

Mary. Will it?

Washington. We'll find you lodging at the inn.

Mary. I tried the inn. It was full of soldiers—and smelled
  rather unwashed.

Washington. No doubt.

Mary. But if I'm unwelcome
  let me find my own lodging.

Washington. There's none to find—
  nearer than Philadelphia.—You can stay here.
  Hamilton's room is empty.

Mary. I thank you, sir.

Washington. It will cause some conversation.—Nothing, I
    hope,
  that can't be weathered.

Mary. What a woman's name
  will bear, a man's should be equal to.

Washington. The sentry
  will show you to your room.
    [*He turns to the door*]

Mary. Sir, I do bring
a word from General Howe. He wishes to see you—
his proposal is general amnesty
with no surrender on either part—the Congress
to receive all it's petitioned for, nothing
reserved, save the king's sovereignty.

Washington. When you see him
tell him we intend to fight while we can. We've asked
complete independence. .

Mary. And still have hopes of it?

Washington. We still have hopes.

Mary. I can say to you truly
there's no hope for you on the other side. If I
have come unasked, and unwelcome, still it can't be said
I go with the wind. We have news to-day from Paris
of the French alliance. This is your losing year!
I was willing to lose with you.

Washington. And your news?
The French will have none of us? Is that your message?

Mary. So the story runs.

Washington. And so I feared. We must take it
in our stride, if we can. I thank you. No doubt I've been
abrupt beyond all warrant.—Forgive it. I carry
a good many burdens.

Mary. I think no less of you.
I'm sorry for us both.

Washington. To be quite frank
you lose no lover in me. I'm old and cold

and given over to soldiering. What love
I have is given.

Mary. Sir, would you teach a woman
the art she's skilled in? I read you by your face
and know how deep you've buried what you dreamed
under your soldiering.
A young man has excess of appetite
and eats at every table. When we're older
the body fires less easily. It waits
permission of the mind and memory,
and these come seldom. Young love we've never had
burns underneath and gnaws the upper ground
ready to flame at a breath. For you and me
we must love one another now, or grow old coldly
and make an end to love.

Washington. It may be so.

Mary. And now, if you'll call the soldier.

Washington. Yes.
    [*He goes to the door*]
Sentry, this lady will occupy Hamilton's room.
    [TEAGUE *comes in for the bags*]

Mary. And good-night.

Washington. Good-night.
    [MARY *goes out.* TEAGUE, *taking up the bags, gives one speak-
ing look at* WASHINGTON's *back and departs, shaking
his head*]

CURTAIN

VALLEY FORGE
ACT TWO

ACT TWO

SCENE ONE

SCENE: *The bunk-house early the next morning. A little light glows from the dying fire in the fireplace. Two or three of the men have risen, but most of them are either trying to keep warm in their frost-nipped bunks or lying like piles of rags as near as they can creep to the fire.*

ALCOCK, TEAGUE and SPAD are absent. JOCK is sitting on the edge of a bunk carefully wrapping his legs with burlap and string. MASON BONNIWELL is kneeling in an upper bunk trying to fill a chink with strips which he tears from the skirt of his coat. ANDREW is washing his face in the basin.

Jock.

[*To* MASON]

Now you're getting it. That's where the whole outdoors came in.

Andrew. The wind was roaring through that east wall all night, like the North Sea down from Rooshia.

Jock. Are ye washing in yesterday's water, ye swine?

Andrew. The bucket's froze solid to the bottom. Not a loose drop in it.

Mason. Give Nick a tap on the feet, will you, Andrew? He's due to relieve Alcock at guard.

Andrew.

[*Looking at the men by the fire*]

There's a heap of feet here, but dommed if I know which from which.

[*He kicks somebody's soles*]

Hi!

Oscar.

> [*Stirring*]

> Ja, ja!

Andrew. Lie still, Scardihoovian. It's Nick's wanted.

Oscar. Mind who you boot then.

> [*He settles back*]

Andrew. How am I to tell fore from aft when you bivouac like a nest of tent-worms?

Nick.

> [*Sitting up*]

> I don't mind you walking on my face, Scotty, only keep moving. Don't stand on it.

Andrew. Your face?

Nick. Yes, that was my face that sort of gave under you when you ground a couple of my back teeth out. Never mind, they'll probably grow in again. Think nothing of it.

Mason. The north side's pointed up with sleet or we'd have a three-foot drift on the hearth.

Nick.

> [*Getting to his feet*]

> Somebody's put gumwood on that fire again, too, and it'll begin to give off heat about the middle of April.

> [*He goes to the fire to rearrange it*]

Mason. We're out of pine, Nick. I lugged that over from Poor's private supply.

> [TEAGUE *enters*]

Marty.
> [*Still half-asleep*]
Shut the door!

Teague.
> [*Stopping in the act of closing the door and leaving it half-open*]
Shut it yourself, and get a whiff of what it's like outside.
> [*He goes to the fire*]

Jock. Shut that door!

Teague. I was about to shut it, but not now.

Mason.
> [*Jumping down to close the door*]
You two noble intellects'd freeze the brainpans right off each other. Only you wouldn't give in.

Teague. Better get over there, son. Alcock's hoofin' it right after me.

Nick. Any breakfast dished out so far?

Teague. I've got a dram of rum left. You'll need it up against that west wall.
> [*He hands over a bottle, which* NICK *pockets*]
You can't soldier around when you're on duty at head-quarters, you know. You have to be there.

Nick. I doubt anybody wants to steal a couple of generals out of bed at this hour in the morning.

Teague. There's a woman there, this time, and you can't tell what might happen.

Mason. How do you mean, a woman?

Teague. What do you usually mean by a woman? Well that's what I mean. Howe sent back a bitch in exchange for his dog.

Nick. A lady at headquarters?

Teague. No, she's no lady. Anyway, if she is I lost a shilling piece on her.

Andrew. How could you lose a shilling? You'd have to find it first.

Teague. I ain't lost it yet.

[Alcock *enters*]

Alcock. Well, boy.

Teague. Well?

Alcock. You'll have to untie that Geordie from around your neck and pay up, Seminole. She slept alone.

Teague. Prove it first, prove it first!

Alcock. Wasn't that her window I set the ladder to?

Teague. Sure it was.

Alcock. Well, I looked in that window—and a charming sight it was, too—only I tell you she slept alone.

Teague. That's your opinion.

Alcock. Opinion? Seminole, a man don't live to be as old as I am without being able to tell at a glance whether there's one or two under a log-cabin quilt. More than that, the lady's scarlet breeches were draped over a chair within reach of my hand—but no others to keep company with 'em—and to judge by what little I saw of her she's not the kind an officer and gentleman would get up and leave before time for morning services.

Jock. What's that about scarlet breeches?

Alcock. She came in a uniform, I tell you—

Mason. What's the bet?

Alcock. Teague, there, bet me a hard shilling General Washington spent the night in the lady's room, and I bet him a hard shilling he spent the night under his own little dormer—and now he's turning Welshman on me—

Minto.
   [*Shivering*]
If anybody slept alone last night he froze to death.

Teague. All I said was, prove it. Maybe I don't know about women, and maybe I can't count through the bed-clothes like some, but when a woman goes brigadiering around the country at night I've got a good idea what she's looking for—

Alcock. Many a woman's looked for it where it wasn't to be had—

Teague. And how do I know what you saw through the window? I don't say you'd lie about it, but, after all, you can't expect a man to pin himself down to facts when there's real money involved—

Alcock. Look for yourself, then—you can climb a ladder—

Nick. Suppose I take a look—I'm going over there, any way.
   [*He goes to the door*]
Only you lost your silver, pappy. Do you think the Gen

eral's a studhorse, covering every mare that jumps his paddock?

[*He goes out. The men have begun to pull themselves together for another day—a process which can hardly be called dressing, since no clothes have been removed*]

Jock. Any orders o' the day?

Mason. Cutting spent the night over at Conway's.

Teague. Cutting's going up on the carpet this morning—and Conway too.

Mason. Up before Washington?

Teague. That's right.

Mason. What for?

Teague. Too much talk, I'd say. I just happened to hear something, going through.

Alcock. In that case this outfit's footloose and fancy-free—and got no more officer than a rabbit.

Mason. Must be some arrangements going on about breakfast somewhere.

Andrew. Not unless Cutting saw to it.

Jock. Why would he see to it? He's fixed for breakfast.

Minto. If it's like the last we had I don't want any breakfast.

Oscar. No, nor me, too.

Jock. Go to sleep, Sweden.

Mason. He who sleeps dines, as they say in France.

Marty. When you can't eat, you sleep.

[*He grins*]

Andrew. Hear that? That's right, moony, you hit it.

Marty. That's right.

Teague. Yeah, and I've heard tell if you don't eat at all over a period of time you sleep forever. I feel it kind of coming over me, and I don't look forward to it.

Alcock. Any cottontail left on Mount Misery?

Mason. Ask Teague.

Teague. Nary one.

Andrew. There's three dead mules floated down the crick yesterday and went aground below the chapel. May be a leetle high by this time.

[*The news is interesting*]

Mason. Thanks.

Alcock. They're gone. A couple of Deutschers been making sausage all night.

Mason. Well, that dashes my hopes.

[*He rises and walks over to* NEIL *who lies quiet, looking at the ceiling*]

How's tricks?

Neil. Good enough.

[MASON *turns toward the fire*]

Alcock.

[*Sings*]

Oh, I'm the son of a unicorn,

I graze the sky, I drink the air,

And many a filly I leave forlorn,
 I leave forlorn,
 In the race of a comet's hair.

[The door opens and Spad *enters, his pockets bulging. The men turn towards him]*

Hiyo!—Here's one bastard that's well fed, anyway.—

Teague. Bit late, ain't you, Spad?

Alcock. The fact is we thought you'd foundered yourself to death on kidney pie—and you can imagine how hard that hit us.

Spad. Gentlemen!

Mason. We look it.

Alcock. Have a good dinner?

Spad. Gentlemen, I had the pleasure of turning down General Howe's dinner—turning it down to his face—

Teague. You saw Howe?

Spad. I did. And his women. And his soldiers. Boys, we can lick him. We can lick him for sour apples. I knocked one of 'em down in his own ballroom! That bunch of wild flowers!

Andrew. You turned down a dinner?

Spad. Oh, I ate—but not with those namby-pambies. Do you know what they are—those—any women present?

[He looks around]

They're hermaphroids, they are. Why, damn it, they're nothing but musicians!

[He pulls some yellow ears of corn out of his pocket, and lays them on the table]

Teague. What the hell?

Spad. There's more where that came from. About six thousand bushels, if I'm any judge. Bust it up and make yourselves a bowl of samp. I had plenty.

[*A few gather round to finger the maize lovingly*]

Help yourselves. It can be chawed. Shell it and parch it by the fire and it makes a damn good imitation of something to eat.

[*The men begin to shell and chew the grains*]

Alcock. Present from General Howe?

Spad. Yes. Only he ain't aware of it. You see, I got pushed off my course by the sentries, and before I knew it I was down around Mud Island—right where they meant to send us. So I lifted somebody's dinghy and got chased by a patrol and had to land in the middle of that God-forsaken slob-land—all to hell and gone. They've got enough hay stacked there to feed through seven lean years and bed down all King Solomon's wives and children. I clawed through that mess like a polar bear for a day and a half, and down at the end of the island I came out on about a dozen corn-cribs full of corn with three soldiers on guard. One of 'em's dead now and two still tied up if I'm any good with a rope. I guess I must have surprised 'em some. My face was dirty at the time. They ain't used to that.

Teague. Where is this?

Spad. That's it. We're going there.

Jock. We're going where?

Spad. We're going over to get that corn. The English—they don't even know it's good to eat. They call it maize and they're saving it for horse-feed. Where's the leftenant?

Teague. We don't seem to have any leftenant any more.

Spad. Fine.

Alcock. You're crazy. We've got no boats and the river's full of ice.

Spad. The current's took all the ice out of the lower end of the island, and there's three old bumboats frozen in at Print's Landing. We can get 'em out, and we can ferry that corn. I tell you there's nobody watching it!

Mason. We ought to report it first.

Spad. Report it and that's the last you hear of it. You're a corporal, Mason. You say go and we'll go.

Mason. A corporal's got no right to order a party out.—I'll go with you, though.

Spad. That's the talk.

Teague. Hell, we'll all go.

> [*The men begin to pick up accoutrements. Each man takes an ear of corn*]

Spad. Only it's devilish cold on the river, I warn you. You'll need more on than a nightshirt.

Alcock. You looking at me?

Spad. I certainly am. You'll freeze off everything you're famous for if you start in that rig.

Alcock. I've stood duty in this.

Spad. Don't try it, old man, don't try it. I'm out of powder. Who's got a full horn?

Andrew. Oh, oh—lay off my stuff—

Minto. I'll divvy with you.

Spad. Somebody take Marty's coat—he don't need to come—

Jock. That's right.

Marty.
[*Shrieking*]

You will not take my coat! You will not take it! I'll claw your eyes out if you touch my coat!

Mason. Let his coat alone.
[ALCOCK, *who has been standing silent, slips out the door.* NEIL *raises himself to watch the preparations*]

Oscar. Ja, but how about der picket lines?

Spad. I'll talk to the pickets. Maybe we'll take a couple along.

Andrew. You going to need your coat, Neil?

Mason. He'll need it to keep warm, won't he? Take it easy, boy, and we'll raid a barnyard for you.

Neil. I'll be all right.

Mason. Tavis'll be over later.
[TEAGUE, *the first man ready, is about to open the door when* CUTTING *walks in*]

Cutting. Morning.

Teague. Morning, sir.

Cutting. What's going on?

Spad. Getting ready for roll call, sir.

Cutting. Looks to me like an unwonted stir of activity for
this hour. Where's Alcock?

Mason. He was here a minute ago.

Cutting. Find him and report on parade ground in half-an-
hour with two squads of the ablest men for morning
drill.

Mason. There's no breakfast issued yet, sir.

Cutting. We're on short rations, and most of the regiment's
going without breakfast this morning.
   [*He turns to the door*]

Mason. I'm sorry, but I'm afraid I can't take the responsibility, Lieutenant.

Cutting. You can't?

Mason. No, sir.

Cutting. And why not?

Mason. I don't know whether they'd follow me.

Cutting. What's in the wind here?
   [*A silence*]
   I want to serve notice about one thing. There's no two
ways to run an army. I'll have absolute obedience or
I'll see a few of you underground.—I think I understand

this early rising. There's been a good deal of desertion the last few days. Personally I don't give a damn whether you desert or not, but officially I do. I'm going to keep my military record clean, and while I'm an officer here I'll put a bullet through anybody that attempts to leave camp without permission. Put down your guns.

[*The men begin to lay down their arms.* CUTTING *has a hand on his pistol butt*]

And just to make certain I'll go with you to drill when the time comes. Mason, I ask you again what was going on here?

Mason. We were stepping out for breakfast, that's all.

Cutting. I thought so. Well, sit down and take it easy. Nobody's stepping out anywhere.

Teague.

[*Lifting his rifle and drawing a bead on* CUTTING'S *back*]

Don't do anything sudden, Mister Cutting, because I'm a nervous man, and liable to spasms in my trigger finger.

[CUTTING *turns toward him*]

If you draw that pistol I'll put a slug through your pump, and I never missed yet with this here iron.

Cutting. Put down that gun.

Teague. Not me. Back over against that wall. Step. Take your hand off that butt.

[CUTTING *moves slowly back to the wall*]

Take that pea shooter away from him.

[SPAD *disarms* CUTTING]

Cutting. They'll stretch your necks for this, you know—
and I'll have the watching of it.

Teague. Don't say things like that, because I never did like
you, and I feel one of my spasms coming on. What shall
I do with him, Corporal?

Mason. Tie him up.

Spad. Right-o.

Cutting. You'll not tie me with your damn dowlas rags!

Spad. Jock!

[JOCK *and* SPAD *leap on* CUTTING *and pinion him.* OSCAR *and*
ANDREW *bring a mass of leg-wrappings to bind his
arms and knees. The others come round to help*]

Cutting. I'll see you all lashed to shreds, you scabby
hounds!

Spad. You won't see us again, you nor none of you! We're
through with your damn camp and your orders! Catch
us if you can!

Cutting. And I will!

[NICK *comes to the door*]

Nick. Lieutenant Cutting's wanted at headquarters at nine
o'clock.

Mason. He'll probably work himself loose about that time.

[*They lay* CUTTING *on a bunk, his boots sticking over the edge*]

Nick. What's up?

Teague.
> [*Who has lowered his gun*]
Grab your stuff, boy. We're going.

Nick. Where?

Teague. We're invited out to eat! Get going, rookies! Come
on, boy, you're in on this!
> [*In silence and haste the men snatch their arms and go out the
> door.* CUTTING *and* NEIL *are left alone*]

Cutting. Get up and untie me, Neil.
> NEIL *gets up from his bunk, buckles his coat around him, takes
> his gun from the corner, and starts for the door*]
You hear me?
> [NEIL *goes out. There is a brief silence, then* ALCOCK *can be
> heard singing as he approaches*]

Alcock.
The unicorn with his turban horn
  And the zebra build behind,
He crops moon-grass in an earthlit pass,
  An earthlit pass,
  And glitters from wind to wind.
> [*He appears in the doorway, wearing Mary Philipse's scarlet
> breeches, which he is so intent on pulling together at the
> side that he fails to see that his companions are gone.*
> CUTTING *wriggles, but the bonds hold fast*]
Oh, I'm the son of a unicorn,
  I graze the sky, I drink the air
And many a filly I leave forlorn,
  I leave forlorn,
  In the race of a comet's hair!

Cutting. Alcock!

Alcock.
[*Looking up*]
Hell, they're gone!
[*He turns toward the door*]

Cutting. Alcock, untie this damn mess! Alcock!
[ALCOCK, *somewhat bewildered, walks over to the bunk and looks at* CUTTING]
The low bastards tied me up.

Alcock. Well, what do you know about it. Somebody left a pair of boots here.
[*He kicks the burlap from his feet, pulls off* CUTTING's *boots deliberately, and dons them*]

Cutting. If I follow you for the rest of my life I'll get you for this!

Alcock. Spew on you!
[*He gives* CUTTING *the Bronx cheer at the doorway, and goes out*]

CURTAIN

ACT TWO

SCENE TWO

SCENE: *Washington's headquarters.* WASHINGTON, *alone, is sitting at his desk, writing with a quill. A soldier enters.*

Washington.

[*Dashing the pen to the floor*]

By God, you'd think there'd be a better contrivance for making marks on paper! Who rode into the yard, Rafe?

Rafe. General Lafayette, sir.

Washington. Back already? He's to come in, of course.

Rafe. Yes, sir.

[*He goes out.* WASHINGTON *picks out another quill and sharpens it.* LAFAYETTE *enters*]

Washington. No luck, I daresay?

Lafayette. Well, good and bad.

Washington. At any rate, you've been on horseback this morning. My life work seems to consist in whittling gray goose feathers and writing letters with them to officials that never answer me.

Lafayette. Mais écoutez, écoutez—I'm here on business. We have a new plan. I've seen General Wayne. We—

Washington. Come then. The sapient General Howe was there ahead of you.

Lafayette. No. Neither Howe nor I has reached the island yet. But he's on his way to it with a large detachment, and I've returned for reenforcements.

Washington. He'll be there before you, even so.

97

Lafayette. You give me too little credit, my friend. He's coming down the river in barges, and General Wayne has blocked the channel.

Washington.

[*Rising*]

Blocked the channel! Well, bully for Anthony! We shall annoy this lady-killer! How much hay has he there?

Lafayette. Some thousands of tons.

Washington. An acutely uninteresting article—but worth having. Is Stirling back with you?

Lafayette. We rather anticipated your consent. He's even now furbishing our expedition.

Washington. From which corps?

Lafayette. His Pennsylvanians. They're fairly well equipped.

Washington. Excellent. Why, this may turn into a major operation.—You'll need a party of horse along the west bank—and I believe I'll lead them myself.

Lafayette. Now, if you would—we'd be insured against surprise.

Washington. If I leave early this afternoon?

Lafayette. You'd be in time—we won't be at the river till a little before dawn. Should you need to reach us we're at the mouth of the Schuylkill—

Washington. And what do you use for boats?

Lafayette. Building rafts—frontier-fashion—

[*He turns to go*]

Washington. Well, luck go with you! I'll cover the northern flank. Oh, you'll see Stirling—tell him I want him here to face the Commissioners with me. He'll catch up with you.

Lafayette. I'll tell him. By the way, the password's Hay.

Washington. Hay?

Lafayette. Just hay. Plain hay. Foin—faire les foins. You know, make hay while the sun shines!

Washington. Oh, pardon! je comprends, je comprends.

   [LAFAYETTE *goes out gaily*]

Rafe!

   [RAFE *enters*]

Rafe. Yes, sir.

Washington. The Commissioners will have a bite to eat with me when they arrive. I want you to serve us here— and serve us on tin—and give us the stuff that was left from the fusiliers' dinner—

Rafe. I guess that stuff was worse'n you know, General. The cookie couldn't pass that off on the cat—

Washington. I know. I tasted it. We'll have it this morning.

   [TENCH *enters*]

Rafe. Yes, sir.

Tench. I've stabled the horses, sir, and have two Congress-men left over. If you can suggest any disposition for them—

Washington. We're giving them breakfast here—and you'll

stay for it, but I warn you to eat sparingly. Heat the
mess, Rafe, heat it just enough to bring out its qualities.

Rafe. Yes, sir.

    [*He goes out*]

Tench. I'm to stay for this?

Washington. Oh, yes—you'll be called on.

Tench. Shall I fetch them in? They're even now scraping
their boots at your door.

Washington. That argues a certain amount of respect. By
all means, fetch them.

    [TENCH *goes out.* WASHINGTON *goes to his desk, takes two let-
ters out of a pigeonhole and lays them on the leaf.*
TENCH, *enters, ushering in* FOLSOM *and* HARVIE,
*Congressmen, fairly young and dressed in the height of
Colonial fashion.* HARVIE'S *boots are soiled a trifle, and
he tries surreptitiously to clean them from time to time*]

Washington. You are welcome, gentlemen. It's long indeed,
since I've exchanged ideas with the Congress
or its committees, face to face.

Harvie. The roads
from here to York are roads only in name.
We arrive somewhat bedraggled.

Washington. But no less welcome
for that. I parted company with my luggage
some two months ago, quite suddenly,
and wear mourning for its loss.—This is Colonel Tench,
my aide, who will hear our discussions. Later, perhaps,
General Stirling will join us.

    [*The men bow*]

Folsom. Must we begin
 so early, General? We've been abroad since seven,
 and damme, I'm starved!

Washington. If you'll excuse a light
 collation, army fare, it's ready.

Folsom. Surely.
 Bring on your light collation. I'll lighten it.
 Groat-bread or what have you.

Harvie. That infernal host
 at the Red Lion—we asked the man for collops
 and he sent us bacon—and bacon sickens me—
 I've a tetchy stomach travelling. I hardly ate—
 not enough to break a fast.

Washington. Then it may be
 our soldier fodder won't do.

Folsom. Oh, yes, it will.
 I'll clean my dish this morning.

Washington. The order's in
 and we'll be served in a moment. Now, will you mind
 if I make bold meanwhile to open the question,
 and say the last letter which I received from you
 concerning food for the troops, has left me dark
 as to how I'd best proceed? This is how we stand:
 The Quartermaster-General was replaced
 against my advice, by Congress. Your new man
 was most unsatisfactory—gave us, in fact,
 almost no co-operation. Food ran low
 and I protested, whereon your man resigned
 and has not been replaced. It's plain that an army

can't run without a quartermaster, and yet
you've left me so this three months.

Folsom. We know it—we know it—
it's most unfortunate, but there's been some quarrel
in Congress over appointments. The North and South
are at odds about the post, each section claiming
the other's had too much. I've done my best
to settle the matter.

Washington. It's not settled yet?

Folsom. God, no,
and I don't know when it will be.

Washington. The resolution
passed by Congress, that we live off the country
until you agree on a quartermaster—if that's
to be taken seriously, I think you'll find
first, there's not that much food within our range,
and second, if you turn men loose to steal
and ravage what they need—

Harvie. Steal? Ravage and steal?

Washington. What else can you call it? Put in a soldier's hands
the right to take what he wants, and where he will,
without reprisal, and how long can you hold him
from rape and wanton plunder? It can't be done.
Better give up at once than sow the country
with foot-pads, armed, insolent and bearing pardons
signed by their officers—

Harvie. Now, now—

Washington. You seemed
   reluctant to advise me before breakfast,
   but within three days you'll have a starving mob
   here—one I can't control—one that could eat
   this country clean as locusts. Every moment
   is precious for our plans.

Harvie. You speak of a mob—
   and truly, it's been rumored here and there
   that discipline is easier to maintain
   under the European code of arms
   than by our backwoods methods. You've preferred
   our native leaders, who fight by hook or crook,
   and win or lose by chance. But you might win
   more regularly if you could bring yourself
   to swallow technical advice. Add to that
   that there are methods known for drilling a mob
   into an army, and holding it to its task
   even under difficulties.

Washington. The art of war
   set down in paradigms, like a Greek declension
   and conned by schoolboys!

Harvie. Shall we say that Gates was a schoolboy
   when he won at Saratoga?

Washington. Oh, it was Gates
   who won at Saratoga? I had supposed
   it was the farmers fighting behind trees
   American-fashion. The art of war's much simpler
   than's set down in the manuals. Get there first
   with superior force if possible, and surprise

the enemy if you can. Any fool knows that.
But before you get there with any force at all
you must write a thousand letters to a thousand fools
begging them for the men, the arms, the food,
the chance to get there late!

Harvie. I beg your pardon!

Washington. Sir, I beg yours,
but if Congress had wanted me to fail, had set
itself to favor the English, it couldn't have played
its hand more neatly! Will you show me a rule
for holding an army together on air?
    [RAFE *enters with tins of food*]

Folsom. I've held
together all morning on little more. This looks
like a very welcome diversion.
    [RAFE *serves* HARVIE *and* FOLSOM, *then* TENCH *and* WASH-
    INGTON]

Washington. We might have sat
at table, but when we're busy we adopt
camp manners—and get used to them.
    [HARVIE *tastes the stuff*]

Harvie. Good God!
Good God in heaven!

Folsom. What's the matter?

Harvie. Help!
Help—I'm strangling!
    [*He reaches out his hands as if falling*]
Have you tried this offal?
In the name of God!

Folsom. Are you dying, man?

Harvie. Look, look!
  Look at your food. It crawls!

Washington. You exaggerate.

Tench.
  [*Eating*]
  This is better than what I've been having lately.
  Not bad at all. It moves about a trifle.
  A weevil's hard to kill.

Folsom. What is it?

Tench. Mostly beans,
  I'd guess. Not what you'd hope for in your beans—
  a little rank, but still—
  [*He eats*]

Folsom.
  [*Regarding his plate*]
  Let me out of here!
  Give me a little air!

Washington. Rafe, Mr. Folsom's
  in need of air.
  [RAFE *goes to* FOLSOM'S *assistance*]

Folsom. I'm all right.
  [*He leans against the wall*]

Harvie. May Christ forgive you!
  [*To* TENCH]
  Damn you, if you taste that plate again
  I'll murder you! Did you mean to poison us?

Washington. Take the plates out, Rafe.
[RAFE *removes the food*]
I'm sorry, gentlemen—
this is the mess we've dealt to several corps
lately, for lack of better. It's pretty bad,
what there is of it, and there's very little left.
That's our predicament.

Harvie. Is that a reason for ladling
Hog-wash to us?

Washington. You're not compelled to eat it,
but the men are, and you sent it—sent nothing else—
They've no choice.

Folsom. Ye gods! Well, it is bad.
I'll admit that.—But give us something else
to clear the air.

Washington. Later. I've eaten nothing
this morning. Suppose we starve till we've thrashed
things out,
just to keep our minds on the commissary.

Folsom. Come, now;
that's hardly necessary.

Washington. Suppose we try it, though.
It may help us to fix on a name for quartermaster
before the morning's over.

Harvie. What would you say
to Conway?

Washington. Why, I'd say if you want Conway
I'll resign.

Harvie. You run things with a high hand,
General Washington! You've set us down to garbage
to teach us ABCs, and you refuse
to serve with an officer you've had no voice
in choosing! You'll learn yet that we were sent here
representing the Congress, and Congress has yet some
    power
over the military! If we name Conway
it's Conway you'll have!
    [STIRLING *enters*]

Washington. You're acquainted with General Stirling,
I believe. He's here to discuss this same question.
It's true that if you name Conway it's Conway you'll
    have,
but I won't have him, under your pleasure, for the reason
that I'll be gone, and none too sad to go.
General Conway's committed himself to an intrigue
to be rid of me and put Gates in my place. It's confined
in the main to officers who have soldiered abroad
and consider my tactics crude. It may be they are,
but certainly if Conway and I were to serve
where reciprocal understanding and regard
were needed, they'd be lacking. Oh, gentlemen,
gentlemen, forget that you're Congressmen, forget
that I'm an officer! Let's put aside
all bickering and rivalries that spring
from personal privilege, take our holds together
and pull out of this slough! If I've been harsh or defiant
or even insulting, I'm desperate, and ready to use

the most desperate means to wake you to what's happened,
what's happening here! Here is our war come down
to a mouldy crust—and you in whose hands it lies
to help, wrangle over ribbons, men dying meanwhile,
our cause dying!

Harvie. Are your own hands clean? You bicker,
I note, over Conway!

Washington. Still Conway. We must settle that first
it seems. Has he arrived yet?

Stirling. He's here with Cutting.

Washington. There'll be no better time
[STIRLING *steps out*]
I had no wish
to humiliate an officer, but if I must
we'll get it over.

Folsom. Is this a trial?

Washington. No, no—
an interrogation. There's something to be explained,
and we'll ask him to explain it.
[STIRLING *ushers in* CUTTING *and* CONWAY]
You gentlemen
are acquainted, I think?

Folsom. We know General Conway.
[*They bow to him*]

Washington. The other's
Lieutenant Cutting.
[*Again they bow*]

Cutting. I hope I haven't delayed you.
 I was a little tardy. The men in my bunk-house
 tied me up about sunrise, and then set out
 for parts unknown.

Tench. Deserting?

Cutting. I imagine so.

Washington. What men were these?

Cutting. The same you were good enough
 to argue with the other night.

Washington. I hope
 you suffered no injury?

Cutting. None.

Washington. Alcock was with them—
 and the other—the leatherskin?

Cutting. Yes, Teague—he led
 the pack, I'd say.

Washington. I'm sorry—if such men leave—
 but another time for it.—General Conway, your name
 has been brought up in connection with an appointment,
 and I must ask you a question.

Conway. Well, put your griphs,
 and I'll make shift to answer.

Washington. I've been informed
 of a letter written by you to General Gates,
 in which you congratulate him on his success
 and indicate that it will not be long
 before he takes my place.

Conway. A letter of mine?
   [*Pause*]
   I've written no such letter.

Stirling. I crave your pardon.
   You wrote and sent such a letter.

Conway. Now, surely, Stirling—
   you haven't turned informer? Why, General,
   men have been known to swagger a bit in their drink
   without meaning all that's said. I do recall
   that Stirling and I sat down to a bowl or two
   and I aired my grievances.—God on the water!
   I don't remember what I spilled, and Stirling
   was in no condition to.

Stirling. I'm clear enough
   on the essentials.

Washington. Do you recognize this letter?

Conway.
   [*Examining the letter*]
   Well, I swear this puzzles me. This is not my writing.
   No, I don't know it.

Washington. You wrote no such letter?

Conway. Never.

Stirling. The reason it's not in your writing's because I made
   a copy of it. But that's your letter to Gates,
   and you damn well know it is.

Conway. You copied it?

Stirling. Took it myself from your courier's saddlebags
   when I overhauled him, made a copy fair as print
   with my own hand, and sent the original
   along to its destination.

Conway. All I can answer
   to that is—this is not my letter. Find
   an original for it if you can. I've never
   trusted a breaker of other people's seals;
   I think his word's hardly evidence.

Washington. I saw
   your letter before it was copied and sent on,
   General Conway. It was as I have said,
   and read like this.
      [*He indicates the copy*]
   It follows I'm rather weary
   of these brummagem excuses and slip-slop
   from men who are not my friends but dare not say so,
   not to my face! It hardly becomes your straps
   to squirm like a hooked eel!

Conway. Very well, I wrote it,
   since you will have it. I believe it's not treasonous
   to hold one man might be better than another
   to lead an army.

Washington. I'm not concerned with that,
   but with another letter which has fallen
   into my hands, unluckily. There have been
   exchanges of prisoners, lately, some of them
   at General Conway's headquarters, as most convenient,
   as indeed it is. In these exchanges letters

have crossed the lines, which is quite allowable,
friends writing to friends on the opposite side. But
  among them
were certain notes which might have contained a cipher,
and a British spy named Jelliffe—oh, you know the
  name—
confirmed them as ciphers, turned state's evidence,
and read them to us.

Conway. This is interesting.
You tell a story well.

Washington. I'll come to my point.
These ciphers were addressed to Lieutenant Cutting
for transmission to General Conway, and through him
to General Gates.

Conway. And they contained—?

Washington. Why, nothing—
nothing incriminating. Only the terms
which would be acceptable to General Howe
and the English crown if the Continental army
were willing to surrender.

Conway. Sir, on my word,
I know nothing of this.

Washington. And I, sir, on my word,
say that you do, and am willing to bring it to trial!
  [*To the* COMMISSIONERS]
You will understand, I think, why I objected
to General Conway's promotion.

Folsom. Perfectly.

Harvie. I
must apologize—

Washington. It's my unpleasant duty
to turn this matter over to the court-martial
and hold you both for it.
[*The* COMMISSIONERS *exchange glances*]

Conway. We shall need your word in this,
Master Harvie.

Cutting.
[*To* FOLSOM]
And yours.
[*A pause*]

Folsom. Why, General—
the truth is, if these officers have acted
with the cognizance of Gates—it's hardly wise
to make a scandal of it—
[WASHINGTON *smiles grimly*]

Tench. Make a scandal!
It's not of our making.

Stirling. Good God, do you imagine
you could whitewash over that?

Harvie. For the good of the service—
at least, we must keep it quiet.

Washington. For the good of the service,
and in all common justice, the officers' court
must pass on the evidence in hand.

Harvie. But reflect, sir.
There are names involved—

Washington. Then they'll be damned as black
as the evidence calls for! What's this sudden concern
of yours for names! The names of these two here
mean nothing to me but two who come sucking around
for favors when they see me, like a couple of squid,
and squirt their ink at my back!

Conway. I give fair warning
if I'm court-martialed I have three words to speak
that'll hush it up!

Washington. Speak them now!

Harvie.

    [*To* WASHINGTON]

    Believe me, sir,
there's more consequence in what you plan than's plain
on the surface—

Washington. What consequence—?

Harvie. I say no more—

Washington. Then we proceed—

Conway. Will you speak up for me
or must I speak for myself?

    [*The* COMMISSIONERS *are silent*]

    Why, these two knew
as well as I of the correspondence with Howe,
and most of the Congress knew it! If I'm a traitor
they're traitors with me! We were commissioned by
    Congress
to angle for Howe's terms! Well, look at me
if you like.—Does it surprise you? When a war's lost

the usual thing's to feel around for bargains
and that's what's being done!

Harvie. What he says is true.
It has not yet been brought to a vote in Congress—
nor did we wish it published, but this is true.
There are those among us who know that a war is worth
what it brings on the exchange, no more. And when
your stock is going down, it's best to sell
before it goes to nothing.

Stirling. What's that? What's that?

Harvie. Why, I'll say it again. A war, my friend,
is a tactical expedient to gain
certain political ends. Those ends being proved
impossible, the war's without excuse,
and should be pushed no further than need be
to gain an advantageous peace.

Stirling. You say it,
and I must believe you've said it, but, death of God,
is this like any other war?

Harvie. The same,
or much the same.

Washington. Sir, I should have supposed
you'd notify me, before negotiations
were begun with the enemy.

Harvie. There was thought of it,
but you and your army have so much of the hot-head
in your composition, it was believed unwise
to open the subject. Besides, there was always doubt

what reply we'd get from the English, and it seemed best
not to call off our dogs till we were sure
we had no need for them.

Washington. Your dogs, you say!

Harvie. Nay, that's a figure.

Washington. Not one I'm inclined to relish!
When did this begin?

Harvie. Some months ago. When you lost at Brandywine
that cooked our goose. Then Gates at Saratoga
made a good talking point in case Sir William
was hard to deal with.

Washington. We might have won—do they know that?—
If they'd given me the shadow of support
behind the lines. It was not too late last fall—
may not be now.
   [*To* FOLSOM]
Sir, you say nothing here.
Are your views his?

Folsom. We had no right to broach
this matter to you, but it's done now. My views
are similar.

Washington. But we might have won! Good God,
do you hear what I say? Have they fudged our cause on
   purpose?
That's the way it sounds.

Folsom. No, no.

Washington. Then why this pother
over Conway and Gates? If we're to lose the war

why not let me lose it? It's hardly like them
to relieve me of that out of kindness?

Harvie. I see no reason
for keeping you in the dark. Gates is in our counsels,
and quite agrees that we might as well give in
while there's still trade on the seas.

Stirling. Wait now! Wait now!
You're putting in Gates because he's agreed to sur-
render!
Is that what you mean to say?

Harvie. It's ruinous
to drag it out further.

Stirling. And who's agreed to this?

Folsom. There's no agreement!

Stirling. Yes, but that was his meaning!
[*He strides over to* HARVIE]
Who's in with you?

Harvie. I have no mind to be pummeled
for answering a question. Answer your own.

Washington.
[*To* STIRLING]
Less ruffling, Stirling.

[STIRLING *steps back*]

Folsom. No more. It's unfortunate
this much has slipped.

Harvie. As for these professional soldiers
who get the bit in their teeth, and insist on fighting
till it's high-water in hell—perhaps they'll learn

sometime, that it's no treason for a government
to consider a peace—even in war-time!

Folsom. No more!

Harvie. Why not? If he wants his answer I'll give it to him.
This war began to protect our trade. The merchants
were being run out of business by subsidies
to English boats! It cut so deep in Boston
there was no more profit in smuggling—and all our trade
was smuggling, anyway! They dumped the tea
in Boston harbor, and raised a hue and cry
of "Freedom!" "Down with the tyrant!" Christ, what
    they wanted
was profits, not freedom. But then the inland boys
took up the yell, and ran together in mobs,
and old Sam Adams made speeches, and cock-a-hoop,
hell-bent, pell-mell—it spread till we couldn't stop,
spread to Virginia, and a pack of oyster-faced
backwoodsmen met and signed a declaration,
and then we were in trouble! Where's our trade now?
Nobody makes money—not even the money-lenders—
nobody but the god-damn farmers selling pork
to the British commissary! It's time to stop it!
We've got to settle down and live, that's all,
and why not under King George? If your fire-eaters
can't make a living in time of peace, why, hell,
the rest can't make one now!

Washington. This sentiment
prevails in Congress?

Harvie. It does, or it will shortly.

Stirling. Then fig your Congress!

Washington. And is this the reason supplies have been
    withheld
  and gone astray—and all our calculations
  upset—to discourage us—and call off your dogs,
  as you put it so tersely?

Harvie. I should say there's been little stomach
  for expenditures that looked to a longer war
  when peace was in the air.

Washington. I understand you.
  Nobody cared to win.

Harvie. What was there to win? We lose more day by day
  than we'll ever gain back!

Washington. Perhaps we've been unaccustomed
  to thinking in terms of money of some things
  men give their lives for. You may find this difficult
  to comprehend, you who have thought beyond us
  and reckon our lives in dollars.

Folsom. But that's not so.
  Harvie forgets himself, and says too much
  and outruns all discretion.

Washington. I think we know
  how to estimate you both. I shall hope no more
  for any help from you. Make your appointments.
  Make any arrangements you like. You need not consult
  with me. Make your plans, and be easy.

Folsom. I'm sorry indeed
  for the turn we've taken. For we had meant to offer
  our full co-operation.

Washington. Had you so?
  Is your report of Congress like your friend's
  or is he in error?

Folsom. Truly, there's a trend toward peace—
  if only for business reasons.

Washington. Then we've heard enough.

  [*The* COMMISSIONERS *bow*]

Conway. And this court-martial that seemed to be in the
    wind—
  is that to go on?

Washington. I beg your pardon, Conway.
  There'll be no court-martial, no, nor for Cutting.

Conway. Thank you.

Washington. It appears the desire to degrade me and put
    Gates
  in charge, so that he might surrender, was patriotic,
  and quite in the fashion. I wish you a very good day,
  you, and the honorables from Congress also;
  may they find good fare on the road.

  [CONWAY *and* CUTTING *exit*]

  Whatever plans
  you have for ending the war in a gradual way
  you may put aside. I'll end the war for you
  and do it quickly.

Harvie. You'll take no steps in that
  without instruction!

Washington. No?

Harvie. You exceed your powers
   if you do. Only the Congress may move in that,
   as you're aware.

Washington. And we've taken orders from you,
   tried to find some patriotic purpose
   in your shifts and denials—you think of lace with no
      guts,
   you essence of Judas!

Folsom. Come, sir—this is raving!—

Washington. And you back him in it—the Congress stands
   behind him
   in this betrayal—

Folsom. A Congress may change its mind!
   It has that right!

Washington. You'll find the army, too,
   has rights that I'll defend! Your dogs of war are yours
   no longer! All further negotiations with
   the British, I'll conduct them! You want the war ended!
   By God, we'll end it then, but in our own fashion,
   and on our own terms! Sir William shall hear from me
   but behind your backs this time!

Harvie. I warn you, sir—
   take no steps without instruction! Your service here
   is under commission from the Continental Congress!—
   Remember it!

Washington. You'll take steps without instruction,
and take them now!

[*He suddenly grasps* HARVIE *by the collar and the seat of the
trousers and turkey-walks him out the door*]

Harvie. You—farmer! Take your hands off me!

Folsom. What's this?
What's this, sir? Will you lose all your friends?

[*A crash is heard outside.* FOLSOM *follows* WASHINGTON *and*
HARVIE *out. A second crash is heard.* WASHINGTON *returns dusting his hands, and sits at the desk*]

Tench. A good beginning.

Stirling. I wanted to do that, and you called me off.
It puts a period.

Tench. Now let them do their worst.
We've no more to fear from them. I've overstayed
my time. I'll be late at the rendezvous.

Washington. True—true—
and I was to ride patrol for Lafayette.
Tench, will you ready a troop?

Tench. If I can find one.

[*He goes to the door*]

It's as I told you. Catch me fighting or dying
for pricks like those. Why should you take it to heart?
All a soldier gets is his pay and his leave
and whatever girls he can catch with a uniform
and never see again. You take no pay

and never see a woman. There's nothing in it
for you. Let them have their war.
  [*He goes out*]

Stirling. Yes. Let them have it.
  Do you know what I think of governments, by and large,
  I mean in general? They're run by pimps
  who get kicked out of hothouses for picking
  the customers' pockets. This one we've got—we made it,
  set it up, picked the best men we could find
  and put them in—and their brains began to rot
  before the year was out. It rots a man's brains
  to be in power, and he turns pimp, and picks pockets;
  the scavengers! At least, when you have a king
  you can chop his head off. I'll be on my way.
  I must be there before sundown.
    [*He goes out.* WASHINGTON *sits moodily at the table.* MARY
      PHILIPSE, *cloaked, bonneted, and ready for the road,
      comes in from the stair. She stands motionless for a
      moment, looking at* WASHINGTON]

Mary. I'm sorry if I disturb you. I'd have gone
  without a word, only I must make my peace
  and ask you to forgive the fool I was,
  for coming here at all.
    [WASHINGTON *does not move*]
  The camp I came from
  is not like this. I drew my notion of warfare
  from the quadrilling officers that dance
  attendance on Mistress Loring, and the bevy
  of officers' darlings with her. How wrong I was
  I've learned through a night of thinking on my ways

and yours. You believe in yourself and what you do
to the verge of martyrdom, and all your men
have cased themselves in some armor of the spirit
to have and hold what's their own. I'm out of place here
with my thwarted love and beribboned misery
where death walks sentry on your night, too near
and real for cavalier fancies. I honor you
and the men you lead, let me say this in saying
farewell, more than I'd thought possible.

Washington. Eh, but it seems
that you were right.

Mary. Not I.

Washington. I've been a gull.
They've led me by a ring, like a circus bear
to fright the children for them. Behind my back
they make their shabby deals, shilling for shilling,
men's lives for copper pennies, marked down, sold off
to die for groats and farthings. The devil drench them,
these talking swine! We're in their way, we've fought on
longer than they intended, and they lose money—
money, by God, hard money! They starve us out
to make us stop—two or three hundred tons
of human beeves, pushed out into the dark
to teach us they lose money, by God, hard money,
and can't afford it.—This is our bright new day,
this is our world well lost! The spirit of the eagle
unconquerable, unconquered! So many crows
over a stinking sheep in a bogged cow-yard
would show more nobility!

Mary. But I'm sure you're wrong—
   disheartened over some check—

Washington. You'll return to Howe;
   tell him he can buy our Congress for tuppence
   if he lays out his money shrewdly. Less; let him save
   his cash, and deal out four or five dozen clerkships
   in so many pawnshops, found; they'll jump at that—
   they were born with the souls of under-secretaries,
   and want no more.

Mary. I shall tell him no such thing,
   but that you are brave men, honest, and dangerous.
   Yes, more than he thinks.

Washington. The revolution's sold out!
   Congress bargains behind my back, asks terms!
   Bargains with Howe!—What's left of the revolution
   you see here, in these windy shacks and starved men
   and the broken boots I wear! What hopes we had
   of the French—you dashed them for me!

Mary. But—are you sorry?

Washington. No. I shall have my life again, and begin
   to fence my land where I left it. I've been the fool!
   It began to get into my blood, this crusading zeal
   pumped up by the counter-jumpers to fill their tills
   and edge out competition! I've lived hard,
   slept hard, drunk water, made my meals on biscuit,
   for some great end!—They've shown me what that's
     worth!
   Six feet of earth, if there's that much left undug.

The corpses crowd in close in this neighborhood—
some get less than that.

Mary. Then this is the end of the war?

Washington. This is the end.

Mary. What will you do now?

Washington. Live again, my dear, live what little's left
to live. Drink at least what wine's in the bottle
before I throw it away. My dancing days
are very likely over, but, looking back,
I'd say I've kept too many rules, and laced
too strait for comfort. I think so when I see
these demi-semi-quavers in their purple coats
and periwigs. There's something in knowing what
you want and taking it. May they die in a ditch
and strangle in ditch-water!

Mary. And yet it's something
to be free—to find yourself free.

Washington. I'd have asked no better
once. But before this quarrel goes out of my hands
I'll make my own bargain with Howe! That satisfaction
I intend to have.
    [*He takes a pen and writes*]
When you see His Excellency
tell him from me that the conference with him
to which you bore invitation waits only on
his pleasure. Let him name his hour and place
in fairly neutral territory. I'll meet him—
and I thank you for the message.

Mary. Sir, I thank you
  for your kindly entertainment at a time
  when you felt less reminiscent than the lady
  who knocked upon your door.—
  Of all men I have known I least like to think
  of you defeated. Defeat seems not for you—
  even in a hopeless quarrel. It's not you that lose,
  but the speech-making mongrels over you. Even now
  you've a king in yourself, unbeaten, one who has within
  what men will follow or a woman serve.

Washington. Aye, once
  I was alive, before so many men
  had died around me. The gray years weigh like a mask
  and set you hard.

Mary. I know.

Washington. And this victory
  called love, adds well to victory, but defeat's
  a dull and lonely thing. I think I've seen you
  only as a brightness lost, something I wished for
  in a happier year, gone now—might wish for again
  if there are years to follow—which I doubt—

Mary. There will be better years—

Washington. I've given myself
  to a footless insurrection, drained out my blood
  on a mock heroic altar, made a monk
  of what might have been a man. And I'll get for that
  what Jack Cade got. Three lines in a history,
  touching a minor figure in a brief uprising
  that died down early in some year of our Lord,

A.D., God quit the beggar. Let us hope
Jack Cade reached out his hand and took what sweets
went by with the years, before they snared him in
and quartered him. Wait for me here. God knows
the years go fast. If I let you leave me now
I'll not see you again.

Mary. And the word to Howe?

Washington. Why, later
will do as well as now.

Mary. No, I must take it—
or you'll change your mind. But we shall meet again.—
If you doubt it—was there ever another meeting
less likely than this we've had?

Washington. No. Then I'll see you?

Mary. I shall manage.
You must leave these things with the woman.
Let's get the soldiering over, and do it quickly.
After that—trust me.

    [TENCH *enters*]

Tench. We're ready to ride, sir.
And damn little good it'll do us.

Washington. Well, let's ride then.
We'll be counted on.

    [*To* MARY]

I've written your passport—
and orders for an escort.

Tench. You leave us, lady?

Mary. Brokenhearted.

Tench. You should have come to me.
I mend these broken hearts.

Mary. Now I believe you.

Tench. This is a poor excuse for a war we're in,
anyway—why, to mend a broken heart I'd leave
at the drop of an eyelash—but, damn it, duty calls,
and, God, we're hounds for duty!

Mary. Good luck!

Tench. Good luck!

Mary. And to you, General.

Washington. Good-bye—

Mary. I betray my cause—
but—don't give up yet—hold on while you can—

Washington. Yes? Dear lady,
this nation's spending its last heart's blood for a package
of liberty. We opened the package today
and it was empty. We ride our last expedition.
And so—good-bye.

Mary. Good-bye.
    [TENCH *and* WASHINGTON *go out*]

CURTAIN

VALLEY FORGE

ACT THREE

ACT THREE

SCENE: *The interior of a barn on Hay Island in the morning light.
The place has been long abandoned and though it was well and
heavily built begins to rot down. The floor is covered with ancient and matted hay, hay hangs from the black rafters, and remains piled in the corners. To the right is a large double door,
one side of it fallen from its hinges; a small door goes out
through a stable at the left. A window has fallen out at the rear.
To the left rear a granary cuts off the corner of the lower floor;
a flimsy door hangs beside its entrance, half-fallen. A few nail
kegs and a barrel are set down-stage to the right.*
ALCOCK, *with a wounded thigh, lies on a truss of hay.* MARTY,
*with a bandage round his head and over one eye, is playing a
jews-harp.* ALCOCK *is still wearing most of the crimson trousers, but now they are stained, ripped and bedraggled from hard
use.*

Alcock. This is the kind of war that as soon as you get a
pair of britches they shoot 'em out from under you.

[MARTY *plays on*]

What's that? Did you hear that?

[MARTY *shakes his head*]

They ought to be across by this time.

Marty. Yeah.

Alcock. Play that again.

[MARTY *plays an air*, ALCOCK *sings*]

For my first love was nothing paid;
  Bright morning caught us where we lay,
Of birchen bark a house was made,
  And bright with silver ran our day.

133

Honey o' dark, honey o' rue,
Where went the kisses I gave to you?

The happy ring I made for her,
That ring was rank with verdigris,
But golden is that's tried with fire,
And golden was her love to me.
Honey o' dark, honey o' rue,
Where went the kisses I gave to you?

[*There is a low detonation in the distance.* ALCOCK *tries to get to his feet, but falls back.* MARTY *starts up*]

That's no musket—that's a long Tom! I told 'em they'd run into something if they stayed past daylight! The damn British have got parties all up and down the river.

Marty. They got howitzers.

Alcock. Boy, they've got everything.

[*They are silent a moment. There is a scattering of distant musket fire*]

Well, we can't do much.

[*He moves his gun toward him*]

That was old Teague's Happy Thought. I know the way she talks.

Marty. Maybe Nick.

Alcock. Yeah, Nick was in it, too—I never feel safe on an island. I can't swim.

Tench.

[*Outside*]

This is the place. It's the only barn in miles.

Lafayette.
  [*Outside*]
  I don't understand this firing to the south.

Alcock.
  [*His gun in his hand*]
  Take hold of your weapon, Marty.
  [*They train guns on the doorway, right*]

Lafayette. It's certainly an exchange, but it's not my men.

Tench. A good mile away, I'd guess.
  [*He enters*]

Alcock. Step into the light, you, where I can see you.

Tench. Easy, easy; who are you?
  [LAFAYETTE *enters*]

Lafayette. There is someone here?

Alcock. You're damn right there's somebody here! Desperate men, too.
  [*He lowers the muzzle*]
  I beg your pardon, Colonel. Drop your sights, lad.
  [MARTY *lowers his weapon*]

Tench. Who are you?

Alcock. It's all right, sir. Virginians.

Tench. Oh, yes. I know them.—Well, friend, for a minute I was in doubt about you. You're wearing British colors on your legs.

Alcock. I got a British bullet through 'em, too. That's why I'm here.

Tench. And now that I reflect on it Lieutenant Cutting said something about being tied up by the men in his bunk-house. I hope I'm not going to find it necessary to make you both prisoners.

Alcock. For what?

Tench. For desertion.

Alcock. We came over here to lift a mess of corn for breakfast. Besides, it was about time somebody tied up Cutting.

Tench. I agree with you about that. Only I wouldn't advise you to go back to Valley Forge.

Alcock. We hadn't figured on going back. And I wouldn't want to get caught here either.

Tench. Well, that's your own lookout. What's the firing downstream?

Alcock. That's our bunch having a little fracas with the English over the last load of corn, if I'm any judge. I told 'em to quit at dawn, but they went right on, and now they've got an army down on 'em.

Tench. What do you mean by the last load of corn?

Alcock. Why, we found Howe had enough ear corn on this island to make a poultice for the state of Pennsylvania. So we commandeered four old monitors below the hook and ferried over a few loads of it in the night. Then we had a brush with some scouts, and Marty and me got clipped. They laid us in here and went back to their navigating.

Lafayette. Why, sir, this was a more important operation than mine; and more successful.

Alcock. We certainly laid in materials for a whale of a lot of corn pone.

[*Musket fire again*]

They're ketching it down there now, though.

Lafayette. We should take a hand in that.

Tench. We will. Now, listen to me. Howe sent out a flag for a parley, and the Generals are meeting here to talk over the revolution and what they fought each other for and all that. But if you've got a fight going we'll look in on it. How do we get there?

Alcock. Follow the shore line south—but keep your eyes open for sharpshooters.

Tench. How far is it?

Alcock. Maybe a furlong to the cribs.

Tench. Where did you dump the stuff on the mainland?

Alcock. Clopton's granary.

Tench. Good enough.

Alcock. Wait a minute—you say the Generals are coming here?

Tench. Where else? It's the only roof visible in these parts.

Alcock. Well, what are we going to do?

Tench. Lie where you are and let 'em step over you. Only don't shoot 'em as they come in—that's all I ask of you.

[TENCH *and* LAFAYETTE *are about to leave by the left door when*
MINTO *enters by it, panting and wet. He sits down, ex-*
hausted]

What's going on?

Minto. They sunk the big scow. With a round shot. But
we got off.
[*A shot is heard*]
The boys are beating back this way.
[TENCH *and* LAFAYETTE *go out left*]

Alcock. You hurt any?

Minto. No. Neil's hurt. Got a splinter through his chest.
Andrew was carryin' him.
[*He rises*]
We'll have to get you out of here.

Alcock. Us?

Minto. The red-coats are coming this way.—Lost my musket in the water.

Andre.
    [*Outside*]
This is the roof we glimpsed beyond the marsh,
I'm sure of it.

Brigadier.
    [*Outside*]
It's what a man might call
an ancient pile. These oafs of pioneers,
how they can handle their tools! They level these sills
and notch the beams with a broad-axe.

[ANDRE *and the* BRIGADIER *enter.* MINTO *has retreated on
    hearing the voices*]

Andre. The arms are quiet
    some hundred years that did this hewing. Basta!
    The roost's inhabited!

Alcock. I'd hardly call it that.
    We're birds o' passage.

Andre. I'm sorry if we intrude.
    The truth is we mistook this for a place
    appointed for a meeting.

Alcock. Well, this is it.
    There's been some officers here.

Andre. And they're returning?

Alcock. That's the idea
    [MINTO *has picked up a fork*]

Brigadier.
    [*To* MINTO]
    Come out,
    fellow—is this an ambush?

Alcock. Put down that pitchfork;
    man, are you daft?

Minto. I won't put down any pitchfork,
    and they won't take me!

Alcock. This is a conversation,
    and nobody wants you.
    [MINTO *leans grimly on his weapon*]
    He won't bother.

Brigadier. Good.

There's an old road comes near the further side.
It may be passable.

Andre. If not, they'll walk.

Now peace be with you, gentlemen; you, most of all,
with the trident yonder. If you're here in half an hour
we'll see you again.

Alcock. Why, drop in any time.

We can do with a little company.

Andre. Thank you, sir.

My prayers for a swift recovery.

[*He goes out with the* Brigadier, *to the right*]

Alcock. Why, you ancient crow-bait, what do you mean
refusing to lay down your arms when addressed by an
officer? How far do you think you're going to get, pitching into a couple of brigadiers with farm machinery?

Minto. How do I know what they're going to do?

Alcock. These are headquarters birds, you stingaree—poll-
parrots from headquarters. Their business is talking, not
fighting. There's a truce on the island, and they're here
to parley voo. If you weren't a thousand years old and
afflicted with all the animal diseases from string-halt to
rinderpest I'd get up and tan your hide off for disregard
of an order!

Minto. I guess you're an officer.

Alcock. Mason's dead, isn't he? He was shot off the boat
right behind you! I'm running this shebang now. Do
you know what I think?

Minto. No.

Alcock. I've got a premonition this war's going to be over to-night.

Minto. To-night?

Alcock. Otherwise why is Washington talking to Howe?

Minto. That's right.

> [OSCAR *and* SPAD *slip in through the left door and turn to look back for possible pursuers.* SPAD *is wearing a dirty bandage on his right hand*]

Oscar. Dey go by Apple Creek, I tall you!

Spad. Damn if they didn't. They missed us. Take a look out that other door.

> [OSCAR *runs into the grain-room*]

They won't try rushing the barn. We could pick 'em off as they came.

Alcock. You ducking out of trouble?

Spad. We led 'em off the wrong way so we could get Neil in here. He's hit pretty bad.

> [*He examines his priming*]

Your gun working?

Alcock. Take Marty's.

Marty. No, sir. Nobody takes my gun!

> [*He hangs onto it*]

Alcock. Mine's all right.

> [SPAD *exchanges guns with* ALCOCK *and goes back to watch the door*]

Spad. Any powder here? I'm about done.

Alcock. I've got half a horn left.
   [NICK *and* TEAGUE *come in quietly, quite at ease*]
   Where's Neil?

Nick. Andrew's fetchin' him over his shoulders.

Teague. Who was that ran down the bank?

Alcock. Tench and Lafayette.

Nick. How come they're here?

Alcock.—Jeez—there's more generals around than you ever see in camp. The woods are full of generals.

Teague. It's pretty hot down that way. They're likely to run into something.

Alcock. It seems there's a truce at the moment, and nobody's supposed to shoot anybody. If you see any Hessians they're out of season. There was a couple of English brigadiers here a minute ago. They went back after more.
   [OSCAR *comes in from the grain-room*]

Teague. More what?

Alcock. Brigadiers.

Oscar. Dere's six mebbe seven red-coats by de vater!

Spad. What do you mean?
   [*He looks out*]
   You say Tench went down that way?

Alcock. They started out to lend a hand in case you needed it.

[*A gun cracks rather near*]

Spad. Sounds to me as if they might want chaperoning.

[*As he starts out*]

Nick?

Nick. Sure.

[*He follows* SPAD]

Spad. Keep your head down! There's musket barrels beyond that hummock!

Nick. Keep your own down!

[SPAD *and* NICK *go out. Three or four shots are fired and bullets rattle on the siding*]

Teague. Spent balls. Wouldn't stop a rabbit.

Alcock. Pretty good for English regulars. First time I ever knew they could hit the side of a barn.

[JOCK *enters from the left, holding the door for* ANDREW, *who comes in carrying* NEIL *on his back. They help him to a heap of straw at the rear and lay him down carefully.* TEAGUE *goes over to look at him and the others watch*]

Andrew. All right, boy?

[NEIL *nods as well as he can, but makes no answer*]

Teague. Was that shooting at you?

Jock. No. They're getting ready to swarm up on this place.

Teague. They are?

[*He goes back to his loophole*]

Andrew. They'd a' got us, too, only Tench turned up from somewhere and held 'em off.

Alcock. Tench wasn't carrying a gun.

Andrew. He borrowed mine.

[Teague *suddenly whips his musket to the crack and fires*]

Alcock. Hey, how many times have I got to tell you there's a truce and you're not supposed to plug anybody?

Teague. They don't know it out there then. They was creeping in on us.

[*He loads his gun.* Oscar *and* Minto *go to his aid*]

I got one.

Alcock. Is that so? Only one?

Teague. One at a time's good fishing.

Minto. They don't want any more. They're making back to the boats.

Teague. That's right. They're leaving us.

[*Two rather distant reports are heard*]

Alcock. That's Nick and Spad.

Teague. Just helpin' 'em on their way, that's all.

Alcock. Maybe if the guests have all departed somebody with a free hand and a couple of legs would share a drink of water with an invalid.

Teague. Listen, can't you walk?

Alcock. No, I can't walk—and I can see where it's going

to be a lot of fun for some of you, carrying me around from now on.

[TEAGUE *brings out a stone bottle of water, and goes to* ALCOCK]

Try Neil, there, first.

[TEAGUE *takes the water to* NEIL, *who drinks thirstily*]

Andrew. Well, they're in the longboat—and pulling out.

Jock. Now that's just too bad. Maybe we didn't treat 'em right.

Teague. I wouldn't want 'em to go away mad.

Jock. We probably hurt their feelings some way. Damn touchy, these English.

Andrew. God grant us mileage between me and them. We've lost enough this day.

Alcock. And that's no lie.

[*The doors at the right are thrust open and* WASHINGTON *and* STIRLING *appear, followed by* RAFE]

Washington. Is this the place?

Rafe. It's where they pointed out.

Washington. I thought Tench had preceded us.

Alcock. He was here, General, but he stepped out to mix in a shindy.

Washington. Sir, it seems to me there's something remarkably familiar and yet remarkably strange about this place. I have seen these faces before.

Alcock. Yes, sir. In the bunk-house at Valley Forge.

Washington. True—I read you a long and I judge rather distasteful sermon on the evils of desertion. Like most advice it went unheeded.

Alcock. Well—not entirely.

Washington. At any rate, you took the first opportunity to pinion your officer and launch out on your own. I had that report from Lieutenant Cutting.

Alcock. Well, what do you expect a man to do—?

Washington. I've no doubt the circumstances might be termed extenuating. No charges will be brought against you, and you may consider yourselves free of all further obligations to the Continental army. However, your presence is damnably inconvenient. I have appointed to meet here with a British officer for a discussion that will hardly concern you. It would mortify me somewhat to usher him into an apartment overrun by renegade Continentals—

Alcock. Cutting's a renegade if you ask me.

Washington
  [*To* RAFE]

Is there any other shelter in the neighborhood to which we might remove our conference?

Rafe. No, sir. We could go back to the boats.

Stirling. The difficulty is that Howe's expected here. I wonder he's not here already.

Alcock. Oh, he'll be along. A brace of periwigs strolled in a while past to look us over. I reckon that's his advance guard.

Stirling. There you are. Would it be possible to move these men into the grain-room yonder?

Alcock. I can be moved. In fact, if I'm renegade I'm glad to get out!

Stirling. Collect your men, then, and post yourselves on guard duty inside. Shut the door behind you and consider yourselves under arrest till you're mustered out.

[WASHINGTON *has pushed a keg into position and sits down beside the barrel to go over papers. The men begin to move uncertainly*]

Teague. General Washington, maybe you didn't get this just the way it was. I was going on leave for the winter that's true, but I didn't go. Far from it.

Washington. It's a matter of small moment what you've done with your time since I saw you, but of considerable importance that we clear this room.

Teague. Yes, sir.

[*He goes to* ALCOCK *and helps* OSCAR *lift him to his feet.* ALCOCK *limps between them toward the granary door, the men following.* VARNUM *enters from the right and goes up to* WASHINGTON]

Stirling. Varnum's here, sir.

Washington. Your report?

Varnum. We took the depot
about three o'clock this morning—with little loss,

for the garrison was asleep. We found some arms
and four or five barrels of powder, but no food.
The food was gone.

Stirling. It's as if they knew what we needed,
and led us on.

Washington. They do know what we need.
> [*The left door opens and* LAFAYETTE *enters with* SPAD]

Lafayette. Death of my soul, man, you're a doughty
fighter—
I wouldn't be here without you!
> [*He gives* SPAD *his hand*]

Spad. There's many of us
wouldn't be here if it hadn't been for trees
and other natural objects.

Lafayette.
> [*To* WASHINGTON]

Your pardon, sir;
this front was not so quiet as it seemed
when we made the assignation.

Washington. I hope you've made
no breach of our compact with the English. We
as well as they were bound to an armistice
for this hour or two.

Lafayette. I assure you they fired at us. It became the part
of wisdom to crawl a little.
whereupon we crawled. This is what you call
in the native parlance, Indian fighting.

Washington. Yes.
I've heard of it. We've other business in hand
with your leave.

Stirling. Stir out, boys. Stir your stumps,
and set a watch, since you're here.

Spad.
[*At the right-hand door*]
By cracky, they're coming
on horseback, his nibs and all. Find your stanchions,
cattle;
They're here with bells.
[*He goes toward the granary*]

Stirling.
[*To* WASHINGTON]
Lord love you, he wouldn't walk!
He must have crossed in state.

Teague. If we move this boy
I'm afraid it'll finish him. Would it dash you much
if he should lie here?
[WASHINGTON *rises and goes back to look at* NEIL, *who lies
with closed eyes.* WASHINGTON *lays a hand on* NEIL'S
brow, then rises]

Washington. Stirling, this is the lad—
you remember him?

Stirling. Aye—this is the one who asked
for what he seems to have got.

Washington. He's badly wounded?

Teague. It won't take long.

Washington. Let him stay there if he must.
Keep an eye on him, Stirling.

Stirling. I will.

A Voice.
　　[*Outside*]
We carry
a flag, friend. Ours is a peaceful errand.

Another Voice. Yes, sir.
They're waiting for you.
　　[*The last of the bunk-house squad, leaving* NEIL *behind, enter
　　the granary. There is a rough knocking on the door at
　　left*]

Stirling. Come in.
　　[ANDRE *and the* BRIGADIER *enter, followed by two or three other
　　Officers and last by* HOWE *and* MARY PHILIPSE, *who
　　wears a soldier's cloak*]
This is poor shelter,
but perfect for our purpose.

Brigadier. It's a spot
that one might refer to as retired.

Washington. I believe
we're unknown to each other, save in name.

Andre. Why, sir,
we carry an interlocutor. This lady—
　　[*He turns to the door.* MARY PHILIPSE *comes forward*]

Mary.
　　[*To* WASHINGTON]
I've been a faithful postman,
you note—rode hard, and caught you a general

in the midst of his strategy. Sir William, this
is General Washington—the tall one, who looks sad—
and, General, this is Sir William Howe—of whom
you may have heard. The rest is entourage
and may be neglected.

Washington.
  [*Bowing*]
  It's good of you to answer
  my word in person.

Howe.
  [*Bowing*]
  Sir, I have long looked forward
  to a meeting with you, though you've avoided it.
  I hope we shall be friends.

Washington. Let's assume we are.
  At least our quarrel's not personal. May I take
  this opportunity to thank a lady
  for bringing us together?

Mary. I have my reward.

Washington. And since life is never as scheduled, I'll be brief
  in apologizing for an exchange of gunfire
  you may have heard as you came. Some lawless spirits
  from my own army had descended on
  this island for their own purposes. There's been
  a skirmish and some casualties, and the men
  are still about, but will keep the truce.

Howe. God, man,
  whoever ordered it, or how it came about

you've had the best of this day's work. I assure you
I'm more than rueful over my good marsh hay
sunk in ten feet of water; and those rascals of yours,
I'm told, have robbed the corn-cribs. I knew of the hay
but I learned of the maize on my way here.

Washington. Well, sir, I fear
it was no great loss.

Howe. Well, it was here and it's gone.
Sic transit horse-feed mundi. I'd sacrifice
much more to make your acquaintance.—Does it meet
your wish that we transact whatever business
we have before witnesses? We can talk alone
if it suits your purpose.

Washington. Sir, I'd a little rather
this discussion were known to my officers.

Howe. Right, right.
And so would I.

Washington. First, let it be understood
that I bind myself to nothing by this meeting,
nor have I altered in my loyalty
to the cause I captain. But you have sent me word
that if a peace were arrived at now, the king
would expunge all statutes over which we differed,
omit taxes of which we complained, and, in simple,
   grant us
all objects for which we fought originally,
except our independence.

Howe. You may add also

complete erasure of all charges made
against you as rebels, so that you're received
freely and brotherly again among us
without writ or reprisal.

Washington. This order would apply
to all, without exception?

Howe. Without exception.
For I'm free to tell you, since it's kept no secret,
we're sick and sore about this war in England,
would to God it had never started, and want you back
on your own terms.

Washington. Well, frankly, my own terms
would mean that we never went back at all, for going
would mean we accept the king, but I'm not alone
in these decisions; we have a government,
and plenty in that government are sore
and sick as in your own. I've lately learned
that some backhanded gesture was made toward you
by members of Congress, and I've come in some pique
    to say
that if any settlement with the king goes forward
it will first go through my hands.

Howe. I would I might
speak freely, as you have, but I confess I'm bound
to secrecy in that matter.

Washington. You may well ask
why I have not gone to Congress, and said to them
what I say to you. I would answer, I've said my say

to Congress in so many different ways
and wasted so much language, that the thought
of speaking to them gives me gumboils. I
have come to you directly as a soldier
to warn you there will be no peace, and no peace
can be made effective, without me.

Howe. How well I knew that
  you can judge from the fact that I asked you for this
      meeting,
  not content to deal elsewhere. I have my spies out.
  There was a time when Congress had control
  of your rebellion. Not now. The city boys
  are weary of it, but all your fighting strength
  is ranked with farmers, and while they follow you
  and you lead them, there's a war. We can begin
  with that as a basis. Your word is good with your army
  and good with me.

Washington. Well, there'll be a storm, but if
  it's peace the Congress wants, peace it shall have,
  only it will be of my making. It's not too easy
  to swallow a king, after your gorge has risen
  against him so long—

Stirling. Now, God forbid this, General,
  must we take back King George?

Washington. God damn you, Stirling!
  Do you think it's easy for me?
      [*A pause*]

Neil. They said it was rain on the roof,

rain, rain, and summer quiet, but it was heartbeat—
heartbeat in the silence—

Stirling. Lie quiet, lad.

Neil. She said lie quiet, too. Who are they here?
They've taken me prisoner! It's articles of war
you can die, but not be prisoner!

Stirling. No, no.

Washington. Forgive us.
The lad was wounded this morning.
[MARY PHILIPSE *goes to* NEIL]

Mary. Does he lie alone,
untended?

Washington. The soldiers cared for him.

Neil. They came in—
oh, you should see them! There were pikes and arms,
and a dying man cried, "Mother of God!" and died,
for they die, too, but not so happy, never
so happy!—They were English bastards!
The bastards of a king! I'm dying, Tavis;
give me your hand.
[MARY *gives her hand to him*]

Mary. Yes, yes.

Neil. You'll have a child.
You must call it by my name. My name was Neil.
Was sometime. You must not carve it. Let it live in a
heartbeat,
yours and mine. You'll remember?

Mary. Yes, Neil.

    [TEAGUE *opens the door, and steps out, thinking he may help.*
    Others appear behind him]

Neil. I'm sorry.

    Something stops my breath. I think I'm dying,
    but if I die you will share my legacy,
    all men will live free in a free land, all men,
    and there will be no more kings. It's hard to believe,
    but I believe it.

Mary. You must believe it.

Neil. I do.

    Hold my hand. This is a dark, dark, morning.

        [*He tries to rise*]

    There's light still—there—

        [*He falls back*]

Teague. Shall we take him?

Mary. Let him lie still. I'll cover his face.

    [*She bends over him.* TENCH *comes in from the left, looks about,*
    and goes directly up to WASHINGTON]

Tench. In regard to certain corn

    which this squad of the First Virginia sacked last night
    from His Majesty's corn-cribs, let me report it stowed
    at Clopton's landing. You'll find it there if you want it.
    If General Howe should miss it, that's where it is,
    but he won't get it.

    [*Nearly all the men have emerged from the granary*]

Howe. I've said good-bye to my corn,
    not without regret.

Tench. As to the losses incurred

in this action, there have been some wounded, and some
   killed,
how many I don't know, but among the latter
Nick Teague and Lucifer Tench. I'm sorry, Teague;
the boy slipped down between the piles. He was hurt
and I couldn't reach him.

Teague. Yes, sir.

Washington. Do you list yourself
   among the slain? It's rather tasteless joking.

Tench. I'm dead enough. My boots are full of blood.
   [*He lays a hand on the barrel for support*]
To die for hay and grain! There's a high death
for a swashing soldier! The devil damn your kings
and Congresses and their hay! Take your hand from me.
I'll walk to where I lie. A dog dies best
in a corner.
   [*He starts toward the granary*]

Stirling. Lucifer!

Tench. I've had my day
   and it's time for another dog. It's exit, midnight,
and alas and alack for Lucifer. Sir, I've loved you,
but if you set your seal to an English compact
my curse on you.—These dying men have visions
and that's the gist of mine. Bring on your burlap,
and the sailor's needle, and sew me in to sleep;
I'm tired and done.
   [*He goes into the granary*]

Washington. Tench, man! Tench!
   [*He follows* TENCH. MARY *lays the blanket gently over* NEIL'S
   face and rises, facing TEAGUE]

Mary. This was your son?

Teague. No, ma'am.
   Nick was different from him. Nick was a boy
   you wouldn't see often.

Stirling. Sir William, it may be
   that you'd prefer to wait elsewhere, and this lady,
   till we're free again.

Howe. Thank you. I'm not unmoved
   at any brave man's passing, but these griefs are private
   and we'll take a turn outside.
      [*He turns toward* Mary]

Mary. I'll stay.
      [Howe *bows and goes out right, with his officers*]

Stirling. Aye?
      [Washington *reenters. There is a pause*]

Mary. I heard what this lad said dying, and I'll betray you
   no further even by silence. The French alliance
   has been signed with the colonies. It was wished, of
      course,
   to keep this from you, but it's true.

Lafayette. It's signed?

Mary. Signed, sealed and made fast by Franklin.

Lafayette. How do you hear this?

Mary. Your letters were on the captured packet.
   Sir William
   had the news yesterday.

Lafayette. Sir, I beg you, before
  you pledge yourself to Howe, you gather your troops
  and make one final effort—

Washington. Gather my troops!
  Have they strength to come together! Gabriel's trumpet
  might rally that vale of bones! Bring me these spectres
  with the wind-fed entrails and mouths that open and
      speak not
  gaping their misery! Summon forth brigades
  and companies from the lazarettes they lie in,
  cry, "Lazarus, arise! On to the field!"
  This is no mockery. The cerements
  are much too tough for miracle. Look about you
  at these remnants of dying and deserting men!
  What could I offer them to follow me?
  What could I say to them? Call them in to me!
  Come in! Come in and hear me—you were some of the
      best,
  you skulkers who run the woods! Come in! I've told you
  no charge will be brought against you. I'll tell you why
  I've come here to surrender. The British staff
  waits outside for my word. And the reason I quit
  is because I've neither a Congress nor an army.
  Congress is through with the war—and the army's
      through
  and running out. Look for them in the woods—
  you'll find them there. They root for acorns and pignuts
  to fill their bellies—and they had good reason to go
  for Congress wanted to quit and sent no food
  and men must eat or die. There was a time

when you had shoes and powder for your guns
and fought to rule yourselves. There was hope in the air
and possible victory. If you starved and died
you died for a purpose. That's gone now. If you die
you die for nothing. We've set our feet down now
on a bed rock of despair, and I promise those
who'll follow me further, no chance of victory,
for, by my God, I see none, no glory or gain,
or laurels returning home, but wounds and death—
cold and disease and hunger, winters to come
such as this you have, with our bloody trail in the snow
and no end to it till you shovel each other in
with those at Valley Forge! Close in and take
your place in my ranks if you like it. If you don't,
and none will blame you, go your road as you have
and find yourselves food, and live!

    [*He turns away*]

Spad. You'll take us back?

Washington. Take you back!

Spad. I'll go with you!

Alcock. Yes, by God!

The Men. Come on, you fellows, you heard what he said!
And so will I.
We'll go with you!
Do you mean you'll take us?
Put me in!
Anywhere you say to go!
That goes for all of us!

Alcock. We thought it was over!
We thought it was falling to pieces, but if you meant
what you said about being plowed under, before we stop,
hell, I'm for being plowed under!

Stirling. Shall I call in the British delegation?
[WASHINGTON *nods assent*]

Andrew. And let them go.

Alcock. Let the English soldiers
take their red-coats back to England where they belong!
They can leave the pants. We can use the pants.

Spad. They won't get me till I get a few of them first!
Let them wash us back to the mountains! When I get
my back to a mountain I'm deadly.

Alcock. And about the commissary—
that corn we ferried over—that's yours, you know.

Washington. What corn?

Alcock. We ferried a thousand bushels last night,
and lost three men doing it. Well, that goes to feed the
army.

Washington. That's what you were doing here?

Alcock. That's what we were doing. And it was cold work,
too,
till the English made it hot!

Washington. The forge was cold
that smelted these fellows into steel—but steel
they are. I know them now. And now I change

my answer! Let one ragged thousand of them
pledge them to this with me, and we'll see it through.

Spad. That's what we want to hear!

Jock. Aye, right!

Spad. Will you do one thing for me, sir?

Washington. Name it.

Spad. I want to shake your hand. That'll be something to
tell the boys.

Washington. My hand—why, lad,
would I keep my hand from my friends? My heart goes
with it
to every man among you. I believe
Sir William Howe is waiting—and now we're ready
to give him his quittance and let him go.
[*There is a movement among the men.* VARNUM *steps out*]

Jock. Aye, aye—now tell him.
[HOWE *and his officers enter*]

Washington. Sir William, I have forgotten
what was last said; something of our accepting
kings or princes. It hardly matters now,
for it's better blank. Gentlemen, I am servant
to these men in the rags of homespun. They've heard
from me
this proposition of the king's, and they
refuse it flatly. This war, to your brief misfortune,
is not mine to end, but theirs. I have my orders
and I'm in your debt for a very fruitless errand
over wild water.

Howe. Your choice of councillors,
  sir, is your own, of course, but may I remind you
  that the people of a country are never open
  to reason in such matters? They're willing to fight
  for the virgin birth, or the freedom of the seas,
  or the tomb of Christ, when nobody knows where it is,
  or your brotherhood of man,—oh, any drivel
  that's clean impossible. But tell them once
  what a war's really for, perhaps, trade advantage,
  or the rights of bankers, and they drop their war like a
     snake.
  This war's for trade advantage.

Alcock. Oh, no it's not!
  It's because we don't like kings, and won't have a king,
  and never will!

Washington. And there we end.

Howe. You'll draw out this tragedy further?

Washington. As far as we must.

Howe. But you've lost, lost now; your government's op-
     posed,
  your men in draglets—the dregs of what's swept up
  to eat—

Washington. We're all too well aware of that.
  And we have lost; we know it; by all rules of the game
  we're beaten, and should surrender. If this war
  were for trade advantage, it would end to-night.
  It was made over subsidies, or some such matter,
  but it's been taken over. Let the merchants submit

if that's any good to you, then come out and find
my hunters and backwoodsmen, and beat us down
into the land we fight for. When you've done that—
the king may call us subject. For myself, I'd have died
within if I'd surrendered. The spirit of earth
moves over earth like flame and finds fresh home
when the old's burned out. It stands over this my
    country
in this dark year, and stands like a pillar of fire
to show us an uncouth clan, unread, harsh-spoken,
but followers of dream, a dream that men
shall bear no burdens save of their own choosing,
shall walk upright, masterless, doff a hat to none,
and choose their gods! It's destined to win, this dream,
weak though we are. Even if we should fail,
it's destined to win! If we could hold on till spring
even now the French would be on our side, and
    beat you.
Have you heard that news?

Howe. I was not aware it had reached you.
    Your work, lady?

Mary. Yes, mine.

Howe. Why, trust a woman
    and tell the world. Sir, I've been more your friend
    than you know in this matter. This is my last winter
    with the British army here. They'll send someone else
    to fight you, but not me. I'm no Quixote,
    to battle with dreams and windmills. But it's not over,
    make up your minds to that. They'll press you harder
    when I'm gone home.

Washington. Sir, we engage to stand it.

Howe. No doubt you will. This spikes our guns for us.
There was a storm promised before we came
and I'd like to beat it back. Come, we must go.
The terms I've offered you will not be offered
by my successor.

Washington. We should hardly expect it.

Howe. No,
for I've been too much your friend. Heigh-ho, I'll get
a drubbing when I face England. Good-bye!

Washington. We wish you good morning,
and a fair voyage, Sir William.
    [HOWE *goes out. The officers follow*]

Washington. We owe you thanks too, madame.

Mary. I hope so.

Washington. And it will be remembered.

Mary. Why, then, I'm glad.
I know my own destiny, little though I may like it,
and it's not high as yours. There are some men
who lift the age they inhabit—till all men walk
on higher ground in that lifetime. God keep you all
and bring you victory.
    [*She goes out*]

Washington. And so we're left
with some years of revolution on our hands.

Alcock. Good God,
you shouldn't have put it up to us. I'm standing

in a man's clothes for the first time in a year.
I'd never say die.

Stirling. We have food for three days.

Washington. And then
for three more if we can find it—and three more—
if we can find it. And now I think we will!
[*He goes toward* NEIL]
Was the brother lost?

Stirling. Yes, Mason.

Washington. Mason and Nick and Neil—and Tench. They
paid
for our three days. You know best who will pay
for days to come. We must bury them here. They died
here
and earned their ground.
This liberty will look easy by and by
when nobody dies to get it.
[*They go toward* NEIL *to take him up*]
Shall we fire a volley
over our dead?

Teague. No, sir. We'll need our powder,
and dead men don't hear volleys.

Washington. So be it, then.

CURTAIN

V · WINTERSET

CHARACTERS

Trock	Carr
Shadow	Herman
Garth	Lucia
Miriamne	Piny
Esdras	A Sailor
The Hobo	Street Urchin
1st Girl	Policeman
2nd Girl	Radical
Judge Gaunt	Sergeant
Mio	

Non-speaking

Urchins

Two Men in Blue Serge

ACT ONE

Scene I

Scene: *The scene is the bank of a river under a bridgehead. A gigantic span starts from the rear of the stage and appears to lift over the heads of the audience and out to the left. At the right rear is a wall of solid supporting masonry. To the left an apartment building abuts against the bridge and forms the left wall of the stage with a dark basement window and a door in the brick wall. To the right, and in the foreground, an outcropping of original rock makes a barricade behind which one may enter through a cleft. To the rear, against the masonry, two sheds have been built by waifs and strays for shelter. The river bank, in the foreground, is black rock worn smooth by years of trampling. There is room for exit and entrance to the left around the apartment house, also around the rock to the right. A single street lamp is seen at the left—and a glimmer of apartment lights in the background beyond. It is an early, dark December morning.*

Two Young Men in Serge *lean against the masonry, matching bills.* Trock Estrella *and* Shadow *come in from the left.*

Trock. Go back and watch the car.

[*The* Two Young Men *go out.* Trock *walks to the corner and looks toward the city*]

You roost of punks and gulls! Sleep, sleep it off,
whatever you had last night, get down in warm,
one big ham-fat against another—sleep,
cling, sleep and rot! Rot out your pasty guts
with diddling, you had no brain to begin. If you had
there'd be no need for us to sleep on iron
who had too much brains for you.

3

Shadow. Now look, Trock, look,
  what would the warden say to talk like that?

Trock. May they die as I die!
  By God, what life they've left me
  they shall keep me well! I'll have that out of them—
  these pismires that walk like men!

Shadow. Because, look, chief,
  it's all against science and penology
  for you to get out and begin to cuss that way
  before your prison vittles are out of you. Hell,
  you're supposed to leave the pen full of high thought,
  kind of noble-like, loving toward all mankind,
  ready to kiss their feet—or whatever parts
  they stick out toward you. Look at me!

Trock. I see you.
  And even you may not live as long as you think.
  You think too many things are funny. Well, laugh.
  But it's not so funny.

Shadow. Come on, Trock, you know me.
  Anything you say goes, but give me leave
  to kid a little.

Trock. Then laugh at somebody else!
  It's a lot safer! They've soaked me once too often
  in that vat of poisoned hell they keep up-state
  to soak men in, and I'm rotten inside, I'm all
  one liquid puke inside where I had lungs
  once, like yourself! And now they want to get me
  and stir me in again—and that'd kill me—

and that's fine for them. But before that happens to me
a lot of these healthy boys'll know what it's like
when you try to breathe and have no place to put air—
they'll learn it from me!

Shadow. They've got nothing on you, chief.

Trock. I don't know yet. That's what I'm here to find out.
If they've got what they might have
it's not a year this time—
no, nor ten. It's screwed down under a lid.—
I can die quick enough, without help.

Shadow. You're the skinny kind
that lives forever.

Trock. He gave me a half a year,
the doc at the gate.

Shadow. Jesus.

Trock. Six months I get,
and the rest's dirt, six feet.

   [LUCIA, *the street-piano man, comes in right from behind the
   rock and goes to the shed where he keeps his piano.*
   PINY, *the apple-woman, follows and stands in the entrance.* LUCIA *speaks to Estrella, who still stands facing
   Shadow*]

Lucia. Morning.

   [TROCK *and* SHADOW *go out round the apartment house without
   speaking*]

Piny. Now what would you call them?

Lucia. Maybe someting da river washed up.

Piny. Nothing ever washed him—that black one.

Lucia. Maybe not, maybe so. More like his pa and ma raise-a heem in da cellar.

[*He wheels out the piano*]

Piny. He certainly gave me a turn.

[*She lays a hand on the rock*]

Lucia. You don' live-a right, ol' gal. Take heem easy. Look on da bright-a side. Never say-a die. Me, every day in every way I getta be da regular heller.

[*He starts out*]

CURTAIN

ACT ONE
SCENE II

SCENE: *A cellar apartment under the apartment building, floored with cement and roofed with huge boa constrictor pipes that run slantwise from left to right, dwarfing the room. An outside door opens to the left and a door at the right rear leads to the interior of the place. A low squat window to the left. A table at the rear and a few chairs and books make up the furniture. GARTH, son of Esdras, sits alone, holding a violin upside down to inspect a crack at its base. He lays the bow on the floor and runs his fingers over the joint. MIRIAMNE enters from the rear, a girl of fifteen. GARTH looks up, then down again.*

Miriamne. Garth—

Garth. The glue lets go. It's the steam, I guess.
It splits the hair on your head.

Miriamne. It can't be mended?

Garth. I can't mend it.
No doubt there are fellows somewhere
who'd mend it for a dollar—and glad to do it.
That is if I had a dollar.—Got a dollar?
No, I thought not.

Miriamne. Garth, you've sat at home here
three days now. You haven't gone out at all.
Something frightens you.

Garth. Yes?

Miriamne. And father's frightened.
He reads without knowing where. When a shadow falls

7

across the page he waits for a blow to follow
after the shadow. Then in a little while
he puts his book down softly and goes out
to see who passed.

Garth.   A bill collector, maybe.
We haven't paid the rent.

Miriamne. No.

Garth. You're a bright girl, sis.—
You see too much. You run along and cook.
Why don't you go to school?

Miriamne. I don't like school.
They whisper behind my back.

Garth. Yes? About what?

Miriamne. What did the lawyer mean
that wrote to you?

Garth.

   [*Rising*]

What lawyer?

Miriamne. I found a letter
on the floor of your room. He said, "Don't get me wrong,
but stay in out of the rain the next few days,
just for instance."

Garth. I thought I burned that letter.

Miriamne. Afterward you did. And then what was printed
about the Estrella gang—you hid it from me,
you and father. What is it—about this murder—?

Garth. Will you shut up, you fool!

Miriamne. But if you know
why don't you tell them, Garth?
If it's true—what they say—
you knew all the time Romagna wasn't guilty,
and could have said so—

Garth. Everybody knew
Romagna wasn't guilty! But they weren't listening
to evidence in his favor. They didn't want it.
They don't want it now.

Miriamne. But was that why
they never called on you?—

Garth. So far as I know
they never'd heard of me—and I can assure you
I knew nothing about it—

Miriamne. But something's wrong—
and it worries father—

Garth. What could be wrong?

Miriamne. I don't know.

   [*A pause*]

Garth. And I don't know. You're a good kid, Miriamne,
but you see too many movies. I wasn't mixed up
in any murder, and I don't mean to be.
If I had a dollar to get my fiddle fixed
and another to hire a hall, by God I'd fiddle
some of the prodigies back into Sunday School
where they belong, but I won't get either, and so

I sit here and bite my nails—but if you hoped
I had some criminal romantic past
you'll have to look again!

Miriamne. Oh, Garth, forgive me—
But I want you to be so far above such things
nothing could frighten you. When you seem to shrink
and be afraid, and you're the brother I love,
I want to run there and cry, if there's any question
they care to ask, you'll be quick and glad to answer,
for there's nothing to conceal!

Garth. And that's all true—

Miriamne. But then I remember—
how you dim the lights—
and we go early to bed—and speak in whispers—
and I could think there's a death somewhere behind us—
an evil death—

Garth.

> [*Hearing a step*]

Now for God's sake, be quiet!

> [ESDRAS, *an old rabbi with a kindly face, enters from the out-
> side. He is hurried and troubled*]

Esdras. I wish to speak alone with someone here
if I may have this room. Miriamne—

Miriamne.

> [*Turning to go*]

Yes, father.

> [*The outer door is suddenly thrown open*. TROCK *appears*]

Trock.

   [*After a pause*]

You'll excuse me for not knocking.

   [SHADOW *follows Trock in*]

Sometimes it's best to come in quiet. Sometimes
it's a good way to go out. Garth's home, I see.
He might not have been here if I made a point
of knocking at doors.

Garth. How are you, Trock?

Trock. I guess
you can see how I am.

   [*To Miriamne*]

   Stay here. Stay where you are.
We'd like to make your acquaintance.
—If you want the facts
I'm no better than usual, thanks. Not enough sun,
my physician tells me. Too much close confinement.
A lack of exercise and an overplus
of beans in the diet. You've done well, no doubt?

Garth. I don't know what makes you think so.

Trock. Who's the family?

Garth. My father and my sister.

Trock. Happy to meet you.
Step inside a minute. The boy and I
have something to talk about.

Esdras. No, no—he's said nothing—
nothing, sir, nothing!

Trock. When I say go out, you go—-

Esdras.

> [*Pointing to the door*]

Miriamne—

Garth. Go on out, both of you!

Esdras. Oh, sir—I'm old—
old and unhappy—

Garth. Go on!

> [Miriamne *and* Esdras *go inside*]

Trock. And if you listen
I'll riddle that door!

> [Shadow *shuts the door behind them and stands against* it]

I just got out, you see,
and I pay my first call on you.

Garth. Maybe you think
I'm not in the same jam you are.

Trock. That's what I do think.
Who started looking this up?

Garth. I wish I knew,
and I wish he was in hell! Some damned professor
with nothing else to do. If you saw his stuff
you know as much as I do.

Trock. It wasn't you
turning state's evidence?

Garth. Hell, Trock, use your brain!
　The case was closed. They burned Romagna for it
　and that finished it. Why should I look for trouble
　and maybe get burned myself?

Trock. Boy, I don't know,
　but I just thought I'd find out.

Garth. I'm going straight, Trock.
　I can play this thing, and I'm trying to make a living.
　I haven't talked and nobody's talked to me.
　Christ—it's the last thing I'd want!

Trock. Your old man knows.

Garth. That's where I got the money that last time
　when you needed it. He had a little saved up,
　but I had to tell him to get it. He's as safe
　as Shadow there.

Trock.

　　[*Looking at Shadow*]

　There could be people safer
　than that son-of-a-bitch.

Shadow. Who?

Trock. You'd be safer dead
　along with some other gorillas.

Shadow. It's beginning to look
　as if you'd feel safer with everybody dead,
　the whole god-damn world.

Trock. I would. These Jesus-bitten
professors! Looking up their half-ass cases!
We've got enough without that.

Garth. There's no evidence
to reopen the thing.

Trock. And suppose they called on you
and asked you to testify?

Garth. Why then I'd tell 'em
that all I know is what I read in the papers.
And I'd stick to that.

Trock. How much does your sister know?

Garth. I'm honest with you, Trock. She read my name
in the professor's pamphlet, and she was scared
the way anybody would be. She got nothing
from me, and anyway she'd go to the chair
herself before she'd send me there.

Trock. Like hell.

Garth. Besides, who wants to go to trial again
except the radicals?—You and I won't spill
and unless we did there's nothing to take to court
as far as I know. Let the radicals go on howling
about getting a dirty deal. They always howl
and nobody gives a damn. This professor's red—
everybody knows it.

Trock. You're forgetting the judge.
Where's the damn judge?

Garth. What judge?

Trock. Read the morning papers.
It says Judge Gaunt's gone off his nut. He's got
that damn trial on his mind, and been going round
proving to everybody he was right all the time
and the radicals were guilty—stopping people
in the street to prove it—and now he's nuts entirely
and nobody knows where he is.

Garth. Why don't they know?

Trock. Because he's on the loose somewhere! They've got
the police of three cities looking for him.

Garth. Judge Gaunt?

Trock. Yes. Judge Gaunt.

Shadow. Why should that worry you?
He's crazy, ain't he? And even if he wasn't
he's arguing on your side. You're jittery, chief.
God, all the judges are looney. You've got the jitters,
and you'll damn well give yourself away some time
peeing yourself in public.

[TROCK *half turns toward Shadow in anger*]

Don't jump the gun now,
I've got pockets in my clothes, too.

[*His hand is in his coat pocket*]

Trock. All right. Take it easy.

[*He takes his hand from his pocket, and* SHADOW *does the same*]
[*To Garth*]

Maybe you're lying to me and maybe you're not.
Stay at home a few days.

Garth. Sure thing. Why not?

Trock. And when I say stay home I mean stay home.
If I have to go looking for you you'll stay a long time
wherever I find you.

  [*To Shadow*]

  Come on. We'll get out of here.

  [*To Garth*]

Be seeing you.

  [SHADOW *and* TROCK *go out. After a pause* GARTH *walks over
  to his chair and picks up the violin. Then he puts it
  down and goes to the inside door, which he opens*]

Garth. He's gone.

  [MIRIAMNE *enters,* ESDRAS *behind her*]

Miriamne.

  [*Going up to Garth*]

  Let's not stay here.

  [*She puts her hands on his arms*]

  I thought he'd come for something—horrible.
  Is he coming back?

Garth. I don't know.

Miriamne. Who is he, Garth?

Garth. He'd kill me if I told you who he is,
that is, if he knew.

Miriamne. Then don't say it—

Garth. Yes, and I'll say it! I was with a gang one time
    that robbed a pay roll. I saw a murder done,
    and Trock Estrella did it. If that got out
    I'd go to the chair and so would he—that's why
    he was here today—

Miriamne. But that's not true—

Esdras. He says it
    to frighten you, child.

Garth. Oh, no I don't! I say it
    because I've held it in too long! I'm damned
    if I sit here forever, and look at the door,
    waiting for Trock with his sub-machine gun, waiting
    for police with a warrant!—I say I'm damned, and I am,
    no matter what I do! These piddling scales
    on a violin—first position, third, fifth,
    arpeggios in E—and what I'm thinking
    is Romagna dead for the murder—dead while I sat here
    dying inside—dead for the thing Trock did
    while I looked on—and I could have saved him, yes—
    but I sat here and let him die instead of me
    because I wanted to live! Well, it's no life,
    and it doesn't matter who I tell, because
    I mean to get it over!

Miriamne. Garth, it's not true!

Garth. I'd take some scum down with me if I died—
    that'd be one good deed—

Esdras. Son, son, you're mad—
    someone will hear—

Garth. Then let them hear! I've lived
  with ghosts too long, and lied too long. God damn you
  if you keep me from the truth!—

  [*He turns away*]

  Oh, God damn the world!
I don't want to die!

  [*He throws himself down*]

Esdras. I should have known.
  I thought you hard and sullen,
  Garth, my son. And you were a child, and hurt
  with a wound that might be healed.
  —All men have crimes,
  and most of them are hidden, and many are heavy
  as yours must be to you.

  [GARTH *sobs*]

  They walk the streets
  to buy and sell, but a spreading crimson stain
  tinges the inner vestments, touches flesh,
  and burns the quick. You're not alone.

Garth. I'm alone
  in this.

Esdras. Yes, if you hold with the world that only
  those who die suddenly should be revenged.
  But those whose hearts are cancered, drop by drop
  in small ways, little by little, till they've borne
  all they can bear, and die—these deaths will go
  unpunished now as always. When we're young
  we have faith in what is seen, but when we're old

we know that what is seen is traced in air
and built on water. There's no guilt under heaven,
just as there's no heaven, till men believe it—
no earth, till men have seen it, and have a word
to say this is the earth.

Garth. Well, I say there's an earth,
and I say I'm guilty on it, guilty as hell.

Esdras. Yet till it's known you bear no guilt at all—
unless you wish. The days go by like film,
like a long written scroll, a figured veil
unrolling out of darkness into fire
and utterly consumed. And on this veil,
running in sounds and symbols of men's minds
reflected back, life flickers and is shadow
going toward flame. Only what men can see
exists in that shadow. Why must you rise and cry out:
That was I, there in the ravelled tapestry,
there, in that pistol flash, when the man was killed.
I was there, and was one, and am bloodstained!
Let the wind
and fire take that hour to ashes out of time
and out of mind! This thing that men call justice,
this blind snake that strikes men down in the dark,
mindless with fury, keep your hand back from it,
pass by in silence—let it be forgotten, forgotten!—
Oh, my son, my son—have pity!

Miriamne. But if it was true
and someone died—then it was more than shadow—
and it doesn't blow away—

Garth. Well, it was true.

Esdras. Say it if you must. If you have heart to die,
    say it, and let them take what's left—there was little
    to keep, even before—

Garth. Oh, I'm a coward—
    I always was. I'll be quiet and live. I'll live
    even if I have to crawl. I know.

  [*He gets up and goes into the inner room*]

Miriamne. Is it better
    to tell a lie and live?

Esdras. Yes, child. It's better.

Miriamne. But if I had to do it—
    I think I'd die.

Esdras. Yes, child. Because you're young.

Miriamne. Is that the only reason?

Esdras. The only reason.

CURTAIN

ACT ONE

Scene III

Scene: *Under the bridge, evening of the same day. When the curtain rises* Miriamne *is sitting alone on the ledge at the rear of the apartment house. A spray of light falls on her from a street lamp above. She shivers a little in her thin coat, but sits still as if heedless of the weather. Through the rocks on the other side a* Tramp *comes down to the river bank, hunting a place to sleep. He goes softly to the apple-woman's hut and looks in, then turns away, evidently not daring to preëmpt it. He looks at Miriamne doubtfully. The door of the street-piano man is shut. The vagabond passes it and picks carefully among some rags and shavings to the right.* Miriamne *looks up and sees him but makes no sign. She looks down again, and the man curls himself up in a makeshift bed in the corner, pulling a piece of sacking over his shoulders.* Two Girls *come in from round the apartment house.*

1st Girl. Honest, I never heard of anything so romantic. Because you never liked him.

2nd Girl. I certainly never did.

1st Girl. You've got to tell me how it happened. You've got to.

2nd Girl. I couldn't. As long as I live I couldn't. Honest, it was terrible. It was terrible.

1st Girl. What was so terrible?

2nd Girl. The way it happened.

1st Girl. Oh, please—not to a soul, never.

21

2nd Girl. Well, you know how I hated him because he had
such a big mouth. So he reached over and grabbed me,
and I began all falling to pieces inside, the way you do—
and I said, "Oh no you don't mister," and started
screaming and kicked a hole through the windshield and
lost a shoe, and he let go and was cursing and growling
because he borrowed the car and didn't have money to
pay for the windshield, and he started to cry, and I got
so sorry for him I let him, and now he wants to marry
me.

1st Girl. Honest, I never heard of anything so romantic!

[*She sees the sleeping Tramp*]

My God, what you won't see!

[*They give the Tramp a wide berth, and go out right. The* TRAMP
sits up looking about him. JUDGE GAUNT, *an elderly,
quiet man, well dressed but in clothes that have seen
some weather, comes in uncertainly from the left. He
holds a small clipping in his hand and goes up to the
Hobo*]

Gaunt.

[*Tentatively*]

Your pardon, sir. Your pardon, but perhaps you can
tell me the name of this street.

Hobo. Huh?

Gaunt. The name of this street?

Hobo. This ain't no street.

Gaunt. There, where the street lamps are.

Hobo. That's the alley.

Gaunt. Thank you. It has a name, no doubt?

Hobo. That's the alley.

Gaunt. I see. I won't trouble you. You wonder why I ask,
I daresay.—I'm a stranger.—Why do you look at me?

[*He steps back*]

I—I'm not the man you think. You've mistaken me, sir.

Hobo. Huh?

Judge. Perhaps misled by a resemblance. But you're mistaken—I had an errand in this city. It's only by accident
that I'm here—

Hobo.

[*Muttering*]

You go to hell.

Judge.

[*Going nearer to him, bending over him*]

Yet why should I deceive you? Before God, I held the
proofs in my hands. I hold them still. I tell you the defense was cunning beyond belief, and unscrupulous in its
use of propaganda—they gagged at nothing—not
even—

[*He rises*]

No, no—I'm sorry—this will hardly interest you. I'm
sorry. I have an errand.

[*He looks toward the street.* ESDRAS *enters from the basement
and goes to Miriamne. The* JUDGE *steps back into the
shadows*]

Esdras. Come in, my daughter. You'll be cold here.

Miriamne. After a while.

Esdras. You'll be cold. There's a storm coming.

Miriamne. I didn't want him to see me crying. That was all.

Esdras. I know.

Miriamne. I'll come soon.

> [ESDRAS *turns reluctantly and goes out the way he came.* MIRIAMNE *rises to go in, pausing to dry her eyes.* MIO *and* CARR, *road boys of seventeen or so, come round the apartment house. The Judge has disappeared*]

Carr. Thought you said you were never coming east again.

Mio. Yeah, but—I heard something changed my mind.

Carr. Same old business?

Mio. Yes. Just as soon not talk about it.

Carr. Where did you go from Portland?

Mio. Fishing—I went fishing. God's truth.

Carr. Right after I left?

Mio. Fell in with a fisherman's family on the coast and went after the beautiful mackerel fish that swim in the beautiful sea. Family of Greeks—Aristides Marinos was his lovely name. He sang while he fished. Made the pea-green Pacific ring with his bastard Greek chanties. Then I went to Hollywood High School for a while.

Carr. I'll bet that's a seat of learning.

Mio. It's the hind end of all wisdom. They kicked me out after a time.

Carr. For cause?

Mio. Because I had no permanent address, you see. That means nobody's paying school taxes for you, so out you go.
[*To Miriamne*]
What's the matter, kid?

Mariamne. Nothing.
[*She looks up at him, and they pause for a moment*]
Nothing.

Mio. I'm sorry.

Miriamne. It's all right.
[*She withdraws her eyes from his and goes out past him. He turns and looks after her*]

Carr. Control your chivalry.

Mio. A pretty kid.

Carr. A baby.

Mio. Wait for me.

Carr. Be a long wait?
[*Mio steps swiftly out after Miriamne, then returns*]
Yeah?

Mio. She's gone.

Carr. Think of that.

Mio. No, but I mean—vanished. Presto—into nothing—prodigioso.

Carr. Damn good thing, if you ask me. The homely ones are bad enough, but the lookers are fatal.

Mio. You exaggerate, Carr.

Carr. I doubt it.

Mio. Well, let her go. This river bank's loaded with typhus rats, too. Might as well die one death as another.

Carr. They say chronic alcoholism is nice but expensive. You can always starve to death.

Mio. Not always. I tried it. After the second day I walked thirty miles to Niagara Falls and made a tour of the plant to get the sample of shredded wheat biscuit on the way out.

Carr. Last time I saw you you couldn't think of anything you wanted to do except curse God and pass out. Still feeling low?

Mio. Not much different.

[*He turns away, then comes back*]

Talk about the lost generation, I'm the only one fits that title. When the State executes your father, and your mother dies of grief, and you know damn well he was innocent, and the authorities of your home town politely inform you they'd consider it a favor if you lived somewhere else—that cuts you off from the world—with a meat-axe.

Carr. They asked you to move?

Mio. It came to that.

Carr. God, that was white of them.

Mio. It probably gave them a headache just to see me after all that agitation. They knew as well as I did my father never staged a holdup. Anyway, I've got a new interest in life now.

Carr. Yes—I saw her.

Mio. I don't mean the skirt.—No, I got wind of something, out west, some college professor investigating the trial and turning up new evidence. Couldn't find anything he'd written out there, so I beat it east and arrived on this blessed island just in time to find the bums holing up in the public library for the winter. I know now what the unemployed have been doing since the depression started. They've been catching up on their reading in the main reference room. Man, what a stench! Maybe I stank, too, but a hobo has the stench of ten because his shoes are poor.

Carr. Tennyson.

Mio. Right. Jeez, I'm glad we met up again! Never knew anybody else that could track me through the driven snow of Victorian literature.

Carr. Now you're cribbing from some half-forgotten criticism of Ben Jonson's Roman plagiarisms.

Mio. Where did you get your education, sap?

Carr. Not in the public library, sap. My father kept a news-stand.

Mio. Well, you're right again.

[*There is a faint rumble of thunder*]

What's that? Winter thunder?

Carr. Or Mister God, beating on His little tocsin. Maybe announcing the advent of a new social order.

Mio. Or maybe it's going to rain coffee and doughnuts.

Carr. Or maybe it's going to rain.

Mio. Seems more likely.

[*Lowering his voice*]

Anyhow, I found Professor Hobhouse's discussion of the Romagna case. I think he has something. It occurred to me I might follow it up by doing a little sleuthing on my own account.

Carr. Yes?

Mio. I have done a little. And it leads me to somewhere in that tenement house that backs up against the bridge. That's how I happen to be here.

Carr. They'll never let you get anywhere with it, Mio. I told you that before.

Mio. I know you did.

Carr. The State can't afford to admit it was wrong, you see. Not when there's been that much of a row kicked up over it. So for all practical purposes the State was right and your father robbed the pay roll.

Mio. There's still such a thing as evidence.

Carr. It's something you can buy. In fact, at the moment
I don't think of anything you can't buy, including life,
honor, virtue, glory, public office, conjugal affection and
all kinds of justice, from the traffic court to the immortal
nine. Go out and make yourself a pot of money and you
can buy all the justice you want. Convictions obtained,
convictions averted. Lowest rates in years.

Mio. I know all that.

Carr. Sure.

Mio. This thing didn't happen to you.
They've left you your name
and whatever place you can take. For my heritage
they've left me one thing only, and that's to be
my father's voice crying up out of the earth
and quicklime where they stuck him. Electrocution
doesn't kill, you know. They eviscerate them
with a turn of the knife in the dissecting room.
The blood spurts out. The man was alive. Then into
the lime pit, leave no trace. Make it short shrift
and chemical dissolution. That's what they thought
of the man that was my father. Then my mother—
I tell you these county burials are swift
and cheap and run for profit! Out of the house
and into the ground, you wife of a dead dog. Wait,
here's some Romagna spawn left.
Something crawls here—
something they called a son. Why couldn't he die
along with his mother? Well, ease him out of town,

ease him out, boys, and see you're not too gentle.
He might come back. And, by their own living Jesus,
I will go back, and hang the carrion
around their necks that made it!
Maybe I can sleep then.
Or even live.

Carr. You have to try it?

Mio. Yes.
Yes. It won't let me alone. I've tried to live
and forget it—but I was birthmarked with hot iron
into the entrails. I've got to find out who did it
and make them see it till it scalds their eyes
and make them admit it till their tongues are blistered
with saying how black they lied!

[HERMAN, *a gawky shoe salesman, enters from the left*]

Herman. Hello. Did you see a couple of girls go this way?

Carr. Couple of girls? Did we see a couple of girls?

Mio. No.

Carr. No. No girls.

[HERMAN *hesitates, then goes out right.* LUCIA *comes in from
the left, trundling his piano.* PINY *follows him, weeping*]

Piny. They've got no right to do it—

Lucia. All right, hell what, no matter, I got to put him
away, I got to put him away, that's what the hell!

[Two STREET URCHINS *follow him in*]

Piny. They want everybody on the relief rolls and nobody
making a living?

Lucia. The cops, they do what the big boss says. The big boss, that's the mayor, he says he heard it once too often, the sextette—

Piny. They want graft, that's all. It's a new way to get graft—

Lucia. Oh, no, no, no! He's a good man, the mayor. He's just don't care for music, that's all.

Piny. Why shouldn't you make a living on the street? The National Biscuit Company ropes off Eighth Avenue—and does the mayor do anything? No, the police hit you over the head if you try to go through!

Lucia. You got the big dough, you get the pull, fine. No big dough, no pull, what the hell, get off the city property! Tomorrow I start cooking chestnuts . . .

[*He strokes the piano fondly. The* TWO GIRLS *and* HERMAN *come back from the right*]

She's a good little machine, this baby. Cost plenty—and two new records I only played twice. See, this one.

[*He starts turning the crank, talking while he plays*]

Two weeks since they play this one in a picture house.

[A SAILOR *wanders in from the left. One of the* STREET URCHINS *begins suddenly to dance a wild rumba, the others watch*]

Good boy—see, it's a lulu—it itches in the feet!

[HERMAN, *standing with his girl, tosses the boy a penny. He bows and goes on dancing; the other* URCHIN *joins him. The* SAILOR *tosses a coin*]

Sailor. Go it, Cuba! Go it!

[LUCIA *turns the crank, beaming*]

2nd Girl. Oh, Herman!

[*She throws her arms round Herman and they dance*]

1st Urchin. Hey, pipe the professionals!

1st Girl. Do your glide, Shirley! Do your glide!

Lucia. Maybe we can't play in front, maybe we can play behind!

[*The* Hobo *gets up from his nest and comes over to watch.* A Young Radical *wanders in*]

Maybe you don't know, folks! Tonight we play good-bye to the piano! Good-bye forever! No more piano on the streets! No more music! No more money for the music-man! Last time, folks! Good-bye to the piano— good-bye forever!

[Miriamne *comes out the rear door of the apartment and stands watching. The* Sailor *goes over to the 1st Girl and they dance together*]

Maybe you don't know, folks! Tomorrow will be sad as hell, tonight we dance! Tomorrow no more Verdi, no more rumba, no more good time! Tonight we play good-bye to the piano, good-bye forever!

[*The* Radical *edges up to Miriamne, and asks her to dance. She shakes her head and he goes to Piny, who dances with him. The* Hobo *begins to do a few lonely curvets on the side above*]

Hoy! Hoy! Pick 'em up and take 'em around! Use the head, use the feet! Last time forever!

[*He begins to sing to the air*]

Mio. Wait for me, will you?

Carr. Now's your chance.

[MIO *goes over to Miriamne and holds out a hand, smiling. She stands for a moment uncertain, then dances with him.* ESDRAS *comes out to watch.* JUDGE GAUNT *comes in from the left. There is a rumble of thunder*]

Lucia. Hoy! Hoy! Maybe it rains tonight, maybe it snows tomorrow! Tonight we dance good-bye.

[*He sings the air lustily.* A POLICEMAN *comes in from the left and looks on.* TWO OR THREE PEDESTRIANS *follow him*]

Policeman. Hey you!

[LUCIA *goes on singing*]

Hey, you!

Lucia.

[*Still playing*]

What you want?

Policeman. Sign off!

Lucia. What you mean? I get off the street!

Policeman. Sign off!

Lucia.

[*Still playing*]

What you mean?

[*The* POLICEMAN *walks over to him.* LUCIA *stops playing and the* DANCERS *pause*]

Policeman. Cut it.

Lucia. Is this a street?

Policeman. I say cut it out.

[*The* HOBO *goes back to his nest and sits in it, watching*]

Lucia. It's the last time. We dance good-bye to the piano.

Policeman. You'll dance good-bye to something else if I catch you cranking that thing again.

Lucia. All right.

Piny. I'll bet you don't say that to the National Biscuit Company!

Policeman. Lady, you've been selling apples on my beat for some time now, and I said nothing about it—

Piny. Selling apples is allowed—

Policeman. You watch yourself—

[*He takes a short walk around the place and comes upon the Hobo*]

What are you doing here?

[*The* HOBO *opens his mouth, points to it, and shakes his head*]

Oh, you are, are you?

[*He comes back to Lucia*]

So you trundle your so-called musical instrument to wherever you keep it, and don't let me hear it again.

[*The* RADICAL *leaps on the base of the rock at right. The* 1ST GIRL *turns away from the Sailor toward the 2nd Girl and Herman*]

Sailor. Hey, captain, what's the matter with the music?

Policeman. Not a thing, admiral.

Sailor. Well, we had a little party going here—

Policeman. I'll say you did.

2nd Girl. Please, officer, we want to dance.

Policeman. Go ahead. Dance.

2nd Girl. But we want music!

Policeman.

[*Turning to go*]

Sorry. Can't help you.

Radical. And there you see it, the perfect example of capitalistic oppression! In a land where music should be free as air and the arts should be encouraged, a uniformed minion of the rich, a guardian myrmidon of the Park Avenue pleasure hunters, steps in and puts a limit on the innocent enjoyments of the poor! We don't go to theatres! Why not? We can't afford it! We don't go to night clubs, where women dance naked and the music drips from saxophones and leaks out of Rudy Vallee— we can't afford that either!—But we might at least dance on the river bank to the strains of a barrel organ—!

[GARTH *comes out of the apartment and listens*]

Policeman. It's against the law!

Radical. What law? I challenge you to tell me what law of God or man—what ordinance—is violated by this spontaneous diversion? None! I say none! An official whim of the masters who should be our servants!—

Policeman. Get down! Get down and shut up!

Radical. By what law, by what ordinance do you order me to be quiet?

Policeman. Speaking without a flag. You know it.

Radical.

> [*Pulling out a small American flag*]

There's my flag! There's the flag of this United States which used to guarantee the rights of man—the rights of man now violated by every third statute of the commonweal—

Policeman. Don't try to pull tricks on me! I've seen you before! You're not making any speech, and you're climbing down—

Judge Gaunt.

> [*Who has come quietly forward*]

One moment, officer. There is some difference of opinion even on the bench as to the elasticity of police power when applied in minor emergencies to preserve civil order. But the weight of authority would certainly favor the defendant in any equable court, and he would be upheld in his demand to be heard.

Policeman. Who are you?

Judge Gaunt. Sir, I am not accustomed to answer that question.

Policeman. I don't know you.

Gaunt. I am a judge of some standing, not in your city but in another with similar statutes. You are aware, of

course, that the bill of rights is not to be set aside lightly
by the officers of any municipality—

Policeman.

[*Looking over Gaunt's somewhat bedraggled costume*]

Maybe they understand you better in the town you come
from, but I don't get your drift.—

[*To the Radical*]

I don't want any trouble, but if you ask for it you'll
get plenty. Get down!

Radical. I'm not asking for trouble, but I'm staying right
here.

[*The* POLICEMAN *moves toward him*]

Gaunt.

[*Taking the policeman's arm, but shaken off roughly*]

I ask this for yourself, truly, not for the dignity of the
law nor the maintenance of precedent. Be gentle with
them when their threats are childish—be tolerant while
you can—for your least harsh word will return on you
in the night—return in a storm of cries!—

[*He takes the Policeman's arm again*]

Whatever they may have said or done, let them disperse
in peace! It is better that they go softly, lest when they
are dead you see their eyes pleading, and their out-
stretched hands touch you, fingering cold on your heart!
—I have been harsher than you. I have sent men down
that long corridor into blinding light and blind darkness!

[*He suddenly draws himself erect and speaks defiantly*]

And it was well that I did so! I have been an upright judge! They are all liars! Liars!

Policeman.

[*Shaking* GAUNT *off so that he falls*]

Why, you fool, you're crazy!

Gaunt. Yes, and there are liars on the force! They came to me with their shifty lies!

[*He catches at the* POLICEMAN, *who pushes him away with his foot*]

Policeman. You think I've got nothing better to do than listen to a crazy fool?

1st Girl. Shame, shame!

Policeman. What have I got to be ashamed of? And what's going on here, anyway? Where in hell did you all come from?

Radical. Tread on him! That's right! Tread down the poor and the innocent!

[*There is a protesting murmur in the crowd*]

Sailor.

[*Moving in a little*]

Say, big boy, you don't have to step on the guy.

Policeman.

[*Facing them, stepping back*]

What's the matter with you? I haven't stepped on any-body!

Mio.

[*At the right, across from the Policeman*]

Listen now, fellows, give the badge a chance.
He's doing his job, what he gets paid to do,
the same as any of you. They're all picked men,
these metropolitan police, hand picked
for loyalty and a fine up-standing pair
of shoulders on their legs—it's not so easy
to represent the law. Think what he does
for all of us, stamping out crime!
Do you want to be robbed and murdered in your beds?

Sailor. What's eating you?

Radical. He must be a capitalist.

Mio. They pluck them fresh
from Ireland, and a paucity of headpiece
is a prime prerequisite. You from Ireland, buddy?

Policeman.

[*Surly*]

Where are you from?

Mio. Buddy, I tell you flat
I wish I was from Ireland, and could boast
some Tammany connections. There's only one drawback
about working on the force. It infects the brain,
it eats the cerebrum. There've been cases known,
fine specimens of manhood, too, where autopsies,
conducted in approved scientific fashion,
revealed conditions quite incredible

in policemen's upper layers. In some, a trace,
in others, when they've swung a stick too long,
there was nothing there!—but nothing! Oh, my friends,
this fine athletic figure of a man
that stands so grim before us, what will they find
when they saw his skull for the last inspection?
I fear me a little puffball dust will blow away
rejoining earth, our mother—and this same dust,
this smoke, this ash on the wind, will represent
all he had left to think with!

The Hobo. Hooray!

> [*The* POLICEMAN *turns on his heel and looks hard at the* HOBO,
> *who slinks away*]

Policeman. Oh, yeah?

Mio. My theme
gives ears to the deaf and voice to the dumb! But now
forgive me if I say you were most unkind
in troubling the officer. He's a simple man
of simple tastes, and easily confused
when faced with complex issues. He may reflect
on returning home, that is, so far as he
is capable of reflection, and conclude
that he was kidded out of his uniform pants,
and in his fury when this dawns on him
may smack his wife down!

Policeman. That'll be about enough from you, too, professor!

Mio. May I say that I think you have managed this whole
situation rather badly, from the beginning?—

Policeman. You may not!

[TROCK *slips in from the background. The* TWO YOUNG MEN IN SERGE *come with him*]

Mio. Oh, but your pardon, sir! It's apparent to the least competent among us that you should have gone about your task more subtly—the glove of velvet, the hand of iron, and all that sort of thing—

Policeman. Shut that hole in your face!

Mio. Sir, for that remark I shall be satisfied with nothing less than an unconditional apology! I have an old score to settle with policemen, brother, because they're fools and fat-heads, and you're one of the most fatuous fat-heads that ever walked his feet flat collecting graft! Tell that to your sergeant back in the booby-hatch.

Policeman. Oh, you want an apology, do you? You'll get an apology out of the other side of your mouth!

[*He steps toward Mio.* CARR *suddenly stands in his path*]

Get out of my way!

[*He pauses and looks round him; the crowd looks less and less friendly. He lays a hand on his gun and backs to a position where there is nobody behind him*]

Get out of here, all of you! Get out! What are you trying to do—start a riot?

Mio. There now, that's better! That's in the best police tradition. Incite a riot yourself and then accuse the crowd.

Policeman. It won't be pleasant if I decide to let somebody have it! Get out!

[*The onlookers begin to melt away. The* SAILOR *goes out left with the* GIRLS *and* HERMAN. CARR *and* MIO *go out right,* CARR *whistling "The Star Spangled Banner." The* HOBO *follows them. The* RADICAL *walks past with his head in the air.* PINY *and* LUCIA *leave the piano where it stands and slip away to the left. At the end the* POLICE-MAN *is left standing in the center, the* JUDGE *near him.* ESDRAS *stands in the doorway.* MIRIAMNE *is left sitting half in shadow and unseen by* ESDRAS]

Judge Gaunt.

[*To the Policeman*]

Yes, but should a man die, should it be necessary that one man die for the good of many, make not yourself the instrument of death, lest you sleep to wake sobbing! Nay, it avails nothing that you are the law—this delicate ganglion that is the brain, it will not bear these things—!

[*The* POLICEMAN *gives the Judge the once-over, shrugs, decides to leave him there and starts out left.* GARTH *goes to his father—a fine sleet begins to fall through the street lights.* TROCK *is still visible*]

Garth. Get him in here, quick.

Esdras. Who, son?

Garth. The Judge, damn him!

Esdras. Is it Judge Gaunt?

Garth. Who did you think it was? He's crazy as a bedbug and telling the world. Get him inside!

[*He looks round*]

Esdras.

[*Going up to Gaunt*]

Will you come in, sir?

Gaunt. You will understand, sir. We old men know how softly we must proceed with these things.

Esdras. Yes, surely, sir.

Gaunt. It was always my practice—always. They will tell you that of me where I am known. Yet even I am not free of regret—even I. Would you believe it?

Esdras. I believe we are none of us free of regret.

Gaunt. None of us? I would it were true. I would I thought it were true.

Esdras. Shall we go in, sir? This is sleet that's falling.

Gaunt. Yes. Let us go in.

> [ESDRAS, GAUNT *and* GARTH *enter the basement and shut the door.* TROCK *goes out with his men. After a pause* MIO *comes back from the right, alone. He stands at a little distance from Miriamne*]

Mio. Looks like rain.

> [*She is silent*]

You live around here?

> [*She nods gravely*]

I guess
you thought I meant it—about waiting here to meet me.

> [*She nods again*]

I'd forgotten about it till I got that winter
across the face. You'd better go inside.

I'm not your kind. I'm nobody's kind but my own.
I'm waiting for this to blow over.

[*She rises*]

I lied. I meant it—
I meant it when I said it—but there's too much black
whirling inside me—for any girl to know.
So go on in. You're somebody's angel child
and they're waiting for you.

Miriamne. Yes. I'll go.

[*She turns*]

Mio. And tell them
when you get inside where it's warm,
and you love each other,
and mother comes to kiss her darling, tell them
to hang on to it while they can, believe while they can
it's a warm safe world, and Jesus finds his lambs
and carries them in his bosom.—I've seen some lambs
that Jesus missed. If they ever want the truth
tell them that nothing's guaranteed in this climate
except it gets cold in winter, nor on this earth
except you die sometime.

[*He turns away*]

Miriamne. I have no mother.
And my people are Jews.

Mio. Then you know something about it.

Miriamne. Yes.

Mio. Do you have enough to eat?

Miriamne. Not always.

Mio. What do you believe in?

Miriamne. Nothing.

Mio. Why?

Miriamne. How can one?

Mio. It's easy if you're a fool. You see the words
  in books. Honor, it says there, chivalry, freedom,
  heroism, enduring love—and these
  are words on paper. It's something to have them there.
  You'll get them nowhere else.

Miriamne. What hurts you?

Mio. Just that.
  You'll get them nowhere else.

Miriamne. Why should you want them?

Mio. I'm alone, that's why. You see those lights,
  along the river, cutting across the rain—?
  those are the hearths of Brooklyn, and up this way
  the love-nests of Manhattan—they turn their points
  like knives against me—outcast of the world,
  snake in the streets.—I don't want a hand-out.
  I sleep and eat.

Miriamne. Do you want me to go with you?

Mio. Where?

Miriamne. Where you go.

  [*A pause. He goes nearer to her*]

Mio. Why, you god-damned little fool—
what made you say that?

Miriamne. I don't know.

Mio. If you have a home
stay in it. I ask for nothing. I've schooled myself
to ask for nothing, and take what I can get,
and get along. If I fell for you, that's my look-out,
and I'll starve it down.

Miriamne. Wherever you go, I'd go.

Mio. What do you know about loving?
How could you know?
Have you ever had a man?

Miriamne.

   [*After a slight pause*]

   No. But I know.
   Tell me your name.

Mio. Mio. What's yours?

Miriamne. Miriamne.

Mio. There's no such name.

Miriamne. But there's no such name as Mio!
M.I.O. It's no name.

Mio. It's for Bartolomeo.

Miriamne. My mother's name was Miriam,
so they called me Miriamne.

Mio. Meaning little Miriam?

Miriamne. Yes.

Mio. So now little Miriamne will go in
  and take up quietly where she dropped them all
  her small housewifely cares.—When I first saw you,
  not a half-hour ago, I heard myself saying,
  this is the face that launches ships for me—
  and if I owned a dream—yes, half a dream—
  we'd share it. But I have no dream. This earth
  came tumbling down from chaos, fire and rock,
  and bred up worms, blind worms that sting each other
  here in the dark. These blind worms of the earth
  took out my father—and killed him, and set a sign
  on me—the heir of the serpent—and he was a man
  such as men might be if the gods were men—
  but they killed him—
  as they'll kill all others like him
  till the sun cools down to the stabler molecules,
  yes, till men spin their tent-worm webs to the stars
  and what they think is done, even in the thinking,
  and they are the gods, and immortal, and constellations
  turn for them all like mill wheels—still as they are
  they will be, worms and blind. Enduring love,
  oh gods and worms, what mockery!—And yet
  I have blood enough in my veins. It goes like music,
  singing, because you're here. My body turns
  as if you were the sun, and warm. This men called love
  in happier times, before the Freudians taught us
  to blame it on the glands. Only go in
  before you breathe too much of my atmosphere
  and catch death from me.

Miriamne. I will take my hands
and weave them to a little house, and there
you shall keep a dream—-

Mio. God knows I could use a dream
and even a house.

Miriamne. You're laughing at me, Mio!

Mio. The worms are laughing.
I tell you there's death about me
and you're a child! And I'm alone and half mad
with hate and longing. I shall let you love me
and love you in return, and then, why then
God knows what happens!

Miriamne. Something most unpleasant?

Mio. Love in a box car—love among the children.
I've seen too much of it. Are we to live
in this same house you make with your two hands
mystically, out of air?

Miriamne. No roof, no mortgage!
Well, I shall marry a baker out in Flatbush,
it gives hot bread in the morning! Oh, Mio, Mio,
in all the unwanted places and waste lands
that roll up into the darkness out of sun
and into sun out of dark, there should be one empty
for you and me.

Mio. No.

Miriamne. Then go now and leave me.
I'm only a girl you saw in the tenements,
and there's been nothing said.

Mio. Miriamne.

[*She takes a step toward him*]

Miriamne. Yes.

[*He kisses her lips lightly*]

Mio. Why, girl, the transfiguration on the mount
was nothing to your face. It lights from within—
a white chalice holding fire, a flower in flame,
this is your face.

Miriamne. And you shall drink the flame
and never lessen it. And round your head
the aureole shall burn that burns there now,
forever. This I can give you. And so forever
the Freudians are wrong.

Mio. They're well-forgotten
at any rate.

Miriamne. Why did you speak to me
when you first saw me?

Mio. I knew then.

Miriamne. And I came back
because I must see you again. And we danced together
and my heart hurt me. Never, never, never,
though they should bind me down and tear out my eyes,
would I ever hurt you now. Take me with you, Mio,
let them look for us, whoever there is to look,
but we'll be away.

[MIO *turns away toward the tenement*]

Mio. When I was four years old
   we climbed through an iron gate, my mother and I,
   to see my father in prison. He stood in the death-cell
   and put his hand through the bars and said, My Mio,
   I have only this to leave you, that I love you,
   and will love you after I die. Love me then, Mio,
   when this hard thing comes on you, that you must live
   a man despised for your father. That night the guards,
   walking in flood-lights brighter than high noon,
   led him between them with his trousers slit
   and a shaven head for the cathodes. This sleet and rain
   that I feel cold here on my face and hands
   will find him under thirteen years of clay
   in prison ground. Lie still and rest, my father,
   for I have not forgotten. When I forget
   may I lie blind as you. No other love,
   time passing, nor the spaced light-years of suns
   shall blur your voice, or tempt me from the path
   that clears your name—
   till I have these rats in my grip
   or sleep deep where you sleep.

   [*To Miriamne*]

     I have no house,
   nor home, nor love of life, nor fear of death,
   nor care for what I eat, or who I sleep with,
   or what color of calcimine the Government
   will wash itself this year or next to lure
   the sheep and feed the wolves. Love somewhere else,
   and get your children in some other image
   more acceptable to the State! This face of mine
   is stamped for sewage!

[*She steps back, surmising*]

Miriamne. Mio—

Mio. My road is cut
in rock, and leads to one end. If I hurt you, I'm sorry.
One gets over hurts.

Miriamne. What was his name—
your father's name?

Mio. Bartolomeo Romagna.
I'm not ashamed of it.

Miriamne. Why are you here?

Mio. For the reason
I've never had a home. Because I'm a cry
out of a shallow grave, and all roads are mine
that might revenge him!

Miriamne. But Mio—why here—why here?

Mio. I can't tell you that.

Miriamne. No—but—there's someone
lives here—lives not far—and you mean to see him—
you mean to ask him—

[*She pauses*]

Mio. Who told you that?

Miriamne. His name
is Garth—Garth Esdras—

Mio.

[*After a pause, coming nearer*]

Who are you, then? You seem
to know a good deal about me.—Were you sent
to say this?

Miriamne. You said there was death about you! Yes,
but nearer than you think! Let it be as it is—
let it all be as it is, never see this place
nor think of it—forget the streets you came
when you're away and safe! Go before you're seen
or spoken to!

Mio. Will you tell me why?

Miriamne. As I love you
I can't tell you—and I can never see you—

Mio. I walk where I please—

Miriamne. Do you think it's easy for me
to send you away?

    [*She steps back as if to go*]

Mio. Where will I find you then
if I should want to see you?

Miriamne. Never—I tell you
I'd bring you death! Even now. Listen!

    [SHADOW *and* TROCK *enter between the bridge and the tenement
      house.* MIRIAMNE *pulls* MIO *back into the shadow of the
      rock to avoid being seen*]

Trock. Why, fine.

Shadow. You watch it now—just for the record, Trock—
you're going to thank me for staying away from it
and keeping you out. I've seen men get that way,

thinking they had to plug a couple of guys
and then a few more to cover it up, and then
maybe a dozen more. You can't own all
and territory adjacent, and you can't
slough all the witnesses, because every man
you put away has friends—

Trock. I said all right.
I said fine.

Shadow. They're going to find this judge,
and if they find him dead it's just too bad,
and I don't want to know anything about it—
and you don't either.

Trock. You all through?

Shadow. Why sure.

Trock. All right.
We're through, too, you know.

Shadow. Yeah?

 [*He becomes wary*]

Trock. Yeah, we're through.

Shadow. I've heard that said before, and afterwards
somebody died.

 [TROCK *is silent*]

 Is that what you mean?

Trock. You can go.
I don't want to see you.

Shadow. Sure, I'll go.
Maybe you won't mind if I just find out
what you've got on you. Before I turn my back
I'd like to know.

> [*Silently and expertly he touches Trock's pockets, extracting a
> gun*]

Not that I'd distrust you,
but you know how it is.

> [*He pockets the gun*]

So long, Trock.

Trock. So long.

Shadow. I won't talk.
You can be sure of that.

Trock. I know you won't.

> [SHADOW *turns and goes out right, past the rock and along the
> bank. As he goes the* TWO YOUNG MEN IN BLUE SERGE
> *enter from the left and walk slowly after Shadow. They
> look toward Trock as they enter and he motions with his
> thumb in the direction taken by Shadow. They follow
> Shadow out without haste.* TROCK *watches them dis-
> appear, then slips out the way he came.* MIO *comes a
> step forward, looking after the two men. Two or three
> shots are heard, then silence.* MIO *starts to run after
> Shadow*]

Miriamne. Mio!

Mio. What do you know about this?

Miriamne. The other way,
Mio—quick!

> [CARR *slips in from the right, in haste*]

Carr. Look, somebody's just been shot.
He fell in the river. The guys that did the shooting
ran up the bank.

Mio. Come on.

[Mio *and* Carr *run out right.* Miriamne *watches uncertainly,
then slowly turns and walks to the rear door of the
tenement. She stands there a moment, looking after
Mio, then goes in, closing the door.* Carr *and* Mio
return]

Carr. There's a rip tide past the point. You'd never find
him.

Mio. No.

Carr. You know a man really ought to carry insurance
living around here.—God, it's easy, putting a fellow
away. I never saw it done before.

Mio.

[*Looking at the place where Miriamne stood*]

They have it all worked out.

Carr. What are you doing now?

Mio. I have a little business to transact in this neighborhood.

Carr. You'd better forget it.

Mio. No.

Carr. Need any help?

Mio. Well, if I did I'd ask you first. But I don't see how it
would do any good. So you keep out of it and take care
of yourself.

Carr. So long, then.

Mio. So long, Carr.

Carr.

> [*Looking down-stream*]

He was drifting face up. Must be halfway to the island the way the tide runs.

> [*He shivers*]

God, it's cold here. Well—

> [*He goes out to the left. MIO sits on the edge of the rock. LUCIA comes stealthily back from between the bridge and the tenement, goes to the street-piano and wheels it away. PINY comes in. They take a look at Mio, but say nothing. LUCIA goes into his shelter and PINY into hers. MIO rises, looks up at the tenement, and goes out to the left*]

CURTAIN

WINTERSET
ACT TWO

ACT TWO

Scene: *The basement as in Scene 2 of Act One. The same evening.*
Esdras *sits at the table reading,* Miriamne *is seated at the left,
listening and intent. The door of the inner room is half open
and Garth's violin is heard. He is playing the theme from the
third movement of Beethoven's Archduke Trio.* Esdras *looks
up.*

Esdras. I remember when I came to the end
  of all the Talmud said, and the commentaries,
  then I was fifty years old—and it was time
  to ask what I had learned. I asked this question
  and gave myself the answer. In all the Talmud
  there was nothing to find but the names of things,
  set down that we might call them by those names
  and walk without fear among things known. Since then
  I have had twenty years to read on and on
  and end with Ecclesiastes. Names of names,
  evanid days, evanid nights and days
  and words that shift their meaning. Space is time,
  that which was is now—the men of tomorrow
  live, and this is their yesterday. All things
  that were and are and will be, have their being
  then and now and to come. If this means little
  when you are young, remember it. It will return
  to mean more when you are old.

Miriamne. I'm sorry—I
  was listening for something.

Esdras. It doesn't matter.
  It's a useless wisdom. It's all I have.

but useless. It may be there is no time,
but we grow old. Do you know his name?

Miriamne. Whose name?

Esdras. Why, when we're young and listen for a step
the step should have a name—

> [MIRIAMNE, *not hearing, rises and goes to the window.* GARTH
> *enters from within, carrying his violin and carefully
> closing the door*]

Garth.

> [*As* ESDRAS *looks at him*]

Asleep.

Esdras. He may
sleep on through the whole night—then in the morning
we can let them know.

Garth. We'd be wiser to say nothing—
let him find his own way back.

Esdras. How did he come here?

Garth. He's not too crazy for that. If he wakes again
we'll keep him quiet and shift him off tomorrow.
Somebody'd pick him up.

Esdras. How have I come
to this sunken end of a street, at a life's end—?

Garth. It was cheaper here—not to be transcendental—
So—we say nothing—?

Esdras. Nothing.

Miriamne. Garth, there's no place
in this whole city—not one—
where you wouldn't be safer
than here—tonight—or tomorrow.

Garth.

  [*Bitterly*]

  Well, that may be.
  What of it?

Miriamne. If you slipped away and took
a place somewhere where Trock couldn't find you—

Garth. Yes—
using what for money? and why do you think
I've sat here so far—because I love my home
so much? No, but if I stepped round the corner
it'd be my last corner and my last step.

Miriamne. And yet—
if you're here—they'll find you here—
Trock will come again—
and there's worse to follow—

Garth. Do you want to get me killed?

Miriamne. No.

Garth. There's no way out of it. We'll wait
and take what they send us.

Esdras. Hush! You'll wake him.

Garth. I've done it.
I hear him stirring now.

  [*They wait quietly.* JUDGE GAUNT *opens the door and enters*]

Gaunt.

[*In the doorway*]

I beg your pardon—
no, no, be seated—keep your place—I've made
your evening difficult enough, I fear;
and I must thank you doubly for your kindness,
for I've been ill—I know it.

Esdras. You're better, sir?

Gaunt. Quite recovered, thank you. Able, I hope,
to manage nicely now. You'll be rewarded
for your hospitality—though at this moment

[*He smiles*]

I'm low in funds.

[*He inspects his billfold*]

Sir, my embarrassment
is great indeed—and more than monetary,
for I must own my recollection's vague
of how I came here—how we came together—
and what we may have said. My name is Gaunt,
Judge Gaunt, a name long known in the criminal courts,
and not unhonored there.

Esdras. My name is Esdras—
and this is Garth, my son. And Miriamne,
the daughter of my old age.

Gaunt. I'm glad to meet you.
Esdras. Garth Esdras.

[*He passes a hand over his eyes*]

It's not a usual name.
Of late it's been connected with a case—
a case I knew. But this is hardly the man.
Though it's not a usual name.

[*They are silent*]

Sir, how I came here,
as I have said, I don't well know. Such things
are sometimes not quite accident.

Esdras. We found you
outside our door and brought you in.

Gaunt. The brain
can be overworked, and weary, even when the man
would swear to his good health. Sir, on my word
I don't know why I came here, nor how, nor when,
nor what would explain it. Shall we say the machine
begins to wear? I felt no twinge of it.—
You will imagine how much more than galling
I feel it, to ask my way home—and where I am—
but I do ask you that.

Esdras. This is New York City—
or part of it.

Gaunt. Not the best part, I presume?

[*He smiles grimly*]

No, not the best.

Esdras. Not typical, no.

Gaunt. And you—

[*To Garth*]

you are Garth Esdras?

Garth. That's my name.

Gaunt. Well, sir,

[*To Esdras*]

I shall lie under the deepest obligation
if you will set an old man on his path,
for I lack the homing instinct, if the truth
were known. North, east and south mean nothing to me
here in this room.

Esdras. I can put you in your way.

Garth. Only you'd be wiser to wait a while—
if I'm any judge.—

Gaunt. It happens I'm the judge—

[*With stiff humor*]

in more ways than one. You'll forgive me if I say
I find this place and my predicament
somewhat distasteful.

[*He looks round him*]

Garth. I don't doubt you do;
but you're better off here.

Gaunt. Nor will you find it wise
to cross my word as lightly as you seem
inclined to do. You've seen me ill and shaken—
and you presume on that.

Garth. Have it your way.

Gaunt. Doubtless what information is required
  we'll find nearby.

Esdras. Yes, sir—the terminal,—
  if you could walk so far.

Gaunt. I've done some walking—
  to look at my shoes.

    [*He looks down, then puts out a hand to steady himself*]

    That—that was why I came—
never mind—it was there—and it's gone.

    [*To Garth*]

    Professor Hobhouse—
that's the name—he wrote some trash about you
and printed it in a broadside.
—Since I'm here I can tell you
it's a pure fabrication—lacking facts
and legal import. Senseless and impudent,
written with bias—with malicious intent
to undermine the public confidence
in justice and the courts. I knew it then—
all he brings out about this testimony
you might have given. It's true I could have called you,
but the case was clear—Romagna was known guilty,
and there was nothing to add. If I've endured
some hours of torture over their attacks
upon my probity—and in this torture
have wandered from my place, wandered perhaps
in mind and body—and found my way to face you—
why, yes, it is so—I know it—I beg of you
say nothing. It's not easy to give up

a fair name after a full half century
of service to a state. It may well rock
the surest reason. Therefore I ask of you
say nothing of this visit.

Garth. I'll say nothing.

Esdras. Nor any of us.

Gaunt. Why, no—for you'd lose, too.
You'd have nothing to gain.

Esdras. Indeed we know it.

Gaunt. I'll remember you kindly. When I've returned,
there may be some mystery made of where I was—
we'll leave it a mystery?

Garth. Anything you say.

Gaunt. Why, now I go with much more peace of mind—
if I can call you friends.

Esdras. We shall be grateful
for silence on your part, Your Honor.

Gaunt. Sir—
if there were any just end to be served
by speaking out, I'd speak! There is none. No—
bear that in mind!

Esdras. We will, Your Honor.

Gaunt. Then—
I'm in some haste. If you can be my guide,
we'll set out now.

Esdras. Yes, surely.

> [*There is a knock at the door. The four look at each other with some apprehension.* MIRIAMNE *rises*]

I'll answer it.

Miriamne. Yes.

> [*She goes into the inner room and closes the door.* ESDRAS *goes to the outer door. The knock is repeated. He opens the door.* MIO *is there*]

Esdras. Yes, sir.

Mio. May I come in?

Esdras. Will you state your business, sir?
It's late—and I'm not at liberty—

Mio. Why, I might say
that I was trying to earn my tuition fees
by peddling magazines. I could say that,
or collecting old newspapers—paying cash—
highest rates—no questions asked—

> [*He looks round sharply*]

Garth. We've nothing to sell.
What do you want?

Mio. Your pardon, gentlemen.
My business is not of an ordinary kind,
and I felt the need of this slight introduction
while I might get my bearings. Your name is Esdras,
or they told me so outside.

Garth. What do you want?

Mio. Is that the name?

Garth. Yes.

Mio. I'll be quick and brief.
I'm the son of a man who died many years ago
for a pay roll robbery in New England. You
should be Garth Esdras, by what I've heard. You have
some knowledge of the crime, if one can believe
what he reads in the public prints, and it might be
that your testimony, if given, would clear my father
of any share in the murder. You may not care
whether he was guilty or not. You may not know.
But I do care—and care deeply, and I've come
to ask you face to face.

Garth. To ask me what?

Mio. What do you know of it?

Esdras. This man Romagna,
did he have a son?

Mio. Yes, sir, this man Romagna,
as you choose to call him, had a son, and I
am that son, and proud.

Esdras. Forgive me.

Mio. Had you known him,
and heard him speak, you'd know why I'm proud,
and why
he was no malefactor.

Esdras. I quite believe you.
If my son can help he will. But at this moment,
as I told you—could you, I wonder, come tomorrow,
at your own hour?

Mio. Yes.

Esdras. By coincidence
we too of late have had this thing in mind—
there have been comments printed, and much discussion
which we could hardly avoid.

Mio. Could you tell me then
in a word?—What you know—
is it for him or against him?—
that's all I need.

Esdras. My son knows nothing.

Garth. No.
The picture-papers lash themselves to a fury
over any rumor—make them up when they're short
of bedroom slops.—This is what happened. I
had known a few members of a gang one time
up there—and after the murder they picked me up
because I looked like someone that was seen
in what they called the murder car. They held me
a little while, but they couldn't identify me
for the most excellent reason I wasn't there
when the thing occurred. A dozen years later now
a professor comes across this, and sees red
and asks why I wasn't called on as a witness
and yips so loud they syndicate his picture
in all the rotos. That's all I know about it.
I wish I could tell you more.

Esdras. Let me say too
that I have read some words your father said,

and you were a son fortunate in your father,
whatever the verdict of the world.

Mio. There are few
who think so, but it's true, and I thank you. Then—
that's the whole story?

Garth. All I know of it.

Mio. They cover their tracks well, the inner ring
that distributes murder. I came three thousand miles
to this dead end.

Esdras. If he was innocent
and you know him so, believe it, and let the others
believe as they like.

Mio. Will you tell me how a man's
to live, and face his life, if he can't believe
that truth's like a fire,
and will burn through and be seen
though it takes all the years there are?
While I stand up and have breath in my lungs
I shall be one flame of that fire;
it's all the life I have.

Esdras. Then you must live so.
One must live as he can.

Mio. It's the only way
of life my father left me.

Esdras. Yes? Yet it's true
the ground we walk on is impacted down
and hard with blood and bones of those who died

unjustly. There's not one title to land or life,
even your own, but was built on rape and murder,
back a few years. It would take a fire indeed
to burn out all this error.

Mio. Then let it burn down,
all of it!

Esdras. We ask a great deal of the world
at first—then less—and then less.
We ask for truth
and justice. But this truth's a thing unknown
in the lightest, smallest matter—and as for justice,
who has once seen it done? You loved your father,
and I could have loved him, for every word he spoke
in his trial was sweet and tolerant, but the weight
of what men are and have, rests heavy on
the graves of those who lost. They'll not rise again,
and their causes lie there with them.

Gaunt. If you mean to say
that Bartolomeo Romagna was innocent,
you are wrong. He was guilty.
There may have been injustice
from time to time, by regrettable chance, in our courts,
but not in that case, I assure you.

Mio. Oh, you assure me!
You lie in your scrag teeth, whoever you are!
My father was murdered!

Gaunt. Romagna was found guilty
by all due process of law, and given his chance
to prove his innocence.

Mio. What chance? When a court
  panders to mob hysterics, and the jury
  comes in loaded to soak an anarchist
  and a foreigner, it may be due process of law
  but it's also murder!

Gaunt. He should have thought of that
  before he spilled blood.

Mio. He?

Gaunt. Sir, I know too well
  that he was guilty.

Mio. Who are you? How do you know?
  I've searched the records through, the trial and what
  came after, and in all that million words
  I found not one unbiased argument
  to fix the crime on him.

Gaunt. And you yourself,
  were you unprejudiced?

Mio. Who are you?

Esdras. Sir,
  this gentleman is here, as you are here,
  to ask my son, as you have asked, what ground
  there might be for this talk of new evidence
  in your father's case. We gave him the same answer
  we've given you.

Mio. I'm sorry. I'd supposed
  his cause forgotten except by myself. There's still
  a defense committee then?

Gaunt. There may be. I
   am not connected with it.

Esdras. He is my guest,
   and asks to remain unknown.

Mio.

   [*After a pause, looking at Gaunt*]

   The judge at the trial
   was younger, but he had your face. Can it be
   that you're the man?—Yes—Yes.—The jury charge—
   I sat there as a child and heard your voice,
   and watched that Brahminical mouth. I knew even then
   you meant no good to him. And now you're here
   to winnow out truth and justice—the fountain-head
   of the lies that slew him! Are you Judge Gaunt?

Gaunt. I am.

Mio. Then tell me what damnation to what inferno
   would fit the toad that sat in robes and lied
   when he gave the charge, and knew he lied! Judge that,
   and then go to your place in that hell!

Gaunt. I know and have known
   what bitterness can rise against a court
   when it must say, putting aside all weakness,
   that a man's to die. I can forgive you that,
   for you are your father's son, and you think of him
   as a son thinks of his father. Certain laws
   seem cruel in their operation; it's necessary
   that we be cruel to uphold them. This cruelty
   is kindness to those I serve.

Mio. I don't doubt that.
I know who it is you serve.

Gaunt. Would I have chosen
to rack myself with other men's despairs,
stop my ears, harden my heart, and listen only
to the voice of law and light, if I had hoped
some private gain for serving? In all my years
on the bench of a long-established commonwealth
not once has my decision been in question
save in this case. Not once before or since.
For hope of heaven or place on earth, or power
or gold, no man has had my voice, nor will
while I still keep the trust that's laid on me
to sentence and define.

Mio. Then why are you here?

Gaunt. My record's clean. I've kept it so. But suppose
with the best intent, among the myriad tongues
that come to testify, I had missed my way
and followed a perjured tale to a lethal end
till a man was forsworn to death? Could I rest or sleep
while there was doubt of this,
even while there was question in a layman's mind?
For always, night and day,
there lies on my brain like a weight, the admonition:
see truly, let nothing sway you; among all functions
there's but one godlike, to judge. Then see to it
you judge as a god would judge, with clarity,
with truth, with what mercy is found consonant
with order and law. Without law men are beasts,

and it's a judge's task to lift and hold them
above themselves. Let a judge be once mistaken
or step aside for a friend, and a gap is made
in the dykes that hold back anarchy and chaos,
and leave men bond but free.

Mio. Then the gap's been made,
and you made it.

Gaunt. I feared that too. May you be a judge
sometime, and know in what fear,
through what nights long
in fear, I scanned and verified and compared
the transcripts of the trial.

Mio. Without prejudice,
no doubt. It was never in your mind to prove
that you'd been right.

Gaunt. And conscious of that, too—
that that might be my purpose—watchful of that,
and jealous as his own lawyer of the rights
that should hedge the defendant!
And still I found no error,
shook not one staple of the bolts that linked
the doer to the deed! Still following on
from step to step, I watched all modern comment,
and saw it centered finally on one fact—
Garth Esdras was not called. This is Garth Esdras,
and you have heard him. Would his deposition
have justified a new trial?

Mio. No. It would not.

Gaunt. And there I come, myself. If the man were still
in his cell, and waiting, I'd have no faint excuse
for another hearing.

Mio. I've told you that I read
the trial from beginning to end. Every word you spoke
was balanced carefully to keep the letter
of the law and still convict—convict, by Christ,
if it tore the seven veils! You stand here now
running cascades of casuistry, to prove
to yourself and me that no judge of rank and breeding
could burn a man out of hate! But that's what you did
under all your varnish!

Gaunt. I've sought for evidence,
and you have sought. Have you found it? Can you cite
one fresh word in defence?

Mio. The trial itself
was shot full of legerdemain, prearranged to lead
the jury astray—

Gaunt. Could you prove that?

Mio. Yes!

Gaunt. And if
the jury were led astray, remember it's
the jury, by our Anglo-Saxon custom,
that finds for guilt or innocence. The judge
is powerless in that matter.

Mio. Not you! Your charge
misled the jury more than the evidence,
accepted every biased meaning, distilled
the poison for them!

Gaunt. But if that were so
  I'd be the first, I swear it, to step down
  among all men, and hold out both my hands
  for manacles—yes, publish it in the streets,
  that all I've held most sacred was defiled
  by my own act. A judge's brain becomes
  a delicate instrument to weigh men's lives
  for good and ill—too delicate to bear
  much tampering. If he should push aside
  the weights and throw the beam, and say, this once
  the man is guilty, and I will have it so
  though his mouth cry out from the ground,
  and all the world
  revoke my word, he'd have a short way to go
  to madness. I think you'd find him in the squares,
  stopping the passers-by with arguments,—
  see, I was right, the man was guilty there—
  this was brought in against him, this—and this—
  and I was left no choice! It's no light thing
  when a long life's been dedicate to one end
  to wrench the mind awry!

Mio. By your own thesis
  you should be mad, and no doubt you are.

Gaunt. But my madness
  is only this—that I would fain look back
  on a life well spent—without one stain—one breath
  of stain to flaw the glass—not in men's minds
  nor in my own. I take my God as witness
  I meant to earn that clearness, and believe
  that I have earned it. Yet my name is clouded

with the blackest, fiercest scandal of our age
that's touched a judge. What I can do to wipe
that smutch from my fame I will. I think you know
how deeply I've been hated, for no cause
that I can find there. Can it not be—and I ask this
quite honestly—that the great injustice lies
on your side and not mine? Time and time again
men have come before me perfect in their lives,
loved by all who knew them, loved at home,
gentle, not vicious, yet caught so ripe red-handed
in some dark violence there was no denying
where the onus lay.

Mio. That was not so with my father!

Gaunt. And yet it seemed so to me. To other men
who sat in judgment on him. Can you be sure—
I ask this in humility—that you,
who were touched closest by the tragedy,
may not have lost perspective—may have brooded
day and night on one theme—till your eyes are tranced
and show you one side only?

Mio. I see well enough.

Gaunt. And would that not be part of the malady—
to look quite steadily at the drift of things
but see there what you wish—not what is there—
not what another man to whom the story
was fresh would say is there?

Mio. You think I'm crazy.
Is that what you meant to say?

Gaunt. I've seen it happen
with the best and wisest men. I but ask the question.
I can't speak for you. Is it not true wherever
you walk, through the little town where you knew him
  well,
or flying from it, inland or by the sea,
still walking at your side, and sleeping only
when you too sleep, a shadow not your own
follows, pleading and holding out its hands
to be delivered from shame?

Mio. How you know that
by God I don't know.

Gaunt. Because one spectre haunted you and me—
and haunts you still, but for me it's laid to rest
now that my mind is satisfied. He died
justly and not by error.

  [*A pause*]

Mio.

  [*Stepping forward*]

Do you care to know
you've come so near to death it's miracle
that pulse still beats in your splotchy throat?
Do you know
there's murder in me?

Gaunt. There was murder in your sire,
and it's to be expected! I say he died
justly, and he deserved it!

Mio. Yes, you'd like too well
to have me kill you! That would prove your case
and clear your name, and dip my father's name
in stench forever! You'll not get that from me!
Go home and die in bed, get it under cover,
your lux-et-lex putrefaction of the right thing,
you man that walks like a god!

Gaunt. Have I made you angry
by coming too near the truth?

Mio. This sets him up,
this venomous slug, this sets him up in a gown,
deciding who's to walk above the earth
and who's to lie beneath! And giving reasons!
The cobra giving reasons; I'm a god,
by Buddha, holy and worshipful my fang,
and can I sink it in!

    [*He pauses, turns as if to go, then sits*]

    This is no good.
This won't help much.

    [*The* JUDGE *and* ESDRAS *look at each other*]

Gaunt. We should be going.

Esdras. Yes.

    [*They prepare to go*]

    I'll lend you my coat.

Gaunt.

    [*Looking at it with distaste*]

No, keep it. A little rain
shouldn't matter to me.

Esdras. It freezes as it falls,
and you've a long way to go.

Gaunt. I'll manage, thank you.

> [GAUNT *and* ESDRAS *go out,* ESDRAS *obsequious, closing the
> door*]

Garth.

> [*Looking at Mio's back*]

Well?

Mio.

> [*Not moving*]

Let me sit here a moment.

> [GARTH *shrugs his shoulders and goes toward the inner door.*
> MIRIAMNE *opens it and comes out.* GARTH *looks at her,
> then at Mio, then lays his fingers on his lips. She nods.*
> GARTH *goes out.* MIRIAMNE *sits and watches* MIO.
> *After a little he turns and sees her*]

Mio. How did you come here?

Miriamne. I live here.

Mio. Here?

Miriamne. My name is Esdras. Garth
is my brother. The walls are thin.
I heard what was said.

Mio.

> [*Stirring wearily*]

I'm going. This is no place for me.

Miriamne. What place
would be better?

Mio. None. Only it's better to go.
Just to go.

[*She comes over to him, puts her arm round him and kisses his
forehead*]

Miriamne. Mio.

Mio. What do you want?
Your kisses burn me—and your arms. Don't offer
what I'm never to have! I can have nothing. They say
they'll cross the void sometime to the other planets
and men will breathe in that air.
Well, I could breathe there,
but not here now. Not on this ball of mud.
I don't want it.

Miriamne. They can take away so little
with all their words. For you're a king among them.
I heard you, and loved your voice.

Mio. I thought I'd fallen
so low there was no further, and now a pit
opens beneath. It was bad enough that he
should have died innocent, but if he were guilty—
then what's my life—what have I left to do—?
The son of a felon—and what they spat on me
was earned—and I'm drenched with the stuff.
Here on my hands
and cheeks, their spittle hanging! I liked my hands
because they were like his. I tell you I've lived

by his innocence, lived to see it flash
and blind them all—

Miriamne. Never believe them, Mio,
never.

[*She looks toward the inner door*]

Mio. But it was truth I wanted, truth—
not the lies you'd tell yourself, or tell a woman,
or a woman tells you! The judge with his cobra mouth
may have spat truth—and I may be mad! For me—
your hands are too clean to touch me. I'm to have
the scraps from hotel kitchens—and instead of love
those mottled bodies that hitch themselves through alleys
to sell for dimes or nickels. Go, keep yourself chaste
for the baker bridegroom—baker and son of a baker,
let him get his baker's dozen on you!

Miriamne. No—
say once you love me—say it once; I'll never
ask to hear it twice, nor for any kindness,
and you shall take all I have!

[GARTH *opens the inner door and comes out*]

Garth. I interrupt
a love scene, I believe. We can do without
your adolescent mawkishness.

[*To Miriamne*]

You're a child.
You'll both remember that.

Miriamne. I've said nothing to harm you—
and will say nothing.

Garth. You're my sister, though,
and I take a certain interest in you. Where
have you two met?

Miriamne. We danced together.

Garth. Then
the dance is over, I think.

Miriamne. I've always loved you
and tried to help you, Garth. And you've been kind.
Don't spoil it now.

Garth. Spoil it how?

Miriamne. Because I love him.
I didn't know it would happen. We danced together.
And the world's all changed. I see you through a mist,
and our father, too. If you brought this to nothing
I'd want to die.

Garth.

   [*To Mio*]

You'd better go.

Mio. Yes, I know.

   [*He rises. There is a trembling knock at the door.* Miriamne
   goes to it. The Hobo *is there shivering*]

Hobo. Miss, could I sleep under the pipes tonight, miss?
Could I, please?

Miriamne. I think—not tonight.

Hobo. There won't be any more nights—
if I don't get warm, miss.

Miriamne. Come in.

[*The* Hobo *comes in, looks round deprecatingly, then goes to a corner beneath a huge heating pipe, which he crawls under as if he'd been there before*]

Hobo. Yes, miss, thank you.

Garth. Must we put up with that?

Miriamne. Father let him sleep there—
last winter.

Garth. Yes, God, yes.

Mio. Well, good night.

Miriamne. Where will you go?

Mio. Yes, where? As if it mattered.

Garth. Oh, sleep here, too.
We'll have a row of you under the pipes.

Mio. No, thanks.

Miriamne. Mio, I've saved a little money. It's only
some pennies, but you must take it.

[*She shakes some coins out of a box into her hand*]

Mio. No, thanks.

Miriamne. And I love you.
You've never said you love me.

Mio. Why wouldn't I love you
when you're clean and sweet,
and I've seen nothing sweet or clean

this last ten years? I love you. I leave you that
for what good it may do you. It's none to me.

Miriamne. Then kiss me.

Mio.

[*Looking at Garth*]

With that scowling over us? No.
When it rains, some spring
on the planet Mercury, where the spring comes often,
I'll meet you there, let's say. We'll wait for that.
It may be some time till then.

[*The outside door opens and* ESDRAS *enters with* JUDGE GAUNT,
then, after a slight interval, TROCK *follows.* TROCK
*surveys the interior and its occupants one by one, care-
fully*]

Trock. I wouldn't want to cause you inconvenience,
any of you, and especially the Judge.
I think you know that. You've all got things to do—
trains to catch, and so on. But trains can wait.
Hell, nearly anything can wait, you'll find,
only I can't. I'm the only one that can't
because I've got no time. Who's all this here?
Who's that?

[*He points to the Hobo*]

Esdras. He's a poor half-wit, sir,
that sometimes sleeps there.

Trock. Come out. I say come out,
whoever you are.

[*The* HOBO *stirs and looks up*]

Yes, I mean you. Come out.

[*The* HOBO *emerges*]

What's your name?

Hobo. They mostly call me Oke.

Trock. What do you know?

Hobo. No, sir.

Trock. Where are you from?

Hobo. I got a piece of bread.

[*He brings it out, trembling*]

Trock. Get back in there!

[*The* HOBO *crawls back into his corner*]

Maybe you want to know why I'm doing this.
Well, I've been robbed, that's why—
robbed five or six times;
the police can't find a thing—so I'm out for myself—
if you want to know.

[*To Mio*]

Who are you?

Mio. Oh, I'm a half-wit,
came in here by mistake. The difference is
I've got no piece of bread.

Trock. What's your name?

Mio. My name?
Theophrastus Such. That's respectable.
You'll find it all the way from here to the coast

on the best police blotters.
Only the truth is we're a little touched in the head,
Oke and me. You'd better ask somebody else.

Trock. Who is he?

Esdras. His name's Romagna. He's the son.

Trock. Then what's he doing here? You said you were on
the level.

Garth. He just walked in. On account of the stuff in the
papers. We didn't ask him.

Trock. God, we are a gathering. Now if we had Shadow
we'd be all here, huh? Only I guess we won't see Shadow.
No, that's too much to ask.

Mio. Who's Shadow?

Trock. Now you're putting questions. Shadow was just
nobody, you see. He blew away. It might happen to
anyone.

   [*He looks at Garth*]

Yes, anyone at all.

Mio. Why do you keep your hand in your pocket, friend?

Trock. Because I'm cold, punk. Because I've been outside
and it's cold as the tomb of Christ.

   [*To Garth*]

Listen, there's a car waiting up at the street to take the
Judge home. We'll take him to the car.

Garth. That's not necessary.

Esdras. No.

Trock. I say it is, see? You wouldn't want to let the Judge
walk, would you? The Judge is going to ride where he's
going, with a couple of chauffeurs, and everything done
in style. Don't you worry about the Judge. He'll be
taken care of. For good.

Garth. I want no hand in it.

Trock. Anything happens to me happens to you too,
musician.

Garth. I know that.

Trock. Keep your mouth out of it then. And you'd better
keep the punk here tonight, just for luck.

[*He turns toward the door. There is a brilliant lightning flash
through the windows, followed slowly by dying thunder.*
TROCK *opens the door. The rain begins to pour in sheets*]

Jesus, somebody tipped it over again!

[*A cough racks him*]

Wait till it's over. It takes ten days off me every time
I step into it.

[*He closes the door*]

Sit down and wait.

[*Lightning flashes again. The thunder is fainter.* ESDRAS,
GARTH *and the* JUDGE *sit down*]

Gaunt. We were born too early. Even you who are young
are not of the elect. In a hundred years
man will put his finger on life itself, and then
he will live as long as he likes. For you and me

we shall die soon—one day, one year more or less,
when or where, it's no matter. It's what we call
an indeterminate sentence. I'm hungry.

[GARTH *looks at Miriamne*]

Miriamne. There was nothing left
tonight.

Hobo. I've got a piece of bread.

[*He breaks his bread in two and hands half to the Judge*]

Gaunt. I thank you, sir.

[*He eats*]

This is not good bread.

[*He rises*]

Sir, I am used
to other company. Not better, perhaps, but their clothes
were different. These are what it's the fashion to call
the underprivileged.

Trock. Oh, hell!

[*He turns toward the door*]

Mio.

[*To Trock*]

It would seem that you and the Judge know each other.

[TROCK *faces him*]

Trock. I've been around.

Mio. Maybe you've met before.

Trock. Maybe we have.

Mio. Will you tell me where?

Trock. How long do you want to live?

Mio. How long? Oh, I've got big ideas about that.

Trock. I thought so. Well, so far I've got nothing against you but your name, see? You keep it that way.

[*He opens the door. The rain still falls in torrents. He closes the door. As he turns from it, it opens again, and* SHADOW, *white, bloodstained and dripping, stands in the doorway.* GARTH *rises.* TROCK *turns*]

Gaunt.

[*To the Hobo*]

Yet if one were careful of his health, ate sparingly, drank not at all, used himself wisely, it might be that even an old man could live to touch immortality. They may come on the secret sooner than we dare hope. You see? It does no harm to try.

Trock.

[*Backing away from Shadow*]

By God, he's out of his grave!

Shadow.

[*Leaning against the doorway, holding a gun in his hands*]

Keep your hands where they belong, Trock.
You know me.

Trock. Don't! Don't! I had nothing to do with it!

[*He backs to the opposite wall*]

Shadow. You said the doctor gave you six months to live—
    well, I don't give you that much. That's what you had,
    six months, and so you start bumping off your friends
    to make sure of your damn six months. I got it from you.
    I know where I got it.
    Because I wouldn't give it to the Judge.
    So he wouldn't talk.

Trock. Honest to God—

Shadow. What God?
    The one that let you put three holes in me
    when I was your friend? Well, He let me get up again
    and walk till I could find you. That's as far as I get,
    but I got there, by God! And I can hear you
    even if I can't see!

    [*He takes a staggering step forward*]

    A man needs blood
    to keep going.—I got this far.—And now I can't see!
    It runs out too fast—too fast—
    when you've got three slugs
    clean through you.
    Show me where he is, you fools! He's here!
    I got here!

    [*He drops the gun*]

    Help me! Help me! Oh, God! Oh, God!
    I'm going to die! Where does a man lie down?
    I want to lie down!

        [Miriamne *starts toward Shadow.* Garth *and* Esdras *help
            him into the next room,* Miriamne *following.* Trock
            squats in his corner, breathing hard, looking at the door.

Mio *stands, watching* Trock. Garth *returns, wiping his hand with a handkerchief.* Mio *picks up and pockets the gun.* Miriamne *comes back and leans against the door jamb*]

Gaunt. You will hear it said that an old man makes a good judge, being calm, clear-eyed, without passion. But this is not true. Only the young love truth and justice. The old are savage, wary, violent, swayed by maniac desires, cynical of friendship or love, open to bribery and the temptations of lust, corrupt and dastardly to the heart. I know these old men. What have they left to believe, what have they left to lose? Whorers of daughters, lickers of girls' shoes, contrivers of nastiness in the night, purveyors of perversion, worshippers of possession! Death is the only radical. He comes late, but he comes at last to put away the old men and give the young their places. It was time.

[*He leers*]

Here's one I heard yesterday:
    Marmaduke behind the barn
      got his sister in a fix;
    he says damn instead of darn;
      ain't he cute? He's only six!

The Hobo. He, he, he!

Gaunt.
    And the hoot-owl hoots all night,
      and the cuckoo cooks all day,
    and what with a minimum grace of God
      we pass the time away.

The Hobo. He, he, he—I got ya!

[*He makes a sign with his thumb*]

Gaunt.

[*Sings*]

> And he led her all around
> and he laid her on the ground
> and he ruffled up the feathers of her
> cuckoo's nest!

Hobo. Ho, ho, ho!

Gaunt. I am not taken with the way you laugh. You should
cultivate restraint.

[ESDRAS *reënters*]

Trock. Shut the door.

Esdras. He won't come back again.

Trock. I want the door shut! He was dead, I tell you!

[*Esdras closes the door*]

And Romagna was dead, too, once! Can't they keep a
man under ground?

Mio. No. No more! They don't stay under ground any
more, and they don't stay under water! Why did you
have him killed?

Trock. Stay away from me! I know you!

Mio. Who am I, then?

Trock. I know you, damn you! Your name's Romagna!

Mio. Yes! And Romagna was dead, too, and Shadow was dead, but the time's come when you can't keep them down, these dead men! They won't stay down! They come in with their heads shot off and their entrails dragging! Hundreds of them! One by one—all you ever had killed! Watch the door! See!—It moves!

Trock.

[*Looking, fascinated, at the door*]

Let me out of here!

[*He tries to rise*]

Mio.

[*The gun in his hand*]

Oh, no! You'll sit there and wait for them! One by one they'll come through that door, pulling their heads out of the gunny-sacks where you tied them—glauming over you with their rotten hands! They'll see without eyes and crawl over you—Shadow and the paymaster and all the rest of them—putrescent bones without eyes! Now! Look! Look! For I'm first among them!

Trock. I've done for better men than you! And I'll do for you!

Gaunt.

[*Rapping on the table*]

Order, gentlemen, order! The witness will remember that a certain decorum is essential in the court-room!

Mio. By God, he'll answer me!

Gaunt.

[*Thundering*]

Silence! Silence! Let me remind you of courtesy toward
the witness! What case is this you try?

Mio. The case of the state against Bartolomeo Romagna
for the murder of the paymaster!

Gaunt. Sir, that was disposed of long ago!

Mio. Never disposed of, never, not while I live!

Gaunt. Then we'll have done with it now! I deny the
appeal! I have denied the appeal before and I do so
again!

Hobo. He, he!—He thinks he's in the moving pictures!

[*A flash of lightning*]

Gaunt. Who set that flash! Bailiff, clear the court! This is
not Flemington, gentlemen! We are not conducting this
case to make a journalistic holiday!

[*The thunder rumbles faintly.* GARTH *opens the outside door
and faces a solid wall of rain*]

Stop that man! He's one of the defendants!

[GARTH *closes the door*]

Mio. Then put him on the stand!

Garth. What do you think you're doing?

Mio. Have you any objection?

Gaunt. The objection is not sustained. We will hear the
new evidence. Call your witness.

Mio. Garth Esdras!

Gaunt. He will take the stand!

Garth. If you want me to say what I said before I'll say it!

Mio. Call Trock Estrella then!

Gaunt. Trock Estrella to the stand!

Trock. No, by God!

Mio. Call Shadow, then! He'll talk! You thought he was dead, but he'll get up again and talk!

Trock.

[*Screaming*]

What do you want of me?

Mio. You killed the paymaster! You!

Trock. You lie! It was Shadow killed him!

Mio. And now I know! Now I know!

Gaunt. Again I remind you of courtesy toward the witness!

Mio. I know them now!
Let me remind you of courtesy toward the dead!
He says that Shadow killed him! If Shadow were here
he'd say it was Trock! There were three men involved
in the new version of the crime for which
my father died! Shadow and Trock Estrella
as principals in the murder—Garth as witness!—
Why are they here together?—and you—the Judge—
why are you here? Why, because you were all afraid

and you drew together out of that fear to arrange
a story you could tell! And Trock killed Shadow
and meant to kill the Judge out of that same fear—
to keep them quiet! This is the thing I've hunted
over the earth to find out, and I'd be blind
indeed if I missed it now!

[*To Gaunt*]

You heard what he said:
It was Shadow killed him! Now let the night conspire
with the sperm of hell! It's plain beyond denial
even to this fox of justice—and all his words
are curses on the wind! You lied! You lied!
You knew this too!

Gaunt.

[*Low*]

Let me go. Let me go!

Mio. Then why
did you let my father die?

Gaunt. Suppose it known,
but there are things a judge must not believe
though they should head and fester underneath
and press in on his brain. Justice once rendered
in a clear burst of anger, righteously,
upon a very common laborer,
confessed an anarchist, the verdict found
and the precise machinery of law
invoked to know him guilty—think what furor
would rock the state if the court then flatly said:

all this was lies—must be reversed? It's better,
as any judge can tell you, in such cases,
holding the common good to be worth more
than small injustice, to let the record stand,
let one man die. For justice, in the main,
is governed by opinion. Communities
will have what they will have, and it's quite as well,
after all, to be rid of anarchists. Our rights
as citizens can be maintained as rights
only while we are held to be the peers
of those who live about us. A vendor of fish
is not protected as a man might be
who kept a market. I own I've sometimes wished
this was not so, but it is. The man you defend
was unfortunate—and his misfortune bore
almost as heavily on me.—I'm broken—
broken across. You're much too young to know
how bitter it is when a worn connection chars
and you can't remember—can't remember.

    [*He steps forward*]

    You
will not repeat this? It will go no further?

Mio. No.
No further than the moon takes the tides—no further
than the news went when he died—
when you found him guilty
and they flashed that round the earth. Wherever men
still breathe and think, and know what's done to them
by the powers above, they'll know. That's all I ask.
That'll be enough.

[TROCK *has risen and looks darkly at Mio*]

Gaunt. Thank you. For I've said some things
a judge should never say.

Trock. Go right on talking.
Both of you. It won't get far, I guess.

Mio. Oh, you'll see to that?

Trock. I'll see to it. Me and some others.
Maybe I lost my grip there just for a minute.
That's all right.

Mio. Then see to it! Let it rain!
What can you do to me now when the night's on fire
with this thing I know? Now I could almost wish
there was a god somewhere—I could almost think
there was a god—and he somehow brought me here
and set you down before me here in the rain
where I could wring this out of you! For it's said,
and I've heard it, and I'm free! He was as I thought him,
true and noble and upright, even when he went
to a death contrived because he was as he was
and not your kind! Let it rain! Let the night speak fire
and the city go out with the tide, for he was a man
and I know you now, and I have my day!

[*There is a heavy knock at the outside door.* MIRIAMNE *opens
it, at a glance from* GARTH. *The* POLICEMAN *is there in
oilskins*]

Policeman. Evening.

[*He steps in, followed by a* SERGEANT, *similarly dressed*]

We're looking for someone
might be here. Seen an old man around
acting a little off?

[*To Esdras*]

You know the one
I mean. You saw him out there. Jeez! You've got
a funny crowd here!

[*He looks round. The* HOBO *shrinks into his corner*]

That's the one I saw.
What do you think?

Sergeant. That's him. You mean to say
you didn't know him by his pictures?

[*He goes to Gaunt*]

Come on, old man.
You're going home.

Gaunt. Yes, sir. I've lost my way.
I think I've lost my way.

Sergeant. I'll say you have.
About three hundred miles. Now don't you worry.
We'll get you back.

Gaunt. I'm a person of some rank
in my own city.

Sergeant. We know that. One look at you
and we'd know that.

Gaunt. Yes, sir.

Policeman. If it isn't Trock!
  Trock Estrella. How are you, Trock?

Trock. Pretty good,
  Thanks.

Policeman. Got out yesterday again, I hear?

Trock. That's right.

Sergeant. Hi'ye, Trock?

Trock. O.K.

Sergeant. You know we got orders
  to watch you pretty close. Be good now, baby,
  or back you go. Don't try to pull anything,
  not in my district.

Trock. No, sir.

Sergeant. No bumping off.
  If you want my advice quit carrying a gun.
  Try earning your living for once.

Trock. Yeah.

Sergeant. That's an idea.
  Because if we find any stiffs on the river bank
  we'll know who to look for.

Mio. Then look in the other room!
  I accuse that man of murder! Trock Estrella!
  He's a murderer!

Policeman. Hello. I remember you.

Sergeant. Well, what murder?

Mio. It was Trock Estrella
that robbed the pay roll thirteen years ago
and did the killing my father died for! You know
the Romagna case! Romagna was innocent,
and Trock Estrella guilty

Sergeant.

[*Disgusted*]

Oh, what the hell!
That's old stuff—the Romagna case.

Policeman. Hey, Sarge!

[*The* SERGEANT *and* POLICEMAN *come closer together*]

The boy's a professional kidder. He took me over
about half an hour ago. He kids the police
and then ducks out!

Sergeant. Oh, yeah?

Mio. I'm not kidding now.
You'll find a dead man there in the next room
and Estrella killed him!

Sergeant. Thirteen years ago?
And nobody smelled him yet?

Mio.

[*Pointing*]

I accuse this man
of two murders! He killed the paymaster long ago
and had Shadow killed tonight. Look, look for yourself!
He's there all right!

Policeman. Look boy. You stood out there
and put the booby sign on the dumb police
because they're fresh out of Ireland. Don't try it twice.

Sergeant.

[*To Garth*]

Any corpses here?

Garth. Not that I know of.

Sergeant. I thought so.

[Mio *looks at Miriamne*]
[*To Mio*]

Think up a better one.

Mio. Have I got to drag him
out here where you can see him?

[*He goes toward the inner door*]

Can't you scent a murder
when it's under your nose? Look in!

Miriamne. No, no—there's no one—there's no one there!

Sergeant.

[*Looking at Miriamne*]

Take a look inside.

Policeman. Yes, sir.

[*He goes into the inside room. The* SERGEANT *goes up to the
door. The* POLICEMAN *returns*]

He's kidding, Sarge. If there's a cadaver
in here I don't see it.

Mio. You're blind then!

[*He goes into the room, the* SERGEANT *following him*]

Sergeant. What do you mean?

[*He comes out,* MIO *following him*]

When you make a charge of murder it's better to have
the corpus delicti, son. You're the kind puts in
fire alarms to see the engine!

Mio. By God, he was there!
He went in there to die.

Sergeant. I'll bet he did.
And I'm Haile Selassie's aunt! What's your name?

Mio. Romagna.

[*To Garth*]

What have you done with him?

Garth. I don't know what you mean.

Sergeant.

[*To Garth*]

What's he talking about?

Garth. I wish I could tell you.
I don't know.

Sergeant. He must have seen something.

Policeman. He's got
the Romagna case on the brain. You watch yourself,
chump, or you'll get run in.

Mio. Then they're in it together!
All of them!

    [*To Miriamne*]

    Yes, and you!

Garth. He's nuts, I say.

Miriamne.

    [*Gently*]

    You have dreamed something—isn't it true?
You've dreamed—
But truly, there was no one—

    [Mio *looks at her comprehendingly*]

Mio. You want me to say it.

    [*He pauses*]

    Yes, by God, I was dreaming.

Sergeant.

    [*To Policeman*]

    I guess you're right.
We'd better be going. Haven't you got a coat?

Gaunt. No, sir.

Sergeant. I guess I'll have to lend you mine.

    [*He puts his oilskins on Gaunt*]

    Come on, now. It's getting late.

    [Gaunt, *the* Policeman *and the* Sergeant *go out*]

Trock. They're welcome to him.
His fuse is damp. Where is that walking fool
with the three slugs in him?

Esdras. He fell in the hall beyond
and we left him there.

Trock. That's lucky for some of us. Is he out this time
or is he still butting around?

Esdras. He's dead.

Trock. That's perfect.

[*To Mio*]

Don't try using your firearms, amigo baby,
the Sarge is outside.

[*He turns to go*]

Better ship that carrion
back in the river! The one that walks when he's dead;
maybe he'll walk the distance for you.

Garth. Coming back?

Trock. Well, if I come back,
you'll see me. If I don't, you won't. Let the punk
go far as he likes. Turn him loose and let him go.
And may you all rot in hell.

[*He pulls his coat around him and goes to the left.* MIRIAMNE
climbs up to look out a window]

Miriamne. He's climbing up to the street,
along the bridgehead.

[*She turns*]

Quick, Mio! It's safe now! Quick!

Garth. Let him do as he likes.

Miriamne. What do you mean? Garth! He means to kill
him!
You know that!

Garth. I've no doubt Master Romagna
can run his own campaign.

Miriamne. But he'll be killed!

Mio. Why did you lie about Shadow?

[*There is a pause.* GARTH *shrugs, walks across the room, and
sits*]

You were one of the gang!

Garth. I can take a death if I have to! Go tell your story,
only watch your step, for I warn you, Trock's out gunning
and you may not walk very far. Oh, I could defend it
but it's hardly worth while.
If they get Trock they get me too.
Go tell them. You owe me nothing.

Esdras. This Trock you saw,
no one defends him. He's earned his death so often
there's nobody to regret it. But his crime,
his same crime that has dogged you, dogged us down
from what little we had, to live here among the drains,
where the waterbugs break out like a scrofula
on what we eat—and if there's lower to go
we'll go there when you've told your story. And more
that I haven't heart to speak—

Mio.

[*To Garth*]
My father died

in your place. And you could have saved him!
You were one of the gang!

Garth. Why, there you are.
You certainly owe me nothing.

Miriamne.

[*Moaning*]

I want to die.
I want to go away.

Mio. Yes, and you lied!
And trapped me into it!

Miriamne. But Mio, he's my brother.
I couldn't give them my brother.

Mio. No. You couldn't.
You were quite right. The gods were damned ironic
tonight, and they've worked it out.

Esdras. What will be changed
if it comes to trial again? More blood poured out
to a mythical justice, but your father lying still
where he lies now.

Mio. The bright, ironical gods!
What fun they have in heaven! When a man prays hard
for any gift, they give it, and then one more
to boot that makes it useless.

[*To Miriamne*]

You might have picked
some other stranger to dance with!

Miriamne. I know.

Mio. Or chosen
some other evening to sit outside in the rain.
But no, it had to be this. All my life long
I've wanted only one thing, to say to the world
and prove it: the man you killed was clean and true
and full of love as the twelve-year-old that stood
and taught in the temple. I can say that now
and give my proofs—and now you stick a girl's face
between me and the rites I've sworn the dead
shall have of me! You ask too much! Your brother
can take his chance! He was ready enough to let
an innocent man take certainty for him
to pay for the years he's had. That parts us, then,
but we're parted anyway, by the same dark wind
that blew us together. I shall say what I have to say.

   [*He steps back*]

And I'm not welcome here.

Miriamne. But don't go now! You've stayed
too long! He'll be waiting!

Mio. Well, is this any safer?
Let the winds blow, the four winds of the world,
and take us to the four winds.

   [*The three are silent before him. He turns and goes out*]

CURTAIN

WINTERSET
ACT THREE

ACT THREE

SCENE: *The river bank outside the tenement, a little before the close
of the previous act. The rain still falls through the street lamps.
The* TWO NATTY YOUNG MEN IN SERGE AND GRAY *are leaning
against the masonry in a ray of light, concentrating on a game
of chance. Each holds in his hand a packet of ten or fifteen crisp
bills. They compare the numbers on the top notes and immediately a bill changes hands. This goes on with varying fortune
until the tide begins to run toward the* 1ST GUNMAN, *who has
accumulated nearly the whole supply. They play on in complete
silence, evidently not wishing to make any noise. Occasionally
they raise their heads slightly to look carefully about. Luck
begins to favor the* 2ND GUNMAN, *and the notes come his way.
Neither evinces the slightest interest in how the game goes. They
merely play on, bored, half-absorbed. There is a slight noise at
the tenement door. They put the bills away and watch.* TROCK
*comes out, pulls the door shut and comes over to them. He says
a few words too low to be heard, and without changing expression
the* YOUNG MEN *saunter toward the right.* TROCK *goes out to
the left, and the* 2ND PLAYER, *catching that out of the corner of
his eye, lingers in a glimmer of light to go on with the game.
The* 1ST, *with an eye on the tenement door, begins to play without ado, and the bills again shift back and forth, then concen-
trate in the hands of the* 1ST GUNMAN. *The* 2ND *shrugs his
shoulders, searches his pockets, finds one bill, and playing with
it begins to win heavily. They hear the door opening, and
putting the notes away, slip out in front of the rock.* MIO
*emerges, closes the door, looks round him and walks to the left.
Near the corner of the tenement he pauses, reaches out his hand
to try the rain, looks up toward the street, and stands uncertainly a moment. He returns and leans against the tenement
wall.* MIRIAMNE *comes out.* MIO *continues to look off into
space as if unaware of her. She looks away.*

Mio. This rather takes one off his high horse.—What I

mean, tough weather for a hegira. You see, this is my sleeping suit, and if I get it wet—basta!

Miriamne. If you could only hide here.

Mio. Hide?

Miriamne. Lucia would take you in. The street-piano man.

Mio. At the moment I'm afflicted with claustrophobia. I prefer to die in the open, seeking air.

Miriamne. But you could stay there till daylight.

Mio. You're concerned about me.

Miriamne. Shall I ask him?

Mio. No. On the other hand there's a certain reason in your concern. I looked up the street and our old friend Trock hunches patiently under the warehouse eaves.

Miriamne. I was sure of that.

Mio. And here I am, a young man on a cold night, waiting the end of the rain. Being read my lesson by a boy, a blind boy—you know the one I mean. Knee-deep in the salt-marsh, Miriamne, bitten from within, fought.

Miriamne. Wouldn't it be better if you came back in the house?

Mio. You forget my claustrophobia.

Miriamne. Let me walk with you, then. Please. If I stay beside you he wouldn't dare.

Mio. And then again he might.—We don't speak the same language, Miriamne.

Miriamne. I betrayed you. Forgive me.

Mio. I wish I knew this region. There's probably a path along the bank.

Miriamne. Yes. Shadow went that way.

Mio. That's true, too. So here I am, a young man on a wet night, and blind in my weather eye. Stay and talk to me.

Miriamne. If it happens—it's my fault.

Mio. Not at all, sweet. You warned me to keep away. But I would have it. Now I have to find a way out. It's like a chess game. If you think long enough there's always a way out.—For one or the other.—I wonder why white always wins and black always loses in the problems. White to move and mate in three moves. But what if white were to lose—ah, what then? Why, in that case, obviously black would be white and white would be black.—As it often is.—As we often are.—Might makes white. Losers turn black. Do you think I'd have time to draw a gun?

Miriamne. No.

Mio. I'm a fair shot. Also I'm fair game.

> [*The door of the tenement opens and* GARTH *comes out to look about quickly. Seeing only Mio and Miriamne he goes in and comes out again almost immediately carrying one end of a door on which a body lies covered with a cloth. The* HOBO *carries the other end. They go out to the right with their burden*]

This is the burial of Shadow, then;
feet first he dips, and leaves the haunts of men.

Let us make mourn for Shadow, wetly lying,
in elegiac stanzas and sweet crying.
Be gentle with him, little cold waves and fishes;
nibble him not, respect his skin and tissues—

Miriamne. Must you say such things?

Mio. My dear, some requiem is fitting over the dead, even
for Shadow. But the last rhyme was bad.

Whittle him not, respect his dying wishes.

That's better. And then to conclude:

His aromatic virtues, slowly rising
will circumnamb the isle, beyond disguising.
He clung to life beyond the wont of men.
Time and his silence drink us all. Amen.

How I hate these identicals. The French allow them, but
the French have no principles anyway. You know, Miriamne, there's really nothing mysterious about human
life. It's purely mechanical, like an electric appliance.
Stop the engine that runs the generator and the current's
broken. When we think the brain gives off a small electric discharge—quite measurable, and constant within
limits. But that's not what makes your hair stand up
when frightened.

Miriamne. I think it's a mystery.

Mio. Human life? We'll have to wear veils if we're to keep
it a mystery much longer. Now if Shadow and I were
made up into sausages we'd probably make very good
sausages.

Miriamne. Don't—

Mio. I'm sorry. I speak from a high place, far off, long ago, looking down. The cortège returns.

[GARTH *and the* HOBO *return, carrying the door, the cloth lying loosely over it*]

I hope you placed an obol in his mouth to pay the ferry-man? Even among the Greeks a little money was pre-requisite to Elysium.

[GARTH *and the* HOBO *go inside, silent*]

No? It's grim to think of Shadow lingering among lesser shades on the hither side. For lack of a small gratuity

[ESDRAS *comes out the open door and closes it behind him*]

Esdras. You must wait here, Mio, or go inside. I know
you don't trust me, and I haven't earned your trust
You're young enough to seek truth—
and there is no truth;
and I know that—
but I shall call the police and see that you
get safely off.

Mio. It's a little late for that.

Esdras. I shall try.

Mio. And your terms? For I daresay you make terms?

Esdras. No.

Mio. Then let me remind you what will happen.
The police will ask some questions.
When they're answered

they'll ask more, and before they're done with it
your son will be implicated.

Esdras. Must he be?

Mio. I shall not keep quiet.

[*A pause*]

Esdras. Still, I'll go.

Mio. I don't ask help, remember. I make no truce.
He's not on my conscience, and I'm not on yours.

Esdras. But you
could make it easier, so easily.
He's my only son. Let him live.

Mio. His chance of survival's
better than mine, I'd say.

Esdras. I'll go.

Mio. I don't urge it.

Esdras. No. I put my son's life in your hands.
When you're gone,
that may come to your mind.

Mio. Don't count on it.

Esdras. Oh,
I count on nothing.

[*He turns to go.* Miriamne *runs over to him and silently
kisses his hands*]

Not mine, not mine, my daughter!
They're guilty hands.

[*He goes out left.* Garth's *violin is heard within*]

Mio. There was a war in heaven
once, all the angels on one side, and all
the devils on the other, and since that time
disputes have raged among the learned, concerning
whether the demons won, or the angels. Maybe
the angels won, after all.

Miriamne. And again, perhaps
there are no demons or angels.

Mio. Oh, there are none.
But I could love your father.

Miriamne. I love him. You see,
he's afraid because he's old. The less one has
to lose the more he's afraid.

Mio. Suppose one had
only a short stub end of life, or held
a flashlight with the batteries run down
till the bulb was dim, and knew that he could live
while the glow lasted. Or suppose one knew
that while he stood in a little shelter of time
under a bridgehead, say, he could live, and then,
from then on, nothing. Then to lie and turn
with the earth and sun, and regard them not in the least
when the bulb was extinguished or he stepped beyond
his circle into the cold? How would he live
that last dim quarter-hour, before he went,
minus all recollection, to grow in grass
between cobblestones?

Miriamne. Let me put my arms round you, Mio.
Then if anything comes, it's for me, too.
    [*She puts both arms round him*]

Mio. Only suppose
   this circle's charmed! To be safe until he steps
   from this lighted space into dark! Time pauses here
   and high eternity grows in one quarter-hour
   in which to live.

Miriamne. Let me see if anyone's there—
   there in the shadows.

   [*She looks toward the right*]

Mio. It might blast our eternity—
   blow it to bits. No, don't go. This is forever,
   here where we stand. And I ask you, Miriamne,
   how does one spend a forever?

Miriamne. You're frightened?

Mio. Yes.
   So much that time stands still.

Miriamne. Why didn't I speak—
   tell them—when the officers were here? I failed you
   in that one moment!

Mio. His life for mine? Oh, no.
   I wouldn't want it, and you couldn't give it.
   And if I should go on living we're cut apart
   by that brother of yours.

Miriamne. Are we?

Mio. Well, think about it.
   A body lies between us, buried in quicklime.
   Your allegiance is on the other side of that grave
   and not to me.

Miriamne. No, Mio! Mio, I love you!

Mio. I love you, too, but in case my life went on
   beyond that barrier of dark—then Garth
   would run his risk of dying.

Miriamne. He's punished, Mio.
   His life's been torment to him. Let him go,
   for my sake, Mio.

Mio. I wish I could. I wish
   I'd never seen him—or you. I've steeped too long
   in this thing. It's in my teeth and bones. I can't
   let go or forget. And I'll not add my lie
   to the lies that cumber his ground. We live our days
   in a storm of lies that drifts the truth too deep
   for path or shovel; but I've set my foot on a truth
   for once, and I'll trail it down!

   [*A silence.* MIRIAMNE *looks out to the right*]

Miriamne. There's someone there—
   I heard—

   [CARR *comes in from the right*]

Mio. It's Carr.

Carr. That's right. No doubt about it.
   Excuse me.

Mio. Glad to see you. This is Miriamne.
   Carr's a friend of mine.

Carr. You're better employed
   than when I saw you last.

Mio. Bow to the gentleman,
Miriamne. That's meant for you.

Miriamne. Thank you, I'm sure.
Should I leave you, Mio? You want to talk?

Mio. Oh, no,
we've done our talking.

Miriamne. But—

Carr. I'm the one's out of place—
I wandered back because I got worried about you,
that's the truth.—Oh—those two fellows with the hats
down this way, you know, the ones that ran
after we heard the shooting—they're back again,
lingering or malingering down the bank,
revisiting the crime, I guess. They may
mean well.

Mio. I'll try to avoid them.

Carr. I didn't care
for the way they looked at me.—No luck, I suppose,
with that case history? The investigation
you had on hand?

Mio. I can't say. By the way,
the stiff that fell in the water and we saw swirling
down the eddy, he came trudging up, later on,
long enough to tell his name. His name was Shadow,
but he's back in the water now. It's all in an evening.
These things happen here.

Carr. Good God!

Mio. I know.
  I wouldn't believe it if you told it.

Carr. But—
  the man was alive?

Mio. Oh, not for long! He's dunked
  for good this time. That's all that's happened.

Carr. Well,
  if you don't need me—

Miriamne. You had a message to send—
  have you forgotten—?

Mio. I?—Yes, I had a message—
  but I won't send it—not now.

Miriamne. Then I will—!

Mio. No.
  Let it go the way it is! It's all arranged
  another way. You've been a good scout, Carr,
  the best I ever knew on the road.

Carr. That sounds
  like making your will.

Mio. Not yet, but when I do
  I've thought of something to leave you. It's the view
  of Mt. Rainier from the Seattle jail,
  snow over cloud. And the rusty chain in my pocket
  from a pair of handcuffs my father wore. That's all
  the worldly goods I'm seized of.

Carr. Look, Mio—hell—
  if you're in trouble—

Mio. I'm not. Not at all. I have
a genius that attends me where I go,
and guards me now. I'm fine.

Carr. Well, that's good news.
He'll have his work cut out.

Mio. Oh, he's a genius.

Carr. I'll see you then.
I'll be at the Grand Street place. I'm lucky tonight,
and I can pay. I could even pay for two.

Mio. Thanks, I may take you up.

Carr. Good night.

Mio. Right, Carr.

Carr.

  [*To Miriamne*]

Good night.

Miriamne.

  [*After a pause*]

Good night.

  [Carr *goes out to the left*]

Why did you do that? He's your genius, Mio,
and you let him go.

Mio. I couldn't help it.

Miriamne. Call him.
Run after him and call him!

Mio. I tried to say it
and it strangled in my throat. I might have known
you'd win in the end.

Miriamne. Is it for me?

Mio. For you?
It stuck in my throat, that's all I know.

Miriamne. Oh, Mio,
I never asked for that! I only hoped
Garth could go clear.

Mio. Well, now he will.

Miriamne. But you—
It was your chance!

Mio. I've lost
my taste for revenge if it falls on you. Oh, God,
deliver me from the body of this death
I've dragged behind me all these years! Miriamne!
Miriamne!

Miriamne. Yes!

Mio. Miriamne, if you love me
teach me a treason to what I am, and have been,
till I learn to live like a man! I think I'm waking
from a long trauma of hate and fear and death
that's hemmed me from my birth—and glimpse a life
to be lived in hope—but it's young in me yet, I can't
get free, or forgive! But teach me how to live
and forget to hate!

Miriamne. He would have forgiven.

Mio. He?

Miriamne. Your father.

[*A pause*]

Mio. Yes.

[*Another pause*]
You'll think it strange, but I've never
remembered that.

Miriamne. How can I help you?

Mio. You have.

Miriamne. If I were a little older—if I knew
the things to say! I can only put out my hands
and give you back the faith you bring to me
by being what you are. Because to me
you are all hope and beauty and brightness drawn
across what's black and mean!

Mio. He'd have forgiven—
Then there's no more to say—I've groped long enough
through this everglades of old revenges—here
the road ends.—Miriamne, Miriamne,
the iron I wore so long—it's eaten through
and fallen from me. Let me have your arms.
They'll say we're children—Well—the world's made up
of children.

Miriamne. Yes.

Mio. But it's too late for me.

Miriamne. No.

[*She goes into his arms, and they kiss for the first time*]

Then we'll meet again?

Mio. Yes.

Miriamne. Where?

Mio. I'll write—
or send Carr to you.

Miriamne. You won't forget?

Mio. Forget?
Whatever streets I walk, you'll walk them, too,
from now on, and whatever roof or stars
I have to house me, you shall share my roof
and stars and morning. I shall not forget.

Miriamne. God keep you!

Mio. And keep you. And this to remember!
if I should die, Miriamne, this half-hour
is our eternity. I came here seeking
light in darkness, running from the dawn,
and stumbled on a morning.

[*One of the* YOUNG MEN IN SERGE *strolls in casually from the
right, looks up and down without expression, then,
seemingly having forgotten something, retraces his steps
and goes out.* ESDRAS *comes in slowly from the left.
He has lost his hat, and his face is bleeding from a
slight cut on the temple. He stands abjectly near the
tenement*]

Miriamne. Father—what is it?

[*She goes towards Esdras*]

Esdras. Let me alone.

[*He goes nearer to Mio*]

    He wouldn't let me pass.
The street's so icy up along the bridge
I had to crawl on my knees—he kicked me back
three times—and then he held me there—I swear
what I could do I did! I swear to you
I'd save you if I could.

Mio. What makes you think
    that I need saving?

Esdras. Child, save yourself if you can!
    He's waiting for you.

Mio. Well, we knew that before.

Esdras. He won't wait much longer. He'll come here—
    he told me so. Those damned six months of his—
    he wants them all—and you're to die—you'd spread
    his guilt—I had to listen to it—

Mio. Wait—

    [*He walks forward and looks casually to the right, then returns*]

There must be some way up through the house and out
across the roof—

Esdras. He's watching that. But come in—
    and let me look.—

Mio. I'll stay here, thanks. Once in
    and I'm a rat in a deadfall—I'll stay here—
    look for me if you don't mind.

Esdras. Then watch for me—
    I'll be on the roof—

    [*He goes in hurriedly*]

Mio.

> [*Looking up*]

Now all you silent powers
that make the sleet and dark, and never yet
have spoken, give us a sign, let the throw be ours
this once, on this longest night, when the winter sets
his foot on the threshold leading up to spring
and enters with remembered cold—let fall
some mercy with the rain. We are two lovers
here in your night, and we wish to live.

Miriamne. Oh, Mio—
if you pray that way, nothing good will come!
You're bitter, Mio.

Mio. How many floors has this building?

Miriamne. Five or six. It's not as high as the bridge.

Mio. No, I thought not. How many pomegranate seeds
did you eat, Persephone?

Miriamne. Oh, darling, darling,
if you die, don't die alone.

Mio. I'm afraid I'm damned
to hell, and you're not damned at all. Good God,
how long he takes to climb!

Miriamne. The stairs are steep.

> [*A slight pause*]

Mio. I'll follow him.

Miriamne. He's there—at the window—now.
He waves you to go back, not to go in.

Mio, see, that path between the rocks—
they're not watching that—they're out at the river—
I can see them there—they can't watch both—
it leads to a street above.

Mio. I'll try it, then.
Kiss me. You'll hear. But if you never hear—
then I'm the king of hell, Persephone,
and I'll expect you.

Miriamne. Oh, lover, keep safe.

Mio. Good-bye.

> [*He slips out quickly between the rocks. There is a quick ma-
> chine gun rat-tat. The violin stops.* MIRIAMNE *runs
> toward the path.* MIO *comes back slowly, a hand pressea
> under his heart*]

It seems you were mistaken.

Miriamne. Oh, God, forgive me!

> [*She puts an arm round him. He sinks to his knees*]

Where is it, Mio? Let me help you in! Quick, quick,
let me help you!

Mio. I hadn't thought to choose—this—ground—
but it will do.

> [*He slips down*]

Miriamne. Oh, God, forgive me!

Mio. Yes?
The king of hell was not forgiven then,
Dis is his name, and Hades is his home—
and he goes alone—

Miriamne. Why does he bleed so? Mio, if you go
  I shall go with you.

Mio. It's better to stay alive.
  I wanted to stay alive—because of you—
  I leave you that—and what he said to me dying:
  I love you, and will love you after I die.
  Tomorrow, I shall still love you, as I've loved
  the stars I'll never see, and all the mornings
  that might have been yours and mine. Oh, Miriamne,
  you taught me this.

Miriamne. If only I'd never seen you
  then you could live—

Mio. That's blasphemy—Oh, God,
  there might have been some easier way of it.
  You didn't want me to die, did you, Miriamne—?
  You didn't send me away—?

Miriamne. Oh, never, never—

Mio. Forgive me—kiss me—I've got blood on your lips—
  I'm sorry—it doesn't matter—I'm sorry—

  [ESDRAS *and* GARTH *come out*]

Miriamne. Mio—
  I'd have gone to die myself—you must hear this, Mio,
  I'd have died to help you—you must listen, sweet,
  you must hear it—

  [*She rises*]

  I can die, too, see! You! There!
  You in the shadows!—You killed him to silence him!

  [*She walks toward the path*]

But I'm not silenced! All that he knew I know,
and I'll tell it tonight! Tonight—
tell it and scream it
through all the streets—that Trock's a murderer
and he hired you for this murder!
Your work's not done—
and you won't live long! Do you hear?
You're murderers, and I know who you are!

[*The machine gun speaks again. She sinks to her knees.* GARTH *runs to her*]

Garth. You little fool!

[*He tries to lift her*]

Miriamne. Don't touch me!

[*She crawls toward Mio*]

Look, Mio! They killed me, too. Oh, you can believe me
now, Mio. You can believe I wouldn't hurt you,
because I'm dying! Why doesn't he answer me?
Oh, now he'll never know!

[*She sinks down, her hand over her mouth, choking.* GARTH *kneels beside her, then rises, shuddering. The* HOBO *comes out.* LUCIA *and* PINY *look out*]

Esdras. It lacked only this.

Garth. Yes.

[ESDRAS *bends over Miriamne, then rises slowly*]

Why was the bastard born? Why did he come here?

Esdras. Miriamne—Miriamne—yes, and Mio,
one breath shall call you now—forgive us both—

forgive the ancient evil of the earth
that brought you here—

Garth. Why must she be a fool?

Esdras. Well, they were wiser than you and I. To die
when you are young and untouched, that's beggary
to a miser of years, but the devils locked in synod
shake and are daunted when men set their lives
at hazard for the heart's love, and lose. And these,
who were yet children, will weigh more than all
a city's elders when the experiment
is reckoned up in the end. Oh, Miriamne,
and Mio—Mio, my son—know this where you lie,
this is the glory of earth-born men and women,
not to cringe, never to yield, but standing,
take defeat implacable and defiant,
die unsubmitting. I wish that I'd died so,
long ago; before you're old you'll wish
that you had died as they have. On this star,
in this hard star-adventure, knowing not
what the fires mean to right and left, nor whether
a meaning was intended or presumed,
man can stand up, and look out blind, and say:
in all these turning lights I find no clue,
only a masterless night, and in my blood
no certain answer, yet is my mind my own,
yet is my heart a cry toward something dim
in distance, which is higher than I am
and makes me emperor of the endless dark
even in seeking! What odds and ends of life
men may live otherwise, let them live, and then

go out, as I shall go, and you. Our part
is only to bury them. Come, take her up.
They must not lie here.

> [LUCIA *and* PINY *come near to help*. ESDRAS *and* GARTH *stoop
> to carry Miriamne*]

CURTAIN

VI · THE WINGLESS VICTORY

CHARACTERS

(In the order of their appearance)

A Girl

The Reverend Phineas
  McQueston

Jared Mungo

Winston Urquhart

Mrs. McQueston

Ruel McQueston

Venture

Faith Ingalls

Happy Penny

Letty

Nathaniel McQueston

Oparre

Toala

Durian

Harry, a Bailiff

Van Zandt, a Sailor

ACT ONE

SCENE: *The living room of a house in Salem, early in the winter of 1800. The place is well, if somewhat sternly furnished, giving evidence of wealth and an eye for design. Over the fireplace a magnificent ship model takes the center of the stage, flanked by two rather restrained religious pictures. There are doors to right and left and a window which looks out over the harbor. The right-hand door leads to the kitchen, the left-hand door to a front hall and stairway. It is evening and the room is just now the scene of an ecclesiastical session. The REV-EREND PHINEAS McQUESTON stands near the fireplace speaking to a GIRL with a BABE in her arms and a shawl over her head who stands near the door. JARED MUNGO and WINSTON URQUHART, elders of the church, are seated facing the GIRL. MRS. McQUESTON, mother of the minister and lady of the house, sits near the fire, her knitting laid in her lap as she listens.*

Phineas. If you had been willing to name this man, sinner with you and equally guilty, we should have been willing, according to our custom, to call you both before the congregation, there to receive castigation fitting your desert and thereafter, the penalties of your guilt borne uncomplainingly, to be readmitted to the body of the church. But you, recalcitrant girl as you are, bring on yourself a heavier verdict through silence. Your case has been considered by the elders of the vestry, and you are to be thrust out from the congregation, neither is there to be entertainment vouchsafed you by communicants. You have chosen your

place with whoremasters and whalers of the water-
front. You are free to go to that place.

The Girl.

> [*Looking up*]

I am free?

Phineas. You are free to seek your own place, for the
old will know you no more.

The Girl. Oh, sir; oh, sir—he will die!

Mungo. You were given a choice. It's still not too late.

The Girl. I can't tell that! Truly I can't tell it!

Mungo. You know his name. You have but to say his
name.

The Girl. But if I were to say it—forgive me—you
would be sorrier than I!

Phineas.

> [*Thundering*]

We know no exceptions and no favorites here!

Urquhart. If the lass wishes to keep her mouth shut let
her keep it shut then. We've no call to drag down a
respected citizen along with her.

Phineas. Guilt is guilt and calls for punishment!

Urquhart. She's willing to take it alone. Let her take it.

The Girl. But if you cast me out—if the congregation
casts me out—me and the babe—we'll have no place

to go. He'll die—there'll not be a crust—and I've had little enough for him where I am—

Phineas. I've spoken to your master and mistress. You'll find it useless to return there.

The Girl. Please, sirs—he's but a bairn and it wasn't his fault. Oh, please, sirs—you couldn't want him to die—

Phineas. We can make no distinction between the sin and the fruits of the sin. It would be as well if he were to die—and better for your soul.

The Girl. Oh, God forgive you, God forgive you—

Mungo. Ask your own forgiveness, woman! You're the one needs it!

The Girl.

[*Timidly*]

Mrs. McQueston—

Mrs. McQueston. I've no part in this.

[*The right-hand door opens and* RUEL MCQUESTON *enters. He pauses.*]

The Girl. But you know how it is when you have a babe and love him, Mrs. McQueston. I've had plenty to bear with him, but I love him. Couldn't you speak to your son, couldn't you ask him—just to let us live—

Mrs. McQueston.

[*Rising deliberately and going to the* GIRL]

Go out! You've heard what was said to you here! Go out. And go far from us.

[*The* GIRL *pauses.* MRS. McQUESTON *spits in her face. The* GIRL *turns, wiping off the spittle with the shawl that is wrapped round the child, and goes to the door, fumbling blindly for the handle.* RUEL *crosses the room, opens the door for her, lets her out and faces the company.*]

Ruel. Sorry to intrude, I'm sure.

[MRS. McQUESTON *returns toward the chair.*]

Phineas. She could have opened the door for herself.

Ruel. Just one of those niceties the cloth could never comprehend, brother. A gentleman opens a door for a lady in distress.

[*He goes to the fire.*]

Phineas. A lady, brother?

Ruel. Do you mean to tell me that in all those rules of the church there's nothing said, absolutely nothing, about common courtesy?—Besides she's a quite personable wench, and I have no doubt a most obliging armful.

Phineas. If you have occasion to use this room we can remove our session.

Ruel. I do have occasion to use the room, God defend me. I came in to get warm—there being no coal fire elsewhere. The family fortunes have fallen so low, gentlemen, that we keep but one fire, and on session days, while you confer so snugly here over the black destinies of man, the rest of the family must needs huddle in the kitchen. I'm loath to speak of this, as it may hurry your already hasty decisions, but my proximity to the kitchen maids tends to undermine their morals. It follows that the more you build up morality in the parlor the more I tear it down below stairs, a regrettable cancellation.

Mungo. We were about to leave, Reverend Phineas.

Mrs. McQueston. Ruel!

Ruel. Yes, mother.

Mrs. McQueston. You've said enough, and you can go.

Ruel. Back to the kitchen, mother?

Mrs. McQueston. You've dishonored us in every tavern on the harbor. Be content with that. I may have hatched a devil, for you speak like one, but in this house I'm mistress and you'll give at least lip service to the things of God!

Ruel. Mother, mother, to make me out a devil you make yourself the devil's dam, which is something of a stain to my progenitors—

Phineas. Must you be taught respect to our mother— you wastrel?

[*He bustles up to* RUEL, *who is amused.*]

Ruel. Come, come, little Phineas. You're at a disadvantage, both in your shoulders and your epithets. However, I'll leave if my errand's unwelcome. I came to tell you news of brother Nat.

Mrs. McQueston. What news?

Ruel. I may stay then? Thanks. Why, it seems you were right in what you heard from New Bedford. Brother Nat is back, he's captain and owner of a five-master, and the damn thing's loaded to the gunnels with spices from the Celebes.

[*To* Mungo *and* Urquhart]

Excuse the language, but our hope is, gentlemen, that brother Nat is returning rich to restore the fading fortunes of our somewhat seedy family. He was treated a bit cavalierly on his exit, being at that time a vagabond sailor, but something tells me he will be received with intoxicating warmth—

Phineas. We can discuss the family fortunes in private—

Ruel. Oh, yes! we will.

Mrs. McQueston. Where did you hear this?

Ruel. You can see the lights of a coasting lugger from the window. When she came in I recognized the *Silver Pennant* of New Bedford. The second mate is a friend of mine, Mr. Happy Penny—I assure you the name's no fiction, though his christened monicker being Merriment Penny we call him Happy for short. Mr. Penny had seen Captain Nathaniel, our distinguished brother, and spoken to him. It's true as Gospel, and perhaps even more reliable, that Nat is rich, healthy and bound for home. He had put into New Bedford only to refit after a storm and is on his way here now. Does this earn me a place among the blest?

Mungo. Mrs. McQueston, I congratulate you.

Urquhart. It's not often a prodigal returns better off than he went.

Mungo. How long has he been away?

Mrs. McQueston. Seven years. Seven years without a word.

Ruel. And seven lean years at that.

Phineas. He's an evil man. Rich or poor, brother or not, he's evil.

Ruel. But you'll forgive him, Phineas, you'll forgive him. Oh, you'll forgive more than you know.

Phineas. And what do you mean by that?

Ruel. Oh, there's a latter end to my story. It has a sting in the tail. I shall retain this sequel until the visitors leave.

Urquhart. Why—in that case—

Mungo. Yes—we shall say good night, Reverend Phineas.

Ruel. Oh, no hurry—the suspense is good for us all.

Phineas. Brother Ruel is not the spokesman for our family, gentlemen. I hope you will disregard his dismissal.

Urquhart. No more words, sir, no more words. You have important matters in hand, and we're off. Bring the

prodigal round to mid-week prayers, Mrs. McQueston. He'll need a little praying after seven years at
sea.

[*He takes her hand.*]

Mrs. McQueston. Thank you. I will.

Urquhart. And good night, sir.

Phineas. Good night, then—since you wish it.

Mungo. Good night. We can find the door.

Mrs. McQueston. Good night.

[MUNGO *and* URQUHART *go out.*]

Ruel. Draw as long a face as you can, dominie—it'll
grow longer while I talk.

Mrs. McQueston. Will you put an end to this, and say
out what you have to say?

Ruel. Indeed I will, mother, and enjoy it. I sat over a
glass with Mr. Happy Penny and he furnished me
with further details of the arrival. Details of a most
scandalous sort. Oh, this world, this world! To what
depths of degradation may a wandering sailor be carried by his passions! Brother Nathaniel brings two
women with him in the after cabins.

Mrs. McQueston. What sort of women?

Ruel. What sort? Well, to tell the truth, they're black.

Mrs. McQueston. Black?

[RUEL *bows.*]

Slaves?

Ruel. Well, the story runs he's married to one or both of them, though on this point Mr. Penny left me dark, being a timid man in family affairs and not liking to put embarrassing questions to Nathaniel.

Phineas. He's married to black women?

Ruel. Now perhaps only to one, and to defend our brother's taste for the moment, perhaps only to the younger and lighter-skinned of the two.

Phineas. Where do these women come from?

Ruel. I don't know. I have only the most alarming suspicions.

Phineas. How long have they been with him?

Ruel. I fear it's not an affair of the moment. There are two children.

Mrs. McQueston. Children!

Ruel. Two children.

Mrs. McQueston. Black children!

Ruel. Well, not black. Shall we say a faint coffee-color?

Phineas. This is an invention—a hoax you perpetrate on us for your own amusement. "Shall we say a faint coffee-color." Faugh!

Ruel. At least it is amusing to speculate. I admit I haven't seen them with my own eyes, and the whole affair may be exaggerated.

Phineas. I rather think so. And I wonder at my weakness of brain in being taken in by you. I'm not usually so open a target.

Ruel. No, Phineas, you're not.

Mrs. McQueston. This was all a fabrication then?

Ruel. Madam, I own I've sometimes permitted my fancy to run away with me in the presence of Phineas. Brother or not, this Phineas is a consummate half-wit, and it's a temptation to lead him on. But in this case I leave all to the great fabricator himself, and scorn to embroider on his matchless doings. I have seen things, madam, in my circumscribed travels, which would lead me to believe anything, quite anything, of the great author of all and what he allows. I say this seriously, madam, speaking though I do to those who cannot understand me.

Phineas. I'll believe none of your preposterous nonsense!

Ruel. It's seldom necessary to encourage a fool in his folly.

Mrs. McQueston.

[*Coming up to* RUEL]

And do you quote that saying to Phineas? You who grew up a mocker in a godly town and a godly household, you who spent more than your share when there was plenty, and bring nothing but grief into the house now we're poor! A friend of rogues and fornicator with street women! A follower of Paris fashions who's never gone out to earn what would buy him a shirt! The shirt you wear was bought by this same brother of yours, who has used his wits to far better advantage for all your fine sayings!

Ruel. All that's quite true. When I was young there was too much money in the house to be good for me, and now that I need it I've an aversion toward going out to get it. Quite true.

Mrs. McQueston. Then keep silent when your brother speaks, out of mere decency!

Ruel. Silent I am, silent I shall be.

Mrs. McQueston. Yes, till you need a shilling. Then you'll speak fast enough.

Ruel. Possession, possession, ah, it's possession makes a man.

Mrs. McQueston. Then you're none.

Ruel. Then I'm none, as you say.

[*He turns out a pocket ruefully. The inner door opens and* VENTURE MCQUESTON, *wife of* PHINEAS, *looks in, followed by* FAITH INGALLS.]

Venture. Phineas!

Phineas. Yes?

Venture. May we come in?

Phineas. Yes. What is it?

Venture. Haven't you heard?

Phineas. Heard? No.

Venture. But here's cousin Faith
and she says Nathaniel's coming!

Phineas. Yes, my dear,
but we've heard that.

Faith. But coming now—this moment—
look out the window—there's a ship warping in
with a star on every masthead—count the lanterns!—
she's a five-master! The whole town's running down
to the harbor front, and everyone I've seen
says it's the *Queen of the Celebes!*
    [*They look out.*]

Phineas. And by
what process of divination can they read
her name at night?

Faith. And who but Captain Nat
would run the shoals in the dark? By the cut of his jib
and his dashing ways you shall know him, cousin
                       Phineas,
and know him I do!

Phineas. Could it be?

Ruel. If he made a quick run
he could be here, yes.

Phineas. It's like him to waste sperm oil
at every masthead.

Faith. Waste it! Now let's allow

one celebration in seven years. He's coming
straight in. He'll dock at your wharf below.

Phineas. He's welcome
to the berth. It's empty.

Ruel. And has been for some time—
and would be?

Phineas. Oh, and would be.

Faith. He said when he left
he'd never cross that bar again till he
could buy the town for cash.

Mrs. McQueston. Have you heard from him
in all this time, my dear?

Faith. Once, only once.
Do I sound possessive? He's forgotten me,
as the fish forgets the hook, only remembering
the cicatrice in his lip.

Mrs. McQueston. I very much fear
he's forgotten all of us.

Faith. What would make you think so?
Isn't he here?

Phineas. He comes to dazzle us,
but he'll go his own way, I doubt, and quite as well
so far as I'm concerned,

Faith. I believe you credit
that absurd story about the blackamoor
he's supposed to have married.

Phineas. No.

Faith. No. I should hope not.
He was nobody's fool. Look, look how they run—
you'd think it was the second coming.

Ruel. Well, in some ways
it was less expected.

Faith. Shall we be on the pier
when he disembarks? Come.

Phineas. If he wants to see us
we shall be here.

Faith. Now, please—if he wants to see you—
Who else would he care to see?

Phineas. I'll make no part
of his triumph!

Faith. But aren't you glad that he's come back—
and glad that he's rich?

Phineas. I shall be more concerned
about the state of his soul. There are better things
in this world than money.

Faith. Oh, not in this world, cousin.
The other world.

Phineas. No, this.

Faith. Oh, but that's tiresome,
really it is, at this moment. Come with me, please,
all of us. Here's a brother of yours returning,

the giddiest, maddest tar that ever followed
the whistling of a wind—and damned his eyes
if he cared where he went—and in he blows
with a fortune reaped on the outlands of the moon
somewhere, anywhere—went out with half a florin
to bless himself, and back now a merchant prince
with gold he coined in a sunset! I may have loved him
once, but so did you I should think, at least
enough to bid him welcome.

Phineas. He'll be happier
if I'm not there with my long face and black coat
to make my comment.

Faith. Ruel?

Ruel. Oh, I'll be along.

Venture. Could I go, Phineas?

Phineas. If it's compatible
that you should walk the road and cling to the palings
with a mob at your heels.

Venture. I'm sorry.

Ruel. They're warping in
at the foot of the street. They'll have the gangplank
down
before we get there.

Faith. Quick, then.

[*A flash lights the room.*]

Ruel. I think they're burning

Greek fire on the point.

[*He turns toward the door.*]

Heigh-ho! Well, anyway
somebody's ship came in!

[RUEL *and* FAITH *go out the outer door.* VENTURE
still stands at the window.]

Phineas. I wish to speak
with my mother, Venture.

Venture. Yes, Phineas.

[*She goes within.*]

Phineas. The ways
of God are strange. The sinner always triumphant;
the babbler and the reveller sit at meat,
while those who serve Him hope for a dinner of herbs
and rise up hungry. It's too much to ask
that I beg of Nathaniel!

Mrs. McQueston. How are we off without him?

Phineas. There's nothing left. You'll lose the house and
the wharf
if it goes much longer.

Mrs. McQueston. He'll not let that happen,
now that he's here.

Phineas. Do you bargain with him then!
It's out of my hands.

[LETTY, *a servant, comes to the inner door.*]

Letty. Madam, there's an officer came to the kitchen door, a Mr. Penny, looking for Mr. Ruel.

Phineas. That will be this Happy Penny then.—Mr. Ruel's gone out.

Letty. I'll tell him. Thank you, sir.

Mrs. McQueston. Ask Mr. Penny if he'll step in a moment. I'd like to see him.

Letty. Yes, madam.
[*She goes in.*]

Mrs. McQueston. He's seen these women of Nathaniel's.
[*She sits.*]

Phineas. I'd rather trade no gossip.

Mrs. McQueston. Listen then, and benefit by it.
[*The door opens and* HAPPY PENNY, *an open-faced young seaman, is ushered in.*]

Happy. Good evening, ma'am. Good evening, sir.
[PHINEAS *bows.*]

Mrs. McQueston. Is this Mr. Happy Penny?

Happy. Yes, Mrs. McQueston.

Mrs. McQueston. This is my son, the Reverend Phineas McQueston.

Happy. Pleased to meet you, sir.

Phineas. And you.

Mrs. McQueston. I'll come straight to the point, Mr. Penny. I'm told you saw my son Nathaniel at New Bedford.

Happy. Yes, ma'am. I did. Aboard the *Queen of the Celebes*. Which is now in below.

Mrs. McQueston. I have heard that he's married. Is that true?

Happy. Now as to that I couldn't say.

Mrs. McQueston. There were two women on board, I hear?

Happy. Yes, ma'am.

Mrs. McQueston. And two children?

Happy. Yes. One of the women was, I should say, a nurse like.

Mrs. McQueston. A black woman?

Happy. Not to say black, no.

Mrs. McQueston. Not of our race?

Happy. No, ma'am.

Mrs. McQueston. Neither of them?

Happy. No, ma'am.—But in turn you couldn't really blame him, I should say.

Mrs. McQueston. Why?

Happy. Because the young one's quite a—a—I wouldn't

know what words you'd use, Mrs. McQueston. You
might not say she was a looker, Mrs. McQueston, but,
in turn, I should say any man would say she was.

Mrs. McQueston. Where does she come from?

Happy. Now that, in turn, I don't know—he not having
said. He not having said a word about her. Not to me.

Mrs. McQueston. I believe that's all I wished to know
then, Mr. Penny. You probably wish to go down to
the dock?

Happy. Yes, ma'am. I was looking for Mr. Ruel.

Phineas. He has preceded you.

Happy. Yes, sir. Yes, ma'am. Thank you. Good evening.
    [PHINEAS *bows.*]

Mrs. McQueston. Good evening.
    [PENNY *goes out the inner door.*]

Phineas. Then he'll not be coming here.

Mrs. McQueston. He might, he might.

Phineas. Would you let him in?

Mrs. McQueston. I think so.

Phineas. And his women?

Mrs. McQueston. He'll not bring them here.

Phineas. If he's dragged his shame
    all this way from the Pacific, why then he means

to flaunt it in our faces. I tell you the man's
a dunghill of evil! Degenerate, eater of ordure,
lower than Ruel because he has more sinew
and daring to carry it through!

Mrs. McQueston. We send over-seas
to wean the pagans of their wood and stone,
and should we do less for Nathaniel?

Phineas. Do you mean that?

Mrs. McQueston. How long is a man enamored of
black flesh
when there's better to be had? I've heard it said
a man might have a lust to do his kind
with a lesser than himself, in his pride of manhood,
despising the thing beneath him, but then to live
his years with this thing despised, I think he'd hate
the flesh he used.

[*There is a pause.*]

Phineas. Where have you heard such things?

Mrs. McQueston. A woman knows them whether she's
heard them or not.
And a woman knows when she's used. And woman or
man,
a black's a slave, and start as high as she likes
she'll sink to be a slave, and be used for flesh
and hate her own flesh for it!

Phineas. You think beyond me.

Mrs. McQueston. Yes. I would hope so. I should like to
think
beyond the immediate disgrace, and find
what lies on the further side.

Phineas. There's disgrace enough.
Even though I disown him, never see him,
think of the fingers pointed at me: there's
that preacher whose brother married a nigger wife
and fetched her home! How much is a man of God
expected to endure?

Mrs. McQueston. Aye, your enduring!
[*She rises.*]

He's my son, bear in mind—and I suckled him
as much as you—the fingers that point, the voices
that rail, they'll cut you only because they touch
your place as a minister—but they'll search me deep,
in an old wound! I have one son already
no mother envies me, and now another
comes home to roost, this with his pockets lined
in gold that might be a stay to my old age,
only he sleeps a heathen whore in his bed,
and I'm cut off for her! Has it crossed your mind
what scalding medicine I'd drench her with
if I had the nursing of her? But that way we
get nothing, and she keeps it all! We'll wait!
Hold down whatever boils inside, and move
when we know what game he plays!
[*There is a distant shout, "Captain Nathaniel!"*]

Phineas. Well, we'll soon know.

[*Straggling voices are heard singing outside.*]

The Men.

[*Outside*]

A-roving, a-roving,
We'll sing once more, to the distant shore,
But we'll go no more a-roving
By the light of the moon!

Phineas. They're bringing him on their shoulders.

The Men.

[*Nearer*]

A-roving, a-roving,
To get dead tight in the dead of night,
But we'll go no more a-roving,
By the light of the moon!

[*A door opens outside.*]

Nathaniel.

[*Outside*]

Set me down, boys, set me down! This is no fitting
way to enter a parson's house!

A Voice. Put him down, lads.

Another Voice. Lower the topsail! Hard a-port now!
We're in!

Another Voice. Reef your jib, Happy!

Another Voice. Son-of-a-gun, you're heavy!

Nathaniel.

[*Outside*]

Feet-first, if you don't mind!

[*There is a trampling on the stoop.*]

Mrs. McQueston. Let him in, Phineas.

[PHINEAS *goes to the door and opens it. There are a
number of men in the hallway, among them*
HAPPY PENNY. MRS. MCQUESTON *goes to a
chair and sits heavily as if half-fainting.*]

Nathaniel.

[*Coming into view*]

Now I'd ask you in, gentlemen, only this is my mother's house, as you know, and I'm home after a long
absence.

Happy.

[*Outside*]

Never apologize to a sailor, sir!

[*He laughs.*]

Phineas. Will you come in, gentlemen?

Nathaniel. Phineas, as I live and swim!

[*He catches* PHINEAS' *hand.*]

Phineas. Come in, sir.

[RUEL *and* FAITH *appear at the door, and enter.*]

Come in, all of you.

[HAPPY *steps inside.*]

Happy. Well, the truth is, you see,
  we know what it's like, coming into port, so we'll leave
                    you,
  and we beg your pardon, ma'am, I'm sure—it's only,
  we had to give a salute.

A Voice. That's right.

Happy. And now,
  in turn, we'll say good night.

Nathaniel. And good night, and thanks,
  thanks for the ride, too!

A Voice. Man, we'll give you a ride
  On any similar occasion!

Another Voice. Right.

Happy. Good night, and to all here.

Nathaniel. Good night. Good night.

The Crowd. Good night, captain. Good night. Good
                    night. Good night.

    [PHINEAS *closes the door.* NATHANIEL, RUEL *and*
       FAITH *remain.* VENTURE *has entered from*
       within. NATHANIEL *looks round the room, his*
       back to the door, and his eye finally comes to his
       mother.]

Nathaniel. And so the sum and substance of it is
  I'm back, yes, and I never believed I'd get here—
  and I hardly believe it now. Damn my two eyes
  but this is a big world, mother!

Mrs. McQueston. You use big words
to tell about it, son.

Nathaniel. Now, there's the girl,
there's the mother! I half expected you'd
rear up and show me the door if I used a word,
and that was why I used it. I'm welcome, then,
damn my eyes and all?

Mrs. McQueston. Where did you think
to find a welcome, if not here?

Nathaniel. Now God
forbid all boasting, but when I chose seafaring,
and went out that door with my extra shirt done up
in a blue bandana, there were no fond farewells
as I remember—and so, one never knows
how he'll be liked coming home.

Mrs. McQueston. You'll find we like you
exactly as you like us.

Nathaniel.

      [*Going to her chair*]
That's good with me,
and then to spare, if you knew how a man could long
for a cool green coast, and maybe a cool green friend
or two, left over from his youth. We never
were much for kissing in this room, but God,
God how I'm glad to see you!
      [*He takes her face in his hands and kisses her brow.*]

Mrs. McQueston. Thank you, son.

Nathaniel.

[*Rising*]

And Phineas, too.

[*He takes* PHINEAS' *hand.*]

In all these seven years
there's a hand's never drawn back from shepherding
his flock, I could swear to that. And Ruel's a man,
by thunder—I hadn't noticed!

Ruel. I'm old enough,
but so far singularly of no account
in the local records.

Nathaniel. Take your time. A life's
a damn sight longer than you think.

[*He looks at* FAITH.]

Faith.

[*Giving her hand, smiling*]

No spark,
no glimpse? But all those fond farewells you said
you missed at the door, I have a faint recollection
they were spoken elsewhere!

Nathaniel. But you were a scrub with pigtails,
and a mamma-washed face! It's Faith!

Faith. Why, so it is!

Nathaniel. And now she walks like a queen, and I didn't
know her!
Give us a kiss for the old-time ways and days,

when we were all younger and less beautiful.
Girl, you've betrayed me!
  [*They kiss.*]

Faith. How?

Nathaniel. Getting out of hand,
  growing up into goddess, and me away!
  Lady, it needs looking into.

Faith. And may I ask
  where you took lessons in blandishment?

Nathaniel. God's truth—
  I'm solemn as an owl. And this will be
  our brother Phineas' wife, and she'll kiss me too
  like a good sister-in-law.

Venture. Yes, sir.
  [*He kisses* VENTURE.]

Nathaniel. And now,
  my hearties, as I said before, I'm back,
  and it turned out better than I thought it would,
  for I own a ship with two hundred tons of spice
  and gums mowed away in her hold. At present prices
  I don't know what it's worth, but when I left
  it would have ransomed the devil out of hell
  and kept the Lord God in pocket money.
  [*A pause.*]

Ruel. Brother,
  they'll tell you I'm no merchant, but two hundred—
  two hundred tons of spices—

Nathaniel. And more than that,
   I know where pepper grows in the Celebes,
   and there's more there. All we want. What's the stuff
               worth here?
   A drug on the market?

Ruel. Man, you're just in time.
   The tea's been getting weaker day by day
   from the McQueston kitchen. Would you take
   two hundred thousand for it?

Nathaniel. No.

Ruel. I thought not.
   Well, it's worth more.

Nathaniel. I've done it, then.

Faith. Oh, yes.
   And you can buy the town, as you said you would
   when you went away.

Nathaniel. Then I can tell you the rest.
   I've had enough of this washing up and down
   across salt waters. There's too damn much salt water
   on our terrestrial pumpkin, and now I'm here
   with two feet planted on New England rock
   I want to shake off my sea legs, sink my pile
   in our old chandlery business—McQueston Sons—
   and take root where I'm remembered. Have you got
               the wharf?
   Can you use the capital?

Ruel. Man, man, oh, man,
    I tell you our tea's been weak.

Nathaniel. Will you take it, mother,
    and take me in?
        [MRS. MCQUESTON *rises and goes to* NATHANIEL.]

Mrs. McQueston. You've come in time. But only
    just in time. There's no business left. The wharf's
    been pledged, and the house.

Nathaniel. Then we'll have them back again.

Mrs. McQueston. You're sure you want it?

Nathaniel. If I was ever sure
    of anything, mother.

Mrs. McQueston. And what must we do for you?

Nathaniel. Why, take me back.

Mrs. McQueston. Will you make it difficult?

Nathaniel. You've heard about her then. It's true I'm
                    married.
    I'm wed to a princess of the Celebes,
    and I'll want you to take her too.

Mrs. McQueston. I've heard it said
    that when men settle in tropic parts they buy
    a native girl to live with. I've not heard
    they bring them home as wives.

Nathaniel. But I've brought mine,
    and she stays with me.

Mrs. McQueston. And she's a black, and worships
some pagan fetish.

Nathaniel. Black? She's a Malay princess,
but one shade darker than I am myself
with too much wind and sun. And she's a Christian,
a damn sight better Christian than I am,
or most of us.

Phineas. But keep her out of my sight
if she comes here!

Nathaniel. She'll take to you, Phineas.
She knows her Bible forward and back as well
as any divine in Salem. Taught herself
her English out of it, runs with Bible talk
like an Old Testament prophet.

Phineas.

   [*Shouting*]
Why are you here?
You mate with some aborigine in a jungle,
beget your children on her, and bring her here,
to spread your baboon kisses on white women
as if nothing had happened!

Nathaniel. I'm sorry. I kissed your wife.
That won't happen again, I thank you. You
should travel, brother. Or read. You'll find some
                    Malays
quite twice as erudite as yourself, and proud
as Lucifer.

Phineas. How do you wipe the smell off
   when you get up in the morning? To lie there tangled
   into an animal's entrails, and you a man,
   and you want to smirch us with it!

Nathaniel. We'll go elsewhere.
   I think we can manage. Eat your cabbage-whey,
   you and your virginal women!

   [*He turns abruptly.*]

Mrs. McQueston. Wait!

Nathaniel. For what?

Mrs. McQueston. There was a man of Salem once who
                                married
   an Indian squaw—and brought her here to live—
   wait till I finish—but they had no neighbors;
   no one spoke to him in the street. He lost
   what work he had. He drank himself to death,
   and the children died. The squaw went back to her
                                tribe,
   and it's said they stoned her. Think well what you do
   before you fetch in this bride.

Nathaniel. These sitters at home
   that think their brain's the only brain there is
   and the rest's all outer darkness! Sending out
   your missionaries to civilizations so old
   and wise they laugh at your Jesus-myth! Believing
   that you're the chosen of Heaven because your skin's
   a half-shade lighter than others! I've seen these
                                peoples

you rank with animals, and I know them. They
can give you cards and spades at any game
except sheer asininity. At that
the Aryan tops the world! I've taken a wife,
from among the Malays, and she's more beautiful,
and has a better head, and sweeter ways,
and higher pride, and makes a better lover
than any celery-top among you! Aye,
and by God I'd trust her farther! That's my choice
and we'll go elsewhere!

Mrs. McQueston. No. You'll bring her here.
I've given you my warning, but if you must
you must, and we'll do as we can.

Nathaniel. I can do without you,
having heard Phineas.

Mrs. McQueston. He's not master here.
He'll keep a civil tongue.

Nathaniel. I'll want more than that.

Ruel. If she's as you say, Nathaniel, she'll be welcome
anywhere, I should think.

Nathaniel. Would you make her welcome,
and let her feel it?

Ruel. Yes, and be happy to.
Where is she?

Nathaniel. I left an order with the mate.
He's to escort them up.

Ruel. I'll go to meet her.

Faith. And so will I.

Nathaniel. You too?

Faith. Why, yes, why not?
     If you love her, that's enough.

Nathaniel. Then thanks for that.
     And I'll go with you.
          [*They start toward the door.*]
     But not if there's any doubt
     how she'll be treated. She's both proud and weary
     and I've offered her a haven.

Mrs. McQueston. I too am proud
     and old and weary, but she shall share my roof—
     since you ask it. Let her come.
          [RUEL, FAITH *and* NATHANIEL *go out the front door.*]

Phineas. With your pardon, mother,
     I'll not be here—nor will my wife. Perhaps
     that will smooth matters.

Mrs. McQueston. You'll be in your room?

Phineas. Yes. And Venture will be, let's say, in the
                              kitchen.
     At any rate not here.

Venture. Yes, Phineas.
          [*She goes out to the kitchen.*]

Phineas. And I'll be quiet.

Mrs. McQueston. It won't be for long.

Phineas. No?

Mrs. McQueston. Not for long.
Come. I must see to her room.

> [*They go out together to the front hall. The room is empty for a moment, then the kitchen door opens and a dark* LITTLE GIRL *of six, very pretty and in Malay costume, comes in. She stands doubtfully a while, looking about, and finally comes to the center of the room to stare at the ship model. She runs a hand delicately over the smooth black arm of a polished chair.* OPARRE *enters, a tall, regal woman, with a noble and beautiful, though somewhat barbaric face. She is also in Malay costume.* VENTURE *follows her.*]

Venture. They were here a moment ago. They may have gone
to meet you. Will you wait here while I find them?

Oparre. It has been said in my country it's an ill omen
to come by the wrong door.

Venture. He didn't know—
the man didn't know. I'll find them.

Oparre. Would you, please?

> [VENTURE *goes out the front way. A* MALAY NURSE *comes in from the kitchen, carrying a* YOUNG CHILD *asleep.*]

Is she asleep, Toala?

Toala. Yes.

Oparre. Sit here.
   We must wait a little.

Toala. Dear Princess, is there any way to go
   from this place to our Celebes, and cross
   no water?

Oparre. No, Toala, there's no way
   but in the ship. Why do you ask?

Toala. Perhaps
   a time might come when one would wish to go,
   and wish for ground underfoot.

Oparre. Yes. It might be.

The Little Girl. Mother, is this our house?

Oparre. It may be, Durian.

Durian. I want to go to our house.

Oparre. Hush, we must wait.
   Kneel at your chair, and listen while I pray.
   I must make a prayer.

Durian. Is it for me too, mother?

Oparre. Yes, for you, too.
      [*She kneels at the window, and* DURIAN *kneels.*]
   Dark oracles of heaven,
   that blaze and burn, swung by an unseen hand,
   forgive me if I give my god no name,
   for men have many. But there is one law only

over the suns and tides, and He sits alone,
giver of laws, and I worship Him, and ask,
under what name is chosen, for those I love,
peace in this house. The terrible sea has been
my child bed, and my children's cradle. Blood
and a black treason lie at their beginning,
and murdered men look down upon our sleep
and curse, and will not live again, and yet
these are the ways of men, and a woman bears them,
forgiving, and a god forgives. What wars
they make, what pitiful scars they leave, what eyes
lie staring at your moon, and will not waken,
this we have seen together, but these men-children
are children still, and loved, and a woman's heart
goes out to them, even guilty. Drive us no more
for the evil we have done, let us eat our bread
beyond the salt of weeping or the sea,
these little ones and him I love, and I,
here on this shore. Yet if a gift is destined
for me alone in years to come, withhold it,
take it again, and pour on that bright head
I pillow in the night whatever meed
has been reserved for me. Forgive me too
that I should worship one who is a man
and hold him dearer than my god. For thus
have you who are my god made me, a woman,
to worship in your image. This is my prayer,
the prayer of the Princess Oparre, spoken in night,
on an unknown coast, among strangers.

[*She rises.* DURIAN *has fallen asleep at the chair.*]

It's silent here.
Not even the wash of water. And Durian sleeps.
I wish we might stay here.

[*She goes to the window.* Mrs. McQueston *comes to
the hall door carrying a candle, sees the visitors
and steps back, her loathing in her face.* Oparre
turns.]

Mrs. McQueston. Who are you?

Oparre. Oparre.

Mrs. McQueston. These are your children?

Oparre. Yes.

Mrs. McQueston. Must she—touch my chair?
[*Her breath comes with difficulty.*]

Oparre. She is clean, madam.

Mrs. McQueston. You are his wife.

Oparre. His wife?
I am the wife of Nathaniel McQueston.

Mrs. McQueston. I am his mother.

Oparre.

[*Smiling, stepping forward*]

Yes, he has your brow.
He's like you. I should have known.
[*A pause.*]

Mrs. McQueston. There's a room ready.
I'll show you to it.

Oparre. But tell me—we intrude here?
We're not wanted?

Mrs. McQueston. Why should you think so?

Oparre. This—
your welcome to me.

Mrs. McQueston. It's my custom to use
few words. You're welcome.

Oparre. I would not have come—
only he asked it.

Mrs. McQueston. It may be that our manners
are not like yours. When I have said you're welcome
I have said all I can.

Oparre.

  [*Wearily*]

Then we are still
no better than wanderers, to be given shelter
and say farewell at morning. I had hoped
for a little respite.

Mrs. McQueston. I'll show you where you sleep.

Oparre. We are your guests.

  [*She bows her head briefly, then takes a step toward the
  sleeping* Durian. Phineas *appears and speaks
  to his mother from the hall.*]

Phineas. There's an odor in the house,
mother, something like incense.

Mrs. McQueston. It's her perfume—

Oparre. Yes. I burned an incense before I came
to sweeten the cabins.

> [PHINEAS *enters and sees* OPARRE.]

Phineas.
> [*Grimly*]

I'm sorry. I didn't know.

> [*He turns to go.*]

Mrs. McQueston. This is Nathaniel's wife.

Phineas. Aye.

Mrs. McQueston. This is my son.
Phineas, my son.

> [*There is a silence.* PHINEAS *stands frozen, with averted*
> *face.*]

Oparre.
> [*Doubtfully*]

There should be no greeting
between us?

Mrs. McQueston. That's as you like.

Oparre.
> [*Softly, stepping toward* PHINEAS]

I wish you well
in all your ways, the brother of my husband.
May there be peace between us.

Phineas. And do you wish well
to Nathaniel?

Oparre. Yes.

Phineas. It would have been far better
if you had never seen him.

Oparre. Do you think so?

Phineas. You must know it.

Oparre. No.

Phineas. Why, keep him then.
You'll know it shortly.

Oparre. You are bitter toward me.

Phineas. Aye, I'm bitter.

> [*The outside door opens.* NATHANIEL, RUEL *and*
> FAITH *come into the hall.*]

Faith.

> [*Outside*]
They're here before us.

Nathaniel.

> [*Entering with* RUEL *and* FAITH]
There, damn it,
we passed on the road, sweet, somewhere. Are we
met?
Has there been exchange of courtesies?

Mrs. McQueston. I've offered
to light her to her room.

Nathaniel. The babes are tired;
that may be best. Another brother of mine,

Oparre—this one called Ruel—and Faith Ingalls,
a good friend now lang syne.

Oparre. You will forgive me.
I am strange to your customs.

Ruel.

[*Coming forward*]
You're welcome, sister,
with all my heart.

[*He takes her hand.*]

Faith. And with mine.

[*She does likewise.*]

Oparre. I thank you, truly.

Nathaniel. And now shall we put these sleepy ones to
bed
before we talk?

Oparre. I must know what your brother means.

[*She looks at* PHINEAS.]

Nathaniel. What brother? Were you speaking, Phineas?
What have you said?

Phineas. I've said all I had to say.

Nathaniel. Repeat it for us. We're at a disadvantage,
having been more or less absent.

Phineas. She asked for it.
I told her only it would be better far
if she had never seen you.

Nathaniel. You told her only—
only so much?—What do you know of her
or me—or our history? The man's an oaf,
my dear. You must make allowances.

Oparre. It was meant—
what he said—and meant darkly.

Nathaniel. He's all made up
of black looks and black sayings. They breed them
that way
to fill our New England pulpits. It's a business.
Let it pass.

Oparre. No.

Nathaniel. I say let it pass
and get the babes to bed. He's a quack prophet
and believes in witches. They're all cracked, these
preachers.
He thinks he's Jehovah.

Oparre. Yet I shall sleep but ill
where there was unkindness toward me. I wished him
well.
Sir, I wish you well still.

[PHINEAS *is silent.*]

Shall I take them up?

Nathaniel. Yes.

[OPARRE *gathers* DURIAN *into her arms and goes out
to the hall followed by the* NURSE *with the*
CHILD. MRS. MCQUESTON *precedes them up
the stair with the candle.*]

And let me warn you, Phineas, the time's
gone by when you're man enough for me. I took
your orders once, but the shoe's on the other foot,
you'll find!

Phineas. You think to own us now because
you've piled up certain quantities of stuffs
in a ship's hold? God is not bought, nor weighs
your value by your having.

Nathaniel. Your church sells out,
like all the others, regularly. Who built
the fold you ply your trade in now? A thief,
that robbed your flock of sheep for thirty years
and paid his way to paradise by standing
the costs of their meeting-house. You reckon without
the power of Mammon, Phineas. For myself,
the deacons will be here tomorrow morning
wanting to sell me a pew.

Phineas. With a pagan wife
and octaroon children?

Nathaniel. Yes, with whatever I have
so long as I have money!

Phineas. Then mind you keep it,
for it's all you have.

Nathaniel. I'll keep it, but if I don't
I'd lose it to one of these holier-than-thous
that pull a long face over their hymns on Sunday
and dismember their victims Monday. They'll after
me

like a flight of buzzards when they smell me out
with silver on me!

Ruel. Hear, hear!

Nathaniel. And you'll be among them
if I'm any judge of medicine men!

Faith. There was once
a man who said to himself in his heart, O soul,
be comforted, we have wealth for many days;
take your ease, be merry—

Nathaniel. I know; it was unfortunate; he died;
there was also a man who had nothing at all; he died,
so that proves very little.

> [MRS. McQUESTON *and* OPARRE *come down into the
> hall.*]

Phineas. Take your choice,
the woman or my friendship! But not both!

> [OPARRE *enters.* MRS. McQUESTON *follows.*]

Nathaniel. Keep your friendship, yes, and your brotherly love,
you damned psalm-singing cur!

Oparre. I have wronged you, wronged you,
my husband, coming here.

Nathaniel. Not an ounce, my sweet.
You're worth the pack of them.

Oparre. You see, for him,
for what was best to him, I'd have stayed away

or drowned myself in the sea—oh, this I speak
you must believe—it is not hard to die
if one should love but a little—to pull the tides
across the eyes and lie quiet to bring rest
to him you love—this is not hard at all—

Nathaniel. You came here at my asking, and I make
no apologies!

[OPARRE *takes courage from him, and smiles.*]

Oparre. Yet seeing he loved me, and I stood
before him flushed with that love, I have dared to say:
I, even I, Oparre, lower in blood,
of pagan nurture, may I not step from darkness
in this garment like a glory he puts round me,
the garment of his love? Wearing this glory,
and proud of it, yet timid in what I am
and know myself to be, I have made my prayer
that I may be found worthy of your god
and your cities and your ways, to walk among you
almost as you—not quite despised. If I
am over-bold in this, my punishment
is sure and deep and mortal.

[*To* NATHANIEL, *pleading*]

You must let them answer.
You must not answer for them.

[*To* MRS. MCQUESTON]

You wept above stairs,
you who are his mother—I saw the tears
wrung from you, when you thought I had not seen,
and you were crying, O my son, my son,

O why were you not caught by your bright hair
among the branches?—You have wished him dead
rather than here with me.

Mrs. McQueston.
    [*Stony*]

I remembered him
asleep in that room where those two of yours are
               lying,
but I'm neither bent nor broken. I won't cry out
again. Not again.

Oparre. What is it that I have done?
How have I hurt you?

Mrs. McQueston. Your blood! The black blood in your
               veins!
Isn't that enough?

Nathaniel. Be silent!

Oparre. Yes. Yes it is.
I feel that it is. But will you pardon me
if I ask a little for life? Where I was born
my father was the sultan of a tribe
of Minahasese. I have heard, before his time,
oh long before, the Mohammedans came down
to teach us Allah with their swords, and all
the tribes fell down to Allah. But in their hearts
they kept the old pagan rites and mysteries—
reverencing them in secret. These too were gods
of blood, revengeful, with their mouths agape

for human flesh, haters of all not ours,
so that to kill an alien in their sight
was grateful to them. My father had no son,
and I was his heir. He took me, a child, to battle,
and once when there were three leaders slain and
                              brought
to the palace gate, he gave me a spear to carry
with an enemy's head thrust on it. The blood ran down
upon my hands and dripped among my tears,
for I'd seen the man die. This was our way of life,
and I dared not let them hear me weep, for I
was to govern, and tears were womanish; were I
as other women I might not rule. But then
when I was grown, a Christian came bound for death
on a certain altar. I saw him, and begged his life
that he might be my slave. This was your son.
—Oh, I had been hard and vengeful too, and taken
life in my hands! Still somewhere I had heard
of a god, the Christ, who had pity—and I asked
for news of this god. He answered mockingly,
your son, no lover of gods, till once, at last,
he gave me this little book of the Testaments,
and I carry it always.—Now pity me for this!
Born in deep cavern darkness, blind, and standing
suddenly in sun! As though a dog,
for worship of a man who was his god
should hunger to be man! As one new dead,
feeling warm tears upon his mouth, might grieve
to lift his heavy clay! Barbarian,
rooted in under jungle, passionate
beyond your knowing, gross in my mind and blood,

still thrusting up toward a memory of light,
not quite forgotten!

Ruel. You bring your light with you lady,
a lamb led in among butchers!

Oparre. No!

Ruel. I can hear
the sharpening of knives on every hearthstone
in this little suburb of heaven!

Oparre.

[*To* Faith]

Your eyes are kind!
Is there hope for us here?

Faith. I don't know.

Oparre. But you,
you have no knife for me?

Faith. What lies between
two women who love one man—that lies between us.
I meant not to tell you, but when I hear you speak
I must be honest, too. Whatever comes,
or whatever I smile and say in after-time,
put no trust in me.

Oparre. You love him?

Faith. Yes.
I've always loved him. But your ways are those
of a princess, or a queen.—I'm touched and sorry,

and because of that I tell you, trust me not,
for I'm your enemy.

Oparre. If I should answer
as when I was a princess, I would say
guard yourself well who take it on yourself
to be enemy of mine! My enemies
have suffered more than I! But in this place,
still carrying in my heart the secret Christ
by whom you live, I answer, I am your friend
who have seen my husband as I see him.—Dark
as your words have been, dark as your looks at me,
evil as you may think you are, your evil
is as the play of children to the world
we two have left behind us. You are gentle
even now in your anger. There is a kindness
even in your abhorrence. Teach me that kindness.
I would live by it, for my soul is sick
of murder and a life that can be lived
only by striking quickly.

Phineas. What murder is this
you speak of? What life was lived by murder?

Oparre. Mine.

Phineas. Tell us what murder then?

Nathaniel. Has it been your notion
that matters are conducted in the South Seas
without an occasional letting of blood?

Phineas. Sir, bloodshed
smells the same here as there!

Nathaniel. Not quite. Oparre
governed a province, and sentenced men to death,
if that's a crime!

Oparre. It was more than that!

Nathaniel. We'll say
no more about it!

Oparre.

[*To* PHINEAS]

Sir, if this winter coast
is tarnished by our footsteps in the snow,
as I feared it might be; if the Christ you worship
gives sanctuary only to his own
lest they be polluted, say this at once, and we
shall rouse the children, and be away. I came
only with a hope.

Phineas. We have no place here for you!

Oparre. I have done what I can. Nathaniel—
we shall go now?

Nathaniel. Yes.

Mrs. McQueston.

[*Coming forward*]

Let the babes sleep.
This has come on us too quickly, and we've said
what we'll regret. It's not been easy for us—
we'll not find it easy—the words come hard—
but take a welcome for this night at least,

and rest,—and let us try.—I fear you, lady,
and fear what's in myself—for I meant to speak
no words but welcome, till a blindness rose
before my eyes, and I cried out, and you heard me—
Oh, my son, my son, and my youth that's gone,
and my high hopes gone! Why then, they're gone,
                    and we're here,
and this is as it is. Let us sleep, let us rest,
those who can rest and sleep. I bid you welcome,
a woman and his wife. A stranger, too,
but one we shall know better.

    [*She offers* OPARRE *her hand.*]

I shall not kiss you,
not yet, perhaps tomorrow.

Oparre.

    [*To* NATHANIEL]

What must I do?

Nathaniel. Take her hand. With Phineas' kind permis-
                    sion
we'll stay the night.

Phineas. Stay then.

Oparre. I'm sorry I came
by the wrong door. Perhaps it can be mended.
Good night.

Mrs. McQueston. Good night.

Ruel. Good night, Oparre.

Oparre.

[*At the door*]

Thank you.
It brings a warm flood round my heart to hear
my name, and gently spoken.—It was one time
the name of a princess, and I remember her
and look for too much honor.

[*She goes out to the stairway.*]

CURTAIN

THE WINGLESS VICTORY

ACT TWO

ACT TWO

SCENE: *The scene is the same as in the first act, on an after-noon of early summer, six months later. Sun streams in through the windows and the outside door, which is open. The place is empty.* DURIAN, *still in Malay cos-tume, comes down the hall stair and slips cautiously into the room, as if venturing into forbidden and unfamiliar territory. Treading softly, not to be overheard, she looks round, then goes to a bowl of calla lilies that stands in the cold fireplace. She smells one of them in her cupped hands and draws back to look at them. The kitchen door opens and* LETTY *enters, passing through on her way to the hall. She sees* DURIAN, *who waits frozen as* LETTY *steps back, horrified, to the kitchen door. As soon as she has gone into the kitchen* DURIAN *runs lightly to the hall and climbs the stairs.* MRS. McQUESTON *comes in from the kitchen,* LETTY *following.*

Mrs. McQueston. Where is she?

Letty. She was there, looking at the flowers.

Mrs. McQueston. Never mind. It's their house now.

Letty. Only she comes and goes like a ghost. It's fright-ening. She was there.

Mrs. McQueston. Never mind. Let it be.

[LETTY *returns to the kitchen.* MRS. McQUESTON *sweeps carefully with the hearth-broom where* DURIAN *stood near the flowers, then goes to the window.* NATHANIEL *and* RUEL *come in from*

the front door, followed by a BAILIFF. NA-
THANIEL *speaks before they enter.*]

Nathaniel. Come in, come in, Harry. To what do we
owe the pleasure of your company?

Bailiff. There's no need to come in. I just had something
to give you.

[*He brings out a folded paper.*]

If you don't mind, sir.

Nathaniel. Not in your professional capacity, I hope?

Bailiff. Yes, sir. It's a service.

Nathaniel. What?

Bailiff. Yes, sir.

Nathaniel. Well, I'll be damned. Where have I run
afoul of the law?

[*The* BAILIFF *comes forward and hands* NATHANIEL
the paper. NATHANIEL *opens it.*]

Bailiff. Yes, sir.

[*He starts out.*]

Nathaniel. Wait a minute! What is this you serve me
with?

Bailiff. It's only that you're to appear before the magistrate, sir.

Nathaniel. For what reason?

Bailiff. I'm sorry—but—it's named there in the paper,
I think.

Nathaniel. Before Justice Urquhart—to show cause why
I've not given bond for two slaves! What slaves have
I?

Bailiff. I don't know, sir.

Nathaniel. I have no slaves!
  [*He tears the paper and tosses it back to the* BAILIFF.]
Take that back to old yellow-face and tell him so.

Bailiff. It's not my province to take it back, sir, having
once delivered it.

Nathaniel. Then tell him yourself! Tell him I've never
owned a slave, and never will, which is more than
he can say for himself!

Bailiff. Good day, sir.
  [*He turns to the door, puts on his hat carefully, looks
  insolently at* NATHANIEL *and goes out.*]

Ruel. From Judge Urquhart.

Nathaniel. Yes. And if he's for bringing me into court
I have a matter of an over-due note I'd like to take
up with him.

Ruel. He was asking for a loan lately. This seems hardly
the way to get it.

Nathaniel. I refused his loan—and this is no doubt his
answer. How deep is he into us now?

Ruel. Seven thousand.

Nathaniel. I should have been watching that. It's a lot
more than he's good for. He sunk his claws in us
once when he had us down, and he'll do it again.

Ruel. It was Phineas let him have the money.

Nathaniel. I was willing to lend a little—to keep him a
friend. And this is my reward. Give bond for two
slaves! Meaning my wife and her servant! Damn
Phineas and his friends! I was too cursed charitable
when I took our reverend brother in as a partner!

Ruel. To say nothing of my unworthy self—

Nathaniel. You've played straight and earned what you
got, but Phineas—and his church members! A thous-
and here for good-will—and a thousand there for
good-will—and their women pass me in the street with
their noses to windward! The well's dry from now
on—and they'll begin to miss the water. I've made
the last voyage I intend to make into the China Seas.
I brought back plenty, and it was enough to set us
up again, but I'll spread no more of it among his
light-fingered elders. It doesn't come so easy as they
might think. And it won't come so easy to them from
now on.

Ruel. Then it's good-bye to Urquhart's friendship.

Nathaniel. It costs too much! He can go—with some
others like him. This town's been run too long for
the overly righteous. It's time we gave the devil his
chance, eh, mother?

Mrs. McQueston. The devil will have his own, no doubt. I've hoped you were not one of them.

Nathaniel. I may be, at that. I met up with the devil once in the South Seas, horns and all, and the old boy was more than gracious. In fact, you owe my presence here to his kindly interest. The children of light were just about to spit me on an altar when the children of darkness intervened. It's a long story, but never speak ill of the devil, mother. He's your son's patron saint.

Mrs. McQueston. As I said, he will have his own. See to it that you are not one of them.

Nathaniel. He'd never hold his own among the God-fearing New England merchants I do business with. Just because I'm not a candidate for heaven they feel a moral obligation to take away my earthly possessions. The pious Urquhart's been running up a thundering bill with the full intention of taking bankruptcy to avoid paying us.

Mrs. McQueston. Have you refused him credit?

Nathaniel. I haven't, but I intend to.

Mrs. McQueston. It's better not to refuse it.

Nathaniel. Why?

Mrs. McQueston. He'll take it.

Nathaniel. You amaze me, mother. How is he going to take credit if I don't give it?

Mrs. McQueston. Never mind. Offer it now or you'll be the one who's asking favors.

Nathaniel. Do you understand this, Ruel?

Ruel. No. But I'm well aware that the appalling moral obliquity of this neighborhood is only equalled by its aptitude for business chicane.

Nathaniel. In other words, give them what they want or they do you out of it.

Ruel. They try to.

Mrs. McQueston. Who was done out of this house, then? Phineas or yourselves?

Nathaniel. Mother, your son Phineas put it up to me— either I got out or he would. Now I might have gone, that's true, but in walking up and down the world, accompanied by my friend the devil, I have made the curious discovery that too much honor is given the medicine men of all nations, and too little respect paid to those who bring home what is grudgingly called the bacon. I am myself a bacon-bringer of a fairly engaging sort. Phineas is a medicine man of the approved variety—sharp-faced, close-fisted, narrow-brained and even a little tight in the hind quarters. As his superior in mind, quality and stature I take my place above him in this world, and I occupy this house because it's the best in town and I like it. I understand that Phineas moved out this morning, bag and baggage, wife and wifeage, and I'm glad to hear it. We can use the room.

Mrs. McQueston. God deliver you from your pride!

Nathaniel. God deliver me from the followers of the lowly Nazarene, and their fake humility.—

[*To* RUEL]

I'll take a look at these vacated quarters.

Mrs. McQueston. If it's convenient for you Phineas wishes to see you here this afternoon.

Nathaniel. Phineas—so soon?

Mrs. McQueston. Phineas and Elder Urquhart.

Nathaniel. I see, a begging errand. Well, let them come.

[*He goes toward the hall door, followed by* RUEL. HAPPY PENNY *enters the hall through the open outside door.*]

How are you, Happy?

Happy. Excellent, sir. Thank you.

Nathaniel. Looking for Ruel?

Happy. Yes, sir. That is—yes, sir.

[MRS. MCQUESTON *goes out to the kitchen.*]

Nathaniel. Well, there he is. Come along when you're free, Ruel.

Ruel. I will.

[NATHANIEL *goes out through the hall.*]

Happy. Fine day.

Ruel. What's on the mind?

Happy. Well—

Ruel. The usual eel-skin appendage?

Happy. To tell the truth—there's more than that.

Ruel. You give me pause, Happy. What's it about?

Happy. As a matter of fact it's about Captain Nathaniel.

Ruel. My brother?

Happy. Yes, sir.

Ruel. Then why didn't you speak to him about it?

Happy. I meant to—that's the truth—but when I saw him—I didn't.

Ruel. Maybe it's something I shouldn't know.

Happy. You should know it. Or he should. It might be better if you told him. You see, it's a little hard for me to talk to him—since he's got so much money. He doesn't make it easy.

Ruel. I see.

Huppy. Not that I don't understand it, what with being overrun with borrowers, and the like. Only I'd rather you passed it on to him.

Ruel. Well, I will. What is it?

Happy. There's been a lot of talk around—underneath, you know—about one of the sailors who came in on the *Queen of the Celebes.*

Ruel. I haven't heard it.

Happy. No, I don't suppose you would. The man's gone now—shipped off for the arctic whaling in the *Levantine Moon*—but he roiled up a lot of stuff before he went.

Ruel. Yes?

Happy. The story is he found a diary on board in the forecastle, all written in Dutch. Now he couldn't read Dutch, and nobody could that saw the diary, but as near as they could gather from it the *Queen of the Celebes* used to be a Dutch boat with a foreign name.

Ruel. That's quite possible.

Happy. Yes, I know it is. In fact, I know she was.

Ruel. You know it?

Happy. Yes, sir. Having a good chance on a fine dark night when I was on watch, I went down under her stern and found out the name'd been painted over. She used to be the *Nike Apteros* out of the Hague. But nobody will know that now because I took the paint right down to the wood and put on the *Queen of the Celebes* again, and nobody ever knew it was done.

Ruel. Wasn't all that a bit unnecessary?

Happy. Was it?

Ruel. It's true she had no ship's papers when she came

in, but then strange things can happen in the Southern Pacific.

Happy. Yes—and the theory is that something strange
did happen.

Ruel. Such as?

Happy. Not that I believe it, remember. But the talk
that goes round is that she's a stolen ship, that her
crew was murdered.—In other words, they say there's
been piracy somewhere.

Ruel. Where is this diary now?

Happy. That, in turn, I don't know. I wish I did—but
I never saw it.

Ruel. Do you suppose the sailor took it with him?

Happy. There's been more talk than ever since he left.

Ruel. Somebody has it, then?

Happy. I'm afraid of it.

Ruel. How serious is it—if this were true of Nathaniel?
Suppose he had stolen the ship and made away with
the crew?

Happy. Why, that's piracy. Only it's not true. Not that.

Ruel. I know. But suppose it were. It's a capital offense
under international law—isn't that so?

Happy. Yes, sir.

Ruel. We must find this diary.

Happy. Yes, sir. That's what I think.

Ruel. And now I know why you didn't speak to Nathaniel. It's not exactly an agreeable subject.

Happy. No, it's not.

Ruel. There's someone coming up the steps. We'll go to my room.

> [FAITH INGALLS *enters from the porch. They meet her at the door.*]

Faith. Are there folk indoors on a day like this?

Ruel. I'm afraid so.
Business, you know. Business goes on as usual—
men must grub for silver.

Faith. Shame on you then—
it's raining gold outside!

Ruel. That's more than it's doing
here within doors.

> [NATHANIEL *returns through the hall.*]

Will you forgive us worms
if we leave to go on grubbing?

Faith. Go mend your nets
if it makes you feel important! I've an errand
the kitchen way.

Nathaniel. We see you here too seldom,
Mistress Faith.

Ruel. Your pardon—

Faith. Yes—

>   [RUEL *and* HAPPY *go out and up the stairs.* FAITH
>   *goes toward the kitchen.*]

Nathaniel. It's not
quite flattering, this haste.

Faith. Why—it was true—
I have an errand.

Nathaniel. But never one to me.
Not for some months. If you'd known I was here
you'd have gone to another neighbor.

>   [*She pauses, then lifts her hand to the door.*]

Faith. You'll excuse me—
the haste was real.

Nathaniel. Am I a shadow then
to be seen through—walked through—like a dog in
                                        the room
through which you need to pass?

Faith. No.

Nathaniel. No. A dog
would get more greeting.

Faith. Was I uncourteous?
I'm sorry if I was.

Nathaniel. When I walk to the wharf
three or four men may pass a word with me,
the rest look the other way—the women sweeping,
drag in their rugs and shut the doors behind them

lest I should catch an eye and speak. You'd think
I carried leprosy. Some half year gone
I had my last good word from you. Your rugs
are hauled in fast enough when I go by,
if you recall.

Faith. But not to be unkind.
Truly.

Nathaniel. It's hard to breathe in a vacuum,
and I've lived in one of late.

Faith. I thought you happy.
You're happy with her.

Nathaniel. Yes.

Faith. Let's say no more.
It's better to say nothing of such things.

Nathaniel. Such things as what?

Faith. We have our separate lives
to live. Let it go at that.—But I could warn you,
if you want a kindly warning, you won't win
the town's good word by lending money to them.
A creditor's always hated.

Nathaniel. I know that.
I've discovered that. A little late.

Faith. Then keep
your fortune for yourself. They laugh at you
behind your back for these loans.

Nathaniel. And you? Do you
  laugh with them?

Faith. No. I make very little use
  of laughter this last year.

Nathaniel. What things are these
  it's better not to speak of?

Faith. Nothing.

Nathaniel. Then
  for God's sake give me a word or two sometimes
  just to water the desert. I begin
  to hate these streets and the people on them. Yes,
  and hate myself.

Faith. I tried to be kind at first—
  to say, we could meet as always, put good luck
  and bad behind.—I had my share of bad,
  but that could be forgotten. Then I couldn't.
  Little by little I couldn't.

Nathaniel. Why? Am I
  so changed?

Faith. Yes.

Nathaniel. I don't feel it.

Faith. Not in yourself.
  But when we think of you we think of her.
  And it's not as if she were one of us. I've never
  thought much about what it was like to be
  an alien—but—if you still loved me, say,

and I'd married a black—how would you think of
                     me—?
would it seem to change me?

Nathaniel. That's it then?

Faith. I tried—
I tried not to have the thought—but it haunted me—
at nights—when you were with her.—It's better, I
                     know,
not to speak of such things.—But we've been friends—
I wanted to be your friend. And I choke on that—
it won't go down.—And if that's true of me,
who wish you well, you know how it is with the
                     others
who wish you all misfortune.—I'm a fool
to let you know of this.—It's you who win.
You have your way in the town—live as you please—
we can't hurt you.

Nathaniel. No. But I can be driven
mad!—And sometimes I think I am mad.—Say
you'd married as I have—for love—and loved him
                     still—
and had two dark-skinned children—and you lived
in a few rooms with this same black love of yours—
and black children, and a black servant—while the
                     town
stepped round you carefully—pointing, whispering,
never to you—always among themselves—
laughing a little when you come down the street—
behind their hands—some excellent jest, no doubt,

at your expense.—It's hard to maintain your love—
you begin to gnaw at this thing you're chained to,
even
hate where you love—curse at it in secret, curse
yourself and all the world equally. That's why
I stopped you here this morning. I must speak
to someone—I must have some touch with the world
outside those rooms upstairs. But now you tell me
you're like the rest.—I'll wake some morning and find
the bed-clothes stained with blood—and know I've
killed her—
her—and the children—and that damned negroid
thing
that waits on us—and not dare to look—but know
I've done it. I thought you might have saved me.
Well—
let it go. You can't.

Faith. Do you love her still?

Nathaniel. Yes, by God, I love her.

Faith. But this is horrible.

Nathaniel. It's everyday. It's all the days there are.
And all alike.

Faith. But it must end.

Nathaniel. There's no end,
except that time goes on, and time makes changes—
time sometimes makes changes.

    [DURIAN *runs down the stair, through the hall and on
into the outdoors.* FAITH *turns toward the win-*

dow. OPARRE *comes down the stair dressed like*
the women of Salem, looks out after DURIAN,
then enters the room.]

Oparre. These children have good eyes! She clung to
                    our room
until today—because, she tells me gravely,
she was afraid of the man in black, but now
he's gone, and she can run!

   [*To* FAITH]

I'm glad to see you.
I had hoped you would come often.

Faith. Thank you.

Oparre. See,
   when she stoops over a rose she touches it
and gives it a child's name. Forgive me, she's
not beautiful to you?

Faith. Yes. Yes, she is.
   She flashes like quicksilver. And changes, too,
I think, quick as quicksilver.

Nathaniel. This dress is new.

Oparre. Yes,
   I have cast my Malay chrysalis
and emerge with little wings! May it be a sign
that I am now New England!

Faith. But did you make it?

Oparre. Yes, from the outside in, I fear, not knowing
the secrets of your needlework. It's wrong?

Faith. It's beautiful.

Oparre. If only this swarthy face
of mine were not above it.

Faith. The best of us
could do no better.

Oparre. You see, Nathaniel,
my handiwork is praised.

Nathaniel. It's a marvel, and
goes marvelous well with you.

Oparre. And the face?

Nathaniel. The face
is still my favorite of faces.

Oparre. Then—
I have done well—I won't be laughed at, truly,
for wearing it?

Nathaniel. You'll be envied.

Oparre.
    [*To* FAITH]
I'll take it off.
You think I shouldn't wear it.

Faith. Oh, please—indeed
it's beautiful—and you must wear it.

Oparre. Yes?
  You are the first to see it. Perhaps the others
  will like it if you like it.

Faith. The others?

Oparre. The women—
  the women of Salem,

Faith. If they judge by the eye
  they'll have no fault to find.

Oparre. But they'll not judge so—
  is that your meaning?

Faith. Not at all.

Oparre. We'll try.
  You could help me if you would.

Faith. I'm afraid—I couldn't.—
  Not I.

Oparre. No? I forget. We are enemies.
  That makes a bond between us. I've heard it said,
  good enemies make good friends.

Faith. I wish you no harm.
  I hadn't meant to stay. I'll go.

Oparre. Yes, surely.
  Surely, if you wish it.

    [*Silent,* FAITH *crosses the room and goes out.*]

  It's that she loved you,
  and it comes to mind.

Nathaniel. Yes.

Oparre. Do you know what I plan?

Nathaniel. No, dear—what is it?

Oparre. To make a change, a great change.
　　I've kept myself a prisoner in my room
　　too long. We shall not win them if I sit
　　cross-legged and brooding.

Nathaniel. No—I know.

Oparre. And—yes,
　　now that the winter's over and the spring
　　warms up my tropic blood, I begin to hope—
　　it's so old a thing, this hope, men cherish it
　　beyond all reason,—and so I dream and wonder
　　whether this Salem has not grown accustomed
　　to my barbaric face and step—may not now
　　almost receive me—

Nathaniel. Almost?

Oparre. I'd be content
　　with a half-countenancing—if the women-folk
　　would say once, Yes, my dear, we sew tomorrow;
　　come, draw a hem with us! Not really caring
　　if I accept, not bothering much about me
　　as I sit there sewing—oh, smiling a little over
　　my odd ways with the needle—but still not angry
　　that I should come—

Nathaniel. Would this help?

Oparre. It would pour oil
  in old and sinister wounds. You know they sew
  for foreign missions. They sit in a circle there
  conversing of the scandals of this world—
  mostly of me—while making decent garments
  for little heathen girls across the seas
  that run stark naked. It's a sweet thought; no, truly,
  it is sweet of them.

Nathaniel. Pardon me. Did I smile?
  Would you sew for their foreign missions?

Oparre. I'm so starved
  for a word with my women-kind—it does no harm
  to clothe the little things—

Nathaniel. Who told you about it?

Oparre. Ruel—and, oh, he brought me a picture, too,
  they passed about the circle to stir their zeal
  for the work in hand. Ten little nudities
  caught somewhere on an island, grouped in a ring
  all innocent of costume. And it's supposed
  they've seen a resemblance, and I was one of these
  with nothing on. Which face they thought was mine
  I couldn't tell, but if I go I'll swear
  that I was one.

Nathaniel. Well, they shall ask you to go
  if you want them to. But I'd rather you went as
                  yourself
  and not as a sample heathen.

Oparre. Oh any way
  that pleases them, take off my clothes, perhaps,

and pose there for their little savage child,
grown older, if it would help.

Nathaniel. Don't shock them, darling;
a lack of clothing is a cardinal sin
in temperate regions.

Oparre. Could I ask something more?

Nathaniel. Why, yes—what it is?

Oparre. I see these men and wives
of Salem, up and down the street, on days
that may be prearranged, go walking out
to visit one another—he in his best,
she in a satin gown—or bombazine,—
and this was most amusing back at first—
when I watched them from my window. Only now
I feel a simple longing to be one
of these same wives, to walk beside my husband
with a gloved hand on his arm,—it's laughable
I know, for me to think it—yet might we, sometime,
or would it be too strange?

Nathaniel. To walk with me—?
You shall certainly take my arm, and wear a gown,
and drink tea with them if you like. It's not
so very entertaining.

Oparre. And sometime, too,
could I pour tea for them—and you'd wait there with
                              me
and sit beside me? If you were there—
    [*She pauses.*]

Nathaniel. I wonder—
   I wonder what my mother'd think of that—
   but we'll persuade her.

Oparre. Is she supposed to pour
   all the tea that's poured in this house?

Nathaniel. No, no. The mistress
   pours her own tea—and you're mistress here.

Oparre. Have you wished
   for another mistress, dear—or been sorry at all
   for the days when you first loved me?

Nathaniel. Never.

Oparre. Because
   if you had I could forgive you, but not her
   and not myself.

Nathaniel. Why think of it?

Oparre. The fire
   that melts down mountain barriers, and runs
   the rock to lava, if it should cool would leave
   only the frozen slag between us, fixed
   with cold, glassy, impenetrable.

Nathaniel. It will cool
   when the great fire under the mountains cools, Oparre,
   not till then. The longer it lies quiet
   the madder it will burn.

Oparre. Does it burn still?

Nathaniel. With the same madness, sweet. So that when
           I touch you
this ground I stand on shifts away from me
and we're alone on a certain coral edge
where you turned to me and I kissed you. A goddess
           rose
from that shallow water, to make me half a god
and keep me so—keeps me still—

Oparre. I've wished
there might be one coast on this earth that was neither
yours nor mine. I'm alien here. You were alien
where I was loved. Is there nowhere a kingdom
that would count us equals? None?

Nathaniel. Could we go back?

Oparre.
    [*Shaking her head*]
  No.

Nathaniel. Then we stay here,
and make them like it.

Oparre. Can we never make them friends?

Nathaniel. We can face them—and face them down! If
           I have to buy
the chattel mortgages of half the town
till we own the dishes they eat from! Whom I choose
I choose, and she I choose shall be equal with them
or set above them!

Oparre. Is it still so desperate?
　That we must buy our welcome?

Nathaniel. They give you nothing
　in this town you don't pay for!

Oparre. I fear my dress,
　and the pretty plans for having them to tea—
　these are hopeless then.

Nathaniel. I'm afraid so.

Oparre. Then we'll go.
　We made a kingdom for ourselves at sea,
　and could again.

Nathaniel. I can't leave. I don't know
　whether they were too foxy for me, or I played
　the game right into their hands—but I've sunk what
　　　　　　I had
　in this damned chandlering business—what with debts
　and capital invested and people owing—
　till I couldn't raise a stiver to go to sea—
　and even the ship's a company matter now—
　not my own!

Oparre. We're fast here.

Nathaniel. Square on the bar
　till the cash comes in again. It's safe enough;
　we're rich if we stay here, but if we go
　we've nothing.

Oparre. I would rather go with nothing
　　than purchase their good-morning—live here on suf-
　　　　　　　　france
　　because they owe us money—

Nathaniel. They'll accept us
　　before the year's out! One at a time they'll come
　　with their hats on their bellies to ask us out to tea
　　or dinner—or what have you!

Oparre.

　　　　[*Putting her hands on his shoulders*]
　　Dearest—I've loved you
　　past worship, and more now since you do this thing
　　to make a home for me—but is it worthy
　　of what we are—what you wished to be?—I've made
　　　　　　　　you
　　less than yourself! To lash and threat and bargain
　　for place and friends! Though we take nothing with
　　　　　　　　us
　　let us go with nothing but our bare hands
　　to live elsewhere as we can.

Nathaniel. Yes, but live where?
　　One town's like another. We're people of substance
　　　　　　　　here,
　　and they're at our feet. But suppose we had to face it
　　with no hold over them? I think you'd find
　　they could make it devilish bitter.

Oparre. It's bitter now.

Nathaniel. But it could be worse. By just how much you
own
  things can be worse if you lose it.

Oparre. I have nothing.
  Nothing but your love. All else I've lost
  or given or flung away. Pitch an Indian camp
  with skins to cover us in a smoking tepee—
  you'd find me loving as here. And proud to love you.
  And happier.

Nathaniel. Let them keep it? Let our Phineas
  swallow it down, what we played with lives to get,
  and won't get again?

Oparre. Yes.

Nathaniel. Well, I can't do it—and won't.
  We stay—and fight it out.

    [RUEL *and* HAPPY PENNY *come to the hall door from
    the stair.*]

Ruel. I beg your pardon.
  Could Penny speak to you a moment, Nat?
  Something important.

Nathaniel. Why, yes—what is it? We've
  no secrets, have we?

Ruel. He'd rather see you alone
  if you don't mind.

Happy. It's nothing about myself, sir—
  something you should know.

Nathaniel. We'll go upstairs.
   Have you heard this?

Ruel. Yes. I'll wait here. You may want me.

Nathaniel. Let's get it over. I'll be back.

   [NATHANIEL *and* PENNY *go up the stairs.*]

Ruel. We've had
   one sunny day at least.

Oparre. Yes.

Ruel. Isn't that Durian
   skittering down the lawn?

      [*She nods*]

   She'll break some hearts
   when she's fourteen and past. Or is it sooner
   with children of the south?

Oparre. Yes—sooner.

Ruel. Then
   I speak for her hand in marriage. She's enchanting—
   just the way she draws breath.

Oparre. Why did he wish
   to speak with Nathaniel?

Ruel. He? I don't know. Oh—Happy—
   nothing in special. Some rumor. Some trade, I guess—
   business, no doubt.

Oparre. You know what it is.

Ruel. I do?
  Yes, but it's nothing.

Oparre. I thought you were my friend.

Ruel. I am, too. If you should ever need a friend
  remember that I am, Oparre. Not
  a summer friend, but one to count on.

Oparre. Tell me.
  We have something to fear?

Ruel. What makes you think so?

Oparre. Only a catch in his voice.

Ruel. I don't know yet.
  It's better not to say it till it's known.

Oparre. Yes—Do you have a legend in your tongue
  of a palace built of words, and how a beggar
  lived there, and drank a magic wine, and ate
  what magic food he wished, and how the floor
  was solid underfoot, the walls were stone,
  the gates were barred with iron—then one day
  because of one word spoken, a casual word,
  all this was suddenly gone; where the palace stood
  a little stream ran through willows?

Ruel. Yes.

Oparre. Suppose
  a whole world built on a word, a sky and stars,
  grass underfoot, sand at the ocean's edge,
  and men and women, and all they have—but this

one word unsaid and the world's not there. Was never
there, has not been, cannot be imagined. This
is a woman's world when she loves. If I should lose
                    him,
if one word were unsaid, the earth's gone. Then
where it rode, there's only a little ailing wind
lost quickly in the night.—He changes here.
He's not as he was. Have you seen it ?

Ruel. No, I haven't.
He's just the same as always.

Oparre. Then it's my fear.
I was afraid he grew more like them, reckoned
too much in dollars.

Ruel. When you've been poor your dollars
mean a lot to you.

Oparre. Then I'm mistaken.

Ruel. Yes.
He's as I've always known him.

> [*There are steps on the porch outside.* PHINEAS, URQU-
> HART *and* MUNGO *come to the door through
> the hall.* PHINEAS *enters, followed by the
> others.*]

Oparre. Yes?

Phineas.

> [*To* RUEL, *ignoring her*]

Is your brother
Nathaniel here?

Ruel. I think so.

Phineas. Would you call him?

Ruel. No.

Phineas. Why not?

Ruel. Sir, the lady of the house
is here, and awaits your greeting.

Phineas. Give her my greeting
if you wish, and call Nathaniel!

    [OPARRE *walks slowly out and up the stairs.*]

Ruel. I hadn't hoped
to see these pleasant faces all together
again in this house. Some other deacon's got
his maid with child, no doubt?

Phineas. Whatever business
you may have to attend to—go tend it.

Ruel. Come—
that's not so bad! I live here.

Phineas. Go or stay—
it's nothing to us.

Ruel. I'll remain.

    [NATHANIEL *comes in from the stair,* PENNY *behind
        him.*]

Nathaniel. Good evening, sirs.
You wished to see me?

Phineas. Yes.

Nathaniel. Well, fire away.

Phineas. In this company?

Nathaniel. It's about a loan, I believe—
   or, at least, an extension of credit. I see no reason
   for privacy.

Phineas. You may wish you'd kept it private.

Nathaniel. Why should I make it easier for you? No,
   we'll out with it once for all, by Judas—make it
   a proclamation to the citizens
   of Salem—Jesus junior here and all
   his sycophant apostles! I've made loans
   and bought up worthless mortgages and made
   investments in your water-logged concerns
   till I've run short of cash and patience! Now
   we face about. It's time for a reckoning!
   I can lend nothing more to Justice Urquhart
   on note or bond or mortgage, signatured
   by whom you please! This goes for the entire town!
   No more! The spring's run dry where you drank your
                        fill
   through this last drouth!

Phineas. Come, brother—

Nathaniel. You're about to say
   you know there's money left in the till. Not much—
   and what there is is needed! More than that,
   I could use some of what you've got already
   and may go after it. There are notes overdue,

mortgages to foreclose, some businesses
I could sell over a ring of godly heads
if I insist on cash. And I shall do it
unless you make my stay here pleasanter
than you made it this last winter.

Urquhart. In what way
can we be of service to you?

Nathaniel. Not by setting
a plague-cross on my door, and scudding by
with heads averted, not by summonsing
my presence to give bond for slaves, when all
my household is my wife and her one servant
and her two children! For that simple insult,
Justice Urquhart, I shall require of you
to the last penny, what shows on my books
as owing me from you! To be paid tomorrow
before the sunset! Or in lieu of that
that your fine wife in her silk neckerchief
invite my wife to tea, and have us there
together, with your whole church-going crowd,
and treat us to your best, and treat us well
as you may wish for mercy!

Phineas. It was of your wife
we came to speak. What was her origin?

Urquhart. And where were you married?

Nathaniel. She's a woman, born of woman, better born
than the best of those you've lived with.

Phineas. Then tell us first
where you purchased the *Queen of the Celebes.*

Nathaniel. The ship?
Is this an admiralty court? My brother,
my history's my own.

Phineas. You'll answer, though—
now or later.

Nathaniel. By what right do you ask
your questions?

Phineas. Sir, as co-sharer in the ship
I'm legally liable if there were fraud
or violence behind your title to her.

Nathaniel. Well, sir, if there were fraud or violence
you'd lose by making it known. But there was none.
Sleep easy. I came by her honestly. How it occurred
I keep to myself.

Phineas. Do you, though? I came by chance
on part of her history. She was once, as you know,
I think, of Dutch registry—and her name, translated,
was *The Wingless Victory.*

Nathaniel. It's news to me.
She was never so called since I've known her.

Phineas. But she was.
• And you'll admit it.

Nathaniel. Why, damn your soul—what cause
would I have to deny it if it were true?

Phineas. Good cause.
  Let me inform you where you took that ship,
  and how and from whom. There were three sailors
                    on her—
  three Dutchmen, all three of them dead now. She
                    lay
  off Singapore at the time. You killed these men,
  took a new crew from the port and changed her name,
  sailed her home with her cargo, and that's the story
  of how you came back to Salem.

Nathaniel. Three mutineers
  tried to take the ship from me, her captain and owner,
  and got themselves killed. That's all there was to it.
                    Hell,
  they earned what they got. And so did I!

Phineas. A sailor named Van Zandt
  who came with you from Singapore, picked up
  a ship's log in his berth. The data's there,
  complete—enough to constitute an indictment.
  There's a translation made. If the facts were published
  your stature might be lessened by a good deal—
  or lengthened by some inches.

Nathaniel. Here's the plain truth:
  I was a prisoner once to a certain sultan
  in the Celebes. He was Oparre's father,
  and refused to trade with foreigners, hated the Dutch
  because they'd burned his villages some years
  before I came there. Well, a Dutch ship came in
  looking for spice, and we persuaded him

to load it up and then capture it. We wanted
to get away, Oparre and I. We took
three Dutchmen who survived and stole the ship
from the sultan—ran toward Singapore—on the way
these three decided to wrest the ship from me
and I shot them down. The rest you know. I managed
to pick up a crew and get home. The ship was forfeit
before I took it. The Dutch had no more claim
than I had to it.

Phineas. A court would hold so?

Nathaniel. What court
will ever hear about it?

Phineas. The courts will hear.
I shall let them know.

Nathaniel. Why, you fool, whatever we own
goes down the drain, ship, business, stock and all,
if the law gets hold of it!

Phineas. Yes, and well I know that—
and so do you. And more than that, you're open
to criminal process.

Nathaniel. For what?

Phineas. For piracy!

Nathaniel. If you care to cut your own throat, bring it
on!

Phineas. I will.
Save on one condition.

Nathaniel. To hell with your conditions!
  I'll make no pact wih you.

Phineas. You see, it happens
  we have the evidence in our hands. If we
  are silent, then there's nothing said; you're safe.
  And we'll say nothing, burn the diary
  and the logbook—if you send the woman Oparre
  back to her people.

Nathaniel. Well, I prefer to hang.
  The woman Oparre! Damn you, when you speak
  of my wife, do so by her title!

Phineas. Is she your wife?

Nathaniel. You have heard me say so!

Phineas. When you put in at New Bedford
  on your way home, you sought out a minister
  and asked him to marry you—but he refused.
  What words you may have mumbled over yourself
  and her, on the high seas, I don't know. But she
  is not legally your wife.

Nathaniel. I owe it to her
  that I'm alive and here. I'm more bound to her
  than book, bell and candle binds you! She betrayed
  her father, coming with me. If she went back
  he'd make short work of her.

Phineas. Send her where you like,
  only far enough. The ship's rigged out and ready
  for a voyage to Indo-China. Let the woman go,

or I swear I'll go through with this. You've held the
whip,
and pushed your black brood on us, and laughed to see
how we took the stench! We'll wipe that laughter out
one way or another!

Nathaniel.

   [*After a pause*]
You'd do that?

Phineas. Yes! We've made
our plans! Make yours!

Nathaniel. Look, Phineas—
this is hardly a question on which a man
makes compromises. You have a wife of your own.
You chose her yourself. You'd brook no interference
in your life with her. I'll stand just as little in mine.
It follows that you ruin us both to wreak
a revenge on me I've scarcely earned.

Phineas. The cases
are not quite comparable, thank you. Then
you've given your answer?

   [NATHANIEL *is silent, then turns away and walks to
   the window.* MRS. MCQUESTON *slips in quietly from the kitchen.* NATHANIEL *turns back.*]

Nathaniel. You're one of them, no doubt?
You've heard of this?

   [*She closes her mouth grimly.*]
Well, speak!

Mrs. McQueston. I've heard of it.

Phineas. We give you a further choice. If it suits **you** better
follow your woman. We'll press no suit against **you,**
if you're both away.

Nathaniel. Leaving the money safe
in your reverend hands!

Phineas. Take with you what you can gather.

Nathaniel. And that's exactly nothing. Well, we'll go.
We'll go together, and leave **you to your** virtue
that undresses under sheets!

Phineas. I'm sorry to hear it—
and you'll be sorry later.

Nathaniel. How do I know
what proofs you have? You'd lie about it. Yes,
and you have lied! Where's this sailor—this **Van**
Zandt
and his record books?

Urquhart. Bring him **in.**

[MUNGO *goes out to the porch and returns with* VAN
ZANDT, *a sailor, who looks about him questioningly, then fixes on* NATHANIEL. *He takes a
small black-bound book from his pocket.*]

Do you wish to hear him?

Nathaniel. No! Take him out! I know what he has **to**
say!
Take him out!

[MUNGO *nods to* VAN ZANDT, *who puts up his book hesitatingly again and goes.*]

And get out, all of you! We can live
without you.

Phineas. Very well.

Nathaniel. But let me tell you
what you're doing, you disciples of the word
and seekers after holiness! You're willing
to compound what you say's a felony, if I'll
accede to your dirty bargain—compound it with you
and send my wife away! But if I don't
then I can either get out of town or hang,
one or the other, while you three line your nests
with stolen goods! Set that in the mealy records
of your mealy-mouthed church of God! It'll look well
                      there,
while you fur your coats with what you thieve from
                      me
and pray for heathen sinners. Money changers!
A money changer's an honest man compared
with these pilfering churchmen!

Phineas. Good-day, then.

Nathaniel. Where are you going?

Phineas. To the custom house. I wash my hands of you.
The authorities will be informed, and can take
whatever steps they wish.

[PHINEAS, URQUHART *and* MUNGO *start toward the door.* TOALA *comes down the stair and looks in, calling* DURIAN. *She steps back apologetically,* NATHANIEL'S *eyes are riveted on her.*]

Nathaniel. Give me a moment.
  You can afford to wait.

Phineas. You have this moment,
  and then no more. We don't trust what you'd do
  if you had more.

Nathaniel. Send her back then. Send her.
  I'll have nothing to do with it.

Phineas. I didn't hear you?

Nathaniel. I say get it over! Send her back! You've wanted
  just that—and you've got it! And what was good in me
  goes with her! Make away with her if you must,
  but you'll not get what I have!

Phineas. You stay in Salem?

Nathaniel. I stay in Salem. What's mine's still mine, by God,
  and you won't get it!

Phineas.

  [*To* TOALA]

  Go find your mistress. Ask her to come here.

  [TOALA *goes up the stairs.* NATHANIEL *sits.*]

Nathaniel. For God's sake—do it yourselves—I can't tell
her—
no—I won't be here—

[*He rises.*]

Mrs. McQueston. You want it yourself.
You've wanted her away. I've seen it.

Nathaniel. Devil!

Mrs. McQueston. Say what names you please. You'll
be glad she's gone.
I knew it would come. Shift the blame on us if you
like.
We'll take it.

Nathaniel. Then you send her back to her death.
It'll mean death to her.

Mrs. McQueston. Women don't die so easy.
They bear pain better than men.

Nathaniel. I'll go.

Mrs. McQueston. No—stay.
She'll listen to no one else.

[NATHANIEL *sits again.* RUEL, *after a look at* NA-
THANIEL, *suddenly crosses the room and signals*
PENNY. *They go out and across the porch to-*
gether. OPARRE *comes down the stair and into*
the room. NATHANIEL *stares at the floor.*]

Oparre. What is it, Nathaniel?

Phineas.
> [*To* URQUHART]
> Speak to her.
> [*He moves away.*]

Urquhart. Lady, the ship is victualed and waiting
to catch the tide in the morning. It's the plan
that you sail with her. You'll need some time, no
> doubt,
for your preparations.

Oparre. What ship is this?

Urquhart. What ship?
The Wingless Victory.

Oparre. I know no vessel
by such a name.

Urquhart. The *Queen of the Celebes,*
if you insist.

Oparre. You spoke of a plan. Whose plan?

Urquhart. It's been agreed upon.

Oparre. By my husband?

Urquhart. He
accedes to it.

Oparre. For myself—I could be glad.
I wished to go, but my husband did not wish it.
How does this come?—Will you not speak to me,
Nathaniel?

Nathaniel. They came on the history
  of how I took the ship, that's all, stumbled on it—
  so they make me out a pirate. Under the law
  perhaps I was.

Oparre.

  [*To* URQUHART]

  Would you make use of this?
  For myself, as I told you, where I go
  will grieve me little, so we're away and clear
  of venomous tongues. But for Nathaniel
  it's bitter—and bitterly unjust. To earn
  a place and fortune in a world where both
  come late or seldom—to earn them young and then
  face exile—for no fault—because he loved me—
  for there's no other reason—this is a sentence
  bred of your malice—

  [NATHANIEL *rises, facing her.*]

Mungo. You misundertand—

Oparre. I've known him
  long and well now. What you have seen in him
  since he came home—his anger, and his pride—
  these are not real.—No, I have known him watch
  a wounded man two days and nights, and nurse him
  tenderly as a child. I've seen a child
  turn toward him in an illness when his hands
  were gentlest and most grateful. He's not hard,
  but kindly, careful, pitying toward those
  who have been hurt or need help. You'll find him so

if there's ever a need among you. This is no man
to banish from your town.

Urquhart. He's not banished, lady.
The plan is you go alone.

Oparre. But, gentlemen,
my husband is accused of piracy.
Of what am I accused?

Mungo. We're satisfied
if you go, and he stays here.

Oparre. Why, then, forgive me,
but you will learn it's not in your power to part
two who would stay together. You may decide
these things for those who love by custom. We
have a world beyond you.

[RUEL *and* FAITH *come quietly to the hall door.*]

Mungo. Damn it, are you deaf
and blind?

Oparre. Deaf and blind to such as you!

Phineas. Then ask him!

Oparre. Then for your satisfaction, but not mine,
I do ask him. They have planned to part us,
my husband. Is there any answer fitting
such men as these?

Nathaniel. We'll go away together.

Oparre. You hear?

Nathaniel. I know
    a certain island where the Netherlanders
    never touch. It's not on their charts, but all
    the natives say it's rank with pepper trees
    down to the water. Give me a ship again
    and capital, and we'll hunt this island down
    and build another fortune. Phineas,
    it may bleed the firm down dangerously but stake me
    with what's left, and I'll try again and pay you back
    twice over. It's too damned little but it might do.

Phineas. No money, no argosy,
    no profit, though it came to a dozen times
    the venture, how would that compensate us for a soul,
    a soul sent forth and lost?

Nathaniel. What soul?

Phineas. Your own.

Nathaniel. Mind your own soul, and I'll mind mine!

Phineas. I take
    small interest in a treasure or return
    that hangs on human sacrifice, a brother
    lost into everlasting fire to snatch
    one poor ship-load of spices. If you go,
    and go with her, back to the ancient witchcraft
    by which she lives, back to her obscene gods,
    you're lost to life forever. Do you think to pay me
    in coin for this?

Nathaniel. By God you've taken coin
    from me before!

Phineas. To hold you here, to break
  her witch's power upon you! For myself
  I want no penny of gain! Yes, if you stay,
  you shall have every penny you've put in,
  for I don't want it, have no use for it,
  want nothing out of it! But the woman Oparre
  has hung her walls with idols, worships them
  in secret, corrupts your heart, blackens your mind
  and snares your body with her flesh! Go with her,
  and you go penniless! Renounce her here
  and take back what was yours!

Nathaniel. You offer freely
  what you'll never be asked to give.

Ruel. The man's gone mad!
  She worships your Christ!

Phineas.

  [*To* OPARRE]

  What is your worship, woman?
  What god do you bow down to?

Oparre. When I came
  I worshipped as you worship, but when I knew you
  there was a kind of blackness in my heart
  for a long time. Sir, there are gods and gods,
  each with his many faces, some of good
  and some of evil, each race with its own,
  but the most jealous are the lesser gods,
  such as you own, of bitterness and wrath
  and eternal fire. And when I try to pray

then all these lesser gods go through my mind
angry and savage, thrusting away the Christ,
and I pray to the unknown god.

Phineas. And who is he?

Oparre. He is the unknown god.

Nathaniel. And that won't do.
I see that by their faces. We take our way
to the other end of the world tonight, foot-loose
and nothing in our pockets.

Oparre. Will it be so hard?

Nathaniel. Hard? To have nothing—no cash—no home
—the ship
gone, too—two children to take care of—just
our hands—beach combers, you and I—a white man
living with a Malay—faking palaver
to get a dollar from a sailor?—Yes,
that's how we'll look to them—and what we'll be
till we can get a start.—When they've sunk to the
beach
they stay on the beach, I've noticed.

Oparre. Is there no way
I could make it easier? If we love enough
we could be parted, even by a world
and yet not lost. If what they want of you
is that you let us go alone, they count
on the great distance and the years to change
your need for me. But I shall not be changed,
nor you.—Would this be sufficient?

Phineas. Quite sufficient.

Oparre. Shall I go alone, Nathaniel?

Nathaniel. It's not safe
for a woman in the Indies.

Oparre. I shall keep safe
if I may wait for you.

Nathaniel. Would you, Oparre?
Would you take what money I have, wait there in the
East
till I can leave?

Faith. Go with her. If you're here
you know what will come of it—you'll stay, and then
you won't forgive yourself. Go with her.

Nathaniel. Christ—
do you know me so much better?

Faith. Yes.

Nathaniel. We've found
a plan, and a way out of it! Let us alone!
Who's to live my life?

Urquhart. You've made your decision?

Oparre. Sir—
will you all pardon if I ask—would you leave me
alone with my husband—for a moment? This—
this should be between us only. I will call you—
very quickly—

[*One by one they go out, leaving* Oparre *alone with*
Nathaniel.]
There's such a thing as a love
that holds the world well lost—I thought it was ours—
perhaps it was only mine.

Nathaniel. I love you enough.
You don't know what they've done.

Oparre. I see it quite well.
They've made you choose between us.

Nathaniel. If you think I choose them—
you're wrong. I want no part of them.

Oparre. What is it—
what is it you choose?

Nathaniel. I love you still—but they've made
our love a torment—it's the world that does it—
it won't have us together.—We touched at ports
before we came here—east and west—and always
I saw them pointing at us—there goes a white man
with a black woman—they think us obscene—somehow
they make it obscene.—They make me ashamed of my
love—
as you were ashamed of me before your father—

Oparre. Never!

Nathaniel. He hated me—as they hate you here—
and he'd have killed me—if we hadn't tricked him
and got away.—I tell you it can't be done—
hard as we've tried!

Oparre. You want me to go alone?

Nathaniel. For God's sake, yes.

Oparre. And will you follow?

Nathaniel. I don't know! I don't know!

Oparre. I should say nothing, I know—
  now that you've said this. I should let it go
  and be silent. Only—if I'm silent now—
  that's the end. One clutches at a pillar
  when the temple falls, though it carry you down.

Nathaniel. It's not
  the money—or the ships—that's something, but
  when we're together we're in an empty world—
  we live nowhere—we're not counted—we're
  some kind of horrible presence they're always trying
  to explain away—

Oparre. Then—only one word more—
  will there be a world—any world—in the midst of
              men
  and houses—or what's to buy and sell—or say—
  if we part here—and the world we had together
  goes down with the sun?

Nathaniel. I don't know. But I know
  I'm beaten, and we're parted. Perhaps a woman
  never knows when she's beaten. They won't have it!
  Nowhere on this earth will they have it! Look—
  I've tried to meet it—every way there was,
  with force and money and flattering—it's no use—
  it was no use from the beginning!

Oparre. I'm to go—
and you're to stay.

Nathaniel. Find another answer for me!

Oparre. Then I've never known you, nor you me.
I've never known you, and I'm alone.

Nathaniel. Good God,
don't you know I'm tortured too?

Oparre. Did you want me to go?
Does this fall in with your plan?—
A man of wood—
a figure-head of pith and straw—an effigy
cut out of paper would feel more! You tortured!
Your feeble rankling! If you felt pain you'd know
what danger you stand in now! Look to yourself!
Speak!—cry out if you're anguished!

Nathaniel. I've done my crying!

Oparre. Cry out, I say! I want to hear you cry!
Are you iron or tin or bronze—to stand and say
I'm to go—and let it go!
    [*She goes toward him.*]

Nathaniel. It's no use.

Oparre. Cry out!
If you're not wood I'll make you cry with my hands!
With my hands! Do you hear me!
    [*She strikes him across the face.*]

Nathaniel. This is not worthy of you.

Oparre. Not worthy of me! He's cut out of stone and his
heart
bleeds water! Will you not cry?
　[*The* MEN *appear at the door.*]
Speak! Weep!
Let me see your tears! Here are mine!

Nathaniel. Be still!

Oparre. Come in!
All these white frightened faces, come in and hear!
We have news for you. I have been misled
a long time by your Christ and his beggar's doctrine,
written for beggars! Your beseeching, pitiful Christ!
The old gods are best, the gods of blood and bronze,
and the arrows dipped in venom! You worship them,
too,
Moloch and Javeh of your Old Testament,
requiring sacrifice of blood, revenging
all save their chosen! You vouchsafe no pity
to the alien, and I'll give none. I have been a princess,
and I remember that gladly now. I come
of a race that can go mad and strike! Why, yes,
you fear me, and you should! Your pallid lips
and pallid hands and hearts, your milky hearts
that know neither love nor hate, your weasel warren
that squeaks and clusters! What could there be between us,
between the eagle and the rat, save death—?
and we've bred together—it sickens me—we've bred—
and I've been brought to bed of you! Your lips

were on my mouth! Your rodent flesh on mine,
in rodent ecstasy! I'll tear you out
from my breast, tear my breast down to bone and hard
till that shame's gone from my people!

> [DURIAN *comes in doubtfully from the porch, looking*
> *for* OPARRE.]

Durian. Mother.

Oparre. Yes.

Durian. Mother,
The sun's gone down.

Oparre. Yes, it's gone down. You, too,
your hands and eyes were made of this, my shame,
a mingling with my enemy. Your lips
speak of him, silent; you are my love and hate
at war, incarnate. Take counsel! Never look
like him if you would live!

> [*She kneels beside* DURIAN]

I frighten you,
my bird, your little heart beats fast. You've played
late in the sun. You're weary. Oh, God, if you
were lost, as he's lost to me! Keep me from that
you pitiless gods.

> [*She rises.*]

We'll sleep on the ship tonight,
and be gone tomorrow.—Over this house the light
darken, the fogs draw down, the evil of graves
seep and flood on you till you know the hell

I walk through living, walk toward when I die,
and will not leave me now!

[NATHANIEL *turns suddenly and goes out.*]

Gazers and fools—
you have seen an end as of mountains torn asunder
to bleed in fire, and still you stand and gape,
witless—with your white witless faces! Go out!
Leave us alone!

[*She sinks to her knees sobbing, her arms round* DURI-
AN; *the others turn to go.*]

CURTAIN

THE WINGLESS VICTORY

ACT THREE

ACT THREE

Scene I

Scene: *A cabin in "The Wingless Victory" which opens into an inner room beyond. It is small and groined with heavy timbers, the wall to the stage right curving to conform to the side of the vessel. At the left a door opens into a central passage-way. There are two port holes in the wall at the right. A small table is built in at the right rear, and there are a few dishes on it, as if for a simple meal. There is a bench along the right wall and a couple of sturdy stools. At the rear and to the left of the entrance to the inner cabin a dark tapestry has been hung, its folds half-revealing the image of a pagan god, embroidered in dull crimson.*

Under the tapestry Toala *lies prone as if felled by a blow, her eyes fixed fearfully on* Oparre. Oparre *kneels in the center of the cabin, her forehead almost to the planking, her hair streaming down, her Malay dress ripped from one shoulder and torn. She holds a dagger in one nerveless hand and her body shakes with sobs.* Toala *begins to crawl slowly toward her. When she has almost reached the dagger* Oparre *rises suddenly, looks down at* Toala, *who presses her head to the ground.*

Toala. Princess Oparre, give me the little dagger.

Oparre.
   [*Dully*]
Why—should I give you the dagger?

Toala. Because it's not safe.

Oparre. What has happened? What have I done?

Toala. You have been in a great fury, Princess, and torn
your hair, and hung the tapestry of the old god. There
was darkness in your eyes. I looked behind your eyes
and saw only darkness.

Oparre. I have been mad.

Toala. Yes, Princess.

Oparre. Why was I mad? What have I said?

Toala. Dear Princess, give me the dagger.

Oparre. I have forgotten—I have forgotten—Yes—

    [*She pauses*]

Aye—aye—aye! Oh, now I remember—!
and now it comes again!—Oh, pity me, save me—
whatever gods there are—it comes in a fall
of fire—I cannot turn but I face it—see—
a desert without shadow—only sun
scalding in fire! I shall go mad again—
take this and keep it from me!

    [*She throws the dagger to a far corner.*]

Let me be mad
and not remember! I cannot bear this thing
he has laid on me. When a woman has a child
the pain comes—and then goes—but this never goes,
never leaves me! I must eat death—I must—
I must die—for he never loved me! Never! Ah, yes,

but not now! Not while I live—not while he lives—
and again, again, the flame!—
   [TOALA *picks up the dagger.*]
Have I hurt them?

Toala. No.

Oparre. Why was this body gathered out of dust
and bitten to my image? Let that day be evil
when a lover took a lover to mould the face
that stares up blind from my agony! Stares up
and cries, and will not be still! Let all women born
take a man's love with laughter, and leave it; take
the coil of animals they give, and rise
in mockery. And you dark peoples of the earth,
cling to your dark, lie down and feed and sleep
till you are earth again; but if you love,
love only children of the dark—keep back
from the bright hair and white hands, for they are
                        light
and cruel, like the gods', and the love that breeds
between us is honeyed poison. Let no flesh
of theirs touch flesh of yours; where they have
                        touched
the welt rots inward! They are unclean, unclean
and leprous to us! To lie with them is sweet,
but sweet with death! I bear that death in me
in a burning tide that rises—choking—Oh, God—
torture me no more!

Toala. You must sleep, dear Princess.
   You must have some rest.

Oparre. Has he come here?

Toala. No.
There's been no one.

Oparre. He will not come. I waited
till the wave broke. I heard a wind in the rigging,
and a clock struck in blackness, and the babes
went supperless to bed. I knew it then—
he would not come—the wind was alive with whips
and my eyes were blind.—The children must be fed.
I'm here now.

Toala. Yes.

Oparre. And we must wake and feed them
that they may live, after I am dead, live out
their lives in the brothels of the East—the place
prepared for half-breeds. Take between their knees
the sewage of old oriental kingdoms
for a little silver. Smiling among the bells,
quick with disease, till they too die, and make
an end of all our love. Why should I live,
or they, when life comes down to a candle-end
to light our crawling? Where is the little knife?
I want it back!

Toala. No, no!

Oparre. Would you have us live?

Toala. Yes, Princess.

Oparre. What god do you worship, Toala?

Toala. Forgive me,
  I worship the old god.

Oparre. Then, in the temples
  of the old god, what is found fitting for her
  who leaves her father's house against his will
  to lie with an alien?—Say it.

Toala.
    [*Whispering*]
  She must die.

Oparre. And for her children—in the old god's temples,
  what is found fitting for them?

Toala. Yes, they too.
  Yes—and the children's slave!

Oparre. When we first came
  from the Celebes you brought a little phial
  of water hemlock, and you have it still.
  Why did you bring it?

Toala. Because I knew I must die!
  Because I knew then I must die! Not you—
  not you, Princess Oparre!

Oparre. You brought it for me—
  foreseeing all these things. Is it not so?

Toala. The men of the West have not been true, dear
                    Princess.
  They are not true to us.

Oparre. You brought it for me!

Toala. Yes, Princess.

Oparre. Why, yes, you knew it,
and I should have known. The laws of the ancient god
will be found best in the end. Why then the pain
goes from my heart, and all the dread is gone—
if I may die! You have been my slave, but now
we are two women of one race, and you
have been the wiser. Choose, then, what you will
          have—
but, as for me and my unwanted babes,
give us to drink of this darkness you have carried
so far for us.—We have borne names too long
across the face of earth, but we shall sleep
and turn back to nameless ground.

   [Toala *kneels and touches her forehead to* Oparre's
     sandal.]

Quick, then—the fire
mounts up in me; quick, lest I should see the sun
of another morning! Lest I should see his face—!
Lest still I should remember—him—

CURTAIN

ACT THREE

Scene II

SCENE: *The ship's cabin, later the same evening.* TOALA *sits on the bench, holding the sleeping infant in her arms, rocking gently.* OPARRE *cradles* DURIAN *on her knee, singing her asleep.*

Oparre.

    [*Singing*]

> Golden eyes, sombre eyes,
> Sleep, now sleep;
> The sun is drowned
> Where the sea is deep.
> The sea is deep
> Where the sun is drowned.
> Darksome eyes, golden eyes,
> Sleep, sleep sound.
>
> Heavy eyes, laden eyes,
> Sleep with me;
> The moon is shattered
> Into the sea;
> The sea is shattered
> Under the moon.
> Darkling eyes, laden eyes,
> Sleep, sleep soon.

When we have first conceived to bear a child
still there's a whisper in the blood, a fear
lest some swart ancient strain look back at us

from opening eyes. But yours were golden eyes
trembling toward amber, and the little one's
shadowed, but sweet and grave. This was happiness.
The little dancing body, delicate
to run the wind, to set a foot on moon-glade
and leave no print—to bear his pointed ears
and sweet blunt hands, but with a grace your own—
how the hard sobs come strangling round my heart,
watching your morning! This was happiness.
In a sea of agony, where one surge follows
after another, to beat us down before
there's a chance to rise, in a sea of fire, where waves
of fire wash over me, I must know that, must still
know we were happy once, and he gave us that
as he gives us torment now! Oh, stubby fingers,
dearer than my own eyes that see them, dearer
because they are like his, he wants us no more,
and we must go! Oh, web of beauty, woven
of his delight, woven in mystery, worn
so proudly, he puts you off, discards you now,
still warm with him. Now to retrace our steps
while the oceaned agony follows, washing down
the sands in fire! Now to go on alone—
now to go on alone. Does she sleep, too?

Toala. Yes.

Oparre. Then we'll lay them down. For the last time.
And we'll lie down, as if to sleep.

Toala. Yes, Princess.

Oparre. Why is it I'm not weeping? I'm wept out
and can weep no more.

> [*They carry the* CHILDREN *into the inner cabin. After
> a moment there is a knock at the passage-door.*
> OPARRE *comes out from the cabin.*]

Yes?

Ruel.

> [*Outside*]
> It's Ruel, Oparre.
> Could I see you a moment?

Oparre. Yes.

> [*The door opens.* RUEL *enters.* HAPPY PENNY *stands
> behind him.*]

Ruel. If we're not wanted
tell us at once, and we'll go. But it's no night
to sleep, we found, and finally we came,
because we'd been walking up and down so long
cursing—

Oparre. I'm a trouble to you—

Ruel. No—
not you—the pack of fiends that drives you, maybe—
and then this luck to fall on you—at this moment—
I tell you we've been cursing—well, we have—
we've cursed the earth black and blind—but there's
nothing to do—

Oparre. Nothing—

Ruel. And almost saved you—Penny here—
　　almost, but they'd found the diary, and the log—
　　and laid their plans—

Oparre. It doesn't matter now,
　　but thank you.

Ruel. No, it doesn't matter now.
　　Now that it's done.—There's an offer I could make.
　　I came to make it. Now that we're here I think
　　it does no good. Where will you go?

Oparre. But that
　　is what we men and women never know
　　of our tomorrow, whither we'll go, what winds
　　will blow across what water.

Ruel. You'll go to your father.

Oparre. No.—

　　　[A pause.]

Ruel. If you'd accept what's left of a life,
　　mine's yours for the taking. It's been small good to me
　　or any one. I've never had a worship
　　till now when I've worshipped you. What help I am
　　or could be—I offer you that.

Oparre. What use could I make
　　of a life?

Ruel. You'll be alone.

Oparre. All life's too long
    when you live after death. Lest I should hurt you, I
                thank you.
  Be happy elsewhere.

Ruel. I tell you I won't have this!

Oparre. Yes, but you will. Such things are borne. Such
              things
    as you have never dreamed are borne. Become
    a custom, meaningless. This stake through my heart,
    I've worn it till it gives no pain. So long
    pain has no meaning. I have seen the jugglers
    walk through fire. It's nothing.

Ruel. You have no place to go.

Oparre. No. But I go.
  You can't help me.

Ruel. Good night.

Oparre. Good night.
    [RUEL *and* PENNY *turn and go out, closing the door.*
        OPARRE *kneels under the tapestry.*]
  The earth rolls toward the dark,
  and men begin to sleep. God of the children,
  god of the lesser children of the earth,
  the black, the unclean, the vengeful, you are mine
  now as when I was a child. He came too soon,
  this Christ of peace. Men are not ready yet.
  Another hundred thousand years they must drink

your potion of tears and blood. I kneel and adore you,
having blood on my hands, having found it best
that evil be given for evil. Receive me now,
one who might once have been a queen, but followed
after a soft new dynasty of gods
that were not mine. I am punished, and must die.
I ask not that my death be easy, no,
for the pain quickens in me like a loved birth
and drowns another pain, too sharp, too sharp
for woman born of women, loving men
as they must love, too well. Let it climb and burn,
this pain, till I forget he was, slip down
the night, a black among blacks, your worshipper,
and unremembering. Being gone from him
I wish no heaven or hell, but only earth
that cannot be hurt again—blind earth, blind dark,
blind water running to silence. This is a prayer
from one who is not, made to an ancient god
who will die as I am dying, when the earth
has passed him and goes on.

> [*She bows her head. The door of the passage opens and*
> NATHANIEL *enters. She looks up, then stands.*]

Why have you come here?

Nathaniel. I find—I must go with you.

Oparre. Some hours ago
    it was too late for that. It's too late now.

Nathaniel. Be bitter as you like. If you have words
    that cut and tear, loose them on me. I know

what hell you've faced here, for I faced it too
walking alone.—I was mad—to think a parting
could ever part us.—

Oparre. And did you dream a meeting
could bring us together now?

Nathaniel. They may have it all,
ship, goods and money—whatever we brought with us,
may it prosper them—because I've nothing left
if I let you go.—A man must keep something within
or it's no use living—

Oparre. Have you found that, too?

Nathaniel. Aye—it's your victory—take it—if I wanted
                    to live
without you, it can't be done.—I know it now,
and you know it.—

Oparre. Because you love me?

Nathaniel. Because your love
and what we'd been together, and all the old days
came tearing at me, and wouldn't let me alone.—
Where you might go, what might happen to you—or
                    the children—
out there in the East! Come, put your arms round me,
                    Oparre,—
say it can be forgotten! All I ask now
is rest from what I've done!

Oparre. We ask for rest,
and sometimes find it in the end. Not here.
Not now.

Nathaniel. For God's sake be kind. I've suffered, too—
and I'll be patient, I swear I will—I've learned
that I must be patient—only be kind tonight—
don't shrink from me.—Do you see that I've come
back,
and it's to be as it was?

Oparre. To be as it was.

Nathaniel. Aye, girl, all as it was. One touch of your
hand
and I'll be healed.

Oparre. Though you should love forever,
and stand before me, pleading, though I should love
you,
and have this love to offer, not once, forever,
will you touch my hand again.

Nathaniel. It's only your anger
makes you say it, Oparre.

Oparre. Not once, forever,
not till the tides of suns, in the infinite years,
wash my reluctant earth by chance to drift
toward earth that hung on you. We are parted. Take
that word for an end.

Nathaniel. But you love me.

Oparre. You've been ashamed
to call me yours—ashamed to say "she's mine"
in any company—and I'm ashamed
to say that you were mine, and my dark body

remembers you. I hold you free of blame.
You're but one of a colorless tribe, a tribe that's said:
those who are black are slaves, to be driven, slept with,
beaten, sent on, never loved. Beyond law, we are,
reptilian, to be trodden. You I forgive,
but not your tribe or race—or the white of your hands;
the insult I have had the blood in me
will not forgive.—It will be no man's slave,
nor will my daughters!

Nathaniel. I swear it—I swear it, Oparre—

Oparre. And though you swear till the night come down
                in fire
to vouch your word, you are not believed, and my
                blood,
my dark blood, richer and prouder than your own,
will pour on the ground before I stretch a hand
to the race you drew from. We are less than you.
You part the earth among you, burdening us
with your labor and your lust. Among yourselves
you think to breed and rule, breed up in men
a race of kings to climb through the centuries
on us who bear you. But your veins turn pale;
your pride is the pride of merchants, crawling; your
                anger—
your very anger's afraid of death, and crawls
lest you should die. You will need us then, your race
of kings will breed water-thin in the after-time
for lack of what we could lend you—fire at the heart,
the word that goes with the hand, a dignity

savage, imperial, choosing rather to die
than live unwanted.

Nathaniel. There's no home left for you
in the Celebes. You'll come there a woman, helpless,
among the Eastern traders —

Oparre. Have you known me helpless
save where I gave my love? But that's gone now,
and I meet my world alone.

Nathaniel. I came prepared
to face this sentence with you. If you won't have it
there's nothing I can offer. But think, Oparre,
we have been happy, and could be.

Oparre. It's burned out.
Only you and yours will cling to a tawdry end
of remembered love, till it's down to rags and habits
hung on your hate.

Nathaniel. Where are the children?

Oparre. Asleep.

Nathaniel. I must see them a moment.
    [*He steps toward the cabin.*]

Oparre. No.

Nathaniel. I won't wake them.

Oparre. No!
They're not yours now!

Nathaniel. I shall see them if I like.

Oparre. As you value happiness, and what was ours
and what may yet be yours—say your farewell
to me and quickly, and go!

Nathaniel. I shall see them, though.

> [*He goes into the inner cabin.* OPARRE *walks unsteadily
> across the cabin as if in a dream, and sinks sud-
> denly beside the bench, her head fallen on her
> arm.* NATHANIEL *re-enters.*]

Oparre! Toala's dead on the floor! The children—
I can feel no heart-beat—! Oparre! Oparre!

Oparre. I know.
There's a black hemlock grows in the Celebes
for which we know no antidote.

Nathaniel. Damn you! What right
had you to kill the children?

Oparre. They're not wanted.
The white men of the East would have made them
whores.
It is not fitting the daughters of a queen
should be whores or slaves. We drank of it together.

Nathaniel. You drank it?

Oparre. Would I let them go alone?
All that was once between us is erased
and has not been, will not be remembered, leaves
no shadow.

Nathaniel. This is your revenge, a fiend's
revenge! It's as well you die! A fiend out of hell
could do no worse.

Oparre. I wanted you—never to know.
Then we'd have gone into silence, and left you free.
I never wanted you to know, oh, truly.
The error has been mine. I loved you enough—
to leave you.

Nathaniel. God forgive me if I love you—
even dying—while they lie dead—

Oparre. Oh, Durian, Durian—
and my babe—not to see you—it will soon be dark—

Nathaniel. Is there nothing to do? Quick, tell me?

Oparre. Nothing. But only
if you would put your hand against my lips.
        [*She stares up blindly.*]
It was all lies I said. I loved you and died
because I loved you. Is any death found better
than to give your life for your love? Oh, quick, your
                                                                    hand
on my lips.

Nathaniel.
        [*Kneeling*] [*His arms round her*]
I murdered you.

Oparre. My sweet, my sweet—
  as it was by the coral edge—in the Indian sea—
  the black wave—out of night—
    [*Her head droops forward. The door suddenly opens
        and* RUEL *enters.*]

Ruel. I'm sorry—I heard
  someone cry out.

Nathaniel. Come in. Oparre's dead—
    [*He rises.*]
  and the children.

Ruel. God! I knew it.

Nathaniel. Will you do this for me—?
  Say nothing of this—the ship will sail tomorrow,
  and I go with it.

Ruel. I'll go too, then.

Nathaniel. Yes?

Ruel. I've had enough of my native town.

Nathaniel. I go
  to be with her while I can. What I've left of life
  I shall know what it is to love one dead,
  and seek her and not find. Let the sands of years
  sift quickly and wash long. I shall have no rest
  till my dust lies down with hers.

CURTAIN

VII · HIGH TOR

CHARACTERS

(In the order of their appearance)

THE INDIAN	A SAILOR
VAN VAN DORN	DEWITT
JUDITH	DOPE
ART. J. BIGGS	ELKUS
JUDGE SKIMMERHORN	BUDDY
LISE	PATSY
CAPTAIN ASHER	A. B. SKIMMERHORN
PIETER	BUDGE

DUTCH CREW OF THE *Onrust*

ACT ONE

Scene I

SCENE: *A section of the broad flat trap-rock summit of High Tor,*
from which one looks out into sky and from which one might
look down a sheer quarter mile to the Tappan Zee below. A
cluster of hexagonal pillared rocks masks the view to the left
and a wind-tortured small hemlock wedges into the rock floor
at the right. Light from the setting sun pours in from the left,
and an ancient INDIAN, *wearing an old greatcoat thrown round*
him like a blanket, stands in the rays from a cleft, making his
prayer to the sunset.

The Indian. I make my prayer to you, the falling fire,
bearing in mind the whisper in my ears
from the great spirit, talking on the wind,
whispering that a young race, in its morning,
should pray to the rising sun, but a race that's old
and dying, should invoke the dying flame
eaten and gulfed by the shark-toothed mountain-west,
a god that dies to live. As we have died,
my race of the red faces and old ways,
and as we hope to rise. I give you thanks
for light, for the coming summer that will warm
my snake's blood, cold and crawling; for the rain
that fed the ripe May apples in the woods
in secret for me; for the waterfall
where the trout climb and pause under my hand,
taken in silence; for quiet on the hills
where the loud races dare not walk for fear
lest they be lost, where their blind hunters pass
peering with caps and guns, but see no game,
and curse as they go down, while the raccoon waits,
the woodchuck stands erect to catch the wind,

3

the partridge steps so lightly over leaves
the listening fox hears nothing, the possum hangs
head down, looking through his hands, and takes no
              breath,
the gray squirrel turns to stone against the rock,
watching the owl, the rabbit holds his ears
steady above the trembling of his heart
and the crow mocks down the shellbark. I am fed
and sheltered on this mountain where their hands
are helpless. But I am old as my race is old;
my eyes hunt day and night along the ground
the grave where I shall lie; my ears have heard
dead women calling upward from the earth,
mother and wife and child: "You are welcome here;
you are no longer welcome where you walk,
but here you are most welcome." I shall go,
and lie and sleep, and I shall give you thanks,
O God that dies, that my last night is dark
and long, for I am tired, but yet I ask
one summer more, that I may be warm again,
and watch the nestlings grown upon the crag,
and hear the wild geese honking south by night,
if this may be, but if it may not be
then is my prayer, that when I lie to sleep
I may lie long, sleep soundly, hear no step,
hear only through the earth your step in spring,
O God of the dying fire!

    [VAN DORN *and* JUDITH *come in from the right.*]

Van Dorn. Evening, John.

The Indian. Evening.

Van Dorn. Had any luck so far?

The Indian. Yes. Plenty of luck.

Van Dorn. Found it?

The Indian. Yes.

Van Dorn. O.K., John, let me know.
  Let me know in time.

The Indian. I will. Good night.

Van Dorn. Good night.

  [*The* INDIAN *slips away through the rocks to the left.*]

Judith. Who is it, Van?

Van. Just an Indian.

Judith. Are there Indians?
  I didn't know there were any Indians left.

Van. Well, there's one. There's not much left of him,
  and he's the last around here.

Judith. He's hunting something?
  You asked him if he'd found it.

Van. Um—yes, you see,
  he's looking for a place to make his grave,
  and he's kind of captious about it—folks get that way
  along toward the end, wanting their bones done up
  in some particular fashion. Maybe because
  that's all you've got to leave about that time
  and you want it the way you want it.

Judith. Did he tell you this?

Van. We've got an understanding. When he feels it
  coming over him he's going to die

he'll let me know, and I'll go dig him in
so the crows and foxes can't get at him. See,
he's all alone in the world. We fixed this up
a couple of years ago.

Judith. But you couldn't Van,
without a permit. A burial permit.

Van. Oh,
I guess you could. This getting old and dying
and crawling into the ground, that was invented
back before medical examiners
and taxes and all that. The old boy's clean.
He'll go right back to dirt.

Judith. But, Van, you can't!
People can't die that way!

Van. I guess they can.
What the hell good's being wrapped in cellophane?
You don't keep anyway.

Judith. You're impossible
to live with! Why do you say such things? If I
should die—you'd get a pine box!—

Van. If you should die
the old boy that drives the sun around up there,
he'd unhitch, and put the cattle out
to grass, and give it up. He'd plumb lose interest
if you should die. Maybe I would myself,
I don't say. Maybe I would.—Fetch out that supper.
We want to see what we eat.

Judith.
   [*Opening a lunch box*]

It's dinner, Van,
not supper.

Van. That's what I said. Fetch out that dinner.
When it gets a little darker what's black's pepper
and what's green's parsley; still you can't be sure.
It might be ants.

Judith. Just the same we'll quarrel.
We'll always quarrel.

Van. Oh, no. We've both got sense.
What's the sense fighting?
[*He looks at a paper that was round the lunch.*]

Judith. And you shouldn't read at table.

Van. I never do. The Nanuet bank's been robbed.
My God, there's not enough money in Nanuet
to buy their gas for a get-away. One night
pap and me sat in on a poker game
in Nanuet and took twenty-seven dollars
out of town. Next day they couldn't do business.
The place was clean.

Judith. There were troopers at the train
tonight, and sirens going through Haverstraw,
but the robbers got away.

Van. They took twenty-five thousand.
How'd twenty-five thousand get to Nanuet?
It's against nature.

Judith. It didn't stay there long.

Van. No—I understand that.
But just to have it there in passing, just

to look at, just to fool the customers,
how do they do it?

Judith. Maybe it wasn't real.

Van. Federal money, that's it. Some of the stuff
Jim Farley prints in Washington with the stamps
to pay you for voting straight. Only now you see it
and now you don't.

Judith. They say it buys as much
as if you earned it.

Van. Bad for the stomach, though
to live on humble pie.

Judith. I'd rather work.

Van. Well, as I said, don't work if you don't feel like it.
Any time you want to move up in the hills
and sleep with me, it's a bargain.

Judith. Van!

Van. Why not?
We'll get married if that's what you mean.

Judith. You haven't any job. And you make it sound
like animals.

Van. I'm fond of animals.

Judith. You shoot them all the time.

Van. Well, I get hungry.
Any man's liable to get hungry.

Judith. Van,
I want to talk to you seriously.

Van. Can't be done.
　Listen, things get serious enough
　without setting out to do it.

Judith. Van, this spring
　you had three weeks' work, laying dry wall.
　You could have had more, but you didn't take it.
　You're an expert mason—

Van. I'm good at everything.

Judith. But you work three weeks in the year—

Van. That's all I need—

Judith. And all the rest of the year you hunt or fish
　or sleep, or God knows what—

Van. Ain't it the truth?

Judith. Last fall I came looking for you once, and you
　were gone—gone to Port Jervis hunting—deer,
　you said on the postcard—

Van. Sure, I was hunting deer—
　didn't I bring you half a venison?

Judith. But not a word to me till I got the postcard
　ten days later—

Van. Didn't have a minute—

Judith. Then last winter there's a note nailed to a tree
　and you're in Virginia, down in the Dismal Swamp
　tracking bear. Now, for God's sake, Van,
　it's no way to live.

Van. Jeez, it's a lot of fun.

Judith. Maybe for you.

Van. You want me to take that job.

Judith. Why don't you, Van?

Van. Porter in a hotel, lugging up satchels,
  opening windows, maybe you get a dime.
  I'd choke to death.

Judith. I'd see you every day.

Van. Yeah, I could see you on the mezzanine,
  taking dictation from the drummer boys,
  all about how they can't get home. You can stand it,
  a woman stands that stuff, but if you're a man
  I say it chokes you.

Judith. We can't live in your cabin
  and have no money, like the Jackson Whites
  over at Suffern.

Van. Hell, you don't need money.
  Pap worked that out. All you need's a place to sleep
  and something to eat. I've never seen the time
  I couldn't find a meal on the mountain here,
  rainbow trout, jugged hare, something in season
  right around the zodiac.

Judith. You didn't like
  the Chevrolet factory, either?

Van.

  [*Walking toward the cliff edge*]

  Look at it, Judy.
  That's the Chevrolet factory, four miles down,
  and straight across, that's Sing Sing. Right from here

you can't tell one from another; get inside,
and what's the difference? You're in there, and you
                              work,
and they've got you. If you're in the factory
you buy a car, and then you put in your time
to pay for the goddam thing. If you get in a hurry
and steal a car, they put you in Sing Sing first,
and then you work out your time. They graduate
from one to the other, back and forth, those guys,
paying for cars both ways. But I was smart.
I parked at a polis station and rung the bell
and took to the woods. Not for your Uncle Dudley.
They plugged the dice.

Judith. But one has to have a car.

Van. Honest to God now, Judy, what's the hurry?
  Where in hell are we going?

Judith. If a man works hard,
  and has ability, as you have, Van,
  he takes a place among them, saves his money,
  works right out of the ruck and gets above
  where he's safe and secure.

Van. I wouldn't bet on it much.

Judith. But it's true.

Van. All right, suppose it's true. Suppose
  a man saves money all his life, and works
  like hell about forty years, till he can say:
  good-bye, I'm going, I'm on easy street
  from now on. What's he do?

Judith. Takes a vacation.

Van. Goes fishing, maybe? I'm on vacation now.
    Why should I work forty years to earn
    time off when I've got it?

Judith. It's not always easy,
    you know it's not. There was that time last winter
    when I helped you out.

Van. Why, sure, you helped me out.
    Why wouldn't you? But if you didn't help me
    I'd get along.

Judith. Yes, you would. I know you would.
    But you don't even seem to want money. You won't
                      take it
    when they bring it to you.

Van. When did they bring me any?

Judith. And what if there was a child?

Van. Why he'd be fine—
    the less they have the better they like it.—Oh,
    you mean the trap-rock company, wanting to buy
    High Tor? They offered seven hundred dollars—
    and they offered pap ten thousand before he died,
    and he wouldn't sell.

Judith. He wouldn't?

Van. They want to chew
    the back right off this mountain, the way they did
    across the clove there. Leave the old palisades
    sticking up here like billboards, nothing left
    but a false front facing the river. Not for pap,
    and not for me. I like this place.

Judith. But, Van Van Dorn!
  Ten thousand dollars!

Van. Well, it's Federal money.
  Damn stuff evaporates. Put it in a sock
  along with moth balls, and come back next year,
  and there's nothing left but the smell. Look, Judy, it's
  a quarter mile straight down to the Tappan Zee
  from here.—You can see fifteen miles of river
  north and south. I grew up looking at it.
  Hudson came up that river just about
  three hundred years ago, and lost a ship
  here in the Zee. They say the crew climbed up
  this Tor to keep a lookout for the fleet
  that never came. Maybe the Indians got them.
  Anyway on dark nights before a storm,
  they say you sometimes see them.

Judith. Have you seen them?

Van. The Dutchmen? Maybe I have. You can't be sure.
  It's pretty wild around here when it storms.
  That's when I like it best. But look at it now.
  There was a Jaeger here from Switzerland
  last year. He took one squint at this and said
  they could keep their Alps, for all him. Look at the
                              willows
  along the far breakwater.

Judith. It's beautiful.

Van. Every night I come back here like the Indian
  to get a fill of it. Seven hundred dollars
  and tear it down? Hell, no.
    [Biggs *and* Skimmerhorn *come in from the right, a bit be-*

draggled, and wiping their brows. SKIMMERHORN *carries a brief-case. It is growing darker.*]

Biggs. Hey listen, Mac, any houses round here?

Van. Guess you're off the beat, buddy; never heard of any houses on the mountain.

Skimmerhorn. Come on, Art; we're doing well if we're down at the road before dark.

Biggs. Look, Mac, maybe you can help us out. You familiar with this region, at all?

Van. I've been around here some.

Biggs. Well, we're all afternoon hunting a cabin that's somewhere along the ridge. Ever hear of it?

Van. Anybody live in it?

Biggs. Fellow named Van Dorn.

Van. Oh, yes, sure.

Biggs. You know where it is?

Van. Sure. You climb down the face of the cliff here and keep left along the ledge about a hundred yards, then you turn sharp left through a cleft up the ridge. Follow the trail about half a mile and there you are.

Skimmerhorn. Down the face of the cliff?

Van. Down through the rocks there, then turn left—

Skimmerhorn. A monkey couldn't go down there, hanging on with four hands and a tail!

Van. Well, you can always walk along back toward Little Tor, and cut down from there through the gulch.

There's a slough at the bottom of the ravine, but if you get through that you can see the cabin up on the side-hill. About four miles that way.

Skimmerhorn. Yeah, we'll set right out. I always did want to get lost up here and spend a night in the hills.

Van. Oh, you'll get lost, all right.

Biggs. Any snakes?

Van. No, you might see a copperhead, or a timber rattler.

Skimmerhorn. Coming back down?

Biggs. Yeah, we'd better go down. Thanks.

Van. Don't mention it.
   [BIGGS *and* SKIMMERHORN *go out to the right.*]

Judith. But they were looking for you?

Van. Yeah.

Judith. Why didn't you tell them?

Van. What?

Judith. Who you were!

Van. They didn't ask about that.

Judith. But out of common courtesy!

Van. Well, you see, I know who they are.

Judith. Who are they?

Van. Art J. Biggs, Junior, and Skimmerhorn, Judge Skimmerhorn.

Judith. But why not talk to them?

Van. Oh, we communicate by mail. I've got
a dozen letters stacked up from the firm:
Skimmerhorn, Skimmerhorn, Biggs and Skimmerhorn,
and maybe two or three Skimmerhorns I left out
printed across the top. They're realtors,
whatever that is, and they own the trap-rock company,
and one of the Skimmerhorns, he's probate judge,
and goes around condemning property
when they want to make a rake-off. Take a letter:
Dear Skimmerhorn—

Judith. But they're the trap-rock men!

Van. That's what I said.

Judith. I'll call them!

Van. Oh, no; oh, no!
I've got nothing to say to those two buzzards
except I hope they break their fat-back necks
on their own trap-rock.

Judith. You take a lot for granted.

Van. Do I?

Judith. You think, because I said I loved you once,
that's the end; I'm finished.

Van. Oh, far from it.

Judith. Oh, yes—you think because a girl's been kissed
she stays kissed, and after that the man
does her thinking for her.

Van. Hell, it's all I can do
to handle my own thinking.

Judith. If we're married
  I'll have to live the way you want to live.
  You prefer being a pauper!

Van. Get it straight!
  I don't take money nor orders, and I live
  as I damn well please.

Judith. But we'd live like paupers!
  And you could have a fortune!

Van. Seven hundred dollars?

Judith. You could get more!

Van. I don't mean to sell at all.

Judith. You see; it's your place, and your thinking! You
                    decide,
  but I'd have to stand it with you!

Van. What do you want?

Judith. Something to start on; and now, you see, we could
                    have it,
  only you won't!

Van. I can't, Judy, that's the truth.
  I just can't.

Judith. They'll get it anyway.
  They've worked right up to where your land begins,
  and they won't stop for you. They'll just condemn it
  and take it.

Van. They'll be in trouble.

Judith. You can't make trouble
  for companies. They have a dozen lawyers

and ride right over you. I've worked for them.
It's never any use.

Van. Well, I won't sell.

Judith. We'll call it off then.

Van. What?

Judith. Between you and me.

Van. Only you don't mean it.

Judith. I know I do, though.
You haven't thought about it, and so you think
I couldn't do it. But it's better now
than later.

Van. You don't know what it means to me
if you can say it.

Judith. It means as much to me,
but I look ahead a little.

Van. What do you see?

Judith. Two people growing old
and having children, running wild in the woods
with nothing.

Van. There's no better place to run.
But I've been counting on you. More than you know.
More than—Judy, this is the kind of night
we've been in love most.

Judith. Yes, we could be in love,
but that's not everything.

Van. Well, just about.
What else do we get?

Judith. I think I'd better go.
It's getting dark.

Van. You could find your way by the beacon.

Judith. I'd better go.

[BIGGS *and* SKIMMERHORN *come back from the right.*]

Biggs. Listen, Mac, would you do something for us?

Van. I don't know.

Biggs. Could you take a paper round to Van Dorn and
leave it with him?

Van. A summons?

Biggs. A sort of notice.

Van. Yeah, a notice to appear. No, I couldn't.

Biggs. It's worth a dollar to me.

Van. I'd be cheating you.

Skimmerhorn. Make it two dollars.

Van. You'd be throwing away money.

Skimmerhorn. Never mind that part of it. Will you do it?

Van. You'll take a running jump over the edge of the
cliff and think things over on the way down before I
serve any papers for you.

Biggs. What's the matter with us?

Van. Might be hoof and mouth disease, for all I know.
You certainly brought an awful stench up here with
you.

Skimmerhorn. Not much on manners, these natives.

Van. My rule in life is keep away from skunks.

Biggs. You'll get the tar kicked out of you one of these days.

Van. Make it today.

Judith. If you gentlemen care to know, this is Mr. Van Dorn.

Biggs. Say, are you Van Dorn?

Van. Sure I am.

Biggs.
> [*Extending a hand*]

Oh, in that case, forget it—you're the fellow we want to see!—Boy, we apologize—
> [*He uncovers*]

and to the lady, too! Listen, I don't know what to say but you've got us all wrong. We want to buy this place!

Van. You like the view, I suppose?

Biggs. Certainly is a view.

Van. You wouldn't spoil it, of course? You wouldn't move in with a million dollars worth of machinery and cut the guts out of the mountain, would you?

Skimmerhorn. We always leave the front—the part you see from the river.

Van. But you take down all the law allows.

Skimmerhorn. Well, we're in business.

Van. Not with me.

Judith. Do you mind if I ask how much you're offering?

Biggs. We said seven hundred. but I'll make it a thousand right here and now.

Skimmerhorn. As a matter of fact, we'll make it two thousand.

Biggs. Yeah, all right. Two thousand for the hundred and seven acres.

Judith. But you offered Mr. Van Dorn's father ten thousand before he died.

Skimmerhorn. His father had a clear title, right down from the original Dutch patroon to the original Van Dorn. But unfortunately the present Mr. Van Dorn has a somewhat clouded claim to the acreage.

Van. My father's title was clear, and he left it to me.

Skimmerhorn. The truth is he should have employed a lawyer when he drew his will, because the instrument, as recorded, is faulty in many respects. It was brought before me in my capacity as probate judge at Ledentown.

Van. And in your capacity as second vice-president of the trap-rock company you shot it full of holes.

Skimmerhorn. Sir, I keep my duties entirely separate.

Van. Sure, but when your left hand takes money your right hand finds out about it. And when there's too much to carry away in both hands you use a basket. You're also vice-president of the power company, and

you stole right-of-ways clear across the county north and
south—

Skimmerhorn. We paid for every foot of land—

Van. Yes, at your own price.

Biggs. Let's not get in an argument, Mr. Van Dorn, because the fact that your father's will was improperly
drawn means he died intestate and the land goes to
his heirs. Now we've found twenty-seven Van Dorns
living at Blauvelt, all claiming relationship and all willing to sign away their rights for a consideration.

Van. The best you can do you'll need my name in your
little paper, and you won't have it.

Skimmerhorn. To put it straight, you'll take three thousand dollars, and I'll hold the will valid.

Van. Oh, it's three thousand, now?

Biggs. You'll say that's crooked, but it's not. It's perfectly
legal—and it's what you get.

Van. I'm still waiting to hear what you do about my sig-
nature.

Skimmerhorn. It's quite possible you'll be held incompetent by the court and a guardian appointed.

Van. Me, incompetent.

Skimmerhorn. But I've got the validation in my pocket,
naming you executor, if you'll sell.

Biggs. And by God, anybody that won't take money when
it's offered to him is incompetent! And you'll take it

now or not at all! I don't go mountain-climbing every
day with a blank check in my pocket!

[*A pause*]

Come on: It's bad enough sliding down that trail by
daylight.

Van. Well, I wouldn't want to make you nervous,
a couple of eminent respectables
like you two—but a dog won't bite a Dutchman—
maybe you've heard that—and the reason is
a Dutchman's poison when he don't like you. Now,
I'm Dutch and I don't like you.

Skimmerhorn. That's a threat?

Van. Not at all. Only don't try to eat me
or you'll curl up. I'm poison to a hound-dog,
and you're both sons-of-bitches.

Biggs. Come on.

[*The daylight is now gone. The airplane beacon lights the scene
from the right.*]

Van. What's more
there's something funny about this mountain-top.
It draws fire. Every storm on the Tappan Zee
climbs up here and wraps itself around
High Tor, and blazes away at what you've got,
airplane beacon, steam-shovels, anything
newfangled. It smashed the beacon twice. It blew
the fuses on your shovel and killed a man
only last week. I've got a premonition
something might happen to you.

Biggs. God, he's crazy.

Skimmerhorn. Yeah, let him talk.

    [*There is a sudden rumbling roar of falling rock.*]

Biggs. What's that?

Van. That's nothing much.
    That's just a section of the cliff come down
    across the trail. I've been expecting it
    this last two years. You'd better go down this way.

Biggs. This way?

Van. Yeah.

Biggs. No, thanks.

Van. Just as you say.
    But there's something definitely hostile here
    toward you two pirates. Don't try that trail in the dark.
    Not if you want to be buried in your vaults
    in Mount Repose. Your grieving families
    might have to move two thousand tons of rock
    to locate your remains. You think High Tor's
    just so much raw material, but you're wrong.
    A lot of stubborn men have died up here
    and some of them don't sleep well. They come back
    and push things round, these dark nights. Don't blame
                            me
    if anything falls on you.

Skimmerhorn. Oh, what the hell!
    Let's get out of here.

    [*Another long rumble of falling rock*]

Van. Another rock-fall.
    Once they start there's likely to be more.
    Something hanging round in the dark up here

doesn't like you boys. Not only me.
Better go down this way.

Biggs. Thanks.

[BIGGS *and* SKIMMERHORN *go out to the right.*]

Judith. What do you mean?

Van. I don't know.

Judith. They'll say you threatened them.
Good-bye, Van.

Van. You'll be up tomorrow?

Judith. No.

[*She steps down into a cleft.*]

Van. You'd better let me see you down.

Judith. Oh, no.
I can climb. Stay here and guard your rock—
you think so much of it.

Van. When will I see you?

Judith. Never.
We'll forget about it. You had a choice
and you chose High Tor. You're in love with your
mountain.
Well, keep your mountain.

Van. All right.

Judith. Good night.

Van. Good night.

[*She disappears down the rocks.* VAN *sits in the shadow, looking into darkness. After a moment a barely perceptible
FIGURE enters from the gloom at the right and crosses the*

*stage toward the rocks at the left. At the foot of the climb
he pauses and his face is caught in the light of the beacon.
He is seen to be young or middle-aged, bearded, and
wearing the costume of a Dutch sailor of the sixteen
hundreds. He climbs the rocks, and* ANOTHER SAILOR, *a
small cask strapped to his shoulders, follows.* THREE MORE
cross the stage similarly, then the CAPTAIN *and* HIS WIFE
pause, like the others, in the light of the beacon. The
CAPTAIN *is like his men, only younger perhaps;* HIS WIFE
*is a tiny figure, with a delicate girlish face looking out
from under the Dutch bonnet. They too pass up the
rocks, and are followed by a rolling* SILENUS *in the same
garments. As they vanish* VAN *rises, looking after them.*]

Uh—huh—going to rain.

CURTAIN

ACT ONE

Scene II

SCENE: *The curtain goes up on complete darkness enfolding the summit of the Tor. There is a long cumbrous rolling, as of a ball going down a bowling alley, a flash of white light, a crackling as of falling pins and a mutter dying into echo along the hills. The flash reveals the outline of the Tor, black against the sky, and on it the figures of the* DUTCH CREW. *Again the roll, the flash, the break and the dying away. The beam of the airplane beacon steals into the scene sufficiently to suggest the bowlers, some of them standing, some sitting about the keg, the* CAPTAIN'S WIFE *a little apart from the rest. Beyond the peak is a moving floor, the upper side of blown cloud.*

The Captain's Wife. I'm weary of it, Martin! When you drink
  there should be one on guard to watch the river
  lest the ship come, and pass, and we must haunt
  the dark another year!

The Captain. To humor her,
  Pieter, old son, climb down and post the Zee,
  and mind you keep good lookout.

Pieter. Ships, aye, ships—
  when the ball's rolling and there's gin in hand
  I go to post. My luck!

The Captain. When you shipped with me
  you signed the voyage.

Pieter. Is this sea or land?
  I'm no foot soldier!

The Captain. March!

27

Pieter. Aye, aye. I'm going.

> [PIETER *detaches himself from the group and goes down the*
> *rocks.*]

The Captain. Are you content?

The Captain's Wife. When the *Half Moon* returns
and we have boarded her, and the wind scuds fair
into the east—yes, when we see the wharves
of Texel town across the Zuyder Zee,
with faces waiting for us, hands and cries
to welcome our returning, then perhaps
I shall be content.

A Sailor. Now God, for Texel town.

Another Soldier.

> [*Rising*]

I'll drink no more.

DeWitt.

> [*The Silenus*]

Drink up, lads, and forget.
It's a long way to the Texel. Drink your drink
and play your play.

The Captain. Drink up and play it out.

The Captain's Wife. Have you forgotten how the cobbled
street
comes down by cranks and turns upon the quay,
where the *Onrust* set sail? The traders' doors
under the blowing signs, bright colors hung
to catch unwary eyes? The bakers' ovens
and the long, hot brown loaves? The red-coal fires
and silver under candles? There your wives

wait for you, their sharp roofs in Amsterdam
cut on a rainy sky.

The Captain. Be quiet, Lise.
You were so much in love you must come with me;
you were so young that I was patient with you,
but now day long, night long you carp and quarrel,
a carping wife.

Lise. We stay so long—so long;
Asher, at first the days were years, but now
the years are days; the ship that set us down
to watch this river palisade becomes
alike with supper-stories round a hearth
when we were children. Was there this ship at all,
was there a sailor-city, Amsterdam,
where the salt water washed the shallow piers
and the wind went out to sea? Will the ship return,
and shall I then see the Netherlands once more,
with sabots clattering homeward from the school
on winter evenings?

Asher. Aye, there was a ship,
and we wait here for her, but she's long away,
somewhere up-river.

Lise. And now you drink and drink,
distill your liquor on the mountain-top
and bowl against the light. But when you break it
these new strange men come build it up again;
and giant shovels spade the mountain down,
and when you break them still the new strange men
rig them afresh and turn them on the rock,
eating the pillared stone. We must go back.
There's no safety here.

A Sailor. We must go back.

Asher. These muttering fools!

Lise. Oh, Asher, I'm afraid!
　　For one thing I have known, and never told
　　lest it be true, lest you be frightened, too,
　　lest we be woven of shadow! As the years
　　have gone, each year a century, they seem
　　less real, and all the boundaries of time,
　　our days and nights and hours, merge and are one,
　　escaping me. Then sometimes in a morning
　　when all the crew come down the rocks together,
　　holding my breath, I see you in the light,
　　and back of you the gray rock bright and hard,
　　seen through figures of air! And you, and you,
　　and you were but cloud-drift walking, pierced by the
　　　　　　　　　　　　　　　　　　　light,
　　translucent in the sun.

DeWitt. Now damn the woman!

Lise. Love, love, before our blood
　　be shadow only, in a dark fairyland
　　so far from home, we must go back, go back
　　where earth is earth, and we may live again
　　and one day be one day!

Asher. Why, then, I knew it,
　　and I have known it, now that you know it, too.
　　But the old Amsterdam of our farewells
　　lies in another world. The land and sea
　　about us on this dark side of the earth
　　is thick with demons, heavy with enchantment,
　　cutting us off from home.

Lise. Is it enchantment?
    Yes, it may be. At home there were tulips growing
    along my bordered path, but here the flowers
    are strange to me, not one I knew, no trace
    of any flower I knew; no, seedlings set
    upon a darkened, alien outer rim
    of sea, blown here as we were blown, enchanted,
    drunken and blind with sorcery.

Asher. And yet
    what we're to have we shall have here. Years past
    the demons of this air palsied our hands,
    fixed us upon one pinnacle of time,
    and on this pinnacle of stone, and all
    the world we knew slid backward to the gulf,
    stranding us here like seaweed on the shingle,
    remembering the sea. In Texel town
    new houses have gone up, after new fashions;
    the children of the children of our days,
    lying awake to think of what has been,
    reach doubtfully beyond the clouds of years
    back to our sailing out of Texel. Men
    are like the gods, work miracles, have power
    to pierce the walls with music. Their beacon light
    destroys us. You have seen us in the sun,
    wraithlike, half-effaced, the print we make
    upon the air thin tracery, permeable,
    a web of wind. They have changed us. We may take
    the fire-balls of the lightning in our hands
    and bowl them down the level floor of cloud
    to wreck the beacon, yet there was a time
    when these were death to touch. The life we keep
    is motionless as the center of a storm,

yet while we can we keep it; while we can
snuff out to darkness their bright sweeping light,
melt down the harness of the slow machines
that hew the mountain from us. When it goes
we shall go too. They leave us this place, High Tor,
and we shall have no other. You learn it last.
A long while now we've known.

A Sailor. Aye, aye, a long while.

Asher. Come, we'll go down.

> [*The* CAPTAIN *and his* MEN *go out, leaving only* DEWITT *with*
> LISE.]

Lise. That's why they drink.

DeWitt. It's enough to drive a sailor-man to drink, by the
great jib boom, marooned somewhere on the hinder
parts of the earth and degenerating hourly to the status
of a flying Dutchman, half-spook and half God-knows-
what. Maps and charts we have, compass and sextant,
but the ships these days are bewitched like ourselves,
spanking up and down the Mauritius with sails struck,
against wind and tide, and on fire from below. Drink?
Why wouldn't we drink? A pewter flagon of Hollands
gin puts manhood into the remnants and gives a sailor
courage to look out on these fanciful new devils that
ride sea, land and air on a puff of blue smoke. They're
all witches and mermaids, these new-world devils, dancing around on bubbles, speaking a language God never
heard, and nothing human about them except when
they fall they break like the rest of us.

Lise. If I had known. It's not too late. The sun
still rises in the east and lays a course

toward the old streets and days. These are my hands
as when I was a child. Some great magician,
binding a half-world in his wiles, has laid
a spell here. We must break it and go home.
I see this clearly.

De Witt. Lise, little heart, the devils are too much for us.
God knows it's a hard thing to say, and I'd help you
if I could help myself, but all hell wouldn't know
where we are nor where we ought to go. The very
points of the compass grow doubtful these latter years,
partly because I'm none too sober and partly because
the great master devil sits on top of the world stirring
up north and south with a long spoon to confuse poor
mariners. I've seen him at it, a horned bull three times
the size of Dundenberg and with more cloven feet than
the nine beasts in Revelations. Very clearly I saw him,
too, as clear as you see the east and a path across the
waters.

Lise. Are we to wait till all the color steals
from flower and cloud, before our eyes; till a wind
out of the morning from the Tappan Zee
lifts us, we are so light, for all our crying,
and takes us down the valleys toward the west,
and all we are becomes a voiceless cry
heard on the wind?

De Witt. We'll see the time, if they continue to work on
us, when we'll be apparent in a strong light only by
the gin contained in our interior piping. The odor itself, along with that of church-warden tobacco, should
be sufficient to convince a magistrate of our existence.—
You tremble, little Lise, and you weep, but look now,

there's a remedy I've had in mind. Fall in love with
one of them. Fall in love with one of these same strange
new-world magicians. I shall choose me out one of their
female mermaid witches, and set my heart on her, and
become a man again. And for God's sake let her love me
strongly and hold on, lest I go down the brook like a
spring freshet in the next pounding rain.

Lise. I gave my love long ago, and it's no help.
I love enough.

DeWitt. Aye, but he's in a worse case than you are, the
Captain. Saving his captaincy, there's not enough belief in him to produce half a tear in a passion of
sobbing. You'll make me weep, little one, and what
tears I have I shall need, lest my protestation turns out
to be a dry rain.

Lise. Aye, we were warned before we came away
against the cabalistic words and signs
of those who dwell along these unknown waters;
never to watch them dance nor hear them sing
nor draw their imprecations—lest their powers
weave a weird medicine throughout the air,
chilling the blood, transfixing body and mind
and we be chained invisibly, our eyes darkened,
our wrists and breasts pulseless, anchored in time,
like birds blown back in a wind. But we have listened,
and we are stricken through with light and sound,
empty as autumn leaves, empty as prayers
that drift in a godless heaven. Meaningless,
picked clean of meaning, stripped of bone and will,
the chrysalids of locusts staring here
at one another.

DeWitt. If it's true it's enough to make a man weep for
himself, Lise, and for all lost mariners, wherever they
are, and for us more than any, here on these spell-
bound rocks, drawing up water from time past—the
well growing deeper, and the water lower, till there be
none.

[*He turns away to go down the path.*]

CURTAIN

ACT ONE

Scene III

SCENE: *Another section of the Tor, in darkness save for the airplane beacon. A large steam shovel reaches in from an adjacent excavation and hangs over the rock, the control cables dangling. VAN is alone on the stage looking at the machinery. He reaches up, catches a cable, and swings the shovel a little. BIGGS and SKIMMERHORN enter from the right.*

Biggs. Hey, what are you doing with that shovel?

Van. Did you know you're trespassing? Also when a man owns land he owns the air above it and the rock below. That means this damn shovel of yours is also trespassing.

Biggs. Oh, it's Van Dorn. We'll have that moved tomorrow, Mr. Van Dorn. Somebody's made a miscue and left it hanging over the line.

Skimmerhorn. By the way, that trail's gone out completely, Mr. Van Dorn; there's a fifty foot sheer drop there now, where it was. Now we've got to get off, if you can think of any way to manage it.

Van. I'm not worrying about it. Spend the night. No charge.

Skimmerhorn. The truth is I have to be in court early tomorrow, and a man needs his sleep.

Van. Afraid you'd doze off on the bench and somebody else might take a trick? Oh, you'd wake up before they got far with anything. The Skimmerhorns are automatic that way.

36

Biggs. You don't know any other trail down?

Van. I showed you the one I knew, and you both turned green looking at it. What am I supposed to do now? Pin wings on you?

[*He goes out to the right.*]

Skimmerhorn. I think I'll swear out a warrant for that squirt. He's too independent by half.

Biggs. On what ground?

Skimmerhorn. He threatened us, didn't he?

Biggs. And where'll that get us?

Skimmerhorn. He might be easier to talk to in jail.

Biggs. That's true.

Skimmerhorn.

[*Sitting on a rock*]

This is a hell of a mess.

Biggs. You're explaining to me?

Skimmerhorn. What did we ever come up here for?

Biggs. Twenty-two thousand dollars.

Skimmerhorn. Will we get it?

Biggs. It'll look all right on the books.

Skimmerhorn. It's not good enough, though.

Biggs. What are you grousing about?

Skimmerhorn. Because I want my dinner, damn it! And because I'm tired of taking forty per cent and giving you sixty on all the side bets! I want half!

Biggs. You're a damn sight more likely to get your dinner. You're overpaid already.

Skimmerhorn. The will's perfectly good. I could find holes in it, but I've probated plenty much the same.

Biggs. What of it?

Skimmerhorn. A judge has some conscience, you know. When he sets a precedent he likes to stick to it.

Biggs. I never knew your conscience to operate except on a cash basis. You want half.

Skimmerhorn. Yes, I want half.

Biggs. Well, you don't get it. Any other judge I put in there'd work for nothing but the salary and glad of the job. You take a forty per cent cut and howl for more. The woods are full of shyster lawyers looking for probate judgeships and I'll slip one in at Ledentown next election.

Skimmerhorn. Oh, no, you won't, Art; oh, no, you won't. You wouldn't do that to an old friend like me; because if you did, think what I'd do to an old friend like you.

Biggs. Well, maybe I wouldn't. Not if you're reasonable. Look, what's the difference between forty per cent and fifty per cent? Practically nothing!

Skimmerhorn. Then why don't you give it to me?

Biggs. Because, try and get it!—

Skimmerhorn. Damn it, I'm hungry.—I ought to telephone my wife, too.

Biggs. Why don't you?

Skimmerhorn. Maybe it's fun for you—nothing to eat, no place to sleep, cold as hell, black as Tophet and a storm coming up! Only I'm not used to it!

Biggs. You're pulling down forty per cent of twenty-two thousand dollars for the night's work. I say it's worth it.

Skimmerhorn. Think we could slide down one of those cables?

Biggs. Maybe you could, Humpty-Dumpty, but not me.

Skimmerhorn. I'm going to look at it.

[*He goes out left,* BIGGS *following. After a moment* THREE MEN *climb in through the rocks at the right, one of them carrying a small zipper satchel. They throw themselves down wearily on the rock. They are, in brief, the Nanuet bank robbers,* ELKUS, DOPE *and* BUDDY.]

Dope. God, I got no wind.

[*A siren is heard faintly, far down on the road.*]

Elkus. Sons a' bitches a' troopers.

Dope. What'd you want to wreck the car for?

Elkus. Want to get caught with the stuff on you?

Buddy. We'll get four hundred years for this.

Elkus. Shut up!

Dope. You didn't need to wreck the car, though.

Elkus. Didn't you hear the trooper slam on the brakes when he went by? You'd be wearing bracelets right now if I hadn't dumped the old crate over the embankment! The way it is he thinks he's following us, and he'll blow that fire alarm all the way to Bear Mountain

Bridge. Only hope he meets something solid head-on at ninety miles an hour.

Dope. What I want to know is where we go from here.

Elkus. Down the other side and pick up a car.
> [*The siren is heard receding.*]

Buddy. We'll get four hundred years for this.

Elkus. What do you think you are, a chorus? Go on back to St. Thomas's and sing it to the priest. You're about as much help as a flat tire.

Buddy. I never wanted to be in it. I was only lookout— you're both witness to that.

Elkus. What good do you think that does you, you poor fish? Brace up and take it like a man. There's twenty-five thousand in that bag and some of it's yours.

Dope. How do you know it's twenty-five thousand?

Elkus. It's the Orangeburg pay roll.
> [BUDDY *looks off left.*]

Buddy. Before God, it's Judge Skimmerhorn!

Elkus. What? Where?

Buddy. There. Coming round the rocks. Judge Skimmerhorn of Ledentown.

Elkus. Does he know you?

Buddy. Sure, he knows me.

Elkus. We're out climbing, see? Hikers, see? On a picnic.
> [*They stand.* ELKUS *holds the satchel behind him casually.* BIGGS *and* SKIMMERHORN *come in.*]

Biggs. Hello.

Elkus. How are you?

Biggs. Out walking?

Elkus. That's right. Climbed up on a bet.

Skimmerhorn. Isn't that Buddy?

Buddy. Yes, sir. Evening, Judge.

Skimmerhorn. You're a long way from home.

Buddy. Yes, sir.

Biggs. Think you could show us a way down? We're stuck up here.

Buddy. There's a path down the cliff. Yes, sir.

Skimmerhorn. No, thanks. I saw that one. Going to camp here?

Elkus. Might as well. Sure.

Skimmerhorn. Bring anything to eat?

Elkus. Matter of fact, we didn't.
    [*He sets the satchel down behind the rock, unobtrusively.*]

Skimmerhorn. Not a thing?

Elkus. Not a thing.

Skimmerhorn. That's funny. Camping with nothing to eat.

Elkus. Yeah, it is kinda funny.

Dope. We ate before we started.
    [*He smiles cunningly.*]

Elkus. That's right. The Dope's right for once. We ate before we started.

Skimmerhorn. Wish I had.

Buddy. You—you staying up here tonight, sir?

Skimmerhorn. Seems that way. We came up looking for somebody.

Elkus. Looking for somebody?

Skimmerhorn. That's what I said.

Elkus. Who was it?

Biggs. That's our business.

Elkus. I see.

Skimmerhorn.

[*Coming near the three*]

Listen, Buddy, you're young and ambitious. Would you do something for me if you got well paid?

Buddy. I guess so, Judge.

Skimmerhorn.

[*Sitting on the rock and incidentally over the satchel*]

We're done in, traipsing around the rocks. Would you climb down the Tor and get to Haverstraw and telephone my wife I can't come home?

Buddy. I guess so, wouldn't I, Elkus?

Elkus. Up to you.

Skimmerhorn. And while you're there will you buy a dozen sandwiches and some beer?

Buddy. Yes, sir.

Skimmerhorn. There's another thing you could do. Call up the state troopers for me, and tell them I'm here and I want them to come up and make an arrest.

Buddy. You—want to arrest somebody?

Skimmerhorn. You get it. What do you say?

Buddy. I—I guess so. Is it all right, Elkus?

Dope. Oh—no. Oh—no.

Elkus. Sure it's O.K. Why not?

Buddy. It'd take about five hours—to get down and back.

Skimmerhorn. Damn it—I'll starve to death.

Dope. What do you want to make an arrest for?

Biggs. That's our business.

Buddy. All right. I'll go.

Skimmerhorn. Here's five dollars for you. And another when you get back. And make it fast, will you?

Buddy. Yes, sir.
   [*He starts out right.*]

Elkus. Just a minute, Bud.
   [ELKUS *and* DOPE *follow* BUDDY *out to converse with him.*]

Biggs. You might have made it two dozen sandwiches.

Skimmerhorn. I guess I will.
   [*He starts to rise, places his hand on the satchel, and jumps.*]

   Christ, what's that?
   [*He kicks the satchel, then flips it up into the rocks.*]

Biggs. Yeah?

Skimmerhorn. I thought it was a snake. Somebody's mouldy luggage. People are always throwing truck around.

[*He calls.*]

Say, for God's sake, get started, will you?

Buddy.

[*Outside*]

Yes, sir. Right away.

[ELKUS *and* DOPE *return.*]

Elkus. I guess we'll all go.

[*He looks nonchalantly where the satchel was.*]

Skimmerhorn. Fine. Will you make it two dozen sand-wiches?

Elkus. What the hell's going on here?

Skimmerhorn. We're hungry, that's all.

Elkus. Are you two finnegling with us? Because if you are—!

Biggs. What are you looking for?

Elkus. Nothing. Who said I was looking for anything?

Dope. Hey, Elkus! They got the troopers up here!

[DEWITT's *broad Dutch hat appears above the rocks in the rear, looking, for the moment, remarkably like that of a state trooper.* ELKUS *and* DOPE *freeze, looking at it.*]

Elkus.

[*Drawing a gun*]

Why, you fat pimps!
[DeWitt *disappears.*]

Dope. Beat it, you fool!
[Elkus *and* Dope *scatter out to the right.*]

Biggs.
[*Looking at the rocks*]

What was all that about?

Skimmerhorn. I hope they bring those sandwiches.
[*He also stares toward the rear.*]

Biggs. Sandwiches? They're not bringing sandwiches for
anybody, those two.
[*He calls.*]

Hey! Hey, you! Anybody there?—What did he mean by
troopers?

Skimmerhorn. Want to take a look?

Biggs. I'm plenty unhappy, right where I am.
[Skimmerhorn *climbs up on the rocks.*]

Skimmerhorn. Wish to God I did see a trooper.

Biggs. Nobody there?

Skimmerhorn. Not a thing. Hey! Hey, you!
[*A silence.*]

Nope. Nobody.

Biggs. Looks to me as if we just missed being stuck up by
a couple of lunatics.

Skimmerhorn. If I can't eat I'm going to sleep.

Biggs. Maybe you've never tried adjusting yourself to igneous limestone.

Skimmerhorn. I'm about to try it now.

Biggs. You have my sympathy.

    ·   [SKIMMERHORN *stretches out on the rock, takes off his coat for a pillow and lies down.*]

Skimmerhorn. Thanks.

Biggs. Beautiful shape you have. A lot of slop tied up with a piece of string.

Skimmerhorn.

    [*Sitting up*]

God it's cold. Listen, we could use one coat for a pillow and put the other one over us.

Biggs. What other one?

Skimmerhorn. Yours.

Biggs. A proposition, huh?

Skimmerhorn. You going to sit up all night?

Biggs. In some ways it might be preferable.

Skimmerhorn. You can't prop yourself on end forever, like a duck on a rock.

Biggs. Pull yourself together, then. You stick out behind like a bump on a duck. All right. Move over.

Skimmerhorn. Your coat's bigger than mine.

    [*They pull* BIGGS' *coat around them and lie down.*]

Biggs. Just a couple of perfect forty-nines. Where the hell am I supposed to put my hip bone?

Skimmerhorn. You juggle your own hip bones.

[DeWitt *appears on the rocks at the rear, looking down.*]

Biggs. If you snore, you probate judge, I'll have you disbarred.

Skimmerhorn. Go to sleep.

Biggs. Wish I thought I could. On bed rock. Wake me early, mother dear.

Skimmerhorn. Shut up.

[DeWitt *meanwhile has opened the satchel and now brings it down into the light to examine the contents. He sits down, takes out five packets of bills, shakes the satchel, then begins to go through the inner pockets. He finds a roll of pennies, which he breaks open into his hands.*]

DeWitt. Copper pieces, by the great jib boom, enough to purchase a new wig, if a man ever got back to a place where money was useful to him. A counting-house full of them wouldn't buy a ship from one of these semi-demi-demi-semi-devils, so that's no good.

[*Two snores rise in concert from* Biggs *and* Skimmerhorn. De-Witt *goes over to them, dropping the money.*]

What kind of demi-semi-devil do you think you are, with four legs and two faces, both looking the same direction? Jesu Maria, it's a kind of centaur, as big one way as another, no arms, and feet the size of dish-pans.

Biggs. What's that?

DeWitt.

[*Backing away*]

It's the rear end that talks, evidently, the front being fast asleep in the manner of a figure-head.

Biggs. Who's there? Did somebody speak?

DeWitt. None too clear in the back thinker, I should say, which would be a natural result of lugging two sets of brains, fore and aft. I'd incline to communicate with the front end, but if necessary I'll converse with the posterior.

Biggs.

[*Sitting up, looking at* DeWitt]

Skimmerhorn!

Skimmerhorn. What's the matter?

Biggs. I'm damned if I know.

Skimmerhorn. Go to sleep, then.

Biggs. Do you believe in apparitions?

Skimmerhorn. No.

Biggs. Well, there's a figure of fun sitting talking to me, right out of a masquerade ball.

Skimmerhorn. You been drinking?

Biggs. What would I find to drink?

DeWitt. If the forecastle wakes now I shall play both ends against the middle, like a marine auctioneer. I want to buy a boat.

Biggs. You've come to the wrong shop, sailor. I'm in the real-estate business, and it's a long mile down to sea level.

[SKIMMERHORN *sits up suddenly.*]

DeWitt. You have no boats?

Biggs. No boats.

Skimmerhorn. What in the hell?—

Biggs. I told you I'm damned if I know.

DeWitt. And the front end has no boats?

Biggs. You're the front end, see. He wants to know if you've got boats.

Skimmerhorn. No, stranger, no boats.

DeWitt. Ah.

[*He shakes his head mournfully, turns him about and goes to the right, still muttering.*]

The great plague on them, the lying, two-headed fairies out of a witch's placket. What chance has an honest man against a two-faced double-tongued beast, telling the same tale—

[*He disappears through the rocks.*]

Biggs. Did you see what I saw?

Skimmerhorn. Not if you saw what I saw. What I saw wasn't possible.—Did you fake that thing?

Biggs. Fake it? I saw it.

Skimmerhorn. Oh, no—! Nobody saw that—what I saw. I didn't either. I've got a family to support. They aren't going to put me away anywhere.

Biggs. Whatever it was, it left a calling card. Looks as if he ate his lunch here, supposing a thing like that eats lunch. Maybe he left some for us.

Skimmerhorn. I don't want any of that.

Biggs.
[*Rising and turning the packages over with his foot*]

There's something in it.

Skimmerhorn. Help yourself.

Biggs.
[*Opening a package, tossing the cover away*]

You know what this is?

Skimmerhorn. Probably a sheaf of contracts with the devil, all ready to sign.

Biggs. No, it's money.

Skimmerhorn. Money!
[*He leaps to his feet.*]

Biggs. Fives and tens.
[*He opens another package.* Skimmerhorn *does the same.*]

Skimmerhorn. Well, bless the poor little Dutchman's heart—after all we said about him, too!

Biggs. Think he left it?

Skimmerhorn. It wasn't there before.

Biggs. No.

Skimmerhorn. Were you born with a caul, or anything?

Biggs. Always before I had to work for it, or steal it. Never till tonight have I been waked up by a little man in a big hat, fetching it to me in packages.

Skimmerhorn. Are you asleep?

Biggs. I probably am, asleep and dreaming.

Skimmerhorn. If you're dreaming, you're dreaming that I found money.

Biggs. Oh, you found it now?

Skimmerhorn. Fifty-fifty.

Biggs. Wait a minute. You know what money this is?

Skimmerhorn. No.

[BIGGS *picks up a discarded envelope.*]

Biggs. It came out of the Nanuet bank.

[SKIMMERHORN *takes the envelope from him.*]

Skimmerhorn. If that little guy's a bank robber he's certainly careless with the proceeds.

Biggs. That's where it came from.

Skimmerhorn. In that case we ought to give it back. For the reward.

Biggs. No reward offered yet.

Skimmerhorn. Maybe we ought to give it back anyway.

Biggs. Think so?

Skimmerhorn. Might be marked bills.

Biggs. No, it's not. I was talking with the president of the bank on the 'phone. Made up for a pay roll. No marks on any of it.

Skimmerhorn. It ought to be returned, though.

Biggs. Sure, it should. Question is, will it be?

Skimmerhorn. I think so, don't you?

Biggs. I'm inclined to think so. Bank robbing's away out of my line.

Skimmerhorn. Mine, too, as a matter of fact. The president of the bank's a friend of yours?

Biggs. Yes, he is, in a way. Oh, he's gypped me a couple of times, same as you would.

Skimmerhorn. He wouldn't lose anything.

Biggs. Oh, no, he's insured.

Skimmerhorn. Has it occurred to you the little Dutchman that was here might not mean any good to us?

Biggs. Did you see a little Dutchman?

Skimmerhorn. I thought I did, there for a minute.

Biggs. I don't believe that any more.

Skimmerhorn. Certainly doesn't sound very likely.

Biggs. We'd better count it. Man never ought to carry money around without knowing how much it is.

Skimmerhorn. Yeah, let's count it. It said twenty-five thousand in the paper.

Biggs. You know, nobody in the world would ever know who had it?

Skimmerhorn. No, they wouldn't.

Biggs. What do you say?

Skimmerhorn. I say fifty-fifty.

Biggs. Damn you, Skimmerhorn, if I hadn't been in business with you for twenty years I'd say you were a crook!

Skimmerhorn. If I wasn't a crook after twenty years with you I'd be slow in the head and hard of hearing!

Biggs. What's fifty per cent of twenty-five thousand? Twelve thousand five hundred? And what's forty per cent? Ten thousand! Are you going to hold up the deal for two thousand five hundred?

Skimmerhorn. I certainly am.

Biggs. All right, take it. Fifty-fifty on this one deal.

Skimmerhorn. And on the Van Dorn deal, too.

Biggs. Why, you fat louse—
  [Van Dorn *comes in from the right out of the shadows.*]

Van. Sorry to bother you gentlemen, but—

Biggs.
  [*As they stuff the bills into their pockets*]
  Where the hell did you come from?

Van. Why, you're not friends of mine, but there's a storm blowing in and it occurred to me I might show you where you could keep dry under a ledge.

Biggs. Thanks. Much obliged.

Van. Want me to go with you?

Biggs. No, thanks—Let's get a little nearer the light.

Skimmerhorn. Good idea.

[BIGGS *and* SKIMMERHORN *go out right.* VAN *looks after them, then picks up one of the discarded envelopes and studies it. He sits.* LISE *comes up the rocks in the rear and stands looking out to the river, shading her eyes from the beacon.*]

Lise. You who have watched this river in the past
till your hope turned bitterness, pity me now,
my hope gone, but no power to keep my eyes
from the mocking water. The hills come down like
        sand,
and the long barges bear them off to town,
to what strange market in what stranger town,
devouring mountains? but never, in all days,
never, though I should watch here without rest,
will any ship come downward with the tide
flying the flag we knew.

[VAN *rises.* LISE *draws back an instant, then comes down a step toward him.*]

Do you hear my voice?

Van. Yes, lady.

Lise. Do you see me in the light,
as I see you?

Van. Yes.

Lise. You are one of those
the earth bears now, the quick, fierce wizard men
who plow the mountains down with steel, and set
new mountains in their sky. You've come to drive
machines through the white rock's heart.

Van. Not I. I haven't.
I hate them all like poison.

Lise. You're against them—
  the great machines?

Van. I'd like to smash the lot,
  and the men that own them.

Lise. Oh, if there were a friend
  among so many enemies! I wish
  I knew how to make you friend. But now my voice
  shrinks back in me, reluctant, a cold thing,
  fearing the void between us.—I have seen you.
  I know you. You are kind.

Van. How do you know?

Lise. When I have been most lonely in the spring,
  the spring rain beating with my heart, I made
  a wild flower garden; none of these I knew,
  for none I knew are here, flowers of the woods,
  little and lovely, nameless. One there was
  like a pink moccasin, another low
  with blotted leaves, wolf-toothed, and many more
  rooted among the fern. I saw you then
  come on this garden, secret as the tears
  wept for lost days, and drew my breath in dread
  that you should laugh and trample it. You smiled
  and then went on. But when I came again
  there was a new flower growing with the rest,
  one I'd not seen. You brought and placed it there
  only for love of gardens, ignorant whose
  the garden you enriched. What was this flower?

Van. Wild orchid. It was your garden?

Lise. Yes. You know
  the names of all the flowers?

Van. Yes.

Lise. But then
you'd teach them to me?

Van. Yes.

Lise. Teach me the names.
What is the tall three-petaled one that's black
almost, the red's so dark?

Van. That's trillium.
Speaking of flowers, tell me your name.

Lise. It's Lise,
or used to be.

Van. Not now?

Lise. I'm weary of it,
and all things that I've been. You have a lover?
She'll be angry?

Van. She's angry now. She's off
and gone. She won't come back.

Lise. Love me a little,
enough to save me from the dark. But if
you cannot give me love, find me a way!
The seas lie black between your harbor town
and mine, but your ships are quick. If I might see
the corner where the three streets come to an end
on sundial windows, there, a child by a fire—
no, but it's gone!

Van. I've seen you on the hills
moving with shadows. But you're not shadow.

Lise. No.
   Could one live and be shadow?

Van. Take my hand.

Lise. I dare not.

Van. Come, let me see your garden.

Lise. No.
   I dare not. It is your race that thins our blood
   and gathers round, besieging us with charms
   to stay the feet of years. But I know you kind.—
   Love me a little. Never put out your hand
   to touch me, lest some magic in your blood
   reach me, and I be nothing. What I am
   I know not, under these spells, if I be cloud
   or dust. Nor whether you dream of me, or I
   make you of light and sound. Between this stone
   and the near constellations of the stars
   I go and come, doubting now whence I come
   or when I go. Cling to me. Keep me still.
   Be gentle. You were gentle with the orchid—
   Take my hand now.

Van. You're cold.

Lise. Yes.

Van. Here on the Tor
   the sun beats down like murder all day long
   and the wind comes up like murder in the night.
   I'm cold myself.

Lise. How have I slipped so far
   from the things you have? I'm puzzled here and lost.
   Is it so different for you? Keep my hand

and tell me. In these new times are all men shadow?
All men lost?

Van. Sometimes I stand here at night
and look out over the river when a fog
covers the lights. Then if it's dark enough
and I can't see my hands or where the rock
leaves off against the cloud, and I'm alone,
then, well I'm damned if I know who I am,
staring out into that black. Maybe I'm cloud
and maybe I'm dust. I might be old as time.
I'd like to think I knew. A man gets that way
standing staring at darkness.

Lise. Then—you do know.
It's better now.—Somewhere along a verge
where your life dips in dusk and my gray days
lift to the light a moment, we walk there
and our eyes meet.—Look, when the wizards come
to tear the mountain down, I'll have no place.
I'll be gone then.

Van. Child, they won't get our mountain!
Not if I have to shoot them as they come
they won't get our mountain! The mountain's mine,
and you're to make your garden where you like;
their feet won't step across it! All their world's
made up of fat men doing tricks with laws
to manage tides and root up hills. The hills
can afford to laugh at them! A race of grubs
bred down from men!

Lise. Is it the light I feel
come flooding back in me? Light or their charms
broken here, seeing your face?

Van. Your hands are warm.

Lise. I'm not cold now; for an instant I'm not cold,
seeing your face. This is your wizardry.
Let me stand here and see you.

Elkus.
[*Outside*]

Somewhere around here it was. Over toward the crane.

Dope.
[*Outside*]

What'd you go and put down the satchel for?

Elkus.
[*Outside*]

How did I know he'd sit on top of it?
[VAN *and* LISE *slip out through the rocks at the rear.* ELKUS *and*
DOPE *come in furtively from the right.*]

Dope. That's where. Under that rock.

Elkus. Keep your eye peeled. They're probably beating
the woods for us.

Dope. What's that?
[*He picks up an envelope.*]

Elkus. They got it.

Dope. God damn the rotten business! Now we will get
four hundred years.

Elkus. Now you're saying it—

Dope. What are we going to do?

Elkus. I'm going to send Buddy back with sandwiches to
see if the Judge got the money. If he did we'll stick
him up.

Dope. Hey, how about the troopers?

Elkus. If that was troopers I'm Admiral Dewey. Troopers would a' used the artillery. Come on.

Dope. O.K. Some pennies here.

Elkus. To hell with 'em.

[DOPE *flings the pennies to the left along the ledge.*]

Dope. Get going.

[ELKUS *and* DOPE *go out right.* BIGGS *and* SKIMMERHORN *come in along the ledge.*]

Biggs. Now it's raining money. I got the price of a morning paper square in the eye.

Skimmerhorn. I've got two thousand five hundred in a breast pocket, five thousand in a side pocket, and five thousand in the billfold.

[*He slaps his rear.*]

How do I look?

Biggs. No different. Just a lot of slop tied up with string. I've got five thousand in each side pocket and two thousand five hundred in the back. How do I look?

Skimmerhorn. You? All you need now's a pair of wings.

Biggs. Wish I could find the little guy with the big heart that gave us the money. Maybe he'd help us down off this devil's belfry.

Skimmerhorn. How about that shovel? Any possibility of making it pick us up and set us down below there?

Biggs. Well—if anybody was running it, sure. If it swung us over on that dump we could slide the rest of the

way. You might wear out that last five thousand of
yours, the five thousand that's bringing up the rear
there.

Skimmerhorn. When do they come to work in the morning?

Biggs. They won't come to work tomorrow. They can't do
any more till we buy this land.

Skimmerhorn. That's fine. That's just dandy.

Biggs. Nice idea though. Somebody might come along
that could run the engine.

Skimmerhorn. You don't think that boy's coming back
with the sandwiches?

Biggs. No, I don't.

Skimmerhorn. The way I feel inside I may never live to
spend the money.

Biggs. Who you going to leave it to?

Skimmerhorn. Yeah?

Biggs. Oh, all right. Nothing personal.

> [*They sit facing the audience. The* CAPTAIN *and* HIS CREW, *in-
> cluding* DEWITT, *seep in through the rocks about them
> and stand quietly looking on.*]

There was something in that—what you said about
needing a pair of wings.

Skimmerhorn. I should say that wings was the last thing
likely to grow on you. You might grow horns, or a
cloven hoof, or a tail, but wings, no. Not unless somebody slipped up behind you and bashed you over the
head.

Biggs. You know, you'd murder me for what I've got in my pockets?

Skimmerhorn. You thought of it first. Who am I going to leave it to, you said.

Biggs. Just the same I wouldn't feel right if you were standing behind me with a rock in your hand.
[*The* CREW *move in a little.*]

Skimmerhorn. You wouldn't?

Biggs. No. At the moment I wouldn't like to think anybody was creeping up behind me.
[*He stiffens.*]

And by God there is somebody behind me.

Skimmerhorn.
[*Without turning*]

What makes you think so?

Biggs.
[*Running a hand over his hair*]

I just feel it. Turn around, will you? Take a look.

Skimmerhorn.
[*Shivering*]

I will not.—Now you've got me worried.—Or else I'm getting light-headed for lack of food.
[BIGGS *ducks suddenly, as if from an imaginary blow.* SKIMMER-HORN *dodges in sympathy, and with their heads drawn in like turtles they creep forward on hands and knees.*]

Biggs. See anything?

Skimmerhorn. There's nothing there, you ass! What are you dodging? Want to scare me to death? Go on, turn around and face it like a man!

Biggs. Now!

Skimmerhorn. Now!

> [*They whirl in concert, on their knees, facing the* CREW. *They look at each other.*]

Biggs. You're crazy!

Skimmerhorn. I certainly am. And so are you.

Biggs. That isn't there at all. There's nothing there.

Skimmerhorn. All right, you go up and hit it. I'll stay right here, and you go punch it in the nose.

> [BIGGS *stands up.*]

Biggs. Uh—how do you do?—Maybe you—wanted to give us something, huh?

> [*To* DEWITT.]

Uh—I see you brought your friends with you.—If you want the money back you can have it, you know. We don't want the money.

> [*He sticks a hand in his pocket.*]

How much was it now?

> [*The* CREW *look at each other gravely, tapping their foreheads.* SKIMMERHORN *rises.*]

Anything we could do, you know, we'd be glad to do. We're just trying to get down off here.

Skimmerhorn. You know what it is, Art; it's a moving picture company. And have they got the laugh on us?

Thinking they're real. It's all right, boys, we're onto
you.

Biggs. Is that so? Say, I guess that's so. Was that moving
picture money, you gave us, you fellows? We thought
that was real. Ha ha! That's a good one. I guess you
must have thought we were pretty funny, backing up
that way and jumping around. You had us scared stiff!
[*The* CREW *shake their heads at each other.*]

Skimmerhorn. Come on, now, you aren't bluffing us at all.
We've seen the pictures work over at Suffern. We were
right out on location there with actors and producers
and everything. Some of those girls didn't care whether
they wore clothes or not. You're probably used to that
where you come from, but I certainly got a kick out of
pictures. Fifty chorus girls changing clothes in the
bushes over there.

 A silence. DEWITT *goes over to the* CAPTAIN *and whispers in his
 ear.*]

Asher. Lay a hand to it.

 [DEWITT *catches hold of the dangling cable.*]

DeWitt. Lay a hand to it, lads. Heave.

 [*The* CREW *catch the rope and haul on it, sailor-fashion. The
 shovel begins to descend.*]

The Crew.

 [*Pulling down*]

   Heave! Heave! Heave! Heave!
   Coming a blow, coming a blow;
   Sea runs black; glass runs low;
   Heave! Heave!

Yardarm dips; foam's like snow!
Heave!
[*The shovel touches ground.*]

Biggs. Say, that's an act if I ever saw one. What kind of
picture you putting on?
[*The* CAPTAIN *points to the interior of the shovel, looking at*
BIGGS *and* SKIMMERHORN.]

What's up, anyway? Want us to go aboard? You know,
we were just saying if somebody could run that thing
we might get across to the dump and slide down out
of here. Think you could swing it across there?
[*The* SAILORS *maneuver behind the two, edging them into the*
machine.]

You might haul us up there and not be able to get us
down, you know. It's mighty friendly of you to try it,
but you'll have your work cut out. Sure, I'll get in. I'll
try anything once.
[*He steps in,* SKIMMERHORN *follows reluctantly. The* CAPTAIN *and*
DEWITT *guard their retreat. The* SAILORS *catch hold of*
the cable.]

Take it easy, now.

The Crew.
Hoist! Hoist! Hoist! Hoist!
Tar on a rope's end, man on a yard.
Wind through an eye-bolt, points on a card;
Hoist! Hoist!
Weevil in the biscuit, rats in the lard,
Hoist!
[*They haul the two up as far as seems necessary, and swing the*
crane out over the abyss. Then they stop to contemplate
their handiwork.]

Biggs. I'll tell you what—if you catch that line over there some of you can hold back while the rest pull and that'll swing it around.—If that don't work you'd better pull it down again and we'll just wait till morning.

[*The* Crew *continue to stare silently.*]

Skimmerhorn. I'm getting sick at my stomach, boys; you better make it snappy. It gives me the megrims to look down this way.

[*He draws his feet up suddenly.*]

Biggs. Hey, don't rock the boat, you fool! It's a thousand miles straight down!

Skimmerhorn. I'm going to be sick.

Biggs. You better take us down, fellows. It's no good. You can't make it.

DeWitt. How about a game of bowls?

[*The* Captain *nods.*]

Pieter. Aye, a game of bowls.

[*Led by the* Captain, *the* Crew *begin to file out.*]

Biggs. Hey, you wouldn't leave us up here, would you? Hey, listen! You! You can have that money back, you know! We don't want the money! What in the name of time?—Listen, what did we ever do to you?—A joke's a joke, after all, but this thing might let go any minute! What's more you're responsible if anything happens to us! There's such a thing as laws in this country!

[*But they have all gone.*]

Skimmerhorn. I'm sick.

Biggs. You'll be sicker before you're out of this mess.— What do you think they meant by that?

Skimmerhorn. I don't know.—Quit kicking me, will you? I'm sick.

Biggs. Well, keep it to yourself.

Skimmerhorn. I wish I thought I could.

Biggs. Help, somebody! Help! We're stuck up here!

Skimmerhorn. What good's that going to do?

Biggs. You don't think they'll leave us here, do you?

Skimmerhorn. I don't know. I don't care. I wish I was dead!—Say, keep away from me, will you? What are you trying to do, pick my pocket?

Biggs. Pick your pocket, you fish? All I ask is keep your feet out of my face.

Skimmerhorn. Well, where in hell's my bill-fold?

Biggs. How do I know? Do you think I took it?

Skimmerhorn. Come on, now. Where is it?
   [*He searches his clothes frantically.*]

Biggs. You're probably sitting on it.—You are sitting on it. There it is.

Skimmerhorn.
   [*Finding it.*]

Jeez, I might have lost it.

Biggs. Now you'd better count it. Just to make sure it's good.

Skimmerhorn. I think I will.
   [*He begins to count the bills.*]

It's good money, Art. Look at it.

Biggs. Not a bad idea, either.

> [*He takes out money and counts it. There is a flash, a long roll and a crash of thunder. Then another and another.*]

Isn't that coming pretty close?

Skimmerhorn. What?

Biggs. The lightning, you fool! Put your money away before you get it wet. You know what I think?

Skimmerhorn. No.

Biggs. There's something up there taking pot shots at us.

Skimmerhorn. There's one thing about money you find. You don't have to pay income tax on it.

Biggs. That's true.

> [*There is a terrific flash, a crash, and the stage is in darkness.*]

That one got the beacon!

> [*Another flash runs right down the crane.*]

Good God, will you quit that? That's close enough!—
Say, do you know any prayers?

Skimmerhorn. I know one.

Biggs. Say it, will you?

Skimmerhorn. Matthew, Mark, Luke and John,
Bless the bed that I lie on.

Biggs. That's not much good, that one.

Skimmerhorn. It's the only one I know.--Hey, catch it--
hey!

Biggs. What?

[*The lightning is now an almost perpetual illumination, the thunder a constant roll.*]

Skimmerhorn. I dropped fourteen ten dollar bills!

Biggs. Do you know we're going to die here?

Skimmerhorn. We're going to what?

Biggs. Will you quit counting money? We're going to be killed! We're going to die right here in our own steam shovel!

Skimmerhorn. Oh, no. I can't die now. I'm not ready to die!

Biggs. I wish you'd put up your money, then, and pray!

Skimmerhorn. I don't know how to pray.

[*A crash*]

Biggs.

[*On his knees*]

Oh, God, I never did this before, and I don't know how, but keep me safe here and I'll be a better man! I'll put candles on the altar, yes, I'll get that Spring Valley church fixed up, the one that's falling down! I can do a lot for you if you'll let me live! Oh, God—

[*A crash*]

Skimmerhorn.

[*On his knees, his hands full of money*]

Oh, God, you wouldn't do a thing like that, hang us up in our own steam shovel, wet through, and then strike us with lightning! Oh, God, you've been kind to us to-

night, and given us things we never expected to get so
easy; don't spoil it now!—God damn it, there goes another batch of bills!

[*He snatches at the falling money, and is hauled back by* BIGGS.]

I don't know how to pray! What makes you think
there's anybody up there, anyway?

[*Another crash*]

Biggs. Say the one you know then, for God's sake—say it!

Skimmerhorn. Matthew, Mark, Luke and John,
Bless the bed that I lie on!

Biggs. Matthew, Mark, Luke and John,
Bless the bed—Oh, God, I've got an old mother de-
pendent on me; please let me live! Why don't you tell
him you'll give the money back?

Skimmerhorn. Because I won't! And you won't, either!

[*A crash*]

Biggs. Now you've done it! Can't you keep anything to
yourself? There's such a thing as being politic, even
when you're talking to God Almighty!

[*Thunder again*]

CURTAIN

HIGH TOR

ACT TWO

ACT TWO

SCENE I

SCENE: *The Tor and the steam shovel as before, only five or six hours later. It's still pitch dark, and* BIGGS *and* SKIMMERHORN *are still in the shovel. They are, however, fast asleep in much the same postures they took formerly on the ground. Under the shovel sits* DEWITT, *picking up and smoothing on his knee a few bills which he has found blowing loose on the rock. The beacon light flashes into the scene.*

DeWitt. There comes on the light again, too, the sweeping light that withers a body's entrails. No sooner out than lit again.—

[*Two snores rise from the sleeping pair.*]

Aye, take your ease and rest, you detachable Doppelgangers, swollen with lies, protected by the fiends, impervious to lightning, shedding rain like ducks—and why wouldn't you shed rain? your complexions being pure grease and your insides blubber? You can sleep, you can rest. You of the two-bottoms. You make nothing of the lightning playing up and down your backbones, or turning in on cold iron, but a poor sailor out of Holland, what rest has he?—

[*He smooths a bill.*]

These will be tokens and signs, these will, useful in magic, potent to ward off evil or put a curse on your enemies. Devil's work or not, I shall carry them on me, and make myself a match for these fulminating latter-day spirits.

[*He pouches the bills.*]

73

I'm hanged if it's not noticeable at once, a sort of Dutch courage infused into the joints and tissues from the mere pocketing up of their infernal numbered papers.

[*He takes out a bill and looks at it.*]

That's sorcery, that's witchcraft, that's black art for you—that's a trick after the old one's heart; why, this stuff would make a man out of a cocked hat and a pair of crutches!

[*He slaps his chest.*]

Now I shall face destiny and take it like a pinch of snuff! Which reminds me I could use a pinch of snuff.

[*He takes out his snuffbox.*]

Snuff? When have I reached for snuff? It would seem to me I haven't gone after snuff in something like two hundred years!

[*He ladles into both nostrils and sneezes violently.*]

Aha, DeWitt! You're a man, DeWitt! A man and a devil! And what shall we wish for now that we have wishing papers in the pockets of our pantaloons? What but a woman, one of these new female furies of theirs, wearing pants like a man, and with nothing to indicate her sex but the general conformation!

[*He draws out bills.*]

Let my woman appear, god of the numbered papers, and let her wear what she likes, so long as a man can make out how she's made. Let her appear within this next three minutes, for God knows how long this mood will last in an old man!

[*He takes another pinch of snuff.*]

Aha! Destiny, present occasions!

[BUDDY *enters carrying beer and sandwiches.*]

Buddy. Hello.

DeWitt. What answer would a man make to that now? That's a strange greeting.

Buddy. Seen a couple of old fat men around anywhere?

DeWitt. Boy, I have seen nothing else all night.

Buddy. Where are they?

DeWitt. You wish to find a couple of old fat men?

Buddy. That's right.

DeWitt. I begin to doubt the supernal powers of these new angel-demons. Here he stands in their presence and asks very foolishly if old DeWitt has seen them.

Buddy. What's foolish about that?

DeWitt. A very cheap, witless little cabin boy unless all signs fail. One who carries packages and lives very badly by the day on half a skilling. A cabin boy.

Buddy. What's the matter with you?

DeWitt. What do you carry in the bag?

Buddy. That's my business.

DeWitt. He has a business then. He is not perhaps so witless as he appears.

Buddy. Are you going to tell me where those two are or do you want me to blow your brains out?

DeWitt. Is my carcass so thin you think to puff my brains out with a breath? Look, 'prentice devil, I am one of you. I bear your signs and symbols. Here you see your own countersign, a cabalistic device of extreme rarity and force. What have you in the bag?

Buddy. Nothing but sandwiches. What do you mean, you're one of us?

DeWitt.

[*Waving a sheaf of bills*]

You should recognize the insignium.

Buddy. Where'd you get it?

DeWitt. It blew away from these same two fat men, 'prentice devil, but now I have it, and it's mine and I obtain power over you. Let me see these sandwiches.

Buddy. It blew away from the fat men, huh? All right, that's what I want to know. It's mine, see? Hand it over.

DeWitt. You reveal yourself a very young and tender 'prentice.

Buddy. Hand it over or I'll fill you full of holes.

[*He sets down his packages and draws a gun, but* DeWitt *is beforehand with two flintlock pistols.*]

DeWitt. You will drop your child's armory on the ground, cabin boy, or I shall pull both triggers at once and blast you halfway to the water.

[BUDDY *drops the gun.*]

I tell you I am now a great devil and violent. When I wish merely I have my way.

[BUDDY *suddenly takes to his heels.* DeWitt *pulls the triggers one after another; the hammers click but there is no explosion.*]

Why, this new world is not so bad. I am left in possession of the field.

[*He picks up the automatic and the bag and retreats to his rock.*]

They fight with the weapons of children. Why, this new world begins to be mine, to do as I please with. Whatever kind of witch a sandwich may be come out and let me interrogate you.

[*He takes out sandwiches.*]

If it be the food eaten by witches and wizards so much the better, for I am now a wizard myself, and by the great jib boom I haven't tasted food in God knows when.

[*He eats.*]

A sweet and excellent morsel, very strong with garlic and salami, medicinal for the veins and bladder.

[*He looks at his pistols.*]

A little glazed powder in the priming now, and these two will speak with more authority if it becomes necessary to defend my position.

[*He opens his powder horn and renews the priming.*]

We have seen the time, these blunderbusses and myself, when we could defend a crow's nest against a whole crew in mutiny.

[*He pushes away the beer bottles with his foot.*]

I will eat your rations, cabin boy out of the new age, and I will master you all, men and maids, now that my strength comes back, but I will not drink your drink. As Pastor Van Dorf observed very wisely before we sailed; you may eat the food of the salvages, said he, when you have voyaged to the new lands overseas; you may share their rations, you may even make up to their females after the fashion of sailors when the flesh is weak, but drink none of their drink, said he, lest it prove to be Circe's liquor and turn you all to hogs.

[*He eats.*]

Now I have small inclination to be a hog, but a man I will be, and a very good man, too, of the fieriest model.

[*He hears* JUDITH'S *step.*]

Take care now, take care! I'm an armed man and a man of blood!

[JUDITH *enters.*]

Judith.

[*At some distance*]

I beg your pardon, sir—

DeWitt. A woman, by the great tropical cross, a salvage woman, come in answer to my unspoken desires.

[*He rises.*]

Your humblest servant, lady salvage; don't run away, please. I'm a poor lost little man, wouldn't hurt a fly.

Judith. Who are you?

DeWitt. I'm a poor bosun, ma'am, but grown, God knows how, to something of a person this last quarter hour.

Judith. Are you lost?

DeWitt. Completely adrift, ma'am, on my own mountain.

Judith. I don't think I've seen you before.

DeWitt. That may be, though I'm by way of being one

of the earliest inhabitants, not counting Indians and Patagonians.

Judith. You live on the mountain?

DeWitt. I maintain a residence here, though the situation eludes me at the moment.

Judith. Then you are acquainted with Van—Van Dorn?

DeWitt. I have seen him about.

Judith. Have you seen him tonight? I want to find him.

DeWitt. A mere blind, I should say, a maidenly defense, not to be too forthright; but sent by the talisman she is.

Judith. You have seen him?

DeWitt. God help him, I have, and in none too sanctified an attitude, saving your ladyship, for the lad was obviously a bit taken with the captain's wife, and she a married woman of some years' standing, young though she appear.

Judith. Where was he?

[*She takes a step nearer to him.*]

DeWitt. I was never one to break in on a budding romance, sweetheart, and out of sheer delicacy I looked the other way.

Judith. No, but where was he, please? I can show you the path.

DeWitt. If you hunt out a very pretty little mistress in a bonnet somewhat behind the fashion, and look under the bonnet, you may chance to find him there.

Judith. Who are you?

DeWitt. Alpheus DeWitt, your most humble, bosun in the King's navy.

Judith. Forgive me—I shall look elsewhere—

DeWitt. Oh, but I assure you the lad's head over ears, ma'am, and loathe you'd be to interrupt him. Now a pretty lass like yourself should have no trouble replacing one sailor man with another in these stirring times. They come and go like a run of salmon.

Judith. Thank you.

DeWitt. I am myself a notionable lad. Salt tears have been wept for me by one and another.

Judith. No doubt.

DeWitt. I'm a blunt man, but constant and of considerable substance on my own wharf. Could you find it in your heart to love me?

Judith. I'm sorry, no.

DeWitt. To save a sad and desperate man from such a death as the lines of frost on a window? This is a kindly face, this of mine, and a kindly heart under a worn jerkin. These are real tears on my cheeks, too, and I weep them for you, lady.

Judith. I've never seen you till this moment.

DeWitt. Yet you could save me from their sorcery, with one touch of your hand. I waited here for you, and you came.

Judith. You're horrible. Your face is horrible!

DeWitt. Is it, truly?

Judith. Ancient and terrible and horrible!—Tell me where he is. I must know.

DeWitt. I don't know where he is.—You will think better of it. You need only pity me a little at first, or even laugh at me—so you do it kindly—

Judith. I'm in no mood for laughing, though you're ridiculous enough in that get-up.

DeWitt. It's not the latest, I know. And I'm a sad and broken man, lady, lost here among the lesser known peaks on the west side of the world, and looking only for a hand to help me.

Judith. I don't think you're lost at all.

DeWitt. Yes, lady, quite lost.—Nevertheless they run from me! You should have seen the lad run when I snapped my pistols at him.

Judith.

[*Stepping back*]

I should think he would.—Isn't there someone coming there now?

[*She points to the right.* DeWitt *faces about, reaching for his pistols.* Judith *slips away left.*]

DeWitt. If there be, watch what soldierly stand old De-Witt makes in defense of a lady! Come out, children of the new Satan, show yourselves in the light!

[Elkus *and* Dope *appear at right.*]

Elkus. Stick 'em up, bo!

[*They train automatics on him.*]

DeWitt. More toys! Stand back, you cheap new devils!

Elkus. Keep your hands down or I'll let you have it!

DeWitt. Watch now how a man holds off the fiends.
[*He lifts his pistols.*]

Elkus. Give it to him!
[*They fire a fusillade at* DEWITT, *who stands unmoved.*]

DeWitt. Firecrackers! You think me a devil like yourselves, to be exorcised with firecrackers?

Elkus. Give it to him again!
[*They fire once more.*]

DeWitt. Look, you puny devils, I'm a patient man, but in one moment I shall blow you both into the Tappan Zee!

Elkus.
[*Stepping up and pouring bullets into him*]

Too bad about you!
[*To* DOPE]

Take the money off him.

Dope. There's something funny about this guy! I can see right through him!

Elkus. No wonder. He's full of holes as a tennis racket.

Dope. No, by God, I can see through him! Look!
[*They step back together.*]

Elkus. What kind of a thing are you?

DeWitt. I'm not a man to be daunted by loud noises and firecrackers, Beelzebub! Go seek your place with the new father of hell before I send you there! Wizards!

Elkus. Where's the money?

DeWitt. I have a talisman and I ate a sandwich, devils!

Dope. Look, he's a moving picture! He's a regular church window! Look!

DeWitt. Disperse or I fire!

Elkus. Keep out of the way of that sawed-off shotgun!
> [DOPE *suddenly runs in and shoots* DEWITT *through the head, then retreats.*]

DeWitt. I warn you I begin to be annoyed!

Dope. It's no use, chief. I blew his brains out, and he's standing right there!

Biggs.
> [*Looking over the side of the shovel*]

It's a war.

Elkus. Who said that?

Dope. Damned if I know.

Elkus. Beat it.

Dope. Yeah, beat it. Let the money hang. I'm for Canada.

Elkus You said it.
> [*They turn tail. As they are going* DEWITT *fires his pistols in the air.*]

DeWitt. Now am I master of the world of things,
a buccaneer, a devil and a rake!
Women love mastery, and they ran from me;
they ran, these minor devils, ran from DeWitt!
Look where they go there, sweetheart!
> [*He turns.*]

God, she's gone!
Lady! New-world lady! Are you lost?

[*He follows her.*]

Look now, I've dispersed them, brats and wizards,
spawn out of hell, they ran! I'm master here,
I'm master of the world! Look, lady!

[*He goes out left.*]

Skimmerhorn. Are you awake?

Biggs. I hope not. I hope this is a nightmare and I wake
up at home in bed

Skimmerhorn. How did we get here?

Biggs. It must have been something we ate.

Skimmerhorn. I didn't eat anything.

Biggs. There's a bag of sandwiches down there on the
ground.

Skimmerhorn. That's a pleasant thought.

Biggs. Look for yourself.

Skimmerhorn. You're right. It's a bag of sandwiches.

Biggs. Didn't we send somebody for sandwiches and beer,
away back there before all this started?

Skimmerhorn. I don't know. I'm all wet, and I'm stuck
to the shovel.

Biggs. You do seem to be kind of going to pieces. What's
the matter with your toupee?

Skimmerhorn. The glue must have melted.

[*He takes off his wig.*]

Now I'll catch cold.

Biggs. If any of your constituency sees you in that condition you're out of office for good.

Skimmerhorn. I don't even care if I fall out. I feel terrible.

Biggs. Might be more comfortable for me if you did fall out.

   [*He shifts his weight.*]

Skimmerhorn. Sit down! Quit rocking the boat!

Biggs. I've got a cramp. O ich!

Skimmerhorn. Don't shove me!

   [*He pushes* Biggs.]

Biggs.

   [*Pushing back*]

You want to pitch me overboard?

Skimmerhorn. Hey! You know I might have gone out?

Biggs. What do you care?

Skimmerhorn. I'll show you what I care!

   [*They lock in a deadly struggle on the verge.*]

Biggs. Wait, Skimmer, look now! If one of us goes down the other goes too. Look at the drop. You don't want to splash on those rocks and I don't either.

Skimmerhorn. Let go then.

Biggs. I'll let go when you do. I'll count three and we'll both let go.

Skimmerhorn. All right.

Biggs. One—two—three.
> [*They let go and catch the ropes over the swinging basket.*]

That's better. Now take it easy, buddy. You woke up feeling like poison this morning. After this you count ten when you get an impulse to push anybody.

Skimmerhorn. Same to you.

Biggs. Fine.
> [*They sit down cautiously.*]

Skimmerhorn. How in hell did those sandwiches get there?

Biggs. How in hell did we get here?

Skimmerhorn. You haven't got a fishing hook on you, have you?

Biggs. No, I haven't.
> [*They sit gloomily looking at the sandwiches.* LISE *and* VAN *come in from the left.*]

Van. Nothing in all the woods
is silent as the owl; you see his shadow
but never hear his wings. The partridge now,
every time he takes off he creaks and cranks
like an old Ford. You never heard such a fuss;
but he's quiet on the ground.

Lise. And is there a squirrel
that flies, bird-fashion?

Van. Well, there's a flying squirrel,
but he's more the glider type. No engine, see,

but he'll do thirty yards. He's on the way
to be a bat if he's not careful.

Lise. How?

Van. He'll leave off tail and put on wing until
he's mostly wing. No doubt the bat was once
some kind of flying mouse.

Lise. Some men have wings.
I've seen them overhead.

Van. That's all put on.
They've no more wings than a goat. When they come
down.

Lise. I've hoped that it was true that men had wings.

Van. Why?

Lise. Oh, they've lived so long, and tried so hard,
and it all comes to nothing.

Van. Having wings,
would that be something?

Lise. Yes, it seems so. And yet
a bird has wings.

Van. And he gets nowhere.

Lise. Yes.
Nothing but just to be a bird, and fly,
and then come down. Always the thing itself
is less than when the seed of it in thought
came to a flower within, but such a flower
as never grows in gardens.

Biggs. Eh—Van Dorn!

Van.

  [*Looking up*]

  What are you doing on the roost, you birds?
  Building a nest?

Biggs. We can't get down.

Van. I'd say
  it ought to be just as easy to get down
  as it was to get up there.

Skimmerhorn. Will you help us out?

Van. You look all right to me. What happened to you?

Biggs. Everything.

Van. How did you get there?

Biggs. God,
  it's a long story.

Van. You've been there all night?

Biggs. Yes, all night.

Van. I wouldn't want to spoil it.
  It's too good to be true. You see those two,
  Lise, there in the scoop?

Lise. They're pitiful.
  Shouldn't you help them?

Van. No. Since time began
  there haven't been two fat-guts that deserved
  a hoisting like those two. In their own machine—
  that makes it perfect.

Lise. What have they done?

Van. They've been
    themselves, that's all. Two thieves, a probate judge
    and a manipulator, hand and glove
    to thieve what they can get. They've got High Tor
    among other things, and mean to carve it down,
    at three cents a square yard.

Lise. These poor old men?

Van. Yes, these poor old men.

Lise. Let them hang there then!

Van. They'll hang there for all me.
    [LISE *and* VAN *turn to go.*]

Skimmerhorn. I'll tell you what,
    Van Dorn, I'll let you have that validation
    if you'll help me down.

Van. That means I'd own the land?

Skimmerhorn. Yes, you'd own it.

Van. Only you'd cancel it,
    once you got down.

Skimmerhorn. To tell the truth I couldn't,
    not if you had the paper.

Van. Toss it over;
    I'd like to see it.
    [SKIMMERHORN *gets out an envelope and throws it to* VAN.]

Biggs. You're a simple judge!
    Now the land's his.

Van. There's a bond goes with this,
    a bond signed by the court. Oh, I looked it up.
    I've read that much law.

Skimmerhorn. Yes, I'll keep the bond
　till we're on your level.

Van. Then I'd advise you both
　to make yourself a nest with two-three sticks,
　like a couple of crows, and settle down to see
　what you can hatch—or maybe lay an egg—
　you'll have plenty of time.

Biggs. Come now, Van Dorn,
　we're in a bad way. It drops off straight down
　a thousand feet here, and Judge Skimmerhorn
　has vertigo. Why, just to save a life,
　out of common humanity, lean on that cable
　and pull us in.

Van. This one?
　　[*He pulls. The shovel dips.*]

Biggs. Oh, no, no! God,
　do you want to dump us out!

Van. You said to pull it.

Biggs. Not that one! This! Pull up on that again!
　We're sliding!

Van. Sure.
　　[*He rights the shovel.*]

　Now you know how it feels
　when you kick out the props from under men
　and slide 'em on the relief rolls. Ever think
　how that might feel?

Biggs. You don't know what we've both
　been through, Van Dorn. Rained on and struck by
　　　　　　　lightning,

no dinner; we're half-crazy; we've had nightmares,
funny people in hats; that's how we got here,
one of those nightmares!

Van. You sound disconnected.
Maybe you've lost your minds; still I'm not melting
down in my shoes with compunction. The fact is
he's clinging to the bond, Judge Skimmerhorn;
he's not too sunk for that. Now here's my bargain:
You're hanging onto life by one steel cable,
but that's much safer than the spider web
most men have to trust to. Toss me the bond,
Judge Skimmerhorn, or I'll give this line a yank
and you won't even hang.

Skimmerhorn. You wouldn't do it.

Van. Oh, wouldn't I? For a two-cent lollipop
I'd pull the chain right now!

Skimmerhorn. You wouldn't do it!

Van. Hang on, then! Just for a taste, how's the incline
now?
A little steep?
[*He pulls the line. The shovel tips as before.*]

Biggs. Pull it up! Take the God damn bond!—
throw it to him!

Skimmerhorn. I will not!

Van. Try this then.
[*He tips the shovel further.*]

Biggs. Give him his bond! I'm slipping!

Skimmerhorn. I will not!

Biggs. I say you will! What good's the money to you
if you're bologny?

Skimmerhorn. What money?

Biggs. You know what money!

Skimmerhorn. Straighten it up.

Van. Do I get the bond?

Skimmerhorn. Hell, yes!
   [VAN *restores their equilibrium.*]

You get the bond if you agree to accept
five thousand for your claim.
   [*He brings out a paper.*]

Van. Don't stall with me!
I'll never have a chance like this again,
and it's hard to resist!

Skimmerhorn. I'm offering you five thousand!
Five thousand! Cash!

Van.
   [*Leaping to the rope.*]

Keep it!

Biggs. Give him his bond!
   [*He wrenches the paper from* SKIMMERHORN *and sails it to* VAN.]

And now you've got it how's five thousand sound?
You settle for it?

Van. Bid against them, Lise. It's a game.
What would you say, Lise?
They offer me five thousand.

Lise. Pieces of silver?

Van. Pieces of silver.

Lise.

[*Smiling*]

But I'll give you more!
Only five thousand for this crag at dawn
shedding its husk of cloud to face a sunrise
over the silver bay? For silver haze
wrapping the crag at noon, before a storm
cascading silver levin? For winter rains
that run in silver down the black rock's face
under a gray-sedge sky? For loneliness
here on this crag? I offer you nine thousand!
To be paid in silver!

Van. You hear? I've got nine thousand;
what am I offered?

Biggs. Make it ten thousand—
and let us down in the bargain!

Van. Yes? Ten thousand?
A mountain for ten thousand? Hear them, Lise,
In their despair they lift it by a grand!
Should it go for ten?

Skimmerhorn. We'll never get it back—
but that's all right.

Van. Yes, Lise?

Lise. Will they pay
no more then for the piling of this stone,
set in its tall hexagonals by fire
before men were? Searching a hundred kingdoms

men will not find a site for lodge or tower
more kingly! A hundred thousand, sir, in silver,
this is my offer!

Van. Come now, meet it boys—
I have a hundred thousand!

Biggs. She's a fraud!
She's no dealer; she's a ringer, primed
to put the price up! What do you mean by silver?
She won't pay silver!

Van. Coinage of the moon,
but it's current here!

Skimmerhorn. Ten thousand, cash, and that's
the last. Five thousand out of my pocket, see,
and five from Biggs!
   [*He pulls out a bundle of bills.* BIGGS *does the same.*]

Take a good look at cash,
see how that operates!
   [*He tosses down the roll.* BIGGS *follows suit.*]

Van. You go well-heeled
when you go mountain-climbing. Is it real?

Skimmerhorn. Well, look it over. Count it.
   [VAN *takes up one packet, then another.*]

Van. Where did this come from?

Skimmerhorn. Where would you think?

Van. I'll say I got a shock.
   [*He studies the bills again.*]

I don't want your money.

Biggs. What's wrong with it?

Van. Didn't I tell you I had a hundred thousand?
   Take the stuff back. We reckon in moonlight here!
   Put up your mitts!
   [*He tosses the bundles back.*]

Biggs. It's yours if you want it.

Van. No,
   oh, no, I thank you. It's no sale. What's more
   I never meant to sell. The auctioneer's
   about to take a walk.

Biggs. Well, look, we're sitting
   right where we were.

Van. You sit there for your health,
   and think it over.

Skimmerhorn. You won't do that, Van Dorn,
   just leave us here.

Van. Watch me, if you don't think so.
   [*He gives an arm to* LISE.]
   Let me tell you about those babes in the wood,
   did I say they were thieves?
   [*They start out.*]

Biggs. Make it fifteen!

Van. Go to sleep.

Skimmerhorn. Well, twenty! and let us down!

Van. Sweet dreams.

Skimmerhorn. We'll run you out of the state, Van Dorn!

Van. You'll have to get down first!

Skimmerhorn. Is he going away
and leave us sitting?

Biggs. Looks like it.
    [VAN *and* LISE *move off.*]

Skimmerhorn. Say, Van Dorn,
will you pitch us up a sandwich?

Van. Sure; they're soggy,
lying out in the rain.
    [*He returns and tosses sandwiches to them.*]

Biggs. Thanks.

Van. Don't mention it.
    [*He goes out right with* LISE. BIGGS *and* SKIMMERHORN *unwrap*
      sandwiches.]

Skimmerhorn. He got away with that bond.

Biggs. Yeah.

Skimmerhorn. Looks as if we wouldn't make anything on
Van Dorn.

Biggs. That's what it looks like.

Skimmerhorn. Christ.

Biggs. Well, we've still got the windfall.

Skimmerhorn. Yeah, we've got that.

Biggs. And here he comes again.

Skimmerhorn. Who?

Biggs. Our mascot, little rabbit's foot, little good-luck
token, little knee-high with the big heart.
[DEWITT *comes in from the left, looks at the place where the
sandwiches were and then at the two in the shovel. He
mutters.*]

DeWitt. Magic again! More devil's work! And the woman
gone, slipped round a turn, and the scent was cold
for an old dog like me. By the mizzen yards,
it's wearing to the temper of a man
even if he's not choleric!—And those two,
those buzzards of evil omen, brooding there
on how they'll cut the mountain like a pie
and sell it off in slices!
[*He looks at his pistols.*]

One apiece.
It should be just enough, and it's a wonder
I never thought of it.
[*He lifts his pistols, the two drop their sandwiches into the
void, and cower down; he clicks the hammers.*]

Damp again! Well, boys,
we'll fix that.
[*He sits down to freshen the priming.*]

They'll brood over us no more,
those two sea-lions. Damn the rain and mist;
it penetrates the priming! Damn the flint,
and damn the spring! A brace of fine horse-pistols,
that's what the Jew said back in Amsterdam;
it takes a horse to cock 'em. Now then, damn you,
blow 'em off their perch!
[*As he rises his eye catches something out on the Zee. He stands
transfixed for a moment, watching.*]

It can't be there!
　　It's there! It's gone! I saw it! Captain Asher!
　　Captain! Captain! Captain! Captain Asher!
　　　　[BIGGS *and* SKIMMERHORN *have ducked down again.* DEWITT
　　　　rushes out to the right, firing his pistols in the air in his
　　　　excitement. BIGGS *sits up, then* SKIMMERHORN.]

Skimmerhorn. Am I hurt? Do you see blood anywhere?

Biggs. It seems there was nothing there.
　　　　[*They contemplate the place where* DEWITT *stood.*]

CURTAIN

ACT TWO

Scene II

Scene: *Another part of the Tor.* Lise *is sitting high up on a ledge,
looking out over the Zee.* Van *stands near her, looking at her
as she speaks. She has his old felt hat in her lap and has woven
a wreath of dandelions around the brim. The beacon light
strikes athwart her face.*

Lise. But nobody likes this flower?

Van. I like it now.
I used to think it was a weed, but now,
well, it's a flower now.

Lise. The dandelion.
Where will you find another prodigal
so merry or so golden or so wasteful,
pouring out treasure down the sides of hills
and cupping it in valleys?

Van. Buttercups
and touch-me-nots. The touch-me-not's a shoe,
a tiny golden shoe, with a hair-spring latchet
for bees to loosen.

Lise. When did you part from Judith?

Van. Judith?

Lise. When did she go away?

Van. Last evening.
But it seems longer.

Lise. Why?

Van. Why, a lot's happened.—
　It's almost morning.

Lise. How do you know?
　　　[*He steps up to the ledge.*]

Van. See that star,
　that heavy red star back in the west? When that
　goes down, then look for the morning star across
　Long Island Sound, and after that the lights
　dim down in the gray.

Lise. You loved her, very much?

Van. Yes.

Lise. I loved someone too. I love him still.

Van. No, you're mine now.
　　　[*He sits beside her.*]

Lise. See the great gulf that lies
　between the heavy red star down the west
　and the star that comes with morning? It's a long way.
　There's that much lies between us.

Van. Not for me.

Lise. Even for you.—You're weary?

Van. Well, the truth is
　I sometimes sleep at night.

Lise. Put your head down.
　I'll hold you.
　　　[*He lays his head on her knees and stretches out.*]

Now I'll wish that I could sing
　and make you sleep. Somehow they're all forgotten,

the old songs. Over and over when the birds
begin at morning I try hard to catch
one tune of theirs. There's one that seems to say:

> Merrily, merrily, chirr, chirr,
> Lueté, lueté, stee—
> Merrily, merrily, chirr, lueté,
> Chirr, lueté, stee.

That's only what it says; for what it sings
you'll have to ask the bird.

Van. I know it, though.
That's the song sparrow.

Lise. Have I come so near?

Van. Say it again.

Lise. I can't. May I ask you something?

Van. Yes.

Lise. There's so much that's changed now men can fly
and hear each other across seas, must men
still die—do they die still?

Van. Oh, yes, they die.
Why do you ask?

Lise. Because I'm still so young,
and yet I can't remember all the years
there must have been.—In a long night sometimes
I try to count them, but they blow in clouds
across the sky, the dancing firefly years,
incredible numbers.—Tell me how old you are
before you go to sleep.

Van. Lying here now
there's not much logic in arithmetic.

Five, or six, maybe. Five or six thousand, maybe.
But when I'm awake I'm twenty-three.

Lise. No more?

Van. No more.

Lise. Tell me why it is I am as I am
and not like you?

Van. I don't know, Lise.

Lise. But tell me.
Have I been enchanted here? I've seen
the trap-rock men, there in the shovel, seeming
so stupid and so pitiful. Could these
use charms and rites to hold wrecked mariners
forever in a deep cataleptic spell
high on a mountain-fringe?

Van. The trap-rock men?
They're no more wizards than I am. They buy
and sell, and when they've had their fill of dust
they die like the rest of us.

Lise. But they laid spells
about us?

Van. There are no wizards and no spells.
Just men and women and money and the earth
the way it always was. The trap-rock men
don't know you're here.

Lise. It's not sorcery then. If I had died
and left my bones here on the mountain-top
but had no memory of it, and lived on
in dreams, it might be as it is. As children

sure we were told of living after death,
but there were angels there, and onyx stone
paving an angel city, and they sang
eternally, no darkness and no sun,
nothing of earth. Now can it be men die
and carry thence no memory of death,
only this curious lightness of the hands,
only this curious darkness of the mind,
only to be still changeless with the winters
passing; not gray, not lined, not stricken down,
but stamped forever on the moving air,
an echo and an image? Restless still
with the old hungers, drifting among men,
till one by one forgotten, fading out
like an old writing, undecipherable,
we lose our hold and go? Could it be true?
Could this be how men die?

Van.

    [*Half asleep*]

  It may be, Lise.
I love you when you speak.

Lise. And I love you.
  But I am dead, and all the crew is dead;
all of the *Onrust* crew—and we have clung
beyond our place and time, on into a world
unreal as sleep, unreal as this your sleep
that comes upon you now. Oh, you were cruel
to love me and to tell me I am dead
and lie here warm and living! When you wake
we shall be parted—you will have a world
but I'll have none! There's a chill falls on me,
the night-dew gathering, or my mind's death chill—

knowing at last I know.—You haven't heard.
You told me this in a half-dream. You've been kind.
You never thought to hurt me. Are you asleep?

Van. I think I was.

Lise. Sleep, sleep. There was once a song,
if only I could call back air and words,
about a king who watched a goblet rising
and falling in the sea. It came to land
and on the rim the king's name was inscribed
with a date many years before. Oh, many years,
a hundred or three hundred. Then he knew
that all his life was lived in an old time,
swept out, given to the waters. What remained
was but this goblet swimming in the sea,
touching his dust by chance.—But he's asleep.
And very well he might be with dull stories
out of old songs.—Sleep, sweet; let me have
your head here on my knees, only this night,
and your brown hair round my finger.

> [*A girl's shadowy figure comes in from the right, walking lightly,
> pauses, as if at seeing them, and turns to go, the face still un-
> revealed.*]

Are you Judith?

Judith. Yes.

Lise. The lad's asleep, but when he wakes
you'll have him back.

Judith. Do you dispose of him
just as you please?

Lise. No. It's not what I please.
It's what will happen.

Judith. I don't know who you are.

Lise. I'm but a friend of his. You left him bitter
  going away so lightly. I was bitter—
  and so we tried to play at being lovers,
  but it won't do. He'll wake, and he'll be yours,
  all as it was. Only if I may hold him
  while he lies here asleep, it helps a little
  and I'll be happier.

Judith. You'll keep him then
  after he wakes.

Lise. No.

Judith. Then why are you crying?

Lise. Am I crying?
  Well, they're not for him, nor you, these tears;
  something so far away, so long ago,
  so hopeless, so fallen, so lost, so deep in dust
  the names wash from the urns, summons my tears,
  not love or longing. Only when you have him,
  love him a little better for your sake,
  for your sake only, knowing how bitterly
  I cried, for times past and things done.

Judith. You're strange—
  the dress you wear's strange, too.—Who are you then?
  I'm—afraid of you!

Lise. Afraid of tears
  and a voice out of long ago? It's all I have.

Judith. No—no—I'm not afraid. Only for him.
  I've done my crying, too.—Shall I come back?

Lise. Don't wake him now. Come back at dawn. You'll
    find him
here alone.

>   [Two *or* Three Sailors *appear on the rocks at the rear, looking
>   out over the Zee.*]

Pieter. Look for yourself.

A Sailor. Aye.

Pieter. Do you make her out?

The Sailor. She's the square top-yards.

Another Sailor. Now, God, if it were she!

Pieter. It's the brigantine! The *Onrust* from up-river
    tacking this way!

Asher.

>   [*Outside*]

Lise! Lise! Lise!

>   [*The* Captain *comes in at the rear with* DeWitt.]

Lise, the ship's on the river! Quick, there's haste!
She must catch the tide down-stream!

Lise. Hush! Hush! You'll wake him!

Asher. But look across the Zee! The *Onrust's* in
    and waiting for us!

Lise. But you say it, Asher,
    only to comfort me. There is no ship,
    nor are we caught in spells here, or enchanted,
    but spectres of an old time. The life we live
    is but a lingering, a clinging on,

our dust remembering. There is no ship,
only a phantom haunting down the Zee
as we still haunt the heights.

Asher. Look! The *Onrust!*
Look, Lise!

Lise. Yes, I see it.

Asher. Will you come?

Lise. Why would I stay? Why would I go? For go
or stay we're phantoms still.

Asher. But will you come?
Who is this lad?

Lise. Her lad. But he was hurt
and fell asleep.
    [VAN *wakes and lifts his head.*]

Asher. Come quickly!

Lise. Yes, for his sake
it's better I should go.

Van. Where must you go?
    [*She rises.*]

Lise. The *Onrust's* on the river
and we must catch the tide.

Van. Would you leave me now?

Lise. Yes, I must leave you.

Van. You'll go back with him?

Lise. Yes.

Van. And was nothing meant of all we said?

Lise. What could we mean, we two? Your hurt's quite cured
and mine's past curing.

Van. Let me go with you then.

Lise. I should have told you if I'd only known
how we stood at the tangent of two worlds
that touched an instant like two wings of storm
drawn out of night; touched and flew off, and, falling,
fall now asunder through a wide abyss,
not to touch again.

    [*She steps back among the rocks.*]

Van. Let them go if they like!
What do I care about worlds? Any world you have
I'll make it mine!

Lise. You told me in your sleep.
There is no witchcraft. Men are as they were;
we're parted now.

Van. Give me your hand again!
They dare not take you from me, dare not touch you
no matter who they are, or where they come from—
they have no hold on us!

Lise. If I could stay!
If I could stay with you. And tend my garden
only a little longer!

Van. Put out your hand!

Lise. There were too many, many, many years.

Van. I'll be alone here—

Lise. No, not alone. When you must walk the air.
   as all must walk it sometime, with a tread
   that stirs no leaf, and breathe here with a breath
   that blows impalpable through smoke or cloud,
   when you are as I am, a bending wind
   along the grain, think of me sometimes then
   and how I clung to earth. The earth you have
   seems now so hard and firm, with all its colors
   sharp for the eye, as a taste's sharp to the tongue,
   you'll hardly credit how its outlines blur
   and wear out as you wear. Play now with fire
   while fire will burn, bend down the bough and eat
   before the fruit falls. For there comes a time
   when the great sun-lit pattern of the earth
   shakes like an image under water, darkens,
   dims, and the clearest voices that we knew
   are sunken bells, dead sullen under sea,
   receding. Look in her eyes.
      [VAN *looks at* JUDITH.]

Asher. Come!

Lise. See, the dawn
   points with one purple finger at a star
   to put it out. When it has quite gone out
   then we'll be gone.
      [VAN *looks at the dawn, then turns back toward* LISE.]

Van. Lise! Lise!
      [*But even as he speaks* LISE *and the* CREW *have disappeared.*]

Lise.
      [*Unseen*]

This is your age, your dawn, your life to live.
The morning light strikes through us, and the wind

that follows after rain tugs at our sails—
and so we go.

DeWitt.
   [*Still half-seen*]

And welcome you are to the age, too, an age of witches
and sandwiches, an age of paper, an age of paper money
and paper men, so that a poor Dutch wraith's more
                              man
than the thickest of you!
   [*He steps back and vanishes. It is now dawn.*]

Van. She never said good-bye.

Judith. There is a ship.

Van. Yes?

Judith. Tiny, with black, square sails;
low and small.

Van
   [*Still looking after* LISE]

She'll be a phantom too
like all the rest. The canvas casts no shadow;
the light sifts through the spars. A moonlight rig
no doubt they call it.

Judith. I think I hear their voices
as they go down the crag.

Van. But you won't see them.
No matter what you hear.

The Sailors.
   [*A wisp of chantey in the distance*]

> Coming a blow, coming a blow,
> sea runs black, glass runs low.

Van. Just voices down the wind.
Why, then they were all mist, a fog that hangs
along the crevices of hills, a kind
of memory of things you read in books,
things you thought you'd forgotten. She was here,
and she was real, but she was cloud, and gone,
and the hill's barren of her.

Judith. There are no ghosts.

Van. I know—but these were ghosts or I'm a ghost,
and all of us. God knows where we leave off
and ghosts begin. God knows where ghosts leave off
and we begin.

Judith. You were in love with her.

Van. She leaves the mountain barren now she's gone.
And she was beautiful.

Judith. I came to tell you
that I was wrong—I mean about the land—
what you have here is better than one buys
down in the towns. But since I come too late
I'll say it and then go.—Your way was best.
I think it always would be.—So, good night, Van—
or, rather, it's good morning.

Van. Yes, it's morning.—
Is it too late?

Judith. Oh, Van, I think it is.
It was for Lise you were calling, not
for Judith. I can't say I blame you much,

because she is more beautiful. And yet
you love her, and not me. You'll say they're ghosts
and won't come back. Perhaps. I'm not so certain
about the way of ghosts. She may come back.
And you still love her.

Van. There's no ship at all.
It faded in the dawn. And all the mists
that hung about the Tor, look how they lift,
pouring downstream with the wind. Whatever it was,
was said, or came between us, it's all gone
now it's daylight again.

Judith. I came to say
if only I could keep you, you should keep
the Tor, or what you wished. I'm sorry I went.
I'm sorry this has happened. But it has.
And so—

Van. Should I keep the Tor?

Judith. Yes, if you like.

Van. God knows they haven't left me much of it.
Look, where the new road winds along the ledge.
Look at the jagged cut the quarries make
down to the south, and there's a boy scout trail
running along the ridge Mount Ivy way,
where they try out their hatchets. There's the light,
and steps cut into stone the linesmen blew
for better climbing. The crusher underneath
dumps road rock into barges all day long
and sometimes half the night. The West Shore tunnel
belches its trains above the dead lagoons
that line the brickyards. Their damned shovel hangs

across my line, ready to gouge the peak
we're standing on. Maybe I'm ghost myself
trying to hold an age back with my hands;
maybe we're all the same, these ghosts of Dutchmen
and one poor superannuated Indian
and one last hunter, clinging to his land
because he's always had it. Like a wasp
that tries to build a nest above your door—
and when you brush it down he builds again,
then when you brush it down he builds again—
but after a while you get him.

Judith. Then you'll sell?

Van. I guess if you were with me then we'd sell
for what we could, and move out farther west
where a man's land's his own. But if I'm here
alone, I'll play the solitary wasp
and sting them till they get me.

Judith. If it's your way
then it's your way.

Van. I'll sell it if you'll stay.
Won't you stay with me, Judith?

Judith. I think I'd always hear you calling Lise
while I was standing by. I took a wrong turning
once, when I left you and went down the hill,
and now it may not ever be the same.
    [*She turns.*]

CURTAIN

HIGH TOR

ACT THREE

ACT THREE

SCENE: *The shovel still hangs over the verge, and* BIGGS *and* SKIM-
MERHORN *still occupy it. The rising sun sends level rays across
the rock, lighting their intent faces as they stare downward.*
BIGGS *has torn a handkerchief into strips and tied them together
into a string. He appears to be fishing for something which lies
below the ledge, out of view of the audience. Over and over
he tries his cast.*

Skimmerhorn. Little to the left.

Biggs. You don't say?

Skimmerhorn. Little to the right.

Biggs. Put it to a tune and sing it, why don't you?

Skimmerhorn. There! Almost!

Biggs. I don't need any umpire.

Skimmerhorn. Let me try it.

Biggs. Oh, no. You always were a butter-fingers.
　　[*The string tightens.*]

　By Golly!

Skimmerhorn. It's on!

Biggs. You're explaining to me?
　　[*He pulls up. A bottle of beer emerges from below.*]

Skimmerhorn. Fifty per cent!

Biggs. What?
　　[*He pauses, the bottle in air.*]

Skimmerhorn. You tore up my handkerchief! Fifty per cent. That's the natural division between capital and labor.

Biggs. Oh, now I'm labor and you're capital.
  [*He pulls up carefully.*]

Skimmerhorn. Fifty per cent!

Biggs. I get the first pull at it. That's all I ask.
  [*The string parts, and the bottle descends silently into the void.*]
That's that.

Skimmerhorn. You should 'a let me handle it.

Biggs. Yeah. No doubt.

Skimmerhorn. Am I thirsty?

Biggs. Wait till the sun gets up a little. We'll be pan-fried in this thing.

Skimmerhorn. Look!
  [*He points down the rocks.*]

Biggs. If it's more of those little people I give up.

Skimmerhorn. It's a trooper.

Biggs. What do you know? Up early for a trooper, too. Listen, about that stuff in our pockets?

Skimmerhorn. Yeah?

Biggs. Do we say anything about it?

Skimmerhorn. Do you?

Biggs. Do you?

Skimmerhorn. No.

Biggs. Neither do I, then.

Skimmerhorn. Beautiful morning.

Biggs. I always say it's worth while being up early just to catch the sunrise.

[*A* TROOPER *climbs in followed by* SKIMMERHORN SENIOR.)

The Trooper. Hello!

Biggs. Hello, Patsy.

Patsy. Say, you boys had the wives worried down in Leden. town. Been looking for you all night. There they are, Mr. Skimmerhorn.

Skimmerhorn, Sr.

[*Winded*]

Good God!

[*He sits, a hand to his heart.*]

And I climbed up here. We thought you were under that rock slide.

Skimmerhorn. I guess you're disappointed.

Senior. The next time you two go on a bat and spend a night up a tree you can stay there and sober up.

Skimmerhorn. We haven't been drinking.

Senior.

[*Pointing to a bottle*]

What's that?

Skimmerhorn. Beer. But we didn't have a drop to drink. I'd certainly appreciate a swallow of that now.

Patsy.

> [*Tossing up bottle*]

Here you are. Hair of the dog that bit you.

Biggs. We're not drunk. We're dry. We didn't have a drop to drink nor a bite to eat.

Patsy. All right. All right. Only the ground's covered with beer and sandwiches.

Biggs. You tell 'em how it was, Skimmer.

Skimmerhorn. You tell 'em.

Biggs. Well, you see, the whole thing's pretty complicated.

Patsy. I know. I've been through it. You wake up in the morning and you can't believe it yourself.

Biggs. I don't mean that. I'm sober as a judge.

Patsy. Yeah, what judge?

> [*He hauls at a cable.*]

Can you lend me a hand with this, A.B.?

Senior. Give me a minute.

> [*The shovel tips.*]

Biggs. Hey, not that one! The other one!

Patsy. Sorry. Not much of a mechanic.

Biggs. Straighten it up again.

> [*Patsy does so.*]

Skimmerhorn. Are we never getting off this? My legs are paralyzed sitting here.

Biggs. So are mine.

Patsy.

> [*Hauling down*]

It's too much for me alone.

Skimmerhorn. Got your wind yet, A.B.?

Senior. I don't know whether I want you down yet. You had your good time, now you can put in a few minutes paying for it.

Skimmerhorn. Oh, we had a good time, did we?

Senior. What were you doing? You came up here to buy Van Dorn's property; you're gone all night, and the whole damn town's up all night hunting for you! And we find you up in a steam shovel enjoying a hang-over!

Patsy. And now I know what a hang-over looks like.

Biggs. I tell you we didn't even have a drink of water!

Senior. I believe that!

Biggs. And we're thirsty! Have you got an opener?

Patsy. No, I haven't.

Senior. Before you open anything tell me what you **were** doing last night. Did you see Van Dorn?

Skimmerhorn. Sure we saw him.

Senior. Well, what did he say?

Skimmerhorn. He said no.

Senior. And I suppose that took all night?

Skimmerhorn. We had an argument.

Senior. And then he chased you up the crane, I suppose?

Skimmerhorn. No.

Senior. Well, how did you get up there?

Skimmerhorn. We were hauled up.

Senior. All right. Who hauled you up?

Skimmerhorn. You tell him, Art.

Biggs. Oh, no. You tell him.

Skimmerhorn. As a matter of fact, I don't think it happened.

Senior. You're there, aren't you?

Skimmerhorn. Yes, we're here.

Senior. Well, if you weren't drunk how did you get there?

Skimmerhorn. Well, you see, first we tried to negotiate with Van Dorn.

Senior. And he wouldn't take the money?

Skimmerhorn. That's right.

Senior. Did you tell him he didn't really own the land? Till the will was validated?

Skimmerhorn. Yes, we told him that.

Senior. And he still wouldn't talk business?

Skimmerhorn. He's stubborn. Stubborn as a mule.

Senior. Did you tell him you could take the land away from him?

Skimmerhorn. Oh, yes.

Senior. And you offered him the twenty-five thousand?

Biggs. We offered him a fair price.

Senior. You were authorized to say twenty-five thousand.

Biggs. We didn't quite get to that. We offered ten.

Skimmerhorn. You see, we thought we'd save the company some money.

Senior. I'll bet you did. You thought you'd make a little on the side, and I'd never know.

Skimmerhorn. Oh, no.

Biggs. Oh, no.

Senior. All right, you offered ten and he wouldn't take it. Then what happened?

Skimmerhorn. Well, we couldn't get down because of the slide, so some sailors offered to let us down in this thing.

Senior. Sailors—up here?

Skimmerhorn. Little men, in big hats.

Biggs. Might have been a moving picture company.

Senior. Yeah? Any elephants? Or snakes?

Skimmerhorn. We're trying to tell you the truth!

Patsy. Certainly sounds like delirium tremens, boys.

Senior. Never mind, you were hauled up by pink elephants, and then what?

Skimmerhorn. Van Dorn came along and started to dump us down the cliff.

Senior. What's Van Dorn look like? Kind of an octopus, with long feelers?

Skimmerhorn. Are you going to let us down out of this basket?

Senior. No. Not till you come across with what's been going on.

Skimmerhorn. All right. I'll talk when I'm down.

Senior. Can a grown man get pie-eyed on beer?

Patsy. Must have been something stronger.
    [VAN DORN *comes in from the right.*]

Senior. Who are you?

Van. Oh, I'm nobody. I just own the property.

Senior. What property?

Van. This.

Senior. Are you Van Dorn?

Van. I am.

Senior. I'm A. B. Skimmerhorn, Mr. Van Dorn, president of Igneous Trap-rock, and I'm glad to meet you.
    [*He puts out a hand.*]

Van.
    [*Ignoring the hand*]
Are these friends of yours?

Senior. One's a nephew and one's a partner. Why?

Van. Because any friend of theirs is no friend of mine.

[JUDITH *and* THE INDIAN *enter at the rear. She is leading him.*]

Patsy. Who do you think you're talking to?

Van. A. B. Skimmerhorn, of Skimmerhorn, Skimmerhorn, Biggs and Skimmerho.n, small-time crooks and petty thieving done. Cheap.

Senior. Now, to be frank, there may have been some misunderstanding, Mr. Van Dorn. Those two were hardly in condition to negotiate. But I can offer you a fair price for your land, and if you don't take it we may have to push you a little, because we want this acreage and we intend to have it.

Skimmerhorn. He's got the validation papers.

Senior. You gave him the validation papers?

Biggs. We had to. He started to trip the machine.

Senior. That puts us in a sweet mess, that does. Will you take twenty-five thousand?

Van. No.

Senior. Will you take fifty thousand?

Van. No.

Senior. Then we go home, and the machinery can rust here. That's the best I can do.

Van. Fine. Let it rust.

Judith. Van?

Van. Yes, Judith.

Judith. There's someone here to see you.

Van. You want to see me, John?

The Indian. But I can wait. I have time enough.

Van. I'll be right with you.

Judith. I had to bring him, Van, because he said
    his eyes were bad. He couldn't see the way.

Van. Thanks, Judith.

Senior. Look, Van Dorn, you know the saying,
    every man has his price. I've heard it said
    God has his price, if you'll go high enough.
    Set a figure.

Van. I'm not thinking of prices.
    I don't want to sell. Hell, fifty thousand's
    too much money for me.

Senior. We'll give you less.

Van. I don't want less or more. It's not a matter
    of money.

Senior. Will you take a partnership
    in the company?

Van. No.

Senior. Good God, what do you want?

Van. I want to have it back the way it was
    before you came here. And I won't get that. I know
    what kind of fool I look to all of you,
    all but old John there. But I'll be a fool
    along with John, and keep my own, before

I let you have an inch. John, fifty thousand
or this old hill-top. Is it worth keeping?

The Indian. No.

Van. No?

The Indian. It's gone already. Not worth keeping.

Van. I thought you'd say it was. I counted on you
to be my friend in that.

The Indian. It's an old question,
one I heard often talked of round the fire
when the hills and I were younger. Then as now
the young braves were for keeping what was ours
whatever it cost in blood. And they did try,
but when they'd paid their blood, and still must sell,
the price was always less than what it was
before their blood was paid.

Van. Well, that may be.

The Indian. I wish now I had listened when they spoke
their prophecies, the sachems of the tents;
they were wiser than I knew. Wisest of all,
Iachim, had his camp here on this Tor
before the railroad came. I saw him stand
and look out toward the west, toward the sun dying,
and say, "Our god is now the setting sun,
and we must follow it. For other races,
out of the east, will live here in their time,
one following another. Each will build
its cities, and its monuments to gods
we dare not worship. Some will come with ships,
and some with wings, and each will desecrate

the altars of the people overthrown,
but none will live forever. Each will live
its little time, and fly before the feet
of those who follow after." Let them come in
despoiling, for a time is but a time
and these will not endure. This little hill,
let them have the little hill, and find your peace
beyond, for there's no hill worth a man's peace
while he may live and find it. But they fought it out
and died, and sleep here.

Senior. Why, this is a wise Indian.
A little pessimistic about the aims
of civilization, but wise anyway.
What do you say, Van Dorn?

The Indian. You too will go
like gnats on the wind. An evening and a day,
but still you have your day. Build monuments
and worship at your temples. But you too
will go.

Senior. You're on my side, so I don't mind,
but you have a damned uncomfortable way
of speaking. I'm a Republican myself,
but I don't go that far! What do you say, Van Dorn?
Can we do business?

Van. Judith?

Judith. I'm out of it.
It's your decision. I'd say keep it though
if you want to keep it.

Van. I'll sell it. Fifty thousand.
On one condition. There's a burying ground
I want to keep.

Senior. Sure. That can be arranged.
It's settled, then. Come down to Ledentown
tomorrow and get your money.

Van. Yes, I'll come.

Senior. Why three cheers, boys. We're out of the woods.
Take hold,
Van Dorn, and swing these topers off the limb.
Then they can sign the pledge.

[*A* TROOPER *appears with* ELKUS *and* DOPE.]

Budge (The Trooper). Help me keep an eye on these
two, will you, Patsy? I've got a confession out of them
on the Nanuet bank robbery, and they say the money's
up here.

Patsy. Up here? Whereabouts?

Budge. They left it in a satchel.

Patsy. There's the satchel, all right.

[*He examines it.*]

Empty.

Budge. Looks like a stall, you guys. You buried it.

Elkus. Didn't keep a cent, officer. Somebody up here got it.

Budge. Well, who?

Elkus. Last time I saw it one of those birds sat down on it.

[*He points to* BIGGS *and* SKIMMERHORN.]

Patsy. You know who they are? That's Judge Skimmerhorn of the Probate Court, and Arthur Biggs of the
Trap-rock Company.

Elkus. Well, one of them sat down on it.

Budge. Why didn't he pick it up?

Elkus. I don't know whether he saw it.

Dope. And then there was a little guy in a big hat that had some of it.

Patsy. Yeah? Who?

Budge. That's right. Buddy said something about a little guy in a big hat.

Patsy. You think he got away with it?

Elkus. He had some of it, and we haven't got a cent.

Budge. So now we have to look for a little guy in a big hat. Any other description?

Elkus. Short and fat, had two sawed-off shotguns, and wore knee-pants.

Dope. And you could see right through him.

    [BUDGE *is writing in a notebook.*]

Patsy. What?

Dope. You could see right through him.

Budge. I'm beginning to think I can see right through you.

Patsy. Check on that. Elkus, you saw him. Could you see through him?

Elkus. Certainly was a funny-looking guy. Looked as if you could see right through him.

Budge. You expect me to send that out over the country: "Look for a short, fat man with a big hat and two

sawed-off shotguns. Dangerous. You can see right
through him.''?

Patsy. They buried the money, Budge. Or else they're
screwy.

Elkus. I thought I was screwy. You couldn't hurt him
with a gun.

Budge. What do you mean?

Dope. We bored him full of holes and he wouldn't even
sit down.

Budge. You mean he kept on running?

Dope. Running? He just stood there and let us shoot him.

Like shooting through a window.

Budge. Must have been wearing a vest.

Dope. I shot him through the head! Two feet away! And
it just made him mad!

Patsy. Take 'em away, Budge. They're nuts.

Elkus. But he had the money! Buddy saw him with the
money!

Patsy. They're all three nuts.

Budge. I never heard a line like that before.

Patsy. Who lives around here?

Van. I guess I'm the only one that lives near-by.

Patsy. Did you hear any shooting last night?

Van. Plenty of it.

Patsy. Did you take a look round?

Van. Yes, I did.

Patsy. Did you see a little guy in a big hat?

Van. Six or seven of them.

Budge. What!

Van. Six or seven of them.

Budge. I suppose you could see right through them?

Van. Once in a while.

Budge. I'm going to quit writing this down. There's enough here to get me fired already.

Patsy. If you saw six or seven where did they go?

Van. Down the river.

Patsy. In a car?

Van. In a ship.

Patsy. Sounds like a motor-boat gang. Well, that's something. They went down the river.

Van. But I can tell you where there's thirty dollars of the money.

Budge. Where?

Van. On the ledge there below the shovel.
    [BUDGE *and* PATSY *step over to look.*]

Budge. There it is. Three ten dollar bills. How did it get there?

Van. I don't know. I just happened to see it.

Budge. Did you try to get it?

Van. No. I thought it probably belonged to the gentlemen up there in the scoop.

Patsy. Did one of you drop some money, Judge?

Skimmerhorn. I don't think so. Not me.

Biggs. Not me.

Patsy. Did either of you see a little man in a big hat?
   [*The two look at each other.*]

Skimmerhorn. Why, yes, we did.
   [PATSY *and* BUDGE *look at each other.*]

Budge. Well, if they say so he must have been here.

Patsy. What was he doing?

Skimmerhorn. He was fighting with those two.
   [*He points to* ELKUS *and* DOPE.]

Biggs. A regular war.

Patsy. Say, listen to that.

Budge. Do you know if he took anything out of the satchel?

Skimmerhorn. Yes, I think he did. He had the satchel.

Budge. Now we're getting somewhere.

Patsy. You don't know where he went?

Skimmerhorn. No.

Patsy. If you saw anything else that might give us a clue—*

Skimmerhorn. No, not a thing.

Patsy. It beats me.

Van. Want me to suggest a question?

Patsy. What?

Van. Ask the Judge if he gained any weight during the
night.

Patsy. What's the matter with you?

Van. Looks to me like he picked up a good deal.

Patsy. I'll think up my own questions, thanks. Might as
well trundle the yeggs back to jail, Budge. Whoever
got the stuff it's gone.

Budge. That's what it looks like.

Van. Aren't you going to help the Judge down before you
go?

Biggs. Oh, don't bother. We'll get down.

Skimmerhorn. No hurry. We're all right. You take care
of your prisoners.

Patsy. Might as well lend a hand while we're here.

Biggs. Run along, boys. We're all right. Don't worry
about us.

Patsy.
    [*To* BUDGE]
    Want to wait a minute?

Budge. Well, I'm due back, if they can make it themselves.

Biggs. Sure.

Van. Oh, don't leave those poor fellows up on that crane! They've been there all night!

Skimmerhorn. We're fine. You run along.

Budge. Well, take a drag on the rope, Patsy. I'll wait.
[PATSY *and* VAN *haul the shovel down.*]

Skimmerhorn. No need to go to all this trouble.

Patsy. No trouble at all.

Van. A pleasure. Why you were asking me all night to get you out of this.
[*The shovel touches ground. The two sit still.*]

Patsy. What's the matter?

Skimmerhorn. Guess my legs are asleep.

Biggs. Mine too.

Patsy. I'll help you up.
[*They are pulled to their feet, staggering. Their pockets are very obvious.*]

Budge. How about it? O.K.?

Patsy. All set. Say, you are loaded down. Carried plenty of lunch, I guess?

Biggs. Oh, we brought plenty.

Van.
[*Tapping* BIGGS' *pocket*]

I told you they gained weight. Something in the air up here.

Elkus. Couldn't be money, could it?

Biggs. As a matter of fact, some of it is. We were carrying cash to pay Van Dorn for his farm.

Patsy. Cash?

Biggs. Yeah, cash.

Patsy. How much?

Biggs. Just what we were authorized to pay. Twenty-five thousand.

Van. Funny thing, too. It's got the Orangeburg pay roll stamp on it.

Biggs. Well, hardly.

Patsy. What makes you think so?

Van. I saw it. They offered me ten thousand.

Patsy. Just for the record, I'd better look at it, Judge.

Skimmerhorn. I wouldn't if I were you. I'm hardly under suspicion of bank robbery.

Patsy. I'll take a look at it.
> [*He holds out a hand.* BIGGS *passes him a package.*]

Senior. I don't get this at all.

Patsy. It's got the Orangeburg stamp on it, all right.

Skimmerhorn. Must be some mistake. They must have got the money mixed at the bank.

Patsy. Sure. Well, if that's all we can easy check on that.

Van. Sure. You'd better check on it.

Skimmerhorn. Are you under the impression that we robbed the bank?

Van. You explain it. I can't.

Senior. You say you drew the money to pay Van Dorn?

Skimmerhorn. That's right, A.B.

Senior. And it's got the Orangeburg label on it?

Skimmerhorn. That's what they say.

Senior. I'll have something to say to the bank about that.

Skimmerhorn. Oh, I'll take care of it. Just a clerical error.

Patsy. I'm afraid I'll have to take the money, though. Oh, you'll get your own money back, but if this is the Orangeburg money—

Biggs. Sure, take it.
[*They unload.*]

Patsy. And I guess I really ought to put you both under arrest.

Biggs. What? Under arrest?

Patsy. Wouldn't you say so, Budge?

Budge. Don't see any way out of it. Doesn't mean anything. Just an examination.

Skimmerhorn. I'd like to keep it out of the papers, if possible, of course. An examination might be very embarrassing—you see, I have political enemies.

Biggs. Always ready to think the worst of a man, and print it, too.

Patsy. Still, I guess we'll have to have an examination. Just for the record.

Skimmerhorn. You know who we are, of course?

Patsy. Yes, sir.

Skimmerhorn. I won't submit to an examination! It's preposterous!

Patsy. I don't see how we can get out of it, though. Because we had a robbery, and here's the money, and we've got to explain it somehow.

Skimmerhorn. I won't submit to it!

Patsy. You got an extra pair of handcuffs there, Budge?

Budge. Yeah.

Skimmerhorn. All right. I'll go.

Biggs. Sure. We'll go. And we'll make a lot of people sorry!

Patsy. Go on ahead, Budge.
    [BUDGE *starts out with his prisoners.*]

Dope. But how about the little guy with the big hat? How about him?

Budge. I'll tell you about him. It's entirely possible there wasn't any little guy in a big hat.

Dope. But we all saw him!

Budge. Oh, no, you didn't see him. You saw right through him. And the reason was he wasn't there.
    [BUDGE, ELKUS *and* DOPE *go out.*]

Biggs. You don't think we made that up, about the man in the big hat?

Patsy. Well, you have to admit it doesn't sound exactly plausible.

[PATSY, BIGGS *and* SKIMMERHORN *go out.*]

Senior.

[*As he goes*]

It shakes a man's faith in evidence.

[*To* VAN]

See you tomorrow.

Van. I'll be there.

[SKIMMERHORN SENIOR *goes out.*]

So now—I've sold the Tor.

The Indian. Yes, but it's better.

Van. Better than living on a grudge, I guess.
It might come down to that.

The Indian. There's wilder land,
and there are higher mountains, in the west.

Van. Out Port Jervis way.

The Indian. Perhaps. You'll find them.

Judith. He came to tell you, Van—this is his death-day.
I'll go now.

Van. All right, John.

The Indian. Could I keep it?
The hand I held? It's a new thing, being blind,
when you've had an Indian's eyes.

[JUDITH *returns and gives him her hand again.*]

Judith. I'll stay a while.

The Indian. When I had lost the path
halfway along the ridge, there at my feet
I heard a woman crying. We came on
together, for she led me. There'll be time
for crying later. Take her west with you.
She'll forget the mountain.

Van. Will you come?

Judith. I'd remember Lise!

Van. Was there a Lise?
I think she was my dream of you and me
and how you left the mountain barren once
when you were gone. She was my dream of you
and how you left the Tor. Say you'll come with me.

Judith. Yes.

The Indian. It's a long day's work to dig a grave
in stony ground. But you're young and have good
                              shoulders.
It should be done tonight.

Van. I'll have it done
even if you don't need it. Tell me the place.

The Indian. There's still an Indian burying ground that
                              lies
behind the northern slope. Beneath it runs
a line of square brown stones the white men used
to mark their dead. Below still, in a ring,
are seven graves, a woman and six men,
the Indians killed and laid there. In the freshet,
after the rain last night, the leaf-mould washed,
and the seven looked uncovered at the sky,

white skeletons with flintlocks by their sides,
and on the woman's hand a heavy ring
made out of gold. I laid them in again.

Van. Seven graves—a woman and six men—
Maybe they'll rest now.

The Indian. Dig them in deeper, then.
They're covered only lightly.

Van. I'll dig them deeper.

The Indian. But you must make my grave with my own
people,
higher, beneath the ledge, and dig it straight,
and narrow. And you must place me in the fashion
used by the Indians, sitting at a game,
not fallen, not asleep. And set beside me
water and food. If this is strange to you,
think only I'm an Indian with strange ways,
but I shall need them.

Van. Don't worry. You shall have it
just the way you want it.

The Indian. Shall we go?

Van. One last look at the rock. It's not too late
to hold out on the bargain. Think of the gouge
they'll make across these hills.

Judith. If it's for me
you sell, we'll have enough without it, Van.
We'll have each other.

Van. Oh, but you were right.
When they wash over you, you either swim
or drown. We won't be here.

The Indian. And there's one comfort.
   I heard the wise Iachim, looking down
   when the railroad cut was fresh, and the bleeding earth
   offended us. There is nothing made, he said,
   and will be nothing made by these new men,
   high tower, or cut, or buildings by a lake
   that will not make good ruins.

Judith. Ruins? This?

The Indian. Why, when the race is gone, or looks aside
   only a little while, the white stone darkens,
   the wounds close, and the roofs fall, and the walls
   give way to rains. Nothing is made by men
   but makes, in the end, good ruins.

Van. Well, that's something.
   But I can hardly wait.

CURTAIN

VIII · THE MASQUE OF KINGS

CHARACTERS

(In order of their appearance)

FRANZ JOSEPH	2ND MAN
KOINOFF	3RD MAN
A SERVANT	RUDOLPH
ELIZABETH	BRATFISCH
TAAFE	A GIRL
BARONIN VON NEUSTADT	MARY VETSERA
BARON VON NEUSTADT	ARCHDUKE JOHN
LOSCHEK	SCEPS
1ST LADY	RAUSCHER
1ST MAN	HOYOS
2ND LADY	

ACT I

SCENE 1

SCENE: *A corner of the study of the Emperor Franz Joseph in the Hofburg, Vienna. It is late at night in January, 1889, but the emperor is
still at work, standing before a high desk covered with letters and
papers. Tapers burn over the desk. There is no other light. Behind
the emperor are a table and a chair, the table also covered with papers.*
CAPTAIN KOINOFF *stands near the table.*

Franz Joseph. Proceed, proceed, man. I can hear you while I
work.

Koinoff. Yes, Your Majesty.

Franz Joseph. Or shall I tell you what you were about to say?
[*He slits an envelope.*]

A well-known oratorical bastard named the Archduke John
of Tuscany—so far right?—

Koinoff. Yes, Majesty.

Franz Joseph. Will confer tonight with the Archduke Rudolph.
In his company will be—let me think—a well-known radical
editor named Sceps, a soft-brained family man with a pro-
found conviction that the whole world can be set right by the
simple expedient of turning everything upside down, including,
I surmise, the imperial navy, the city reservoir and his own
gravy boat.—The presence will also be graced by an obscure
young expert in military affairs, Koinoff by name, yourself in
fact, and the meeting will take place at—shall we say the residence of the Archduke John?

Koinoff. No, Majesty—the apartments of the Crown Prince Rudolph.

Franz Joseph. Dear me, in the Hofburg itself.
[*There is a knock at the door and a* SERVANT *parts the curtain.*]

You know, of course, that I am not disturbed here at this hour.

Servant. Yes, Your Majesty.

Franz Joseph. There is someone dead—or dying?

Servant. No, Your Majesty.

Franz Joseph. There has been a calamity in the kingdom of which
I must be apprised instantly?

Servant. No, Your Majesty.

Franz Joseph. Then henceforth remember your orders.

Servant. Your Majesty, the Empress wishes to speak with you.

Franz Joseph. The Empress. Where is the Empress?

Servant. In the reception room, Your Majesty.
      [*A pause.*]

Franz Joseph. I will see her at once.
      [*The Servant goes.*]
   Go out through my room. I understand then that the three
of you will take up the question of modern government?

Koinoff. That's the whole story, Your Majesty.

Franz Joseph. This way.
      [*He ushers Koinoff out. The servant ushers in the* EMPRESS *and with-
      draws.*]
   I'm more than honored.
   You see before you a workman at his labors,
   a bit dusty, I fear, and worn.

Elizabeth. You've always worked
   while others slept, dear Franz.

Franz Joseph. You wish to sit?
   I'll stand, myself. It's all my exercise—
   stooping for papers.
      [*He stoops to retrieve a fallen letter.*]

Elizabeth. Thank you.
  [*She sits.*]
    I'm afraid
I'm quite inopportune.

Franz Joseph. It's thirteen years
  as I remember it, since you've come through
  this doorway. At that time you said, if I
  recall correctly, you would not see me again,
  you would not see me any more alone
  till I answered you a question. It's not answered.
  But I should be very busy indeed, dear Cissie,
  If I'd no time to give you.

Elizabeth. Let the question go.
  And the quarrel. It's too late to rescue now
  what the flood carried with it to the sea
  so many years ago. All our deaths and loves
  go down the wash.—No it was something else
  I wanted to save now—I've passed your door
  some thousand nights, and listened, and gone by—
  it was never the moment.

Franz Joseph. Something I could grant you—
  something to ask? Among all petitioners
  you would stand first.

Elizabeth. Still?

Franz Joseph. Yes. You no longer love me,
  I know, but I love you still, and will, no doubt,
  while the pump goes. This has been our misfortune,
  yours more than mine.

Elizabeth. I've been too fortunate
  in many things. Or was when I was young.
  As we grow older and need our luck it fails.

Perhaps we take it for granted, and the gods,
the non-existent gods, are angry with us,
having spoiled us earlier.

Franz Joseph. Non-existent?

Elizabeth. There—
let's not quarrel about it—let's believe
what we believe. When you took me and made me Empress,
long ago, that was luck, unbelievable luck
for a younger daughter of the Wittelsbachs,
a footless, scandalous tribe, with nothing to offer
but my footless, scandalous ways, and a little beauty
that faded under the lamps.

Franz Joseph. It's not faded, Cissie,
and I think it never will.

Elizabeth. Well, beauty or not,
you found me out for the ne'er-do-well I was,
and I found you more emperor than mine,
and things have happened that won't be forgiven
on either side, no matter how you love
or how thick the years mulch over.

Franz Joseph. Yes. It's true.—
This was what you wished to say?

Elizabeth. No. Oh, I'm clear
in my mind, Franz, though I may have given you cause
to wonder these last years. I know how strict
you guard your time, and wouldn't waste it. Here's
my business, stated plainly, quite without grief
or a woman's art. We have two things left to us
out of the wreck of years and youth: the empire,
and Rudolph, our son, who will rule it by and by,
if all goes well. I think we shall lose them both
if things go as they are.

Franz Joseph. Yes?

Elizabeth. I gave you an heir—
  my one gift to the kingdom, but a noble one;
  such a prince as an emperor, dreaming of sons,
  could wish no happier issue. Magnanimous, wise,
  beyond his years, gentle but manly, eager
  to serve, a lover of justice. This was true?

Franz Joseph. Yes.

Elizabeth. But now he's thirty years old, and this last two years
  the furies begin to tear at him. Perhaps
  my ways and yours at war in his blood. Perhaps
  inaction, and the cynicism of courts
  corrode more readily when a mind's been brought
  to a delicate perfection. A peasant brain
  resists and keeps right on. It's an evil court,
  but it doesn't touch you—nor me.

Franz Joseph. Come then—our Rudolph?

Elizabeth. I'm troubled over the news from Hungary.
  It's a freedom-loving people, never ours
  except by conquest. There's but one way to keep them—
  that's to extend the suffrage, rule them gentler
  than they can rule themselves—give without asking
  more than they think to ask.

Franz Joseph. This is like old times.

Elizabeth. It's as true now as then.

Franz Joseph. Proceed. I'll listen.

Elizabeth. Partly because he's my son, and they believe
  I've been their friend, partly because he speaks
  for all their hopes, the Hungarians have loved Rudolph,
  and he could hold them in the empire for you.

You were emperor at eighteen. It's a discipline
that Rudolph needs; power in his hands; we grow
by what we have to do. I've thought of this
a long while now. Divide your empire. Set
our Rudolph over Hungary.

Franz Joseph. As king?

Elizabeth. As king of Hungary.

Franz Joseph. I'm growing old then?

Elizabeth. No, but he'll have it in the end. You'll live
for many years, I hope.—Is he to come
to full dominion in a late middle age
when he's been burned out hollow with idleness
and lusts—all his fine faith soured to mockeries
with waiting—?

Franz Joseph. Have you spoken with Rudolph?

Elizabeth. No.

Franz Joseph. You've never told me a lie, and I believe you—
else I should think you must have spoken with him.
When have you seen our son?

Elizabeth. Why, yesterday.

Franz Joseph. To talk with him? As a mother might with a son?
I think not within the year.

Elizabeth. It may be—longer.

Franz Joseph. Then let me enlighten you concerning Rudolph.
I have a message here from His Holiness
that enlightened me this morning. Our son's petitioned
the Pope to set him free of his present marriage,
free to marry again. I have no doubt
he has in mind the same Vetsera harlot

who shares his bed at present. Even you should grant
this would make a kingly stench for the new-born court
of a new-born kingdom in Europe.

Elizabeth. Yes.

Franz Joseph. That's first.
Second, the state of Hungary's aflame,
of late, and I think our Rudolph set the fire—
with plots to make him king, blow me aside
like the old dodderer over desks I am,
oh, leave me Austria if I care to keep it,
but Hungary for Rudolph, Rudolph for Hungary,
caps in the air, the old men in their places—
somewhat to the rear, or slightly underground
if they're in the way—a young man on the throne,
and let the bugles blow! You knew of this?

Elizabeth. No.

Franz Joseph. Well, I've known—perhaps as much as any,
and more than they know I know. If you'd be kind
to Rudolph, tell him this; that his hot friends
would better cool their heads or they'll cool their heels;
they're too hot by half.

Elizabeth. Rudolph began this?

Franz Joseph. I don't know. I can't swear it. It seems likely,
judging by what he's written, by the friends he hugs
and the rendezvous he keeps. But to be just
I don't know how far it's his.

Elizabeth. If it were so
that Hungary does wish it—wish him for king—
you would oppose it still?

Franz Joseph. A state will wish
what it's told to wish. It has no will of its own.

Elizabeth. But what I've asked—could so easily be done—
without loss, even with gain to you. When we
were young together, you lightened your hand one day
over Hungary for my sake—and in time,
for I think it won them—

Franz Joseph. I should oppose it still.
Not that it's treason to me—all these things
are words—faith, treason, honor—behind them lie
realities of government which I face
daily here at my desk. No—let me go back.
When I first saw you you were not seventeen,
and beautiful in some sad crystal fashion
that's quite beyond the phrasing of an old man
who's made himself book-keeper to an empire
and sloughed the graces. If I told you then
I came too short in the telling—by some worlds
I came too short. I loved you instantly,
beyond recking costs, must have you; we were married,
the year went by like summer lightning, then
I looked behind the laughter on your face
and found an anarch, a laughing devil, stronger
than I was, quicker of wit, a child in purpose,
a demon in desire. You never once
put out your hand but to tear down the kingdom,
riddle authority, and with that seraph's face
and seraph's tongue seduced me to betrayals
that bind me yet. And still I loved you, still
I could not tear you out, and Rudolph came,
his mother's child, an archangel's face and tongue
again, with a devil's will, a Wittelsbach
as they've been from the beginning. But I loved him—
as I loved you—almost as I loved you.
He hates me and betrays me—and I love him.
All my life long I tread my own heart down

here in the dust and silence of this room
where no one enters. I shall defend my kingdom
and hold it, and send it on despite you, yes,
despite my love for you and him. Go now.
I have work to do.

Elizabeth. I shall not ask again.

Franz Joseph. I have been patient with Rudolph, and shall be
  patient.
He may be a son to me yet—but as for you
when you loved elsewhere, when you took your body,
the body of the Empress, and laid it down
beside another man, and took him to you—
when I heard this I heard my own death walking
the palace hallways, stepping off my days
and no other step to wait for.

Elizabeth. You were the first
  in that, remember.

Franz Joseph. A man may be unfaithful,
  but not a woman, and not an empress.

Elizabeth. No?
  Well, that has been changed, I think.

Franz Joseph. It has not been changed.

Elizabeth. You've chewed on your revenge these many years.
  Surely it's been enough, Franz. Where is Imry?

Franz Joseph. Where you'll not see him,
  where you would hardly care to see him now,
  no place for lovers.
    [*She steps back.*]

Elizabeth. Goodnight.

Franz Joseph. Goodnight.

Elizabeth. This step
  you hear in the halls, it may not be your death
  but only a girl you loved one time, grown old
  and sleepless, hurrying now a little toward
  a too-long corridor's end. You're of tougher grain
  than I—or Rudolph. You'll outlive us; when
  you bury us the halls will be quieter.

> [*She goes out through the curtain. Franz Joseph takes up the paper-weight on his desk, as if to resume his work, puts it down and sits, his eyes on the floor.* COUNT TAAFE *enters.*]

Taafe. Your Majesty.

Franz Joseph. Yes? Yes, Taafe.

Taafe. You asked me to come in without announcement
  when it was certain the Vetsera girl
  had come alone to Rudolph.

Franz Joseph. She's with him?

Taafe. Yes.

Franz Joseph. We must be sure.

Taafe. There's a serving maid who watches
  about Prince Rudolph's door. I'll wager on it;
  so far she's made no errors.

Franz Joseph. Then we'll go.

> [*He takes a step, then puts out his hand to the table.*]

One moment.

Taafe. Your Majesty's not well?

Franz Joseph. It's nothing.

> [*He sits*]

Nothing, I shall wish you to come with me.
They'll be alone together?

Taafe. For a time.
 However, I have also information
 the Archduke John may visit him tonight,
 and it seems reliable.

Franz Joseph. The Archduke John.

Taafe. That's the Hungarian business.
 I should have thought the woman was enough,
 but when we're young we take it in our stride,
 amours and intrigue after midnight.—Sleep?
 Sleep later on, while the alarm rings. Still,
 we may find it awkward.

Franz Joseph. Say nothing of Hungary.
 One thing at a time, and the woman first.

Taafe. Very well.

Franz Joseph. What do you think of Rudolph, Taafe, frankly,
 forgetting I'm his father?

Taafe. Frankly, sire,
 he's a rebel and a rake.

Franz Joseph. I'd give these arms
 here at the shoulder, I'd step down in a grave
 tonight, let them stop my mouth and ears with earth
 to have another son. It may be I
 won't live forever. God send me the wit I need
 to save my empire from the son I have.
 I'm better. We can go.
  [*They go out.*]

     CURTAIN

ACT I

SCENE 2

SCENE: *A room—half living-room and half study, in the apartments of the Crown Prince Rudolph of Austria, at the Hofburg. A door to the right leads to a reception-chamber, a door at the rear to the interior of the apartment and the bedroom. To the right rear a desk stands under a shelf of books, a skull grinning among the writing materials. At the left rear a fire burns in the fireplace. In the left wall are high French windows. Over the desk hangs a portrait of Rudolph's mother, the Empress Elizabeth, as a young girl, her hair crowned with stars. It is after midnight, the room ablaze with light.*

THREE MEN *and* THREE WOMEN, *dressed for a masked ball, lounge and stand about the room, as if waiting. Among them are the* BARON *and* BARONIN VON NEUSTADT. *A domino lies across the couch, ready to be donned.*

Baronin von Neustadt. Your question, then, sir. Your question. I am ready for your question.

[*She seats herself before one of the men.*]

Baron von Neustadt. My dear, where were you yesterday afternoon?

The Baronin. At home, my love. Proceed.

von Neustadt. Be more specific. Where, definitely where?

The Baronin. In my own bedroom, heart's darling.

von Neustadt. Ah, and your occupation?

The Baronin. I was burning—old letters.

1st Lady. Yes, that's true, she told me. She was burning old letters.

1st Man. All afternoon?

The Baronin. My dear Fritzi, all afternoon.

1st Man. A bale of letters.

The Baronin. Oh, quite a bale. At least.

14

von Neustadt. Ah—ah!—Then how did it happen, my only love—
   I call you to witness, d'Orsay—how did it happen that Mimi
   waited for you all afternoon in your bedroom, and saw nothing
   of you—no wraith of you, no glimpse, from two till six—

1st Man. What, saw no flame, smelled no smoke, no burning?

von Neustadt. There was nobody there—!

The Baronin. The slut lies.

2nd Lady. Oh, no, darling. I tell the truth.

von Neustadt. Rudi—Rudi!

The Baronin. He's about to complain to royalty.

von Neustadt. By God, I shall buy a whip! Rudi! Rudi!

Loschek.
   [*Entering from the bedroom*]
   The prince will be with you in a moment, sir.

The Baronin. And now will you answer my questions, sweetest
   of the sweet?

von Neustadt. No.

The Baronin. Come, I give you the witness chair. And to begin,
   where were you, my lord and master, yesterday afternoon?

2nd Man. In church. He told me.

3rd. Man. In medias res.
   [RUDOLPH *enters in a dressing gown.*]

Rudolph. Why the outcry?

von Neustadt. Rudi! She refuses to tell me where she was!

Rudolph. She? Who, dear baron?

von Neustadt. That one there! My wife there!

Rudolph. Must you take up our time with these domestic details?

von Neustadt. But it's incessant! No matter where I expect her to be she's always somewhere else!

Rudolph. But how fortunate you are in your family arrangements, and how some men would envy you!

von Neustadt. You think so?

The Baronin. My love, you exaggerate!

von Neustadt. Not at all.

2nd Man. You are coming with us, Your Highness?

Rudolph. I meant to, but some servant of the state has left a pile of documents on my desk—you see?

1st Man. They must be signed?

Rudolph. They must be signed—tonight.

1st Lady. And you must read them?

Rudolph. I must read them.

1st Lady.
Shall we do him the honor of believing him?
1st Man.

[*Looking up at the portrait of the Empress*]

I swear there's never in the history of the world been a woman as beautiful as the Empress.

2nd Lady. Isn't it true? And she's still beautiful.

2nd Man. God knows where Rudi got his looks.

The Baronin. There was a certain master of horse much favored of the Empress about our Rudolph's time. An oaf, but ingratiating. Methinks a resemblance has been traced—

Rudolph. Trail your slime where else you will, you rout of bitchery, but keep your tongues now and forever from my mother! [*A pause.*]

1st Lady. Come, come, darling, you attack the succession.

The Baronin. Yes,—I'm sorry. After all, a prince's mother is sacred. Will you forgive my offending?

Rudolph. Some other time, shall we say? Tonight I find you not so much offending as offensive.

The Baronin. You will make enemies.

Rudolph. I have made them—many and terrible.

The Baronin. Do you wish to add me to the list?

Rudolph. There was once a grandam, you may remember, who added water to the sea?

The Baronin. I do remember.

Rudolph. Ponder it.

The Baronin. I would much rather be friends with you, Your Highness. And you'll need friends. You are playing a deep and devious game in the Hungarian elections. You are involved far beyond safety with the Baroness Vetsera. You have offended your father on both these counts, and there is a limit to the tolerance even of an emperor.

von Neustadt. For God's sake, darling!

Rudolph. Not because you are dangerous, but for your honesty, I will be friends with you, my dear Baronin, and I will admit that the court of Vienna is a high and slippery place, whence a breath, a reaching out, may send one down the escarpments to oblivion. But for myself I have leaped, I have slid, I have positively dived over the parapets, only to find myself replaced

with miraculous celerity upon the topmost point of this distasteful pinnacle, I loathe the court of Vienna, I despise the
people who inhabit it, I despise myself for making a part of it,
yet here I am and have been, any time this thirty years. What
you say of my relations to Hungary and to the Baroness
Vetsera, these are lies, rumor, scandal, what you like, but repeat
them infinitely, I beg of you—give me what push you can from
this glassy eminence, and you will be a friend indeed.

The Baronin. But you're in earnest, your Highness.

Rudolph. Is that a capital crime in your circle?

The Baronin. It always makes me a little uncomfortable.

Rudolph. Oh! that's beyond pardon!

The Baronin. But do you actually despise the court of Vienna?

Rudolph. And loathe it.

The Baronin. Then I'm saved from boredom for another fortnight. I too shall despise the court of Vienna. I shall wither it
with scorn, I shall drench it with adjectives. Children, we shall
make this the latest thing. The Habsburg court! Its incredible
morals! Its perfervid asininities! Despise it? I loathe it! It's—
putrid!—Rudi! Rudi! We shall make you the height of fashion!

Rudolph. Be off with you, all of you. You're late, and so am I.

The Baronin. Nevertheless I'm more your friend than you guess.
I have had the confidence of a certain person, but hush, we say
nothing.

2nd Lady. Are we going?

1st Man. Come, you rout of bitchery!

1st Lady. That's the word.

von Neustadt. But we'll see you, Highness?

Rudolph. In half an hour.

The Baronin. Come, refuse! Excrescences of a tawdry royalty! Come!

von Neustadt. Your word, Rudi!

[*They go out, leaving Rudolph alone. He waits for a moment, then calls.*]

Rudolph. Loschek.

Loschek.

[*Entering*]

Your Highness?

Rudolph. Look in the little passage, and bring Bratfisch to me.

[*Loschek bows and returns through the inner rooms. Rudolph sits at his desk, lifts a paper from the pile and leafs through it, then thrusts it back. Loschek returns with* BRATFISCH, *and stands waiting.*]

Bratfisch. There was something, sir?

Rudolph. Yes.

[*He draws his hand over his eyes wearily.*]

Loschek—there are too many lights.

[*Loschek bows and begins to extinguish the candelabra, leaving two candles that burn under the portrait of the Empress.*]

What's the weather tonight?

Bratfisch. A light snow, Your Highness. It may fall an inch or two.

Rudolph. You're to wait at the postern till the lady comes, Bratfisch. Afterward Loschek will take your place. You understand?

Bratfisch. No, sir.

Rudolph. He will take your place because you will assume this domino—this—the arms here—the eyes here—

Bratfisch. Yes, sir—

Rudolph. And will be driven to the Baltazzi palace, where you will be announced as the Crown Prince Rudolph.

Bratfisch. Very well, sir.

Rudolph. Comport yourself accordingly, with grace, with dignity, above all with fitting reserve. Remain not more than a quarter of an hour. I should not suggest any passages with the ladies— beyond a discreet compliment here and there.

Bratfisch. Yes, sir.

Rudolph. Go now and take the domino with you.

Bratfisch. If you'll pardon me, Highness, there's a little man at the area-gate offering to sell chestnuts.

Rudolph. Did you make a purchase?

Bratfisch. I'm his only customer so far.

Rudolph. An agent?

Bratfisch. He's been posted there by somebody—to see who goes out and in.

Rudolph. Then he'll follow my domino. See that my domino makes a night of it, Bratfisch. A little of everything disreputable, and back here at dawn or thereabout.

Bratfisch. Yes, Highness.

> [*Bratfisch bows, takes up the domino and goes out with Loschek. Rudolph looks up at the picture of Elizabeth.*]

Rudolph. We live too long—is that what you say, my mother, with the stars in your hair? A woman outlives her beauty, a man outlives his dreams. When they painted you so, with the stars, there was brightness on your earth— dew on the lawns in spring. But now you walk

the long cold Hofburg corridors at night—
silent—and if you meet me there—your son—
you look at me as if you walked the moon
and men were strange. But then you're all courtesy:
you murmur "Rudolph, darling" and go on
and it's the moon again. We're lost and damned
here in the Hofburg. You know it; you know I'll find it—
why tell me before my time?—

[*The clock strikes twice outside.*]

   Count it out, count it,
you bells that turned back Atilla! I'm in
my thirtieth year. There's half a life left yet
before I'm cold. Would it be something gained
if I'd put roads and water enough between
my corpus and Vienna, before I die,
to evade that damned Capuchin church? It reeks
of Habsburgs and rotted kings. Must you rest there,
dear mother, when you're dead? You tell me yes—
they have plucked out the stars from your eyes and hair
and made you ready.

[*He sits, hidden in the shadow. The place is quiet for a moment, then
a* MAID *tiptoes in gently and goes to the fireplace. She busies
herself with the fire, pausing meanwhile to listen. Rudolph
moves. She rises quickly.*]

The Girl. I'm sorry—I thought—everyone was gone.

[*She starts out.*]

Rudolph. Wait.

The Girl. Yes, Your Highness. I'm sorry.

Rudolph. Who sent you here?

The Girl. No one, sir. It's—something I'm supposed to do.

Rudolph. Yes, of course.

The Girl. I may go, sir?

Rudolph. Yes.

The Girl. Thank you.

Rudolph. Wait again. Wait one moment. I know you.

The Girl. No, sir.

Rudolph. From many years ago.

The Girl. No, sir.

Rudolph. Oh, yes! I troubled your innocence, I believe,
and gave you money, and let you go. I'm sorry.
But why are you here?

The Girl. It—happened. I earn my living
here in the palace.

Rudolph. Who hired you?

The Girl. The major domo.

Rudolph. And by what pretense of duty do you prowl
my rooms after midnight?

The Girl. To see that—there's no disorder—
and they said you were gone—

Rudolph. This is the seventh.
One after another I uncover them,
these household spies they set on me. And this,
this they thought was clever—a girl I'd known,
one with a pretty face—I might slip again,
and you'd pick secrets between kisses—yes,
and tattle to the Emperor.

The Girl. No, no!

Rudolph. Why not? He pays preposterously. When you're used
and full of secrets you'll be silenced with
a pension and well guarded! Who set you here
and what were your instructions?

The Girl. But it's not—true—

Rudolph. You have a brain! You know what happens when
they hang a spy on the ramparts! Tell me who's
your master, where you give your reports, who pays
at the end of the week, or you'll go back in a basket
to this same major domo!

The Girl. Your Highness—

Rudolph. No lies—
for I tell you I'm sick of this spying; they crawl in
the walls
like typhus-lice at plague-time! By God, I'll hang you
in sheets from a bedpost!

The Girl. No, my lord—no, truly.
I'm only here in the palace to earn my way—
I've said nothing about you.

Rudolph. But I'm not wrong.

The Girl. Oh, you are. Please let me go. You've hurt my hand—
please, will I lose my place?

Rudolph. No. I was wrong.
Forgive me. It gets under the skin and into
the blood, the business of being a prince. In the end
you fancy yourself a god, and all other flesh
an offering to you.

The Girl. I know.

Rudolph. How do you know it?

The Girl. It was so before.

Rudolph. Was it so even then,
   when I was twenty-three? Perhaps it was—
   I took you, and paid you off. But it grows with the years,
   even though you know your flesh is grass like the rest,
   even though you swear it daily, still when they bring you
   food on gold, and armies tread the night
   to ensure your sleep, and when you stretch out your arm
   they run to make a garden—it taints the mind,
   this mindless service, till what you wish you must have,
   no matter how many bleed for it. I'm unjust,
   and violent, and revengeful—they've made me so—
   they'd make you so in my place. And so, forgive me.

The Girl. I—forgive you?

Rudolph. Yes.

The Girl. Yes, if you wish, Your Highness.

Rudolph. I say this for myself—
   not for you, my dear. I've schooled myself
   to live my birth down, make apology
   where apologies are due, though I writhe within
   to say the words. I thank you for your forgiveness.
   We'll let it end there.

The Girl.
   [*Falling on her knees, taking his hand*]

   My lord, let me thank you—

Rudolph. No!
   Keep off your knees!

   [*Loschek enters from within.*]

   Yes?

Loschek. You're not at liberty,
  Your Highness?

Rudolph. What is it? Yes.

Loschek. There's someone waiting.

Rudolph. Go now.
  [*The Girl bows and slips out.*]

Loschek. The Baroness Vetsera's here.

Rudolph. Let her in quickly.

Loschek. If I may mention it,
  we suspect this girl—this that was on her knees.

Rudolph. I know—I think you're wrong. But follow her,
  look through the hall.
  [*Loschek goes out after the Girl. Rudolph goes to the inner door.*]
  Marie!

Mary Vetsera.
  [*At the door*]
  May I come in?

Rudolph. How did you come?

Mary. Does it matter? It's snowing, sweet,
  and I walked through the snow. I wasn't followed.
  I'm sure I wasn't.

Rudolph. It doesn't matter now—
  now that I have you. Here's a whole snowflake yet
  caught in your hair. Your cheeks are cool. Good God,
  how you transform a room!

Mary. Don't you want to kiss me?

Rudolph. Does one make love with an angel, darling? Wait—
  surely one should worship a little first,

light a fire on an altar, or burn incense,
and kneel in prayer.

Mary. But not to me.

Rudolph. Yes, sweet,
to you.

Mary. Then all the gods grant all your prayers,
as suddenly.
[*She lifts her lips and he kisses her.*]
Have you been well?

Rudolph. Well enough.
I saw you once in the Prater.

Mary. I know. I saw you.
[*Loschek comes back unobtrusively through the room.*]
God in heaven, these two weeks! Oh, Rudi,
have you been lonely?

Rudolph. I've been miserable,
creeping about on trains, listening to welcomes,
fat mayors of fat towns making fat speeches
unto eternity, no word from you—

Mary. I couldn't manage. Verily, I'd have died
only for your black blessed raven Loschek
and the little note he dropped like manna in
my prayer book. Then I took up heart and lived
to see you.

Rudolph. Do you love me so much?

Mary. And more,
more than I tell you.

Rudolph. How long will it keep on?

Mary. Oh, easily till I die.—And afterward—
  I doubt that it will be much different then.

Rudolph. Oh, child, child.

Mary. Oh, truly, Rudi! I'll die
  when you die—even if you should be away
  I'd know if you were dead, and I'd die too,
  yes, where your earth was mine would find yours out
  and lie there with you.

Rudolph. Pretty.

Mary. And keep you warm—
  for there'd be such a burning in the dust
  that used to be my heart, I'd keep you warm
  deep under ground. You'll know me by the fire
  there in the dust, and then we can make up
  for never having spent a whole night together—
  lying quite still, a long while.

Rudolph. You speak too well.

Mary. Well, but I've never spoken well before,
  and never will again. It's now, for you.
  And then that's all.

Rudolph. Surely you know, dear Mary,
  this is a profitless passion for a girl
  whose family looks to her to marry the Indies
  and make her face their fortune.

Mary. Have I asked for money?

Rudolph. No. God knows I've none to give.

Mary. But then—
  my family does well enough.

Rudolph. Some time
  there will be reasons of state why I can't see you.
  My wife will rattle the gates of the Vatican,
  and bring the emperor down on us. Somehow
  they'll ship me off to the east and you to the west
  and no amount of loving will help. You'll find
  you have to wed a banker. Then your price
  will have gone down, after the scandal here,
  and I'll have spoiled your name.

Mary. If it must be,
  it must. But if I marry, still I'll love you—
  even if you go back to the Fleming—even—
  if—you should want to.

Rudolph. Would you love me then?

Mary. Yes.—This is a bitter welcome—after
  so long away.—Do you wish me to go now?

Rudolph. No.

Mary. Will it be soon?

Rudolph. I don't know.

Mary. Yes.
  I won't ask for more than I can have.
  Only—let me see you while I can.—
  It can end—when it ends.

Rudolph. May I be eaten
  of worms before my time for this! Look, sweet,
  this is a letter I wrote two weeks ago
  to the sacred nose in Rome—and here's a ring
  I've carried in my pocket this two weeks
  to give you when you came! But my damned soul
  has been so cursed and crawled upon with punks

and serving men and women I feel the itch
in every palm I touch, and taste the greed
in every kiss!

Mary. But I'm greedy, too. Too greedy.

Rudolph. Look at the letter.

Mary. What is it?

Rudolph. A petition,
drawn up formally, wherewithals and flourish,
requesting that the Pope annul my marriage
with the Princess Stephanie, on sufficient grounds,
that I may marry again.

Mary. Must you marry again?

Rudolph. This ring's to be yours.

Mary. But it's a wedding ring.

Rudolph. Perhaps if you should study it a little
and look inside the circlet you might find
a date graved. Now the dark blood climbs in your throat
remembering.

Mary. This is worse than mockery;
it's torment, Rudi. Were you free as fire
we could never marry.

Rudolph. No?

Mary. With an empire waiting?
Marry a Baltazzi out of the east,
a daughter of peddlers?

Rudolph. Why then goodbye to the empire!
They may keep it. And luck to them who get it.
It's been no luck to me.

Mary. Goodbye to the empire?—
Now I know you mock me. I'm a girl,
foolish, and easily gulled, but this I know—
no prince throws up an empire for a woman
who's been his for the asking.

Rudolph. Oh, Vienna!
The wisdom of Vienna! All her daughters
have eaten it with their porridge! But it's true
that I'm no jingling poet, to sell a crown
for love and a pair of shoes. If I wanted empire,
I'd have the empire, and you, and Stephanie,
and anything I whistled for! But when
I say the Habsburg crown's an ancestral curse
and I won't wear it, then the bars go up
around me, and I feel my father's hand
closing on what I do and where I go,
till the Hofburg's a prison, the street's a prison
where I ride, with yielding walls, but iron
and not to be broken through. Crown Prince I am,
Crown Prince I must be. This is my answer to them:
either I take the road free as a beggar,
or from now on my life's my own. I've played
their game, kept my intrigues hidden, held my tongue
from comment on injustice, let myself
be dangled like a golden calf on strings
till I'm at the end of my tether. I married once
to barricade the throne, a Habsburg stallion
led to a Leopoldine filly for
the act of royal generation. That's
accomplished. Generation's possible
between whichever two of opposite sex
they lock in a room together, young enough
to have more appetite than brain. But now
I shall marry where I please, say what I please

in private or in public, and the storm
I rouse may drive me either up or down,
but I shall have my way.

Mary. And this ring's for me?

Rudolph. This ring's for you.

Mary. How have I earned it, Rudi?

Rudolph. I don't know. There have been other women
here in this room, a handsome company,
I give my word, and where they went afterward
concerned me only mildly. When you've gone
I hear your laughter dying down the hall
and think you're gone, but then you run in my veins
like sun on Danube water, and your hair
comes down between me and the book I write,
and I curse you for a witch. This is for boys,
this spring-sap madness, this magic in a feather,
the one red feather in one girl's dark hair,
this dreaming at windows, memory of a perfume,
this is for boys and girls, and not for me,
but with you it's mine again. And so we'll keep it.
Let them try to take it from us.

Mary. It's what I've wanted
too much to dare to wish, but now I'm trembling—
I don't know why. What will come of us, Rudi?
What will they do?

Rudolph. Why, for a time you'll hear
such a concaterwauling of horrid shrieks
you'll think Walpurgis night has broken out
in all the embassies. Little men will trot
through palace doors with black brief-cases packed
with facts and papers. Hands will be upraised,

friends estranged, lips bitten, beards gone white,
hair turned gray on diplomatic heads,
and a long growl will stem from the father walrus
to crack like thunder down the Hofburg stairs
and maybe split that curtain. Unseen hands
will write on walls—prophetic cries will rend
the midnight—vendors, likely, calling the news—
but we can't listen to stuff like that forever,
so we'll go to sleep.

Mary. I hope it comes to no more.

Rudolph. Would you be happy?

Mary. You know that.

Rudolph. And not frightened
when the wind comes up and the sacred elder statesmen
begin to rake the clinkers out of hell
to roast the two of us?

Mary. If you still want me
I won't blench at hell.

Rudolph. Then they can't hurt us.
They need me. I don't need them. But I need you—
and Q.E.D., it follows. Make your peace
at home, as best you can, for I'm not content
with these stolen interviews. We shall appear
as often as we like together.

Mary. Then—
I must tell you—there's an arrangement made—
lawyers and seals and signatures—I'm not
quite sure what all—it's covert yet, but I'm
supposed to marry—

Rudolph. Yes?

Mary. You see, I thought
  you'd tire of me. They put me up for sale,
  no doubt, for so much cash. And I said yes,
  sometime—next year, perhaps. But now I'll break it.

Rudolph. Yes, break it.

Mary. I had to tell you. You might have heard.
  Will you forgive me?

Rudolph. Who was the man?

Mary. Braganza.

Rudolph. Oh, the Duke. Well, tell the charming Duke—
  what will you tell him?

Mary. That I was passing a palace
  when a prince came out who asked me to marry him,
  and suddenly, there in the midst of winter,
  it was spring, and so I'm very sorry
  but—Rudi, Rudi, you're angry!

Rudolph. No. It's just
  the ancient masculine aversion to
  the fact of other males in the world. But break it,
  tomorrow.

Mary. Yes.—And it's true about the spring.
  I feel it like a trembling in the earth,
  this spring in winter. If I die of it
  I die of too much miracle.

Rudolph. It's not death
  to love me.

Mary. There'll be a storm—worse than you say.
  The birds' nests will come down.

Rudolph. I've never yet
    stood up before the emperor and said:
    this I intend to have! but when I do
    it may rain birds' nests in the Wienerwald
    but I shall have it.

      [*The* ARCHDUKE JOHN *of Tuscany comes in from the rear,* Loschek
        following, KOINOFF *and* SCEPS *behind them both.*]

John. It will rain birds' nest soup
    in Pesth before you rule if you can't keep
    your women out of conference!

Rudolph. Loschek!

John. Christ,
    don't blame Loschek! I walked in. We have
    an appointment here tonight—

Rudolph. No doubt you've met
    the Baroness Vetsera—the Archduke John
    of Tuscany—a man who hides his brain
    under his lack of manners.

      [*Loschek lights the candelabra and goes out.*]

John. I've heard of her.

      [*He bows.*]

Rudolph. Behind him Captain Koinoff, behind him
    Herr Sceps of the Tageblatt.

      [*Koinoff and Sceps bow. She acknowledges the salute.*]

Mary. Shall I leave you?

Rudolph. No. You can hear this.

John. Then we go back again.
    Pick up your boots, my friends, and set them down
    outside. Whatever it was we had to say

can't wait, and we can't either.
  [*He starts out.*]

Rudolph. I think you can.
  Sit down, my Salvator. The Baroness
  is in my confidence.

John. But not in mine,
  if I can help it. I've stuck my precious neck
  into a noose some dozen times this fortnight,
  all for your damn fool Highness, and got it out
  by some fool luck each time. There's such a thing
  as tempting the old lady with the shears
  just once too often.

Rudolph. The Baroness Vetsera
  will be my wife when it can be arranged.
  If you trust me, trust her.
  [*The men bow. John returns.*]

John.
  [*To Mary*]

  I beg your pardon.
  [*To Rudolph*]

  This will take some doing, though. Your current wife
  has a king to her father.

Rudolph. Yes. That's occurred to me.
  She can go home to her father.

John. Give me your hand.
  I like you better.
  [*He takes Rudolph's hand. To Mary*]

    I was burdened once
  with one of these royal frumps. She's back with mama
  and I've gone human with a chorus girl.

But you might have helped yourself to a sweeter portion
than you'll share with the prince, my dear.

Mary. I'll chance it.

John. Oh,
    I don't doubt it. Where there's purple blood
    a woman's apt to chance it. Come, kiss her hand,
    captains and editors, before it's royal—
    She'll be more distant then.
        [*Sceps and Koinoff come forward.*]

Koinoff.
        [*Kissing Vetsera's hand*]

    May you be happy,
    Baroness.

Mary. I thank you, Captain.

Sceps.
        [*Bending over the hand*]

    May
    you make him happy. For he hasn't been.

Mary. Thank you, too.

John. I have this one half-hour,
    and things have happened since you galloped off
    on your trumpery progress. We've talked a lot this year
    of liberties, rights, broken pledges to the people,
    what pressure we could bring on your father. Well,
    while we talked, there were rather more forthright fellows
    up and doing. It seems the Hungarians
    were eighteen jumps ahead of us—they're on
    the verge of a revolution.—It's not wild talk—
    I don't exaggerate—the train's been laid
    for such a major explosion as might lift

our sister state right out of Franz Joseph's precinct
and lay it in your lap.

Rudolph. Were these the lads
   called on the carpet for circulating pamphlets
   bearing my name?

John. No, no—that's another thing
   though they meant business. That article you wrote
   for the Tageblatt, the authorship leaked out
   and several universities went berserk
   in Hungary—you know, boys yelling for blood,
   French style, the Marseillaise, and organizing
   under the Rudolph banner. The pedagogues
   were scandalized, but their innocents ran wild,
   got out of hand.

Rudolph. And so they were expelled?

John. Right.

Rudolph. And that ends it.

John. For the children, yes—
   but not for some others. Sceps, relate.

Sceps. Your Highness,
   you know how carefully I've preserved my head,
   believing, as I do, that a head's essential
   even to a journalist. Your father's way
   with traitors is a mild decapitation,
   minus publicity. And I want to live
   and raise my family and use my voice
   on the side of justice, so I've walked warily
   and I'm alive. But after this upheaval
   in the universities, when it had all died down,
   a young Hungarian noble came to see me
   here in Vienna, and questioned me point blank

about your writings and yourself. I told him
what I thought safe, and when he thought it safe
he talked to me. He told me what we knew,
that Hungary's sick of the Empire, sick of your father,
ready for fireworks.—He is himself the head
of a band of young aristocrats, all sworn
to separate from Vienna or die trying,
and they don't expect to die. They mean to win;
they've organized by cities, laid their plans—
they're ready to strike now—and what he wanted
was to get word to you. They've set themselves
to make you king of Hungary. Oh, yes.
Koinoff and I went off to Buda-Pesth
to look them over, and it's true—the town's
like a hive ready to swarm—with a royal word
to lead them they'd be on the wing tonight—
tomorrow—when you say.

Rudolph. And your advice, Sceps?

Sceps. This is one time, Your Highness,
when I would risk my head. I've fought oppression
all my lifelong, and got nowhere, your father
being the man he is. We might at least
see an enlightened and liberal Hungary
break off from Austria.
Rudolph. Tell me the name
of this young noble.

Sceps. Szogyeny. You know him.

Rudolph. Yes.
And Captain Koinoff?

Koinoff. I'm somewhat less dismayed
by the word treason, Highness, than Herr Sceps,
who has a family and a paper. I

have nothing but a life that I'd exchange
for, say, a thought more freedom in the world—
and we won't get it while the emperor
sits where he sits in comfort.

Rudolph. As for the Archduke,
  I know his mind.

John. God knows I've nothing to lose
  but a starveling dukedom and a gangling neck,
  whereas you have imperial prospects, likewise
  an imperial rack of bones on which to hang
  a crown if you should get one. But your crown
  won't be worth having if you wait long for it,
  in my opinion. Five or six more years
  as things go now and the Habsburg coronets
  will rate with barrel-hoops on the market.—This
  is not our plot, this blaze in Hungary;
  it burst out ready made; it's real, it's hot,
  it's simple; it began when your mother took
  her first trip to their capitol, and begged
  some mitigation of the penalties
  your father laid on independent speech
  when he was young and brash. She got her way
  because he was in love, and since that time
  the Magyars worship her and you because
  they think you're two of a kind. No doubt you are,
  and you could give them the government they want
  and they'd follow you through brass. But take it now
  or never; a revolution grows like fruit
  and you pluck it when it's ripe or not at all.
  It won't keep on the tree.

Rudolph. You think it's ripe?

John. I know it is.

Rudolph. What would you have me do?

John. Talk with Szogyeny.

Rudolph. And then I'd be committed.

John. No. Not at all.

Rudolph. How does your word go, Mary?

Mary. You shouldn't ask me.

Rudolph. Why?

Mary. I know too little.

John. It's pretty plain if you two want to break loose
and live together, this is your chance for it.
They won't allow it here.

Rudolph. But you flatter me,
you lads, when you assume that if I ruled
the Magyars they'd be compensated for
a war, a bloody war—yes, and a lost one—
with a loss of liberties, and the fees imposed
by victors on the vanquished. I don't list
my set of bones and necessary features
among the major risks—but as a fact
I fancy them as they grow, all in one piece,
and I'd fain, fain keep them so.

John. Then I'm off for Rome
and a boat, and the South Seas! Save your fat neck
and I'll save mine!

Rudolph. If your nobility
implies that what you've told me will go further
you hardly do me justice. I'll be silent.
Yes, if the project smelled a little less
of the moon and more of the earth, I might be tempted
to listen further.

Koinoff. It's not lunacy,
　　Your Highness, truly. As a student of tactics
　　I should say, with the disposition of troops
　　as it was three days ago, when I left Buda,
　　there's little room for doubt that we could snatch
　　control of Hungary. It just so happens
　　that three of this pledged band we told you of
　　are generals—two of them in command
　　of two main key positions. A sudden movement
　　made by night and both the capital cities
　　would be ours, the approaches under our guns,
　　and all Austria couldn't budge us.

John. You will write,
　　you will talk, you will singe the old man's beard
　　with words, but when we need an eagle dropping
　　like thunder on the lambs, you perch on your eyrie,
　　in other words your rump, and gaze at the sun
　　and make snide comments on the smell of the moon
　　around our enterprise! You talk to soldiers,
　　and it's you that's moonstruck! Back through recorded time
　　no prince was ever offered such a kingdom
　　on such a platter—they had to fight for theirs,
　　the Alexanders and the rest!

Rudolph. I'm not
　　an Alexander. What he stood for slipped
　　down the black hills in a very bloody sunset
　　when the first Napoleon died. There are two reasons
　　why I might wish to rule in Hungary;
　　let us look at them calmly. First, if the empire
　　drifts as it's drifting now, it will smash up
　　and I'll be left nothing to rule. Second, if I
　　were king I might inaugurate reforms
　　which I've worked all my life for, and which might

be in time to stave off ruin. Well, they're both
fallacious, both these reasons. If I seize
on Hungary, there'll be a war, and all reform
wiped out for a decade, what advance we've planned
toward tolerant government will be ridden down
not only in Austria, but by my orders
in Hungary, and the empire will break up
for the same sweet reasons we have now—dragoons
on every peasant's back—the forms of law
with absolutism behind them. Add to that
that I, on whom you pin your hopes of freedom
would go the way of all the Habsburgs, lose
my liberal principles one by one, be driven
to give them up to hold a realm together,
and once committed to the adventure, doomed
to be my father over again, I'd catch
at desperate expedients, fill the gaps
in the falling walls with more and more lives of men;
acts of oppression, made to stiffen the line,
would harden into policies, we'd mix
our mortar out of the shambles of the dead
to build new bastions where more men might die
defending me, and my throne! If you're a soldier
you should know this.

John. Have you read in history
of any age when men have not been forced
to fight for freedom?

Sceps. There are times, Your Highness,
when the means are rendered gracious by the end,
though the means be evil. No war lasts forever,
nor would you change so much.

Rudolph. And that's fallacy!
A government will end as it begins,

and if it builds on slaughter it will stand
on slaughter till it falls!

Sceps. But they all begin so!

Rudolph. And they all end so! But I'll not begin
with murder that breeds murder to the end,
and whip my conscience into a corner with
"But this was needed for the ultimate good
of my dear subjects." When this same ultimate good
is but to die in a corner with my conscience
to make me a dull king! For no other purpose,
for nothing would be gained!

John. Why, then you mean
that men should sit and bleat because the butchers
have sharp knives, like a batch of calves and lambs
in the slaughter-yard! Bleat and then run away
to get their throats slit later!

Rudolph. It sounds to you
like cowardice, and it may be all thinking
has the effect of making us less apt
to spit at danger. Insofar as he thinks
a man is much more cowardly than a lion,
but he may live longer, may even get his way
more surely. Something a soldier wouldn't know,
but I offer it.

John. You have a plan?

Rudolph. Why only
this—that I know a bad plan when I see it,
and I'd rather wait. There have been instances
of men who stalked the forces of the dark
and caught them napping, men in whom indirection
and a long patience stood them in better stead

than force of arms. I'm not a patient man,
but I'm trying to learn patience.

John. By God, you've learned it!

Rudolph. Not yet I haven't—but you give me practice,
with your half cock schemes! I tell you I've looked beyond you
and caught a vision of what a man might do
if he were king. And having that vision in me
I've set myself to make myself a man
and unlearn kingliness, shed it like the rag
it is, till a king stands up a man, but a man
with power to make men free!

Mary. May I speak now,
now that I've listened, Rudolph?

Rudolph. Yes.

Mary. I've heard
you talk of danger, all of you, but it seems
you don't know what the word means. It means dying—
cruelly—dungeons without air.—For Rudolph,
if one least whisper of this goes beyond
the room, who could answer for it, who could guess
how long he'd live? You say we might be happy
in Hungary. It's not true. The emperor
watches these things, and knows them before they happen,
and hears them in the walls!

    [*There is a knock at the door.*]

Rudolph. Loschek!

    [*Loschek enters, crosses to the right, opens the door and steps out for
a moment. He returns somewhat shaken.*]

Loschek. Your Highness,
the emperor is here and wishes to see you.

Rudolph. Very well.

> [*He dismisses his guests with a gesture.*]

Loschek. And asks, particularly
that your friends remain here with you. For he wishes
to see them also.

Rudolph. Good. My friends remain.
Will you open the door for the emperor?

> [*Loschek opens the door, bowing.* FRANZ JOSEPH *enters, dusty and
> humble.* TAAFE *follows.*]

Franz Joseph. I intrude
at a ghoulish hour, my son. This end of the night's
for revelling when we're young. I too kept revel
late, in my day, and understand it—yes,
and grieve to interrupt you. When your years
begin to dwindle like the coins a child
takes in his hand to carnival, you'll know
why days are precious to me, till I work
long in the night, and break in on your game
with what seems deadly urgent.

Rudolph. You're quite welcome,
Your Majesty. And we're not, as you call it,
revelling. A listener might have guessed
that we were serious.

Franz Joseph. A symposium!
Well, I can't add to that. My thinking's done.
We get that over early, we of the Habsburgs,
I'm afraid, and then we settle down
to take things as they come. They come so fast
there's little time for thinking.

Rudolph. Am I in error
or did you ask that these my guests remain
to hear our conference?

Franz Joseph. It's no conference!
  I merely wished to see you and your guests—
  these guests you have. No blenching, gentlemen!
  Be easy! I don't ask you why you're here
  nor what's been said! God's love, we talk a lot
  back in our twenties when our heads are light
  with such a lack of birthdays!

Rudolph. Do you wish
  to make the acquaintance of those present?

Franz Joseph. No—
  I know them. We won't spend our time in greetings
  but say what we came to say. I have in hand
  a copy of your missive to the Pope,
  sent without consultation. May I ask
  the meaning of it?

Rudolph. I thought the meaning plain.

Franz Joseph. You wish to marry again?

Rudolph. I do.

Franz Joseph. Your friends
  have heard of this from you?

Rudolph. They have.

Franz Joseph. But I—
  I have not. You are aware, of course,
  that marriages within the Habsburg line
  are subject to imperial control
  without exception?

Rudolph. Yes.

Franz Joseph. It should be apparent
  that you have made your prayers to the wrong throne.

This is a temporal matter. One in which
I take an interest. One that concerns the state
which I have undertaken, under God,
to lead and guide, while I have strength to do it,
and which I must not suffer to be torn
by minor loves and whims.

Rudolph. This is no whim,
 sir, and no minor love.

Franz Joseph. I thought it was.
 Your pardon. Where has your fancy fallen then,
 in its latest phase?

Rudolph. Outside the conventions, sir.
 I've chosen the Baroness Vetsera.
 [*The Emperor bows to Mary.*]

Franz Joseph. Yes.—
 And so I had supposed. And I must still
 be blunter than I like. It's known that you've
 received the lady's favors in advance
 of bell and candle. Or at least your wife
 has so informed the cardinal. These things
 are winked at. You will tire of her, and she,
 I hope, will tire of you. Play out your play.
 As for divorce and marriage to her, that
 I utterly refuse. A child in arms
 should have more foresight.

Rudolph. If Your Majesty
 will fix it in your mind that we are not
 quite children here, it may be possible
 to find some common ground on which our wills
 can meet! I am not sorry for this visit.
 For I have wished to tell you for some time
 what I have in mind to do.

Franz Joseph. You'd have been wiser.

Rudolph. Not only in regard to my divorce,
    but in a graver matter. For my wife,
    I was too much a child when I allowed
    your word to bed me with a well-intentioned
    but very dull young princess. Being grown,
    and somewhat more, I shall arrange details
    of this sort for myself.

Franz Joseph. Forgive me.—And
    as to the graver matter you speak of?

Rudolph. Why,
    this Austria, this kingdom of the east,
    the Oestereich, you govern it, you bred
    this son of yours, myself, to govern it,
    set me to some five hundred tutors, one
    behind another, till I'd crammed my skull
    with usage and prerogatives and law,
    till I was read blind on usages and trash
    and like a fool I turned to drink, or women—
    the easy women you presented me
    to cut my man's teeth on, and keep me quiet
    when I was less than docile. Now I'm sick
    of this your training, and I've spewed it up,
    and it's not pretty what was stored inside
    my carcass. What have I found instilled in me
    to make me king—to fit me to be king—?
    the morals of a wolf in a court of wolves
    and bitches, such a pride in decorations
    as might become an ape, no truth, no honor,
    no faith in a man's word or a woman's, stealth
    and craft in brigandage, hyena's appetites
    for flattery that smells, resentment of
    all honesty lest it should cut too deep

and show me what I am, the tongue of a bootblack
licking out coins, but underneath a cold
analytical fury, a knowledge that all friends
are dangerous, all men enemies—

Franz Joseph. But thus—
thus is mankind, at heart.

Rudolph. This is myself
and you—no other man in the world excepting
those who are trained like you and me to rule
this outpost of disaster, Europe!

Franz Joseph. Well,
kings do not grow on bushes. They are made
as well as born, like poets. In the process
if they must pass through fire, like steel the blade
is sharper for it. And harder.

Rudolph. Sharp and hard,
and withered at the entrails, like a headsman
bred up to deal out death, and never flick
an eyelid with his shoes awash in blood
from crying children!

Franz Joseph. What child have I sent to death?

Rudolph. Too many!
    [*A pause.*]

Franz Joseph. May I ask that you state briefly
what meaning you may wish me to attach
to these hot cries from your heart? For you do mean them—
but I have not understood.

Rudolph. If it were quite plain
to me, I might make it so to you. But I wish

to leave the court, live like a commoner, choose
some obscure village where I'll touch the earth
from time to time without these damnable footmen
to spread rugs on it. I want no guards round me,
no authority, no rank; I want to sink
my roots outside this hot-house, where I'm kept
at even temperatures and if I joke
all men laugh like madmen. Because I had
a brain one time, but under this contagion
of flattery and power and sycophance
a brain can't live. I break down cell by cell,
day by day, toward that quick ulcerous growth
men call a king, a tumor on the lives of men,
with no other function than to spread, grow and eat,
rot into the body politic, spraddle out,
a witless fungus, a running sore, an evil
on what men have and are!

Franz Joseph. And you would take
  this lady with you to the obscure village
  for contact with the soil?

Rudolph. I would.

Franz Joseph. But then—
  you would return?
Rudolph. If ever I were needed
  I would return.

Franz Joseph. Do you not comprehend
  that knowledge, skill and use are necessary
  in managing a realm? An untried horseman
  on an unbroken colt might yet stick on,
  but Austria, where we ride wild horses tandem,
  Austria would trample down an unpracticed rider
  before he was well mounted.

Rudolph. And is this practice
  that I get now?

Franz Joseph. Count Taafe and I are here
  tonight to ask that, from tonight, you take
  a place on one of those hard stools that face
  his desk, and share our councils. We're not young,
  the Count and I. We need you as apprentice
  to take the business over when an old king
  says goodnight to an old kingdom.

Rudolph. Then—
  I shall seem most ungrateful, but it's true
  that I would rather never reign at all
  than reign as you have reigned.

Franz Joseph. We need new blood,
  a fresh voice, modern ways. What you have to say,
  we'll listen to it.

Rudolph. My first advice would be
  to grant autonomy to Hungary,
  open the franchise to all men of age
  to vote, rescind restrictions on free speech
  and press throughout the empire, wipe out clean
  all laws that make political crime, swing open
  the gates of political prisons. Sign away
  to parliament the power to make and change
  all laws, keep for yourself executive
  and advisory functions.

Franz Joseph. You have read too much.
  This is an empire, not a democracy.
  No king has ever given till he must
  what you ask me to toss away.

Rudolph. Our Habsburg house
  has been a cancer on mankind, a fluke

that eats till the host dies! Its power's cancerous,
destroying what it lives on, yes, and itself,
as it's destroyed your brain and eats at mine
to make me also what all emperors
have been, blind parasitic poisonous mouths
sucking at arteries. When you came to the throne,
the day you came to power, you signed and sealed
four hundred warrants of execution, death
to four hundred men, your enemies. Since then
you have continued as that day began,
feeding your strength on blood, your tentacles
sinking in deeper, spreading out further, till
no man dare whisper in an empty room
lest you should reach and touch him. And what for?
To build for you an arrogant machine
in middle Europe that will feel its way,
crushing and grinding men, to a larger greed,
more tributary lands, extensions of
degenerating tissue and disease
of which you make the center! This machine
is under way, and moves colossally
inch by inch, and every inch it crawls
it nears a precipice over which we'll go
and all of Europe with us!

Franz Joseph. And now indeed
I understand you, though your flux of figures
takes some unravelling. Still my dull old head
asks further enlightenment. How would one rule better
if one ruled better?

Rudolph. As if the lives of men
were precious things, as if men's happiness
was precious as your own. Under your hand
men tend toward maggots, with like mouths and brains

as grow in their masters—such cheese-loving souls
that one could curse the high permitting stars
that give them leave to crawl! For your machine
has but one purpose, to iron and discipline
till men and lives are so much mud and death
in a game in which the stakes are mud and death
for enemies and friends!

Franz Joseph. And under your rule
there would be no national rivalries, no wars,
no enmities?

Rudolph. Who gains by wars but the kings?
Let the people choose war or peace.

Franz Joseph. But there's no choice.
There was a time when plagues and famines kept
the populations down, but in our wisdom
we have dispensed with famines and with plagues,
and nations press against their boundaries
incontinent, spawning more children on both sides,
till they knock the chips from one another's shoulders
and snatch the food from one another's mouths
and fight for standing room. Those who fight best
will live, and those who will not fight will die.
Shall we choose to die? Will you choose it when you're king?
The kaiser of Germany is just your age,
or nearly, William the Second, a crafty boy
but not your equal. What he dreams there in Prussia
is dominating Europe. His machine
is building up like ours. The time will come
when he will set his foot down on your lines
and two great empires, equal in wealth and men,
will lock in one mortal year. Your destiny
is war, not peace, our Rudolph against their William,
our Habsburg against their Hohenzollern. Then

the outcome hangs on who's the better man,
and there the Habsburgs have it. Not in my time
has any prince in Europe shown a promise,
a quickness, a grace, an aptness in all arts
of war and peace, such as in you, my son,
recalls an ancient glory. It rests with you
whether Austria shall live.

[*A pause. There is a clatter of rifle-butts on the floor outside.*]

A Voice.

[*Outside*]

Halt!

Another Voice.

[*Outside*]

You must wait here, madame.

A Third Voice.

[*Outside*]

The emperor is here, and you must wait.

Elizabeth.

[*Outside*]

The emperor is here—and I must wait?
I am the Empress Elizabeth, if you please,
and I will not wait.

The Third Voice.

[*Outside*]

Let her pass.

[*Loschek has slipped in from the inner rooms. At a nod from Rudolph
he opens the door. Elizabeth enters. The men bow. Rudolph
goes to her, bending over her hand.*]

Rudolph. You are welcome, mother.

Elizabeth. Thank you.

> [*To Franz Joseph*]

I came to bring a word from you to Rudolph,
but you're here before me.

> [*Loschek goes within.*]

Franz Joseph. I've little more to say,
and I'll be gone.—-When a man's old as I am,
suddenly all he wagered on his youth,
his dreams, what he tried to do, transfer themselves
to the person of his son. You may not love me;
whether I love you I don't know, it may
mean much or little, this clutching at the throat
where you're concerned. But surely what I've dreamed
and hoped, and poured my passion and my days
to serve and rescue, these are holy things:
the honor of the Habsburgs' thousand years,
which now devolves on you, the circle of ground
which we call Austria, held toward east and west
through many bloody, endless, desperate wars
down to this hour. These you must help me keep.
And you must take my word that keeping them
requires you keep your name quite clear and free
of slander, such as would come of this divorce
and contemplated marriage. You must not
impugn your place. You must not leave the court
for mad *al fresco* venturing. It's fatal
ten thousand different ways. And so I ask
your word on both these matters.

Rudolph. You ask my word
that I'll not leave Vienna, will not divorce
my wife, will not remarry?

Franz Joseph. Yes.

Rudolph. It's easy
     to say that for the honor of our race,
     and to preserve our fatherland, men's blood
     must be poured down the old dynastic rat-hole
     as in the past. I say if that were true
     I'd have no interest in the government,
     nor in our fatherland, nor the tapestry
     of wars and madness our mad ancestors
     the Habsburgs wove, and in which their acts and features
     are doubtful decorations. What's the way out,
     how men are to save themselves from repetitions
     of that same tapestry in still more wars
     and blood down the same damned rat-hole, I don't know;
     but I might find out, in some other atmosphere
     than this. I shall leave the court. The Baroness
     goes with me where I go. And I shall ask,
     publicly, for a divorce.

Franz Joseph. I'm very sorry.

Rudolph. I'm sorry that we must differ.

Franz Joseph. I'm very sorry
     that to maintain much more than discipline
     I must interfere with your wishes. I know this lady
     better than you do. She must be shut away.
     Oh, in her mother's house, where she'll feel at home;
     and to put her more at ease, perhaps her jailor
     should be the man she's pledged to marry.

Rudolph. Sir,
     you grow childish.

Franz Joseph. When we deal with children,
     with wilful children, we must sometimes adopt
     a childish method. I have known your mother

to glance off at these tangents in her time,
and thank me later for restraints.

Elizabeth. A woman's
easily broken. Take care how you anger Rudolph.
You won't break him so easily.

Franz Joseph. My dear,
where our treasure is—you've read it in Holy Writ.
Rudolph will stay in Vienna.

Rudolph. From this hour
I do and say and go as I please.

Franz Joseph. Why then—
it's as I said. Taafe, the guard was needed,
and you were right after all.

Taafe. Shall I call them?

Franz Joseph. Yes.
        [*Taafe steps to the door and opens it.*]

Rudolph. The royal guard!

Franz Joseph. I do regret it, Rudolph.

Rudolph. You will regret it.

Taafe. Come in. You're to make an arrest.
        [Two or Three Soldiers *enter, an* Officer *following.*]

Franz Joseph. This lady goes with us.

Rudolph. Your Majesty,
this is opera bouffe! To arrest her in my rooms!

Franz Joseph. It will not be printed. You may trust our discretion,
Herr Sceps and me. Even the Archduke John
will curb his tongue. You were lately in Buda-Pesth,
were you not, sir?

John. No, Your Majesty.

Franz Joseph. Good. We'll say nothing
   of that, nor of this either.
   [*To Mary*]
   Will you come?

Rudolph. She'll stay where she is.

Franz Joseph. Oh, now I beg of you,
   no words, no violence!
   [*To Mary*]
   My guest for the evening
   only, and then your mother's. As I've said
   I know you better than Rudolph.

Mary. Yes. I'll go.
   [*She looks once at Rudolph, then walks out through the soldiers. The
      Officer and the soldiers go with her.*]

Rudolph. You count on your gray hair
   and greasy words too much! You've never seen me
   angry—but by your own everlasting God
   you may find such a change in me as we'll
   regret—both of us—if you let her walk between soldiers
   three steps farther—!

Franz Joseph. I should think less of you
   and the metal in you if you showed no temper
   at such a moment. Be angry. It will pass,
   and you'll think better of it. There are matters
   much more important than the boiling-point
   of turbulent princes. You spat out your defiance
   lightly, across my face. No man, since I
   was crowned, has spoken so to me, nor will
   and go unpunished.

Rudolph. But I have, and will,
   and will again! What do you gain by this?

Franz Joseph. Time—and your presence
   here in Vienna—on which we set a value.
   But mainly time—the only cure I know
   for adolescent ills. I wish you well.
   I'm cruel to be kind. But when to be kind
   I must be cruel, I use no half-measures.
   Reflect on that. And when you're cooler try
   if there's a way to my clemency.

     [*He bows and goes out with Count Taafe.*]

Rudolph. This is the ultimate in degradation—
   to come here ready with a squad of soldiers
   and take her like a criminal! It's second childhood,
   and empty posturing.

Elizabeth. It wasn't empty
   once when a squad of soldiers visited
   my lodging in Madiera. Oh, it's known
   that I was then a rebel, rebel enough
   to fall very much in love. The man was Imry.
   We thought we'd kept it secret, but this rank
   of guardsmen came—in their comic opera fashion—
   without warrant or warning, and what was done with him
   I never knew. Perhaps the Baroness
   will not be seen again.

Rudolph. But that's not possible!

Elizabeth. It's happened. Oh, to make a hole in the earth
   and lay an unwanted body in it, that's
   quite possible. What we call civilization
   is built on dead men's silence.

Rudolph. What can be done?

Elizabeth. Nothing. He has his way.

Rudolph. But not with me!

Elizabeth. I hope not.

John. Now will you take this Hungary
we offer you, and pay him back in his coin,
or will you sit here still in your fine detachment,
contemplating destiny?

Rudolph. What in God's name
do I want with Hungary?

John. Make her queen of it,
make yourself king. Look, Rudolph, if you strike
before he's warned we'll have the Baltazzi palace
and Mary out of it and be off across
the border, to a new kingdom, while he's still
awaiting your apology!

Rudolph. We have
no arms, no plans, no men—

John. I'll find you fifty
within six hours!

Elizabeth. And now I could almost hope.

Rudolph. For what?

Elizabeth. That he'll be broken.

Sceps. He has information.
He knew we'd been in Buda.

Elizabeth. He has little.
He sent me here with a bit of cold advice
for Rudolph's ear, that some of his hot-head friends
might find their heads in danger.

Sceps. That's enough.

Elizabeth. No, no! It only means he plays for time
and isn't ready for you.

Rudolph. It's a madman's scheme,
incredible as a nightmare. No sane man
would believe it might be tried, or might succeed,
unless doors open of themselves and walls
come down on hinges. Yet it may be they do
after this nightmare we've lived through, his guards
set in the halls, and an emperor at large
with paranoia. Find your fifty men,
and we'll raid the Baltazzi palace.

John. There's fire in the man!

Rudolph. Do you think I'm tame?

Sceps. I'll drop out. I've given
too many hostages.

John. Save yourself and your paper.
You say we'll raid the palace—and after that
what happens?

Rudolph. What else could happen—then we'll try
for Hungary.
    [*John takes Rudolph's hand.*]

John. Koinoff, come in. Your hand on this.

Koinoff. Oh, count on me.

John. The devil drink his eyes
that breaks this pact.

Sceps. Put me in too. Good God,
we die sometime.

John. That's better. That makes our circle.

Rudolph. And now I set my hand to it I'll go
as far as your best madmen. If he wants war
he shall have war. Mother, you're one of us.

[*Elizabeth steps toward the circle of men and then pauses.*]

Elizabeth. I wish I might. But my heart's in your enterprise
too far to touch it with my hand. The lips
and hands I've aided in rebellion, they're
all cold. There's an old fatality in me
that I outlive all those with whom I league
against him. Make your compact, you who are young
and may be lucky. I am a wraith of things
long dead and buried. I must not burden you
with griefs past sounding.

[*She turns to go.*]

CURTAIN

THE MASQUE OF KINGS

ACT TWO

ACT II

Scene i

SCENE: *The following evening in the study of Franz Joseph. This time the room is fully revealed and is seen to be of ample size and exquisitely furnished. An inner door at the left leads to the Emperor's apartments, the outer door is at the right. Near the entrance at the right sits the* MAID *who has been seen previously in Rudolph's room. The* BARONIN VON NEUSTADT *stands near her.*

The Baronin. My dear, it would hardly do if you were to be found sitting when the Emperor entered, would it, now?

The Girl. No, madam.
[*She rises.*]

The Baronin. On the other hand, the Baronin von Neustadt, for ineffable reasons, may be found seated, even by royalty, on condition that she rises immediately to meet such an august occasion.
[*She sits.*]

The Girl. Yes, madam.

The Baronin. Pardon me these hornbook lessons in deportment, but as you rise higher in the state you will find them more and more to your advantage, perhaps even obligatory. You have not been summoned previously to this Holy of Holies?
[*The Girl is silent.*]

There—the fault was mine—you must not violate a confidence. —And yet, I know your business here very well, since it's the same as my own, perfidious wretch that I am. I sell information for pin money, my husband being sometimes a little to the windward of lavish, and you do the same for bread and butter— therefore your secret's safe with me and mine with you.

The Girl. I have no secret, madam.

The Baronin. Excellent! And so dewily, so fragrantly, so honestly said! And so we wait here cheek by jowl, petticoat to petticoat, the above-stairs smothering its knowledge in words, the below-stairs in silence—but still in perfect understanding, baronin and parlor-maid, for next to death there is no leveller of classes like espionage.—But what levels us is that we find it a rather despicable business, and despise ourselves and each other in our hearts.

The Girl. Despise ourselves?

The Baronin. Don't you?

The Girl. No.

The Baronin. No? Come, come, my dear, there are a half-dozen of us waiting to clear up some minor doubt that balks the imperial will in respect to Rudolph. A very nasty occupation; and we take money for it.

The Girl. I hate him.

The Baronin.
 [*Rising*]
Truly? But then you have a reason. No doubt he has given reasons, though none to me. No, my interest is purely mercenary, and I sink below you in my estimation. Occupy the chair, my dear, and I shall stand.

The Girl. Thank you, madam.
 [*She remains standing.*]

The Baronin. Strange, strange, how a woman will love a man for robbing her of youth and filling her with innumerable children, while she will hate him forever if he gives her back to herself with her good looks intact and only a memory of pleasure to remind her of him! There, there—I meant nothing by it. My remarks, as usual, are for the ambient air, and by no stretch treasonous.
 [*The inner door opens, and Count Taafe enters.*]

Taafe. You will oblige me by waiting in the anteroom for a moment, Baronin von Neustadt. I have a word to say to this young woman.

The Baronin. Surely, Taafe, surely. Ah, my child, you will go far. You already take precedence.
[*She goes out right.*]

Taafe. What was she saying to you?

The Girl. Only, sir, that she knew my business very well, because it was the same as her own.

Taafe. Very true, and quite democratic of her, though indiscreet. However, she's a mistress of indiscretion, and makes it serve her ends. Whatever you do don't attempt to emulate her in that direction.

The Girl. No, sir.

Taafe. So far, and so far as I know, you've been close-mouthed under strong temptation. Remain so, and we shall continue to be pleased.

The Girl. Yes, sir.

Taafe. Your instructions this evening are very simple. There is, or is likely to be, somewhere in the Prince Rudolph's apartments, a list of Hungarian officers and noblemen. If you can lay your hand on it, copy what you can without risk, or memorize as much of it as you have time for. The list may not be there at all, as I say. Someone else may have it, or he may carry it upon his person. But we need it quickly and desperately, and you may happen on it if you try.

The Girl. Yes, sir.

Taafe. That's all.

The Girl. Thank you, sir.

[*She goes out.* A LITTLE MAN IN A CAP *enters.*]

Taafe. I suppose you know, Rauscher, that the Crown Prince was in his apartments last night while you were amusing yourself at the Tzigan dancer's?

Rauscher. I followed his domino, sir, and it was a man of just his build. What's more, he must have been imitating the prince's walk. You'd have sworn to it yourself.

Taafe. I hope you know who it was?

Rauscher. I know now. It was Bratfisch, the coachman.

Taafe. As it happens it doesn't matter this time, because we had other information. But for the future, you have your instructions. Don't be misled again.

Rauscher. No, sir.

Taafe. That's all.

[*Rauscher bows and goes out. The Baronin reenters.*]

The Baronin. Your most humble servant.

Taafe. My dear baronin, your extremely agile and provocative tongue may sometime dig you a bear-pit so deep and wide that God and man will not be able to extricate you from it.

The Baronin. Ah, luckless that I am, what have I said now?

Taafe. You'll find it just as well to avoid communication with others of our—shall I say our under-cover staff? As you must be aware, ideas are poisonous to the unsophisticated mind, and you are unfortunately not devoid of certain helter-skelter philosophic concepts—

The Baronin. Oh, you do me too much honor!

Taafe. Concepts of a corrupting character which pervade your very charming conversation, and which do you no harm, but might well pervert a simple faith or taint an untutored devotion.

The Baronin. I love that.

Taafe. Curb yourself, my dear baronin. No further remarks of any kind to the little serving-maid. It may not have occurred to you, but there are only two ways out of the ranks you entered when you consented to employ yourself on our little missions. One of them is an honorable discharge after years of undeviating and scrupulous fidelity. The other we shall not speak of, but it would entail the loss of many things which at present make life endurable to you—first and least among them your freedom to go and come.

The Baronin. And I may not resign?

Taafe. There is no third alternative. And let me say that the mere suspicion that you wish to resign is enough to place you in a most precarious position.

The Baronin. I have no wish to do so. I merely asked.

Taafe. Good.—The rest is business. You have seen the Baroness Vetsera?

The Baronin. Yes.

Taafe. She is still rather disconsolate, no doubt?

The Baronin. I should guess so, though you will agree that she has her reasons for being fairly monosyllabic toward me—knowing me as she does.

Taafe. There is no possible manner in which she might correspond with Rudolph?

The Baronin. There's but one door to her room, dear count. It's locked, and the Duke of Braganza keeps the key. No servants are allowed to enter, her mother being thoroughly on your side in this business.

Taafe. The Duke, I hope, is a jealous man?

The Baronin. Jealous, tyrannical and exacting. He will make her an excellent husband. He is, for the moment, an excellent jailor.

Taafe. It was he who admitted you to see her?

The Baronin. At your request, yes.

Taafe. It would be annoying if she hanged herself, or threw herself from the window.

The Baronin. Oh, but she's young, passionate and full of hope. She will be quite as passionate in another direction once she's married to the Duke.

Taafe. These women are cynical about each other.

The Baronin. We have reason to be.

   [*Franz Joseph enters from the left. Taafe turns to him deferentially, the Baronin bows.*]

Franz Joseph. Have you heard from Koinoff?

Taafe. No, Your Majesty. I've expected him since three o'clock.

Franz Joseph. Will you ask the baronin whether she knows of any faint suspicion that Captain Koinoff may be less than wholehearted in our cause?

Taafe. You know, my dear baronin, that Koinoff has been entrusted with a delicate commission in connection with Rudolph. He has appeared admirably diligent and we had a report from him this morning, but now, just when we stand in dire need of further information, he has failed an appointment to meet us, and is all of six or seven hours behind-hand—with no word from him.

The Baronin. Oh, but he may be entangled in such a fashion that it would give his hand away to leave—

Taafe. True, but for seven hours, and when we depend on him utterly.—How much did you know of him when he was first recommended to us?

The Baronin. Only that he was clever, needed money, and looked honest.

Taafe. But now we find that he was employed in Berlin under Prince Bismarck before coming to Vienna—in some quasi-secretarial capacity. He left Berlin under a fairly noxious cloud. In fact, it's probable that he's had a startlingly wide experience in double-tonguing and quick exits. That his schooling was with the Jesuits has not added to our confidence.

The Baronin. I had no notion of all this.

Taafe. When it's added that the Vetsera girl was also your recommendation you will comprehend why we grow slightly uneasy about the character of your friends.

The Baronin. But that—nobody could foresee. She fell in love.
   [*There is a knock at the door, and a Servant enters.*]

The Servant. Captain Koinoff is here, Count Taafe.

Taafe. Ah, that alters matters. Send him in at once.
   [*The Servant goes out.*]

We excuse the baronin, thoroughly re-instated in our good opinion.

The Baronin. Exonerated by accident, Your Majesty—in the casual manner of this world we live in.

Franz Joseph. My dear, the appalling amount of accident in the best-governed dominions is hardly flattering to a king.
   [*The Baronin bows and goes out.*]

And yet we must get rid of this woman. Her tongue is like an open razor in the hands of a child.

[*Koinoff enters and bows.*]

Koinoff. Your Majesty—Count Taafe—

Taafe. You are late, sir.

Koinoff. Indeed I am, and I've been bleeding inwardly over it ever since the clock went past the hour.

Taafe. You have the list?

Koinoff. No. I expect to get it this evening.

Taafe. But you have gathered the most important names?

Koinoff. Only Szogyeny.

Taafe. Come, come, Captain Koinoff, you have Rudolph's entire confidence, you are acting as military advisor to the leaders, there is an all-important list of rebelling Hungarians on the table before you, and you fail to memorize one additional name.

Koinoff. But the list has not been displayed, it has not been discussed in my presence, and I can't ask for it, as you must realize.

Taafe. You could angle for it, and if you were adroit you would have got it long ago. In your capacity of tactical expert you can express doubt of their strength in the west—they will answer by identifying their allies in that region. You can demand specific information as to their support from ranking officers in Buda-Pesth—they will reply by enumerating certain members of the clique—

Koinoff. They have given that information in a general way. But there seems to be a tacit understanding among them that their confederates are to remain anonymous till they're ready to strike—

Taafe. And when will that be?

Koinoff.

[*Smiling*]

We plan to rescue the Baroness Vetsera from the Baltazzi palace and leave for Hungary tonight.

Taafe. A sufficiently hare-brained project.

Koinoff. And easily prevented.

Franz Joseph. But it must be apparent to you, Captain Koinoff, that before we move openly to prevent it we must have in our hands the names of my sworn enemies in Hungary. Otherwise I may never know them. And until I know them I can take no steps to forestall a much more serious thing, a major and well-planned revolution in Hungary, with or without Rudolph

Koinoff. Yes, Your Majesty.

Franz Joseph. Then I shall expect you here with at least a portion of that list before midnight. If we have some of them we can get the rest. No doubt your heroic little band is even now in a fever of preparation?

Koinoff. Yes, it is, Your Majesty.

Franz Joseph. Then go and we shall wait for you.

[*Koinoff bows and goes out.*]

Taafe. The movement of troops into Hungary has been taken care of. Several trains left at seven this evening and others will follow during the night. I was obliged to entrain the Seventh Corps, because no other could be got ready on short notice. It leaves Vienna almost entirely unprotected, but I felt that the emergency required it, and we run no risk here.

Franz Joseph. It may be all these things come home to roost, sometime, what we've been and done. I see them camp

round us tonight. There's a shadow of black wings
between me and the candles. Well, my ways
have not been pretty always.

Taafe. That's the voice
of a man who needs his sleep.

Franz Joseph. I could use some sleep
if I could sleep. But that's not what it is.
It's that this ruling as I've ruled is like
a child's sand castle by the sea. It stands
with flags and soldiers till the sea licks at it
gently, a little at a time, and then
in one great wash it's gone. Perhaps the tide
is due now. We've both seen it on the flats
in Hungary, and it's not turned yet.

Taafe. My king,
this is a morbid strain, and baseless. There's
no danger in these youngsters.

Franz Joseph. It's their world,
and we're old men, hanging on by our last half-hours,
alive by a legal fiction. There's something forgotten,
something we've overlooked that makes it fatal,
and I don't know what it is.

CURTAIN

ACT II

SCENE 2

SCENE: *A small section of Rudolph's room, including the portrait of the Empress, the desk beneath it, and a number of chairs which have been pulled up to the desk for a study of maps and schedules.*

RUDOLPH *and* SCEPS *bend over papers under the light. Rudolph is in military uniform.*

Rudolph.

[*Reading a note*]

"She will escape. Wait for her." And you found this on your
desk?

Sceps. With no envelope, just the sheet
of plain note paper.

Rudolph. Every move one makes
recorded and transmitted under ground
as if by seismograph. But it's from a friend.
It may come from her. We'll wait till midnight—
no longer.

Sceps. Shall I draw the proclamation?

Rudolph. It was Napoleon Bonaparte, the runt,
who first worked out the formula still used
for consolidating conquest. Caesar, before him,
cut him a crop of kings, and then went on,
more or less bored to discover that new kings
sprang up behind him. But the young scrub Napoleon,
with a heart like that of a cheap Swiss watch, and the brain
of a coffin salesman, set out to sell his wares
by getting one foot indoors, and then proclaiming
his stuff was free, guaranteed, and a hundred years
to pay. He tried it first in Italy,

offering liberty, also fraternity,
equality gratis, and all they had to do
was let him buckle their shoulders into a collar
and the world was theirs. Our aim is not the same,
but the formula's still good. Our first six words
in Hungary tomorrow must be these:
We come to set you free.

Sceps. But is this model
apt for your purpose, Highness?

Rudolph. If it works
when it's but a trick, it should be more effective
when we mean to carry it out. We must weld the nation
in one day, in one hour. Is policy
the peculiar possession of thieves?

Sceps. It's so considered.
But it may be superstition. I'll try a draft
and show it to you.

Rudolph. Make it brief and simple.
Brief as a boy's prayer, simple as its answer.

Sceps. I'll try it.

Rudolph. Yet at the very best, not all
will follow us. There are men in Hungary
who have no interest in our freedom. Some
who'd rather die than see their revenues
reduced three groschen. Some of them will die,
no doubt.

Sceps. My lord, I hope——

Rudolph. I know your hope.
You hope this revolution won't come **down**
to what the history of revolutions

predicts too clearly: a struggle for what's there
on the part of those who want it. That's my hope, too.
And yet I fear that certain men must die
if we're to win. And we must win.

[*Loschek enters.*]

Loschek. Your Highness.

Rudolph. Yes.

Loschek. The Archduke is here with Count Joseph Hoyos.

Rudolph. Cover these papers. We'll see him at once.

[*Loschek goes out. Sceps lays a newspaper over the confusion of maps.
John of Tuscany comes in with Count Hoyos.*]

John. I beg your pardon, Rudolph, a visitor,
if you have a moment's time.

Rudolph.

[*Giving his hand to Hoyos*]

I'm glad to see you,
never more so.

Hoyos. God and the Archduke John
know why I'm here. We had some talk in a corner,
and he told me you were up. That is, the Archduke;
so far God's said nothing.

Rudolph. Don't wait for him.
He hasn't spoken since Moses.

Hoyos. Well, my lord,
I don't know what's in the wind. John spoke in riddles,
very darkly, of some black inner ring
fed up with tyranny.

Rudolph. No doubt there are
such groups. I'm not acquainted with them.

John. Oh,
    but Hoyos made an answer.

Rudolph. Yes?

Hoyos. I said
    that my digestion was somewhat impaired
    by the same diet. So we chatted on
    still quite obscurely, led from one thing to another,
    till I found myself led here.

Rudolph. This Salvator
    will swear to a good deal more than he'll live up to,
    and nobody minds. He's not serious.

Hoyos. I see.
    We'll wipe it out. Let's talk about the hunting.
    I shall try Mayerling this year.

John. Good God,
    I took my soundings! You can back my word
    Count Hoyos is as safe a man to talk with
    as any of us!

Rudolph. Keep your head, my cousin.
    The count is trusted by the emperor
    for excellent reasons. Likewise he commands
    the imperial troops in Vienna. I know him loyal
    as I am. If you're meditating treason
    try somewhere else.

Hoyos. This is the truth, Prince Rudolph;
    there's been but little said, but it's enough
    so that if I were colored all the way through
    like this imperial uniform, I'd buzz
    a bee in the emperor's ear, but as it is
    my insides are my own when I take my clothes off
    and probably much like yours. Whether I'm with you

or not, no man shall hear of you from me,
either now or later. We're mutually aware
of a singular danger in frankness. Drop pretence,
and I'll drop it too.

Rudolph. I've known you a long time.
I'll take your word for bond on any subject.
This is a graver matter than you think,
not to be entered lightly.

Hoyos. I'm grave enough.
And I have my grievances, Rudolph.

Rudolph. And could you
afford to lose royal favor?

Hoyos. I have lost it. I'm to lose my command.
I might get it back again, from you.

Rudolph. Our plans
don't touch Vienna.

Hoyos. Aye—aye, Buda-Pesth.
Yes, I'd be useless there. That leaves me out.

Rudolph. I thought it would.

Hoyos. But you have my good wishes, boy.
Go on and take it from him, if you can.
Only why not make a real revolution of it,
go after all or nothing?

Rudolph. We're not ready.
Hungary's organized. And add to that,
I want no more than comes to me of itself:
I make no bid for Austria.

Hoyos. That's a pity,
because you could certainly have it.

Rudolph. You think so, Hoyos?

Hoyos. Hell, I could almost give it to you myself!
Your father has no friends he doesn't pay for,
and there are installments overdue among
some folk I know.
[*Loschek enters.*]

Loschek. Your Highness was expecting the Baroness Vetsera?

Rudolph. Can she be here?

Loschek. She is here, sir.

Rudolph. Then at once—

Loschek. Yes, Highness.
[*He goes out. Mary enters.*]

Rudolph. Mary—

Mary. Don't touch me—don't touch me till I've told you—
is Koinoff here?

Rudolph. Not yet.

Mary. Then when he comes
put a knife in him! He's in the Emperor's pay,
and has been all along!

Rudolph. Koinoff?

John. Oh, no.
We went to Koinoff first. We picked him out
because he was our kind.

Mary. But I know! I know!
It wasn't easy to come and tell you this;
don't question it, and don't wait! Whatever's said
to him goes straight to the Emperor!

Rudolph. How have you learned this?

Mary. From the Baronin von Neustadt. She told me to get you word
of that, and remind you that she'd promised once
to be your friend. I couldn't send, so I came.
Oh, I know it's true.

Sceps. That blocks our expedition
before it starts.

John. She may have lied to you.
She's not to be trusted on either side.

Mary. Oh, yes,
in this—she is.

Rudolph. We heard that you were guarded.
Have they let you go?

Mary. I found my way round that.
The Duke of Braganza thinks he can trust me now.
He's been somewhat misled.—You need never touch me,
never, because I can feel his kisses on me,
his fat-toad kisses, till I'll never be clean,
never; Oh, all I'll ask of you is haste,
lest you be too late, for he was here, this Koinoff,
and heard the plans!
    [*Rudolph goes to Mary. She steps back.*]

    Oh, Rudi, Rudi, it's ended,
you and me, too!

Rudolph. I think not, not you and me,
see, thus we wipe it out, whatever it was.
    [*He kisses her.*]
I'll take you, and let the world go. I'll maybe have to,
for this news of yours, it brings our balloon to earth,

so much rag. It may even mean my days
as prince of the blood are over. Gentlemen,
we're warned in time so that if we're quick about it
and clever we may save the firing-squads
unnecessary labor.

John. I doubt the story,
the Koinoff story.

Hoyos. I think the lady's right.
Why were they shipping troops to Hungary
this evening?

John. Were they?

Hoyos. Yes, train-loads of them.
Nobody knew why.
[*A pause.*]

Rudolph. If you wish to leave, Count Hoyos,
we're not very healthy company.

Hoyos. No, you're not.
[*He rises.*]
If that snake Koinoff crawls in while I'm here
I'm damned with the rest of you.
[*He starts out.*]
In case you find
two or three dozen horses would come handy
for any purpose, there's a cavalry stable
near the Mall. The doors will be unlocked
and no guard set.

Rudolph. Thanks, Hoyos. We may use
some of your nags.—If any of you should wish
to leave at once, they'll watch the west roads, so—
we'd best go south for the winter. For myself,

I have an account to settle. I shall wait
a few moments more.
   [*Hoyos turns away.*]

John. So shall I.
   [*Koinoff enters through the shadow.*]

Koinoff. I give you greeting,
   gentlemen.

Hoyos. Koinoff?

Koinoff. Yes, general. It's Count Hoyos, is it not?

Hoyos. Right, right.

Koinoff. I'm unannounced, your Loschek
   waved me in, as expected.
   [*Hoyos returns.*]

Rudolph. Come, sit down,
   we need you, Captain. There's a road here, look,
   nobody seems to know.
   [*He bends over a map.*]

Koinoff. I was not aware
   Count Hoyos was one of us.

Hoyos. You sometimes find
   a red-wing among blackbirds.

Koinoff. All the better.
   Why, this road, we talked of it yesterday.
   The Baroness Vetsera!

Mary. Yes.

Koinoff. Good Lord,
   that simplifies our problem.

Rudolph. We pick things up
  as we go along.

Koinoff. Yes, sir.—There was a question
  about this road?

Rudolph. It shows on this one map
  but not on the other three. Are you sure it's there—
  for we'll need it?

Koinoff. It's a military road,
  built two years ago, and never used
  for commercial traffic. But it's there.

Rudolph. You have
  these things at your finger tips.

Koinoff. I've studied them.

Rudolph. Hungary, too—you know it
  as well as Austria.

Koinoff. Yes, sir.

Rudolph. We were speaking of you
  before you came, Captain Koinoff. There's no man
  among us but yourself who knows this maze
  of forts and arsenals and guns. Count Hoyos
  is out of it. He's studied Austria
  but not the west. The rest of us grew up
  with politics and statecraft. We shall want
  a general we can trust, one of ourselves,
  to lead the Hungarian armies. Would you accept
  the commission from me?

Koinoff. Your Highness, it's beyond
  my hope or my desert.

Rudolph. But would you take it?

Koinoff. I'm inexperienced in handling men—
except by companies.

Rudolph. But you know tactics
and strategy, you're acquainted with the field,
at least the Hungarian border?

Koinoff. Yes.

Rudolph. Would this
make up to you for the small weekly stipend
you draw from the emperor?

Koinoff. From the emperor? I?

Rudolph. You. From the emperor.

Koinoff. Surely, Prince Rudolph,
you know me better. Tell me who's whispered this
and I'll refute it.

Rudolph. It wasn't whispered, captain.
It's known. But we're inclined to say no more
about it, since we need you, and your heart's
on our side more than his. An old arrangement,
made with Count Taafe for your laundry bills,
it happens with lieutenants. They make out
perfunctory reports for a week or two,
then let it drop. If that was true of you
what of it? It's gone now.

Koinoff. It was never true.
Tell me who's said it!

Rudolph. It will be evident,
if you reflect, that though we want and need you,
we shall regard you with less confidence
if you're not open with us. I know quite well
it's a usual slip with these cadets. I've seen

their schoolboy writings. Come, man, make confession
and get your absolution.

Koinoff. It was years ago.
I'd almost forgotten it.

Rudolph. That's more like a man.
Then it was true?

Koinoff. Yes.

Rudolph. But you've broken it off?
You make no more reports?

Koinoff. It was as you said,
Your Highness, a schoolboy business. I'm heartily sorry
that it should trouble you now.

Rudolph. Can you explain
why troop-trains were departing from Vienna
for Hungary this evening?

Koinoff. No, I can't.
I didn't know it.

Rudolph. Then I'll tell you why.
Because a hybrid snake named Koinoff truckles
from one suite to another in this palace
conveying news! Stand away from him! We shall end
this custom of wearing swords among ophidians,
at least by one! I'm good with my rapier,
even by candle-light! Try how you are!
Quick, for we're short of time!

Koinoff. I won't fight with you!

John. I'll cut your throat, you hound!

Rudolph. Let me deal with him!—
I have a strain of cruelty in me,

and it comes out when I look at vipers. Yes,
and on you I'll turn it loose. Sit on that chair!
And now you're there let me assure you, sir,
you'll never rise from it.

Mary. Rudi!

Rudolph. Let me alone
till I've disemboweled the rat!

Koinoff. I'm innocent!
I'm not to blame!

Hoyos. There's often a use for rats,
Rudolph. Don't waste him.

Rudolph. What experiment
would you suggest?

Hoyos. Ask him what regiments
were left here to guard Vienna.

Koinoff. I can tell you!
Whatever you want to know!

Rudolph. Our adventure's done!
We have no further use for information
concerning guards and troops.

Hoyos. Our choice lies now
between a very chancy dash for the border
and the capture of Vienna. The latter sounds
more likely to succeed.

Koinoff. As God's my judge,
there are three regiments left here, and Count Hoyos
commands them!
     [*He points at Hoyos.*]

Rudolph. Hoyos?

Hoyos. It's past all doubt I do
    command three regiments. If that's what's left,
    and it may be, it's your city, and your kingdom.
    I make you a present of it.

John. Take it then.
    You seem to have some question in your mind.
    Boy, it's better than hanging.

Rudolph. Perhaps it is.

John. Perhaps! Perhaps! Man, the great wheel goes round—
    and we go up, and the emperor goes down!
    Seventeen's our number, and it shows!
    Quick, man, quick like a rat, rake in your fortune
    before it changes!

Sceps. We have luck at last!

Rudolph. I'm sorry they pulled me off. My fingernails
    are white to the bone with an itch for murder! I'd give
    a kingdom or two to have the carving of you
    when I remember how you came and went
    and smiled in our faces! Where was the emperor
    when you last saw him?

Koinoff. Waiting in his study.

Rudolph. For what?

Koinoff. I'd promised him a list of names,
    the Hungarian nobles.

Rudolph. Must I still let him live?

Hoyos. These rats are useful. In a war, my God,
    there's nothing like them!

Rudolph. Then stand up, and put
    your wrists behind you. Tie them together, someone.

If I should touch him he might come apart
in my hands, and lose what usefulness a rat
may have.—And so he's waiting for a list
of our Hungarian friends. We'll take it to him.
He can eat it for supper.

Hoyos. One word first! How far
do we go in this? It's safer yet to run
if we're not set to smash the whole way through
and come out on the other side!

Rudolph. What side?

Hoyos. Beyond
the emperor's power to touch us! If you leave
one shred of kingship to him, or influence,
he'll build it up so craftily, we'll all
make mincemeat for him!

Rudolph. We shall leave him nothing!
The man has one strength only, and that's to weave
his webs around you till he binds you down
with one strand after another. Let him weave!
Tonight we pitch his checkerboard in the moat
and all the pieces with it! The game's over
and we start a new one!—Pull it up till it cuts—
we want no slipping!—Step on ahead. Yes, you,
you with your arms tied.—

  [*Koinoff goes toward the hall.*]

CURTAIN

ACT II

SCENE 3

SCENE: TAAFE *and* FRANZ JOSEPH *are sitting in the study over a chessboard. Taafe moves a piece.*

Franz Joseph. Mate, then.

Taafe. What will you play?

Franz Joseph. Pawn takes knight, sir.

Taafe. I hadn't seen it. I thought you beaten.

Franz Joseph. I was.
 Then suddenly it unfolded. The ancient brain's
 not quite dead for sleep. We'll give our Rudolph
 a run for it yet.

Taafe. It's midnight, and no news.
 What shall we do?

Franz Joseph. Wait.
 [*The Servant enters.*]

The Servant. Captain Koinoff's here,
 Your Majesty.

Franz Joseph. Send him in.
 [*The Servant goes out.*]

Taafe. I don't trust Koinoff.
 He fancies himself.
 [*Koinoff enters, his hands behind him. Taafe leaps up.*]
 Your hands, sir! Why are your hands
 behind you?
 [*Koinoff shrugs.*]

Koinoff. They're tied there.

Taafe. Tied?

Koinoff. Why, look for yourself.
    I don't care for the fashion. If you'll undo them
    I'll wear them somewhere else.
        [*Taafe looks out through the curtains.*]

Taafe. You're alone?

Koinoff. Not quite.
    Prince Rudolph's on his way. I'm sent ahead
    as avaunt courier.

Franz Joseph. Sir, explain yourself.
    Has Rudolph sent you to ask audience?

Koinoff. Yes.

Franz Joseph. Then why are your wrists bound?

Koinoff. Sir, he did it,
    or it was done at his order.

Franz Joseph. Unlace his hands.
    You will return to Rudolph and say from me
    his audience is granted. You seem to have bungled
    your business badly.

Koinoff. They knew before I came,
    and were ready for me.

Franz Joseph. They knew?

Koinoff. No doubt of it.
    Also there's little use in sending back
    because he's coming. And will enter when he likes.
    And bring whom he pleases.

Taafe. There's a guard in the hall.

Koinoff. It's gone.

Franz Joseph.
> [*Roaring*]
> The guard?

Koinoff. Your Majesty, it's gone.

Franz Joseph. See what he means.
> [*Taafe steps out.*]

Koinoff. Your Majesty, I'll offend,
whatever I do, but somehow between the time
I left them and returned, they'd learned about me,
yet what they sent me here to say I cannot
and dare not say.

Franz Joseph. Deliver your message, sir.

Koinoff. I dare not, truly. In this room, where you
are most a king, I dare not.

Franz Joseph. It's from Rudolph?

Koinoff. Yes.

Franz Joseph. He makes demands?

Koinoff. Yes.

Franz Joseph. Are you more afraid
of Rudolph than of me? For if you're not
why do you mention it at all? The lad
has frightened you!
> [*Taafe returns.*]

Taafe. Your Majesty, Prince Rudolph,
accompanied by some two or three, is here
asking admittance.

Franz Joseph. And the guard?

Taafe. The guard
may have been changing. But it's set as usual.
I know the men.

Franz Joseph. The captain exaggerates.
Who's with Rudolph?

Taafe. Herr Sceps, the Archduke John,
and Mary Vetsera.

Franz Joseph. Vetsera? The boys are quick!
They've been bird's nesting!

Taafe. Yes.

Franz Joseph. I'll see Prince Rudolph.
Not the others.
    [*Rudolph enters.*]

Rudolph. You were not so delicate
when you led an expedition into my rooms
and over-ran us with soldiery.

Franz Joseph. Come in.
You meant it as an affront, the officer
you sent me pinioned?

Rudolph. A minimum return
for many similar favors. He's your man;
you may have him back. He's of the stuff you like
in councillors and statesmen—two parts crawling
and three parts venom.

Franz Joseph. Still, without him, sir,
I should have fared but badly. You'd have got
just half my empire. That, if I may presume,
should be your first lesson in government. When you're
crowned king, leave scruples at the chancel door

with the holy water. If you keep them by you
they'll trip you up.

Rudolph. I'm not here for instruction.
  Moreover the demands I made before
  are altered now.

Franz Joseph. Suppose we speak in private.
    [*Taafe and Koinoff go out.*]
  Looking out over the conflicts of the world
  I have observed that winners make demands,
  losers take what they get. You've made a play
  for Hungary, and lost. You have in tow
  the little Vetsera, and no doubt for you
  that constitutes victory. But you may keep her
  only at my pleasure. You have little reason
  to raise your voice, more than a cockerel has
  for his first mezzo crowing.

Rudolph. If you look
  from the outer window, you'll see men ranked four deep
  around the palace. No one goes out or in
  without permission.
    [*Franz Joseph pauses, then goes to the window.*]

Franz Joseph. Quite unusual. Tell me,
  is there some celebration?

Rudolph. These are our men.

Franz Joseph. You have no force in Vienna.

Rudolph. Try to leave.
  Order your carriage. Call a servant. Ring.
  You'll get no answer.

Franz Joseph. Count Taafe!
    [*John of Tuscany comes to the door.*]

John. Count Taafe is my prisoner, Your Majesty,
  but if you wish him—
  [*Taafe enters.*]

Franz Joseph. Then whose prisoner am I?

Rudolph. Shall we avoid the word? My terms are simple.
  Shall I state them to you?

Franz Joseph. You run great jeopardy
  for a trollop and a farm!

Rudolph. I'm not a novice
  in such scurrility. I could pass it back,
  but it hardly becomes us.

Franz Joseph. You have scooped up brigands
  among the socialist witlings—such as read
  Herr Sceps, his garbage, and your own—but wait.
  Wait till this slight disorder is perceived
  by authorities in the city. Hold the Hofburg
  against regulars if you can.

Rudolph. Do you recall
  what general commands in Vienna?

Franz Joseph. More than one.

Rudolph. There's been a thundering exodus tonight
  toward Buda-Pesth. Can you have been so blind,
  with all your policy, as to lock the stable
  and leave the house doors open? It's Count Hoyos
  commands Vienna. You've offended him
  in some major way.

Franz Joseph. Where is Count Hoyos?

Rudolph. Here.
  But he's been busy. It was he gave orders
  to isolate the palace.

Taafe. Hoyos too?

Franz Joseph. This may be much more serious for you all
than I had guessed. May I look at this rebellion
face to face?

Rudolph. Surely.

Franz Joseph. Bring them all in.
And our little frightened captain, bring him too.
I've something to ask him.
   [*Rudolph nods to John, who steps out.*]

   This should make history,
what with so much nobility in one room.
and so little mother wit!
   [*John, Hoyos, Mary Vetsera, Sceps and Koinoff enter.*]

   The good Count Hoyos,
Vetsera, the enchanting, the truant Archduke
who never sees his Tuscany, Herr Sceps
of the trenchant pen, silent in council, Rudolph,
the heir apparent. And not among them one
to say, when they knock at my door, let the lion sleep,
lest he be dangerous still? I am dangerous,
and never more so than now. If you will turn
and take your way to your homes through the silent snow
as silently as you came, I'll not remember
what faces I saw here, nor once remind you
by word or act there was snow on the streets tonight
and you left traces in it.

Hoyos. It's a little late
to say that nothing's happened. Some of your friends
have questioned our activities enough
to make a stand against us. Where they stood
the snow is somewhat bloody.

Franz Joseph. An execution?

Hoyos. No, a clash. However, not of our seeking.
Some companies on a street corner.

Franz Joseph. How many dead?

Hoyos. That's not known yet.

Franz Joseph. And this was done, Count Hoyos,
on your authority?

Rudolph. No, on mine.

Franz Joseph. Even that
might be hushed up and pardoned. I engage
to hush and pardon it if you end it here.
Not otherwise.

Rudolph. The victors make the terms!
That was your word!

Franz Joseph. And you are the victors?

Rudolph. Ring!
Call your people! I saw a servant lying
across the threshold of your hall. It seems
he cared more for your safety than his own
and got his throat cut.

Franz Joseph. So the boy's dead. One more
to be explained.

Rudolph. We explain nothing. We've taken the city and hold it.

Franz Joseph. It's not a grateful task to brush the dew
from such a gleaming dawn, but you're misinformed
about the forces in our capital.
There's a reserve of more than twice your numbers,
Count Hoyos, at the arsenal. They'll be sent

to settle this night-brawling in the streets
and cut your lines outside. You'll reign but briefly.
Count Taafe, testify to this.

Taafe.
  [*To Rudolph*]
  Your Highness,
  I have been hoping you'd withdraw your men
  before you're crushed here. It's inevitable
  if you wait longer.

Franz Joseph. Perhaps you don't quite trust
  the word of the captain here, and yet he's expert
  in all these matters. He can state exactly
  what regiments are stationed in the city
  for emergencies.

Koinoff. They're lying! They're both lying!
  There are no troops at the arsenal!

Franz Joseph. Koinoff! Koinoff!
  The weathervane should make certain of the wind
  before it whirls.

Koinoff. But that's the truth, Prince Rudolph,
  there's no guard there.

Franz Joseph. Do you remember, Taafe,
  I said there was something overlooked? Even so.
  It was Count Hoyos who had slipped my mind
  when we stripped Vienna down. And so we've lost.
  At least we've lost this hand. And I accede
  to your terms, Prince Rudolph. Much against my will
  and judgment, choose out your village farm and dangle
  your lady with you. You'll rue it, and so will I,
  but take the disease with the cure.

Rudolph. It was my plan
   to take only Hungary, leave you Austria,
   but now you've pushed your stakes across the table
   and thrown your dice and lost, I win them both,
   and keep them both.

Franz Joseph. Both? Not only a farm,
   but Hungary—and not only Hungary,
   now, but Austria, too.

Rudolph. Yes.

Franz Joseph. Come. I'm to abdicate?

Rudolph. It's necessary—in cases of this sort.

Franz Joseph. You've studied them?

Rudolph. I have.

Franz Joseph. You hold a palace,
   and one old man in his room. Outside the empire
   sleeps peacefully, but when it wakes and asks
   what has been done with the emperor, you'll have
   no ready answer.

Rudolph. Tell me then what answer
   you made when in your youth you took your crown
   from the man who wore it? What's been done before
   can be done again.

Franz Joseph. Boy, you'd be followed only
   by those who stand to gain by you! The gifts
   you give to some you must take away from others!
   Could you ride a civil war?

Rudolph. Sir, by all rules
   of immemorial Austrian intrigue you
   would have the better of me. But the earth

goes steadily round the sun, and men and customs
die out or change. Shut here in your darkened room
you've seen all Europe as one static night
inhabited by spiders that sit still
mending their webs, eating their flies, and watching
each lest another spring. But, could you see,
you have not stayed the wheeling of the stars
nor held the tide piled on one longitude
by bandaging your eyes. Were I not here,
were there no men about your palace, still
your sun went down the Simplon twenty years
before tonight. What you came offering
when you were crowned, men want no longer.

Franz Joseph. Son,
they never wanted it.

Rudolph. If I offer now
what a new day demands, they'll come to me,
and the old dog's forgotten. It's no pleasure
to say this to my father, but it seems
that in these matters sentiment's not used.
You taught me that.

    [*Franz Joseph turns away for a moment, then comes back.*]

Franz Joseph. It might be done. If you turned orator,
and spread the butter thick where the logic's thin
and acted swiftly, and somewhat brutally
while the spell was on them, you could sew them up
before they caught their breath. But it's not your way,
my Rudolph. No, you'd mean it while you said it,
and trust in righteousness to bring you through
and they'd have you by the throat.

Rudolph. I'd mean it all.

Franz Joseph. No doubt. But when an actor plays a part

he's much more moving to the audience
if he's not taken in by what he's doing
enough to weep real tears. The trick of the onion's
more effective.

Rudolph. Sir, you may hear my creed.
There's been no king, since the half-mythical figures
of medieval times, who took for his motto:
Nothing for myself. But I shall take it.
I'm tired of having. Let me drink plain water
and eat plain food, and turn what mind I have
to an instrument of justice, clean of greed,
despising politics. The first steps we take
may seem arbitrary or tyrannous,
but when we're once entrenched we'll lighten all
oppression from above, and let the garden
grow, for it will!

Franz Joseph. Suppose I abdicate.
What is your first step, being king?

Rudolph. To remove
political restrictions.

Franz Joseph. Oh, but first, I know,
say two or three hundred men in Hungary,
say three or four hundred men in Austria,
who must die if you'd be king. Oh, yes, they **must**.
And I'm among them.

Rudolph. I'd think there were not so **many**.
Shall we say—imprisonment?

Franz Joseph. Oh, no—they're like
the little servant who was killed outside.
While they're alive they'll fight, and they'll have friends.
Koinoff will live, the snakes will shed their skins,

but those who can't crawl must die—that's absolute,
if you're to last ten days.

Rudolph. Very well. Let them die.

Franz Joseph. Yes, a few—you'll say—men nobody wants,
but for your real antagonists, the men
with power and will and courage, you'll respect them
and let them live, because your heart's too soft
for more than a moderate slaughter. And being alive,
and having no inhibitions of your sort,
they'll rip you up.

Rudolph. And since that must be prevented
I'll be thorough.

Franz Joseph. I beg your pardon?

Rudolph. Sir,
interpret it as you please. I shall be thorough.

Sceps. This is a strange beginning, Rudolph!

John. Yes,
but logical. There's no escape from it.

Mary. Rudi—it's not the way—

Rudolph. It's the road we've taken
and can't retrace—

Sceps. Yet we'll have much the look
of the French guillotine that came, my lord,
to set men free!

Hoyos. When men make revolutions
they put their enemies to death or die.
That's beyond argument.

Rudolph. Little as we like it
some few must die.

Sceps. I don't go with you in it!
  Moreover, in matters serious as this
  you owe it to us all to ask our word
  before you make decisions!

Rudolph. I shall ask
  your word, later on, but at the moment this
  is a military action. One strong hand
  must guide it.

Sceps. If you begin, Prince Rudolph,
  with these wholesale proscriptions, my tongue and pen
  are useless to you. I'm no facile journalist.
  What I believe I'll write and publish. These
  are murderous tactics, unnecessary to
  the establishment of authority.

Rudolph. You'll no longer
  cooperate with us?

Sceps. No.

Rudolph. Why, in that case
  you'll publish nothing till we give you leave.

Sceps. You'll establish censorship? You?

Rudolph. Until it's clear
  who governs—till we're quite past being shaken
  we dare brook no opposition.

Sceps. Dare not! Dare not!

Rudolph. You heard my order!
  This is no moment for a descent of doves
  and apocalyptic revelations! Take
  your place among us or leave!
   [*Sceps is silent.*]

Franz Joseph. Your reign begins
    to shake off dreams, and may in time emerge
    as the age of iron. We agree on my demise.
    And what will you do next?

Rudolph. With Your Majesty's pardon
    our time grows short, and we have much to do.
    I can give you no more answers.

Franz Joseph. To put it plainly
    you wish to see this remnant of a monarch
    encased behind stone walls?

Rudolph. Of necessity.
    And further speech is useless. In this hour
    I'm responsible to myself alone.

Franz Joseph. It's best
    when you're in company to make pretense
    that there's a God, and you're responsible
    to Him on high. But there, I take your time.
    If I might put one question more I'll swear
    to eternal silence.

Rudolph. What is it?

Franz Joseph. When you've killed
    these seven hundred men, and they've been ushered
    solemnly under ground, what disposition's
    planned for their property? Will it be given
    to friends of yours?

Rudolph. Sir, not to my enemies.

Franz Joseph. Why, fairly answered.
    Count Taafe, stand erect. We've had the watching
    of many gallant gentlemen who passed
    this doorway for the last time. Our admiration

went with those few who took it in a stride
and laughed as they went out. I say goodnight,
adding, with the fine old piety of kings,
a hope that we meet in heaven.

Rudolph. Goodnight.

Taafe. Goodnight.

Hoyos. Shall I call a guard?

Rudolph. Yes. Take the emperor
and Taafe in your keeping. As for Koinoff
have him shot when convenient.

Koinoff. Your Majesty!

Rudolph. I want no such allegiance! Wipe him out,
and let his death come first! Let it stand as omen
over what follows!

Franz Joseph. In your place I'd keep him,
but that's a minor matter. Before I go
may I congratulate your cabinet
on the accession of an emperor
who'll give my reign, in retrospect, the air
of a golden age, in which the headsman's axe
fell as light punctuation.

John. Why do you say so?

Franz Joseph. When you grind my friends
for fertilizer, and plant your friends in their dust
I know your history.
    [*Franz Joseph and Taafe step toward the door.*]
    Now may I ask
one final favor?

Rudolph. Yes.

Franz Joseph. When the good Count Hoyos
  finds me a cell, will he see that this cell's furnished
  with pen and ink and paper, paper enough
  to hold seven hundred names? It just so happens
  that I, of all men living, can tell best
  the names of my fast friends. For a legacy
  I'll leave the list to you.

Rudolph. Leave it if you like.
  I'll not trust it.

Franz Joseph. It will be full and accurate. One name
  will be omitted, that of Count Taafe here,
  because there are, say, ten or a dozen matters
  he can inform you of, unfinished business
  that carries over. What you may do with him
  or with his information, when you have it,
  that of course rests with you. Will you mind, Count Taafe,
  if we leave you delegate among the living
  from the kingdoms of the dead?

Taafe. At Your Majesty's service.

Rudolph. And for your information let me state
  that no unfinished business carries over
  from your régime to mine. I want no links
  that tie us in with your machinery
  for the exploitation of underlings. No doubt
  you leave ten thousand questions at loose ends,
  matters of foreign correspondence, matters
  of internal discipline, taxes, legislation
  to stop fresh gaps in the walls where liberty
  begins to wear through stone. But all these questions
  will go unanswered till we get to them
  and answer them our own way. Our way's not yours,
  has no relation to it.

Franz Joseph. You could trust him.
  I am myself too dangerous a chattel
  to keep about, but Taafe knows as much
  as I, and will serve you quite as well.

Rudolph. Have you failed
  to hear me? What in God's name is Taafe to you
  that you should plead for him?

Franz Joseph. Lad, nothing, nothing.
  I don't ask this for Taafe, but for you!

Rudolph. And I don't want him, won't have him at any **price**—
  want none of your retinue, nor plans nor fragments
  left over from your ruins!

Franz Joseph.
    [*Almost to himself*]
  It may be wise.
  It may be the way to win them. Yet at first
  you'll go so far astray. Well, let it go,
  Taafe comes with me.

Rudolph. Why this is kind of you.
  I thank you both.

Franz Joseph. You'll think I delay for a purpose,
  but one more word. A revolution's won
  or lost on its first morning, all depending
  on how your people take it, and your people
  depend on the press entirely. Before one word
  sifts out on your revolution, the journalists
  of both the capitals must be informed
  firmly of what to print. A censorship's
  inevitable. Herr Sceps is an indication
  of what you must expect.

Rudolph. Must I say again
    that nothing you have ever said or done
    is necessary as a precedent
    to what we have to do? You came to enslave!
    We come to set men free!

Hoyos. But if you're worried
    about the censorship, we thought of that.
    The papers have been silenced. That was my job,
    and I saw to it first.

Franz Joseph. You've seen to it! I see.
    You have two hands; with one you set men free,
    with one you shut them up. That's as it should be.
    That's as it always is.

Rudolph. Does your catechism
    draw to a close, or will you indulge us further
    with reminiscences of triumphs over
    the people you have ruled?

Franz Joseph. You have left one weakness,
    though only one. The Princess Stephanie
    is still your wife. If you should break with her
    you will get tardy recognition from
    the powers of Europe; your support at home
    will be confused. Temper your blood a while;
    postpone your union with Vetsera, or
    your kingship's mortally wounded.

Rudolph. I'm aware
    of your feeling on that question. We'd not be here
    tonight if the tempering of my blood had lain
    in your imperial hands.

    [*He turns to Mary.*]

Franz Joseph. You turn for solace
  to a rather doubtful bosom—I know this lady
  better than you—

Rudolph. Damn you, will you bring this maundering to an end?
  why all this kindly interest in me? Why,
  to poison what I'm to do, with your last breath
  infect us with your leprosy! Take them out!
  Let it end! I've listened too long!
    [*He turns his back and walks away. A pause. Taafe steps toward the
     door. Koinoff, a dagger in his hand, leaps across the room to-
     ward Rudolph.*]

Franz Joseph. Rudolph! Rudolph!
    [*He throws himself between Koinoff and Rudolph and is hurled to the
     floor. Hoyos and the Archduke John pinion Koinoff's arms
     and his knife falls. Rudolph bends over Franz Joseph, helping
     him as he gets to his feet slowly.*]

Koinoff.
  [*To Franz Joseph*]
  Why did you stop me? Do you want to die?

Franz Joseph. You mistake me, sir!
  Was I too quick for you? It's not for nothing
  I've learned to watch men's eyes! These weathercocks
  blow east and west.

Rudolph. Why do you risk your life
  to save mine?

Franz Joseph. Why, because you've forty years
  of life in you, and I have ten or twelve—
  and we're alike. I shall have no other son,
  but you may breed a dozen Habsburgs yet
  to send the name on.

Rudolph. Sir, have you joined my rebellion
  against yourself?

Franz Joseph. Why, lad, I've won! I've won!
What I want most is to leave a king behind me
such as I see you are!

Rudolph. You wanted this?
You played for it?

Franz Joseph. How often what we've wanted
comes to us in the night, a little early,
too unexpected, and we put it by,
and it never comes again. I take my way
quite happily into what darkness you prescribe,
my son, knowing now I leave behind a king
after my heart, a better than myself,
but a king, and a Habsburg king! He will chew on iron
who tries to eat you, now that your salad days
are over. When you speak you speak the words
of Wittelsbachs and fools, but when you act
then you're my son, and the long quarrel in your blood
between the Empress and myself, the quarrel
that lay in your conceiving, it's now ended,
and I shall win, by dying.

Rudolph. I shall not rule
as you have.

Franz Joseph. You'll try reforms, and then you'll learn
that all reforms are counters in the game
of government, played to get what you want;
a trick of management. I tried it too,
and found it useful. We have said goodnight—
the guard is ready, you have things in hand,
and I'm sorry to have kept you. Before you sleep
look in that little black book on your desk—
and read three words of it. I think you'll find
it's worth your time.

> [*The prisoners are taken out, Koinoff between Hoyos and John. Mary
> and Rudolph are left together.*]

Rudolph. I am the thing I hate!
　　Among us all we've made of me the thing
　　I shall hate most till I die. The thing I do,
　　caught on this bayonet of time, and driven,
　　repeats in word for word and death for death,
　　his coronation.

Mary. Once I heard you say
　　a king might be a man, but a man with power
　　to make men free.

Rudolph. I've come to this point in anger,
　　but standing here, looking out on what's behind
　　and what's before, I see in one blinding light
　　that he who thinks of justice cannot reach
　　or hold power over men, that he who thinks
　　of power, must whip his justice and his mercy
　　close to heel. My anger brought me here
　　and ruthlessness will hold me where I am
　　and those who are my friends are gainers by it
　　but nothing's changed. I knew this as a child
　　knows what's in books, as words, and I believed
　　that by some ardent miracle of the mind
　　I'd give my own mind wings. But what was anger
　　I must now keep, and make a code, and live by,
　　or be torn down.

Mary. One moment since you said it,
　　let the garden grow.

Rudolph. I said it. But in this light,
　　this blinding light that beats on you and me
　　now as we stand here, robbing those who have
　　of what they robbed from others, tell me what rule,
　　what guide, what standards, human or divine,
　　can possibly direct a man or king

toward justice? Is it just that men shall keep
what they already have? It was not gained justly.
The titles to possession all run back
to brigandage and murder. What men own
is theirs because they have it, remains theirs
while they can keep it. There's no other proof
of any man's deserving. I set up
my title now on murder, as my father
set his up long ago. And I take over
an old concern, maintained by fraud and force
for traffic in corruption. The rest is perfume.
A government's business is to guard the trough
for those whose feet are in it.

Mary. How can you know this?

Rudolph. I have been taken up on a crest of time
and shown the kingdoms of the world, those past,
those present, those to come, and one and all,
ruled in whatever fashion, king or franchise,
dictatorship or bureaucrats, they're run
by an inner ring, for profit. It's bleak doctrine,
it's what the old men told us in our youth,
but it's savagely true.—I know it true for me,
for when I entered this room, and knew I owned it
and knew I'd touched Franz Joseph's power, then virtue
went out of me to him; I was not the same,
and any man who sits here in his place
will be as he was, as I am.

> [*He sits at the table, placing his hand on the notebook. Mary comes
> forward and lays her hand over his.*]

Let the man live.
Let the old man live.

Mary. Don't read it.

Rudolph. No. I won't read it. I won't need it now.
I know what I have to do.

Mary. Not for that reason.
You'd know the writing.

Rudolph. Yes?

Mary. Because it's mine.

Rudolph. What's written in it?

Mary. It's a diary,
Of where we went, and what we did, at first,
when I first knew you.

Rudolph. How does it come here, Mary?

Mary. I was a little fool, and I had seen you
somewhere at a ball—and worshipped you—
as they all worship you, perhaps, not thinking,
just whispering to each other in the night
about the Crown Prince Rudolph. Then one day
the Baronin von Neustadt took me aside to say
she could arrange a meeting. All she asked
was that I keep a record of my day,
and where we went—

Rudolph. These are reports to him?

Mary. Yes.

Rudolph. This is how you came to know me?

Mary. Yes.
Only at first—

Rudolph. I think I might forgive
anything else you'd done, but to think of you
along with Koinoff! Did you know Koinoff?

Mary. No.
    I warned you when I knew. Oh, Rudolph, please,
    it's nothing. There's nothing here you couldn't see
    if you wish to read them. And when I loved you, then
    I sent no more. You can believe it, truly,
    knowing how much I love you.

Rudolph. I do believe you.
    And I have loved you, but it is like Koinoff.
    These Koinoffs. They're the woman in your arms.
    They're the love she brings you. They're your love for her.
    You hear them in the music, taste them in
    the drink. It seeps and rains and drizzles Koinoffs.
    I think I must have loved you more than I knew.
    More than I knew.
        [*Hoyos and John re-enter.*]
    There was little enough left walking on this earth
    to hold a man from spitting! That's gone now!
    This was to be my lover and my queen,
    and he sent her to me, to sleep with me and tell!
    Even that was his! Let him keep it! Let him have his earth
    where men must crawl and women must crawl beneath them
    and all their words are lies! I'm sick of it,
    sick, and sick to my death!—Hoyos, the guard
    that's round the palace—send them all home to bed.
    Our revolution's over.

Hoyos. Yours may be,
    not mine. I have no wish to send myself
    the last six feet downstairs.

John. Walk out if you like,
    but I'm not through.

Rudolph. Take it. You're next in line.
    Take Austria and welcome.

John. Will you let us die
    like so many bitch's pups?

Rudolph. Why, who are we
    that we shouldn't die? Have we more reason to live
    than our seven hundred? But you won't die, you'll fix it
    or get away.

Hoyos. Is this definite?

Rudolph. Quite definite and final. But you'll live.
    And Koinoff, he'll live, too. It's an ill wind
    that brings nobody salvage. Make your arrangements,
    Hoyos, and cross the border. It's snowing still,
    and the blood we shed's been covered. The little groom
    that fell on my father's threshold, see that he's
    removed, so folks won't stumble when they enter
    and raise an outcry. I think you said the shooting's
    good at Mayerling. I shall try it. If
    you want me, look for me there.
        [*To Mary*]
            You've managed nicely
    to take my last faith from me.
        [*He turns away.*]

Mary. Am I to stay?

Rudolph. You'd better go with Hoyos. Take care of her
    for my sake, Hoyos. Look that she's safe away.
        [*He starts out the door.*]
    The devil take these dead men. I shall see
    his eyes forever.

Mary. Rudolph!
        [*Rudolph goes out.*]

                    CURTAIN

THE MASQUE OF KINGS

ACT THREE

ACT III

SCENE: *Rudolph's apartment in the shooting lodge at Mayerling. The room is plainly furnished, containing little more than a writing table, a gun-rack and a number of chairs. There is a fireplace at the rear, also a door to the bedroom; the entrance to the hall is at the right. At the left two curtained windows. It is dawn of the next day, just beginning to lighten toward sunrise. Three shots are heard in the distance, at varying intervals, then two more, as if a covey of birds had been flushed. There is a tap at the hall door, a pause, and LOSCHEK enters. He pauses, looking at the open bedroom door.*

Loschek.

[*Softly*]

Your Highness.

[*Rudolph comes out in a dressing gown, a packet of letters in his hand.*]

You wished me to call you at dawn, Your Highness.

Rudolph. Yes. It's dawn already?

Loschek. Nearly six.

Rudolph. Is Hoyos about?

Loschek. I think he's shooting in the lower copse with the others. They went out at five.

Rudolph. Yes. I heard them banging. There's nothing like fire-arms to amuse a soldier. I've been writing letters, Loschek.

Loschek. Yes, Your Highness.

Rudolph. I have addressed them in my own tangled chirography, but you've had experience with it, and I trust them to you.

Loschek. Yes, Highness.

[*He takes the letters.*]

Rudolph. Also I think your face is my earliest memory, Loschek, except perhaps for my mother's. You'll say your face is nothing much to remember, I know—

Loschek. Yes, Your Highness—

Rudolph. But the point is you've never failed me in any commission—nor in anything whatever—except for brief periods when you restricted my allowance of spirituous liquors—

Loschek. Oh, sir—

Rudolph. Thereby lengthening my life toward some highly dubious conclusion. Which conclusion, if it should be sudden, I have anticipated by penning certain laborious notes to my friends. You will keep them for me, and you will keep them where nobody will find them unless—and until. You understand me?

Loschek. Too well, Your Highness.

Rudolph. Oh, but there's nothing immediate, nothing in the least immediate. Only the news has reached me that we all die sometime. Azrael, the angel of death, came to me in the night and told me I bore a resemblance to my father. I felt a feather fall from his wing, and where it touched my temple the hair was gray this morning. As they say in the Old Testament, Selah.— When we know that we're to die what's the difference whether we're dead or not, Loschek?

Loschek. The greatest difference in the world, my lord.

Rudolph. And yet no difference at all.—In fact, I don't know yet what future my dear father plans for me, if any. I await his pleasure. Nobody knows what may go on at the back of the old man's mind. Hence the premonitions. Let me see Count Hoyos when he's finished with the partridges.

Loschek. Yes, Highness.

[*He goes out. There are a few scattering shots from the copse and Rudolph goes to a window. Mary Vetsera opens the rear*

*door and enters in a nightgown. She pauses a moment, then
speaks softly.*]

Mary. Rudi.

Rudolph. Yes.

Mary. I was half awake, and reached for you with my arm,
      but you were gone; then suddenly I felt
      such deadly terror—I'd have died of it
      if I hadn't found you.

Rudolph. Or gone back to sleep
      and waked to ask for breakfast.

Mary. Rudi, please
      don't mock me—my blood's cold with it—as if
      the author of the experiment put out
      a hand and took the sun—and from then on
      it would be dark and cold. It was a dream.
      One can't tell dreams.

Rudolph. You tell them very well—
      you do everything well—perfect, finished,
      adept, accomplished—that's the woman of it;
      God knows where they learn.

Mary. Is it dawn on the windows?

Rudolph. Yes.

Mary. The sun's not gone then. But it's cold
      as if it would never be warm.

Rudolph. Go back to bed.
      I'll have them light a fire.

Mary. Whose lover were you—
      last night when you loved me?

Rudolph. I can pay.

> [*He holds out his hand with coins in it.*]

No doubt you'll recognize the sum. It's usual
here in Vienna.

Mary. Is this the wage they set
for prostitutes?

Rudolph. You recognize it?

Mary. No,
but I've heard, I think.

Rudolph. I've heard men say it was little
for a woman's soul in the night. It seems her soul's
worth more then than by day. For scrutinize it
under broad daylight and it's plainly dirt
like the rest of us. Take the money.

Mary. You want to hurt me?

Rudolph. These little hurts! They're fiction, like your souls,
and they wash out like rain. With a new dress
they're half-healed—add half a dram of starlight,
three kisses and a ring, and they're gone clean,
better not spoken of.

Mary. What have I done?

Rudolph. Women are realists, my dearest dear,
loving the sun like flowers, but if one sun
goes headlong down the sky, with Phaethon,
they weep a little under dewy lids
and wait for the next sun's rising. I've gone down
and you will weep your most becomingly
and swear it's the end, the last, and so it is
until the next sunrise.

Mary. Why should you hurt me?
    Is it because you hate the whole earth so much
    you want to hate me too?

Rudolph. If you'll go stop
    three tradesmen on the street, and ask the three
    what it is they live by, they'll reply at once
    bread, meat and drink, and they'll be certain of it;
    victuals and drink, like the rhyme in Mother Goose
    makes up their diet; nothing will be said
    of faith in things unseen, or following
    the gleam, just bread and meat and a can of wine
    to wash it down. But if you know them well
    behind the fish-eyes and the bellies, if
    you know them better than they do, each one
    burns candles at some altar of his mind
    in secret; secret often from himself
    each is a priest to some dim mystery
    by which he lives. Strip him of that, and bread
    and meat and wine won't nourish him. Fish-eyed,
    pot-bellied, standing over counters, still
    without his chuckle-headed hidden faith
    he dies and goes to dust. The faith I had
    was baseless as a palace of the winds
    anchored in cloud, a faith that I had found
    a use for kings, a faith that with skill and wisdom
    and infinite tolerance, infinite patience, I,
    the heir of all the Habsburgs, might strike out
    a new coinage of freedom, cut new dies for the mind
    and lift men by their bootstraps till they walked
    the upper air. This is the faith of fools,
    but I had it, and I lost it. One by one
    the holds I counted on to take us up
    turned out to be the ancient clanking irons
    that bind men to the rock. Till one by one

I could trust no one—could not trust myself,
and stretched out blindly at the end to rest
on a love I had—a woman's love—not much
to ask when your world comes down about your ears
after your faith. And then I saw it there,
a little, dirty, calculating love,
smelling of stale champagne and cigarettes
and girls'-school lushing. Fit to go to bed with,
and offer coins for.

Mary. I know it. I said it once.
And now you see me as I see myself,
a baggage, the sort that might have sold you flowers
or cleaned your rooms. Once when we walked in line
out of the school, thirty girls in line, you rode
with your princess, down the Prater—and we looked
and gasped and worshipped. That's when I saw you first,
among these females in the egg, adoring
their king of men. I loved you after that,
even when I had a nasty small affair
with the officer, that, too, was in your world,
and I was almost proud. I know it's silly
to be young, to be love-sick, to make a portrait-shrine
of someone far-off, above you; but to have
the sudden offer of a meeting with him
if only you'll bring word of where he goes,
and then to find that he's incongruously
in love with you, as you with him, to know
that you're a little fool, no more, no more,
and one of the great masters of the world,
the highest, wisest, godliest, looks down
and loves this empty face of yours—oh, Rudi,
I could have wished you better than to love
where there was nothing! Then I took my soul
between my hands, and said, if this is his

it must be worthy of him; watched your ways
and listened when you spoke, and loved, and listened
till I knew better than you knew yourself
what your dreams were; yes, till it sometimes seemed
that something nobler grew here in my breast
than the heart of a gypsy's daughter. Words came to me
to say what I had never thought nor said,
and pride came, and reserve. But these are yours,
not mine, for I was moulded in the womb
after a slighter pattern. Made for dancing
or for light loves. And now you look on me
and see it. What was yours you take away
and what you leave of me will dance again
because that's all it knows, but not be happy
because it loved you once.

Rudolph. Why were you here
last night?

Mary. Was it wrong? I've nothing that's my own.
I followed you. I came because you came,
not even thinking. Why did you let me in
if I wasn't wanted?—But it was wrong. I know;
I come between you and your father. Once
I'm gone he'll take you back. Rudi, I swear
I didn't think of it.

Rudolph. Think of this then, my dear;
my date's run out; I'm no more king of men
than Loschek. I've a pocket-full of silver,
and certain braid on my coat, and a name I hate,
and a strong inclination toward the dark
like a cur dying. It's a woman's place
to fix her to some bastard that goes up
and set her heel on faces that go down
as mine is going. All the rest is words,

the weeping interim, the sweet despair
before you dance again.

Mary. I'll go if it helps you.
I'll try never to see you.

Rudolph. Try? Oh, child,
look in your heart. Your hands still cling to me,
but if you're a woman, if you're human, while
you cling, your mind's alive with circling wings
searching this way and that—one man who smiled,
one man who asked you boldly for a night,
ten men who came a-wooing—of them all
which of them all shall make his bed with me
when Rudolph's gone? The treacherous, savage mind
knows betters than our words. And I know this
because my mind's more savage than your own,
filthy, desperate, faithless, hopeless of faith
in men or women or myself.

Mary. Is there no way
I could still see you, any creeping way,
so low the emperor would never know
that I was there? If I could be your dog,
even your dog—

Rudolph. You're shivering. It's cold here.
We must have a fire.
    [*He lights the fire in the grate.*]

Mary. I read a story once
about how all men vanished from the earth
after some pestilence, and a race of dogs
grew up where men are. Their religion was
that there had once been gods who walked upright,
built fires, and knew all things, and gave commands
and still lived, but invisible. I think

> when I have lost you I'll remember you
> as the dogs remembered man.

Rudolph. For the fires I build?

Mary. No. One must have a god. Was I faithless, Rudi?
> Why did I speak when you'd have had an empire,
> and warn you not to take it?

Rudolph. Because you knew
> you'd lose me if I were emperor.

Mary. Would I have lost you?

Rudolph. Yes.

Mary. Yes, I would. And that was selfish, too.
> Either way I must lose you. Very well.
> I lose you either way.—What will you do?
> Where will you go?
>> [*Rudolph is silent.*]
> You'll be crown prince again.
> Go back to your father.

Rudolph. Yes.—It's all one now
> which way I go.

Mary. Yes. Surely.
> You'll be forgiven if you give me up,
> but with me you're a beggar, as I am.
> You were too chivalrous to say it out,
> but that's the way it's left us.

Rudolph. As for you
> the world's young yet. If you should never see me,
> isn't it true, another love comes by
> and whistles at your window, and it's spring,
> and the great wound you thought would never heal
> leaves not a scar in time—? oh, a few months

or years and all the paths that led to grief
are stopped with green-briar, overgrown and lost,
past finding when we hunt for them.

Mary. Why, yes,
oh, yes. I shall not like the thing I'll be
when that has happened.

Rudolph. When it's happened, then
we think no more about it.

Mary. Yes, but now
I'd rather be a statue to my love,
a statue in a forest, lost and unseen,
cold, too, and white, and hardly once remembered,
but changeless just the same.—Oh, but I'll go!
When feet are made for dancing they must dance
unless the heart stops.

[*A couple of random shots are heard from the woods.*]

Rudolph. Hearts are durable;
they wear out all the rest. You're still trembling.
Come near the fire.

Mary. No, I'll go back to bed.
I think I'm tired.

Rudolph. Forgive me?

Mary. As a dog
forgives his god, see, I forgive you wholly,
and worship what you do. Only forgive me
if I should never change.

[*She kisses him.*]

Rudolph. Yes. Rest well.

Mary. I'm happier now, and I'll rest.
> [*She goes into the bedroom and closes the door. There is a tap at the hall entrance and Loschek looks in.*]

Loschek. Count Hoyos, Highness.

Rudolph. Let him in.
> [*Loschek withdraws and Hoyos enters.*]

Hoyos. Greetings, Your Highness.

Rudolph. It seems
you never sleep.

Hoyos. I haven't your inducements.
I hear you sent for me, but I was coming
with a bit of news. A coach just topped the rise
bearing the royal arms. It looks to me
as if you had early visitors.

Rudolph. You saw it?

Hoyos. On the other side of the gates. He should be here
by this time.

Rudolph. It's the Emperor.

Hoyos. No doubt.
It struck me you'd do well to wash your face
and hide your woman.

Rudolph. How do you stand with him?

Hoyos. Well, as I said, he put us out like lightning,
gave us our pardons with the back of his hand
and combed his whiskers. I was out of favor—
I'm still out, that's all.
> [*A single muffled shot is heard.*]

Rudolph. Why is he coming?

Hoyos. Oh, just to get you back. Put in a word
for your humble servant.

Rudolph. I will. That's what I sent
to tell you now.

Hoyos. You'll kiss and make up?

Rudolph. Why not?
Between the black wolf's jaw and the lamb's hind-quarters
I'd rather play the wolf.

Hoyos. That's sensible.

Rudolph. I was born half wolf, half sheep, God pity me;
one tears the other.

Hoyos. If it's that way with you
make your terms, man.

Rudolph. Terms? When wolf eats lamb
that's terms—and peace. Wait for me.
> [*He goes into the bedroom. Hoyos walks to the fire. After a moment
> Rudolph comes out with a small revolver in his hand.*]

Hoyos.

Hoyos. Yes?
> [*Rudolph shows the revolver. Hoyos goes into the bedroom. Rudolph
> sits unsteadily. Hoyos returns.*]

When did it happen?

Rudolph. This moment. She was here.

Hoyos. I must tell the emperor.

Rudolph. No! Tell no one! Their damned kites
will take her from me!

Hoyos. What will you do?

Rudolph. I don't know yet.
  Keep them away.—She's dead?

Hoyos. She died instantly.

Rudolph. I can't believe it. Hoyos, she was here,
  before you came.

Hoyos. I must tell some story. Quick,
  what is it?

Rudolph. Keep them out. Let them leave me alone.
  She wanted to be changeless. I heard the shot
  and thought it was the hunters. Tell the king
  the Crown Prince Rudolph came to Mayerling
  to seek seclusion. Hold them off with that
  and tell them nothing.

Hoyos. Lad, I know it's awkward
  to see a pretty woman that you've known
  with a bullet through her head. But don't let that
  mislead you. It's an embarrassment the less
  once you've run dry of tears. Suppose we're quiet
  till I can smuggle her quietly under-ground.
  Then if she's travelling in Italy
  or Turkestan and never does come back
  at least she's gone.

Rudolph. Damn you, what do you mean?

Hoyos. Only that we say nothing. You yourself
  suggested it.

Rudolph. Then do as I suggest,
  and leave me with her.
      [*Hoyos goes toward the door. As he approaches it there is a knock and
        he opens to Loschek.*]

Hoyos. Who is it?

Loschek. The Empress, sir.
She asks me to tell Rudolph that she begs
on her knees to see him.

Rudolph. Why should she beg of me?
She may come if she likes.

  [*Loschek steps back, and after a moment the Empress Elizabeth
   enters.*]

Elizabeth. What is it, Rudolph?
What's in your face?

  [*She goes across and kneels beside him.*]

Rudolph. The black jaw's at the flock,
that's all.

Elizabeth. What is it, Hoyos?

Hoyos. We've both been rebels;
maybe we're sorry for it.

Elizabeth. It's something more.
As if you'd watched a pageant cross the night
with horror at the end.

Rudolph. Oh, mother, mother,
so many, many times, I needed you
when I was a child, but you were never there,
and now we're strangers.

Elizabeth. They kept me from you!

Rudolph. Yes.
And now we're strangers. What you'd have me do—
all that was worth the saving in me, that
was you, and I've betrayed it.

Elizabeth. But all we've lost,
all the lost years, we'll have them now. Look, Rudolph,

your father's with me. This night long he wept,
a pitiful, shrunken king, because his child
despises what he does. Come back to him.
I've been against him always, as you have,
but we've grown old together, and his son
means more to him than kingdoms. He's forgotten
whatever it was that happened, forgives it, pardons
all that took part, asks nothing, only to have
his man-child back again.

Rudolph. Yes—as before.

Elizabeth. Will you see him?

Rudolph. Yes.

Elizabeth. He's waiting, Hoyos.

Hoyos. Yes, madam.
    [*He goes out.*]

Elizabeth. You haven't slept.

Rudolph. No.

Elizabeth. It's quite useless, Rudolph,
to fight against what we are. It's broken me.
It will break you too.

Rudolph. You have gone over to them.

Elizabeth. Only to help you.
    [*There is a short pause, then Franz Joseph enters. They rise.*]

Franz Joseph. Lest you should think I deal
in crocodile promises, Rudolph, I have here
three long state papers, drawn in a sleepless night,
and signed and sealed. One is full pardon for
your friends and you, another's a commission
left blank that you may choose what place you'll take

in the Austrian government—and this, the third,
will place you on the throne of Hungary
three years from now, even if I live so long
and you're not there before. I offer these
as humbly as I can. Lose you I cannot.
Let you go I cannot. If I've been
too politic, too stern, forgive me, Rudolph,
I went to a bitter school.

Rudolph. What else?

Franz Joseph. I hold
to one condition only. The Vetsera's
a light, designing woman, bought and sold,
loving by instinct where she lies, but quick
in trade, like the trader's daughter that she is,
where a kiss will mean advantage. She's no queen
for you. The mirror on her wall has kept
as full a record as her heart of those
she'll reach her arms out for.

Rudolph. I told her that,
and have her answer that she'll never change
after this morning.

Franz Joseph. You believed her?

Rudolph. Yes.

Elizabeth. There should be something regal in a queen,
Rudolph; she's small and cheap.

Rudolph. But she'll not change,
after this morning. A statue in a wood
runs more in the rain, yields more to the frost, than she
in this last mood.

Elizabeth. Is she here?

Rudolph. Yes.

Elizabeth. May I see her?

Rudolph. Mary! Mary Vetsera!
  [*There is a pause.*]

Elizabeth. She's asleep?

Rudolph. Yes.

Elizabeth. Shall I wake her?

Rudolph. Wake her if you can.

Elizabeth. What is it, Rudolph?
  [*She looks at Rudolph's face, then crosses to the bedroom and enters.
  Returning, she leans heavily against the door-jamb, her eyes
  fixed first on Rudolph then on the Emperor.*]

Franz Joseph. I understand.
  [*He walks to the door, looks through it briefly, then turns to Elizabeth.*]

It will be necessary to conceal
our visit here. Hoyos will bring us word
of what has happened to the Hofburg.—You
will come with us.

Rudolph. I shall stay here to make
the necessary arrangements.

Franz Joseph. It must not be known.
that you were with her. Nothing in the world
could clear your name of scandal, or suppress
the story if you remain.

Rudolph. She's quite immune
to scandal now, and I shall not greatly mind
what's said of me.

Elizabeth. Rudolph, Rudolph, it's your name,
    your name before the people! Say you loved her,
    still nothing you do or say can hurt her now,
    and you have a life to live!

Rudolph. If I go back
    this morning, and leave her lying in this room
    alone, then hour by hour you'll win me from her,
    and in the end it will be my hand that guides
    all Europe down to hell. I know myself
    and what you'll want of me, and what I am,
    and my black destination. But I've learned
    from the little peddler's daughter, the Vetsera,
    how to keep faith with the little faith I have
    quite beyond time or change.

Franz Joseph. For the love of God!

Rudolph. You have no God, nor I! When a man lies down
    to sleep, he sleeps!

Elizabeth. My child, my child, don't think it!
    It tears my heart!

Rudolph. My mother was a rebel,
    and she used all her beauty and her brain
    to check the darkening evil of a house
    that thrives and grows by evil. She's here now,
    an angel still, but fallen, holding out
    to me the bloody symbols of the trade
    by which we've lived too long. And if I live
    I'll wear them, as she wears them, till my mind's
    a charnel house, and men remember me
    as the breath of pestilence! I had thought, indeed,
    of going back with you, but I'll die young
    and pleasanter to remember.

Franz Joseph. Must we believe
   that the first prince of Europe, in his pride
   of mind and hope, will die for love—the love
   of a basket-woman's child?

Rudolph. Sir, in your sanity
   you'll never glimpse what thin partitions part
   our life and death, to a dweller on the threshold.
   This prince is only a walking apparatus
   for oxidation, a web of water, spun
   to last one morning. A morning more or less
   will hardly count.
      [*A burst of gun-fire is heard from the wood.*]

Elizabeth. Let me have this, at least,
   out of my sacrifice, that the son I bore
   to be a Habsburg king, will be a king;
   let me have this! Whatever else I had
   when I was young is gone now, melts beneath
   a finger's touch, like the tapestries they lift
   into air from a Pharaoh's tomb. When I have walked
   the Hofburg rooms, this alone was real, that you
   were Rudolph, and my son, and would be king
   though the very walls dissolve, and I dare not speak
   to those I pass lest there be no one there
   but my imagining.

Rudolph. We are all ghosts, we three,
   walking the halls of Europe in a dream
   that's ended, a long masquerade of kings
   that crossed the stage and stumbled into dark
   before we came. We are the shadows cast
   by medieval conquerors, a rout
   of devil-faces, thrown up long ago
   by the powers beneath erupting, but long dead
   and gone to slag. Now the earth boils up again

and the new men and nations rise in fire
to fall in rock, and there shall be new kings,
not you or I, for we're all past and buried,
but a new batch of devil-faces, ikons
made of men's hope of liberty, all worshipped
as bringers of the light, but conquerors,
like those we follow. I leave the world to them,
and they'll possess it like so many skulls
grinning on piles of bones. To the young men
of Europe I leave the eternal sweet delight
of heaping up their bones in these same piles
over which their rulers grin. To the old and dying
I leave their dying kingdoms to be plowed
by the new sowers of death—fools like myself
who rush themselves to power to set men free
and hold themselves in power by killing men,
as time was, as time will be, time out of mind
unto this last, forever. We are all ghosts,
we three, but from today I shall not haunt
the Hofburg halls, Habsburg or Wittelsbach,
wolf, sheep or shadow. So saying, light of heart,
I lie with the Vetsera.

> [*He makes one of his stiff little bows, steps into the bedroom, with-
> drawing from royalty, and closes the door. Elizabeth runs to
> it.*]

Elizabeth. Rudolph, Rudolph—
you cannot, cannot—Rudolph, open to me,
your mother!

> [*There is a shot within the room.*]

Franz Joseph. We have no son.

> [*Hoyos enters.*]

Elizabeth. Hoyos, here—quick,
It's Rudolph—

Hoyos. What has he done?

Elizabeth. Break down the door!
   He went in—he may be only hurt!
   Hoyos—Hoyos!

Hoyos. I shall need help with this.

Elizabeth. Help him, Franz.

Franz Joseph. Help him? We have no son.
   Leave this pawing of doors. He was too much
   a prince not to die if he wished. And he is dead.

Elizabeth. You wished him dead!

Franz Joseph. I loved him. I must think now
   how to go on without him.

Elizabeth. How to go on!
   What could we go toward now?

Franz Joseph. Toward that same darkness
   he prophesies, perhaps—Oh, Rudolph, my son,
   would I had died for you. Would I had died.—
   This must be covered up. We have not been seen here.
   Hoyos will bring us word to the palace. Get
   the girl in the earth tonight. An accident—
   a hunting accident—

   [*There is faint gun-fire in the distance.*]

   Toward that same darkness
he prophesies—

CURTAIN

IX · THE FEAST OF ORTOLANS

CHARACTERS

(In the order of speech)

POMPIGNAN	CHENIER
BEAUMARCHAIS	GENERAL CUSTINE
CHAMPFORT	LAFAYETTE
DUCHESS DU GRAMONT	A SERVANT
CONDORCET	BAILLY
MLLE. DE SOMBREUIL	ANOTHER SERVANT
PHILIPPE OF ORLEANS	DESMOULINS
LA HARPE	ROUCHER
MALESHERBES	THE CHEF
THEROIGNE	LIEUTENANT CUSTINE

THE FEAST OF ORTOLANS

In the year 1789 a group of writers, artists, intellectuals, and, mingled with them, a scattering of Nobles, are seated round the great dinner table in the residence of the Duke of Pompignan, not more than twenty miles from Paris. The occasion is the Feast of Ortolans, a ceremony observed once a year by the Pompignan Family during the reigns of the last three kings who bore the name of Louis. It is a ceremony which has grown out of the family custom of serving a special and remarkable dish of ortolans once in the year to the most intimate as well as the most distinguished friends of the family. This gallant and famous dish has not yet been brought in, but the guests have already whetted their appetites on hors d'œuvres and the first wine.

Pompignan. And things shall be thus in that great day, my masters: there shall be five quarters in the year, seven feet to the ell, ten days in the week, and all days pay-days; the ounce shall be equal to the pound in every scale, the half-crown equal to the crown, the rod to the mile, the woman to the man. The king shall be Marie Antoinette, and Marie Antoinette shall be the king—

[*There is a burst of laughter from the table*]

Beaumarchais. And more—

Champfort. More and no miracle—

[*More laughter with an undertone of conversation*]

Duchess du Gramont. Gentlemen, gentlemen, not all together, please. You drown each other with wit, and we poor women are left wondering what was said—

Condorcet. Forgive us, Madame la Duchesse, but for this once you were not supposed to hear—

3

The Duchess. Not to hear—and why?

Condorcet. To spare your cheeks, madame, lest those who blush easily should never blush again without art, and lest those who blush by technique, as say, by holding the breath, or by pressure on the jugular, should do themselves a mischief.

Mlle. de Sombreuil. But I've heard nothing really scandalous for years. I'm quite out of practice with my blushing!

Pompignan. At the feast of ortolans, my dear, we expect the men to be ribald and the women to be indiscreet, but when our ribaldry outruns your discretion, as it will, at times, we cover the words with untimely laughter.

The Duchess. Ah, but women are to be equal with men in that new day, are they not, Vergniaud?

Mlle. de Sombreuil. Equal or above them!

Pompignan. But not equal in wickedness, surely?

The Duchess. Oh, above them in wickedness, as indeed they are now. All the Encyclopedists say so. Women have a natural genius for wickedness, whereas men are naturally moral, even docile, clinging to the Decalogue as a drowning man clings to his chicken coop—

Mlle. de Sombreuil. Yes, man, man—a creature of good habits, broken to harness by the mere offer of sweetmeats—

Philippe of Orleans. Not all of us—

Mlle. de Sombreuil. Not the soldiers, no—but all the rest—

Philippe. And not the artists—

Mlle. de Sombreuil. I grant you—not the soldiers or artists—

Champfort. But here tonight we are all soldiers or artists—

Mlle. de Sombreuil. And when have we married any of you here tonight? No, no, we women know a manageable man by his occupation. A solid Breton with a fur business in the Rue Vaugirard, a bald and ageing banker with an estate at Versailles and a house in the city, these we lead with a show of sugarplums to the altar of Saint Eustache—

Pompignan. But all this too will vanish in the new era, in the light of freedom and reason, Mademoiselle. In that glorious dawn there shall be no marrying or giving in marriage, and man will doff his gyves.

The Duchess. Then I begin to have my doubts of the wisdom of revolution altogether.

La Harpe. Would you have things go on as they are, dear lady?

Malesherbes. They cannot go on as they are. As time goes on men become wiser, and they must apply their wisdom to the state.

Mlle. de Sombreuil. But not to the state of marriage!

Pompignan. To marriage, to religion, to law—there is even talk of reforming the calendar—and the multiplication table is to be rearranged so that what a man has in his pocket will always equal what he needs to live on.

Theroigne.

> [*Aside to Chenier, while another conversation proceeds in an undertone*]

Who is the pale, grave gentleman who wears the order of the Golden Fleece and takes no part in the conversation?

Chenier.

> [*Aside*]

Are you caught by the noble profile, Theroigne? Never mind, he's no ladies' man, and you may abandon the idea at once. He is the Marquis de Lafayette, hero of the revolution in the new world, friend of Washington, a saint in private life, much in love with his wife and beyond temptation.

Theroigne.

> [*Aside*]

And the patrician with the burnished bronze face, to the left, his breast covered with orders?

Chenier. You look high, my darling. You have an instinct for impossibilities. He is only Philippe d'Orleans, prince of the blood and heir to the throne of France.

Theroigne. Ah.

Chenier. No more?

Theroigne. Yes—the tall, imperious-looking one, who could be more witty than any if he tried?

Chenier. To the right of the prince?

Theroigne. Yes.

Chenier. Beaumarchais. The playwright, the author of Figaro. The fellow who made a fortune on paper out of the American revolution, but has not yet been paid, and who hopes to make a fortune out of a revolution here.

Theroigne. He's very handsome.

Chenier. Oh, and a devil with the women. Come, darling, are we unhappy already that you begin to cast about for another?

Theroigne. You'll tire of me, you know.

Chenier. You anticipate.

Theroigne. And when you have tired of me, surely it would be better to go up and not down.

Chenier. Too candid to be flattering.

Theroigne. Dear Andre, I love you so very much, and I shall not quit you. You will quit me—and when that happens it would be as well to have a foothold—

Chenier. A step higher—

Theroigne. If possible a thought higher—

Chenier. There, I understand you. And I've watched many a pretty woman climb to a pretty career on the shoulders of successive lovers. But never before has one confided her plans to me in advance. This too is revolutionary.

Theroigne. The candor, perhaps, not the method.

Chenier. The method is as old as the world. And for women perhaps the best.

Gen. Custine.

> [*Loudly*]

But look at the conditions, Monsieur Condorcet, look at the conditions! It may all come out well as you say, but the disorders are becoming insupportable! There was a mob stopping carriages on the Pont Neuf this evening, merely for the fun of making well-to-do folk cry "Down with the King!" They were harmless enough, and quite good-humored, but they insisted on "Down with the King!"

Beaumarchais. And did you cry "Down with the King!", General?

Custine. I did, indeed; otherwise they would have turned the horses quite around and sent me back whence I came.

The Duchess. But that's marvelous!

Custine. Isn't it? And my friend Revillon, the manufacturer, was actually besieged in his house for having said a workman could live on fifteen sous a day.

Pompignan. Besieged? When?

Custine. Yesterday. He was a fool to say it, no doubt, but a man should be allowed to speak his mind. And a man's house and carriage should be his own. There should be no interference with private property.

Pompignan. The police should deal with such matters.

Custine. I have no expectation of real violence, of course. We are a gentle, submissive, peaceful folk, we people of

France. But at present there's no discipline. The government allows the workmen to do as they please.

Lafayette. To be quite frank, gentlemen, the lower classes are badly paid and heavily taxed. Much of the present disorder arises from your refusal to accept a levy on your estates.

Pompignan. Come now, the nobles of France couldn't support the government half a year, if they gave all they have—

Beaumarchais. It's that confounded national deficit that swallows everything. Year after year we're promised a balanced budget, and year after year the deficit grows— it's up beyond all calculation now, insatiable, and rocketing every day into astronomical figures!

Pompignan. But how's the budget to be balanced when the government's so easy with money on every hand? Money goes out right and left—

Lafayette. Haven't you had your share?

Pompignan. Yes, my share and more. Others were holding out their hands and so I held out my hat. It was filled. It made no difference!

   [*Laughter*]

Service, lads, service!

   [*He claps his hands*]

There seems to be some delay in changing the plates.

A Servant. I'm sorry, monseigneur.

Pompignan. Pray why is it? There has been no such hiatus

between courses since my ancestors purchased Pompignan.

The Servant. Monseigneur, if I may explain, there has been some quarrel between the house-servants and the wood-cutters—

Pompignan. And why should that affect us here?

The Servant. Monseigneur, the proper baking of the ortolans requires a white-hot oven, which is possible only with wood seasoned under cover. But the woodmen brought green faggots today and would bring no more— and in consequence the chef has quarreled with them—

Pompignan. Never mind, your explanations are tiresome, and my friends are hungry. Let the ortolans be made ready and brought at once.—

The Servant. Yes, monseigneur.

Pompignan. And if there are further quarrels in the kitchen I myself will come to settle them.

The Servant. Yes, monseigneur.

[*He withdraws*]

Pompignan. This is a maddening contretemps, but let us ignore it, guests and lovers! Your glasses! I pledge the revolution, and Philippe d'Orleans! Philippe, heir to the throne and friend of the revolution!

Voices. The Prince!

Philippe. Let me assume that though I am pledged in jest, dear fellows of the feast, I may answer seriously. There has never reigned in France a juster, nobler, wiser, more

lovable king than our Louis. A king who welcomes reform, who gives with both hands, who hears the humblest petition, who suffers with the poor, and understands all classes alike. May the throne never devolve
upon me at the expense of his most generous majesty.
Yet if it should devolve upon me, things would not go
on as they are going. I should convene the States-Gen-
eral. There should be representation in France, and a
new way of life. I see about me many who would be my
ministers.—Whatever the human mind has conceived in
the way of freedom of the spirit or of the mind should be
inaugurated, even the more experimental. Jean-Jacques
Rousseau has given us our religion of liberty, and we
should carry it out, even to the recognition of the social
contract, the responsibility of the state for the people's
welfare. And all, even the woodcutters, should be heard,
should air their grievances.

[*There is some applause*]

The Duchess. Let us hear the woodcutters tonight!

Pompignan. Yes, let us hear them. Let us demonstrate.

Philippe. But not in a spirit of levity, gentlemen. The
woodcutters are men of the soil. Their service is an
ancient and sacred function. They are men such as we
might wish to become, men living with nature and made
wise by her laws. They are man himself, innocent, unspoiled by courts, the natural savage, the epitome of
Rousseau's gospel, virtue incarnate.

Bailly. Let us, by all means, have in the woodcutters. And
treat them with grave respect.

Pompignan. Sirrah, fetch us a woodcutter.

A Servant. Into this presence, monseigneur?

Pompignan. Into this presence.

The Servant. But monseigneur, it may be necessary to wash him—

The Duchess. No, no, unwashed—bring him unwashed!

Pompignan. You hear! An unwashed woodcutter!

The Servant. But, monseigneur, if he should not wish to come?

Pompignan. Bring him, and no more words.

The Duchess. He shall taste the ortolans!

Pompignan. He shall indeed. And so shall we all if this kitchen feud has been resolved.

The Duchess. I shall set my cap for this woodcutter.

Chenier. But this is mockery.

Pompignan. No, quite serious.

Lafayette. The lad's right. It is mockery. You've played
     With the thought of revolution. While you jest
     And the Prince talks of his States-General,
     The fires roar underneath, and the old injustice
     Runs too deep to be cured with summoning
     A Parliament. I tell you we now stand
     On the threshold of a world in which all men
     Are equal under law as in the sight
     Of God Himself. You say it and laugh! I say it,
     Knowing that when the clothes of rank and power

Are shed, and all men naked in the light
Of inner godhood, this will not be the world
We know—of privilege, greed, and subterfuge—
But a world of liberty and reason! Nay,
You smile, ready to mock again. Good form
And social usage in this company
Require that one be serious in jest
Only, and jest in earnest. Purge yourselves
Of that spirit, gentlemen, and make what haste
You can toward a citizenship you've never dreamed,
Citizenship in a world made just and pure
By the abolition of chains!

Pompignan. Oh, Lafayette,
You shame us all!

Beaumarchais. No chains, no jails, Marquis?
Men free to do as they please?

Lafayette. If there are criminals
They will be those of us whose privilege
Has given us too much power. Men in themselves,
Unspoiled, are men of good will. The natural passions
All tend toward justice and mercy.

Beaumarchais. Oh, that's yourself.
Not all men.

Lafayette. All but the few whose trade it is
To live by their wits on others. Parasites
By birth or training. That's you and me, my friend,
And we must learn from our betters who cut wood
To cook our ortolans.

The Duchess. I have a glimpse
  How men might live like angels in a heaven
  Without distrust.

Lafayette. What is it that makes criminals?
  A lack of bread; the winter in clay huts
  With little fire; children who have no shoes;
  Taxes to maintain luxury; we've lived
  Too long by others' weeping. Say three words
  And this is changed—freedom, equality,
  Brotherhood among men. When men are free
  They are men, not animals, reasoning men,
  Loving their peace, keeping a pride of manhood,
  Holding no envy.

Pompignan. So said the good Rousseau.

Malesherbes. Well, let it come. I shall hope.

La Harpe. Yes, let it come.

Chenier. And may I add a word?

Pompignan. Let the poet speak.
  Speak, Chenier.

Chenier. A nation lives and dies;
  It runs its course and dies, and what it is
  Is known in the end by what it leaves behind
  For other men to see. Music and song,
  Painting and poetry, these tell our story
  When there's nothing left but records. A free people
  Sings at its labor and leaves song behind,
  Loves what it does in handiwork and sets
  Its dream down in such color and design

As make all ages wonder. Let us have that
For the people of France, set free.

Pompignan. Let that come too.
I shall hope for it.

The Duchess. And I.

Beaumarchais. But, Lafayette,
What will our world be like when the revolution
Has really come? What are the fruits of it?
How will men live?

Lafayette. You will laugh when I say it,
Beaumarchais. For you finance rebellion
And laugh at it, while you cheer it on, and yet
You build better than you know. There will be no kings,
No capitalists, no nobles, and no armies.
Men will keep their own peace. Loving his land,
Each citizen of France in that new day
Will farm his frugal acres, grind his corn,
Dress his own meat, and bring wood for his fire;
Returning, happily wearied, when night falls,
To a simple cottage, where his wife has spun
And woven through the day, and where his children
Tend to their lighter tasks. Sitting together
At a plain supper, earned and prepared and grown
In their own fields, each family will make
Its little Eden, its own paradise,
Without shame or rancor. Those will be the fruits
Of our revolution.

Beaumarchais. Adam and Eve in the garden.

Lafayette. Yes, if you like. Adam and Eve.

Beaumarchais. This time—no snake, no Cain, no murder?

La Harpe. Murder enough.

Beaumarchais. Did you speak, La Harpe?

La Harpe. I think not—no.

Beaumarchais. You said "Murder enough."

La Harpe. Did I say that? Then the rest's better unsaid.

Beaumarchais. La Harpe, the silent. Shall we not hear
from him?

The Duchess. If it's something better unsaid, why then,
beyond all,
We wish to hear it.

La Harpe. I speak quite doubtfully,
But it comes to my tongue that you shall live to see
This revolution you hope for. Be content
With that. The rest's not cheerful.

Condorcet. Say it, man.

Beaumarchais. Come, out with it.

La Harpe. Then, I repeat, you shall see it,
This revolution; but do you wish to know
What will come of this revolution, for us all here,
Before it's done?

Condorcet. Do you know?

La Harpe. I think I know.

Beaumarchais. A prophet, ho! Bring locusts and wild
honey!
We have a prophet!

La Harpe. I've been troubled lately
   With a strange aberration, not a thing
   One cares to boast about. On a certain morning,
   Looking up from my shaving toward the mirror,
   I saw how I should die.

Beaumarchais. A pleasant death?

La Harpe. No, not pleasant.

Condorcet. But how, then, how? A prophet
   Should be more definite.

La Harpe. Let it suffice
   That my aberration troubles me tonight
   Again, and looking round me at the table
   I see your deaths in your faces.

Condorcet. All men die,
   How shall I die? Of too much or too little?
   Diet or gout?

La Harpe. You will die, Monsieur de Condorcet,
   On the pavement of a prison cell; you will die
   Of a poison you will carry with you always
   To escape the headsman's axe. Yet not a headsman,
   No, but a new mechanical contrivance
   For cutting off men's heads, a thing designed
   To save the axe-man labor in a time
   Of numerous executions.

Mlle. de Sombreuil. Ah—

Pompignan. Enough.
   This is a stupid jest.

The Duchess. What does he mean?

Beaumarchais. He's mad. The good La Harpe sat so long
silent
He's gone mad like a hermit.

Condorcet. You could have made
A much better story of it. Let me have
An inkling of romance. Let me die to save
A lady compromised. What was my crime?

La Harpe. Your crime will be that you once sat at dinner
with
Philippe d'Orleans.

Philippe. He sits with me now.
We are all at dinner together, I believe.
But is that a crime?

La Harpe. It will be.

Philippe. Against whom, La Harpe?

La Harpe. Against the revolution.

Beaumarchais. But our Philippe is a friend of the revolution,
And we are all at dinner with him.

La Harpe. Yes,
And more than one will die for it.

Beaumarchais. Come now,
You say it will be a crime to sit at dinner
With d'Orleans. But why he?

La Harpe. It will be a crime
To be an aristocrat, to have spoken with one,

To give him shelter. It will be a crime
To oppose the government, to write a pamphlet,
To fail in battle, to hold unorthodox
Or irregular opinions, to have more money
Than any of your neighbors, to wear silk
Or keep a carriage, yes, even to be named
Or suspect of these things. And for these crimes
The punishment will be death.

Condorcet. And what has all this
   To do with the revolution or the rule
   Of reason?

La Harpe. It is exactly as I tell you.
   In the name of reason and philosophy;
   As part of the program of humanity
   And liberty—you will end thus. Oh, but the reign
   Will veritably be one of reason, for
   There will be temples of Reason throughout France;
   There will be no other temples at that time
   Save those to Reason. The people will go mad
   In the name of tolerance, and cut men down
   In the streets for advising tolerance; to write
   Or read will be a crime. To speak too well,
   To have kept books in a counting-house; to buy
   Too cheap or sell too dear will bring you death
   And no appeal.

Champfort. Dear, dear, I should like to know
   How I shall die?

La Harpe. You, Monsieur de Champfort?
   You will cut your veins a dozen times

With a razor in your cell; yet you will linger
And die hard later on.

Champfort. If we do have
A revolution, I shall have friends in it.
I shall be one of the leaders. I've worked for it
Night and day, and though, as you say, I jest,
I jest to some purpose. This will not be forgotten
Even in troubled times.

La Harpe. It will be forgotten.

Malesherbes. And I? My fortune, please, La Harpe!

Bailly. And I?

Desmoulins. And I?

Roucher. This way, La Harpe! My fortune, too.

La Harpe. The revolution will devour its children,
And those who fostered it. You, Malesherbes,
Who have done all you can to bring about
A change in the state, you will die on the scaffold.
You, Monsieur Bailly, friend of the people,
Proponent of their rights, you on the scaffold;
You, Desmoulins, who have edited and spoken
For the rights of man, you on the scaffold, too.
You, Monsieur Roucher, on the scaffold.

Roucher. Heigh-ho;
Shall we be inundated by the Turks
And Tartars?

La Harpe. No, as I said, you will be governed
By philosophy and reason. Those who rule
Will be philosophers, and will repeat

All you have said about the bright new world
In which all men are free; in that world's name
You and your children will be put to death,
Till the executioners are wearied out
With chopping, and they fling you into rivers,
Your arms tied, singly and in groups, and men
Are thrown to the mobs for butchery.

Pompignan. You forget
Your host, La Harpe! Shall I die by fire or water,
Singly or in groups?

La Harpe. I can tell you nothing.

Pompignan. Why, man, why?

La Harpe. There's nothing in your face,
Nothing beyond tonight.

Pompignan. No future, nothing?

La Harpe. Nothing beyond tonight. You will die young.

Pompignan. Gad! I shall have to hurry!

Beaumarchais. Miracles,
Nothing but miracles, and am I too
Without a future?

La Harpe. You will escape to England. First,
However, you will hide in a linen closet,
And then in a well. And, not the least miracle,
You will turn Christian.

Champfort. Now I am relieved.
If we're to die when Beaumarchais turns Christian,
We're all immortal!

The Duchess. As for us poor women,
    It's our good fortune not to count for much
    In revolutions. They won't trouble about us,
    Or our ideas.

La Harpe. And yet this time your sex
    Will not protect you. No, not age nor beauty,
    Youth nor desire will succor you. You spoke
    Of marriage. There will be a new kind of marriage,
    The marriage of the revolution. Men and women
    Bound with their lips together, will be tossed
    Into the sea, saints, sinners, good and bad,
    Heroes and courtesans, brigands and nuns,
    To swim the Styx in company. This will go on
    Till people tire of it. You, Madame la Duchesse,
    You will be led to the scaffold in a cart,
    Your arms tied behind you; many will weep
    Of the ladies who must take that journey with you,
    And you will comfort them.

The Duchess. But that's heroic!
    You leave me that much, though denying me
    Absolution and a confessor.

La Harpe. Oh,
    There'll be no absolution or confessors—
    Only reason and terror. The last victim
    Who as a royal favor is confessed
    Will be—

Beaumarchais. Well—who?

La Harpe. Will be the King of France.
    Nor will Philippe succeed him.

Philippe. I shall be dead?

La Harpe. Not long after.

Philippe. And when will all this be?

La Harpe. Within six years.

Beaumarchais. Ha, ha, ha!

La Harpe. Chenier will die on the scaffold,
   The poet of the revolution. Lafayette
   Will be driven into exile, having tried
   To save the king. Marie Antoinette will die
   Quite beautifully, on the scaffold.

Theroigne. But me—you don't speak of me!

Chenier. Theroigne! Theroigne!

La Harpe. You will lead a revolt of women, and the men,
   My dear, will cut your head off.

Theroigne and Beaumarchais. Ha, ha, ha! Ha, ha!

La Harpe. The dead will lie in the streets. The dogs will
      sicken
   On the meat of men. You will hear the people cry:
   The voice of the people is the voice of gods,
   And the gods are athirst! Give them your blood to drink!
   Mademoiselle de Sombreuil will pledge
   The crowd in blood, drinking the blood of friends
   To save her father's life. And this will come
   Of our reasonable, philosophic emancipation
   By revolution.

Pompignan. And the end?

La Harpe. Why, toward the end
  The noise of tumbrils on the cobblestones
  Will not slacken all day long, loaded with suspects,
  With nobles, all condemned, going their way
  To the Place de Greve to die. You will be among them,
  The eloquent, the brave, the wise, the fair,
  Author and artist, prophet—I myself
  Will be among them. There will not be in France
  Three men of note left living, whom we've known
  In this our time. New leaders will ride in
  On the tide of blood. Then one man bloodier
  Than all the rest, small, and without illusions,
  Will set himself to master all the world
  By preaching our own doctrines, such as freedom
  From kings and slavery, till he make himself
  An emperor, and all his brothers kings,
  And that's the end.

Beaumarchais. Ha, ha, ha! Are you frightened?
  Will you let him scare you with jests? Come, laugh with
    me,
  Give him his due, he's a first-class romancer,
  And he's earned a laugh! Ha, ha, ha!

The Whole Table. Ha, ha, ha! Ha, ha!

Condorcet. A real ghost-story—and we the ghosts!

The Table. Ha, ha, ha!

  [*The laughter mounts, hysterically, into a roar. As it dies
     down it merges with confused angry voices outside the
     windows*]

The Voices. They shall not have a hostage!

Not one man!
Not one!
Let them eat their ortolans raw!
Raw!
Show us this cook who cooks ortolans!

Lafayette. What can this be?

Pompignan. An altercation in the courtyard. *Peste!* These carters shall be hung by the thumbs!

The Voices. But he wishes only one as a guest!
An honored guest!
Guest, eh?
An honored guest!
He wants a hostage!
We've seen that before!
He shall not have one!
Not one man this time!
Let him come out and take us!
Let him bring his ortolans!
And his guests!

    [*A servant enters*]

Pompignan. Silence that rabble in the court! And bring me the ringleader!

The Servant. Monseigneur, they will not send a man to you.

Pompignan. Who are they?

The Servant. The woodcutters. They are afraid of punishment and refuse to send even one, thinking you mean to hold him as a hostage!

Pompignan. A hostage? Is this a war we wage? I have

asked for a woodcutter. My guests wish to be joined by a woodcutter. He will be treated kindly. Tell them so.

The Servant. Monseigneur, I have told them—

Beaumarchais. Ah, the cook himself.

[*The chef enters from the kitchen, white and stumbling*]

The Duchess. Come to explain.

Pompignan. Perhaps we shall have our ortolans at last— Why are you here, sirrah? What do you want with us?

The Chef. For three generations we have served you, we of my family, at the feast of ortolans. It has been my office alone to prepare this dish—and I had hoped never to fail you—

[*He sits*]

Pompignan. Why are you here? Why do you sit in my presence?

The Chef. But I have failed you. I shall never cover a dish for you again, nor stand at your fire—

Pompignan. Rise! Stand up!

The Chef. Yes, monseigneur.

[*He rises*]

Pompignan. Have you left your senses? Why are you not to cook for me again?

The Chef. Because I am dying.

[*He falls to the floor*]

The Duchess. He's ill, Pompignan. There is blood about him on the floor. Do not be angry with him.

Pompignan. Remain here, gentlemen. There has been a quarrel in the kitchen. Remain here while I attend to it.

[*To the servants*]

Take this fellow out.

[*He goes to the kitchen*]

The Duchess. But lift him gently.

Philippe. Yes.—See, he has a knife wound.

Mlle. de Sombreuil. Oh!

The Duchess. Gently. Gently, please. Tell them to lift him gently.

The Chef. And now I shall not serve you—any more.

[*He is carried out*]

Custine. It seems we are to have nothing but disorder this evening. Rioting on the Pont Neuf, feuds in the kitchen, ill omens at table—

A Servant.

[*Announcing*]

Lieutenant Custine, monseigneur.

Custine. My son has come. I wondered.

[*Lieutenant Custine enters*]

Why were you late, my son? The place was set for you.

Lt. Custine. Forgive my uniform. I had no time to change. —Gentlemen, had any of you intended returning to Paris this evening?

Philippe. Many of us, I think. Perhaps all.

Lt. Custine. Then I advise you to take carriage in another direction. Paris has gone mad. Saint-Antoine is a seething mob. Many have been killed on both sides. None of the roads is safe. I came through on horseback with difficulty.

Gen. Custine. You are injured?

Lt. Custine. No, no, but I fear I may have injured others. It was necessary to ride them down.—General Lafayette, I have a message for you. The king asks that you rally a regiment to form a special guard.

Lafayette. For what purpose?

Lt. Custine. To protect the queen and him.

La Harpe. Ah! It begins to come true! It begins already.

Lt. Custine. Something has begun indeed. There has been an attempt on the Bastille.

Lafayette. By whom?

Lt. Custine. By the Paris rabble. I heard that it had fallen, but one hears many things, and that's impossible.

Lafayette. The Bastille is impregnable.

Lt. Custine. Yes. At any rate to a mob armed with scythes and hatchets. But the city's unsafe.

The Duchess. What must we do?

Lt. Custine. Take what roads you like. But not toward Paris.

    [*A cry is heard in the distance*]

Where is our host?

The Duchess. In the kitchen.

Lt. Custine. Are you jesting?

The Duchess. No. There was some trouble between the servants and the woodcutters. He went to settle it.

Lt. Custine. Have you let him go alone? The whole country is in flame, and his workmen with the rest.
[*He strides to the kitchen entrance*]

Lafayette. I'll go with you.
[*They go out*]

Gen. Custine. The lad has never seen service. It may be that he exaggerates.

Beaumarchais. He cannot have seen it with his own eyes. The Bastille has not fallen, I assure you.
[*There is another cry from the kitchen*]

Philippe. Where are the servants? They seem to have disappeared.

The Duchess. I feel suddenly oppressed here. As if we were surrounded by invisible things, hemmed in. Someone cried out.
[Lafayette *returns*]
Where are the servants? We are left unattended here.

Lafayette. They are all gone.

Philippe. And our host?

Lafayette. We found him alone in the kitchen. Dead. A poniard between his shoulders. Face downward in the great dish of ortolans.

La Harpe. This is the last feast of ortolans. The gods are athirst. We shall not meet again.

CURTAIN

X · SECOND OVERTURE

CHARACTERS

REVEL

GENERAL PLEHVE

KRUG

PRINCESS

COLONEL LVOV

ROSTOV

GREGOR

KATERINA

OLGA

ANDRE

ADAM

LUGAH

A GUARD

CHARASH

CAPTAIN

A SERGEANT

KRASSIN

THE VOICE

SECOND OVERTURE

A Play in One Act

*The scene is a square cellar in the village of Tiumen, east of Moscow.
The whitewashed walls and low ceiling are lighted by two candles
that burn on a table near the center of the room. Armed guards
stand more or less at ease, but alert, along the wall at the left.
At the right huddled together, some refugees await disposition
at the hands of the authorities who have taken them prisoner.
Among them are the* Princess Thalin *and her two daughters,*
Olga, *fifteen and* Katerina, *thirteen; their butler,* Krug;
Lugan *a peasant;* Colonel Lvov, *a young officer;* Adam, *a
bearded lawyer;* Rostov, *former lieutenant in the Russian
army;* Revel, *a lad of twenty;* General Plehve, *a retired
officer;* Bishop Andre; *and* Gregor, *an exile escaped from
the Siberian mines. It is an evening in January, 1918. Revel
slips to the floor in an agony of fear.*

Revel. Why does it have to be me? Why does it have to be
me? The others got away—the whole trainload—and
they'll live—oh, yes, they'll all live; only we get it—
we get it—and I did nothing—nothing—

Gen. Plehve. It would be kinder, both to yourself and to us,
my son, if you would refrain from baring your soul in
that manner.—

Revel. Do you want to die!

Plehve. Look about you, my son. I myself am old, but there
are those among us who have as much to lose as you.
They are not weeping. There is an ancient stoicism cus-
tomary among those who face death by violence. It has
its use, for it lends an air of dignity to scenes which

3

might otherwise disgust us with the race of men. If we must die we must die.

Revel. You'll die all right, and so will I. I know! I used to live across the street from such a place as this in Moscow. You'd hear the truck idling in front, and then you'd hear muffled shots—and then they'd load the truck and drive away.

Krug. There is a truck idling outside. I hear it.

Princess.

   [*To the guards*]

What is this place? You there, the guard there—why are we all ushered together into one basement room—with no fire, no furniture, no privacy? Is this a courtroom—or an execution chamber?

   [*There is a silence*]

We are guilty of no crime. We are merely fellow-travelers, largely unknown to each other, leaving Moscow and all we possessed behind us in the hope of finding a refuge in some foreign country. Now we are taken from the train without warrant or warning, ignorant of the accusation against us. By whose command are we held?

Col. Lvov. They have orders not to speak.

Rostov. There's blood on the wall behind us.

Princess. Shall we not have a trial?

Col. Lvov. The officer said we should be given a hearing. Of course, it may have been only to keep us quiet, but he stated positively that the Commissar would see us before any action was taken.

Gregor. My friends, since you are guilty of nothing that would demand punishment, you distress yourselves unduly. I take it upon myself to promise you that there will be no injustice done. It must be that you have misunderstood our revolution.

Lvov. Your revolution? Are you one of them?

Gregor. In a way, yes. No doubt you remember the uprising of 1905. I was arrested and sentenced as one of the leaders. It may be that you and I were opponents at that time. You wear a uniform.

Lvov. I have conveniently forgotten my military record.

Gregor. No matter. I bear no grudge. But I assure you that what we fought for in 1905 we have now won.—We fought for free speech, for civil rights, for the abolition of arbitrary and tyrannical power, such as was exercised by the Czar, such as was carried out, perhaps, under your orders. But the safety from oppression which was never vouchsafed us under your regime you shall receive under ours.

Lvov. Then, if you are a revolutionary leader, why are you here?

Gregor. By mistake, naturally. Any administrative officer makes his mistakes from time to time, and all the more in such times as these. It follows that you are here through error also—and I shall certainly testify that there was no conspiracy among you.

Princess. Why, it may be true. It may be that we are detained through some stupid official blunder. God knows we meant only to escape, my children and I.

Gregor. I am certain of it, and I am certain that it will be proved.

Katerina. There are names here on the wall.

Lvov. Names?

Katerina. Yes. Written here in the whitewash. Names and messages. Look, Olga.

Olga. Look where you've stepped. Your shoes are ruined.

Plehve. Are there messages on these walls, too? Everywhere, everywhere, on the hoardings, on the lintels, on the platforms, names and hopeless messages. "Look for me at Tobolsk." "If you find this, Shura, follow me to Minsk." "Forgive me—I haven't forgotten—Tatiana is with us—come after us toward Harbin." Always signed, always hopeless. But what kind of hope did they keep who'd leave a message here?

Katerina. This one says, "We are the brothers Golitzin, Sergei and Alexander, not ashamed of noble blood, and we have come here for trial, on the last day of the last year of the empire. Whoever reads this, have a mass said for our souls."

Andre. I shall see to it.

Revel. You'll see to it in hell then!

Andre. Neither in hell nor heaven—here on earth.

Adam. He's about to prophesy again.

Lvov. Let him alone. It's bad luck to annoy a priest. Besides, he's old and ill.

Adam. He's brought us his bad luck already! It's nothing to me what he thinks about the Czar and the revolution, but he might at least keep his mouth shut in front of Communist officers! It was his gabble brought us here! Maybe the revolution is the Beast out of Revelations but he picks a very funny time to talk about it.

Andre. I bear on my soul the blame for the revolution;
I alone turned the great Beast loose, this Beast
Of the Apocalypse; no ear save that of God
Shall hear how I was guilty; yet my sin
Brought on these bloody penalties; my faith
Must expiate them.—Listen, our God is with us!
I've stumbled on their plans.—We here—we few,
Banded like iron, sworn here to silence, we
Could release the Czar!

Adam. Will someone shut him up, or shall I strangle him?

Andre.

   [*Almost whispering*]

Yes, but these hands, these few; it would need no more
—it would need no more—

Lugan. Why are you pointing your gun at me, comrade of the guard?

A Guard. Keep away from the door.

Lugan. Ah, I see, I was too near the door. Very well, don't fire at me. I'm a poor peasant, quiet and peaceable. It was my intention to stuff up the crack at the sill, and keep out a portion of the winter, but if it's against the rules I shan't trouble you. In my province the jails are better built, and less riddled with drafts. But you will forgive me.—

Katerina
  [*Whispering*]
  Ah! Olga!

Olga. What is it, Katerina?

Katerina. Our father's name!

Olga. Where?

Katerina. Here on the wall. See. It's the way he prints.

Olga. Be quiet. Don't tell Mother.

Katerina. He died here.

Olga. Yes, he died here.

Lvov. What are you looking at?

Olga. There have been executions here—not long ago. See, there's a date in blood—under a name.

Lvov. May I read it?
  [*A pause*]
  I'm sorry. General Plehve?

Plehve. Yes.

Lvov. The girls have found their father's name printed here in the whitewash. He preceded us by three days. We must keep it from the Princess, of course, but it has a very definite meaning for us.

Princess. Why are you crying, Katerina? Let me see your face. You haven't cried before.

Olga. It's nothing, Mother.

Princess. Was there a message for us?
   [*There is a pause while she reads*]
Oh, Sergei, Sergei! This is where we meet!

Revel. Then we are here to be shot, and I knew it!

Lvov. Wait! Wait! There may be something yet to be done!
We shall see the Commissar. There is a lawyer among
us, who has already prepared the arguments for our
defense—

Plehve. The Commissar of Tiumen is named Charash.

Lvov. What of that?

Plehve.
   [*Gently*]
Have you never heard of Charash? Let me prepare you
for him. He is an intellectual, a man of gentle presence,
friendly and understanding. But it is his faith that the
earth must be purged of the old regime before the prole-
tariat may flower. It is said that he turns over the slay-
ing of aristocrats to a drunken captain, Krassin by name,
because he himself dislikes the shedding of blood. But
he is nevertheless an advocate of the terror, and its fore-
most evangel in the provinces east of Moscow.

Lvov. Will you answer me one question, you of the guard:
Is your Commissar named Charash?
   [*A silence*]

Plehve. But it is Charash, I know.

Gregor. Then you are mistaken about him. Charash and I

were friends in the revolution of 1905. We were sentenced the same day, he to prison, I to exile. There is nothing I dare not ask him, nothing he would fail to grant. As to what you have heard about him, it is all lies! I've known him too well! He would not kill for revenge, nor to aid any cause save that of justice! No doubt there have been necessary executions! They occur in every state, under the mildest of governments; but under Charash you will find no terror, no unnecessary cruelty. This is not hearsay; all this I know, because he was my friend!

[*There is a heavy knock at the inside door*]

A Guard. Open the door. It's the Commissar.

[*The door is opened and* COMMISSAR CHARASH *enters with* A CAPTAIN]

Charash. Tell me briefly as you can who they are, when and where they were arrested, and the charge against them.

Captain. I have here a list of the names as they gave them. They are fugitives from Moscow, mainly aristocrats. They were taken this evening from a cattle-car in which they were attempting unauthorized passage through our lines. Among them is Bishop Andre, twice convicted of conspiring against the Soviets, and twice escaped from custody. The charge against them is counter-revolutionary activities and sympathy.

Charash. If they have no answer there is nothing more to be said.

Princess. Indeed we do have an answer, sir. We are not

guilty of any activity against the existing government. The presence of Bishop Andre among us is purely accidental. We have only one wish—to save our lives by departure from your territory.

Charash. These are statements without proof.

Adam. Sir, I have drawn up our defense in writing as well as I could without facilities. May I present this memorandum?

Charash. Take it from him. You are a lawyer?

Adam. I am.

Charash. We have neither time nor use for legalistic forms. Where is the Bishop Andre? Quickly. The Bishop Andre.

Andre. Here.

Charash. Why are you here in Tiumen?

Andre. Tell me first for whom you speak?

Charash. For the Soviet government.

Andre. I speak for my God, who brought me twice through your hands
And will again! They think me mad, these about me,
Because my God speaks through me in the night
And rends my breast, and I cry out! Even now
His voice is in me, like a tongue of fire,
Saying: He who was set above my people,
He who has fallen, shall arise, and build
His justice on the blood of little men
Too soon triumphant. Touch me if you can!
I am the chosen instrument, to build

No less than to destroy! Keep your hands clean
Of evil toward me, and these with me, lest
You taste his punishment!—No, I have spoken badly—
And now I forget why we are here, or why
I have been angry.—You, sir, you are the captain—
Must I speak further?

Princess. You see, sir, he is mad.

Charash. Madness can be assumed. It is assumed,
No doubt, in this case. We know Bishop Andre,
And know his record. I must confirm the sentence
As it has been recorded.

Adam. We were not sentenced,
Nor even tried.

Charash. You have been sentenced.

Princess. Wait—
You were his friend—speak now!

Gregor. Do you remember
A man named Gregor, Charash?

Charash. Are you Gregor Lirod?

Gregor. Yes.

Charash. Have you turned against the revolution?

Gregor. No.

Charash. Then why are you here?

Gregor. I must ask you that.
I am a simple traveler, on my way
To meet my wife at Tobolsk, having escaped

From the northern mines. You have arrested me,
And now it seems, I'm sentenced.

Charash. Why do you travel
In company with aristocrats?

Gregor. Why, simply,
There was no choice. I travel as I can,
Having no money. Luckily for me
I meet you here.

Charash. Captain, this man's dismissed.
We were together in 1905. Come with me.
The sentence stands for the others.

Gregor. Charash, Charash—
They are not guilty.

Charash. Come with me.

Gregor. They are not guilty!
Can it be that means nothing?

Charash. Look at me, Gregor.
I have not slept for twenty-four hours. I'm in
No mood to be patient. In this city of Tiumen
I dare trust no man but myself to make
One final decision. With my own hands I've held
The mobs back, fought for mercy, had my way,
Kept order here. It means no sleep, no rest,
Till I'm driven half mad. And now at our first meeting
After these years, you turn on me and arraign me
As an unjust judge. What justice there has been
In Tiumen has been here because I give
My days and nights to it!

Gregor. But I tell you plainly
  These people were arrested without cause.
  Send them on their way, and then take your rest
  With a good conscience.

Charash. They are aristocrats,
  In flight from Moscow; every soul among them
  Traitor to us, ready to join the Whites
  When they've crossed the border.

Gregor. What is their crime?

Charash. Their crime
  Is what they are. Yes—what they mean in the world!

Gregor. And what was ours when we heard a sentence read
  That sent you off to prison, me into exile,
  Under the Czar? Our crime was what we were—
  And what we meant to have was a government
  Of equal justice! And now, by some strange chance,
  You are the government, but our equal justice
  Is far away as ever! It's murder
  To kill men for opinions! It's the terror
  And tyranny back again!

Charash. I must forgive you.
  You have been out of the world, up there in the salt
    mines,
  And missed a dozen years. This revolution
  Of ours is no reshuffling of the cards
  For the old game. We're sick of that game. We want
  A nation new from the ground up—rebuilt
  Without one stick of the old materials
  In the whole structure. The race has looked too long

On a vision of heaven in the clouds, to be
Attained by faithful service with these masters
We've driven out. We want our heaven here and now
In a world set free of nobles, free of profit,
Free of oppression, free of armies!

Gregor. Yes—
And that's what I want, too. But to free a world
Of the old oppressions, to set up a heaven on earth,
You use the methods we learned long ago
To hate under all the Czars!

Charash. Yes, we do use them.
We do use them, Gregor. We have caught
A vision of the earth, with men set free,
Such as no nation, back through all known time,
Has seen in our world before. A vision of an earth
Where men share equally and humbly all
The fruits of labor, no man starves, no mother
Need prostitute herself to feed her child,
Where men have time for beauty, and the sunlight
Of what is learned of wisdom and of truth
Falls to all men by right. Against this vision
The old creeds, and the members of those classes
Who lived by selfish interest, will fight
Forever, as they fight us now, will wage
The war against us till they die. We know that,
And they have said it. All these in this cell,
Fugitives, madmen, broken nobles, one
And all, given a half chance, would return
To load us with the chains of the old empire,
Even the children among them! They must die

Or they'll win against us yet, against the world
That's so far only glimpsed, of tolerance
And equality and good-will. I say to them:
Though it be hard to die, and all men cling
To the scrap of life we have, yes, though it's sweet
To live, even basely, you should be proud of death
In such a cause. For you are carriers
Of the ancient plague, the leprosy of the spirit,
That blights the hope of justice in mankind
With each beginning. Until you are dead
Or burnt and scattered in the holocaust
Of terror, the black pestilence that runs
In all your veins will poison what we do
With the rot of the old order. You are unclean,
Uncurable, and must die! Though we writhe within
To say it, though we turn our eyes away
From the judgment and the bloodshed, though your
   deaths
Haunt us by day and night, still you must die
Or we lose all we hoped to gain!

Gregor. I have heard this
   From others, but never believed it. You strangle with
     your own hands
   All hope for the revolution. Your aspiration,
   Your faith, and your nobility go down
   The drain with this unnecessary blood—
   Shed as a military measure. Justice—
   To attain justice you revoke all justice—
   To attain mercy you repudiate
   The principle of mercy.—Blood will breed murder,

Murder breed blood—the evil means we use
For a good end, will bring down only more evil
And curses at the end. There was a time
You knew this, Charash. You must dismiss these pris-
    oners,
Or your regime will emulate the Czar's,
Only bloodier and less honest.

Charash. I'm sorry, Gregor.
    Those who are not for us are against us.
    We have no love of the means at hand, but **we**
    Must use them now or lose.

Gregor. Better to lose
    Than lose your faith.

Charash. I shall not lose my faith.
    But we shall win, and after we have won
    There will be time for justice. The task now
    Is a cleansing of the empire of the filth
    Of a thousand years. I have no more time
    And this is a fruitless argument. Come with me.
    I have my orders and my own convictions.
    You will not change them.

Gregor. I shall stay here.
    [*A pause*]

Charash. Very well.
    Your name is on the roll. It has not been erased, as **yet.**

Gregor. I have heard it said here, Charash,
    That you yourself have never dared to look
    On what you do here, that you delegate the killings

To a drunken underling, who kills and drinks,
Drinks to forget his murders, and then drinks
Again to forget them, and then drinks to kill
And drinks again to forget.

Charash. It may be true.
I am no captain of a firing squad,
Yet the thing must be done. Must be.—For our old
    friendship
I ask again, come with me.

Gregor. Now that I know you
I am against you.

Charash. Goodnight, then.

Gregor. Goodnight, Charash.
    [*The door is opened*]

Adam. May I remind you of the memorandum,
Commissar?

Charash. All useless, all quite useless.
I can only say, as I said before,
That you do well, dying.
    [CHARASH *goes out with the* CAPTAIN, *and the inner door is
    closed*]

Adam. You were the man, I believe, who said he'd deny
you nothing.

Gregor. Yes, I was the man.

Plehve. No recriminations.

Princess. What can be done now?

Gregor. I can think of no desperate measures worth trying now.

> [*There is a knock at the inner door.* A GUARD *opens it*]

A Sergeant.
> [*Outside*]

Captain Krassin.

Guard. Come in.

> [CAPTAIN KRASSIN *enters with the* SERGEANT, *who carries a number of papers*]

Krassin. Put them down on the table. Push that box a little nearer.

> [*He sits*]

Are they all ready there?

A Guard. Yes, sir.

Krassin. Are you all ready over there?—Well, why don't you answer?

Plehve. We are, sir, as you see us.

Krassin. Have you been told?

Plehve. We have been told.

Krassin. Good. It's all settled then.

> [*He fumbles with his papers*]

Lvov. He seems to be drunk.

Lugan. He is drunk.

Krassin. General Plehve.

Plehve. Here, captain.

Krassin. Charged with illegal communication with the enemy. Stand over there.

Plehve. Yes, sir.

Krassin. Bishop Andre.

Andre. Yes.

Krassin. Conspiring against the revolution. Stand over there.

    [PLEHVE *and* ANDRE *take their places in line*]

The Princess—the Princess—why don't they write the names so a man can read them?

Princess. Is it the Princess Thalin?

Krassin. It is. The Princess Thalin and her two daughters. Stand over there.

Princess. But is this our trial?

Krassin. There is no trial. You've had your trial. I thought you'd been told.

Princess. We have.

Krassin. Then take your places.

    [*They do so*]

Illegal communication with the enemy.—Gregor Lirod.

    [*A silence*]

Conspiring against the revolution. Well, where is he? Gregor Lirod.

    [*Another silence,* KRASSIN *rises*]

Answer and use your tongue, Gregor Lirod, because you won't have much more chance to use it.—Sergeant, which one is Lirod?

Sergeant. I don't know, captain.

Krassin. You—which of you is Lirod? Speak.

Gregor. Gregor Lirod is not here, sir.

Krassin. His name's here.

Gregor. Are you sure?

Krassin. Damn you, why wouldn't I be sure?

Gregor. You don't see very well, you know. You hold the
paper at a peculiar angle, and the letters move before
your eyes—

Krassin. Be quiet! I have called the name of Gregor Lirod,
and this court is conducted in order. We condemn no
man without a record containing his name and his offense! This name is on the record and the man is here!
[*He smashes the box on which he has been sitting with a blow of
his fist*]
You see that? I shall do the same to this Gregor!

Gregor. Softening of the brain is sometimes brought on by
drinking. I have seen a case like it before.

Krassin. What's that?

Gregor. You're drunk, you know.

Krassin. Are you Gregor Lirod?

Gregor. Gregor Lirod is dead.

Krassin. You lie!

Gregor. He has been dead three days. You had him shot
three days ago, and ever since then you have had his
name on the brain. Night after night you have come in

here roaring for Gregor Lirod. You are not only drunk
but crazy. You are haunted by those you have killed.
And since the others are afraid to tell you this, I tell you.
 [*He rises*]

Krassin. Who are you?

Gregor. I am one of those you shot against that wall! What
does my name matter?
 [*He levels an arm at* KRASSIN]
But as for you, you have drunk and you have killed
until your mind is gone, and night after night you come
in here calling the names of dead men, long lists of dead
men, men shot a month ago, a week ago, and when their
phantoms rise before you, you have them shot. Have us
shot if you like. We are all ghosts here on this side of
the candles, all dead, and you are mad. Tomorrow you
go to the asylum. Tonight they let you shoot at phantoms to keep you quiet, but tomorrow you go to the
asylum.

Krassin. I say you lie!

Gregor. All the others lie to you, but we are dead; we have
nothing to lose. We tell you truth. Your brain is gone.
You have killed too many and drunk too much—and
from that little window the officers watch you and laugh
—watch you as you rave up and down calling on ghosts
and shooting against an empty wall.

Krassin.
 [*Looking blindly at his papers*]
But I saw the name—Gregor.

Gregor. Yes—Gregor—a dead man!

A Guard. That's not so.

Gregor. Yes, say I lie. They have orders to humor the mad-man. Six days a lunatic and not one to tell you.

Krassin. Stand in that line. Stand in that line, whoever you are! We shall shoot him first and see whether he falls down!—No. Wait. I must do everything in order. Come near me. Let me see you.

Gregor. Shall I show you that the candle shines through my hands? See—these are the hands of a man long dead and buried—a phantom of your mind—

Krassin. Keep away, then! To hell with you all—

[*He turns away uncertainly.* GREGOR *overturns the table and steps on the candles*]

Gregor. The door! Smash the door! Seize the truck! They dare not fire in the dark!

[*There is a rush of feet and a crash*]

Again! It will go down!

[*Another crash*]

Krassin. A light, someone! Strike a light! You hear?

[*A voice is heard outside giving orders*]

The Voice. Throw him off! Take the wheel! Kill him! Kill him!

[*The truck roars and starts*]

Krassin. Shoot, you fools! Shoot! Will you let them get away?

[*There are a few scattered shots*]

Where is the door? Where are they?

Sergeant. This way, men! Head them off!

Krassin. Who's master here? I give the orders here!

Sergeant. Then give your orders.

> [*A pause*]

Krassin. I have killed too many. Let them go.

Sergeant. You're drunk.

Krassin. Yes, I'm drunk, and a fool, and I've killed too many.

> [*There is a knocking at the inner door*]

Sergeant. It's the Commissar. Open it.

Charash.

> [*Outside*]

Bring the lantern.

> [*He enters*]

What has happened here?

Sergeant. The prisoners broke down the door, Commissar Charash. But it's not too late to pursue them.

Charash. Let them go. There's a body on the ground. The Bishop Andre.—It appears that you've outlived your usefulness, Captain Krassin. However, let the prisoners go. I had a friend among them.

Sergeant. Your friend's here.

Charash. Gregor? You should have escaped with the others.

Gregor. Yes, I know, Charash. But whatever meaning my life has had derived from the revolution we made together. If the revolution's dead I'm happy to die with it.

XI · KEY LARGO

CHARACTERS

(In the order of their appearance)

VICTOR D'ALCALA	PRISCILLA
NIMMO	KILLARNEY
JERRY	MR. AARONSON
MONTE	MRS. AARONSON
KING MCCLOUD	MR. WHEELER
SHERIFF GASH	MRS. WHEELER
D'ALCALA	OSCEOLA HORN
ALEGRE D'ALCALA	1ST MAN TOURIST
GAGE	1ST WOMAN TOURIST
CORKY	2ND WOMAN TOURIST
MURILLO	JOHN HORN
HUNK	SAM

Prologue

SCENE & & Bright moonlight comes down across a rocky hill-top in northern Spain, revealing four young men on outpost guard duty. They are Americans, dressed haphazardly in nondescript uniforms, zipper overalls and mufti, well-worn and uncared-for. At the extreme left a pup-tent gapes open. One lad sits above, writing on a pad on his knee, occasionally looking off to the right and singing softly to himself. The others are rolled in their blankets near the tent or within it. There is a flash of light against the sky, followed, after an interval, by a far-away detonation.

Victor.

    [*Singing softly*]

             Au clair de la lune,
             Mon ami Pierrot,
             Prête moi ta plume
             Pour écrire un mot.

    [*He rises, looks out left, then sits to finish his song.*]

             Ma chandelle est morte,
             Je n'ai plus de feu.
             Ouvre moi ta porte
             Pour l'amour de Dieu.

Nimmo. All right, howl, you dog. Howl the moon. Who cares if I sleep?

Jerry. Let him sing. It keeps him awake.

Nimmo. Me too. Isn't that a French song about the moon?

Victor. It is.

Nimmo. Well, why do you whine in French, you whelp of old Castile? You said your folks were Spanish.

Victor. Cradle songs are international, O Son of Chicago! I was writing a letter to my sister and she used to sing that song.

Nimmo. I hope she sings it better than you do.

Victor. She does. But I'll be quiet.

> [*There is a silence for a moment, then* MONTE *rolls over on his back, looks up at the sky, and murmurs the song.*]

Monte. Ma chandelle est morte,
Je n'ai plus de feu—
It has absolutely no meaning, that song. It's completely without meaning. But excellent poetry.

Nimmo. That's fine. Now can we just let the whole thing drop?

Victor. They had every chance to make it good poetry, with no meaning to worry about.

Monte.
> [*Sniffing*]

We'll have to move the tent, Victor. Those Moors stink like murder.

Victor. The wind'll change tomorrow.

Monte. This is what it means, really. In prose:

> Out in the moonlight,
> My friend Pierrot,
> Lend me your pen
> To write a word.

There he is, out in the street, you observe, asking for writing materials. But then it goes on:

My candle is dead—
I have no more fire—
Open your door to me
For the love of God.

Still out in the moonlight, apparently, only now he's worrying about modern conveniences—and thinks maybe he'd better move in with his friend. The whole situation's baffling.

Nimmo. Are you really writing a letter to your sister, Victor?

Victor. I really am.

Jerry. You know, as near as I can remember, I never wrote to my sister in my life. I'm not bragging about it, but—

Victor. There are only three of us, and we've been alone a good deal, down there on Key Largo.

Jerry. Where's Key Largo?

Victor. In Florida.
  [*He lies flat with his gun.*]
There's something climbing up the rocks.

Jerry. It's probably King and Shippy.

Victor. Last time we thought it was the patrol it wasn't.

Nimmo. God, I'm hungry!

Jerry. This living is a hand-to-mouth business. I certainly miss my dinner when I don't have it.

Monte. Give them the owl.

Victor.
[*Imitating*]
Huh-who, huh-who-oo!

King.
[*At a distance*]
Huh-who-oo.

Nimmo. Good! We can eat!
[*He stands up.*]

Monte.
[*To* VICTOR]
Satisfied?

Victor. That owl had an American accent. It's King, all right.
But he seems to be alone.
[*Two or three boys look over the crest. Again the flash, the interval of silence, and the sound of the shell.*]

Jerry. Now why the hell would they keep a poor guy up all
night shooting at the side of a mountain?

Nimmo. Maybe he can't hit it.

Monte. There's nobody with King.

Victor. No.
[*He stands upright.*]
Where's Shippy?

King.
[*Outside*]
Don't stand up there, boy. The moon's behind you, and
that Greek profile of yours is visible at a hundred yards.

Monte. Get down.

> [VICTOR *does so*.]

King. Get down and stay down, all of you. From here you look like so many ducks in a shooting gallery.

Victor. There's nobody between here and the road.

King.

> [*Appearing, burdened with two heavy sacks*]

There wasn't this morning, but there is now.

> [*He leaps down among them.*]

I saw two trucks parked on the road without lights, just south of the turn. Somebody must have come in them.

Monte. Where's Shippy?

King.

> [*Opening a sack*]

That's right, that was this morning, wasn't it? It seems like a week ago. That big gun laid one down right outside the village. We both dropped and Shippy didn't get up. He's in the hospital, but he won't live. I didn't want to leave him alone, but I had to get your damned grub up to you.

Victor. Is he conscious?

King. No. And he won't be any more.—This is mostly dry-pack—chocolate and biscuits.

> [*He hands out packages; the boys take them in silence. One or two begin to eat.*]

There's one cut of salami.

Nimmo. That's my meat.

King. Cut in five equal portions and distribute.
[*He hands over the sausage.*]

Nimmo. Five? That's right, it's five now. Eight, seven, six, five.

Monte. We've been lucky, comparatively. Whole companies have been wiped out, not a man left to turn in a report. We're used to being lucky and it hits us hard when somebody goes.

Victor. You're sure he won't come to enough to talk?

King. Positive.

Jerry. This is the God damndest loneliest mountain this side of hell.

Nimmo. Well, take your section. Salami's salami whether it's in six cuts or five.

Monte. Aren't we beginning to talk like a lot of drafted men with a choice between prison and the front line? We volunteered, mind you. It isn't our fight, and it never was our fight, but we made it our fight. We said that to each other before we came over here—we said if a lot of good, healthy men don't die for Spain right now there won't be any place on earth where a free man can live in a couple of years. Well, we're in Spain, and three of us are dead in Spain—and will stay dead for the rest of time. Maybe we'll all die and stay dead—but the original proposition remains unchanged. I admit it's getting pretty close, and I don't find it very comfortable, but if I can manage to keep my food down maybe I'll stick it out.

Jerry. To say nothing of the fact that you'd damn well better stick it out now you're here. Because if you don't they'll stand you up against an outhouse and shoot you.

Monte. I guess we all know the honeymoon's over.

Nimmo. It's not that so much. It's mostly you don't like yourself as much as you did—or respect yourself. When you're in a fight it doesn't count how you got in it, or what you're out to get. You have to crawl on your belly and rip up the other fellow's guts just the same. And it does something to you. Because it's a stinking business, and it makes you stink.

King. Quit talking, and eat your food. You'll need it before the night's over.

Jerry. But the worst is you don't know what you're out to get.

Nimmo. We thought we did before we started. We said, no matter what they do with their freedom, they have a right to keep it. But suppose the first thing they do with their freedom is assert their right to put on chains? We believe in the rights of minorities, don't we? Well, there are fifty-seven minorities in Loyalist Spain, all pretty sharp with each other, but willing to drop the arguments while they deal with Franco. They're Anarchists, Communists, Leftists, Rightists, Leftist-rightists, Rightist-leftists, Socialists, Leftist-Socialists, Rightist-Socialists, Anti-clericals, Clerical-Communists, Loyalist soldiers, police, crazy people, and once in a while just a plain farmer, all fighting Franco! But if they won and it came to a vote, and one party was in power, would it make hash of the other fifty-six varieties! They're very intense about politics, these Spanish. Once

they get in an argument, they don't care how long they
live, and they don't think it matters about you, either. Each
one of them intends to live as he God damn pleases, and he
intends to see to it that everybody else lives the way he
wants them to!

Victor. They may be somewhat intolerant, but after all freedom's fairly new to them. They don't know how to use it.
And if there's a good fight anywhere in the world it's here.

Nimmo. Franco's low enough, God knows. When you think
about Franco you think any man ought to be proud to die
fighting that complete son-of-a-bitch, but then you think
about the bloody mess on this side, and you wonder.

Jerry. You wonder, for one thing, why the Red Ogpu's running our Brigade, and why you're likely to disappear if you
can't pretend you're a Communist. Are we fighting for a
democratic Spain or to make the world safe for Stalin?

Monte. The Loyalists wouldn't have got this far without
Stalin—and naturally the leaders take help wherever they
can get it.

Jerry. He charges a high price for his help. I don't like the
Ogpu any more than Franco. The question is whether
Spain would be free even if the Loyalists won.

Monte. She won't be free if the Loyalists lose, of course.

Victor. Hasn't it always looked the same, the fight
for freedom? It's never respectable. It's led
by unscrupulous fanatics, each one eyeing
the others' throats. They're followed by a rabble
that pulls down all the walls and lets the roofs

fall in on them. A lot of people die,
good and bad, but there is more freedom later,
for the next generation, there is. If you want a clean,
Armageddon battle, all the beasts of hell
against the angels of light, you won't get that,
not in this world.

Nimmo. No.—Well, I'm not complaining,
except about the food.—Will you look at King,
working away with a needle and thread by moonlight,
on his old gabardine. Did you meet a girl
in the village, you lug, and did she have black eyes,
and did they find that hole in your coat?

King. I'm not sewing—
I'm—as the old women say—I'm ripping out.

> [*He pulls a tag loose.*]

That's what they look for first—your tags.

Monte. How come?

King. When you've had enough to eat pack up what's left
to go along, get out your razor blades
and rip off labels—for we're changing names
and seeping out of here.

Monte. Are we ordered out?

King. No.
But I led you here. I'm responsible,
and I mean to get you out.

Jerry.
> [*Saluting*]

As you say, commandante.
Here's to hell or Paris. But I prefer Paris.

Monte. Remember, King,
  this is a democratic army, and even
  anarchistic in spots—we'd want to know
  what's on your mind, because we have minds of our own,
  all of us.

King. Why certainly. Take a vote.
  I was at that wine-shop back of the convent
  waiting to hear how Shippy came out, when in
  walked a couple of officers, spread out their maps
  and went to work. I guess they didn't see me.
  I was up in the alcove. Well, there's to be
  a general retirement along this line;
  our ridge is being abandoned; they're falling back
  three miles to the rear.

Victor. When?

King. Tonight and part of tomorrow.
  There's a lot of stuff to move, and it takes time;
  they want to be out before Mr. Franco's scouts
  begin to notice. Have we had marching orders?
  Are we going anywhere?

Monte. Not that I know of.

King. No, and you won't get any.
  We're left to hold the ridge.

Monte. How do you know?

King. I heard something vague about Hill 4—
   how it would take them anyway twenty-four hours
   to blast us out of here, and by that time
   they'd be dug in three miles back.

Monte. They're leaving us
   to cover the retreat?

King. That's what I gathered.
   And why not? It's good strategy. This salient's
   way out of line, and never could be held
   in a general assault. But if they withdrew
   without a rear-guard action they'd be caught
   in the valley and massacred. They have to choose
   between losing a lot of men and losing a few,
   and we're picked for the few. Personally I don't take it.
   I'm fed up with the war, and the whole damn setup
   from God and Chamberlain on down. I'm ripping
   a few identification marks and labels
   off my clothes and leaving. And so are you.

Jerry. How about passports?

King. Well, I hold my passport dear,
   and I've hugged it pretty close, but not so dear
   and not so close as my life.

Jerry. Could a man get through
   without one?

King. He could try. He might live. But he won't
   if he sits here and waits.

Monte. How sure is this?

King. From what I heard I'd say it's certain.

Nimmo. God—
> [*He crosses the stage to* KING.]
> wait a minute! We're going to die here?

King. Boy,
> you're thick, but when a notion penetrates,
> there's a reaction!

Monte. We're stationed here, you know.

King. And I know what for.

Jerry. We have orders to hold the hill.
> There's no getting out of that.

King. There may not be,
> but we can leave it, and try.

Monte. And the companies
> moving back, who's going to cover them
> if we're not here?

King. It's going to be tough for them,
> almost as tough for them if we're not here
> as it is for us if we are.

Nimmo. And if you're caught
> they shoot you.

King. Without doubt. If they know who you are.
> But the poor ragged sons of bastards that run
> this war, how can they keep track of the other bastards
> that fight it for them? We'll get up some sob story
> on the way down—and, by the way, if we're going

we'd better hump it. I want to be ten miles
from here by morning. Once the trouble starts
it'll be too late. Get ready with your packs
if you're coming with me.

Monte. An ignominious exit
from our crusade.

King. Was there ever a crusade
without an ignominious end? Before
we came to Spain we should have thought of that.
The knights in rusty armor crippling home
with an increment of blood and bone diseases
from Palestine—leaving the infidels
in charge as usual. Or the A. E. F.
over-seas for democracy, and winning—
along with other diseases—
this Mussolini and Hitler. Yes, and Franco,
very likely.

Victor. Isn't this a graver matter
than you pretend, King?

King. It's running for your life.
That's grave enough.

Victor. If we go it's more than an end
to our crusade. It's an end to everything
we were, everything we talked of in your room
under the skylight, an end to all the meaning
you found in the world. We haven't talked much lately.
I thought it was only because there wasn't time,
but maybe you've changed and haven't told us.

King. I have.
    I was trying to hold on. When you've believed
    that right wins in the end it's a little hard
    to turn round suddenly on a battle-front
    and say the hell with it.

Victor. But you've turned round now,
    and said it?

King. Yes.

Victor. But right does win in the end.

King. Only if you believe whoever wins
    is right in the end. Because we're losing here—
    and dying here!

Victor. You have been our leader, King.
    Certainly you've been mine. We haven't been cowards,
    any of us, but we've let you show the way
    most of the time. Are we suddenly afraid
    to die, when suddenly it's necessary?
    Are you afraid? If you are then it's come about
    between tonight and this morning.

King. Nobody's afraid
    to die when he sees good reason for it. Hell,
    we're not here for fun! We came believing
    there was some use in it! Maybe some of us think
    there still is use. I've been trying to hold on
    this last half-year—I've been trying to believe
    the whole world would rise up and step on this evil
    that crawls over Spain—and it has risen up,

and stepped on us. And now I'm beginning to wonder
if a cause is sacred when it's lost. Did we volunteer
to die in a lost cause?

Victor. What's gone? What's changed
since yesterday?

King. Our cause is lost, that's all.
Maybe because there isn't any God
and nobody cares who wins. Anyway if you win
you never get what you fight for, never get
the least approximation of the thing
you were sold on when you enlisted. No, you find
instead that you were fighting to impose
some monstrous, bloody injustice, some revenge
that would end in another war.

Monte. Why do you say
our cause is lost, and Franco will win in Spain?
Is there news of Franco? Is the war lost for us?
We've told ourselves we couldn't lose.

King. Well, we can.
This was between the lines of what they said—
the officers—the war's at an end in Spain—
this withdrawal, it's part of a larger movement—
falling back on Madrid, getting ready to ask for terms;
I don't know what else—but the end.

Monte. Then I understand you.

King. I should think you would.

Jerry. And the war's over.

King. That I can't swear to. It was never said,
   only by hints, indirectly, but I got it,
   enough to convince me.

Nimmo. I never thought of the end.
   I never thought of that part.

Monte. So it's not only
   we cover a retreat—but the war's lost
   and we die for a lost cause.

King. So get your duffle,
   and we'll move out. Look, we were children,
   suckled in one of these nutmeg Alma Maters,
   and Spain was a bugle call. Up and to Spain
   and save the world! Byron went out to Greece
   about a hundred years ago and died
   in a swamp of the fever. Don Quixote
   went out against the windmills. It was a Spaniard
   who knew his Spain well enough to write Quixote—
   and we should have read it.—I know I'm a turncoat;
   it was my romantic notion to save Spain,
   and I was eloquent about it. Yes,
   maybe I thought I talked like Rupert Brooke—
   for all I know maybe I thought I looked
   like that poor Galahad of Gallipoli,
   saving heaven for the angels.—The best I can do now
   is be fairly honest about it, and get you out
   and get myself out. They say there's just one test
   for whether a man's a fool—it's how long he lives
   and how well.

Jerry. There's not much to carry. It won't take long.
   Shall we pack up?

Nimmo. I think so.

Monte. And those three hundred
on the ridge to the south—if we're not here they're caught;
they'll be wide open crossing the valley. Look,
couldn't we get word to them?

Nimmo. Not before morning.

Jerry. Well, let it go.

Victor. Is it decided?

Nimmo. Yes. What can we do?

Victor. Then I'll play anarchist
tonight. I'll stay here.

Monte. Alone?

Victor. I like company—
but if I'm alone, I'm alone. Don't think I blame you.
You went into it for any number of reasons,
mostly perishable, as King says. You could leave
and go on living, but I couldn't. I'm a Spaniard,
or my father is, and all my blood and belief
are in this fight here. I was brought up to think
of Spain and freedom first in the morning, and first
at night. It took the place of prayers with us;
but that's because my father's a little crazy,
according to the neighbors, and I'm infected—
not that I mind.

King. Wait a minute, Victor!
You can't stay here alone.

Victor. Oh, yes, I can.
That's the anarchist angle of this army—
every man his own captain. I can stay
if I wish, and those who wish to go, can go.
So I'll sit here.

King. You can't hold them alone, you know.
You'll die for nothing. They'll walk right over you.
Won't even pause.

Victor. Well—

King. Then why do it? Why sit here
and get yourself murdered?

Victor. Because there is no God.

King. What do you mean?

Victor. Because the sky's quite empty,
just as you said. The scientists have been over it
with a fine-tooth comb and a telescope, and the verdict
is, No God, nothing there. Empty and sterilized,
like a boiled test-tube. But if there's no God there
and nothing inside me I have any respect for
then I'm done. Then I don't live, and I couldn't.
So I stay here to keep whatever it is
alive that's alive inside me.

King. It's not only the sky
that's empty, remember. They've looked us through pretty
well,
and men and horses are pure chemistry
so far as anybody knows. The soul—
or psyche—has the same composition
as eggs and butter.

Victor. It's too late
to change. I know what I live by, and I'll die by it.
It's more important than living.

King. What you live by?

Victor. Yes.

King. Then what is it? Tell us.

Victor. I'd rather not.

King. If it's like all the other faiths I've ever known
it's nothing you can put your finger on,
or say in words, or put any trust in, and so
it's nothing. A pocket of air under the vest.
That's why it can't be stated.

Victor. I have to believe
there's something in the world that isn't evil—
I have to believe there's something in the world
that would rather die than accept injustice—something
positive for good—that can't be killed—
or I'll die inside. And now that the sky's found empty
a man has to be his own god for himself—
has to prove to himself that a man can die
for what he believes—if ever the time comes to him
when he's asked to choose, and it just so happens
it's up to me tonight.—And I stay here.
I don't say it's up to you—I couldn't tell
about another man—or any of you—
but I know it's up to me.

King. Is it up to us still,
after all the betrayals, after the game's changed

and we're cheated on both sides? After the Russian
secret police taking over our own brigade? And Munich,
and Czechoslovakia, and this last betrayal
of Spain by France and England? We should know
by this time—we've looked at Europe long enough
to know there's nothing to fight for here—that nothing
you win means freedom or equality
or justice—that all the formulas are false—
and known to be false—democracy, communism,
socialism, naziism—dead religions
nobody believes in—or if he does believe
he's quietly made use of by the boys
who long ago learned better, and believe
in nothing but themselves. Let it end—let them end it—
these idiot ideologies that snarl
across borders at each other. Stalin walking
his swamps in blood, Hitler's swastikas
in blood above the lintels, the English and French
desperate because everything has failed,
because life itself has failed, and capitalism,
and they may even lose their colonies,
unless God can be revived. And here in Spain,
Franco will win in Spain, they'll see to that—
but if he didn't, Stalin would win in Spain,
and it's one blood-purge or the other, but never justice,
only the rat-men ratting on each other
in a kind of rat despair.—I tell you it was a dream,
all a dream we had, in a dream world,
of brothers who put out a helping hand
to brothers, and might save them.—Long ago
men found out the sky was empty; it follows
that men are a silly accident, meaningless,

here in the empty sky, like a flag on the moon,
as meaningless as an expedition led
to take possession of it—in the name of Marx—
or maybe democracy—or social justice!
Why should we die here for a dead cause, for a symbol,
on these empty ramparts, where there's nothing to win,
even if you could win it?

Victor. Yes, but if I die
   then I know men will never give in;
   then I'll know there's something in the race
   of men, because even I had it, that hates injustice
   more than it wants to live.—Because even I had it—
   and I'm no hero.—And that means the Hitlers
   and the Mussolinis always lose in the end—
   force loses in the long run, and the spirit wins,
   whatever spirit is. Anyway it's the thing
   that says it's better to sit here with the moon
   and hold them off while I can. If I went with you
   I'd never know whether the race was turning
   down again, to the dinosaurs—this way
   I keep my faith. In myself and what men are.
   And in what we may be.

King. Well—

Victor. Oh, I know all this
   sounds priggish—it's the manly thing to joke
   in extremis—but just for the record let it stand,
   and now we'll forget it.

King. If you won't argue
   there's no arguing. I only wish
   we could all stick together. Are we ready?

Jerry. One minute.

    [NIMMO *and* JERRY *pick up to go.*]

Monte. I guess I'll stick with Victor.

Jerry.

    [*Stopping suddenly*]
    Yes. I'll stay.
    I'll stay, too.

King. It's Nimmo and me then.

Nimmo. I can't go.
    With the four of us we might hold them. Long enough—
    while the shock troops got away.

Jerry. By God, we might—
    with the four of us.

King. It seems I was wrong
    and nobody needs advice. I could have saved
    the walk up here and down. Why, you God damn fools,
    what do you care what the Sunday-school teachers say
    if you can live?

Jerry.

    [*Tremulously*]
    That's all right.

    [KING *picks up his gun and pack and steps to the embankment by
    which he entered. As he stands silhouetted he turns to them.*]

King. It's not cowardice, you know,
    It's plain, common, everyday horse-sense;
    it's not me that's crazy.

    [*They are silent, looking up at him.*]

Don't you see I can't save you,
but you can save yourselves, and if you don't
I'll run from you all like a pack of ghosts?

Victor. But you shouldn't.
You shouldn't, King. Why can't you think of us
as among the fortunate few whose lives have had
a meaning right up to the end? And not as heroes—
just ordinary fellows who ate breakfast
on a certain morning—and then ate lunch and dinner
and slept exceptionally long that night—
as why shouldn't they?

King. Well, anything I can do?
You were writing a letter.

Victor. It isn't finished,
and it wasn't important. Give me your hand, though.

King. Good-bye.

Victor. You're doing what you believe, and that's all that
matters.

[KING *comes down and takes* VICTOR'S *hand, then turns and goes
down the hill.*]

Monte. Has it occurred to you—here in the moonlight—
there's a resemblance between these Spanish mountains
and the mountains of the moon?

[*Again the flash, and the detonation.*]

CURTAIN

KEY LARGO

ACT ONE

Act One

SCENE & & *The scene is a wharf on Key Largo from which one looks north and west across the Gulf of Mexico. The planks end at the water, and the blue sea runs out into a blue sky, with a sharp blue demarcation along the horizon. At the left is the wall of a one-story house, thatched with palm branches and Spanish bayonet. A section of porch faces the audience and a door opens on to the wharf from it. At the right a summer house, thatched and partially sided with the same materials, covers an outdoor table and some chairs. A line or two of boat rigging is visible above the wharf. It is morning.*
SHERIFF GASH, *a tall, middle-aged man in leather boots, comes in from the left, in front of the house, and knocks on the door. It is opened by an elderly man who wears dark glasses.*

Gash. Your name's d'Alcala?

d'Alcala. Bruno d'Alcala, yes.

Gash. This is your place?

d'Alcala. Yes.

Gash. I was about to ask you—
    is something the matter with your eyes?

d'Alcala. I'm blind.

Gash. Yeah, I was about to ask you if you'd seen
    a couple of run-away Seminole boys; I guess
    you're the wrong man to ask. Another thing,
    you have a son called Victor?
    [*He takes out a little book.*]

d'Alcala. I had a son
    called Victor. He was killed in Spain last winter—
    early this year.

Gash. He was killed?

d'Alcala. Yes, sir.

Gash. I see.
    The reason I asked, there's something on the books
    about a charge against him, maybe two years
    or so ago—giving aid or sheltering
    a fellow from a road gang. That's why I came in.
    But the boy's dead?

d'Alcala. I wish he were alive
    to answer for himself. But since I must say it,
    he's dead, and I answer for him.

Gash. Who's hereabout
    that might have seen these Indians passing through?
    I'm Sheriff Gash of the Star Keys, in case
    you should want to know.

d'Alcala. Sir, if you'll ask my daughter—
    she's here, I think. I heard her set the rake
    against the house.

    [ALEGRE *comes round the corner of the house, wearing a wide
    sun-hat and carrying a basket.*]

    This is Sheriff Gash, Alegre,
    wanting to know about some Seminole boys
    that might have passed this way.

Alegre. I haven't seen them.
    No, I've seen no one.

Gash. Part of a road gang—
    been gone two days and a half—might have got rid
    of the stripes by this time—one of them middle-aged,
    but looks young, one a boy.

Alegre. I haven't seen them.
  No one's been by.

Gash. Who's staying here? Any transients?

Alegre. Just one party. Professional people—at least
  that's what they call it. Now that you're here, Sheriff
    Gash,
  what's the procedure when a little group
  of professional gamblers rents all the rooms you have,
  sets up its paraphernalia on the wharf
  and refuses to leave?

Gash. What's the complaint against them?

Alegre. They're gamblers. And not honest.

Gash. They pay their rent?

Alegre. Yes, but they'll ruin our trade.
  They fleece the tourists
  and give the place a bad name.
  Haven't we the right to choose
  what kind of people stay here?

Gash. No,
  not if there's nothing against them. Just at present
  this whole county's lenient and wide open
  when it comes to any kind of gambling. No,
  you've got to take what comes.

Alegre. The games are rigged
  and faked—it's all mechanically done—
  they boast of having purchased the devices
  by mail, show you the catalogues.

Gash. They're taking a chance,
but that's their own affair. Now I've got to go;
you'll let me know if you hear of those fellows—?

d'Alcala. Yes,
we'll watch out for them. But before you go
one word about the gamblers. If you wish them well—
if you have any personal concern—

Gash. I have none.

d'Alcala. If you know anyone who has, then tell him
they've burned out their welcome here, and it's high time
they leave the Key. There's misfortune in the wind,
particularly for Murillo.

Gash. You don't want him here,
and I don't blame you, but that's hardly news.
The law can't deal with prophecy, you know;
only with facts.

d'Alcala. If I should have to wait
for what you'd recognize as facts, your friend
might not thank you.

Gash. Who said he was my friend?

d'Alcala. I beg your pardon.

Gash. When you've information
to lodge, produce it. When you start prophesying
it sounds too much like a threat. Good day to you.
Good day, ma'am.

d'Alcala. Very well, I'll tell you plainly,
I think you take money from them.

&⅋ 32 &⅋

Gash. And that kind of talk
  doesn't make for friendship!
    [*He goes out.*]

Alegre. Murillo will leave, no doubt.
  It must be dangerous for him when he's known,
  and he'll soon be known here.

d'Alcala. Give me the basket.

Alegre. I'll carry it.

d'Alcala. Let me be useful in my darkness—
  or seem so.—Yes?

Alegre. Those Indians and this sheriff—

d'Alcala. Yes?

Alegre. I lied to him. There are two Indians hiding
  under water in the mangrove swamp. I saw them
  from the clam-flats yesterday, and again today—
  I've just come from there.

d'Alcala. Well, that's God's lie,
  as your mother would have said. And modern science
  is less and less insistent on the truth,
  seeing there is none.

Alegre. But we're so constructed,
  what with our antique conscience, and whatever
  makes us blush, that we can't prevaricate
  without a sense of fear. It was worse than I told you.
  I put some of Victor's old clothes in my basket

when I went for clams, this morning, and left them there
out of reach of the tide. They'll find them, because I saw
where they'd been digging clams.

d'Alcala. May they find them, and Godspeed
to all poor fugitives. We've seen no one and nothing,
and you were quite right to say so.

Alegre. Then that's all clear—
For a moment I thought it might be sacrilege
to let his clothes go walking down the beach
on some lost vagrant. They were all he left
and had his shape still in them.—

d'Alcala. It doesn't help
to hang things in a closet, and take them out
on rainy days when you're lonely. I tried that
and it doesn't help.—The Indians are still there,
still hiding among the mangroves?

Alegre. Yes. They must be.
They won't dare leave till dark. Only two black heads
bobbing behind the roots. They won't be seen
even if there's a search.

d'Alcala. Would they do something for us?
Would they do us a favor? A favor in return?

Alegre. I think they would.
Yes, I saw their faces.

d'Alcala. If I had my eyes
I wouldn't need an Indian or anyone else
to teach this sheriff! God, if I had my eyes!

Alegre. If I could see for you—

d'Alcala. You could take a message
and leave it with the clothes.

Alegre. The truth is, father,
I meant to put some breakfast in a basket
and take it down later on. What shall I tell them?

d'Alcala. Only that I must talk to one of them,
tonight, if it's possible. But go instantly.

Alegre. I must make up a basket.

d'Alcala. It may be
even a blind man can see beyond them.

[*He goes in, she follows.* GAGE *and* CORKY *come in from the right, carrying some scaffolding and a table-top which they proceed to set up on the wharf.*]

Gage. Set it square in those bolt-holes or the nuts won't draw up.

Corky. Yeah, bo, I know about that. My uncle kept a hardware store. I know about nuts and bolts, male and female.

Gage. What do you mean male and female?

Corky. Just like the human race, these nuts and bolts, Gagey. Male and female created he them. It's a technical description useful in the trade. Some stick out and some recede, that's all.

Gage. Well, pull them up tight, because if they're loose the control won't work.

[ALEGRE *enters with a basket, pauses, and then crosses to the summer house.*]

Corky. Not much traffic this morning and what there is is Florida natives exploding along on ten-cent gas.

Gage. Any liquid that's more than ten cents a gallon a Florida cracker just naturally considers it's a beverage and drinks it.

Corky. Imagine a cracker about to visit St. Augustine. He stands beside the jalopy with a gallon jug in his hand. "Wife," he says, "do I pour it in the tank, or do we drink it and push her?" (*To* ALEGRE) Listen, Winsome, will you do me a favor?

Alegre. What is it?

Corky. Take a spin down the Long Bridge and have a coconut rum with me tonight. One of those and you can almost see the Southern Cross from Key West. Two of them and you can see it but you don't care.

Alegre. Thank you.

   [*She goes out round the house.*]

Corky. How long do you suppose it would take for a guy to make that dame? Three days?

Gage. I saw the boss looking at that girl. You haven't got a chance.

Corky. Mussolini? Listen, he better keep out of my way or I'll make a non-aggression pact with him.

Gage. Well, anyway, if it's going to take three days you might as well give up. We won't be here three days.

Corky. Mussolini said a week.

Gage. Don't make any plans in this neighborhood.

Corky. What do you know?

Gage. We're in trouble.

Corky. Something wrong with the protection?

Gage. You can't be protected for what happened last night

Corky. No? There's only one thing you can't be protected for.

Gage. That's right.

Corky. Who got it?

Gage. You remember the big fellow that lost all the expense money and made a play for the boss's girl?

Corky. Yeah.

Gage. Now I didn't see this—and I don't know anything about it if anybody asks me, but I'm willing to bet he's sunk out there in forty feet of water with a turn of steel clothesline around his arms, a bag of coral hung on his feet, and a school of these tropical fishes taking little bites out of his ears.

Corky. Don't be so graphic.
[*He rubs his ears.*]

Gage. I don't know anything about it from now on.

Corky. You mean the guy came back last night?

Gage. I heard a little brawl, and a few other noises. So I say we're not going to be here very long.

Corky. You don't know Mussolini. He's been followed by dead meat before and it never catches up with him. He never even worries about it. He wouldn't think of pulling out on account of dead meat in the water.

Gage. Well, I would.

Corky. So would I.

Gage. If you should ever think of going somewhere else let me know, will you?

Corky. Maybe I will. Yeah, I will.
[*He reaches a hand to* GAGE.]

Gage. Because I've been thinking about it for some time.
[MURILLO *and* HUNK *enter, followed at some distance by two girls,* PRISCILLA *and* KILLARNEY.]

Murillo. Listen, everybody, I'm changing the set-up. Hunk, you're on the porch, watching, and you play deaf and dumb, you understand?

Hunk. I get you.

Murillo. Now put your minds on this because what you say's different. Killarney, when you win, and I put down your money, you cross over to Corky, and you say, "Mac, I won eighty dollars! Look!"

Killarney. "Mac, I won eighty dollars! Look!"

Murillo. That's right. And Gage, after I lose the first time to the monkeys you go up to the fellow with the most money and say, "Look, this bird's an amateur! He's been losing money to the whole crowd hand over fist."

Gage. Yes, sir.

Murillo.
> [*To* HUNK]
> Did a car turn in?

Hunk. Naw—I been watching the roaa.

Murillo. And Corky—Hey—somebody says you've been calling me Mussolini.

Corky. Me? Maybe in fun, boss. Just in fun. Just because you're the boss.

Murillo. I don't think it's funny. My name's Murillo, in case you want to know.

Corky. I get you.

Murillo.
> [*Inspecting the wheel-of-fortune*]
> Let me see it spin. And tune your mouth down from now on. Stop it on red. Again. Stop it on black. I said on black! Was the wheel wrong or did you foozle it?

Corky. My foot slipped.

Murillo. I thought so. I'll work the control myself! Turn it around. If I didn't need you, baby face, you'd start back tonight for wherever you were born!

Killarney. Lay off the boy! He talks well and he's good looking, and some of us like him even if you don't.

Murillo. Any time you want to start more trouble, baby, just put in your nominations.

Killarney. Haven't you got enough hanging over you now? For no God damn reason at all?

Murillo. I had my reasons.

Killarney. For no God damn reason at all! And how long do you think anybody's going to stick with you with that around your neck?

Priscilla. What's the argument about?

Hunk. Damn if I know.

Murillo. Let it end where it is, then! And no more talk, you fool!

Hunk.
   [*To* MURILLO]
One from the north, walking.
   [*He stops the wheel.*]

Murillo.
   [*Hard*]
Looking for something, neighbor?

King. Can you tell me who lives here?

Murillo. We all live here.

King. Thanks.
   [*He glances again at the contraption, looks at the door, decides **not** to knock, and goes out around the far side of the house.*]

Murillo. See where he goes.
[HUNK *follows and looks after* KING, *then returns.*]

Hunk. Just strolling.

Priscilla. Whatever kind of uniform is that?

Gage. Whatever kind it is there's a gun goes with it.

Hunk. It ain't no variety of state trooper I ever saw. And I've seen several.

Gage. Think he's snooping on us?

Murillo. Why would he walk here if he's an officer? I never knew an officer to walk anywhere he could ride. I'd say he was a soldier out of a job.

Hunk.
    [*Watching*]
What the hell?

Murillo. Yeah?

Hunk. He's taking off his shoes.
    [*A pause*]
His feet must be tired. He's fixing to wash his feet in the Gulf of Mexico.

Murillo. I guess we don't worry about him.

Gage. There's a car on the way in. Packard sedan. Two women and two men. Just looking around. Packard Twelve, by God. Got plenty of money, and look as if they carried it.

Murillo. Get ready.

[*They all gather round the wheel-of-fortune as if interested in a game.* MURILLO *spins the wheel.*]

Get around to that side, you girls. Spread out a little. And this time no off-hand remarks, if you don't mind. Nothing except what's been rehearsed, and if you can't remember your lines keep quiet. I run this show alone, and you can count on it anything you think of to say is wrong. It just so happens you never queered anything yet, but you will if you go on trying.

[MR. *and* MRS. AARONSON *and* MR. *and* MRS. WHEELER *come round the corner.*]

Mrs. Aaronson. What a darling place! But really darling! It's an inn, too, you know. Rooms and special dinners the sign said.

Mrs. Wheeler. Don't you love it?

Mrs. Aaronson. I want to stay here all the rest of the time! Can't we stay here, darling?

Aaronson. I haven't asked yet.

Mrs. Aaronson. It's perfectly lovely.

Murillo.

[*As the wheel stops*]

Well, there you are, ladies and gentlemen! Red again! Forty dollars for this gentleman, fifty dollars for this other gentleman; am I right, please—? Correct me if I'm wrong! Seventy-five dollars for this lady, and eighty dollars to the lady in red! Count your winnings, ladies and gentlemen, count your winnings! I want to see everybody satisfied!

A satisfied customer is the best advertisement to an established house! Correct, sir, correct, madam?

Corky. Absolutely.

Killarney. Mac, I won eighty dollars! Look!

Corky. Don't throw it around, now!

Murillo. That's right, lady. Money saved is money earned, as the old saying goes. Looks like the house was the big loser today, but we'll have to take it and smile, ladies and gentlemen. When I bought this machine they told me the house makes a percentage in the long run—and I'm depending on that, ladies and gentlemen. So far the house is a big loser, but you can count on it, win or lose, lose or win, we play the game square and pay up in the end. Count your money, lady.

Priscilla. Yes, sir. Look, John!

Mrs. Aaronson. This is where I spend the day! Oh, darling, it's a betting machine. Where's my money!

Aaronson. Wait a minute! Wait a minute!

Mrs. Wheeler. Look at the funny home-made wheel!

Mrs. Aaronson. Please, don't let them start till I've got my money down!

Wheeler. What do you call this game?

Murillo. Does anybody else wish to join in our backwoods pastime? This, sir, is a wheel-of-fortune, the rural version of what they call roulette in the gilded halls of Monaco!—

Only here we play it straight, gentlemen, on a home-made contrivance, absolutely uncontrollable and honest; anybody can spin it, anybody can win! Everybody does win, as these folks will tell you! Round it goes like this, ladies and gentlemen—that's right, the lady may spin it if she wishes—and every time it stops on red you get double your money! Every time it stops on black we double the bet! You can't lose; you honestly and truly can't lose! Only a dollar to get in the game, folks; anybody can afford a dollar! Here's a lady put down a dollar and picked up eighty—here's a gentleman put down a dollar and picked up seventy-five! A little hard on the house, friends, but we can still pay!

[KING *returns around the house and joins the crowd.*]

Put down one dollar each; you're gambling on the red— I'm gambling on the black! And just to make it more attractive if it comes up red the first time I pay five to one! Five to one, friends and neighbors, if it comes up red on the first spin.

[*The newcomers put their dollars down.* KING *puts down his dollar, getting a sharp look in return.*]

Mrs. Aaronson. But you can't lose!

Murillo. Exactly! You can't possibly lose! Wait now, wait now! It's a good spin! It's an honest wheel, I tell you! It's coming red, it can't miss that red now! Red! The house pays five to one—here you are, friends.

[*He pays* MR. *and* MRS. AARONSON, MR. *and* MRS. WHEELER, *cnd* KING.]

Who goes with me on another little spin—the house pays five to one if it stops on red? Who's in on it?

Corky.

[*To* Aaronson]

Jeez, this bird's an amateur. He's been losing money to the whole crowd, hand over fist.

Mrs. Wheeler. I don't see how we could lose.

Murillo. Right-o! You can't lose, as the little lady says. There you are, everybody back in for the second spin at five to one; you play red, and I play black! Wish to play, sir?

King. Right.

[*He puts down his five.*]

Murillo. All down? Everybody in that's coming in?

[*He spins.*]

Five to one, ladies and gentlemen! If it comes up red you win twenty-five dollars each—and red it is!

[*He pays.*]

Red it is! What the hell! It's Roosevelt money, anyway, fiat money, unsupported by specie, badly inflated and negotiable only because Barnum was right! Take the money! Who wants to try one more spin at five to one? You can't lose, friends—you've got one dollar invested and if it comes up red you win a hundred and twenty-five!

Mrs. Aaronson. Here's mine! Put your money down, darling.

Murillo. Everybody down! We're playing in bad luck, ladies and gentlemen—the house is losing money fast, but we're still good for it. Wish to play, sir?

King. Not this whirl.

[*He sits down and counts his money.*]

Murillo. Very well. The gentleman's out. He doesn't want a chance at easy money. Does the lady wish to spin the wheel? A good spin, lady! Not too hard, not too easy, a professional hand in every way! It's coming red again, it's coming red, watch the indicator, it's creeping, ladies and gentlemen—it's creeping. Luckiest wheel you ever saw in your lives! It'll make red yet, just a little more, just a little more! Let me call your attention to the fact that there's three times as many red as black spaces! Come now, come —creep, creep a shade more—Sorry, ladies and gentlemen, it's black, and the game's five to one. I'd much rather it came out the other way, because I took a liking to you at once, but there it is, and nothing we can do about it. Pay the house a hundred and twenty-five.

Wheeler. What?

Murillo. Pay the house a hundred and twenty-five.

Wheeler. I don't see that.

Murillo. It's a very simple game, sir. If it had come up red, I'd have paid you a hundred and twenty-five. It came up black, which means you pay me a hundred and twenty-five.

Mrs. Aaronson. Each of us?

Murillo. Naturally, each of you.

Mrs. Wheeler. But how did this happen?

Mrs. Aaronson. I simply don't follow you.

Aaronson. I won't pay it. It's a gyp, by God!

Murillo. I think you will. It's a perfectly fair and honest game, sir. You came into it of your own free will. You took my money without question. I think you'll all pay.

Aaronson. Then you've got another think coming. Come on, everybody.

Murillo.

[*His hand on* AARONSON'S *arm*]

It'll be much better if you don't make trouble. I've got a partner here I never know what he's going to do, see?

Aaronson. Take your hand off my arm!

Murillo. Certainly. But take care what you do! If you don't want to gamble you should keep out of gambling games.

Aaronson.

[*Looking about and finding himself surrounded*]

By God, it's a gang! The whole damn thing's a frame-up! We walked into a trap.

Murillo. I'd advise you to pay, sir, before my partner makes trouble.

Aaronson. All right.

[*He takes out his wallet.*]

Mrs. Aaronson. Well, I won't pay!

Mrs. Wheeler. And I won't!

Mr. Wheeler. Oh, yes, you will—or I will for you.

[*He counts out bills and gives them to* MURILLO. AARONSON *does the same.* KING *slips casually out to the right. In grim silence the party of tourists troops toward the left.*]

Aaronson. Four hundred dollars! Jesus Christ, what a nest of banditti!

[*He goes.*]

Murillo. Give me the currency.

[*They hand him back the money they won in the fake game.*]

Where's that son-of-a-bitch that took the thirty from me?

Hunk. He was right there a minute ago.

Murillo. He's too God-damn smart for his uniform! We're going to get that thirty out of him if we have to melt it out of his teeth!

Priscilla. They always say the same dumb things: "What a darling place! But really darling!" "I want to stay here all the rest of the time!"

Gage. "By God, it's a gang! We walked into a trap!"

Killarney. Don't I keep any part of this?

[ALEGRE *comes back around the house and goes in.*]

Murillo. No. You watch me take in four hundred, and you think Christ has risen!

Killarney. I merely asked.

Murillo. I give you fair warning, girl, you ask too often, and I'm getting sick of you!

Killarney. I merely asked.

Murillo. Keep out of sight for a few minutes, just in case those New Jersey clucks come back.

[*They go out right, leaving* MURILLO *alone for a moment. He pulls out a wallet, folds in four hundred fresh dollars with the rest, and starts to go.* ALEGRE *enters with a tray to re-set the table.*]

You know, when I look at you I get all starry-eyed and impractical. For a thin dime, one-tenth of a dollar, I'd put on a pair of overalls and go in the fishing business with your father.—Did you hear what I said?

Alegre. Yes.

Murillo. Well, do I get an answer? Did you take it in? You can't be as dumb as you are beautiful! That would be too good to be true.

Alegre. I understand very little of what you say, and what little I do understand I dislike.

Murillo. I'll tell you what I'll do, I'll cut your old man in on the gambling take, an honest five per cent. You'll make more money than you ever saw in your life. We're doing well here and we want to stay. There's plenty in it for all of us.

Alegre. If we could have got rid of you legally you'd be gone now, but it seems the law protects you. It seems that we can do no more than say that you are unwelcome. You are unwelcome, and any percentage you might offer, large or small, would be quite unacceptable.

Murillo. Listen, do you think, for God's sake, there's anything I want I can't have? I'm offering to pay because I'm a gentleman, but look at the situation, baby. Your old man's blind, and you haven't got so much as a gun in the house, and if you had one you couldn't use it. I can have this place, and I can pay what I like for it, and I can have you too any time you look good to me! What's more I

probably will, so come down to earth and talk my language
and maybe we can make a deal!

[KING *slips in from the left and stands listening.*]

Alegre. You're mistaken about the fire-arms. I have a revolver, and I have a rifle, and I handle them both very well.

Murillo. Now you're talking. Now I have some respect for
you.

Alegre. But I have none for you.

Murillo. You will have, baby. You will have. It's the same
with women as with nations, baby; the fellow with the
most guns and the most money wins. Always. Because
that's what the nations want! And what the women want!

Alegre.
[*Turning on him*]
Don't count on it too much.

Murillo. Why not?

Alegre.
[*More gently*]
I don't know what you've wanted—or what you want now
—but whatever it is you'll never have it.

Murillo. They all come round in time, girl, every one of them
comes round in time.

Alegre. But not to you. Nothing will come to you.

Murillo. If you mean you'll make a noise, lady, and people
will come—and I'll be in trouble, don't rely on it. That's
all different now. You go ahead and scream and if anybody

hears you he'll turn over and say, "That's Murillo and his woman; why the hell can't he keep his women quiet?" And before long you won't mind; before long you'll be asking me to come home early nights. That's the way it goes with a man and his women.

[*He follows his group out to the right.* ALEGRE *sets the table and comes back toward the left with the tray in her hand. She sees* KING, *and stops.*]

King. I beg your pardon.—I was just passing by. I won't trouble you.

[*He goes out with a gesture of despair. She steps back from him, then goes toward the house.*]

Alegre. Father!

[D'ALCALA *comes out to meet her.*]

d'Alcala. You called me?

Alegre. Here in broad sunlight, just a moment ago, I saw someone from Spain!

d'Alcala. He's here now?

Alegre. No, he's gone now.

d'Alcala. Who was it, Alegre?

Alegre. It was King. King McCloud, the boy who went out with Victor, or it may be I've begun to see his ghost— but I thought I saw him—between me and the water. My eyes still dazzle with it. And I heard his voice, or thought I heard it.

d'Alcala. There was definite word?
Wasn't King reported dead?

Alegre. Yes, with the others.

d'Alcala. And you've never seen him?

Alegre. Only his picture. Never
his face till now. Never till now. Perhaps
not even now.

d'Alcala. Why should you see a ghost
of this one lad that we never knew?

Alegre. The old reason.
The same old reason one has for seeing ghosts.
Because there was someone that I wanted to see,
and never could. When Victor went away
there was a little snapshot of King left lying
somewhere in his room. I picked it up,
and put it in a frame—and as years went by
and there was nothing to love among the faces
that passed along the Key—the picture and frame
became an altar where I could say a prayer
at night and morning—something to give a meaning
to a girl's day. He was the gayest, the proudest,
the one they all loved most, and who figured most
in all the letters. I'm punished for it now
wanting him too much—and seeing him
between me and the sky.

d'Alcala. Whoever you saw,
it was no ghost.

Alegre. There was someone?

d'Alcala. I heard him,
heard his step. The same step that went by
a little while before—it's a man who played
a round with the gamblers—and won money, and quit
and made them angry.

Alegre. But that couldn't be King.

d'Alcala. I don't know.
But I know he's real, and no ghost.

Alegre. Would you leave me here—
just for a moment?

d'Alcala. Yes.
[*He goes in.* KING *comes round the corner of the house again, and
pauses, looking at* ALEGRE.]

King. You're Alegre d'Alcala?

Alegre. Yes. Is there no one with you? Have you come alone?

King. I've come alone.

Alegre. Why is it only you?

King. Out of those who went to Spain?

Alegre. Yes.

King. Perhaps because I'm the only one alive.

Alegre. You're alive then?
[*A pause*]

King. My name's King McCloud. Your brother Victor
and I joined up with the Loyalists in April,

nineteen thirty-seven. He was killed, as you know.
I sent his letter to you.

Alegre. Yes. It came.
Unfinished, and the superscription written
in a strange hand.

King. That was my writing.

Alegre. Yes.

King. There were eight of us who went out together,
as you know, no doubt. I was the one survivor,
and I've taken it on myself to bring back reports
personally to the nearest of kin of each,
to say how it was they died. No one else could know—
  [*A pause*]
If it's not too close to you—or too far away—
or something you'd rather not hear.

Alegre. It's one of those hurts
one would rather have. Much rather. It's good of you
to come so far.

King. I had my own reasons for that.
I feel myself responsible in part—
having led the boys to Spain. Having recruited.
And having escaped alive. It's for that reason
that I'm here now. Because it came to a choice,
to a question of illusion or disillusion,
and Victor and I were not of the same mind—
no, that's not it—
I came because there's little that's worth doing
in the world we live in now—and to say a last word

for certain gallant men who died gallantly
in an unselfish cause seems to make more sense
than merely to earn a living.

Alegre. Yes. I understand.
It's more than we hoped for.

King. I've come here last. The others
were mostly from New England—and this seemed
a long way south, almost out of the world—
at least the world I've known. But it was Victor
whom I'd known best, and loved most, and felt surely
had been most loved at home.

Alegre. We did love him, and knew
that he'd know how to die well if it came
to dying. But to know just how and where
is something—almost as if you'd saved a trace
of life for him too. And that's a thing so precious
one can hardly give thanks.—My father will want to hear.
Shall I call him?

King. There's something—it would be easier
if I spoke to you for a moment—

Alegre. Yes, surely.

King. I've told
this all so often—and yet the oftener told
and the longer in between—the harder it is
to bring myself to begin. I can't help knowing
that it's a shock to see me. Wherever I go
(and I can't blame them, mind you)

they look at me and say, he's above the earth,
he walks about and breathes—and my boy's dead—
and might have been alive like him—no older—
not so old by a year or two, but dead—
underground and beginning the long cycle
of being dead forever. You thought of that
when you first saw me. You looked about for Victor,
and then looked back to me.

Alegre. No, for at first
  I thought you were a ghost.

King. I've learned this much—
  that I'm not easily forgiven.

Alegre. Forgiven?
  But it's not your fault—and couldn't have been your fault
  that some came home and others stayed in Spain.
  No one could hold it was.
  Have the others been cruel, or silent? Or only silent?
  For that would be cruel.

King. The home I came to first
  was in New England. I can see it now,
  the elm, the honey-locust, and the sea,
  the twelve-foot tide lapping up and down the piers
  and I watching from the red diner across the common
  afraid of the blind door.—Then, after that
  I looked them all up, one by one, the homes
  of all the boys that died there on Hill 4:
  only each time it took longer to steel myself—
  and I'd wear my shoes out pacing up and down
  across from every house. Then suddenly I'd go in

and tell them. One by one I told them all,
how the boys came to die—and how I was alive—
and I can see now it was natural
they'd give me little thanks.
There in New England a man goes down with his ship
or he's not a man. And so at last, in the end,
it came down to Key Largo. That was the name
on Victor's letter. I had some reluctance
about deciding on so many miles,
on foot—and I hesitated. Then a month ago
I noticed there were buzzards overhead
along the road I took, and the pine was slashed
for turpentine, and I knew I was drifting south
to see you. Then I followed the buzzards down
and left the turpentine and followed the palms—
and watched the moss grow thick and the shacks grow thin
and came on down the keys.

Alegre. Do you mean you came
without quite knowing what roads you had taken
nor why you took them?

King. Something like that.

Alegre. As if
some compulsion lay over you?

King. Have I said so?

Alegre. No,
but, how have you lived?

King. It's not so hard to get money
if you don't care how you get it.

Alegre. If this is a story
  that harrows you to tell—or if you're weary
  and would find it easier later—come in now
  and be our guest—and let it all go till evening
  or as long as you like. Victor wrote me about you
  long ago, and nothing you can say
  will alter your welcome.

King. I'd better say it now.
  It's fair to tell you there was an argument
  that night before the last battle—and I held
  that the war was lost, and everything was lost,
  and it was better to abandon Spain
  and save our lives. And it was true; we lost,
  and the war's lost, and the others are all dead—
  and they might be alive if they'd followed me—
  yet Victor said I was wrong, and even now
  he'd say I was wrong, and that's what tortures me—

Alegre. But why should you be tortured? When men differ
  they must follow what they believe. Victor believed so
  and would have said so.

King. Yes, he said so then.
  And over and over I say it to myself—
  that I meant their good and mine—that I tried to save
      them—
  could have saved them if they'd only followed
  when I left the lines. And it's true. I was cool and sane
  and chose to live. But some insanity
  came over them there in the moonlight, and they chose
  to stay and die. They chose it, and all I could say

meant nothing to them. Why should I feel a guilt
or be looked upon as guilty?

Alegre. You shouldn't.

King. No,
and yet I do. Something within myself
accuses me. They accuse me. Without warrant,
without reason, day and night, incessantly,
till I look at a bed with horror, as a place
where a man can't sleep, and look at a road with horror
as something I must walk along forever
followed by the dead!—Will you forgive? All this—
this is just raving—

Alegre. If there was something said
or done that tortures you—

King. Something done, perhaps.

Alegre. And if what you seek's forgiveness, then pass it over
in silence, and consider it forgiven.
Forget it utterly. It won't help to remember
some fatal awkwardness.

King. But I have to say it
and say it honestly, and then wait to hear
a verdict from you.

Alegre. Shall I call my father?

King. Not yet.—Yes, do call him. He must hear it now
or I go through it again.—I'll put it off
while there's excuse. But call him.

[D'ALCALA *enters from the house.*]

Alegre. This is my father.
This is King McCloud.

d'Alcala. You're welcome, sir.

King. You lost your eyes in Spain?

d'Alcala. How did you know?

King. Victor told me.
I shouldn't be here! I should be anywhere else
but here! I of all men! But I had to come!
I tried everything else—and everywhere else in the world
before I came here!

d'Alcala. God knows you're welcome here.

King. This was all pretense, this tale
of having come here out of sentiment
to let you know how Victor died! I came
to make my peace with myself, or you, or someone,
maybe with those who died—came here for penance
and expiation—as I went the rounds
in the north, in New England—driven by an evil
that must see the light or strangle me to death
working inside!

d'Alcala. You'd rather I were not here?

King. I'd rather you were. Only I find it hard
to meet men. You're the one I feared most to meet.
Victor's father. Sometimes I've found myself
on an empty street somewhere in a little town
perhaps on a Sunday morning. Then if a man
came walking toward me I'd cross over quickly

and turn my face away—study the windows
to keep his eyes from my face—and meet my own eyes
there in the glass—running away from him—

d'Alcala. How can we help you?

King. Maybe you'll find a way.
It was all right, you know, when I came from Spain,
when I first came. Eight of us had gone out
and one came back—and I was that one. All right,
but it wouldn't let me alone. I sent you the letter,
the one Victor wrote, and took a job and was fired,
for this thing was on my chest,
and I had to get it off—money or none—
shoes or none.—I've been going ever since
from one address to another, but no better,
worse if anything,—but not insane—
remember that, not shell-shocked, perfectly sound,
except for a little trembling in my hands!
But I can't stand men!
It seems that I'm allergic to the race
of men and their women! Damn them when they talk!
I hear them talking in the stores, I hear them
talking in comfort-stations; I walk three times
around a block, till the fellow that gives service
is giving his God damn service somewhere else
and I don't have to hear him saying yes, sir,
this way, sir, and I don't have to see him smiling
his comfort-station smile.—Till I get desperate,
and I think, by God, they're all of them thin-skinned,
only they make an effort. And I barge in—
Give me a cup of coffee! How's tricks, pardner!

What a day! Hot damn, what a day! And they all come
    back—
Boy, oh, boy, what a day! —That's how it was
when I put my dollar down with the gamblers here—
I must do it somehow, must break in, must speak—
must learn again how my voice sounds—must practice a
    little
before I can speak to his sister.

Alegre. I'm afraid, too. Of men.

King. No, not as I am.
    [*A pause*]
When I left Victor
there on the hill with the others, I went through
an orange-grove and a pasture in the valley
and climbed the cliff beyond. Then I could see
the enemy playing star-shells over the ridge
where the boys were, getting ready to attack,
not even waiting for dawn. I couldn't stand it,
not to be in the fight, and I started back
again, to join them—but it was done like lightning—
before I was down the hill the Franco men
had lifted over the ridge and came rolling through
the valley in a sheet of steady flame,
ten thousand of them, so that our three or four hundred
never had a chance—anyway they were caught—
trapped there between the hills. When I came on them
it was still moonlight and the enemy
had gone straight on, leaving them lying there,
three or four hundred faces draining white,
under the moon. No prisoners and no wounded,

everything made certain and sure forever—
that's Franco's way. When I climbed up Hill 4
I found the boys there with a ring of dead
in front of their machine-gun, and the boys
dead too, lying in that dead white light
from the dead moon. I gave them what last rites
I could to keep them from the buzzards—then
it was morning, and I was a prisoner. What comes next
you won't believe, and I don't. But I fought
the rest of the war out with the Insurgents.

Alegre. Joined them?
  [D'ALCALA *rises.*]
Joined the Insurgents?

King. Just so they wouldn't kill me.
Something broke inside me. My nerve, maybe.
I was willing to eat dirt and be damned
if I could live. I ate dirt, and I'm damned.
I had to tell them I was one of them—
and then there was no way out. And now you know me.
I deserted, and left my friends to die alone—
and fought on Franco's side—and I'm alive—
and better men are dead.
That's why I'm here, why I've gone from door to door.
Not because I deserted, and left the lines
when the fighting was no use, for I was right
there on Hill 4—but once having saved my life
by slipping away, there never came a time
when I could say to myself, make a stand here,
this is too low—even to save your life
this is too low. So I went on and down

keeping myself alive, till the very maggots
cleansing the earth, took more pride in their work
than I in mine—or in myself.

[*A young* INDIAN *in slacks and shirt comes softly round the corner
of the house, listens for a moment, and comes forward.*]

Alegre. It's Osceola. One of the Indians.

Osceola. Please,
my father says, whatever it is you wish,
we will do it. Only he asks you please
it can only be at night.

d'Alcala. Do you know the second buoy,
the second glass buoy beyond the second weir
outside the beach?

Osceola. Yes.

d'Alcala. There's a body sunk
beside that second buoy. It's not my murder,
mind you, but I'd like to bring it home
to the man who did it. If you'll bring up that body
when the tide turns tonight,
and disengage the weight, and let it float
to the bar below, that's ten times over pay
for anything you've had. If it's too hard
and you can't do it, why then it was too hard
and forget I asked you. You understand?

Osceola. Yes, surely.

d'Alcala. Then don't be seen here. Every minute's a risk,
And that's the whole story.

[OSCEOLA *disappears silently.*]
[*To* KING]

And still
I don't know why you're here.

King. Because my mind
  says even now I was right, that I should live,
  that one's better living on carrion, beast among beasts,
  than dead in the earth's shell. But I have a demon
  that won't hear any of this, that lives in my soul
  and cries out day and night—that I should have died
  before I gave the lie to what I was
  there with the rebels! This demon tore me inside,
  saying, very well, let them decide it
  whose sons died on Hill 4! Tell your tale to them
  and if one answers, yes, it was well done,
  lift up your head and go on. But they said nothing,
  and the demon drove me here.

d'Alcala. I have my own demon.
  There was some kind of hell took fire in me
  when I was young in Spain, that sent me out
  to fight against the tyrants of that day
  in that sad country—to give my wealth and youth
  and then my eyes, and then my son, to trap
  the rats that ate my country to the bone—
  yet now my country's dying, and the rats
  feed on the carcass.—And you've come from there—
  from where I left my eyesight and lost my one son—
  and you fought there against us—accepted life
  and took money and took food, and slept beside them!—
  God knows in what blood your feet have walked, God
    knows
  who's dead by your hand!—and I struggle to hold out

my hand to you, but the demon of my youth
says, no, he's your enemy by blood, let him die
and go, before you touch him. As for Spain,
the Moors held Spain eight hundred years one time,
and thought it was permanent, but we took it from them,
as we'll take it back again!

King. I knew you must say it.

d'Alcala. Whether a man should live when his own demon
cries out in the night, and drives him across the hills,
and his bed becomes a torture, and he fears
men's eyes, I can't tell you that—if he still finds it
palatable to live, then I can't answer!

King. I hadn't hoped
to have your friendship. But I'm desperate, too,
and I won't go yet. I had another hope—
that I've never admitted, even to myself,
but all the way down through the south, these months,
I've been remembering what Victor said
in a long night in Spain—about his sister:
that there was no one else in all the world
to whom a man could go with a man's crime
and say, I did this, and get understanding
for the lowest he could do. Get even forgiveness
for what a man does, and never dares tell. He said
that she was named Alegre for the town
in Spain where she was born. And you're Alegre?

Alegre. Yes.

King. Here's something else to forgive me then.
Out of a desperate loneliness and fear—

out of an outcast's life, with no God to pray to—
and never having seen your face—I've dared to love you—
have even imagined you from knowing Victor—
and find you as I knew you'd be. Never saying,
never admitting it even to myself,
I've put what little hope was left on you
and kept on south toward you. Now you owe me nothing
except a parting curse, and I ask for nothing,
but I have said it at last, and said it to you.
If I said more I'd go beyond all begging.—

Alegre. Why must you tell me?
About this betrayal—and then about—this love?
Why should you tell me, and make me live through it, too?
How could a woman love you?
We're all less for it, the whole world's less because
of what you are! A woman can hesitate
forever—but a man must be something sometime
bright and clear, like a plowshare in the sun
or a mountain above the cloud!

King. Well, look, out there
the dusty roads go trailing away in the sun,
and fork out east and west—that's where I live—
on those interminable branching highways
that reach on out into nothing.

Alegre. Don't go yet.

King. I'll take—
any kindness—yes, any usefulness—just to be wanted—
a shadow of the welcome that you gave
when I first came.

d'Alcala. Stay if you will. If you stay
  it's safer for my daughter.
  We're alone here and beset.
    [*He goes in.*]

King. Then I am wanted.
  Yes, the gamblers. Even that's better than nothing.
  I came to be forgiven, to be shriven,
  and maybe to be cured. I can't have that—
  and yet some kind of easiness to the heart
  comes over me with this. I can face them now,
  as I couldn't before. Having told my story
  and let the winds blow through me.

Alegre. Will you come in?—
  And we'll try to forget that any of this has happened.
  You're tired, and you should rest. It's all too easy to
    lengthen out misery.

King. You have your own misery?

Alegre. Yes. I have my own.

King. If it's only love it's something you get over—
  not like mine.

Alegre. One can get over love—
  oh, any kind, except for someone dead—
  that doesn't end.

King. For someone dead in Spain?

Alegre. For a boy who went to Spain and won't come back.
  One of the leaders. With a beauty on his face
  that comes to a man with being more a man
  than other men.

King. What was his name?

Alegre. Never mind. Why are you shivering?

King. Oh, just the cold wind from between the worlds,
the inter-stellar wind.
    [*He rises.*]
And human footsteps.
The smell of the human race.
    [MURILLO *comes back with his group, ready to go to work again.*]
Forgive me—I'm—
I've got to get out of here.

Murillo. The travel's light
this morning, and what little there is of it's running
on ten cent gas. Keep an eye on the road
and don't slip up again. Wait a minute, big gambler,
I want to talk to you.
    [KING *has tried blindly to go out through the palm lattice and missed
    the exit. Finding himself caught he turns.*]

King. What about?

Murillo. I'd like to have my thirty dollars, gambler.
You walked off with thirty-one, but one was yours
in the first place, so you can keep it. A neat trick
that was, dipping in and out of a come-on game,
only I want my money.

King. You don't get it.

Murillo. Whatever's mine I get.

King. I heard you say,
if you don't want to gamble keep out of gambling games—
that goes for you!

Murillo. Who the hell are you?

King. A soldier.
   I came out of Europe in a bad year—
   say 1939—and I'm engaged
   like all men alive, in hunting for my grave.
   No doubt I'll find it, along with a bag of gold,
   at the foot of a rainbow—or right here where I'm standing,
   by the way you look at me. Only I carry a gun
   and it's loose in the holster.

Murillo. Why did you raid my game
   and walk off with the sucker money?

King. I needed it—
   and you didn't need it—and it was easy to get—
   and so I took it.

Murillo. Look, I've been in this business
   fifteen years, and nobody ever yet
   got away from me with sucker money.

King. No?
   Then this is new for you.
     [MURILLO *puts a hand to his pocket.* KING *lays a hand on the butt of his revolver.*]
   I know your kind.
   I've watched a dozen like you, up and down
   the fairs and carnivals—sneaking into town
   and sneaking out—setting up three-card monte
   and disappearing like a bad smell when they try
   to get their fingers on you—always just three jumps
   ahead of the police—always an eye on the exit—
   a species of gangster rabbit! Don't threaten me

with that hand on your pocket. You know your shifty game
too well to make a noise!

Murillo. Well, it just happens
you've got me wrong. I know the kind you mean,
but personally I've used a gun before
and I'll maybe use it again, because it gets
to be a kind of thirst, and maybe a soldier
knows what that means. I want my money back
and I'm going to get it.

> [*He reaches slowly into his pocket and takes out an automatic.* KING
> *extracts his revolver at the same time.*]

Look, bo, that was your chance
to shoot, and you didn't do it. In my game
you learn that there are just two kinds of men,
those who are not afraid to die, and those
who are. A man who's not afraid to die,
he's dangerous. The others you can handle.
You have to learn to pick 'em out in a crowd
and pick 'em fast—and you can't make mistakes—
so I don't make any—

King. Maybe I underestimated you,
Mr. Whoever-you-are. You looked cheap to me
and I took you for cheaper than you are.

Murillo. Give me your gun.

> [KING *doesn't move*]

This is trained on your belly, see; if you
kill me, you die. I'm not afraid to die,
and you are. And please remember
that's a delicate trigger on those army models,
so let go easy.

King. I've been in tighter places
   than this, and I've had better chances to die,
   and didn't take them. You'll think that's cowardice.
   But there are more than two kinds of men.
   And I belong to a kind you haven't met
   and wouldn't know about.
   [*He lets* MURILLO *take the gun*]

Murillo. You're afraid.
   You're all afraid, all your lives,
   afraid of gods and churches and the law—
   but if a man gets up who's afraid of nothing,
   and he'll kill you as soon as look at you,
   well, men do what he tells them. Now give me the money.
   [KING *hands the money over.*]

And now you can start back north.
I don't want you here.

King. But I shall stay.

Murillo. I wouldn't advise it. Not if you want to be sure
   of getting up in the morning.

King. I wouldn't be sure
   in any case. I'll stay here.

Murillo. You should have tried that
   before you gave me your gun! There's a champion!
   There's a hero! I've paid up my protection
   another two weeks. And there's two more weeks' rent.
   We're staying on.
   [*He turns away, tossing* ALEGRE *two ten dollar bills.*]

Corky. There's a party of monkeys walking in. Two men
   and two women, Packard sedan. Flash tourists.

Murillo. Get ready!

> [*The gangsters gather round the machine.*]

Listen, you, I won't need you here!
Get going, and if I find you within ten miles
you won't be worth much to yourself.

> [KING *goes toward the house. Two couples enter.*]

1st Woman. What a darling place! But really darling!

Murillo. The house loses, ladies and gentlemen. Loses heavily but we're still game. Eighty dollars to this lady. Eighty dollars to the two gentlemen.

> [*He pays off in bills.*]

2nd Woman. Harry! An outdoor casino! Where's my purse? I left my purse in the car!

CURTAIN

KEY LARGO
ACT TWO

Act Two

SCENE & & The interior of the house on the wharf, late the same evening. There is a couch to the left—a door to the rear of it. A desk and a large wooden chair are set under a window along the rear wall. There are several chairs to the right, and a downstage entrance. A small dining table stands near the center of the room. The walls are weathered board, decorated with sharks' teeth, shells, and a blue, bright painting of the house and the bay as seen in the first act.

Kɪɴɢ *is lying on the couch, his face to the wall.* ᴅ'Aʟᴄᴀʟᴀ *and* Aʟᴇɢʀᴇ *sit talking quietly. She is looking at the harbor out of the rear window. Both doors stand open.*

Alegre. What do you hear?

d'Alcala. The breathing of our guest—
    a man sleeping lightly.—His face is toward the wall
    by the way the sound comes to me.

Alegre. Yes.—

d'Alcala. The tide's
    three-quarters out, by the clanking of the chain
    where the boat's tethered. Murillo and the others
    are holding some kind of conference in his room;
    one of the women's crying. Out on the gulf
    there's a government cutter heading in this way—
    no, it may be a fisherman; but a Chrysler engine,
    too new for a fisherman. A mother porpoise
    blew at the wharf a moment ago, and the calf
    came up after her. The eyes can look
    only one way at a time, but the ears reach out
    in every direction. It makes for a full world.
    Do you love him still?

Alegre. Yes. He must never know it.

d'Alcala. When you love, is it better the man should die
and keep his faith, or lose his faith and live?

Alegre. I can't answer that.

d'Alcala. Can you wish him dead—
only nobly dead?

Alegre. Oh, why do you ask me?

d'Alcala. Because I don't know. I've thought so long about it
that I don't know. Because I lost my eyes
fighting against Rivera in our Spain,
and now Rivera's dead, and I'm alive,
only another and a worse dictator
rules in Spain—and Victor's bed stands empty,
and we've lost and we're here alone.
   [ALEGRE *rises suddenly.*]
What did you see?

Alegre. A man went past this window.

d'Alcala. You're sure it was a man?

Alegre. Yes, but bent over—
bent completely double—and without a sound.
I can't believe now I saw him.

d'Alcala. Don't be frightened.
He'll appear in a moment in the doorway—
this one, behind me—and no doubt he's wearing
Victor's old slacks. It's the two Seminoles
that you befriended.

Alegre. How can you know?

d'Alcala. An Indian
Walks that way. Nobody else. Come in.
[JOHN HORN *appears in the doorway to the left, his son* OSCEOLA *behind him.*]

Horn. We're sorry to disturb you.

d'Alcala. Come in if you wish.

Horn. We'll stand here out of the light. It's not good manners
to say your thank-you and ask another favor
all in one breath.—We're thankful for the clothes
and they saved our lives, but we must get off Key Largo
or our lives aren't worth much. There's an old boat in the
inlet
beyond the beach, and it's probably yours. We've caulked it
with Spanish moss, and we think it may hold water
as far as the Everglades.

d'Alcala. It's yours, man. Take it.
We'd forgotten it was there.

Alegre. But you have no oars.

Horn. Now there it is again. If we had a knife
we'd soon have oars. I hope that's the end of begging.

Alegre.
   [*Bringing one*]
There was one here—these are all unused things,
and better you should have them.

Horn. Before we go
we floated the body, and it went down the tide

two hours ago. It would have missed the bar,
but we swam after it and shoved it up
by hand where the flashing light shows off the reef.
It will be seen by the fishermen.

d'Alcala. It's my turn
to wonder how I'll thank you. This may save us.
Is there anything else?

Horn. Nothing. We'll have to start.
The night's not long enough.
> [*He turns to go.*]

Alegre. There's a boat with a flashlight
playing on the house. Had you better wait
till it's gone by? Sit down.

Horn. Thank you. We'll wait.
> [*He sits.*]

d'Alcala. Some stranger's rowing west along the Key.
It's not a stroke I know. Whoever it is
he's not coming here.

Horn. Out in Oklahoma
there are ten thousand Seminoles cooped up
on a reservation. It was Andrew Jackson
moved them there—those he could get his hands on.
I was born there; I taught there twenty years
in the Indian schools—till my wife died and my boy
was a man grown. But all my life I've wanted
to join the poisonous remnant of our tribe
in the Everglades that Jackson couldn't catch
and had to leave here. The Oklahoma Indians

sit and look at the reservation fence
and take their hand-outs from the government
and die out like the buffalo. Good riddance
of an obsolete animal. There are too many men
even when they're white, and an Indian's just too much;
feed him, God damn him, and let him die! We left
to find our brothers here in the Everglades,
and shake the Indian Office. All my life long
I've taken charity, and seen my race
take charity from a race it hates, a race
that hates it. I named my boy Osceola
because Osceola struck back in his way,
the only way he knew, and couldn't be conquered,
and left his sons here in the Florida swamps
unconquered. They live badly here, no doubt
but they live as they please.
Tell them, Osceola, what is it to be an Indian?

Osceola. It's to be a dead man erect among the living.
It's to be a ghost bred in a tribe of ghosts
that haunts its murderers. It's to be a symbol
of all lost causes—and how soon they're forgotten. It's
to be what I am.

d'Alcala. But why were you on the roads?
What do they have against you?

Horn. We were out of money;
they picked us up as negro vagrants and sent us
to work in the gang.

Alegre. Do you know the Everglades?
Is there anyone there you know?

Horn. No, but we'll live.
We'll live on what there is.

d'Alcala. The conference
seems to have broken up, and some of the gamblers
are on their way here.

Horn.
[*Rising and going to the left door*]
We start tonight.—Good night.
I won't try to thank you.

d'Alcala. We're even with thanks. Good night.

Alegre. Good night.

King.
[*In his sleep*]
The Everglades.
[*He wakes and turns.*]
Yes, now I know who I am.

d'Alcala. Were you dreaming, sir?

King. Yes. There's the rat-tail end of a long dream
just slipping over the lip—into that grand canyon—
where we lose what we don't remember.—
I dreamed there was an Indian
running away to the poisonous Everglades
so he could be free there—and then in my dream I knew
this Indian was myself.—And when you think of it
the Everglades are exactly what a man wants;
if ever there was a refuge where they can't find you,
and there's always something to eat, and it never freezes,

and the wild white birds nest silently, unobserved
ten thousand years—it's the Everglades—that's the end
of dreaming. That's our home.

d'Alcala. Only it happens
there was an Indian here who was escaping
into the Everglades.

King. And it wasn't a dream? But then when the dream went
on
I think Alegre was the Everglades,
silent, with white nesting birds, and I'd
come south to find her. But the oars were gone
and the only knife was one that once was Victor's
and cut me off from her.
[*There is a knock at the right-hand door.*]

d'Alcala. Come in.
[CORKY *and* GAGE *and* HUNK *enter.*]
Sit down.
[*They sit.*]

King. This is a delegation. The three rats.

Hunk. Oh yeah?

King. Excuse me.
I've lost my right to insult his underlings,
now that I've been insulted by the satrap,
and I've taken money from him, and done his work.
No, I'm referring to the human race
in general. As rats. Remembering
the research fellow in the laboratory
who tested the rat-brain. You remember him?

He put a rat in a cage with little doors
that didn't go anywhere—except for one
that had a circle on it. Behind that one
there was food—and so the rat learned if he jumped
at this one door with the circle he could eat—
no other door would do—and he jumped at that
without a mistake for a year, and ate, by God,
and then the experimenter fixed that door
so it wouldn't open. The rat jumped and banged his head
till he was bloody around the top, and sick;
and when there was never anything to eat,
and the circle was always wrong, he lost his mind,
his poor rat-mind, because it was just beyond him—
the circle should be right—always had been right,
and there should be something to eat, and it wasn't there—
so he went mad. All up and down the room
white rats in cages, butting the wrong doors
and bleeding at the ears,
and going mad because the problem set
baffled the small rat-brain. They ran in circles
and bit themselves, and were quiet. After that
they just lay there; men did what they pleased with them—
they'd had enough.

Hunk. We came about the new rules.

Alegre. What rules?

Hunk. The rules here from now on.
　　He's got 'em down there. Corky's got 'em.

Corky. Nobody's to leave the place without permission.

Alegre. Tonight?

Corky. From now on. And after sunset
  nobody's to leave the house without permission.

Alegre. Permission from whom?

Corky. The boss. Murillo.

King. Curfew.

Corky. That's what it amounts to. Curfew.

King. Why, yes, curfew—
  and concentration. Let's look at this a moment;
  maybe these rules aren't feasible. Suppose
  the commissary wanted to send out
  to get supplies?

Corky. You make a list. We'll do
  the buying, and all that.

Alegre. I'm to make a list?

Corky. Yes. And we do the buying. You stay here.

Hunk. And one more thing.

Corky. Yes—one more thing. The boss
  likes the accommodations in the house.
  He'll sleep and eat in the house, and the stranger here
  he'll move on.

King. You'll run out of doors, you know.
  Those with a limited intelligence
  never see more than two or three doors, and those
  shut up on them young. You've jumped at the one with
    the girl,
  and that's a little stale now, that's no answer,

and now you're jumping at the dollar sign,
and easy money sign; you live by that;
but when the author of the experiment
nails that door up, and you jump and break your head,
and then you jump again with blood in your eyes
and end up breaking rock—then all doors are shut,
then they're made of steel and it's no use jumping—
then they bring you your beans—and you're a little sick,
and nothing matters.

Gage. What are you trying to do?
Trying to make us jittery, the way you are?

King. That's the idea.

Hunk. Go tell your own beads. There's nothing biting us.
We're working perfectly legal and straightforward.
Go back and serve your time if you've been tagged
and get it over.

King. It must be obvious
if two hundred pounds of Irish beef can look
and put his finger on it—or his foot.
Look—about those rats—size doesn't count—understand?
Big and little, it gets them.

Hunk. We'll see about that;
you and me, we'll see if size counts. So that's all.
We're going.
  [*The three rise.*]

d'Alcala. Will you take back a word from me
for the man you call Murillo?

Hunk. That's his name.

d'Alcala. It's also what you call him.

Hunk. There's no need
for any word back.

d'Alcala. But tell him if you will
that his conditions are acceptable
and we make no objection—except to the last.
The stranger, as you call him, will continue
to eat and sleep in *this* house. The man Murillo
will remain where he is.

Hunk. You tell him that. Not me.
What he says goes.

d'Alcala. But take the message.

Hunk. Hell,
I can tell him what you said, but take it from me,
he does what he wants.

d'Alcala. I leave you that illusion.
And he may keep it, too. Good night.
[*The three go out silently.*]

King. What must I do now?

d'Alcala. Sleep in your bed,
because it's yours.

King. But you see what you've done?

d'Alcala. It was done deliberately.

King. You accept the conditions
only that I'm to eat where he wants to eat
and sleep where he wants to sleep.

d'Alcala. He won't sleep here.

King. Don't think I won't stand up and do what I can
against him! He wants Alegre, and my blood can burn
like yours when he looks at her—burns in me now
and I can feel it.—But, God, how can I explain?
If it came to dying I don't trust my brain,
my busy, treacherous, casuistic brain,
presenting me with scientific facts
and cunning reasons. It's separate from myself,
separate from my will—a traitor brain,
an acid eating away at all the faiths
by which we live, questioning all the rules,
and leaving us bare—naked white animals
without poetry or God.

Alegre. But say these things.

King. I lived with the worms so long
and ran away so often, that my mind's trained
to find excuses, like a poacher's ferret
finding himself a warren underground
and running wild among the rabbit-holes,
sleeping among the bodies, and forgetting
the master above ground.

d'Acala. If we ask too much
it's possible a man could slip away
to the west of the house, in the shadow.

King. I couldn't do that,
and wouldn't try. But could we all go together
or are we watched?

d'Alcala. We're watched quite carefully.

King. If you stay here
then I must stay.

d'Alcala. Then it won't come to dying.
If we can only hold him off tonight
someone will find the evidence on the point
and Murillo will move on. Perhaps even this evening.
The mullet fishermen are out at night
this time of year.
  [*A pause*]

Alegre. What does your mind
think traitorously underneath sometimes to betray you
when you're in danger?

King. I can't tell you that.

Alegre. Does it begin by saying that we live—
all of us—on illusions? That we live
and lay our lives down for things unsubstantial
as a sunrise or a rainbow?

King. That's how it begins.

Alegre. Then I have it too. It's not peculiar
to soldiers out of Spain, or even to men
who've left a line against orders. It's all of us
in this age of dying fires.

King. Do you wish to live
by truth or by illusion?

Alegre. By the truth.
Always by the truth.

King. But that's an illusion.
Because by the truth no man can live at all,
even a day. We die when we look at truth.
And one by one the illusions
wear themselves out.

[MURILLO *appears in the entrance at the right.*]

Murillo. It seems that you want to hear it from me
that I'm moving in here tonight, and you're moving out,
sort of synchronized. If there's any objection
I want to have it now.

[*He goes to* KING.]

Do you object?

[KING *makes no answer.*]

All right, you don't object. Then when do I move,
because I go early to bed?

King. Listen, I'm not
supposed to be here. I'm supposed to be dead,
and I have reasons for travelling under a name
that's not my own. But I'm Alegre's brother.
My name's Victor, and I'm back from Spain.
The only extra bed in this house is mine,
and you can see I'll need it for myself—
and I can't let you in here with my sister,
not without trouble. You didn't know this, of course—
nobody knew it, and I don't hold it against you,
but a man's sister's his sister. He has a right
to say hands off.

Murillo. I didn't know that. Now,
if it's as you say, and your name's Victor and she's

your sister, hell, I know how it is; I know,
because I had sisters of my own; nice girls,
went to school, got married, asking for money
sometimes when you see them, but not much,
respectable girls.
[*Sharply to* KING]
Where were you born?

King. In Alegre,
Spain.

Murillo. That's your sister's name?

King. Alegre, yes.

Murillo. When did you come to this country?

King. In twenty-four.

Murillo. Where are your passports?

King. We have none. We came in
through Cuba and South America.

Murillo.
[*To* ALEGRE]
He's your brother?

Alegre. Yes.

Murillo.
[*His hand on* D'ALCALA'S *shoulder*]
What's this young man's name?

d'Alcala. Victor.

Murillo. He's your son?

d'Alcala. Yes.

Murillo. What's the color of his hair?

d'Alcala. Black.

Murillo. How tall is he?

d'Alcala. Five-ten.

Murillo. There's a scar on his face.
　Where is it?

d'Alcala. He had no scar when he went away.

Murillo. What's the color of his eyes?
　　　　[D'ALCALA *hesitates.*]
　You should have told him that
　before you lied to me. You're no more Victor
　than I am.
　　　　[SHERIFF GASH *comes to the right-hand door.*]

Gash. Murillo—come out a minute.

Murillo. What for?

Gash. I said come out a minute!

Murillo. Damn it, give orders
　where you're owed money! Let me finish this
　and then I'll see you!

Gash. I can talk from here.
　Would you maybe want to know what we found, Murillo,
　washed up below on the bar with a gag in his mouth
　and tied with wire?

Murillo. What?

Gash. That road gang boss.
Dead about twenty-four hours. It seems he was tangled
with a cray-fish line.

Murillo. Who?

Gash. That boss of the road gang
that disappeared yesterday. You may know the fellow.
I heard some talk he'd been seen gambling here—
yesterday sometime. And there was some kind of quarrel
over the game and a woman.

Murillo. Not to my knowledge.
I can't keep track who gambles.

Gash. Well, all I say, I wish whoever did it
had sunk him deep enough so he wouldn't come floating
around to cause a stink.
We've got a body, and it was certainly murder,
and when a fellow's working for the state
and drawing checks you can be God damn sure
he's got connections somewhere. He'll be missed,
and there'll be an investigation. It'll come to me—
I've had to swear in extra deputies
already—and, Jesus, there was enough to explain,
without explaining murder.

Murillo. Don't look at me,
for Christ's sake! It's not my murder!

Gash. Who said it was?
I said I wished to God whoever did it

had sunk him deep enough so he wouldn't wash up
in my territory!

[*He goes to the door and calls in a* DEPUTY.]

Hey, Sam, take these three out,
and hold them on the porch. They're all of 'em suspects.
I'm questioning Murillo.

[*To* D'ALCALA]

If you don't mind,
we'll use this room.

[*To the* DEPUTY]

Shut the door.

[*The door is closed and* GASH *and* MURILLO *face each other.*]

Murillo. You're serious.

Gash. You're God damn right I'm serious.

Murillo. But what about?
You're not accusing me?

Gash. It's not my business
to accuse anybody, mind you. But I'm supposed
to make arrests of suspicious characters
found near the scene of a crime!

Murillo. Good God! I hope
I'm not a suspicious character.

Gash. Get me right,
Mr. Murillo, what I think about you
or anybody here, won't matter a damn—
but if other people think you should be arrested
and I didn't arrest you, then I begin to worry
about my job! You have to hold the votes

to get re-elected sheriff, and most of the time
you can just play along, and it's easy, but when it's murder
you've got to watch your step, for they're watching you.
They're watching me now. Watching both of us.

Murillo. I shouldn't be here.

Gash. No.
You should have left. When anything suspicious
happens, you should trek it. Innocent or guilty.
For your own protection—and mine. And the trouble is
this stink's bigger than you are, and bigger than I am,
and you're right here in my hands, and the deputies
want to know who you are.

Murillo. I'm getting out.

Gash. You can't.
Not now. But why the hell you aren't in Georgia
or Alabama gripes me. You could have been,
easy, by now.

Murillo. I had something particular here.

Gash. She must have been pretty. They hang in this state,
you know.
They don't burn or smother.

Murillo. Are you holding me up
for money?

Gash. Son, if I take my hand away
and you start running, you'll never get off this Key,
you won't get fifty yards! I wish to God
I could get you out of this, and into Cuba,

because you're around my neck! And you'll cross me up
if you ever get in the dock.

Murillo. I wouldn't say that.

Gash. Well, I would.

Murillo. Then, for Christ's sake, use your head,
    and pin this on somebody.

Gash. Meaning who?

Murillo. Has it slipped your mind already about those niggers
    you were hunting before breakfast? Where were they
       running
    and who were they running from?

Gash. From his own gang.
    From the fellow that was killed.

Murillo. Then, you stupid ass,
    they killed him, and ran.

Gash. It does no good whatever
    to pin suspicion on two runaways
    that we can't find. To get you out of it
    I've got to arrest somebody. Find those niggers,
    and that's all I want. They murdered him in escaping,
    and I'll say it's perfect. But I couldn't find them this morn-
       ing,
    and I can't find them now!

Murillo. They were here this evening.

Gash. They were? When?

Murillo. Not half an hour ago.
   Here, near the turn.

Gash. Now, look, boy, it all hangs
   on this—if it's accurate.

Murillo. Hell, Corky saw them!
   They came to the house.

Gash. Came in?

Murillo. Came in and stayed
   say half an hour.

Gash. By God, that gives us something!
   [*He goes to the door.*]
   Before I call them, who's this boy?

Murillo. He says
   he's the old man's son, says his name's Victor, says
   he's the girl's brother. Poppycock—that's all
   to get me out of the house.

Gash. Let him say it, though
   Let him say he's Victor.
   [*He opens the door.*]

   Come in. Let them all come in.
   And shut the door again.
   [ALEGRE, D'ALCALA *and* KING *enter.*]
   There were two negroes
   here this evening. What have you done with them?
   Where are they now?

d'Alcala. There were two Indians here,
   no negroes.

Gash. Just as you like. We'll call them Indians.
  Where are they now?

d'Alcala. What do you want with them?

Gash. Just murder, that's all.

Alegre. They escaped three days ago
  and the murder occurred last night. It's impossible
  to connect them with it. Once they were free and away
  why would they kill a guard?

Gash. Why did they come back?
  What were they doing here? And just how much
  do you know about it, sister? You said this morning
  you hadn't seen them.

Alegre. This is this evening.

Gash. Yes,
  but I don't trust you. And there's one among you
  who was cited before on a charge like this.
  Your brother Victor. Aiding a getaway.
  Is your name Victor?

King. Yes.

Murillo. He said it was Victor
  not ten minutes ago. He'd better keep it.
  It's a good name.

Gash.
    [*To* D'ALCALA]
  I'll remember that, too.
  Now I begin to see a little daylight.
  Now I begin to think we'll get somewhere.

The Indians did the killing to get away
and Victor helped them—on that theory
he's an accessory, and can be arrested,
so that's one in the bag!

d'Alcala. He came back from Spain
only this morning; the murder took place last night,
when he wasn't here.

Gash. And you told me just this morning
that he was dead. So where and when he came
and what he was doing when the murder happened,
whenever it was, and I don't know yet when,
that's all to be explained.

d'Alcala. Then I'll explain it.
You have no need for suspects, because I know
the murderer and what happened. The gambler, Murillo,
who sits there, in that corner, even now,
because I hear him breathe,—this man Murillo
(by God, I should have learned to shoot by ear)
surprised the road gang boss and the girl who's called
Killarney, and struck him over the head, and tied him
with wire from our clothes-line. This was near the wharf-
    end
at two o'clock. He made Killarney help him
and they dragged the body to the rowboat, towed it
some fifty yards or so out into the gulf,
weighted it with pockets full of stones,
or so I judge, and let it sink.

Murillo. God damn you,
who told you that?

d'Alcala. Told me? I knew so well
 where you had sunk that body that today
 at my direction it was fished to the surface,
 and freed of weights and floated to the bar
 where it was found to use against you!

Murillo. Damn you,
 I say who told you this? For he can't see!
 He's blind as dirt!

Gash. He's drawing you out, you lunk
 and you fall in the trap! Where did you get this story?
 Can you substantiate it?

d'Alcala. I hear better
 than most men see.

Gash. You mean you heard all that,
 and nobody told you?

d'Alcala. Heard it, just as I said,
 and know what happened.

Gash. That's not evidence.
 That could be manufactured by the yard
 and no check on it. No court in Florida
 would take a blind man's word for a thing like that,
 and no court should, unless there's corroboration,
 and there isn't any.

Alegre. But we know who's guilty.

Gash. Do you, lady? That's to prove in court,
 according to court rules. I'd like to hear more
 of this story of yours. Who fished the body up

and set it afloat? You said you told them where
and how to find it. Who were they?

d'Alcala. I can't tell you.

Gash. You don't know who they were?

d'Alcala. Yes. I can't tell you.

Gash. But I think I know. There were two Indians here
according to what I hear. They fished him up
and set him afloat.

d'Alcala. Yes.

Gash. Could they have reason
for wanting to involve Murillo here,
or do you have some reason?

d'Alcala. Sir, I have some!
I wanted to send his murder home to him
because he's fixed himself here on my house
like a cancer on the heart!

Gash. That's a possible version.
But I tell you what it'll sound like to a jury:
It'll sound as if two convicts killed a foreman
to get away—and then got scared, and towed
the body down to the doorstep of a man
who'd had a quarrel with that foreman, and as if your son
was in on it somehow, because you knew exactly
where the body was sunk, and because the boy
was mixed up in a very similar business
some years ago. That sounds to me like sense.
How does it sound to you?

d'Alcala. Like the lie it is,
and you know it is.

Gash. That's how it all adds up
for any jury, I tell you. And the truth in court
is what sounds like the truth in court, and not what happened,
not necessarily.
Give me your gun.
[*He takes* KING's *revolver.*]

Alegre. But he's not Victor, and he didn't help them,
and they didn't kill the guard!

Gash. He said he was Victor.
And the rest they can argue.

Alegre. But look what you're doing!
Doesn't it matter who's guilty?

Gash. That comes into it. As a matter of fact
I'd much rather have the Indians than your brother,
and you know where the Indians are. So think it over,
maybe we can make a deal.
[*He opens the door.*]
Come in here, Sam.
[SAM *enters.*]
The boy's under arrest. I'm searching the house.
Just keep an eye on this room.
[*He goes out left with a flashlight.*]

Murillo.
[*After a pause*]
God, it's hot in here.

If I didn't know that you were guilty, I'd know
by looking at you—it shows in the way you sit,
and the way you speak, and the way you turn your head!

[GASH *re-enters carrying a rifle and a revolver in one hand, a small
box and a photograph in the other. He lays the articles on the table.*]

Gash. By God, a snake
couldn't hide in this bungalow. There's nothing here
to crawl behind. What's this?

Alegre. Letters.

Gash. And here's
a picture of this bird that said his name
was Victor, or wasn't Victor, I forget
which he said last. Maybe he is your brother;
either that or you've known him a damn long time,
because there's a date here on the picture—May,
1936. Whose guns are these?

Alegre. Mine.

Gash. We'll give them back when the trouble's over.
Listen, Sam, tell Mac to get organized
on board the cutter. We'll have to search the beach
and do a little scouting along the coast.
I'm looking for two Indians.

[SAM *goes out, closing the door.*]

Now here's my proposition. Give me the Indians
and I'll let Victor off. You'll find my word's
as good as an honest man's, and it's a good bargain—
better than you'll get in court. I keep my word
because if I didn't I couldn't stay in business,
but once you get in a District Attorney's office

hell can't save you.—So tell me where they are
and I'll do without your brother.

Alegre. They'd be hanged.

Gash. I wouldn't be surprised.

Alegre. Then why do you protect
one man, whom I won't name, who might be tried,
but evidently won't be?

Gash. Lady, I told you.
I keep my word. If I keep my word to you
I have to keep it elsewhere.

Alegre. And you dare admit that?

Gash. Ma'am,
if I was to deny it people would laugh.
That's just politics and government.
I've been in politics here all my life,
and I don't like it myself, and I didn't invent it,
but what you have to do is sell protection
to people that can pay, and then protect them
the best you can.

Alegre. Even from murder?

Gash. No,
not from murder. But if it comes down to murder
you give them what breaks you can.

Alegre. You could be honest.
You know that?

Gash. No, lady, I couldn't. It's been tried;
  you have to have a machine to stay in office,
  and nothing runs a machine but money. Now
  I've never been off the keys, but I've heard it said
  there's honest government elsewhere, here and there,
  by fits and starts. Maybe there is. I don't know.
  I don't see how it could last. It might come in,
  but it wouldn't be natural. There's a John Chinaman
  runs the laundry down at Star Key. He says
  in China the same word that means to govern
  means to eat. They've worked it out in China.
  The government eats you, but it protects you first,
  because if it didn't you wouldn't get fat enough
  to make good eating.

Alegre. But if they knew about you—!

Gash. Lady, they know, and nothing you could say
  would mean a thing.—For your own good, and his,
  and his—I tell you, give me a line on those Indians
  and from now on we're friends.

Alegre. We'd be dishonored
  by such a friendship.

Gash. Well, give me the information,
  and friends or not, I'll keep my word.

Alegre. Look for them
  below the lower beach, under the mangroves.
  They sleep near there at night. They were planning to
    catch the tide,
  but it's not turned yet, and they'll be there still.

Gash. I'll post
  a guard here, so don't try to leave the house.
  If I find them, then we're all free and clear.
  If I don't, if you've sent me on a cold trail,
  then I'll need Victor. Murillo comes with me.
    [*He goes out, carrying the guns and letting* MURILLO *precede him.*]

King. But they'll be there. You told him where they are.
  They're not gone yet.

Alegre. No.

King. This was for me?

Alegre. I can't let you go out to die for them—
  nor send them to die for you. He'll bring them here
  and then—it may be—you must choose—

King. Yes, he'll bring them here—
  and they'll stand before me—and this big-mouth Gash
  will ask are these the men—

Alegre. Yes.

King. Will you say they are?
  Could you say that?

Alegre. Yes, if you say it. Yes,
  if you say they're guilty, I'll say it too.
  It must be your decision.

King. I'll choose to live then!

Alegre. No one can choose for you.

King. Why shouldn't I choose it?
  What else could be expected?

Alegre. You'll do what you must
   I've always heard one does what's generous
   in danger. Saves others first and then oneself.

King. Only it isn't a question of who's saved first,
   it's a question of which is saved. It's one or the other
   but it's not both. There has to be a scape-goat,
   and either the Indians pay for Murillo's fun
   or I pay for it.

Alegre. Yes.

King. Then what you mean is
   I should strike an attitude of what the hell
   and walk off gallantly to a death on the gallows
   to save two drones from a reservation?

Alegre. No,
   I haven't said that. But can you stand face to face
   with two innocent fugitives, and stand there silent
   and load them with a crime to save yourself?
   How could one do it and live? Would you wish to live
   after they were gone?

King. How else can I live?

Alegre. Any way that squares
   with what a man, waking, may think of himself in the night
   and not want to die before morning.

King. But no way squares—
   no way I could possibly think of, squares with the rules;
   you're thinking of the old rules, the ancient code
   established by the knights in the middle ages,

the old authentic code. And men don't live
by faith or honor or justice. That's revoked.
They live as they can, as the animals they are,
because it's impossible to arrange a life
by these fantastic, inexcusable rules.
Look at these laws of chivalry as they're laid
upon my soul tonight. Half an hour ago
I'm asked to die to protect a woman's choice
of the man she'll have. That's understandable.
All right, one can die for that. But now I'm asked
to forget about you, because that was less important,
and die for a couple of Indians out on the beach
that I don't know—meanwhile leaving the woman
to the mercy of the same scoundrel it was my job
to save her from before. Isn't it a question
whether I'm more useful here, and alive, and trying,
at least, to ward off Murillo?

Alegre. But we cannot choose,
either you or I, to purchase your safety or mine,
by offering up those two poor, wandering children
to Murillo and the sheriff. We simply can't,
whatever happens to us.

King. Whatever happens?
Have you envisioned that?

Alegre. I have a revolver,
and I can use it.

King. And would you?

Alegre. Do you doubt it?

King. Then we both die—as a sacrifice to the rules.
  It would be something to know who it is arranges
  these little ironies.
  I came here running from a civil war
  where madmen and morons tore a continent
  apart to share it, where death and rape were common
  as flies on a dead soldier, and alien men
  were weary of native women. I ran from that storm
  of rape and murder, because I couldn't help
  and nobody could help, and I wanted at least
  to save my life, in any crawling way,
  and the great master of the laboratory,
  (wearing spectacles, probably) drives me down
  to this bloody wharf, where I must choose again
  between death and the rape of a woman, between death
  and the murder of innocent men. I made my choice
  long ago, and ran, and left them bleeding
  there in the field. And I say it's better to live—
  if one could live alone in the Everglades
  and fill his stomach with fish, and sleep at night,
  and knock his oysters from the mangrove roots,
  and let the dead bury their dead, for there's no faith sure,
  no magnanimity that won't give way
  if you test it often enough, no love of woman
  or love of man, that won't dry up in the end
  if the drouth lasts long enough, no modesty
  that isn't relative. There's no better than you
  among all women—and yet when you envisioned
  the choice between Murillo and your death
  there was a flash when your mind asked itself,
  must it be death? Is even the man Murillo

worse than death? And if you can ask the question
then there's more than one answer.

Alegre. How did you know that!

King. Because the mind, the bright, quick-silver mind,
has but one purpose, to defend the body
and ward off death. Because it's the law of earth
where life was built up from the very first
on rape and murder—where the female takes what she gets
and learns to love it, and must learn to love it,
or the race would die! Show me one thing secure
among these names of virtues—justice and honor
and love and friendship—and I'll die for it gladly,
but where's justice, and where's honor, and where's friendship,
and what's love, under the rose?

Alegre. Then you've never loved.

King. Not as you've loved, perhaps, for you assume
that it's forever, and I've known, and know,
that it's till the fire burns down, till the stimulant
of something new or something stolen's gone,
till you know all the intimate details
and the girl's with child, and cries. And if that's true
of love, it's true of all the other doors—
the doors of all the illusions, and one by one
we all jump at them. We jump first at the door
with Christ upon it, hanging on the cross,
then the door with Lenin, legislating heaven,
then the emblem of social security, representing
eighteen dollars a week, good luck or bad,

jobs or no jobs—then the door with the girl expectant,
the black triangle door, and they all give meaning
to life, and mental sustenance, but then
there comes a day when there's no sustenance,
and you jump, and there's nothing you want to buy with
    money,
and Christ hangs dead on the cross, as all men die,
and Lenin legislates a fake paradise,
and the girl holds out her arms, and she's made of sawdust,
and there's sawdust in your mouth!

Alegre. But if this were true,
    then why would one live—woman or man or beast,
    or grub in the dark?

King. To eat and sleep and breed
    and creep in the forest.

Alegre. Answer him, father, answer,
    because it sounds like truth—but if it were true
    one couldn't live! There is something in women
    that is as he says, and there is something in men
    that merely wants to live, but answer him!
    We're not like this!

d'Alcala. Why, girl, we're all alone,
    here on the surface of a turning sphere
    of earth and water, cutting a great circle
    round the sun, just as the sun itself
    cuts a great circle round the central hub
    of some great constellation, which in turn
    wheels round another. Where this voyage started
    we don't know, nor where it will end, nor whether

it has a meaning, nor whether there is good
or evil, whether man has a destiny
or happened here by chemical accident—
all this we never know. And that's our challenge—
to find ourselves in this desert of dead light-years,
blind, all of us, in a kingdom of the blind,
living by appetite in a fragile shell
of dust and water; yet to take this dust
and water and our range of appetites
and build them toward some vision of a god
of beauty and unselfishness and truth—
could we ask better of the mud we are
than to accept the challenge, and look up
and search for god-head? If it's true we came
from the sea-water—and children in the womb
wear gills a certain time in memory
of that first origin—we've come a long way;
so far there's no predicting what we'll be
before we end. It may be women help
this progress choosing out the men who seem
a fractional step beyond sheer appetite—
and it may be that's sacred, though my values
are hardly Biblical—and perhaps men help
by setting themselves forever, even to the death,
against cruelty and arbitrary power,
for that's the beast—the ancient, belly-foot beast
from which we came, which is strong within us yet,
and tries to drag us back down. Somehow or other,
in some obscure way, it's the love of woman
for man, and a certain freedom in her love
to choose tomorrow's men, and the leverage

in the interplay of choice between men and women,
that's brought us here—to this forking of the roads—
and may take us farther on.

King. And where are we going?

d'Alcala. To a conquest of all there is, whatever there is
among the suns and stars.

King. And what if it's empty—
    what if the whole thing's empty here in space
    like a vast merry-go-round of eyeless gods
    turning without resistance—Jupiter
    and Mars and Venus, Saturn and Mercury,
    carved out of rock and trailed with cloud and mist,
    but nothing, and in all the constellations,
    no meaning anywhere, nothing? Then if man gets up
    and makes himself a god, and walks alone
    among these limitless tensions of the sky,
    and finds that he's eternally alone,
    and can mean nothing, then what was the use of it,
    why climb so high, and set ourselves apart
    to look out on a place of skulls?

d'Alcala. Now you want to know
    what will come of us all, and I don't know that.
    You should have asked the fish what would come of him
    before the earth shrank and the land thrust up
    between the oceans. You should have asked the fish
    or asked me, or asked yourself, for at that time
    we were the fish, you and I, or they were we—
    and we, or they, would have known as much about it
    as I know now—yet it somehow seems worth while

that the fish were not discouraged, and did keep on—
at least as far as we are.—For conditions
among the fish were quite the opposite
of what you'd call encouraging. They had
big teeth and no compunction. Bigger teeth
than Hitler or Murillo.
Over and over again the human race
climbs up out of the mud, and looks around,
and finds that it's alone here; and the knowledge
hits it like a blight—and down it goes
into the mud again.
Over and over again we have a hope
and make a religion of it—and follow it up
till we're out on the topmost limb of the tallest tree
alone with our stars—and we don't dare to be there,
and climb back down again.
It may be that the blight's on the race once more—
that they're all afraid—and fight their way to the ground.
But it won't end in the dark. Our destiny's
the other way. There'll be a race of men
who can face even the stars without despair,
and think without going mad.

King. And a man who's lost
    the very light from his sky, sits here in his sky
    and can say this yet.
        [*A light flashes across the window.*]

Alegre. They're turning back.
    They've called the flashlights in and got aboard,
    and they'll be here soon.
        [KING *picks up the picture from the table.*]

❦ 114 ❦

King. Why is my picture here?

Alegre. It was Victor's and he left it for me.
Let me have it.

King. There's something written beneath.
May I read it?

Alegre. If you like.

King.
[*Reading*]
Let me not to the marriage of true minds
Admit impediments. Love is not love
Which alters when it alteration finds,
Or bends with the remover to remove.
Oh, no, it is an ever-fixed mark
That looks on tempests and is never shaken;
It is the star to every wand'ring bark
Whose worth's unknown, although his height be taken.
[*He looks away from the picture and speaks from memory.*]

Love's not time's fool, though rosy lips and cheeks
Within his bending sickle's compass come;
Love alters not with his brief hours and weeks
But bears it out even to the edge of doom.
If this be error, and upon me proved,
I never writ, nor no man ever loved.

I learned it once in school and it still stays with me.
Why is this written here, under my picture?

Alegre. I wrote it there.

King. Three years ago?

Alegre. One spring
    when I felt most alone, the spring when Victor
first went away, I wrote it then; but not
because I was in love. It was much more than love,
it was a worship,
and I had a ritual I said before it
for matins in the morning, and for vespers
before I went to bed. He'd talked about you
and you were the singing hero of their venture
into the world, leading the great crusade
to make over the face of things. It was on your face—
this light of the future. It's on your face there yet,
on the picture in your hand.

King. Have I changed so much?

Alegre. You've changed.

King. And all this happened in the spring
    three years ago.

Alegre. It happened in the spring
    and lasted till this morning.

King. You said you loved
    someone who died in Spain.

Alegre. You died in Spain.
    And now I see that everything you said
was true, and the poem's rhetoric, for love
does alter when it alteration finds,
or I'd love you still.

King.

[*After a pause*]

Yes. I did die in Spain.
And maybe this was what I came looking for,
this picture of the athlete who died young,
the portrait of one dead. I came a long way to get it
and tried to stay away, but now I have it
and I'll know what to do.

[*Another pause*]

And yet it's unfair somehow.

Alegre. Is it unfair?

King. It doesn't come to us all. It comes to many
in certain generations, comes to only a few
in others; and it says, if you want to live
you must die now—this instant—or the food
you eat will rot at your lips, and the lips you kiss
will turn to stone, and the very ground you tread
will curl up under your footsteps like a snake
and hiss behind you.—Yet if you're chosen out,
or choose yourself, and go out to die, you die
forever after, and that's farther away
than one can say in light-years;—and the thing
you die for is as far away as that.
You die to bring about a race of men
who'll walk the heavens on a rope of sines
and cosines, looking like Wells' Martian polyp,
and operating on the womb of night
with a long sharp equation. It's no fun
to perish in your own person, when you're young,
for this remote eventuality—

even if it were attractive, which it's not;
and so in the last analysis one dies
because it's part of the bargain he takes on
when he agrees to live.—A man must die
for what he believes—if he's unfortunate
enough to have to face it in his time—
and if he won't then he'll end up believing
in nothing at all—and that's death, too.

d'Alcala. They're here
and they're bringing the Indians with them. And so perhaps
that part of it's settled.

[*The right-hand door opens and* SHERIFF GASH *enters with*
MURILLO, *the* DEPUTY *and the two* INDIANS. HUNK, KILLARNEY,
CORKY, GAGE *and* PRISCILLA *follow them in.*]

Gash. Go in, go in!

d'Alcala.

[*To* HORN, *putting out his hand to him*]
I'm sorry, sir. This wasn't our intention.

Horn. No doubt, no doubt!
The white man gives, the white man takes away.
Blessed be the name of the white man.

Gash. You keep your bargains to the letter, ma'am,
and I'll do the same by you. It seems the Indians
were moving on tonight, but we came in time,
and your brother or your friend, whichever it is,
can sleep at home. Also here's your weapons,
but what you're doing with a forty-five
I wouldn't be sure. This thing'll break your wrist
if you ever shoot it.

Alegre. It was my brother's.

King. Yes,
> [*Taking the revolver*]
You won't need it now.

Gash. Now I understand
there's been some trouble between Murillo here
and the people of the house. I'm mentioning it
because you're all here, and listening, and right now's
the time to say, forget it—because there's one thing
no business anywhere can afford to have
and that's trouble with the authorities. There's been murder
here on this point, but I can tell you now
it was nobody's fault here locally. We've caught
the likely suspects, and the thing to do's
go back to work, and whatever quarrel there was
put it out of your minds.—I'll be watching you
from now on—and listening to reports—
and I want to hear it's all peaceful here on Key Largo,
and doing business as usual.

King. Do I understand
that these two Indians are in custody
charged with the murder?

Gash. It looks as if they did it,
so they're under arrest, and you're discharged.

King. I'm sorry
to have let things go so far. When you went out
to hunt the Indians I was silent because
I couldn't bring myself to face what I'd done

and take the consequence. I thought—two Indians—
let them die—and nobody knows I'm guilty,
so it won't matter. But now I see their faces
I can't let them die for me.

Gash. What are you guilty of?

King. I murdered the foreman. They knew nothing about it.
I did it alone.

Killarney. The boy's crazy!

King. Oh, no, I'm not—
though I think I know why you say it. And I thank you.
Still—I'm guilty. Confession's difficult
at first, as you can imagine, but now it's out
there's a kind of relief, a kind of satisfaction
in getting it over.—I can recommend it
to anybody here who goes about
with an old crime searing his soul. Perhaps Murillo
has something on his conscience. If you have
get it off and you'll feel better.

Killarney. But he is crazy!

Gash. Son, if you go on I'll have to arrest you.
So keep your mouth shut.

King. You'll arrest me, naturally,
and let the Indians go, since I'm confessing
the crime, and without accomplices.

Gash. Very well.
Is this on the level?

d'Alcala. I think so.

King. Let me point out
   my advantage as a defendant. I'm a good witness
   and I'll convict myself, whereas the Indians
   will probably protest their innocence—
   being innocent, as they are. I recommend
   that they be shown the door, and set afloat
   as quickly as possible.

Gash. Well, no, they're wanted
   as runaways.

King. They'll make poor witnesses.
   They have another theory of this crime
   as you probably know. Let's spare Mr. Murillo
   any unnecessary mention.

Murillo. Get the Indians out. They know too much.

Gash. All right.
   Take the handcuffs off them, and let them go.
     [*The* INDIANS *are released.*]
   You're sure you want it this way? There are witnesses
   and they've heard what you said.

King. I'm certain of it.

Gash. Let them go.
     [*The* INDIANS *go out.*]

King. If they'd been allowed to talk
   do you know what they'd have said? That Murillo did it.
   Murillo there, who wouldn't injure a flower,
   or step on your hand, he's so chicken-hearted! Yes,
   but they'd have accused him!
     [*He draws the forty-five.*]

Look, atom-smasher,
we played a game this morning, you and I;
revolver-on-the-belly or atom-smash-atom,
and it seems to me you won—

Gash.
[*To his* DEPUTY]
Take that gun from him!

Murillo. Wait! Don't move, for God's sake! The fool means
it!
Don't move or he'll kill me!

King. Yes, I certainly would!
If anybody jumps at me you're done
because the triggers on these forty-fives
are tender as young love. I think you said
you weren't afraid to die, but what you meant
was that you knew I didn't have the guts
to shoot you. And I didn't. Only tonight
I have, and strangely enough, it's the other way round,
and I'm not afraid to die!

Gash. What are you trying to do?

King. Once in a thousand years a mortal man
gets the same chance twice. Where we stood this morning
we stand now again. Give us elbow-room.
[*The others draw slowly back from them.*]
And now, my friend,
let me explain that we won't either of us
emerge from this predicament. This is curtains
for me and you. Black curtains and the end
as sure as you're a gambler. To save my soul

I have to get rid of you, and if you're to go
you'll certainly want me along.

Murillo. Listen, boy, I'm licked.
I know when I'm licked. Put up your gun for God's sake
and I'll put mine up.

King. Not at all. What I want now, atom-smasher,
is that you back out gently through that door,
putting out your hand behind you so you won't stumble
and die before your time. We'll go together—
always the gun-point on your belly-button—
and then we'll climb together into your car—
you first, climbing in backwards—and then we'll drive,
or rather you'll drive, Mr. Murillo, turning
to right or left as indicated, the gun
still on your unathletic periphery.
You may begin,
one foot behind the other, very softly;
and as we go, I'd like to say that for sheer
unadulterated pleasure to the heart,
for a happiness that beats against the side
and almost makes you weep, this game of yours
is tops with me. There was another door,
and one I never leaped at, and there's food
for the soul and mental sustenance, and mirth
to last out all the long night after dying
in the winning of this last hand. And thanks where they're
    due:
I thank you, Mr. Murillo, from my teeth,
for appearing out of the darkness of that hell
which is probably your home, to teach me the game,
and take me with you to earth!

Murillo. Hold it, for God's sake!
Don't shoot at him!

[HUNK *shoots* KING *and* KING'S *gun fells* MURILLO, *who falls half
outside the door.* KING *staggers to a chair and sits.*]

Gash. God damn you, have you no brains?

Hunk. I had to do it!

King. Oh, you lunk, you lunk-head,
I knew you couldn't stand it! You must be shooting.
I counted on you—and you did it!—Nevertheless
it looks as if you might have to do it again!
That first wasn't enough!

Gash. Sam, get those Indians
before they get away. No, wait a minute,
I can't use them now.

King. Right, right, Mr. Sheriff;
now that Murillo's gone, there's not much point
in proving he was or wasn't. Let the Indians go.
Give them a chance at their happy hunting grounds.
They waited long enough for it!

Alegre. King, I was wrong!
You didn't have to die!

King. Is this dying, Alegre?
Then it's more enviable than the Everglades,
to fight where you can win, in a narrow room,
and to win, dying.

Gash. Where's he hurt? Get him down here
flat, so he won't lose blood.

King. No, let me alone.
Let me sit up and look him in the face
whoever he is. They say when they bury an Indian
they bury him seated upright in his grave
with his weapons around him. That's very sensible.
Very sensible.

[*He slumps down.*]

Gash. You can't be sorry
for a man that planned it, and it all worked out,
and he got what he wanted.—
Just for the record, sir, this was your son?

D'Alcala. He was my son.

CURTAIN

DATE DUE
